MW01257304

North Carolina English, 1861–1865

North Carolina English, 1861–1865
A Guide and Glossary

Michael Ellis

Foreword by Stephen Berry

The University of Tennessee Press / Knoxville

First Edition.

The paper in this book meets the requirements of American National Standards Institute / National Information Standards Organization specification Z39.48-1992 (Permanence of Paper). It contains 30 percent post-consumer waste and is certified by the Forest Stewardship Council.

Library of Congress Cataloging-in-Publication Data

Ellis, Michael E., 1949–
North Carolina English, 1861–1865: a guide and glossary / [compiled by] Michael Ellis; Foreword by Stephen Berry. — First Edition.
pages cm.
ISBN 978-1-62190-002-3 (hardcover)
1. English language—Dialects—North Carolina.
2. English language—North Carolina.
3. North Carolina—History—Civil War, 1861–1865—Correspondence.
4. North Carolina—History—Civil War, 1861–1865—Personal narratives.
5. Americanisms—North Carolina.
6. North Carolina—Languages.
7. North Carolina—History—Civil War, 1861–1865.
I. Title.

PE3101.N76E55 2013
427'.9756—dc23 2013018585

Camp near bunker hill [Virginia]
July the 19th 63

Dear Wife I take
the pleasier of writing you a fiew lines which
will inform you that I am not well at this
time I have a bad cold and I am waried out
a marching but we are stoped at this time
but we dont no for how long we will stay hier
they is Some talk of our going back in
mayerland but I am in hopes that the war will Soon
end for I tired of mayerland I hope that we will
not go back thare we marced through PN and
we had a hard fight thare we lost all of our
boys nearly thare charly got kild and he suferd
a graideal from his wound he lived a night and
a day after he was woundid we sead hard times
thare but we got a nugh to eat ther but we
dont now as to my Self I git a nugh for I
dont want nothing to eat hardly for I am
all most Sick all the time and half crasy
I never wantid to come home so bad in
my life but it is So that I cant come
at this time but if we come down South
I will try to come eny how for I want
to come home so bad that I am home sick
I want you to kepe charlys pistol and if
I ever git back I will keep it
Thomas and Robert Ramsy both got woundid
and they was left with the
yankes but I hope that we will
live to come home without a wound
for I have Seen So many woundid
and died I staid with Charly untill he
died he never spoke after he was woundid
untill he died I never was hurt So
in my life I had reather that it
would of bin my Self as my apertunity
is bad of writing I will close So
nothing more only I Stil remain
your kinde and afectionet husband

John Futch

Futch Letters, North Carolina State Archives

Contents

Illustrations

Gallery of Civil War Letters

Maps

Foreword

Forty million people watched Ken Burns's documentary *The Civil War* when it first aired in September 1990. Most of them had been hooked by the first night's closing drama: the recitation of an obscure major's final letter home before his death at Bull Run. "Dear Sarah," Sullivan Ballou intoned from a few million televisions. "My love for you is deathless. It seems to bind me with mighty cables that nothing but Omnipotence could break; and yet my love of Country comes over me like a strong wind and bears me unresistibly on with all these chains to the battle field. . . . If I do not [return] . . . Sarah, do not mourn me dead; think I am gone and wait for thee, for we shall meet again."

The Civil War generation is justly famous not only for what it said but also how it said it. North and South, the war's elites spoke in a sublime high tongue, less embroidered than the speech of their colonial forebears but still inflected with the signature cadences of Shakespeare and the King James Bible. The master practitioner of this hauntingly spare, Romantic-cum-modern rhetorical style was Abraham Lincoln, and whole shelves have been filled with paeans to the lilt of his language. But as Civil War historians have long recognized, the war produced a thousand prose-poets yet unsung, men and women whose letters and diaries pulse with passages so searingly beautiful they seem somehow *more true*. "Oh that my heart was a fountain of waters," Amanda McDowell lamented in 1861, "that I might weep it away for this my ruined country."[1]

The voluminous letters that Michael Ellis and his team painstakingly collected and transcribed to create this glossary were written not in the war's high tongue but in what we might call its common tongues. Inked by semiliterate men and women who wrote as they spoke, the letters capture invaluable traces of their authors' ethnic and dialectal heritage. The result is a linguistic bonanza, a glossary that allows us to really *hear* the Civil War's common soldiers for the first time. Leafing through the entries, we eavesdrop on men as they complain to their "Mars" and "Pars" about "musketeers" (mosquitoes) and "tackies" (poor white trash) and "this tornel war" (eternal war). We listen in as they tell the boys they're "well as common" having just "drempt" about "flying a round" with their "jularkys" and "duncys" and "widders" whose "lipps" need "bussin" "pawrrful Bad."

Since the "linguistic turn," historians have been sensitive to the notion that language structures experience, which makes this glossary as much a historical bonanza as it is a literary one. Civil War historians have consistently tried to get inside the heads of the conflict's common soldiers, with mixed results. The tradition is often traced back to Bell Wiley and his legendary portraits of Johnny Reb and Billy Yank, published in the 1940s and 1950s. But it was men such as Mark Twain and Sam Watkins who first profaned the High Church of the War to let in a little air. Both men had been "high privates" in their day, and both knew the real reason the "real war" would never get in the books: The "better men" would never be honest about all the bleak and blasphemous absurdities they'd committed and seen. "The histories of the Lost Cause are all written out by 'big bugs,'" Watkins complained in 1882. "Of course, [their] histories are all correct. They tell of great achievements of great men, who wear the laurels of victory; have grand presents given them; high positions in civil life; presidents of corporations; governors of states . . . and when they die, long obituaries are published, telling their many virtues, their distinguished victories, etc. . . . But in the following pages I propose to tell of the fellows who did the shooting and killing, the fortifying and ditching . . . the drilling, the standing guard, picket and videt, and who drew (or were to draw) eleven dollars per month."[2]

To tell the privates' story, Watkins instinctively knew that he would have to use the privates' language. He and his fellows had met the war's violence and drudgery with their own argot, a language more raw and wry than that of their officers, and it was a language Watkins believed had as much legitimacy, and perhaps more honesty, than the war's high tongue. Indeed, from the first page to the last, Watkins staked a claim for his memoir that was at once historical and linguistic: "Like the fellow who called a turtle a 'cooter,' being told that no such word as cooter was in Webster's dictionary, remarked that he had as much right to make a dictionary as Mr. Webster or any other man; so have I to write a history."[3]

If North Carolina's real war is ever to be written, it must be written out of Michael Ellis's glossary, for here is the English of the Tar Heel masses. Here are idiosyncrasies of spelling and syntax that ring true; here is a language incapable of misdirection. The war's high tongue may be justly famous for its artistic flourishes, but such filigree can obscure as much as it reveals. The war's common tongues strip out the rhetoric to capture a war lived closer to the bone by people whose expression and experience are left sparer, barer, and balder. "Please lette me now in your next letter whether it can talk or not and whether it still sucks titey yet," Isaac Lefevers asked his wife about their baby just before Valentine's Day in 1863. "Mag i can tell yow wee hav a heep of sort of men her thay hav the cl. an po. [clap and pox] an all complaints," T. F. Baggarly wrote home just before Christmas 1862. "That is thay git drunk an run after negroes an mien white women bwt i can till yow with a clare concience i tak no part with them." Lefevers and Baggarly were no Sullivan Ballou. But they weren't unromantic either; they just spoke as they lived, directly and without pretense, as did their womenfolk. "I have got a sore throat," Rhoda Bateman wrote her brothers in November 1864. "I have lost my baby she lived nine days the rest of the famaly is well hopeing this will find you boath well we have nothing new to wright about."

Full of such "directness," the letters Michael Ellis has excavated and made available on the University of Tennessee Press website—letters that form the first installment of the larger Corpus of American Civil War Letters (CACWL) project—themselves have enormous potential for scholars. What other source, for instance, could give us so compelling a glimpse into common white conceptions of heaven? Very few of the letter writers describe the hereafter as a place where sins are forgiven and enlightenment bestowed, or where believers sit at the right hand of God. Most describe it simply as a place where families meet to part no more. They got such ideas from their preachers, obviously. But they cleaved to them because they struck a chord. For many poorer white families, the Civil War marked the first and only time they weren't together. Absence, as much as violence, defined what war meant. "I never new what It was befor to bee from home," one soldier wrote his family, "but I [k]now some thing a bout it now." "I hope we will meet agin in the world," wrote another, "but if we should not I want to meet you in haven whar we wont have to part aney more." This yearning for family *permanence* is only different from Ballou's in its language, but *language matters.* Imagine, for instance, if Burns had ended the first night of *The Civil War* with this scene:

> *Narrator:* Isaac Lefevers, a sergeant in the Forty-Sixth North Carolina, wrote his wife in mid-May 1864, after the Battle of the Wilderness had disabled half his regiment.
>
> *Voice actor:* Dear wife. . . . I most tel you that I have neaver saw such a site in no Battle as I have in this I have saw lots of Dead bod[i]es Burnt in to a crips [crisp] and I have no Eyedea but what some of the wonded was burnt of both sides but the most that I saw was of the enemy I saw one man that was burnt that had the picture I Suppose of his little Daughter in his pocket it was all burnt only the glass it loocked to be the Sise of Ida a very sick little girl I neaver saw enny thing that made me feel more sorrow. . . . I could not tel you how glad I would be to See you and the Dear little childrean this morning. . . . Dear wife we neave[r] new the pleasure that we Enjoyed to geather before this war come now we can see Corrows [sorrows] but my life is in the lordes handes and I am willen that he shal Dispose of it as he thinks beast. . . .
>
> *Narrator:* Isaac Lefevers died of wounds sustained three weeks later, at the Battle of Petersburg.[4]

Surrendered to the bodily brutalities of war, Lefevers offered no mitigating references to "honorable manhood" or "love of country." His version of war seems less romantic than irredeemably sad.

Historians of soldier motivation, desertion, Southern Unionism, Confederate nationalism, foodways, folklore, medicine, gender, family, and race relations among the nation's relatively poor will all hail the phenomenal new resource that has been systematically assembled, transcribed, and annotated by Michael Ellis of Missouri State University and Michael Montgomery of the University of South Carolina. Indeed, their CACWL project offers nothing less than the best chance historians may ever have had at reconstructing the world of the common soldier.

Stephen Berry
University of Georgia

NOTES

1. Amanda McDowell diary, June 15, 1861, quoted in Joan Cashin, ed., *Our Common Affairs: Texts from Women in the Old South* (Baltimore: Johns Hopkins Univ. Press, 1996), 285. For more on the lilt of Lincoln's language, see Garry Wills, *Lincoln at Gettysburg: The Words That Remade America* (New York: Simon & Schuster, 1992); and Douglas Wilson, *Lincoln's Sword: The Presidency and the Power of Words* (New York: Knopf, 2006).

2. Sam Watkins, *"Co. Aytch," Maury Grays, First Tennessee Regiment; or, a Side Show of the Big Show* (Chattanooga, Tenn.: Times Printing, 1900), 11.

3. Watkins, *"Co. Aytch,"* 11.

4. For more on mobility, not violence, as the defining experience of the Civil War, see Yael Sternhell, *Routes of War: The World of Movement in the Confederate South* (Cambridge, Mass.: Harvard Univ. Press, 2012).

Acknowledgments

The present volume has been a journey in a variety of ways. It began in 2007 when friend and colleague Michael B. Montgomery asked if I would be interested in transcribing some photocopies of Civil War letters from western North Carolina. One of the first collections Michael sent consisted of letters written by John W. Reese of Buncombe County, and it was not long before I was hooked. The linguistic treasures contained in the Reese letters were incalculable and left me eager for more. This began a journey through time to the 1860s and a Civil War seen through the eyes of common soldiers and their families and written in the words they used.

It also has been a literal journey in the form of three trips to archives and libraries in North Carolina, as well as side trips to other parts of the country. I want to thank the staffs of the Rare Book, Manuscript, and Special Collections Library of Duke University, the Southern Historical Collection at the University of North Carolina in Chapel Hill, the North Carolina State Archives in Raleigh, the Special Collections Department of the Hunter Library at Western Carolina University, and the Special Collections Department of the Joyner Library at East Carolina University. I would especially like to thank Janie Morris, who was so helpful during my first trip to Duke, and George Frizzell of WCU. Thanks are due to George Rugg of the Special Collections at the University of Notre Dame, who generously provided photocopies of the excellent Jackson Family Correspondence and Shipman Family Correspondence of Moore and Henderson counties respectively. For late additions to the glossary, thanks are due to Richard Sommers of the Military History Institute at Carlisle, who told me about the remarkable Constantine Hege Letters. The August 2012 visit to Carlisle, which will continue to bear fruit for years to come, was made possible by a Ridgeway Research Fellowship.

I must also thank W. D. Blackmon, head of the English Department at Missouri State University. Dr. Blackmon has been an enthusiastic supporter of the project from the beginning, and the Corpus of American Civil War Letters would have been difficult to bring to complete without his consistent encouragement and support.

Collecting photocopies and digital images of the North Carolina Civil War letters was a time- (and gasoline) consuming endeavor, but the real challenge was to transcribe the two-thousand-plus letters so that they could be transformed into citations for this book. I must recognize the efforts of the research assistants who spent hundreds of hours helping me transcribe the collections of North Carolina letters from the summer of 2008 through the fall of 2011. Those research assistants include Andrea Cudworth, Jennifer Fields, Casey White, Gemma Bellhouse, Toni Mitchell, and Andrew Albritton. My most recent assistant, Shiloh Peters, proofread the glossary. I also must recognize the graduate students in my linguistics seminars in the spring of 2009 and the spring of 2011 who transcribed North Carolina letters. They include Antonina Paver, Jamie Young, Chaz Miller, Nicole Teghtmyer, Holly Corbett, Brett Young, Duane Gilson, Heather Cook, Genevieve Vallentine, Jessica Sneeringer, Allen VanNess, Judith Bridges, Sarah Pasquale, Catherine Pettijohn, and Barbara Jones.

Thanks are also due to historians John Inscoe and Stephen Berry of the University of Georgia, who offered advice about sources of information for the historical, social, and sometimes geographic background for nineteenth-century North Carolina. I want to thank Brandon Cooper of the University of South Carolina, who took the time and trouble to photograph several North Carolina letter collections at Duke University and at the North Carolina State Archives.

I want to thank my son, Matt Christy, who kept my various computers operating over the last few years and who responded to my regular pleas for help with a generosity and competence that continue to amaze me. I also want to thank my wife, Gay, for proofreading the introduction, for holding down the fort during my frequent research trips, and, most of all, for responding to my frequent requests to offer a second opinion on a particularly difficult reading. Gay is also a master of tracking down arcane information on the Internet.

Finally, I must express my deepest gratitude to Michael Montgomery, friend and mentor for over twenty years, and in every respect the godfather of this project. Michael has long been my chief advisor in all matters linguistic and lexicographic, and his *Dictionary of Smoky Mountain English* has served as both a constant resource and a model. He also has been generous with his time by reading and commenting on two earlier drafts of this book, and without his help this volume could never have been completed.

Map of North Carolina, 1861-1865

By Betsy Johnson

Revised by Charles L. Price and John Conner Atheson, Jr., 1980

This map locates the principal forts, towns, railroads, and engagements fought in the State during the Civil War.

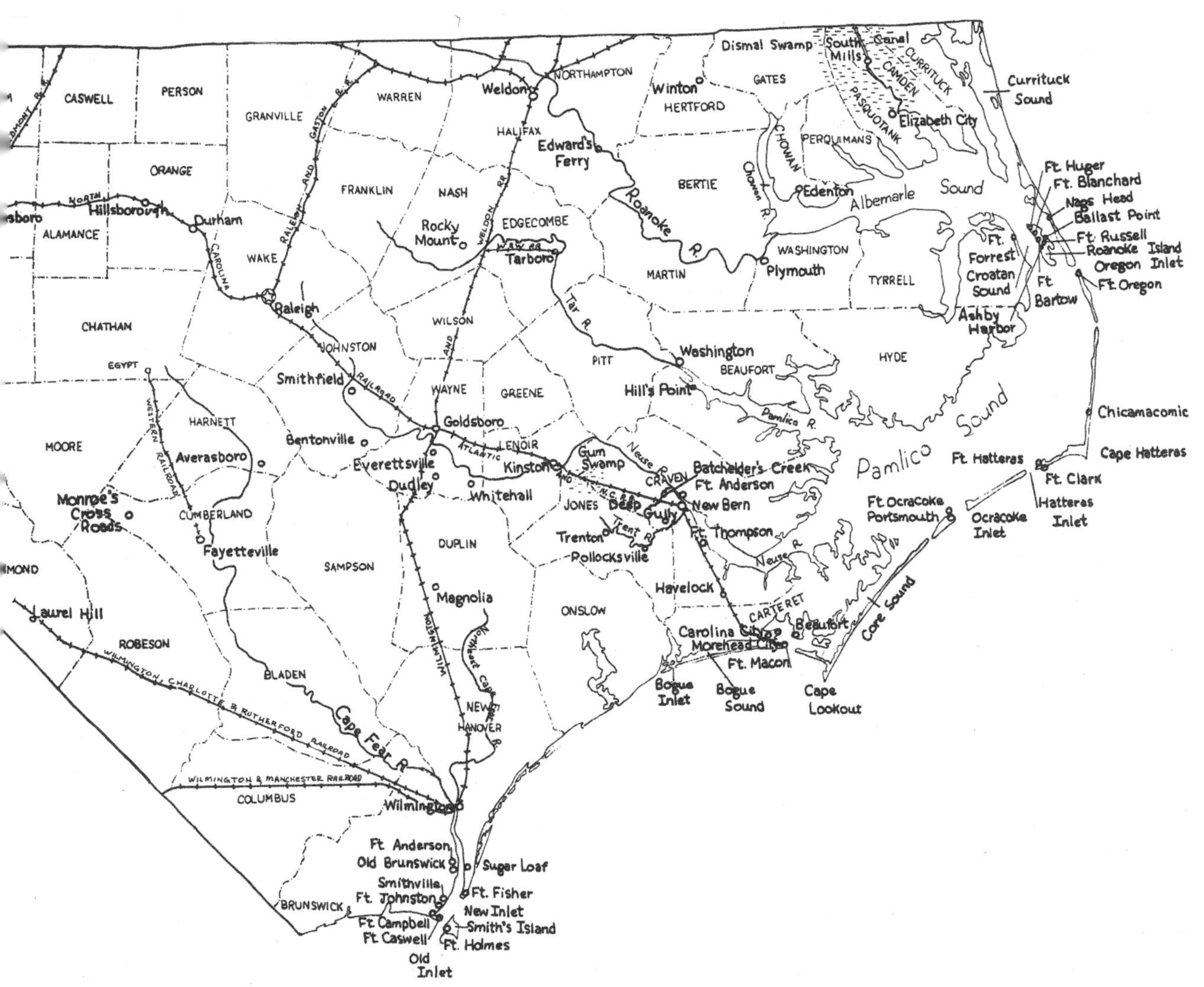

Introduction

In June 1852, Neill McGregor, who had recently left his native North Carolina and settled in Barbour County, Alabama, wrote to a cousin back home:

> this is a fine county. its Said to bea the most Sivel county in the State and the people is veery kind. we have verry good neighbours. thay hav bin verry good to us. thay are all principly Scotch and N.C.[1]

McGregor's letter not only provides insight into how the out-migration of North Carolinians in the nineteenth century spread their English far to the west but also introduces one of the groups of Europeans who immigrated to North Carolina during the colonial period. Neill McGregor's ancestors were among the large number of Highland Scots who began settling in the Cape Fear River valley in the mid-eighteenth century and arrived in North America speaking Scottish Gaelic rather than English as their first language.[2] At about the same time, large numbers of German and Scots-Irish settlers were migrating southward from Pennsylvania through Virginia and into the Yadkin and Catawba river valleys, where they joined other settlers, mostly of English ancestry, moving westward from the Coastal Plains. Therefore, the European element in much of North Carolina at the end of the colonial period and into the early nineteenth century was both linguistically and culturally diverse.[3] Add to this the thousands of African Americans, mostly slaves, who populated the state, particularly in the eastern half. By 1861, however, the descendants of those early Gaelic or German-speaking immigrants were using dialects of English largely indistinguishable from their neighbors of English or Scots-Irish ancestry.[4] In 1872, Gotthardt Bernheim wrote that a visitor forty or fifty years earlier to German-speaking communities in several Piedmont counties "would have been greeted with sounds of the peculiar dialect of the Pennsylvania-German language." But by 1872 that had changed, and Bernheim admitted:

> This language, however, has almost become extinct in North Carolina; a few aged persons may still be found, who are fond of conversing in that kind of German with those who are acquainted with it, but in a few more years the last vestige of Pennsylvania-German will be sought in vain in this State, where once even many of the negro slaves of the Germans spoke no other language.[5]

While traces of Gaelic or German influences might have lingered in intriguing phonetic spellings, expressions, and perhaps grammatical forms, by 1861 the only significant language left in North Carolina other than English was that of the Eastern Band of Cherokees, who lived in the Smoky Mountains on the western border of the state. This does not, however, mean that there was a single, uniform North Carolina dialect of English in the 1860s. Indeed, there is evidence of numerous variant linguistic features, not only between different parts of the state but also within communities and even within the speech of individuals.

This volume is a description of the English Language in North Carolina as it existed in the mid-nineteenth century. It is based on a sample of more than twenty-two hundred letters written by North Carolinians, mostly during the period 1861–65. The sample also includes several letters written in the decade before the beginning of the Civil War by North Carolinians who had migrated westward to Alabama and Arkansas, to western Kentucky and southern Indiana, and to Illinois and Missouri. These letters, like the one written by Neill McGregor, suggest North Carolina dialects must have had an impact on the formation of regional Englishes in the states where these migrants settled. What is needed is a better understanding of what North Carolina English was like in the mid-nineteenth century. What variations existed in the state in the 1860s? In what ways may North Carolina English have changed since the 1860s?[6] Norman Eliason's 1956 *Tarheel Talk: An Historical Study of the English Language in North Carolina to 1860* does an excellent job of introducing North Carolina English in the colonial and antebellum periods, but Eliason's book ends on the eve of the Civil War.[7] North Carolina fieldwork for the Linguistic Atlas of the Middle and South Atlantic States (LAMSAS) included a substantial number of informants who were born in the 1850s and 1860s, and the publications based on that project provide invaluable information about North Carolina

English as it was from the late nineteenth and into the twentieth century.[8] The present volume seeks to fill the gap between Eliason's work and the LAMSAS fieldwork by taking advantage of an extensive and neglected body of linguistic evidence: the many thousands of letters written during the Civil War.

The Corpus of American Civil War Letters

The North Carolina letters upon which this volume is based are part of a much larger project, the Corpus of American Civil War Letters (CACWL), a collaborative effort undertaken by Michael Montgomery and Michael Ellis in the summer of 2007 with the aim of gathering evidence about American regional English in the nineteenth century. Since then, we have accumulated over eight thousand letters and diaries written by soldiers and their families during the Civil War, and these documents have proved to be a remarkably rich source of information about American English as it was spoken 150 years ago. The letters collected for the CACWL project were written by individuals with limited education who knew little about the formal conventions of punctuation and capitalization and tended instead to write "by ear." These are the writers who are most likely to reproduce characteristic features of their spoken language in the form of phonetic spellings, regional words and usages, and, particularly, nonstandard grammatical forms. This evidence is of great value from the standpoint of the history of American English. Although linguists have had considerable success in describing the structure and features of American English and its dialects in the twentieth century and beyond, our knowledge of nineteenth-century American dialects is still very limited, and we must rely largely on the writing of those who, because of a lack of formal education, are most likely to reproduce the features of their spoken language in their writing.

Why Civil War letters? During that conflict the sheer number of letters written by soldiers and by family members on the homefront was unprecedented in American history. More than three million soldiers served in either the Union or Confederate army, and most of these soldiers were away from home for the first time, eager for news from home and eager to share their experiences. Many of these soldiers became regular correspondents for the first time in their lives, often writing home weekly while in camp and leaving behind a body of evidence exceeding, by far, anything that existed before. Further, the American Civil War was such a powerful event in our history that any documents relating to the war were more likely to have been preserved by the descendants of the soldiers who served in it. Though once private keepsakes, especially among the families of the several hundred thousand soldiers who never came home, many of these letters have found their way into libraries and archives. These are mostly the letters of little-educated privates, who were not writing for posterity but were desperate for news from home. Letters from privates provide entirely different perspectives on such daily experiences of war as morale, disease, privation, and sheer loneliness. In so doing, these letters are frequently more powerful than those written by the privates' more educated counterparts. The long-term goals of the CACWL project include creating an extensive and accessible corpus of documentary evidence in the form of transcriptions of letters and diaries, producing a linguistic atlas of nineteenth-century American regional dialects, and compiling lexicographical collections which will complement existing dictionary resources.

The CACWL North Carolina Sample

Along with the Chesapeake Bay areas of eastern Maryland and Virginia and the coastal areas of South Carolina and Georgia, North Carolina in the early and mid-nineteenth century would have been an important representative of the earliest forms of English in the American South. North Carolina English in the mid-nineteenth century was not far removed from its colonial roots. Indeed, several letter writers included in the sample were born in the last two decades of the eighteenth century. Many others, including parents of soldiers serving in the war, were born in the first two decades of the nineteenth century. The largest number of letter writers, including soldiers serving in the Civil War, were born in the period 1825–45.

As CACWL developed, it became clear that archives and libraries in North Carolina held a very substantial number of letters written by native North Carolinians during the Civil War. This large number of letters may be attributed, in part, to the number of North Carolina soldiers who served in the war. North Carolina supplied, by one estimate, 133,905 soldiers for state or Confederate service. Of these, nearly 20,000 were killed in battle or died of wounds, about one-fourth of all battle deaths among Confederate troops. Another 20,000 died of disease while in service, bringing the total number of soldiers who did not survive the war to a little over 40,000, or nearly one out of every three North Carolina soldiers who served in the war. In addition to the many soldiers in Confederate service, over three thousand white North Carolinians and five thousand black North Carolinians served in the Union army.[9]

The North Carolina sample consists of 2,299 letters and three diaries. Of these, 2,174 letters and two diaries were transcribed from digital images, photocopies, or microfilm printouts of the original documents. The remaining 125 letters and the third diary came from published sources.[10] The sample includes letters written by 633 individuals, with about half of the writers represented by a single letter.[11] On the other hand, the sample includes fifty-seven letters John Hartman of Rowan County wrote to his wife, Partha, between April 1862 and April 1865. Constantine Hege wrote nearly a hundred letters home to his family in Davidson County. There are more than forty family collections numbering between twenty and eighty letters and another twenty-three collections numbering between ten and nineteen letters. The shortest letters contain barely one hundred words, while the longest letters contain twelve hundred words or more. In all, the North Carolina sample totals over a million words.

Of the 633 North Carolina letter writers (see Appendix A), 362 served in the Confederate army and 9 (6 whites and 3 African Americans) served in the Union army.[12] Eight of the Confederate soldiers and one of the Union soldiers served in regiments from other states. There are 123 females among the letter writers, the majority of these being wives, mothers, or other relatives of soldiers. A total of 18 African Americans are represented in the sample, including slaves and former slaves. Obviously, African Americans are woefully underrepresented, given that the 1860 population of slaves (not including free blacks) in North Carolina was 331,059 out of a total population of 992,662.[13] No doubt, additional Civil War–era letters by African Americans from North Carolina are yet to be uncovered in the National Archives and elsewhere. We also had hoped to find letters by Cherokees who served in the Confederate army, but we were not successful in locating any.[14]

Every effort was made to make the sample geographically inclusive, and, in fact, seventy-nine of the eighty-nine North Carolina counties that existed in 1861 are represented. There are more letters from the Piedmont and western counties of the state, but eastern North Carolina is represented, with major collections of letters from the southeastern counties of New Hanover, Onslow, and Duplin and the northeastern counties of Martin, Bertie, and Washington.[15]

Most of the copies of letters were obtained during three visits to North Carolina, first in December 2009, then again in August 2010, and finally in August 2011. The institutions in which the letters are held include the North Carolina State Archives in Raleigh; the Rare Book, Manuscript, and Special Collections Library at Duke University; the Southern Historical Collection at the University of North Carolina, Chapel Hill; the Special Collections Department of the Hunter Library at Western Carolina University; and the Special Collections Department of the Joyner Library at East Carolina University. Additional collections of letters were obtained from libraries and archives outside of North Carolina, although the bulk of the North Carolina letters came from institutions within the state.

Existing Studies of North Carolina English

North Carolina English before the Civil War is described in some detail by Norman Eliason in *Tarheel Talk*. Eliason found his examples of antebellum North Carolina speech in a variety of historical documents he examined at the Southern Historical Collection while he was a faculty member at the University of North Carolina. His work is particularly valuable since it records numerous words and usages from the eighteenth century. The account books and other examples of record keeping he studied were especially rich in nouns denoting tools and equipment of all kinds, furniture and other household goods, and commodities in general. Church records, letters, diaries, journals, and even writing by children and students rounded out the various kinds of texts Eliason mined for his book, making *Tarheel Talk* is an important starting point for the study of English in colonial and antebellum North Carolina. His word list, which comprises Appendix A in his book, contains about five hundred words and usages, many of which were around in North Carolina speech decades before they appeared in the Civil War letters: *bull tongue* (plow), *candy stew, corn shucking, coon's age, fixing to,* and *fly around.*

Beginning in 1949, the linguistic diversity of the states along the eastern seaboard was documented in publications resulting from fieldwork conducted by two subdivisions of the Linguistic Atlas the United States and Canada (LAUSAC) project: the Linguistic Atlas of the Middle and South Atlantic States and the Linguistic Atlas of New England (LANE). LAUSAC director Hans Kurath authored the first of these publications, *A Word*

Geography of the Eastern United States (*WGEUS*). In *WGEUS*, Kurath proposed three primary speech areas: the "North" (New England, New York, and the northern parts of Pennsylvania and New Jersey), the "Midland" (the lower two-thirds of Pennsylvania and New Jersey, the northern parts of Maryland and Delaware, all of West Virginia, the western and southwestern parts of Virginia, the western half of North Carolina, and the northwestern parts of South Carolina), and the "South" (the Delmarva Peninsula, southern Maryland, eastern Virginia and North Carolina, and most of South Carolina). These areas and various subdivisions can be seen in *WGEUS* figure 3.[16] The North Carolina field work for LAMSAS was carried out Guy Lowman between 1934 and 1937 and involved interviewing informants and employing a lengthy questionnaire designed to elicit regionally significant linguistic features. There were 155 informants in North Carolina, and these were spread out across seventy-one

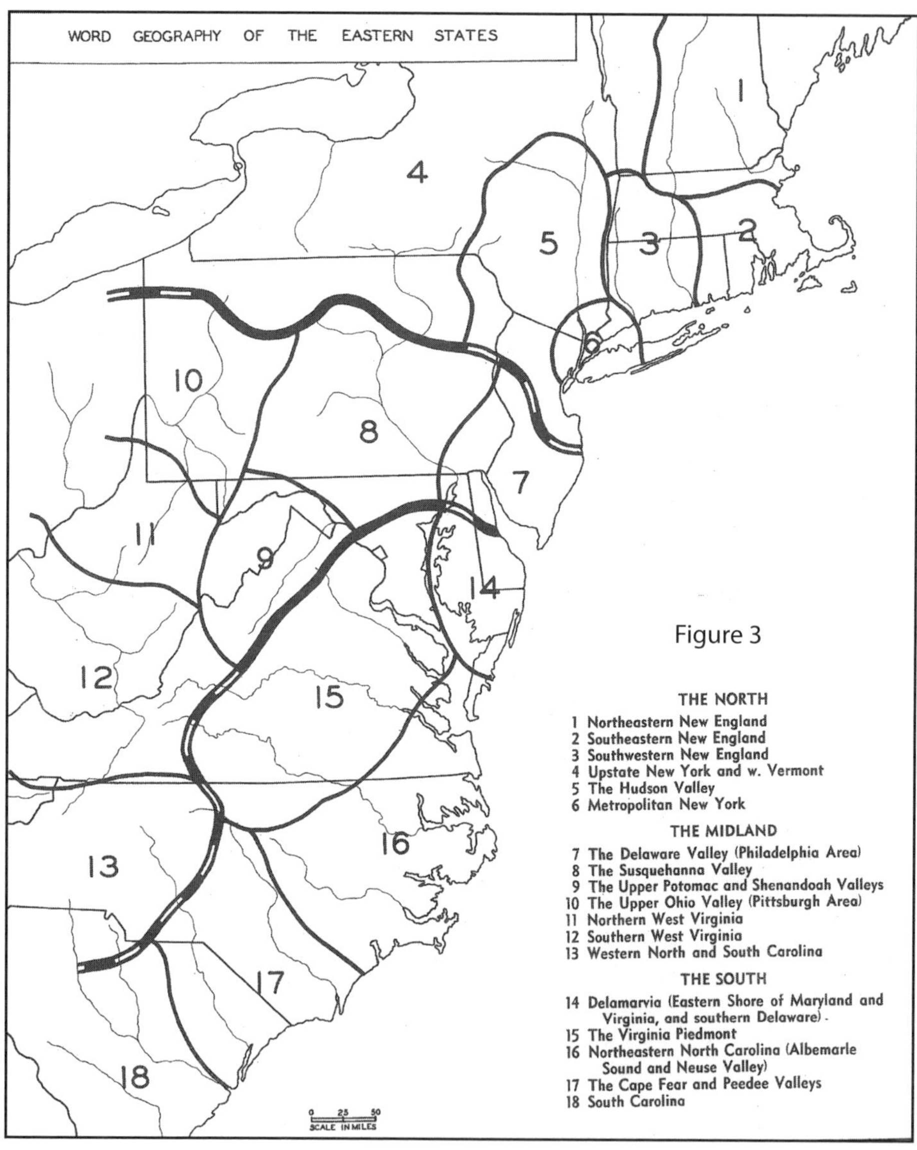

From Hans Kurath, *A Word Geography of the Eastern United States*, ©1949 by the University of Michigan Press. Reproduced by permission of the publisher.

counties of the state in order to produce a geographically representative sample of North Carolina English. Nearly 70 of the informants were born in the 1850s and 1860s, and nearly all of these resided in rural areas. Of the 155 North Carolinians interviewed for the project, fewer than 10 were under forty years old.[17] More than 70 of the informants were labeled as Type IA: "Little formal education, little reading, and restricted social contacts" and "Aged and/or regarded by the field worker as old-fashioned."[18] *WGEUS* was followed in 1953 by E. Bagby Atwood's *Survey of Verb Forms in the Eastern United States* and in 1961 by *The Pronunciation of English in the Atlantic States*, coauthored by Kurath and Raven McDavid.[19] The maps in these publications, complete with the locations of informants, make it possible to compare linguistic features found in the North Carolina Civil War letters with those collected by LAMSAS. For example, figure 114 in *WGEUS* shows occurrences of second-person plural pronouns *you all, you'ns,* and *yous* not just in North Carolina but throughout the Midland area. There are also maps indicating the overall regional distribution of North Carolina words such as *corn pone, light bread, middling meat, poke* (a bag), *roasting ear,* and *salat* (greens). The maps based on the LAMSAS field work can provide information about regional differences within North Carolina as well as what may have changed in North Carolina English between the 1860s and 1930s.

In 1985 the first volume of the *Dictionary of American Regional English* (*DARE*) was published, and with it, scholars possessed a new and, as additional volumes were produced, ever-growing resource on regional dialects.[20] In addition to more conventional lexicographic methods, which drew citations from published sources, the *DARE* project carried out fieldwork in North Carolina between 1966 and 1970, interviewing ninety informants.[21] However, the real value of *DARE* lies in its remarkably comprehensive treatment of American folk vocabulary, including words, usages, grammatical forms, and pronunciation spellings drawn from written sources going back through the eighteenth century (and occasionally the seventeenth). Linguistic atlas studies, like LAMSAS, can cover a significant number of regional words and usages, but only a comprehensive dictionary like *DARE* can cover the thousands of words, including rare and archaic forms and usages, that are likely to be encountered in nineteenth-century letters. *Dog pelter, freestone water, glant, gollop, grass nut, grass widow, ground pea, josie, jewlarker, rusty bacon,* and *sad bread* are a just few examples of the many words that appear in the North Carolina Civil War letters and for which *DARE* was able to supply essential information. Another invaluable dictionary resource is the *Dictionary of Smoky Mountain English* (*DSME*), which includes words from parts of western North Carolina.[22] The *DSME's* value is due, in part, to its in-depth regional focus, which makes it particularly useful for the study of southern dialects in general and dialects of the southern Highlands in particular. This dictionary is also concerned with the more conservative speech of the region and combines fieldwork (going back to 1937) with evidence taken from a wide variety of written sources dealing in one way or another with the language of the region.

Goals and Methods of the CACWL North Carolina Project

The primary goal of this volume is to help people better read, understand, and appreciate letters written in North Carolina during the Civil War. The collection of North Carolina words and usages contained in this glossary will hopefully provide a better sense of how North Carolinians spoke in the 1860s and what words they actually used to describe their experiences in the war. The glossary draws from only one kind of source: more than two thousand letters and diaries written during the Civil War era. As such, it can provide more information than other lexicographical resources about the currency of words and forms, especially those that have a high frequency of occurrence. For example, *you all* occurs 1,447 times in the North Carolina Civil War letters, while the other second-person plural forms of the term, *youns* and *yous,* occur only 18 and 40 times respectively. Moreover, most of the writers who use *youns* or *yous* also sometimes use *you all.*

There is no reason to assume that North Carolina English, like other American regional varieties, has not continued to evolve over the last 150 years. Words that are both common and distinctive to the state's speech today may have been uncommon or nonexistent during the 1860s. For example, among the many words used instead of *father* in the North Carolina letters, *daddy* and *dad* are the rarest and are only used by two letter writers; *pap, pappy, pa,* and *papa* are all considerably more common (*pap* occurs seventy times, *daddy* only four). On the other hand, words and usages that may have been fairly common in the 1860s have disappeared entirely over time. The word *slips* for men's underpants appears a total of eighteen times in the North Carolina letters and is used by thirteen different writers, all from the western half of the state. However, there is no reference to this word in *DARE*, in the *English Dialect Dialect Dictionary* (*EDD*), in the *Oxford English Dictionary* (*OED*), or in any other resource, even though CACWL has found examples in North Carolina and neighboring states.

As the CACWL project grows to include a comprehensive collection of linguistic features from other states and other regions of the country, the North Carolina sample will help establish a baseline for understanding how southern linguistic features migrated westward, as well as how southern dialects resembled or differed from northern dialects. *You all*, for example, was found throughout North Carolina but so far has proved rare in Civil War letters from northern states. *Youns* and *yous*, on the other hand, are found only in letters from the western half of North Carolina, but both are common in Pennsylvania Civil War letters.

The methods used for the North Carolina sample gathered for CACWL follow, at least in part, those employed in twentieth-century linguistic atlas studies. We have attempted to create a representative sample, both in terms of the number of letter-writing "informants" and in terms of geographical coverage. Besides place of residence, we also recorded essential demographic information contained in census and military records, including the age, occupation, family, and socioeconomic status of the letter writers. The basic criteria for including letters and letter writers in the sample were as follows:

1. Erratic spelling and capitalization, lack of punctuation, and nonstandard grammatical features are all clues that a letter or collection of letters may reflect a writer's speech, as are the presence of high-frequency words that reflect regional variation. Examples are the noun *a heap* (a great deal), the adverb intensifier *mighty* (very), the adverb qualifier *tolerable* (fairly, somewhat, rather), and the interjection and noun *howdy*. Nonstandard past tense forms such as *knowed, drawed, tuck* (took), *taken, seed,* and *seen* are all good indicators that letters may contain rarer forms.
2. Letter writers had to be North Carolina natives, and the county of residence, as well as other essential demographic information, needed to be determined by using the federal census of 1860, supplemented in some cases by military records.
3. Letters had to be written during the years 1861 through 1865, although if a specific collection included some letters of linguistic value written before the war (as did the Neill McGregor letter quoted above), they were included in the sample.

Finding the letters proved to be less of a challenge than one might imagine, though the search required a great deal of preparation and considerable time spent in libraries and archives examining documents. The quotes from letters contained in the work of Civil War historians and the lists of primary sources and bibliographic information contained in endnotes proved invaluable for identifying collections of potential interest.[23] Beyond that, the finding aids and online catalogue information contained in the websites of every institution visited as part of this project made it possible to compile long lists of collections to be examined. For example, the "Catalogued Collections in the Manuscript Department" of the Perkins Library at Duke at present contains 5,991 entries and is searchable.

The selection of potential collections was guided by the following criteria: First, as mentioned above, the letters had to be from the relevant time period. Second, as nearly as could be determined from catalogue descriptions, the letters had to be written by individuals who were most likely to fulfill our criteria for "vernacular" writers. Soldiers who were identified as privates and individuals who made a living by farming were sure to make the list, but that kind of detail was not always available, either at the institutions or in their online catalogues. Ultimately, it was necessary to examine large numbers of collections to find letters of linguistic interest. Collections of all sizes were examined, and since larger collections usually contained letters written by several individuals who possessed varying degrees of literacy, it was often necessary to spend time reading through very large collections in order to find a small number of relevant letters. Once preliminary lists were compiled, the archives or libraries were visited and photocopies or photographs of the letter were obtained, the letters were transcribed, proofread, and corrected twice, and citations containing significant features were extracted from the letters for inclusion in the glossary. We then searched the transcription files for quantitative analysis of selected, usually high-frequency forms (for example, verbs, pronouns, kinship terms).[24]

Scope of the Glossary and Principles of Inclusion

It is important to make it clear at the beginning what this glossary is *not*. It is definitely *not* a collection of Civil War military terminology, although there are some terms dealing with soldiering and the war. Their inclusion in this glossary is intended to illustrate how they were actually used by soldiers during the war. The entry for the common word *ration*, for example, is included primarily for the many variant forms soldiers used in their letters (for example, *rashing*). The same is true for the many variant forms of *skirmish* and *cavalry* (for example, *scrumish* and *calvary*). The familiar noun *fight* and the verb *whip* are included because they represent characteristic nineteenth-century usages. Inclusion in the glossary is entirely limited to words, usages, and grammatical features found in the more than twenty-two hundred letters of the North Carolina sample. Criteria for inclusion are as follows:

1. The word, usage, or grammatical form has regional significance as determined by reference to established dictionary sources, especially the *Dictionary of American Regional English*, the *Dictionary of Smoky Mountain English*, the *Oxford English Dictionary*,[25] or the *English Dialect Dictionary*.[26] Examples of these include *roasting* ear (sweet corn), the conjunction *against* (before, by the time), and the adjective *smart* (well behaved, hard working). Not surprisingly, most of the words in this glossary that also are included in *DARE* are identified as belonging to South and/or South Midland dialect areas, which include, respectively, the eastern and western halves of North Carolina.
2. The word, usage, or grammatical form is characteristic of earlier English and may currently be uncommon, archaic, or obsolete. The word or usage may have been common in earlier, especially nineteenth-century, American English regardless of region or it may have been limited to a particular region of the country. Examples of this kind include *without* (unless), *shant* (won't), and *tapister* (a peddlar).
3. The word, usage, or grammatical form is not found in any of the authoritative dictionary resources, but the context suggests that the occurrence is an authentic linguistic feature. Typically, such a word or form must have multiple occurrences to be included in the glossary. Examples of this kind include *slips* for a pair of men's underpants, *necklace* for a knitted scarf, and the expression *all to,* meaning *except for.*
4. The frequency, or relative infrequency, of a word in comparison with contemporary regional American English merits the word's inclusion in the glossary. The term *daddy,* mentioned above, is an example of this.
5. The word is of special significance because it illustrates the experiences of soldiers during the Civil War. The word *box* falls into this category. What were these boxes like? How were they shipped? What kinds of items did soldiers request? (Common items included pies, cakes, bread of various kinds, butter, molasses, honey, chicken, sausage, ham, whiskey or brandy, fresh or preserved fruit and vegetables, or anything else to supplement a meager diet and the monotony of rations issued to the soldiers.)

Limitations and Utility of the Glossary

No book of this kind can capture more than a fraction of the total vocabulary, since the limitations of the documentary evidence are simply too great and we can only report what we find in the letters we have located and transcribed. However, this glossary is based on a collection of North Carolina letters that amounts to more than a million words and five years of work. Certainly, they contain plenty of rare, obscure, or obsolete words and usages, including some not found in either of the two most comprehensive dictionary resources available, the *OED* and *DARE*. Beyond these lexical rarities, this volume represents a comprehensive list of the most common words and usages in 1860s North Carolina, along with citations extracted from the letters to illustrate how the words were used. The glossary, which makes up the bulk of this volume, contains nearly twelve hundred entries, a collection not quite extensive enough to be called a dictionary. It is also not a glossary in the conventional sense, in that the meanings of many of the words may be transparent to the reader. The word *box*, mentioned above, is not going to be a source of confusion for most readers, but the citations supply information about the kinds of things boxes contained and what these things meant to the soldiers to whom they were shipped. Even for words that are in common use today, the meanings may have shifted in ways that create misunderstandings. For example, the adjective *smart* for North Carolinians and other Southerners in the 1860s did not mean "intelligent, bright" or "fashionably dressed." Applied to children it generally meant "helpful, obedient, well behaved" (*be smart children and mind your mother till pap gets home*). Applied to adults, it generally meant "productive, hard working." The Southern and South Midland *smart* also contrasts with the common New England usage of *smart*: "healthy, well, recovered from an illness or injury." Battles (most commonly called *fights*) did not usually *start* or *begin*; they *commenced*. If a person *started* a letter it meant it had been mailed. The glossary, therefore, is intended to be a record of usage as well as a record of common grammatical forms and significant variant spellings. Perhaps most important are the quotations found in the glossary. These quotations provide the best record of what it was like to be alive during the Civil War, whether as a soldier far from home or a family member on the homefront dealing with the challenges the war created.

Finally, as conversational as the letters often seem, it would be a mistake to consider the evidence they contain as representing the actual speech of North Carolinians in the 1860s. As a medium, letters impose limitations beyond their formulaic salutations and closings. Prewar letters typically contain news about the weather, the productivity of crops, the litany of prices for essential commodities, and the recitation of births, marriages, and deaths. Wartime letters take on different themes: long-term and enforced separation of husbands from wives and children, deprivation of a kind never experienced before, death from disease and battle, war weariness, conscription, desertion, and execution. The grammar might be the same, but the war brought some changes to the vocabulary, and the circumstances under which letter writers lived controlled, to a large extent, the kinds of things they wrote about and the *hard times* they endured.

A Note on Method

The editorial method employed in this book has been to preserve the original capitalization, spelling, and grammatical forms of the letters. Although the majority of the North Carolina Civil War letters have little or no punctuation, we have silently inserted a minimal amount of punctuation to aid the reader. Word division in the letters has also been preserved as long as these do not interfere with readability. Missing letters and words are provided, when necessary, in square brackets. Translations of difficult words have been added in square brackets following the equal sign.

NOTES

1. Neill McGregor to A. A. Jackson of Moore County, N.C., June 13, 1852, Jackson Family Corr., Notre Dame.

2. Duane Meyer, *The Highland Scots of North Carolina, 1732–1776* (Chapel Hill: Univ. of North Carolina Press, 1961), 102, 117–119. A search of some of the most common Highland Scots surnames (for example, McLeod, McGregor, McDonald, Campbell, McNeill, McLean, and Morrison) in the federal census of 1860 for North Carolina located more than seventy individuals who were born in Scotland, some as young as thirty years old. Obviously, immigration of Highlanders to North Carolina continued well into the antebellum period. The only foreign-born letter writer included in the North Carolina sample is Anguish (Angus) Darroch, who was born in Argyll about 1835. Individuals in the 1860 census who were born in Scotland resided mainly in the counties of Moore, Harnett, Cumberland, Richmond, and Robeson.

3. Guion Griffis Johnson, *Ante-Bellum North Carolina: A Social History* (Chapel Hill: Univ. of North Carolina Press, 1937), 4–14; Harry Roy Merrens, *Colonial North Carolina in the Eighteenth Century* (Chapel Hill: Univ. of North Carolina Press, 1964), 53–81; H. Tyler Blethen and Curtis W. Wood Jr., "Scotch-Irish Frontier Society in Southwestern North Carolina," in *Ulster and North America, Transatlantic Perspectives on the Scotch-Irish*, ed. H. Tyler Blethen and Curtis W. Wood (Tuscaloosa: Univ. of Alabama Press, 1997), 213–226.

4. For a good introduction to the Scots-Irish and English influences on the dialects of the region, see Michael B. Montgomery, "The Scotch-Irish Influence on Appalachian English: How Broad? How Deep?" in *Ulster and North America: Transatlantic Perspectives on the Scotch-Irish*, ed. H. Tyler Blethen and Curtis W. Wood (Tuscaloosa: Univ. of Alabama Press, 1997), 189–212. For a comprehensive treatment of Scots-Irish features in American English, see Michael B. Montgomery, *From Ulster to America: The Scotch-Irish Heritage of American English* (Belfast: Ulster Historical Foundation, 2006).

5. Gotthardt D. Bernheim, *History of the German Settlements and the Lutheran Church in North and South Carolina* (Philadelphia: Lutheran Book Store, 1872), 148. Bernheim writes about the close contact and "friendly terms" between the Scots-Irish and Germans, both in

Pennsylvania and, later after both groups had migrated southward, into the western parts of North Carolina (151–152). A search of more than one hundred German surnames (including anglicized forms) in the 1860 census for North Carolina located only five individuals who were born in Pennsylvania, and the youngest of these was sixty-eight years old. This suggests that, unlike the migration of Highland Scots, new migration of Pennsylvania Germans to North Carolina decreased significantly by the early nineteenth century.

6. A particularly influential model for new dialect formation is that developed by Peter Trudgill in *Dialects in Contact* (Oxford: Blackwell, 1986) and, more recently, *New-Dialect Formation: The Inevitability of Colonial Englishes* (Oxford: Oxford Univ. Press, 2004).

7. Norman E. Eliason, *Tarheel Talk: An Historical Study of the English Language in North Carolina to 1860* (Chapel Hill: Univ. of North Carolina Press, 1956).

8. Raven I. McDavid Jr. and Raymond K. O'Cain, *Linguistic Atlas of the Middle and South Atlantic States*, fascicle 1 (Chicago: Univ. of Chicago Press, 1980); for more information about LAMSAS, visit the website at the University of Georgia, http://us.english.uga.edu/.

9. William S. Powell and Jay Mazzocchi, eds., *Encyclopedia of North Carolina* (Chapel Hill: Univ. of North Carolina Press, 2006), 235–236.

10. Published sources include Joe M. Hatley and Linda B. Hufman, eds., *Letters of William F. Wagner, Confederate Soldier* (Wendell, N.C.: Broadfoot's Bookmark, 1983); H. Douglas Pitts, ed., *Letters of a Gaston Ranger* (Richmond: Museum of the Confederacy, 1991); Ira Berlin, Joseph P. Reidy, and Leslie S. Rowland, eds., *Freedom: A Documentary History of Emancipation, 1861–1867*, ser. 2, *The Black Military Experience* (Cambridge: Cambridge Univ. Press, 1982); Ira Berlin, Steven F. Miller, Joseph P. Reidy, and Leslie S. Rowland, eds., *Freedom: A Documentary History of Emancipation, 1861–1867*, ser. 1, vol. 2, *The Wartime Genesis of Free Labor in the Upper South* (Cambridge: Cambridge Univ. Press, 1993); William Whatley Pierson Jr., *The Diary of Bartlett Yancy Malone*, James Sprunt Historical Publications, vol. 16, no. 2 (Chapel Hill: Univ. of North Carolina, 1919).

11. The sample includes 217 transcriptions of letters sent to Governor Zebulon B. Vance from November 1862 through October 1863. Of this number, 209 were written by individuals who wrote only one letter.

12. One of the six white Union soldiers had deserted from the Twenty-ninth North Carolina Infantry before enlisting in the Thirteenth Tennessee Cavalry (Union). The other five were East Carolina Unionists (known as "Buffalos") who enlisted in the First or Second North Carolina Infantry Regiments (Union). There were an additional three Confederate soldiers who were captured and later became "galvanized yankees" by swearing allegiance to the United States and enlisting in regular U.S. Army units for service on the western frontier. Lucinda Tweed of Madison County wrote to Governor Vance in December 1862 requesting a "pasport" to join her husband and oldest son in Kentucky, where they had enlisted in the First Tennessee Cavalry (Union). Another son enlisted in the Second North Carolina Mounted Infantry (Union).

13. Historical Census Browser, 2004, University of Virginia, Geospatial and Statistical Data Center, http://mapserver.lib.virginia.edu/collections/ (accessed Feb. 8, 2012). The North Carolina sample includes African American soldiers who served in the Thirty-fifth, Thirty-sixth, and Thirty-seventh U.S. Colored Infantry Regiments, regiments that consisted primarily of soldiers who were former slaves recruited in the eastern counties of North Carolina. The source for the texts of these letters is Berlin, Reidy, and Rowland, *Freedom*, ser. 2. For a description of the recruitment and service of these four regiments, see Richard M. Reid, *Freedom for Themselves: North Carolina's Black Soldiers in the Civil War Era* (Chapel Hill: Univ. of North Carolina Press, 2008).

14. William Holland Thomas recruited four companies of Cherokees to serve in his composite unit of infantry, cavalry, and light artillery, called a "legion" because it was somewhat larger than a regiment. The 1860 census records 1,158 "Indians," the largest number (1,062) residing in Jackson County, with much smaller numbers recorded for Macon and Cherokee counties. Historical Census Browser, 2004 (accessed Feb. 8, 2012). For treatments of Thomas and his legion, see Vernon H. Crow, *Storm in the Mountains: Thomas' Confederate Legion of Cherokee Indians and Mountaineers* (Cherokee, N.C.: Press of the Museum of the Cherokee Indian, 1982); and E. Stanly Godbold Jr. and Mattie U. Russell, *Confederate Colonel and Cherokee Chief* (Knoxville: Univ. of Tennessee Press, 1990).

15. No other county, however, can quite approach Catawba in terms of the number of letters and letter writers. Catawba County, on the western edge of the Piedmont, is represented by fifteen different family collections, fifty-five letter writers, thirty-seven different surnames, and a total of 405 letters.

16. Hans Kurath, *A Word Geography of the Eastern United States* (Ann Arbor: Univ. of Michigan Press, 1949), 27–49. For detailed treatment of dialect areas in the United States, see also Craig M. Carver, *American Regional Dialects: A Word Geography* (Ann Arbor: Univ. of Michigan Press). The term "Upper South" is often used by cultural and linguistic geographers as an alternative to "South Midland."

17. McDavid and O'Cain, *Linguistic Atlas*, 10–11; see also the University of Georgia website.

18. McDavid and O'Cain, *Linguistic Atlas*, 6.

19. In addition to Kurath's *Word Geography of the Eastern United States*, these publications include E. Bagby Atwood, *A Survey of Verb Forms in the Eastern United States* (Ann Arbor: Univ. of Michigan Press, 1953) and Hans Kurath and Raven McDavid, *Pronunciation of English in the Atlantic States* (Ann Arbor: Univ. of Michigan Press, 1961).

20. Frederick G. Cassidy and John H. Hall, eds., *Dictionary of American Regional English*, 5 vols. (Cambridge: Harvard-Belknap, 1985–2012). It is fortunate that volume 5 of *DARE* became available before the North Carolina project was completed.

21. *DARE* 1:cxxv–cxxvi, cxlix.

22. Michael B. Montgomery and Joseph S. Hall, *Dictionary of Smoky Mountain English* (Knoxville: Univ. of Tennessee Press, 2004). The linguistic study of North Carolina English is extensive, as a review of past issues of *American Speech*, the journal of the American Dialect Society, will attest.

23. Among the first works we consulted were the two volumes of Christopher Watford's *The Civil War in North Carolina: Soldiers' and Civilians' Letters and Diaries, 1861–1865*, vol. 1, *The Piedmont* (Jefferson, N.C.: McFarland, 2003), and vol. 2, *The Mountains* (Jefferson, N.C.: McFarland, 2003). Watford's books, which feature transcriptions of letters, led us to a number of collections in North Carolina archives. Among other works that led us to collections of North Carolina letters were Reid Mitchell's *Civil War Soldiers* (New York: Viking, 1988); James M. McPherson's *For Cause and Comrades: Why Men Fought in the Civil War* (New York: Oxford Univ. Press, 1997); and J. Tracy Power's *Lee's Miserables: Life in the Army of Northern Virginia from the Wilderness to Appomattox* (Chapel Hill: Univ. of North Carolina Press, 1998).

24. Transcription of the North Carolina letters was carried out by me and by my students at Missouri State University. Work began in December 2007 and January 2008 with photocopies of the Councill and Reese collections obtained from Duke University. The volume of North Carolina transcriptions increased significantly after my December 2009 trip to North Carolina and continued through January 2012.

25. For this project the online version of the *Oxford English Dictionary* was used (available through the Missouri State University, Meyer Library website).

26. Joseph Wright, ed., *English Dialect Dictionary*, 6 vols. (London: Frowde, 1898–1905).

The Social Background

Establishing the county of residence for each of the North Carolina letter writers was important because of this study's geographic dimensions. However, in order to correlate social factors with language use, it was also important to record other kinds of demographic information, beginning with age, occupation, and socioeconomic status. In the 1860 federal census, the place of birth is typically recorded as a state, but sometimes a specific county within the state is listed, and in cases of immigrants, the country in which they were born is noted. With very few exceptions, the letter writers were natives of North Carolina. Two elderly people were born in Virginia; Harnett County overseer Anguish (Angus) Darroch was born in Scotland. In addition to basic information, the 1860 census also lists each family member who lived in the household (with name, age, gender, and place of birth), the value (in dollars) of real estate and personal estate owned by the head of household, as well as the education and literacy of family members.[1]

There are, however, several challenges in working with the census, beginning with the spelling of surnames. How writers spelled their names frequently differed from how those names were recorded in the census or in military records. For example, the surname of the Bleckley family of Catawba County is spelled Blakely in the 1860 census, and the surname of Marcus Hefner, also of Catawba County, is recorded as Huffman. This situation often requires searching under a variety of alternative spellings in order to locate an individual or a family in the census. It is also helpful to know the names of wives and children in order to confirm the identities of soldiers.

The majority of unmarried males in 1860 were living in the households of their parents and can only be located by finding the record for the head of the household, typically the father but occasionally a widowed mother. Half of the North Carolina soldiers who were located in the census of 1860 lived in the households of their parents, and often the full names of parents are not given in soldiers' letters. Fortunately, letter writers regularly headed a letter with both the date and the place where the letter was written, and in collections which include letters by family members at home, names of family members and places of residence can be determined from this evidence.

Further, soldiers often identified their companies and regiments in the heading of their letters or at the end of letters in directions to the folks at home about how to address or *back* their letters. The county of residence, as well as the age and occupation of soldiers, was also generally recorded in military service records, and these can be found in *North Carolina Troops, 1861–1865: A Roster*, an invaluable resource for tracking down information about soldiers.[2] Besides census and military records, finding essential information about letter writers requires consultation with a variety of other resources and not a little detective work of the kind genealogists, no doubt, know well.[3]

Occupations and Socioeconomic Status

A total of 241 of the North Carolina soldiers in the sample have been identified in the federal census of 1860, and from these census records we can obtain some basic insight into who these people were, how they made a living, whether they were married and had children, and their socioeconomic status (see Appendix B). Among occupations listed in the 1860 census, farming was by far the most common, with over two hundred heads of households listed as a farmer, farm laborer, laborer, or farm hand. There were also six millers, four carpenters, three blacksmiths, three turpentine distillers, two millwrights, two coopers, two house carpenters, and two overseers. Additional occupations included a carriage maker, a mechanic, a miner, a harness maker, a tailor, a painter, a shoemaker, a school teacher, a Methodist minister, and a dentist. It is an overwhelmingly rural sample, with the majority of individuals dependant, directly or indirectly, on farming. Although his occupation was listed as "miller" in the 1860 census, the letters that Buncombe County native John W. Reese wrote home to his wife make it clear that the family also supported themselves by raising corn, livestock, and garden produce on their small patch of rented or loaned land. Part-time school teacher Alfred N. Proffit also worked on the family's Wilkes County farm. Others listed in the 1860 census as farmers supplemented their income by working as artisans. John Peterson of Catawba County, besides farming, worked as a gunsmith, and fellow Catawba Countian Isaac Lefevers operated a pottery shop in addition to farming. In other words, the letters themselves provide more information about how individuals made a living than the census of 1860 can. Of the 241 soldiers listed in the 1860 census, just over half (121) were not heads of households, and these were mostly sons in their teens or early twenties living in the households of their parents (the youngest was eleven-year-old Carr Setzer; the oldest was thirty-five-year-old F. A. Bleckley). In an age in which unmarried males generally remained in their parents' households, a total of 56 of the 121 were twenty years old or older in 1860. Of the 120 soldiers listed as heads of households, 95 were married and 82 of these were fathers.

The soldiers in the sample can be divided into two broad groups: those who owned land and those who did not. Yeoman farmers, those who owned the land they farmed, represent the largest group and make up about two-thirds of the 241 soldiers listed in the census (this includes sons living in household of a landowning parent). However, the value of the real estate reported in the census varies considerably from farmer to farmer. Wilkes County farmer William Walsh occupies the bottom of the list with land valued at only ten dollars, and four others owned real estate valued at less than one hundred dollars. At the other end of the scale is Cherokee County farmer and slaveholder Stephen Whitaker, whose land was valued at ten thousand dollars and whose personal property (including slaves) was worth another ten thousand dollars. Whitaker was one of just four whose real estate was valued at more than five thousand dollars. An additional nine soldiers owned land but had occupations listed that were other than farming. In all, the number of soldiers owning land or residing in landowning households totals 169:

Value of Real Estate	Households
Less than $100	5
$100–499	42
$500–999	33
$1,000–5,000	85
Over $5,000	4
Total	169

The personal property of these yeoman farmers and other landowners also varied widely, from the ten who reported less than one hundred dollars in personal estate (four reported no personal estate) to one who lived in a household reporting more than twenty-five thousand dollars. No attempt has been made to determine how many of the soldiers in the North Carolina sample were slave owners or came from slaveholding families, although some writers make specific reference to slaves they or their families owned. However, since the value of slaves was included in personal property, only those at the higher end of the list, such as Henry Bowen of Washington County and Stephen Whitaker of Cherokee County, were likely to be slaveholders. Washington County farmer Henry Bowen possessed $2,000 in real estate and $5,470 in personal estate (including slaves). Job Cobb of Edgecombe County lived in a household which listed $11,700 in real estate and $26,250 in personal estate (including slaves). The following is a list of the personal property of landowning soldiers and the personal property of heads of households whose households included soldiers:

Personal Estate	Households
Less than $100	10
$100–499	63
$500–999	46
$1,000–5,000	37
Over $5,000	13
Total	169

Landless farmers, farm laborers, and others who owned no real estate make up about 30 percent of the 241 soldiers. Of these, 31 owned less than one hundred dollars in personal property, and another 33 reported personal property valued at between one hundred and five hundred dollars.[4] While most of these were landless farmers with personal property amounting to $500 or less, there were exceptions, including Macon County dentist and slaveholder Alfred W. Bell, who reported $3,090 in personal property but no real estate in 1860. Since many of the landless soldiers were farmers by occupation, we may assume they were tenant farmers who either rented their farmland or were employed by landowners for wages or for a share of the farm's produce. The following list indicates the personal property reported by those who owned no real estate:

Personal Estate	Households
Less than $100	31
$100–499	33
$500–999	2
$1,000–5,000	5
Over $5,000	1
Total	72

To put some kind of perspective to these figures, one of the soldiers in the list, John Whitfield, was employed as an overseer in Warren County and reported no estate, either real or personal. One of his neighbors, listed on the same page in the 1860 census, had one hundred thousand dollars in real estate and six hundred thousand dollars in personal estate. Other neighbors were similarly wealthy, and no doubt Whitfield was employed by one of them. While it is difficult to make generalizations about all the soldiers on the list, it is clear that the majority lived in rural areas and made their livings from agriculture. Several of these were at the bottom of the socioeconomic order, though most owned the farms on which they worked and could list at least some personal property in the form of livestock, tools, provisions, and household goods.[5]

Service Records

Among the Confederate soldiers in the North Carolina sample, the median age at the time of enlistment was twenty-six. The oldest soldier on the list is William Newell of McDowell County, who was fifty-one when he enlisted in September 1861. The youngest soldier was John Boyett of Duplin County, who was fifteen when he enlisted in March 1862. James K. P. Shipman of Buncombe County and William C. Featherston of Henderson County both enlisted in May 1861 at age sixteen. Featherston was discharged in July 1862 for being underage but reenlisted in October 1863 and was wounded at Drewry's Bluff in May 1864. "Polk" Shipman was captured in September 1863 and confined at Point Lookout, Maryland, where he died on October 22, 1864, at the age of nineteen. Among civilian letter writers in the North Carolina sample, the oldest were born before 1790, the youngest around 1850.[6]

The enlistment dates for 302 of the 354 Confederate soldiers serving in North Carolina units are listed in the *North Carolina Troops* volumes (this is a different, larger group than that used in the "Occupations and Socioeconomic Status" section above, which is based on the 1860 census). Of the 302 soldiers, 125 enlisted in 1861, 154 in 1862, and 23 in 1863 or 1864.[7] Their service records indicate that forty-eight were killed on the battlefield or died of wounds. Another fifty died of disease, including seventeen who perished while prisoners of war at Point Lookout, Maryland; Elmira, New York; or Camp Douglas, Illinois. One soldier died in a railroad accident. Twenty-six soldiers deserted, and several of these later returned to their units. Two of the letter writers, John Futch and Job Redmond, were executed for desertion. In all, 101 of the 354 soldiers (about 29 percent) did not survive the war.[8]

Companies within a regiment were typically recruited in a single county, and soldiers who avoided enlistment ran the risk of being conscripted into a company or regiment from a different county or a different part of the state (in which case they would be serving with strangers). The papers of Governor Zebulon B. Vance contain numerous requests for transfers by soldiers who were in just such a predicament:

> I have bin in Survice 12 Months the 15 of this Month. I am A conscript. the Regt I have bin in is the 21 Regt Co G. I noed no body in the 21 Regt when I was sent to it. I have got one Brother in the 17 Regt Co K. the Capt in Co K wants me and if you pleas let me go to Capt Wiswall Co K. I am not vary far from the Regt at this time.[9]

Intha McCraw of Polk County wrote Governor Vance on behalf of her son, James, in an attempt to have him transferred to a regiment where he could serve with his brothers:

> I hope you will send orders to let him go to were he volenteerd at. if you do I would be glad if he could come by home to get his Clothes. I would of rote sooner but I keep thinking the war would stop but I have got out heart so I humbly hope you will grant my petition an send him to the Company whare his brothers an friends is. he is in the 50the regt NC troops in Care of Captin Ford an wants to go to the sixty fourth regt in Care of Captin Jones.[10]

The ties of kinship within a military unit reflected the complex social networks to which soldiers belonged. Since companies were typically raised in a single county, in some ways the social structure of the company was a reflection of the home community. Brothers and cousins often enlisted together, and the mess to which one belonged was usually made up of individuals from the neighborhood. County and community solidarity could and often did outweigh all other factors:

> we Elected a new Lieutenant last Thursday. we elected Hector McEachern. orderly [sergeant] Boon run but Hector beet him be cause Hector was a Robeson [County] man and orderly Boon was a cumberland man. if Boon had bin a Robeson man he would beet Hector but the Robeson boys woundt Elect a cumberland [County] man.[11]

The North Carolina letter collections contain numerous examples in which several family members served in the same regiment, usually in the same company. Brothers Thornton and Marion Sexton of Ashe County both served as privates in Company A, Thirty-seventh North Carolina Infantry; brothers Charley and John Futch of New Hanover County both served as privates in Company K, Third North Carolina Infantry; brothers Alfred N. and Andrew J. Proffit of Wilkes County served as privates in Company D, Eighteenth North Carolina Infantry; brothers Thomas, Elbert, Wyett, and James Carpenter of Chatham County served in Company D, Sixty-first North Carolina Infantry; Kinchin, Joseph, James, and Jonathan Coghill of Granville County served in Company G, Twenty-third North Carolina Infantry; and William H. Brotherton served in Company K, Twenty-third North Carolina Infantry with several of his Howard and Allen cousins from Lincoln County. A sense of community is often strongly reflected in the letters, as letter writers regularly provided information to the folks at home about the health and well-being of relatives and neighbors serving with them in the same unit. Letters became means of relaying news beyond the immediate family, whether it was a soldier sending *howdy* or making a request through the medium of another soldier's letter, or the folks at home sending news or greetings to a larger audience consisting of more than soldier in camp. Letters were routinely read aloud and the news they contained shared with members of the extended family, with in-laws, and with neighbors:

> Dear wife I take the oppoituny of writing you a few lins to in form you that I am well at this time and I hope this Letter May find you and your Letter Sharers all well.[12]

Education and Literacy in Antebellum North Carolina

There is no way to state with any certainty how many North Carolina soldiers and their family members were literate in 1861, other than to say that the percentages were probably larger than many have assumed. The term "literate" is rather vague and did not necessarily mean the same then as now. In *For Cause and Comrades*, James M. McPherson notes that "Civil War armies were the most literate in history to that time. More than 90 percent of white Union soldiers and more than 80 percent of Confederate soldiers were literate, and most of them wrote frequent letters to families and friends."[13]

The federal census of 1860 indicates whether members of a household could read and write, as well as whether individuals in a household had attended school in the previous year. The North Carolina Education Act of 1839 certainly provided a boost for public education, as did the establishment in 1852 of a state superintendent of common schools. Guion Griffis Johnson credits Greensboro lawyer Calvin H. Wiley, who held the office of superintendent from 1853 through 1865, with revolutionizing the public school system in North Carolina. In the decade before the beginning of the war there was a steady increase in the number of schools and school districts, of children attending school, and of licensed teachers.[14] This surely must have had an impact on literacy rates among soldiers and their families, although for many of limited economic means, educational opportunities remained limited. Moreover, educational reform came too late to benefit many older soldiers. For most African Americans, free or slave, educational opportunities were nonexistent, and laws existed during the antebellum period which prohibited their education.[15] This injunction, however, must have been ignored by some slaveholding families, since the North Carolina sample includes letters written before and during the war by slaves to their masters. One of the most remarkable, and most literate among all the letters in the sample, is one written by Washington Wills, a slave in the household of William H. Wills, a Methodist minister in Halifax County. In a condolence letter to the family, Washington Wills writes about the death of son and brother Lt. George W. Wills, who was killed in September 1864 at the Third Battle of Winchester:

> the day before he was killed, he shaved up nicely, looked so promising for life, as likely to live as any body else. Was very busy the week before he was killed, on monday, he settle up any debt he owed any one in the Regt. I reckon you understand how the battle was at the time he was killed. our army was falling back. he was walking up and down the line laughing and smiling. it seems that all fear had been banished from him. through all I am glad to tell you his coat was buttoned up in the prettiest style of uniform and in his breast pocket was his little Testament.[16]

Presumably Washington Wills received his education from the Wills family. However, whether altruistic or practical motives account for his literacy there is no doubt that he and they were aware of his social position. He was a servant to George Wills and consistently addresses or refers to members of the Wills family as "Master."

Education and levels of literacy vary widely among the letter writers and are no doubt tied to an individual's socioeconomic status and occupation. A few, such as Macon County dentist Alfred Bell, who served as a captain in the Sixtieth North Carolina Infantry, are fairly literate, but even Bell's letters to his wife reveal evidence about his spoken language. However, a considerably larger proportion of letter writers, and those of the greatest linguistic interest, represent the "strata of Southern society" described by Bell Wiley:

> It is a significant fact that during the Confederacy a large portion of the middle and lower strata of Southern society became articulate for the first time. Certainly from no other source can so much first-hand information be obtained of the character and thought patterns of that underprivileged part of Southern society often loosely called "poor whites."[17]

Nevertheless, a large percentage, including yeoman farmers and landowning artisans, among the letter writers would not be considered "poor whites." What is also apparent in the letters is that by the 1860s, although literacy was not quite taken for granted, it was assumed by most North Carolinians in the sample that literacy was becoming an economic and social necessity. Even soldiers belonging to landless families or families on the lower end of the socioeconomic scale still managed to attend school and acquire the ability to read and write. Indeed, many individuals took advantage of what educational opportunities existed regardless of age. Forty-two of the 241 soldiers in the 1860 census are listed as having attended school in the previous year, and of these 8 were age twenty or older (William A. Carter of Chatham County was twenty-seven). Several others were eighteen or nineteen. According to the census, forty-five-year-old Margaret Holder of Randolph County attended school the previous year, along with her thirty-year-old son and her twenty-year-old daughter.[18]

Many soldiers were aware of their limitations as writers, commenting on and apologizing for their "badly wrote" and "porely spelt" letters, but that did not stop most from making the effort. Some soldiers, however, either could not write or lacked so much confidence in their writing skills that they had others write letters for them. Most of the time, this practice worked reasonably well, but having others write letters could pose problems, as William Pickney Cline of Catawba County discovered after receiving a troubling letter from his wife, Mary, to which he responded:

> you rit to me like you diden Care mch A bote mey. i didnot rite them lise to you i will rite my one [= own] leters my self after this. i dont now What the[y] put in my leter. if you get mad fore that i cannot hep that . . . the boys had rote nasty leter for mey. after dis i will rite my one leters. i rote dis leter my self.[19]

Like many other soldiers who were insecure about their writing abilities, Cline recognized his limitations as a writer but was determined to write his own letters in the future, if for no other reason than to avoid the kind of prank that had been played on him.[20] Cline was not the only soldier in the sample who lacked confidence in his writing skills and dictated some of his letters to more literate comrades serving in the same company. The questions of authorship, location, and language are important to consider, and our basic assumption has been that soldiers generally served with others from the same community and would have shared the same dialect. Some soldiers learned to read and write while in the army or practiced their penmanship and perfected their spelling enough that they felt confident that their writing was readable:

> our chaplin does not suite the men but I think he is doing all he can. he has just got back from richmond and is going to teach the men in the regiment. he gives them choice to study all branches from the alphabet up. he laid in spelling books grammer & paper. he says he thinks he can do some good and can learn them to read & write.[21]

Despite the often difficult conditions under which soldiers wrote their letters, despite the poor quality and scarcity of writing material, and most of all, despite their lack of education and experience writing letters, soldiers felt compelled to become regular correspondents.

NOTES

1. The census of 1850 and the census of 1870 were also consulted on occasion, especially in cases in which a letter writer could not be located in the 1860 census. Besides problems with the spelling of names, the ages recorded by enumerators should be considered only approximate. This is especially true among older letter writers. For example, Isaac Miller of Davidson County claimed to be eighty-eight in a letter he wrote to Governor Vance in 1863, although the 1860 census records his age as seventy-five. The 1860 census records whether or not each family member attended school in the previous year and whether or not each family member could read and write. County of residence in this study was based on where individuals were living at the time of the 1860 census. Isaac Lefevers, for example, was born and raised in northern Lincoln County, but in 1860 he resided in neighboring Catawba.

2. Louis H. Manarin and Weymouth T. Jordon Jr., *North Carolina Troops, 1861–1865: A Roster,* 18 vols. (Raleigh: North Carolina Department of Archives and History, 1966–2011). I was very fortunate to have access to this series in the research library at Wilsons Creek National Battlefield. Information about soldiers in *North Carolina Troops* generally includes the date of enlistment, age at time of enlistment, as well as information about when and where a soldier was wounded, captured, confined, released, and/or exchanged, killed, died of disease, or deserted.

3. The National Park Service's online Civil War Soldiers and Sailors system is another invaluable resource for tracking down soldiers and their units and confirming the spelling of the names of comrades mentioned in soldiers' letters. The regiment and unit summaries included in the website also contain information about counties in which individual regiments were recruited as well as information about battles in which these regiments were engaged, places they located during the war, and names of field officers. For identifying place names in North Carolina, *The North Carolina Gazetteer: A Dictionary of Tar Heel Places and Their History,* 2nd ed., ed. William S. Powell and Michael Hill (Chapel Hill: Univ. of North Carolina Press, 2010), has been among my constant companions for the North Carolina project. Another useful resource for background information is the *Encyclopedia of North Carolina,* edited by William S. Powell and Jay Mazzocchi (Chapel Hill: Univ. of North Carolina Press, 2006).

4. Two of the more prolific letter writers among the soldiers were John W. Reece of Buncombe County and Francis M. Poteet of McDowell County. Both were married and had children, and both reported no real estate or personal property in the 1860 census.

5. For detailed treatments of the socioeconomic background, see, for example, Bill Cecil-Fronsman, *Common Whites: Class and Culture in Antebellum North Carolina* (Lexington: Univ. Press of Kentucky, 1992); Charles C. Bolton, *Poor Whites of the Antebellum South: Tenants and Laborers in Central North Carolina and Northeast Mississippi* (Durham, N.C.: Duke Univ. Press, 1994); and Martin Crawford, *Ashe County's Civil War: Community and Society in the Appalachian South* (Charlottesville: Univ. Press of Virginia, 2001). Also of interest for western North Carolina, before and during the war, are John C. Inscoe, *Mountain Masters: Slavery and the Sectional Crisis in Western North Carolina* (Knoxville: Univ. of Tennessee Press, 1989); and John C. Inscoe and Gordon B. McKinney, *The Heart of Confederate Appalachia: Western North Car zolina in the Civil War* (Chapel Hill: Univ. of North Carolina Press, 2000).

6. Martha Phelps of Brunswick County was born about 1785, Jemima Thomas of Iredell County was born about 1790, Pleasant Black of Rockingham County was born about 1792. The age of Elizabeth Nance of Randolph County is recorded in the 1860 census as ninety, but in a January 1863 letter to Governor Vance she states that her age is "about 70."

7. Many of those who enlisted in 1863 or 1864 only reached military age later in the war. Charles A. Walker of Cherokee County, for example, was an enthusiastic recruit when he joined William Holland Thomas's legion on January 1, 1864, shortly after his seventeenth birthday.

8. Among the North Carolina soldiers serving in the Union army who are included in the sample, the only known death is Alfred E. Cowand of Bertie County, who served in Company B, Second North Carolina Infantry (Union). Cowand was taken prisoner at the Battle of Plymouth in April 1864 and later died at Andersonville. Alfred Cowand's Bertie County cousin, Joseph J. Cowand,

served in the Confederate army, in Company G, Thirty-second North Carolina Infantry, and was killed on July 3, 1863, at the Battle of Gettysburg.

9. Berry Thomas to Governor Z. B. Vance, July 23, 1863, Vance Papers, NCSA. Thomas was from Pitt County.

10. Intha McCraw to Governor Z. B. Vance, June 14, 1863, Vance Papers, NCSA.

11. Ervin Q. Davis to Mary Margaret McNeill, Apr. 26, 1863, McNeill Papers, Duke. Having to serve with strangers caused some soldiers to desert, as did Jacob Herring: "wee wais tuck prisoners at Roan oak. after the perroal wais out I went Back to the old Co[mpany] again and tharee wais only one man in the Campany that I ever sawe bee fore and hit seamid like the[y] had a spite at ous as wee wais from Columbus [County]" (Jacob Herring to Governor Vance, Oct. 12, 1863, Vance Paper, NCSA).

12. John W. Joyce to Francis Joyce, Feb. 22, 1865, Joyce Papers, MHI. In a letter W. M. Patton sent to his parents back home in Bencombe County, Patton relays a somewhat accusatory message from neighbor and relative John R. Petillo, who comments indirectly about his lack of communication from home: "J R Pittillo send his respects to you all & says he is not ded" (W. M. Patton, Feb. 22, 1863, Patton Family Letters, SHC).

13. James M. McPherson, *For Cause and Comrades: Why Men Fought in the Civil War* (New York: Oxford Univ. Press, 1997), 11. McPherson does not state how he arrived at this figure, but I suspect it is not too far off the mark.

14. Guion Griffis Johnson, *Ante-Bellum North Carolina: A Social History* (Chapel Hill: Univ. of North Carolina Press, 1937), 266–282. Attendance did not become compulsory until 1913 (Powell and Mazzocchi, *Encyclopedia of North Carolina*, 379).

15. Powell and Mazzocchi, *Encyclopedia of North Carolina*, 378.

16. Washington Wills to Richard Wills, Oct. 30, 1864, Wills Papers, SHC.

17. Bell Irvin Wiley, *The Life of Johnny Reb: The Common Soldier of the Confederacy* (Baton Rouge: Louisiana State Univ. Press, 2005), 192.

18. Wives of soldiers sometimes learned to read or write by attending school and/or practicing at home while their husbands were away: "I am more than glad that you have got so you can rite yore letters yore self. I never had a letter from you or any body that I thought more ove than I Dough [= do] ove this last one that you rote me, you named something a bout going to school. if you will take yore penn and rite a bout three times a Day at home you will lern faster than you will at school" (W. D. Smith to Angeline Smith, Jan. 22, 1865, W. D. Smith Papers, Duke).

19. W. P. Cline to Mary Cline, Apr. 14, 1862, Cline Papers, SHC.

20. Cline's amanuensis had written that Cline had visited a house of prostitution.

21. J. W. Lineberger, Sept. 11, 1863, in *Letters of a Gaston Ranger*, ed. H. Douglas Pitts (Richmond: Museum of the Confederacy, 1991), 6.

Reading Civil War Letters

There is no way to know approximately how many letters were written by soldiers during the Civil War, but the total must be in the millions. Of course, a much smaller number would have survived the war and the hundred-plus years that followed, but there must be hundreds of thousands in libraries, archives, museums, and private collections, as well as in the possession of descendants. James McPherson maintains that he has read more than twenty-five thousand in the course of his long career (in addition to about 250 diaries).[1] Indeed, Civil War letters have long been an invaluable resource for Civil War historians, as well as a source of personal interest for descendants.

There is probably no better introduction to Civil War letters and letter writing, especially by Southern soldiers, than the chapter titled "Dear Folks" in Bell Irvin Wiley's pioneering work, *The Life of Johnny Reb*. Wiley was perhaps the first to make extensive use of primary sources in the form of letters written by ordinary soldiers for whom letter writing was a new experience. "Dear Folks" covers a wide variety of topics associated with letter writing, including the language (and erratic spelling) of little-educated privates, the difficult conditions under which the letters were written, the chronic lack of writing materials, and the kinds of topics that found their way into the words that soldiers and their families recorded in their letters.[2] There is something of a learning curve for those reading (and transcribing) Civil War letters. Besides the unfamiliar, often idiosyncratic handwriting styles, letter forms, even abbreviations, there are the many eccentric spellings and rare or archaic words and phrases. Often, reading a letter aloud will illuminate some of the mysterious spellings, and reading aloud to an audience will often render the lack of punctuation and the most idiosyncratic kind of spelling completely invisible for the audience. Names, both place names and personal names, can be particularly challenging, and those who want to correctly identify these must resort to maps and atlases, census records, military records, regimental histories, and unit rosters. Sometimes we must simply give up and move on, leaving some details and identities unknown for the present. The challenges, and sometimes frustrations, are nevertheless worth the effort, as the treasures (whether historical, social, or linguistic) contained in the letters are revealed.

"I am afraid you cant half read my letter"

Letters from soldiers often contain comments about the difficulties they faced writing their letters, even in camp. Excessive cold, insufficient light, lack of any kind of flat surface on which to write, extreme fatigue from forced marches, frequent overnight picket duty, and the like, as well as a lack of time and lack of news, all made letter writing a challenge. And yet most kept on writing at every possible opportunity:

> **Oct. 12, 1862:** I can inform you that I am tired and sleepy at this time and the wind is very high it is Most imposibel to rite. you Can see the dust on the paper. (Marcus Hefner, Hefner Papers, NCSA)

Often soldiers had to make do with substandard ink, paper, or pens, and these can result in faded ink or ink that is blotchy. Letters written in pencil can present problems for readers, but fortunately for modern readers, the majority of letters were written in ink. Pencil-written letters must have caused problems even for the original audience since soldiers sometimes apologized for writing in pencil:

> **Sept. 24, 1861:** John pray for me an i will for you for i feal the nead of prair. this is the sorys [= sorriest] paper you ever saw. (Lewis Thomas, Williams Papers, Duke)

> **Apr. 23, 1864:** My dear wife this paper blotches So bad that I cant hardly rite on it. (John Hartman, Hartman Papers, Duke)

> **Dec. 4, 1864:** I rite with a pencil because this paper is so thin it dont rite good with a pen and ink. (Henry Bowen, Bowen Papers, NCSA)

Scarcity of papers and decent ink and pens was not limited just to soldiers. Family members, particularly those who resided in relatively remote, rural areas sometimes found it difficult or impossible to acquire writing supplies:

> **June 4, 1863:** Sally you must excuse this paper for it was the Best I could do for there is no paper to Be Had about Hear and i wanted to hear from you so Bad I thought i woul write on any thing. (Elizabeth Wagoner, Hundley Family Letters, SHC)

> **Feb. 18, 1864:** my ink is so pail I am afraid you cant half read my letter but I will try and do better next time. (Molly Tesh, Tesh Papers, Duke)

When times were good, soldiers bought their stationary by the *quire*, a quire of paper consisting of twenty-four or twenty-five sheets.[3] Prices for paper varied depending on circumstances, but typically it became scarcer and more expensive as the war progressed. Early in the war, soldiers, who frequently listed the prices of items they had to buy, could purchase a quire of paper for a dollar or two. Toward the end of the war, the price had increased to five dollars or more, and soldiers were reduced to buying paper one sheet at a time. Often paper could not be found at any price, and letter writers had to make do with any scrap of paper they could find. Writers made use of every part of a page, and if a writer ran out of space at the bottom of a page, he or she often continued writing sideways in the right or left margin or upside down at the top of a page. The ultimate challenge for readers is probably the practice of "cross writing," in which a writer would write across a page as usual, then turn the paper ninety degrees and write across the text that was already written. Fortunately, this was a practice rarely used by privates. A Confederate victory was often followed by a period of time in which Confederate soldiers wrote on paper "liberated" from captured yankees or plundered from abandoned camps. More than one collection in a library or archive has been misidentified as having been written by a Union soldier because it contained letters written on "patriotic" Northern stationary featuring color-printed illustrations of U.S. flags or eagles or the goddess liberty, along with a patriotic motto or verse. Paper cut from unused ledger books was also commonly used for writing paper, and the North Carolina letters include some written on hotel registers, and even one written on a Baltimore and Ohio Railroad bill of lading:

> **July 20, 1862:** Dear Sister. As Papa are going to leave in the Morning I take from my portfolio Some yanke paper to drop you a few lines to inform you all that Iam well as usual and all the rest of the Boys. (K. W. and J. F. Coghill, Coghill Papers, Duke)[4]

> **May 13, 1863:** This is yankey paper I am writing on. we capterd A good eal of yankey paper. (Hardy Matthews, McLeod Letters, SHC) Moore County

Whatever problems "pail ink" and blotchy paper may have created for the original readers, the passing of 150 years has compounded those problems so that many letters or parts of letters are no longer legible. Some letters are stained, torn, or otherwise damaged, or so badly creased at folds that words and sometimes whole lines are unreadable. Proper lighting and a magnifying glass can be of some help, and digital images can be manipulated in ways that can sometimes help recover difficult readings, but there are times when the reader must simply give up and move on. There are too many other letters out there waiting to be read. However, the real challenges for reading Civil War letters often have less to do with the condition and legibility of letters and more to do with handwriting and the language itself.

In the first half of the nineteenth century, students were taught cursive handwriting styles that developed from eighteenth-century roundhand or "copperplate" script. For most letter writers, the way they formed their letters was just as important, if not more important, than how they spelled their words. Even little-educated writers often took great care with their handwriting. Indeed, the handwriting of many poorly educated letter writers is sometimes more readable than that of their better-educated comrades. Many fathers away from home in the army communicated concern about the education and writing skills of their children, as illustrated in the following two passages:

> **May 27, 1863:** I will Send Margaret and Ann a coppy [= copy text, the alphabet] home and I want you to give them my pen ink and paper and let be a writing every chance the[y] have and I want them to send me some of theire wr[i]teing in two or three weeks. I want you to indulge them in it as much as. you can. (Daniel Murph, Murph Papers, Duke)

> **Mar. 6, 1865:** I wil now tel haret about her riteing. She dus toleable wel. all the falt She has She Scatters them a little two much. i want Sophrena to take more panes and rite as plane as She can and dont Slant her Letters quite So much. (Franklin Setzer, Setzer Corr., UVA)

It takes first-time readers of Civil War letters time to be able to recognize some of the letters and other graphic conventions of nineteenth-century handwriting.[5] A prime example of this is the so-called long *s*, a form still in use by many letter writers in the 1860s. The long *s* is used as the first element in pairs (the "double" *s*), as in *Miss*, *Mississippi*, and *sickness*. The long s closely resembles the letter *f* and can be mistaken by neophytes for that letter, as in *Mifs, Mifsifsippi*, and *sicknefs*. For purposes of transcription, it is better to simply render the letter as *s* rather than to create confusion by attempting to approximate something resembling the long *s*.

Other complications encountered include some writers confusing the letters w and u, the practice of dotting an upper-case *I*, and difficulty differentiating between *i* and *e* and *o* and *a*. Readers unfamiliar with nineteenth-century handwriting may have difficulty recognizing the letter *x*, which in some cases resembles a small capital *H* or two letters *c*, the first facing backwards and the other facing the usual way. It may also be difficult to recognize the common abbreviation for *and*, the ampersand (*&*). There are so many variations on this symbol that it is difficult to make a useful generalization about it. Sometimes it looks more like a cross or a cross with a small loop joining the two parts. An ampersand followed by a *c* (*&c*) represents *and et cetera*, and this abbreviation is sometimes doubled (*&c &c*) for *and et cetera, et cetera*. These are usually found at the end of a text or section of a letter (*Verry Respectfuly yours &c*):

> **Apr. 25, 1864:** Cerby Smith & Dick Taylor has whipt Bankes in 2 fights & has made large capture of men & Canon guns &c (Stephen Whitaker, Whitaker Papers, NCSA)
>
> **Mar. 16, 1863:** we will Remain youre friends &c &c. (John L. Johnson, Vance Papers, NCSA)

The "Gallery of Letters" included in this volume contains photographs of letters, accompanied by transcriptions, which contain examples of these problematic letter forms and abbreviations.

"I remaine as ever your Sincer and affectionated Brother"

Most of the writers in the North Carolina letter sample used one of several formulaic salutations that were a popular convention of nineteenth-century letter writing. Most of these salutations date back to the eighteenth century and were learned either in school or from fellow soldiers reading letters aloud. There were at least three basic formulas with endless variation: *I seat myself to write you a few lines, I take* (or *avail* or *embrace*) *the present opportunity of writing you a few lines, I am once again permitted to write you a few lines*. Often *drop* is substituted for *write*. The writer then makes some brief statement about his or her health (good or bad) before *hoping that these* (sometimes *those*) *few lines come(s) to hand* (or *reaches you* or *may find you*) *well and harty* (or *enjoying good health* or *enjoying the same blessing*). Sunday must have been a good time to write letters, given the number of letters including *this beautiful* (or *blessed*) *Sabbath morning*:[6]

> **Apr. 18, 1862:** Dear and mos afection mother I avail mi self the preasent oprtunity of droping you afew lines to in form you that we ar all well at presant hoping when those fu lines reach you they will find you enjoying the same greate blessing of health. (Elizabeth Mock, Tesh Papers, Duke)
>
> **Jan. 10, 1863:** Dear wife with pleasure I am pur mited to drop you A fue lins to let you no that I am still A liv and on top of the ground. (J. W. Reese, Reese Papers, Duke)
>
> **Jan. 22, 1863:** Dear wife I take this present opportunity of riting you a few lines to let you no that I am Stil living though not well at this time though I think that I am improveing alittle at this time. I hope when these few lines reaches you they will find you well and harty. (Daniel Abernathy, Abernathy Papers, Duke)
>
> **Nov. 22, 1863:** My Dear Wife and Children I seat my self this Blesed sabath morning to Rite you afew lines to let you now that I am only tolarabel well. I hav got A very Bad Cold and A very Bad Cough. (F. M. Poteet, Poteet-Dickson Letters, NCSA)
>
> **Jan. 24, 1864:** Dear Sister I seat my self this evning to drop you a few lins to let you no that I am in the land of the living yet and in very good health at this time and I hope that these lins my find you injoying the like blesing and find the famly all well. (J. A. Smith, J. A. Smith Papers, Duke)

Following the salutation, soldiers often reported that they had nothing of any importance to write, nothing that would be of interest to the reader, or nothing *strange*, that is, newsworthy to communicate. Sometimes this was true, but just as often the conventional disclaimer was followed by news of a recent battle or the death of someone known to the addressee or some other dramatic and indeed newsworthy event. Consider this passage from a letter written by Catawba Countian Laban Cline:

> **Apr. 20, 1857:** I have nothing very strange to rite. Corn sells at 75 cts Ruffnus [= fodder] is verry scerce. Anderson Sherrill froze to Death the 1st Day of march. Catherine Rosemon and John Moser is married. Henry Shook and Barbara Miller is maried & Wilton Douglas wife was beried the 18th of April. Julees Douglas and mag Sharp is maried and thare is a great many more weddings than what has been expecting. (Laban Cline, Hefner Papers, NCSA)

Cline, an apparent master of understatement, ends his missive with "Rite as soon as you get this. Nothing more untill Death. . . . Laban Cline. I am Maried."

Not surprisingly, letters written to Governor Zebulon B. Vance often follow a very different set of conventions and a much higher level of formality in their salutations, depending of course on the level of education and relative social status of the correspondent. This more-or-less official correspondence frequently begins with *To His Excellency* or something similar. However, mixed in with official communication from members of the Confederate cabinet, generals, the governors of neighboring states, and representatives of the political or social elite are hundreds of letters from the common folk of North Carolina. Unlike letters written between soldiers and their families, people writing to the governor were writing to someone they most likely did not know personally, and they were writing to the chief executive of their state, usually to make an important request. Writers asked for discharges, exemptions, or transfers for themselves or for family members serving in the army. Vance was generally powerless to grant these requests. Wives of soldiers petitioned the governor for relief in the form of provisions or supplies for making clothing, and these letters often illustrate the plight of families on the homefront. Fortunately these were requests that Vance had the power to grant. The governor apparently read every letter himself and had a clerk or aid reply to each of them. While salutations in these letters usually follow one of the standard formulas, there are sometimes attempts at a higher level of formality, as in the citation below in which the writer addresses the governor as "your Worshapry." Nevertheless, there is a kind of directness, a tendency to get to the point, that is generally missing from more educated letter writers. In his letter to Vance, Macon County farmer Abraham Corpening opens with what reads like a paraphrase of Thomas Paine's famous line from *The American Crisis*:

> **Nov. 9, 1862:** Governor Sir These are times that pesters the mind of a man to know where he should stand as a law abiding man. (Abraham Corpening, Vance Papers, NCSA)

> **Apr. 11, 1863:** onarbel Z B Vance Govner of the State. pleas your Worshapry as i this day seat my self to inform you of my Husband situation Which is Bad Helth. (Mahata Bell Boykin, Vance Papers, NCSA)

> **Apr. 27, 1863:** Gov. Z. B Vance Dear Sir. I This day avail my Self To Rite To you my present Condition. That I am here in This hospital afflicted with The Rheumatisms also from A fall off ov A Bridge and A mule falling on me and Cripeled my hip. (James R. Duncan, Vance Papers, NCSA)

> **Oct. 12, 1863:** To Govner Vance. Sir I Drope you a few lines To in form you that my sone William Lury is in Raleigh in Jail fore Deserting. Sir I hope that you Will Try to have him not Shote as he has not Got very Goode sence. (Betsey Lury, Vance Papers, NCSA)

Often there is also a sense of familiarity in the letters, even a conversational tone, as if the writer was personally acquainted with Governor Vance, as in this passage written by M. P. Lytle on behalf of his neighbor, Alcey Crook:[7]

> **Mar. 25, 1863:** my object of riting to you is This. a young man bey Name of Jasper crook was taking sick an sent to Ralegh NC an was put in tha houspitatal a bout 7 weaks a goe and his pople has not heard from him sence. he is from Bumcombe co in J. R. Young companey in tha 11 Reagment of state Troops of .N.C volenteers an Mr vance his Mother qu<??>hes [= inquires?] of you if tha is a man bey tha name of Jasper crook in tha Houspital at Roligh. she wants you to you to make an inqury a bout him an if he is thar she wants youe to goe an see him an see how he is a making out an rite what you thinck is the matter with him. (M. P. Lytle, Vance Papers, NCSA)

The closings of letters, while typically shorter than salutations, also tend to follow conventional formulas: *if we meet no more on earth may we meet in heaven where parting is no more . . . give my best respects to all inquiring friends and save a portion for yourself . . . I remain your affectionate (husband, wife, brother, son) until death.* The unfamiliarity of letter writers with some of the words used in formulas (*opportunity, inquiring, affectionate*) leads to some interesting spellings as well as morphological forms. *Affectionate* frequently becomes *affectionated* and often simply *affection. Your loving husband* sometimes becomes *Your lovely husband.* North Carolina soldiers often include *howdy* as part of the closing, for example, *Tell my poor old mother howdy for me* or *I send howdy to all the children*:

> **Aug. 7, 1861:** So nothing more at present only Remanes your loving Brother till Death. So farwell. Peter Poteet to F.M. Poteet And famley Mother and all inquirnes [= inquiring] friends. (Peter Poteet, Poteet-Dickson Letters, NCSA)

> **Jan. 1, 1863:** Pray for mee that I may returne home to you all. tell All my friends houdey for mee tell mother Eller houdey for mee I want to see hur vary bad. J W Reese to Ct [=Christina] V Reese Kiss my Boys and Reserv one for mee. (J. W. Reese, Reese Papers, Duke)

> **May 9, 1863:** I must bring my letter to a Close by asking you to write to me as Soon as this Comes to hand and give me all the news. no more at present. I remaine as ever your Sincer and affectionated Brother untill death. (Joshua Carter, Murph Papers, Duke)

> **Jan. 21, 1864:** if we Meet no moor in this world Ihope we will Meet in heaven to part no moor. May the Lord bless save you is my prayer for Christ sake. write soon and often. farwell. Martha A. E. Poteet to her loving husband Francis M. Poteet. God bless you my husband. (Martha Poteet, Poteet-Dickson Letters, NCSA)

Bell Wiley remarked on the common practice of including a bit of verse in their letters, the most common example, by far, North and South alike, being *When this you see remember me, though many miles apart we be.* Young, unmarried soldiers, especially early in the war, were the writers most likely to include verse in their letters. Mary Davison of Gaston County had several young admirers sending letters to her while they were serving in the army. J. T. Hamilton included this verse in a September 1, 1861, letter:

> Shoar as the grape grows on the
> vine i will be yours if you will be mine
> Shoar as the vine grows round the
> Stump i Chose you out for my Sugar lump
> the world is wide the see is dee[p] and in
> your dear armes i wish to Sleep (J. T. Hamilton, Davison Papers, Duke)

In a January 23, 1862, letter, Hamilton includes some verse that is considerably more morbid and ominous in tone, particularly so when we learn that he died of disease just a few weeks later:

> When I am dead and in the grave and
> all my Bones are Rotten, look at this
> and think of me or I might Be forgoten

In addition to short verses, soldiers also copied out long "song ballets" to send home to wives and sweethearts, like this one T. F. Baggarly of Iredell County sent home to his wife, Margaret:[8]

Lovers Departre. 1862.

1 So fare yow well my darling
So fare yow well my dear
Dont griev for my long absents
While i am presant her
2 Since its been my fortune
a sowldier for to bee
o try an live contented
an Do not grieve for mee
3 i am going a way to morrow
to tarry for a while
so fair from my Dier Darling
a bowt five hundred miles
4 she rung her lilly white hands
an so mournfully did Cry
yow listed an bee a soldier
an in the war yow will Die
5 in the battle youl bee wounded
an on the field slain
yowl burst my heart a sunder
if i never see yow a gain
6 The canons lowdly rowering
The bullets Come whislin by
The fife and Drum ar soundin
To Dround the soldiers Cry

In the same letter, Baggarly asks his wife, "Mag make mee a plat to go a round my rist out of your hair an pwt [= put] it in a letter an send it to me."[9] Hair, especially that of wives, must have had important cultural significance, judging by the number of requests for plaits or delicately braided rings of hair from wives, sweethearts, children, or sisters. Soldiers included a wide variety of small items in letters sent home: papers of pins, needles, pen points, pen knives, sewing scissors, buttons, and jewelry, especially rings.[10] In their spare time, soldiers fashioned rings from silver dimes and other small coins. Some also made rings from the bleached bones of yankees that lay about on old battlefields, like the one Joseph Cowand sent to his cousin Winifred Cowand back home in Bertie County:

> **Oct. 11, 1862:** this is a yanky Bone Ring. som of my one manufacture. this is A Present to you for remembrance sake untwel I return home again And if I never return you may Have it for life. (Cowand Papers, Duke)

There is no record of what Winifred thought of this *memento mori* or whether she kept it after Joseph was killed at Gettysburg. In a March 1862 letter to his wife, Jonas Bradshaw included one of his teeth: "here Nancy is my tooth it hert me so bad I had it pulled out."[11] If Nancy kept the tooth it would prove to be her only tangible remains of Jonas, who was wounded and captured at Gettysburg and died at the Point Lookout prisoner-of-war camp in August 1864. Fortunately, artifacts such as those sent by Cowand and Bradshaw were much less common than other items included in letters. For example, Amanda Murph of Catawba County sometimes used the mail to keep her husband, Daniel, supplied with tobacco while he was away in the army, while Rowan Countian John Hartman sent his wife, Partha, instructions for sending a kiss through the mail:

> **May 17, 1863:** I would send yo some money if I node that yo would get it and I will send yo another chaw of to baco in this leter. (Amanda Murph, Murph Papers, Duke)

> **Nov. 11, 1863:** My dear wife I Supose you laught at me about Sending kisses and you Sead you wonted me to lern you how I will now tel you how to do it when you get your letters rote. Just put your mouth on the paper and then take apensyl and mark round your mouth and in marking give the paper asweat kiss and then when you thake your mouth away thair will be the kiss. thats the way to Send kisses but I dont Suppose you can do it with out help. you will hafto get Some person to mark while you primp your mouth. thats a yankey trick. (John Hartman, Hartman Papers, Duke)

"Father I have Saw a rite Smart of the world Sence I left home"

Early in the war, young soldiers from rural areas in North Carolina often sent home reports about the wonders they encountered in Raleigh and Richmond. For the first time they traveled on railroads to get to these places, crossed great bridges over rivers, and saw steamboats and sailing ships, factories, and public buildings of a size and construction they could scarcely have imagined before. For farm boys like Catawba Countian William H. Brotherton, who harvested his wheat with a scythe, among these wonders were mechanized agricultural implements. Brotherton sent word home that he had seen "more than ever I Saw before I Saw a thrasher that was on awagon an it thrash and clean both at once I have Saw more than I Cood tell yow in [a] month."[12] Young men from the mountains of western North Carolina found themselves stationed on the Carolina coast and saw the ocean for the first time. Others stationed in the camps around Raleigh and Richmond, like Granville Countian Joseph Coghill, were able to see in person the *big men*, the politicians and generals, they had only read about:

> **July 18, 1861:** I never saw the like before nor nether did I ever expect to experians such atime here you can only imagion the excitement but we know the excitement. Petersburg is a prety plase. it is. situated upon the Apomatoc River. but here is a River. it is James river and the greatest Brig I ever saw or I ever expect to see. it is about one mil long and 30. Ft high. they tel me this place is 8 Mils squar an Petersburg 6. here at Richmon we see Ships an Steam-boats and it seams like every thing else. [. . .]I have just been walking. looking over the city of Richmon. I saw Houses Ships Steamboats of an enormos size. this is the rufest and most hilly cuntry for a city to be prtch upon I ever saw. here is a hill that we can go upon and vew the magnificent city. (Joseph W. Coghill, Coghill Papers, Duke)

> **Sept. 25, 1861:** I went down town the other eavining. I went in the state house [in Raleigh] and

went all through it. it is three store high. all made out of stone and I think it has got the most rooms in it of any house that I ever saw. (J. W. Williams, Williams Papers, Duke) Onslow

Nov. 16, 1861: I saw several saile vesels flat bottom & one steeme boat which was right smart for me to see. went to the paper mill saw them making paper. Richmond is a great place for any body to see that has never seen no more than I had. you may gow out look all arand and see buildings 2 or 3 miles every way. (Isham Upchurch, Upchurch Papers, Duke)

June 12, 1862: I had the plasure of seeing our Noble president Some few days ago. I Nead Not try to gave you a discription of him. if you Will Look at a postedg Stamp he is fully pictured thare. (Alfred Walsh, Proffit Family Letters, SHC)

Nov. 6, 1862: I was a garden Genrl Long Streets head Quarters. the man you have heard sow much talk a bout. he is a bout the sise of J. W. Bandy only a heaver man. he wais about 2 hundread 25 lbs. he has Large whiskers & mostach. fair complection & blew Eyes. we air all under his command at this time. I just thought that I would tell you what for a loocken man he is as you have heard sow much talk a bout him. (Isaac Lefevers, Lefevers Papers, NCSA) Catawba County

Soldiers also saw more people in one place than they had ever seen before, including thousands of other soldiers, and at times it must have seemed like all the young men of North Carolina and the rest of the South had gathered to whip the Yankees. But reality soon set in. By September, Joseph Coghill had died in camp of one of the diseases that ravaged the troops, and Alfred Walsh was killed on July 1, 1862, at the Battle of Malvern Hill. The wonders of the larger world began to fade in the face of hardship and death, and, after all, there was indeed no place like home:

Nov. 10, 1861: Father I have Saw a rite Smart of the world Sence I left home But I have not Saw any place like Buncomb and henderson yet. (John B. Lance, Lance Papers, LSU)

Soldiers began to long for the time when the war would end and they could be reunited with families. Hard times soon became a common refrain in the letters—not only for the soldiers but also for their families at home:

Feb. 5, 1862: i have nothing new to rite as i now of only *hard times* an wors a coming i fear. (Roxy Sandlin, Williams Papers, Duke)

Oct. 5, 1862: this is a hard place to live here. a soldiers life is a hard one. no man nose what he has to go thrught when he a way from home. you all thincke you have hard times ther but you dont now what hard times un less you wase here. I thought I seed hard times when I wase at home but I did not see any thing to Whate I see here. (Isaac Copeland, Copeland Letters, NCSA)

Feb. 5, 1863: Father it is hard times here Shore. nothing to Eat nor to drink but I hope this war will not last all ways. (John Futch, Futch Letters, NCSA)

Aug. 30, 1864: I want you to keep out of them fights as much as you can. they say that pease will be made before 3 Months. I hope and pray that it will be made so that you can come home. you know that I see hard times with out you. (Martha Poteet, Poteet-Dickson Letters, NCSA)

As soldiers began to desert in large numbers, letters received by the folks at home often contained descriptions of executions witnessed by their husbands or sons in the army:

Aug. 13, 1862: I saw a Site yesterday that I never saw before nor I never want to see no more. I saw a man Shot for deserting and trying to go to the yankes. they Shot 5 balls threw him. (Neill McLeod, McLeod Letters, SHC)

Mar. 1, 1863: Francis I sead a man Shot yester day for runing way. he had run away three time in the time of fighting. the hole brigade was muster out and then tha fetch him out with his coffin and tha tide a white honkercheif over his eyes and tuelve men shot him. (J. W. Joyce, Joyce Papers, MHI)

June 9, 1863: thear was A man that had run A way six times in our regment and he was shot yisday when we got to peters burg. i tel you that it looks hard to see A man neal don And have t[w]eelv balls put thru him. (W. P. Cline, Cline Papers, SHC)

> **Mar. 21, 1864:** it is very cold here now and geting colder every minit. I saw a man shot l ast Fryday and I dont want to see ary other one. (Peter J. Peterson, Mar. 21, 1864, Peterson Papers, Duke)

Letters were not censored during the war, and writers generally described what they witnessed, as well as their opinions (often negative) about Jefferson Davis and the Confederacy. As the war progressed, the soldiers letters became increasingly pessimistic in outlook. The hardships of life in camp or in the field, the dangers of battle, and the loss of so many comrades caused many to lapse into despair. Lorraine W. Griffin of Rutherford County had already lost two brothers in the war when he wrote the following to his sisters back home:

> **Oct. 18, 1864:** you sed the dogs was no count. they ar like me they ar in low sperits. if iwas thar I cood cher them up for I wood go hunting with them. I dont know when iwill git home for they ar fur lowing so slow & thar is 5 or 6 befor me. maby I will git home next spring if I live but that is so unserting. I may be with the yanks befor then. I come very ner agoing to them the other knight. (L. W. Griffin, Griffin Papers, NCSA)

Griffin never deserted, but more than twenty of the other letter writers did, including several married soldiers who were concerned for the welfare of their families at home. Most of these eventually returned to their units. Thornton Sexton deserted in February 1863, returned to his regiment, and endured several months of punishment before rejoining his company. He was mortally wounded at the Battle of Cold Harbor in June 1864. Sexton's brother, Marion, deserted three times. Daniel Setzer of Catawba County was mustered into the Forty-sixth North Carolina Infantry early in 1863 when he was about forty years old. He deserted in August of that year and eventually rejoined his company, where he remained until he was captured in March 1865. While Setzer was serving out his sentence in the guard house, his wife, Susan, wrote to him about her fears for his safety:

> **Dec. 19, 1863:** Dare loving husban I received yor kind letter last evning and was very glad to hair from you that you was well and I a sorrey too to hair you was in the gard hous yet but I hope and pray to god tha wont cill you for coming home to see us. sum thinks tha will cill youns yet. (Susan Setzer, Setzer Papers, Duke)

Fortunately, Daniel Setzer survived the war and returned home, as did his teenage son, Carr, who had joined his father's company late in 1864. However, many of the North Carolina soldiers who wrote the letters used in this project did not survive. Some died of disease in camp, others were killed or mortally wounded in battle, and some were captured and later died in Union prison camps. There are a number of letters that inform the families at home that a loved one has either been killed or died of disease. When John Futch returned to Virginia following the battle of Gettysburg, he sent several letters home to his wife describing the death of his brother, Charley, and his own inability to recover from the loss. At least one of the letters was written for John by someone else, a letter much more "standard" than letters John wrote himself and filled with the kind of sentimental platitudes that soldiers often wrongly felt were superior to what they wrote themselves. By comparison, the letter John wrote on August 2, 1863, contains a kind of raw emotional power that no one else could convey:

> Dear wife I take the plesher of riting you a few lines to in forme you that I am well at present hopen thos few line May reach and find you well. Dear wife I receved you kind leter august the 1 and was glad to hear from you and to hear that you was well. I havent got Mutch to write at present only it is harde times hear with us and Mity hot and we haft to March very harde. I havent sean no plesher sence charley got kild. he got wounded the 2 and died the 3. he was shot in the head and sufered Mity Bad before he died. I toted him of of the feald and stade with him tel he died. I am at a grate lost sence I lost charley tel I am all Most crasey but I hope that I will get a long with it the [best?] I can. I was Mity glad that you taken the honey as long as it was sitch a god price. I wish that you had a taken both gumes. I want to sea you the worse I ever did in My life. I want to sea you all the worse I ever did. if we get dwn a bout fredricksburg I want the father to come and sea Me. I have got a heap of talk for him. I have had one Mes of beanes and squashes but I had to pay 1 dollar for them. I havent drod no Money in fore Month but I have got some Money as yet. I am a comin home the first chance I can get. I think that this war will end before long for I think that the yankes will whip us before long. charley never spoke after he got wounded and he wanted to go home Mity bad before he died.

he was kild at getties burg P N. pore feler he got kild a long wase from home. I was very sory that I codent get a cofen to bearey him but I beared him the best I cod. it was somthing that I never expected to haft to do but we dont know what we will do tel he gets in the war. Nothing More at present only I remain your lovley hosban tel Deth.

John Futch
to wife Marth Futch

In the same letter, John also addressed his mother-in-law, Catherine Ramsey:

Dear Mother i will rite you a few lines to in form you that i am well at present hopeing those few lines May reach and find you and famley well. i want to come home to sea you Mity bad. i have got a heap of talk for you if you i cod sea you. i have rote to you sevrl times but i havent got No anser as yet. i haft to go bear footed. the botom of My foot is as thick My thome and sores that i ever had. we sea hard times and haft to March Mity harde and it is the hotes wether that i ever saw in My life. Several of our Men fanted yesterday on the March. i want you to com and sea Me and fetch Me a warter Milin and rite Me word how your garden is and how your crop is. Me and charley bothe amed to come home crismas if we both had a lived but charley pore feler got kild. but i will come if i can which i hope that i can come to sea you all and have some for it is pore fun to Me Now hear in this war. Nothing More at present only i remain yours as ever.

John Futch to C Ramsey[13]

Sometime after he wrote this letter, John Futch deserted. He was soon arrested, and on September 5, 1863, he was shot for desertion. The language John Futch and the many other soldiers and their families used in their letters have "a heap" to tell us about the war and how people did or did not survive it. Their words tell us what crops and livestock they raised, what kind of clothes they wore, and what things in life were most important to them. It would be difficult, if not impossible, to identify any single linguistic feature that could be characterized as an exclusively North Carolina usage. Most words in the letters are either shared with neighboring states or not found everywhere in North Carolina. However, anyone who reads the North Carolina letters may be struck by the common use of the greeting *howdy* in the closing parts of letters:

Billy & Eliza sends howdy to you & wants to see you very bad

I want you to give John hemphill houdy for me

girls you most tell Hugh A houdy for me

To *tell, send,* or *give howdy* conveys so much about language as a kind of social interaction, even if carried out at a far distance. Indeed, the letters often have an uncommon conversational feel about them, a familiar, informal, even intimate quality which makes them such a rich and compelling source of information into these long-gone Americans and their language.

NOTES

1. James M. McPherson, *For Cause and Comrades: Why Men Fought in the Civil War* (New York: Oxford Univ. Press, 1997), 11–12.

2. Bell Irvin Wiley, *The Life of Johnny Reb: The Common Soldier of the Confederacy* (Baton Rouge: Louisiana State Univ. Press, 2005), 192–216. For an interesting treatment of Civil War soldiers and their letters, see Robert E. Bonner, *The Soldier's Pen: Firsthand Impressions of the Civil War* (New York: Hill and Wang, 2006).

3. Letters are written in two basic formats. Either the letter is written on each side of a sheet of papers, making two pages, or the sheet is folded down the middle to make four pages. These folded sheets are typically unfolded by archivists, so the first and last page are side by side and the second and third are together on the opposite side. Because this arrangement is regularly reproduced in photographs and photocopies, and because writers rarely numbered pages, this format may cause confusion for readers unfamiliar with it. Letter writers will sometimes add "turn over" or simply "over" in the lower right corner of page one, which may cause confusion for first-time readers until they realize the words mean to turn the sheet over.

4. At some point the Coghill collection was divided. Some of the collection is at Duke, some at the Southern Historical Collection.

5. Readers unfamiliar with nineteenth-century handwriting will benefit from works such as Kip Sperry's *Reading Early American Handwriting* (Baltimore: Genealogical Publishing, 1998). There are numerous online images of early American school texts which feature examples of the alphabet in the various cursive handwriting styles. See for example, images from George Fisher's 1786 work, *The Instructor; or, American Young Man's Best Companion Containing Spelling, Reading, Writing, and Arithmetick,* http://dohistory.org/archive/doc039/.

6. For these formulas, see especially Francis Austin, "*Heaving this importunity:* The Survival of Opening Formulas in Letters in the Eighteenth and Nineteenth Centuries," Historical Sociolinguistics and Sociohistorical Linguistics 4, 2004, http://www.let.leidenuniv.nl/hsl_shl/heaving_this_importunity.htm/. See also Lucille M. Schultz, "Letter-Writing Instruction in 19th Century Schools in the United States," in *Letter Writing as a Social Practice,* ed. David Barton and Nigel Hall (Amsterdam: John Benjamins, 1999); and William Merrill Decker, *Epistolary Practices: Letter Writing in America before Telecommunications* (Chapel Hill: Univ. of North Carolina Press, 1998).

7. Lytle and Vance were both natives of Buncombe County.

8. The song is sometimes identified with the title "The Soldier's Farewell," although that title is also applied to several other nineteenth-century songs.

9. T. F. Baggarly to Margaret Baggarly, Oct. 6, 1862, Baggarly Papers, Duke.

10. Soldiers typically bought ready-made envelopes, which were smaller than they are today, measuring about five and a half by three inches. Given the small size of envelopes, it is a wonder what soldiers and their families were able to stuff into them.

11. Jonas Bradsaw to Nancy Bradshaw, Mar. 30, 1862, Bradshaw Papers, Duke.

12. William H. Brotherton to his parents, Sept. 14, 1862, Brotherton Papers, Duke.

13. John Futch to Martha Futch and Catherine Ramsey, Aug. 2, 1863, Futch Family Papers, NCSA.

Overview of North Carolina English, 1861–1865

I. Vocabulary

Before discussing the vocabulary of the North Carolina letters, it is necessary to recognize the limitations inherent in the medium. Writing is not the same as talking, and the words soldiers used, especially some nouns and verbs, may not have always been words they commonly used at home. Their new experiences in the military are reflected in words such as *cavalry*, *ration*, and *skirmish*, which commonly appear in the letters, often in variant forms such as *calvary*, *rashing*, and *scrumish*. Interestingly, the most common verb (other than *be* and *have*) in the North Carolina letters is *write*, with 7,568 occurrences. It seems highly unlikely that *write* would have occurred as commonly in the everyday speech of letter writers, but the compelling need to communicate with loved ones at home meant that there is hardly a letter in which that word does not appear at least once. Take, for example, the way Jonas Bradshaw ends a letter to his wife early in the war:

> **Jan. 26, 1862:** Dear Wife it would do me good if you would **write** to me. I have long loked fur a letter from you my Dear and have not seen one sence I left home. if you have **wrote** thay have bin miss placed and has not reached me. **write** to me Dear Wife and let me hear from you and my little baby. I do want to hear from you. I must close my letter by saying **write** Dear Wife, from J. N. Bradshaw in the camps to his Dear Wife at home. (Bradshaw Papers, Duke) Alexander County

In many ways the war transformed the written vocabulary of North Carolinians, whether they were soldiers serving in the army or their families back home. Words that would have been rare or unknown before the war become commonplace in letters; phrases like *on the march*, *on a scout*, *in camps*, *in line of battle*, and *throwing up breast works* appear regularly, as do words and expressions like *grape (shot)*, *cannister*, *bomb* (usually as *bum*), *minie ball*, *cap box*, *furlough* (spelled *furlow*), *whip*, *whip out*, *kill dead*, *kill up*, *skeddadle*, *descriptive list*, and *commutation money*. In the letters, the verb *draw*, including the variant past tense and past participle *drawed*, is quite common in the sense of being issued pay, rations, weapons, or clothing (see section II.4.1.3 below). Before the war it is unlikely that this would have been a common usage among largely self-sufficient yeoman farmers or even landless farmers. On the homefront, wives of soldiers often *drawed* some kind of subsistence payment or commodities from the state. Reference to specific models of weapons are very rare. If soldiers mention weapons at all, it is usually simply *pistol*, *musket*, *rifle*, or *gun* (rarely *rifle gun*). There are, for example, only two references to the British Enfield rifled musket, including one by William Tesh:

> **May 25, 1862:** Father you wanted to Know What Kind of Guns we have. we have the old United States muskets. they are two companys has the enfield Rifels that will Shoot 800 yards. They are the Flanking Companies. (William Tesh, Tesh Papers, Duke) Yadkin County

The *old United States muskets* mentioned by Tesh may refer to the Model 1842 smoothbore musket produced at the Harpers Ferry and Springfield armories and commonly used by both sides early in the war, or it may refer to older models of muskets, flintlock or percussion, that were still around in Southern armories at the beginning of the war. There are two references to *Mississippi Rifle*, the Model 1841 Harpers Ferry rifled musket (see glossary entry). In a letter home, John W. Reese describes what is certainly a Henry repeating rifle taken from a drunken Union soldier who mistakenly crossed into Confederate lines and was captured:

> **July 9, 1864:** J J wevear got A gun. A Rifle tha[t]s A hed of any thing I Ever saw in the way of A gun in my life. it shoots sixteen times with out loding. (J. W. Reese, Reese Papers, Duke) Buncombe County

However, as was usually the case, Reese never mentions the name the weapon's manufacturer. There also two references to an artillery piece nicknamed *Long Tom*, including one used for the defense of Fort Fisher (see glossary entry).

Among soldiers, the act of leaving home to enlist voluntarily or to avoid conscription is described as *going to the army* or *going to the war.* Once in the army, soldiers belonged to a *ridgement* and to a company typically made up of men from the same county, but the ultimate social group was a soldier's *mess,* made up of relatives and neighbors who were generally known to the folks back home:

> **Apr. 14, 1862:** you wonted to now what **mes** i was in. i can harly tell you thare is too meny in A **mess.** J L huit. a huit. f huit. w huit. C goo[d] mon. S Parker. C Parker. J s[h]ronc. J Props. W Props. C set[z]er. h Parkins. J Miller. C Cobb. And W P Cline. (W. P. Cline, Cline Papers, SHC) Catawba County

> **Aug. 13, 1862:** the **mess** is well except James vaughn. he went to the hospital yesterday at golsburough. he is purty bad of[f] with relaps of mesels. (R. C. Love, Love Papers, Duke) Henderson County

After the Conscription Act of April 1862, those who remained were *in for the war* with no possibility of serving out a specified period of enlistment and no chance of discharge unless so seriously disabled by wounds or disease as to be of no further use as soldiers. Soldiers who experienced battle or the hardships of campaigning could write that they had *seen the elephant* (or *the monkey*). They were often *wore out, broke down, barfooted, worsted, famished,* or *perished.* The war was also hard on the homefront. Not only were citizens beset by lawless gangs of *outliers, bushwhackers, tories, Lincolnites,* and *rogues,* but they were also harassed and plundered by the *homeguards* and *details* sent to *take up* (arrest or apprehend) conscripts and deserters, who would *lie out, dodge, take to the bushes, runaway,* or *go to the yankees*:

> **Apr. 14, 1863:** they are giting no deserters nor conscripts scarcley and are layin a bout here in the way of Sivil peapel and in truding on them and eating up all the Serpelas provision from they pore Soldiers wives and Childern which had a hard time to git along at best without being run over and troden down with such lawless mob company as tha have for the last two monts **pressing** the provision that they aught to have for there pore little childern. ("meny Citizens," Vance Papers, NCSA) Randolph County

The verb *press* regularly appears in complaints by wives and others on the homefront, either in letters to Governor Vance or to family members in the army. It was used in the sense of forcibly *pressing* men into the military through conscription, as well as in the sense of soldiers or other government representatives requisitioning, confiscating, or otherwise taking grain, livestock, and other commodities from citizens, including the families of soldiers:

> **Dec. 26, 1863:** tha Sa tha are a goint to **press** all our things and if tha Dow I Dont no how wee will live. (Susan Setzer, Setzer Papers, Duke) Catawba County

> **Feb. 4, 1864:** all the honest men is gone and a set of speckalating dogs is left to **press** the lives out of the poor Women and children. (Martha Poteet, Poteet-Dickson Letters, NCSA) McDowell County

Those responsible for instigating and continuing the war and those who profited from it, the *big men, big bugs,* and *secesh men,* became objects of ridicule. The growing sense of hopelessness among soldiers toward the end of the war is expressed in the phrases *gone up* and *gone up the spout*:

> **Feb. 2, 1865:** the **sesesh men** dos hate to own that we are whiped. they wont talk about it if they can help it. it dos me good to tell it to them but they hav to own it. (Martha Poteet, Poteet-Dickson Letters, NCSA) McDowell County

> **Feb. 26, 1865:** it looks like the confedercy is **gone up** to evry bodey in the armey at this time. (Henry Bowen, Bowen Papers, NCSA) Washington County

> **ND [1865]:** this confederacy is **a going up the spout**. money is hard to get holt of and after a man gets it he cant by nothing with it, this ware canot last longer than till Spring I Dont think. (W. D. Smith, W. D. Smith Papers, Duke) Davie County

Some words in the letters first appeared during the war: *secesh, Lincolnite, copperhead* (in the political sense). The verb *skedaddle* and the term *Tar Heel* are first recorded during the war. The origin of some of these, such as *Bull Run trot,* are fairly transparent, while others, such as *take highlow* for "to desert" and *go up the spout* for "to die, perish, be ruined" are obscure. Some idioms are particularly inventive, as is J. W. Reese's use of *the owls has caught him* to describe those who have disappeared at night (and presumably deserted):

> **July 9, 1864:** A compney out of the 54 verginia Regmant Belonging to ouer Bregad one nite whil on picket the liutenant in Command of the Companey he went over an mad airraingmet with the yankeys pickets and Cum Back and tuck the Companey over with him and sum has went sence and sevril has went out of the 58 N C Regmant. the Boys Calls this when on[e] Runs A way or is miss ing that **the owls has Cout him**. (J. W. Reese, Reese Papers, Duke) Buncombe County

I.1. Semantic fields

Words belonging to a particular area in the vocabulary, such as terms having to do with the war, belong to a *semantic field,* a group of words which share a common domain under a more general topic, for example, kinship terms, words having to do with food or eating, words having to do with illness or death, agricultural terms, clothing terms, and so on. Since soldiers serving in the army and their families at home wrote about the things that were most important to them, it is not difficult to group terms by one or more of these topics.

I.1.1. Kinship terms

Kinship terms represent one very important semantic field in Civil War letters, and among common words occurring in the letters are the different words that are used for a male parent. Not surprisingly, the formal forms father (and variant *farther*) are the most common, especially in the salutations of letters (*Dear Father and Mother*). Some writers use the form exclusively; others vary between the formal usage and the more informal forms *pa, pap, pappy,* and *papa*. The term *pap*, for example, is uncommon in salutations but occurs in every other possible context including direct address (*Pap, I want you to . . .*) and indirect communication (*Tell your Pap . . .*) or other third-person reference (*Tell me how is pap getting along . . .*). Perhaps the biggest surprise has been how uncommon the terms *daddy* and *dad* are in comparison with present-day usage in North Carolina and in the South in general. There are other factors as well which point to the importance of context. The form *pappy* (but not *pap*) appears to be an affectionate term when used by adult children, and it is also used in self-reference by fathers in parts of letters addressed specifically to young children (*tell them to be good children and pappy will bring them a pretty . . .*). The term *papa* is also favored by children and as a form of self-reference by fathers. Below is a list of all the terms for *father* in the North Carolina sample by frequency of occurrence:

father	783
farther	75
pa, par, paw	74
pap	70
pappy	61
papa	43
old man	5
daddy	4
dad	2
Total	1,117

Terms for *grandfather* are much less common in the letters, with only eighteen occurrences of all forms. The formal forms *grandfather, granfather,* and *granfarther* occur a total eight times; *grandpa, granpaw,* and *grandpar* a total of four times; *granpap* three times; and *granpappy, grandaddy,* and the archaic *grandsire* one time each. Terms for a female parent tend toward the more formal *mother* in all contexts, while the familiar term *mamma* is the least common of all. The following is a list of terms for *mother* in the North Carolina sample by frequency of occurrence:

mother	878
ma, mar, maw	44
mam	13
mammy	6
mamma	4
old lady	3
Total	948

Of the terms for the female grandparent, the formal *grandmother* and *granmother* predominate with fifty-three occurrences. There are thirteen occurrences of *granny* and seven of *grandma* or *grandmar.* The totals for the *father* and *mother* terms, while suggestive of predominant forms, do not tell the whole story, since some terms may predominate in a single family or by a single writer. For example, letters written by the Coghill family of Granville County account for forty of the *pappy* occurrences and twenty of the *papa* occurrences, as well as twenty-five of the examples of *ma,* suggesting that these were especially popular names within one family. William Brotherton of Catawba County frequently wrote letters to his grandmother, Polly Howard, who lived in neighboring Lincoln County. His letters account for twenty-one of the examples of *grandmother* and all but two of the occurrences of *granny.* Edgar Smithwick, who regularly wrote to his widowed mother back in Martin County, uses the term *mother* a remarkable 157 times in his letters.

On the other hand, there does seem to be a possible regional significance to some terms used for parents and grandparents. The term *pappy* occurred only in the Piedmont and eastern counties, while *pap* was only found in the western half of the state. The term *daddy* also may have some regional significance as it was only found in letters by writers from Catawba, Davie, and Stokes counties. The writer who used *dad* was also from Stokes County, and the single occurrence of *grandaddy* was used by a writer from Henderson County.

Readers of Civil War letters, especially those written by Southerners, will notice the common practice of referring to a sibling by using *brother* or *sister* rather than the person's name, as in this citation for a letter written by Robert T. Conley of Jackson County, reporting the circumstances of the death of his only brother, James, after the Battle of Piedmont in June 1864:

> **June 28, 1864: Brother** was wounded, Shot through the bladder at 9 o'clock Sunday evening 5 inst.[= day of the month] & fell in the hands of the enemy who carried him to Mr Isac Myre's & dressed his wound. (R. T. Conley, Conley Letter, ADAH) Jackson County

This distinctive usage is typically limited to contexts in which the person referred to is the only brother or sister, or in some cases, the only brother present or serving in the same unit as the letter writer. Lorraine Griffin of Rutherford County had several brothers, but only his brother James served with him in Company D, Sixteenth North Carolina Infantry:

> **Nov. 24, 1861:** you think hard of me for not writin to you when **Brother** was sick. I wrote the day after he was taken and the day I got the leters from you and tildey. **brother** was so lo[w] that I had no hart to writ. (L. W. Griffin, Griffin Papers, NCSA) Rutherford County

This usage, however, varied from family to family, as in this citation from a letter by Jonathan Fuller Coghill to his three brothers, Kinchin W., Joseph W., and James Norphelet, all serving together in Company G, Twenty-third North Carolina Infantry. In this particular case, *Brother* refers specifically to the eldest brother, Kinchin:

> **Sept. 2, 1861: Brother** Joseph and Nophlet. Pappy and ma sais that they wants you all to be good boys. [. . .]Jo tell **Brother** and Nophlet to wright to us. one of you three must wright every week. (J. F. Coghill, Coghill Papers, Duke) Granville County.

Sadly, the kinship terms applied to the Coghill brothers became less ambiguous after both Joseph and J. N. died of disease in camp in Virginia the same month the letter was written. Within a few months, the youngest brother, Jonathan Fuller, joined his surviving brother in Company G, and in his letters home continued to use the term *Brother* in reference to Kinchin W. Coghill.

Most of the letter writers in the sample lived in rural areas and belonged to extensive social networks that included their neighbors and, especially, people to whom they were related by blood or marriage and to whom they were bound by ties of social and economic interdependence. The expression that letter writers in North Carolina and neighboring states most commonly use to describe this relationship is *connection,* with *connection* treated as a collective noun and describing a group that includes aunts, uncles, cousins, in-laws, and so on, as well as those who have moved to distant places, usually states to the west, but stay *connected* through occasional visits before the war or through the medium of letter writing. The words *relative(s)* and *relation(s)* are much less common, and *kin* and *kinfolk,* which one might expect to encounter frequently, are surprisingly uncommon, with only two examples of *kin* and one of *kinfolk* occurring in the North Carolina letters.

I.1.2. Food

Soldiers write about food more and use a wider variety of terms than their counterparts on the homefront. Words associated with food include general terms used to describe food supplies: *provision(s), rashings, victuals, vittles, eatables, eating(s),* and *fare* (but never the Northern term *grub*), as well as specific kinds of food they would like to have either at home or shipped in a box: *cowcumbers, roasting ears, Irish taters, yam potatoes, goober peas, ground peas, mush melons, muscadines, kraut, june apples, sallet, middling meat, ham of meat, souse, hash, spare ribs, backbones,* and *chicking.*

Although comments about rations are mostly positive early in the war, as time went by soldiers began to complain more and more about the monotony of their rations. Soldiers missed the variety of food they had at home, particularly fresh fruit and vegetables, among the most commonly requested items to be included in a box sent from home:

> **Dec. 29, 1861:** if you have plenty of cabage I would be glad that you would Send me Some heads by Tilmon Heartly when he comes or some other person. Clint Lee will be at home in a few days you could send them by him. you need not be surprised at my wanting cabage for a most any thing is good down here. (Robert Blair, Blair Letters, NCSA) Caldwell County

On occasion, food could be purchased locally or from sutlers in camp, but the prices of these items were generally beyond the means of Confederate privates, who were paid eleven dollars a month in steadily devalued currency. Soldiers grumbled about the quality of the rations, with complaints about *blue beef* and *rusty* (rancid) bacon and rotten meat infested with *skippers*. In the closing months of the war, soldiers regularly complained of *small rashings* and of consuming a day's rations, and sometimes two days' rations, in a single meal.

The largest group of food terms in the North Carolina letters refer to a wide variety of bread: *bake oven bread, cake bread, crackling bread, flour bread, light bread, loaf bread, pone bread, sad bread, sponge bread, corn cake, (corn) pone, (corn) dodger, fritter, ginger cake,* and *raised biscuits*. The importance of bread as the principal staple in the diet of the common people is reflected in the frequent complaints addressed to Governor Vance that people will suffer for the lack of bread because of high prices and scarcity of supplies. They are likely to *famish* (starve) because of speculation in *bread stuff,* the flour and corn meal necessary for making bread. There is even a verb form, *to bread* (to supply with bread).

I.1.3. Illness and death

The second most common topic in the letters concerned illness and disease, among both soldiers and the folks at home. Mortality rates from disease were particularly high among soldiers in camps, and letters frequently inform folks at home of the deaths of brothers, cousins, and neighbors from home:

> **Mar. 11, 1863:** I have the sad and hart brakeing news to write you of the death of our beloved brother C.L.P. [= Calvin Luther Proffit]. he departed this life March the 25. the doctor who attended him in his last hours said it was an inflamationn of the brain. he had not been sick but 3 or 4 dayes and had not been bad of[f] untill a few hours before he died. (Alfred N. Proffit, Proffit Family Letters, SHC) Wilkes County

Entries in the glossary for illnesses or conditions from which people suffered include *ager* (ague, usually malaria), *biles* (boils), *bilious fever, bloody flux* (dysentery), *the bowel complaint, brain fever, the each* (itch), *(yellow) janders* (jaundice), *piles, putrid sore throat, quinsey, a rising* (an abscess), *thrush, the weak trembles,* and the *white swelling*. They might have felons on their hands or runarounds on their fingers. They might be *bad off, down sick, puny, poorly, fittified, in the gants,* or simply *low*. They might *get well* of an illness and be *on the mend* only to have a *backset* and have to go to the *horse spitle* and be *doctored* by a *physicianer*. If they were fortunate they might *mend up* and once again be *well and hearty, fleshy, stout,* and *peart*. If not, they might end up in the *dead house* and go to their *long homes* (graves). The families at home were especially concerned that loved ones were prepared for death and *in their right minds* before passing away:

> **June 28, 1863:** I think he was in his right mind to the last. a bout two hours I recon it was be fore he died he called me to him and said he wanted me to stay with him for he should die but I tried to encourage him. (John Bachelor, June 28, 1863, Brown Collection NCSA) Duplin County

News of the death of a loved one was not limited to soldiers but also included family members at home. In November 1864, Martha Poteet wrote her husband in Virginia what must have been the most devastating kind of letter a father could receive:

> **Nov. 2, 1864:** I seat My Self this evning to try to write you a few lines to let you know what has happend at home. poor little Francis Emmer is dead. she died the 29 of oct last saturday a little while before sundown. [. . .] when it got so that it couldent talk it would point its little finger for what it wanted and the day before it died it would look at me and then point with its little finger towards the loft. I think it saw the Angels that come to take it to heaven. it tried to show it to me but

> I couldent see nothing. (Martha Poteet, Poteet-Dickson Letters, NCSA) McDowell County

I.1.4. Farming

Since the majority of soldiers made their living from agriculture, perhaps their greatest concern while away from home was the productivity of their livestock, truck patches, and, most of all, corn and wheat crops, which were the primary source of sustenance for their families. Without corn, oats, and fodder, there would be no feed for livestock. Without corn and wheat, there would be no bread, that article which for many North Carolinians meant the same as food. Therefore, the letters from soldiers are filled with questions about livestock and crops, as well as detailed instructions for planting what crops in which fields, about getting help from family members or neighbors, and about disposing of surplus livestock or grain:

> **Aug. 3, 1861:** I wod like to know how much wheat you maid and how the corn looks. (L. W. Griffin, Griffin Papers, NCSA) Rutherford County

> **Oct. 16, 1863:** i wont you to sel all the wheat that you Can. tel the old man that i am well. tel me if you have getherd youer Corn yet ar not. (W. P. Cline, Cline Papers, SHC) Catawba County

The productivity of crops is also a common topic in letters from home, as wives and other family members report on the success they are having:

> **July 5, 1863:** I am laying by my crop. they old field looks tolerbul well consider[ing] the ground. the sweet potatoes looks well as tha did last yeare. the wheat was as good as ever yo saw. I made 20 shocks. the oats is wast high to any boday. (Amanda Murph, Murph Papers, Duke) Catawba County

Nouns referring to land, crops, equipment, and livestock include *beast, bee gum, bottom* (land), *bull tongue* (plow), *check line, cradle* (scythe), *a cut* (for a portion of cultivated land), *garden truck, gearing, jack* (a donkey), *mole* (plow), *muley* (cow), *newground, old field, plow stock, roughness* (coarse fodder), *shoat, slip* (sweet potato sprout), *swingle tree,* and *truck patch.* Verbs include *break up, grub up, lay by, lay off, make garden, maul rails,* and *pull fodder.*

I.1.5. Clothing

The semantic field for clothing is smaller than the semantic fields for food, illness, or farming, but clothing terms frequently appear in letters, and some of these are either regionally distinctive or obscure. Soldiers, especially early in the war, often report on clothing they have been issued as part of their uniforms. Soldiers also request articles of clothing from home as well as mention articles of clothing they are sending home:

> **Mar. 20, 1863:** wee drawn clothing yester day. I drawn 2 shirts an 2 par of slips an one military coat an pants. (T. F. Baggarly, Baggarly Papers, Duke) Iredell County

> **Apr. 4, 1863:** Dear Wife I send my Comfert and wolen shirt and neckless and gloves and one litle hat for Elfonso. (W. F. Wagner, *Confederate Soldier,* 44) Catawba County

These citations include two clothing terms which do not appear in *DARE, OED,* or *EDD*: the word *slips* for men's underpants and *necklace* for a woolen scarf. The word *slips* probably has the same meaning as the more common *drawers.* The North Carolina letters contain more than two dozen examples, all from western counties of the state. Additional examples have been found in letters from western Virginia, East Tennessee, northern Georgia, and the northwestern corner of South Carolina. *Necklace* is even more obscure and regionally restricted. The dozen examples we have collected all come from Catawba County, with the exception of a single occurrence from neighboring Davie County. All the writers who use the word are of German ancestry. Other terms for clothing, or material for making clothing, include *britches, flannen, frocktail* (coat), *gambadoes, galluses, gambadoes* (leather leggings), *janes, josie, linsey, neck comfort* (a woolen scarf), *pantaloons, roundabout* (a jacket), and *wamus* (a work coat).

I.2. Variation in North Carolina English

Not surprisingly, most of the words in the North Carolina letters that are regionally distinctive are designated South and/or South Midland in the *Dictionary of American Regional English,* as well as in publications based on the Linguistic Atlas of the Middle and South Atlantic States, including *A Word Geography of the Eastern United States* and *A Survey of Verb Forms in the Eastern United States,* both of which also incorporate material from the Linguistic Atlas of New England. What follows is a list of words collected from the North Carolina letters which appear in the *WGEUS* maps:

South
piazza (porch) and *snap beans*

South Midland
a little piece (a little way), *dodger* (a cake made from cornmeal), *green beans, plum* (completely), *poke, skillet, turn of corn, youns,* and *yous*

South and South Midland
bottom(land), branch (creek), *carry* (take), *Christmas gift!, clean* (completely), *comfort* (quilt), *granny* (midwife), *light bread, middlin (meat), (corn) pone, right smart, roasting ear, salat, (corn) shucks, snack, swingletree, turn* (a load), and *you all*

Overall, few words appear to be limited to the South Midland and fewer still to the South only. The largest number are shared by both the South and South Midland. The western half of North Carolina is in the South Midland speech area, which runs from about Rockingham County southward through Randolph County, then southwest through Union County. The LAMSAS data are, however, limited to the questionnaire items, so overall there are relatively few words that can be directly compared to the vocabulary of the North Carolina letters. *DARE,* on the other hand, draws on a much larger reservoir of lexical and grammatical evidence. Although there is no absolute agreement among authorities, North Carolina is conventionally divided into three regions, the Coastal Plains, the Piedmont, and the western counties, based primarily on physical geography. Linguistically, however, where there are regionally distinctive forms within the state, these distinctions are primarily between the eastern and western halves of the state. The somewhat higher number of South Midland features in the lists above may be accounted for in the fact that the western half of the state is more heavily represented in the North Carolina sample in terms of both numbers of letters and numbers of letter writers.

WGEUS map 114 (see p. liii) contains the various forms of second-person plural pronouns, including *you all, youns,* and *yous,* and the North Carolina portion of the map is in substantial agreement with the North Carolina letters. The very distinctive Southern form *you all* is found throughout North Carolina, while *youns* came southward with Scots-Irish settlers from Pennsylvania and is limited to the western half of the state. *Yous* has an even smaller regional domain than *youns,* being found primarily in the letters of writers of German ancestry and especially in Rowan and Catawba counties. That *yous* came to North Carolina with German settlers from Pennsylvania will probably come as a surprise to some readers since yous has long been attributed to Irish immigrants. With only two instances of *yous* collected by the LAMSAS fieldwork in the 1930s (in Rowan and Mecklenburg counties), it is likely that the form was declining in the late nineteenth and early twentieth centuries, replaced by the more universal southern *you all.*

In the North Carolina Civil War letters, there are two variants for the common conjunctions *before* and *by the time* and prepositions *by* and *before.* One is the Scots-Irish *against* (sometimes as *again* or *agin*) and the other is *till* in the English of Pennsylvania Germans; both of the words likely came to North Carolina with settlers from Pennsylvania. The CACWL collections indicate that *against* was very widespread through the Midland and South during the nineteenth century. In the North Carolina Civil War letters, *against* is restricted to the western parts of the state, although *WGEUS* map 160 suggests a wider distribution. In the North Carolina Civil War letters, *till* is restricted to writers of German ancestry and those parts of the state where Pennsylvania Germans settled in the second half of the eighteenth century. With only one North Carolina instance of *till* in WGEUS map 160, this word, like *yous,* appears to have been on the decline well before the LAMSAS fieldwork was conducted.

As stated in section I.1.1. (kinship terms), *pap, daddy,* and *dad* are limited to the western half of North Carolina. Other primarily "western" words include *kraut, hash, souse, kin, kinfolk,* and the pronunciations *Canetuck, Canetucky* for Kentucky (see glossary entry for variants). As noted above, both *slips* for underpants and *necklace* for a knitted scarf are particularly restricted to the western counties and the western Piedmont. The word *wamus* for work coat is a Pennsylvania German term and is limited to individuals of German ancestry in the western Piedmont, specifically Catawba and Lincoln counties. For the influence of Pennsylvania German on pronunciation, see section III.2.7.

In terms of grammar, another east-west distinction found in the North Carolina Civil War letters is the variant forms of the past tense of *see* (see section II.4.1.7. below). The nonstandard past tense *seed* is found throughout the state, while past tense *seen,* which may have come to North Carolina with immigrants from Pennsylvania, occurred most heavily in the western half of North Carolina, with only a few scattered instances in the southeastern part of the state. Among the various patterns of subject-verb agreement, an adjacent pronoun with *is, has,* or a verb + *-s* (*we is, I has, I sends, we wants*) is limited to the eastern half of North Carolina. For additional distinctively South and South Midland words, forms, and usages, see individual entries in the glossary.

II. Grammar

Among the linguistic features in the North Carolina letters that are the most compelling are those having to do with syntax (for example, subject-verb agreement, multiple negation) and morphological forms of verbs (past tenses and past participles). Because of their high frequency and consistency of use among letter writers, grammatical features in general have a higher degree of reliablity than most lexical features. Writers may have been concerned with penmanship and spelling, but they seem to have had little, if any, self-consciousness about using grammatical forms that were part of their native speech, even if these were often included in lists of prohibited usages in their school texts.[1] The following section is a catalogue of grammatical features with a minimum amount of commentary.

II.1. Nouns

II.1.1. Unmarked plurals of count nouns following a numeral

Mar. 23, 1863: he Sold five or six **pound** of his butter. (W. H. Brotherton, Brotherton Papers, Duke) Catawba County

May 23, 1863: I dont know when I will get home. there is Sum men here that hant bin home in fifteen **month** now. (R. C. Caldwell, Caldwell Collection, ECU) Cabarrus County

July 30, 1863: the do[c]ter said this moring that I wold note Be fite for Servis in thirty **day**. (J. W. Joyce, Joyce Papers, MHI) Stokes County

Aug. 24, 1863: Mother we hav got two Gunes at Wilimington that will carry a Eight hunard pound Ball they weigh fourty four thousand **pound** Each. (Edgar Smithwick, Smithwick Papers, Duke) Martin County

II.1.2. Nouns ending in *-s* or similar sound treated as a plural

Jan. 12, 1862: I will tell you what we have to eat. beef and bread an Rhy Coffee. some time **a few molasses** an some none. (James Keever, Keever Papers, Duke) Lincoln County

Apr. 18, 1864: my dear I can inform you that we have one case of the **Small pocks** in camp James trexler has got **them**. (John Hartman, Hartman Papers, Duke) Rowan County

II.1.3. Unmarked possesives of nouns

Sept. 7, 1862: tell **grany** peple that I am well at present and uncil William and uncil John. (W. H. Brotherton, Brotherton Papers, Duke) Catawba County

Apr. 13, 1863: they come to my house and take en my **son** saddle after thay hade killed him and takein one of my best horses i hade. (Isaac Miller, Vance Papers, NCSA) Davidson County

Sept. 2, 1863: your **Farther** family ar all well. (Thomas Brann, Tesh Papers, Duke) Yadkin County

Jan. 20, 1864: Leathham wants to know what become of **Joseph** money and things he had with him. (Thornton Sexton, Sexton Letters, Duke) Ashe County

II.2. Pronouns

II.2.1. Personal pronouns

II.2.1.1. Second-person plural forms *you all, youns, yous*

Plural *you all* is, by far, the most common variant second-person plural, with 1,447 occurrences in the North Carolina letters. There are 40 occurrences of *yous* and 18 of *youns*. *You all* is a very distinctively Southern form (see map on p. liii) and is rare north of the Mason-Dixon line. In North Carolina it is found throughout the state and used by writers who also use *yous* or *youns*.

II.2.1.2. Third-person singular *hit*

There are 244 occurrences of *hit* among fifty-two different North Carolina writers from every part of the state:

Oct. 12, 1862: your hogs are dwoing vry well that was spaid but won and **hit** is dead. (Serepta Revis, Revis Letters, NCSA) Henderson County

Dec. 21, 1862: Cousin **hit** wuld take me a some time time to rite **hit** doun and I have to gow to put on some of old Nead [= pork] to cook to pursurve life. (Phillip Shull, Councill Papers, Duke) Watauga County

II.2.1.3. Object pronouns in subject position with compound subjects

Jan. 1, 1862: me and **him** and tolliver had a pretty smart singing Last night. (G. J. Huntley, Huntley Papers, WCU) Rutherford County

Jan. 15, 1863: me and Causey is working close together now. (James Hackett, Hackett Papers, Duke) Guilford County

Mar. 18, 1864: hit was rote her in John Blacks letter that **him** and alen carter had Swore ilye [= a lie] a gin calvin. (Thornton Sexton, Sexton Letters, Duke) Ashe County

June 16, 1864: me and the children will be bound to suffer. (Martha Poteet, Poteet-Dickson Letters, NCSA) McDowell County

II.2.2. Possessive pronouns ending in *-n* rather than *-s*

See also glossary entries for *hern, hisn, ourn, theirn, yourn*.

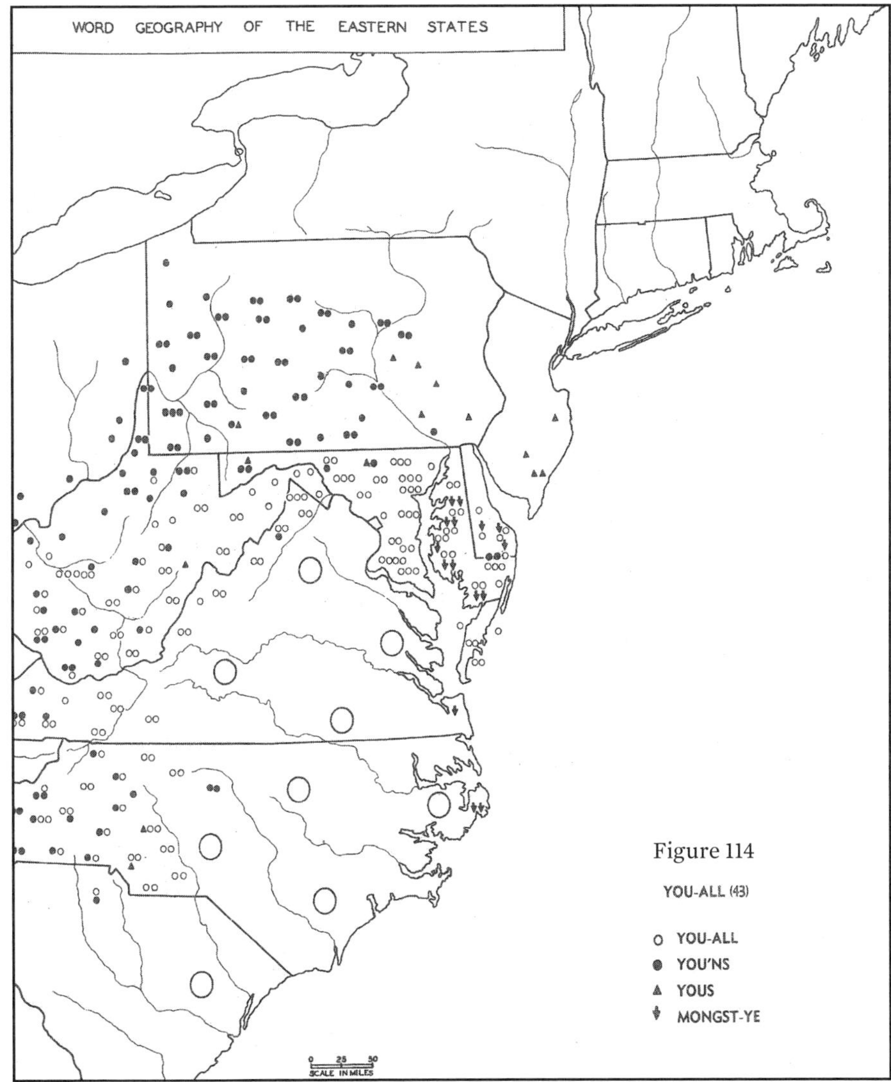

From Hans Kurath, *A Word Geography of the Eastern United States,* ©1949 by the University of Michigan Press. Reproduced by permission of the publisher.

Aug. 14, 1862: I hante never hern [= heard] ner I dont now how many of **ourn** is lost. (Austin Brown, Brown Family Papers, Duke) Johnston County

Nov. 8, 1862: you Rote to me that you had done broke one of you <???> teath and mary Eetter had fell dow[n] broke out some of **hern**. you and hear must take care of you teath better than that. (J. W. Joyce, Joyce Papers, MHI) Stokes County

Apr. 12, 1863: Dear wife the reason I hant ancerd yours letter yett I had jest started one that same day I Got **yourn**. (Daniel Brown, Brown Collection NCSA) Duplin County

II.2.3. Reflexive pronouns

II.2.3.1. *hisself, ourselfs, theirselves*

Aug. 9, 1862: J W Hutcheson is well if he will take care of **his self**. he is so he can walk all A Bout. (J. W. Love, Love Papers, Duke) Henderson County

May 28, 1863: I ame in a lo Stat of helth. I hav lost one of my eyes and I Cant Sea good out of the other an my folks is a Sufering an they ant nary one able to help **ther selvs**. (John Brock, Vance Papers, NCSA) Wayne County

II.2.3.2. Personal dative (personal pronoun forms used instead of forms marked with *-self* or *-selves*)

Sept. 5, 1861: he will never get **him** A wife. (J. W. Williams, Williams Papers, Duke) Onslow County

June 12, 1862: you had better get **you** some wooll before it gets all hunted up. (Isaac Lefevers, Lefevers Papers, NCSA) Catawba County

June 23, 1863: I want you to come home as soon as you can get the chance try to get **you** afurlow and come home. (Sarepta Revis, Revis Letters, NCSA) Henderson County

Nov. 22, 1863: Mother I Bought **me** apocket knife to day and giv ten dollars for it. (Edgar Smithwick, Smithwick Papers, Duke) Martin County

Nov. 24, 1863: we had orders to build **us** cabins. I have got **me** one all ready dun. (William Tesh, Tesh Papers, Duke) Yadkin County

II.2.3.3. Reflexive pronoun in subject position (with compound subject)

Feb. 15, 1863: I Can informe you that **my self** and family is all well as comon. (Samuel Phillips, Confederate Misc., Emory) Yancy County

Sept. 29, 1863: This lieves **my self** & Burjes well except he is taking of a Cold which causis him to feel dull. (A. A. Jackson, Jackson Family Corr., Notre Dame) Moore County

II.2.4. Demonstratives

II.2.4.1. *them* as a modifier in a noun phrase

Apr. 6, 1863: tell Delia I will write to her after I get **them** things. (W. B. Lance, Lance Papers, LSU) Henderson County

Jan. 17, 1864: Well Mag I want hen to make rails cut his timber along Side of the nuground Gap cut **them** big trees where the wood was piled. (R. C. Caldwell, Caldwell Collection, ECU) Cabarrus County

II.2.4.2. *them* as a demonstrative pronoun

July 16, 1862: Brother France [= Francis] got kill in the Battle. Wilson Walker got kill an John Willhelmm. **them** is all that got kill on the feel [= field] as wee know off. (Leonard Alman, Alman Papers, Duke) Cabarrus County

Aug. 15, 1863: I heard Mack younts company in the 38th Regt had all Runaway but 9 and **them** would go too before long. (W. F. Wagner, *Confederate Soldier,* 65) Catawba County

II.2.5. Indefinite pronouns

See glossary entries for *all, ary, ary one, nary one, one, t'other, what all,* and *who all.*

II.2.6. Relative pronouns

II.2.6.1. Relative pronoun *what* instead of *that, which,* or *who*

Aug. 5, 1862: I want you to make me Some Shirts outen tha[t] Calico **what** I got at germington. (A. J. Spease, Zimmerman Papers, Duke) Forsyth County

Sept. 25, 1863: I will Say to you that mi things **what** I left is her yet all but mi drawers and lewis is awarein [= a-wearing] them. (Daniel Setzer, Setzer Papers, Duke) Catawba County

II.2.6.2. Reduced form *at* for *that*

July 24, 1864: Jim i have bin on every raid **at** the yankees has maid this summer. (Thomas B. Litten, Fisher Papers, Duke) Catawba County

II.2.6.3. Relative pronoun *which* with a human referent

Jan. 4, 1863: I am 48 years old in Febuary next and has 4 litle children and My wife **which** is vary weekly. (J. C. M. Justice, Vance Papers, NCSA) Cumberland County

II.2.6.4. Relative pronoun *as* instead of *who, whom, which, that*

July 31, 1861: I am agoing to send you some buter and some pickles **as** I made a purpes [= especially] for yu. (Letty Long, Long Family Papers, SHC) Alamance County

II.2.6.5. Relative pronoun deletion (indicated with Ø)

Nov. 13, 1861: I am not very well but it is the bad Cold I think **Ø** ails me. (James Fisher, Fisher Papers, Duke) Catawba County

Feb. 6, 1862: wee ar not uneasy. I think their is the best hops of peace **Ø** has ever bin. (J. A. Shipman, Shipman Family Corr., Notre Dame) Henderson County

II.3. Articles and Adjectives

II.3.1. Articles

II.3.1.1. Indefinite article *a* before words starting with a vowel

Oct. 6, 1864: the Assosiation has past over. there was 14 or 15 preachers there. your couisen bob Moody was there. he preached on Sunday. it rained So Much that they dident hav Much of **a** assosiation. (Martha Poteet, Poteet-Dickson Letters, NCSA) McDowell County

II.3.1.2. Definite article *the* used before illnesses, place names, and *most*

Nov. 24, 1861: I must quit this is the last leter that I will write from **the Hot Springs**. prehaps it is the last one that I will ever wright. (L. W. Griffin, Griffin Papers, NCSA) Rutherford County

Oct. 13, 1862: I herd today that he is at home and has **the tifored fever** and is verry low. (J. W. Lineberger, *Gaston Ranger,* 23) Gaston County

Nov. 29, 1862: my freinds ar all in the army and **The moast** of them ded. (Jemima Thomas, Vance Papers, NCSA) Iredell County

II.3.2. Indefinite adjectives

See glossary entries for *ary* and *nary.*

Mar. 21, 1864: I saw a man shot last Fryday and I dont want to see **ary** other one. (Peter J. Peterson, Peterson Papers, Duke) Catawba County

June 22, 1861: I have not been down Sick **nara** day since I have left home But I have been Some what puny several thimes. (J. N. Cunningham, Cunningham Letters, NCSA) Haywood County

II.3.3. Comparatives

II.3.3.1. redundantly marked with both *more* and comparative suffix *-er,* for example, *more healthyer, more happier*

Aug. 15, 1862: I am inhopes we are getting into a **more healthyer** climate than we have been: for the country looks more lik old buncombe: and the watter is more pure: and the aire is fresher. (W. M. Patton, Patton Family Letters, SHC) Buncombe County

Apr. 23, 1863: I am in hopse that the future will bring forth **more happier** moments than has ben for the last two years. (J. F. Coghill, Coghill Papers, Duke) Granville County

II.3.3.2. Irregular forms with suffix *-er,* for example, *faireder, worser*

Sept. 17, 1860: your cotton is **farrieder** than it wours [= was] last year but I dont think it is So ful of boles. (Thomas Harding, Blount Papers, NCSA) Beaufort County

Nov. 28, 1861: he new that he had to go. the longer they put it [off] the **worsser** it is. (Dena Stack, Confederate Papers, SHC) Union County

II.3.4. Superlatives

II.3.4.1. Redundantly marked with both *most* and superlative suffix *-est.*, for example, *most handsomest, most happiest*

Aug. 10, 1861: we are at Camp wigfall one mile from manassa in a **most Hansomist** place you Ever saw sur rounded by mountains large Clover fields And Bact by a Great number of Southern Soldiers Large stout & well Drilled men. (W. R. D. Bost, Gibson Papers, Duke) Catawba County

Jan. 17, 1863: I tell you it was the **most happ[i]est** move that we have ever taken since we have bin out. everyone was hope up to think that we was a getten Back to our good olde state. (Isaac Lefevers, Lefevers Papers, NCSA) Catawba County

II.3.4.2. irregular forms with suffix *-est,* for example, *badest, blessedest, disablest, helplessest, pitifullest, powerfullest, lonesomest, roguishes*

May 17, 1863: we air at fair feeld in 4 miles of war trace in 18 or 20 of murfrees Boro on one prong of duck River. this is A good Country hear grate land and the **powrfulst** plac I Ever Saw for pasture. (J. W. Reese, Reese Papers, Duke) Buncombe County

July 13, 1863: this is to inform you Dear Sir how the Surgent Doctor acted when the militia was cald oup to forty five [years old]. he Discharged the Men Seems like that was his friends and the **Disablest** Bodyed Men that wasent he Dident. (William Martin, Vance Papers, NCSA) Burke County

Aug. 20, 1863: Sis I am the **loansomest** chicken you ever saw. no pirson to stay with or talk with of my acquaints. (Alfred N. Proffit, Proffit Family Letters, SHC) Wilkes County

Jan. 9, 1865: she would have slight chills and some times high fevers and ache so bad she couldent ly but a little while. she dident have pain but ache and sore she was the **helplessest** person I ever saw. (Ann Bowen, Bowen Papers, NCSA) Washington County

II.3.5. Adjective phrase *all the,* "the only"

June 12, 1862: I want you to try and come to see mee as that will bee **all the** chance that I will have to see you as longue as times keep they way their now. (Isaac Lefevers, Lefevers Papers, NCSA) Catawba County

Mar. 30, 1863: I am a very pore man. old and unable to work. I have raisd three Sons to be men. tha are **all the** help I had able to doo enny thing hardley. (Henry Johnson, Vance Papers, NCSA) Forsyth County

Apr. 25, 1864: they yankes loss 3 Captured & 30 kild & wounded among the kild 1 mager & 1 Capt. hour men faught well. [The] Thomas legion was **all the** forces her[e] except a small co of Tenn cavelry. (Stephen Whitaker, Whitaker Papers, NCSA) Cherokee County

II.4. Verbs

II.4.1. Verb principal parts

A wide variety of nonstandard past tense and past participle forms of verbs appear in the North Carolina letters. In some cases irregular (strong) verbs have become regular (weak) verbs by analogy: *blowed, catched, drawed, drived, growed, knowed, runned, seed, throwed.* A few have resisted analogy and retain their earlier, irregular past tenses and/or past participles: *cotch, fotch, hope* (helped). Still others have a reduction in the number of principle parts (a process known as *leveling*), some with past tenses identical with the present tense: *come, eat, give, run,* some with the past tense taking the form of the past participle: *done, gone, seen, taken, written,* and others with the past participle taking the form of the past tense: *drew, went, knew, saw, took, wrote.* There is a considerable amount of variability among the verb forms, even in the writing of individuals. The verb *see* follows a variety of patterns in the North Carolina letters, including the form *seed* for past tense and past participle, as well as two different leveled forms, *seen* as past tense and past participle and *saw* as both past tense and past participle. Below is a list of the principal parts of common verbs in the North Carolina letters, including standard and nonstandard forms:

Verb	Past Tense	Past Participle
attack	attacked, attackted	attacked, attackted
blow	blew, blowed, blown	blowed, blown
break	broke	broke, broken
bring	brought, brung	brought, brang, brung
catch	caught, cotch, catched	caught, cotch
come	came, come	come
do	did, done	done
draw	drew, drawed, drawn	drew, drawed, drawn
drive	drove, druv, drived	drove, druv
eat	ate, eat, et	eat, et, eaten
fetch	fetched, fetch	fetched, fetch, fotch
fight	fought, fit	fought
give	gave, give, given	gave, give, given
go	went, gone	went, gone
grow	grew	growed, grown
help	helped, hope	helped, hope
know	knew, knowed	knew, knowed, known
run	ran, run, runned	run
see	saw, seen, seed	saw, seen, seed
set	set, sot	set, sot, sat
take	took, tuck, taken	took, tuck, taken
throw	threw, throwed	thrown, throwed
write	wrote, written	wrote, written

Other, less common verbs that have nonstandard past tenses/past participles with a redundant *-ed* suffix include: *borned, bursted, costed, drownded, freezed/frozed.* Less common verbs following the irregular pattern include past tense *drunk, sunk, druv* (drove), *shuck* (shook) *sot* (sat), *tetch* (touched). The sections below provide frequency counts for different morphological forms of some verbs in the North Carolina Civil War letters.[2]

II.4.1.1. *ask*

There were fifty-two examples of the past tense of *ask* in the North Carolina letters. Of these, twenty-nine (55.8%) were the standard form *asked,* twelve (23.1%) were the variant form *ast,* and eleven (21.1%) were of the variant form *ask* without the *-ed* suffix. No examples of past tense *ax* were found, and only one each were found of infinitive, present tense, and present participle forms to *ax, ax, axing.*

II.4.1.2. *catch*

There were relatively few past tense (eighteen) and past participle (nineteen) forms of *catch.* In both cases the standard form *caught* predominated, with two occurrences of variant past tense *cetched* and one of past participle *catched.* There was also one past tense *cotch* and one past participle *kotch.*

II.4.1.3. *draw*

The variant form *drawed* for the past tense and past participle of *draw* predominated, with forty-five (81.8%) of fifty-five past tense forms and sixty-three (73.3%) of eighty-six past participle forms. There were also five examples of past tense *drawn* and five of past participle *drew.*

II.4.1.4. *eat*

Although there were 674 occurrences of the verb *eat* in the North Carolina letters, there were relatively few past tense forms (37) and past participles (25). In both cases, the leveled form *eat* predominated, with 32 (86.5%) of the past tense forms and 23 (92.0%) of the past participle forms. There only a single occurrence of the standard past tense *ate* and a single occurrence of the standard past participle *eaten.* There were 2 examples of the past tense *et* and 2 of the past tense *eaten.* There was also a single occurrence of past participle *et.*

II.4.1.5. *help*

Past tense and past participle forms were not very common in the sample, but of the past tense forms, *hope* accounted for ten (58.8%) of seventeen total occurrences of the past tense. The past participle *hope* accounted for seven (43.8%) of sixteen past participles.

II.4.1.6. *know*

The regular (weak) form *knowed* occurred thirty (32.3%) times out of a total ninety-three past tense forms; the standard *knew* accounted for the remainder. The past participle knowed occurred only six times (23.1%) out of a total of twenty-six past participles. The variant past participle *knew* occurred three times.

II.4.1.7. *see*

The verb *see* is unusual in that it has North Carolina variants that reflect both leveling and regularization of past tense and past participle forms. In the past tense, the standard form *saw* predominated, with 365 (80.8%) of 452 occurrences. The regular (weak) past tense *seed* occurred 60 times (13.3%) and the leveled form *seen* occurred 27 times (6.0%). The standard past participle *seen* occurred 76 times (50.3%) of 151 total occurrences of past participles. The variant past participle *saw* accounted for 41.1% of the total, with 62 occurrences. There were only 13 examples (8.6%) of the weak past participle *seed*. The North Carolina letters contained only a single example of past tense *see* (from Duplin County).

II.4.1.8. *take*

The standard form *took* accounted for 267 (61.2%) of 452 past tense forms. The leveled past tense *taken* occurred 118 times, for 27.1% of the total, while the variant *tuck* occurred 51 times (11.7%). The standard past participle *taken* predominated, with 369 (92.5%) of 399 past participles. Variants *took* and *tuck* accounted for only 3.8% each.

II.4.1.9. *throw*

Although *throw* was not a particularly common verb in the North Carolina sample, the regular (weak) variant past tense *throwed* was the most common past tense form with twenty-four out of a total of thirty-six occurrences (66.7%). There were only ten examples of past participles, three *throwed,* two *threw,* and five *thrown.*

II.4.1.10. *write*

There were 7,568 occurrences of write in the North Carolina letters, including 1,145 past tenses and 592 past participles. In the past tense, the standard form wrote predominated with 1,127 (98.4%) occurrences. The remaining 18 examples were the leveled form written. Of the past participles, the leveled form wrote accounted for 471 (80%) of the total, with the remaining examples all being standard written.

II.4.2. *be*

See also the glossary entry for additional examples.

II.4.2.1. *be* in a subordinate clause introduced by *if* or *unless*

> **Oct. 13, 1862:** their haint no chance to get a Furlow now unless a man **be** sick. (William Tesh, Tesh Papers, Duke) Yadkin County

II.4.2.2. *are* with first-person and third-person singular subjects

> **Apr. 18, 1862:** the draft did not hit eather **won** of mi brothers. it hit three of the reveses boys. won of them **ar** gone and too of them ar gone an i dont no whear. (Elizabeth Mock, Tesh Papers, Duke) Yadkin County

II.4.2.3. *is* with an adjacent pronoun subject

> **Aug. 4, 1862: we is** ancious to no if B.C. is a wating on you. (Dicy Ann Jackson, Jackson Family Corr., Notre Dame) Moore County

II.4.2.4. *is* with a plural or conjoined noun subject

This particular pattern is very common, occurring 374 times (75.9%) out of 493 possible occurrences. It is also regionally distinctive of the South and South Midland:

> **Mar. 20, 1862: I and Mathew is** well and all of my mess is well. (J. W. Love, Love Papers, Duke) Henderson County

> **Nov. 29, 1862: paps folks is** well as far as i know. times **is** mity hard here. (J. T. Revis, Revis Letters, NCSA) Henderson County

II.4.2.5. *is* with a non-adjacent (remote) pronoun subject

> **Oct. 2, 1860:** Dear Sister. I take my pen in hand to let you know **I** and all **is** well. (J. W. Love, Love Papers, Duke) Henderson County

II.4.2.6. *was* with a plural subject

This particular pattern was (and still is) very common throughout the country. In the North Carolina sample the pattern occurred 113 (85%) out of 133 possible occurrences with nonpronoun subjects and 316 (88%) out of 356 possible occurrences with pronoun subjects:

> **Sept. 7, 1862:** I have nowthing partictoler to write only this is a wright smart place hear. I have Saw Some yankees hear. I Saw two yankees doctors scienc I come hear. **they was** mighty nice looking men. (W. H. Brotherton, Brotherton Papers, Duke) Catawba County

II.4.2.7. *were, war, ware* with a first- or third-person singular subject

This pattern was very uncommon in the North Carolina sample, with a total of six occurrences (four of these in letters by J. F. Coghill of Granville County):

Oct. 28, 1862: Dear sistor you dont now how glad **I wer** to hear from you and to hear that John had got home. (Jonas Bradshaw, Bradshaw Papers, Duke) Alexander County

Mar. 28, 1864: wee had to cross on the Railroad bridge which was very high from the ground so wee fought on the bridge and **I ware** the one to go in front when wee advanced and in the rear when wee retreated. (J. F. Coghill, Coghill Papers, Duke) Granville County

II.4.2.8. Negative past tense *weren't, want, warnt* with a singular subject

This pattern is uncommon and only occurs seven times in the North Carolina letters:

Aug. 14, 1862: Bardin is gon to the horsepittle. **he want** verry bad of[f] when he left us. (Austin Brown, Brown Family Papers, Duke) Johnston County

Nov. 12, 1862: i warnt fit for servies nor never wold bee a gain. (Samuel J. Guy, Vance Papers, NCSA) Cumberland County

II.4.2.9. Deletion of linking verb *be*

Dec. 27, 1862: I take the present oppertunity to Let you know that I **Ø** well at present. (W. H. Brotherton, Brotherton Papers, Duke) Catawba County

II.4.2.10. Deletion of auxiliary *be*

Oct. 10, 1862: we **Ø** laying by waiting amovement of they yankees. (W. H. Brotherton, Brotherton Papers, Duke) Catawba County

II.4.3. *have*

See also the glossary entry.

II.4.3.1. *has* with a plural or conjoined subject

Nov. 26, 1862: it seemes that my **friends has** fogoton me. (Daniel Revis, Revis Letters, NCSA) Henderson County

Mar. 26, 1863: I feel stiff in my Joints yet but the **Pains has** abated considerable. (A. A. Jackson, Jackson Family Corr., Notre Dame) Moore County

II.4.3.2. *have* with a third-person singular subject

Oct. 1, 1861: Fes is with us. **he have** ben a Brother to me and I love him as a Brother. I never can forget him for what **he have** don. (K. W. Coghill, Coghill Papers, Duke) Granville County

Oct. 8, 1863: my **husband have** ben in servise going on two years and my dependenc is in him. (Sallie Carter, Vance Papers, NCSA) Hertford County

II.4.3.3. Deletion of auxiliary *have*

Mar. 22, 1862: they took .100. prisners and if the road had not Bin so muddy they would **Ø** run them to Bulls Run. (J. A. Shipman, Shipman Family Corr., Notre Dame) Henderson County

Feb. 8, 1863: Jane says she wishes you had bin here to **Ø** seen that fellow fly around. (Molly Tesh, Tesh Papers, Duke) Yadkin County

Aug. 8, 1863: the wheat must **Ø** bin mity bad. that hant half as much as it made too yares ago. (Daniel Setzer, Setzer Papers, Duke) Catawba County

Mar. 12, 1865: Mas[ter] Eddy is on his way from Kinston to goldsboro and expect him her soon in the course of an hour or so. he may **Ø** wrote to you himself but may not have time when he gets her. (Washington Wills, Wills Papers, SHC) Halifax County

II.4.4. Modal auxiliaries

II.4.4.1. *shall, should, shan't*

In the mid-nineteenth century, *shall* was still in use with first-person subjects to indicate the future. *Should* and *shan't* were also used with first-person subjects where present-day English usually employs *would* and *will not/won't*. All three are less common than *will, would,* and *will not/won't*.[3]

Apr. 19, 1863: Mag live contented for i think i **shall** come home this summer yet. (T. F. Baggarly, Baggarly Papers, Duke) Iredell County

May 25, 1863: I **shal** start [= send] this letter to morow. (Neill McLeod, McLeod Letters, SHC) Moore County

July 9, 1861: I **should** be the glades in the World to com an stay with you a week or to but I cant get off for we shal hav to leave shortly I think. (G. T. Beavers, Upchurch Papers, Duke) Chatham County

Dec. 22, 1862: I **should** like to be with you all at home a Christmas. (James Zimmerman, Zimmerman Papers, Duke) Forsyth County

Dec. 8, 1861: we are bilding houses to live in. I hope when we get them don we **shant** sufer so much with cold. (George Williams, Williams-Womble Papers, NCSA) Orange County

May 10, 1863: dear wife I have lot more to wright than I could right in a week bwt I **shant** right much now for I cant right. I have Got the trimbles so bad I doant feele like setting up. (Daniel Brown, Brown Collection, NCSA) Duplin County

II.4.4.2. *mought* and *might + could, would*

See glossary entry for *might*. The common multiple modal *might could* in present-day English in the South and South Midland was not found in the North Carolina letters. For a possible connection, see *might* in the glossary. See also *maybe can*.

Aug. 9, 1862: it is A mistry to me to see how the close got of the bag and never took any thing elce. probly they **mought**. (J. W. Williams, Williams Papers, Duke) Onslow County

II.4.5. *A*-prefixing

See also the glossary entry. The CACWL data indicate that *a*-prefixing was very widespread in nineteenth-century American English. This feature occurs a total of 664 times before present participles in the North Carolina letters. It is uncommon before past participles. Most of the examples of a-prefixing are before stressed syllables beginning with a consonant. The most common present participle to which the *a-* is attached is going, but the number of different verbs found with the prefix is extensive and sometimes exceptional: *a beginning, a complaining, a court martialing, a deserting, a eating, a improving,* and *a speculating.*

II.4.5.1. Added to a present participle

Oct. 29, 1861: allison is **a working** for mea and epects to work 10 or 12 days. (Elizabeth Watson, Watson Letters, WCU) Jackson County

Mar. 1864: we are **a driving** wagons in the general Army Supply train. (W. H. Horton, Councill Papers, Duke) Watauga County

Apr. 13, 1864: I have been **afishing** here several times. (C. A. Walker, Walker Papers, WCU) Cherokee County

II.4.5.2. Added to a past participle

July 1862: the enemy was throwing ther grape Shot at us By the Bushel and Thousands Shooting at us with ther mus kets where you would a thought that if a mans hat had **a Bin** hel up in the air that it was Bound to Be Shot to pieces (P. S. Whitner, Whitner Papers, Duke) Catawba County

II.4.6. Infinitive marker *for to*

See also glossary entry.

June 5, 1863: in the eavning we stopt **for to** camp for the nite. (B. Y. Malone, June 5, 1863, *Malone Diary,* 34) Caswell County

June 19, 1863: all you must Writ to me often for We are in a bad place **fore to** get any letters here (John Futch, Futch Letters, NCSA) New Hanover County

II.4.7. Phrasal verbs

A phrasal verb consists of a verb and a verb particle (*turn up, turn down, turn in*) which are joined to create a complex, often idiomatic verb. A few phrasal verbs have more than one particle. The English language is unusual among related languages for the large number of phrasal verbs it contains, and the North Carolina letters are particularly rich in phrasal verbs that have regional or historical significance. There are about eighty phrasal verbs included in the glossary. Some of these may be familiar to many people, although the variant grammatical forms may not be. Others may look familiar, but their meanings may be quite different in present-day usage. The following is a list of the phrasal verbs in the glossary: *blow up, bob around, break open, break up, come clear, come off, come on, come up, eat out, fall off, feel to, fly around, fool with, fork over, fun at, get about, get awake, get to, give in, give out, give over, give up, give way, go for, go to, go up, go with, grub up, happen to, hear say, hear tell of, hold out, hold up, keep clear, kill up, knock about, knock along, knock around, lay by, lay off, lay up, lie out, light with, look for, look out for, look over, make out, meet up with, mend up, pitch in, pitch into, play off on, play on, play out, press out, prevail with, pull down, put away, put off, put over, put up, run out, run over, set in, shet up, sit up, start up, swop off, take down, take on about, take up, tear down, tear up, think hard, throw out, throw up, turn off, turn out, wait on, whip out,* and *work on.* The following are examples of some of these phrasal verbs:

> **July 5, 1856:** the people has bin faithful an dutiful to mee an to thare work and all have agreed togather Sence master left home. I am glad that tha have **helt out** So well in thare health all Saving oncle charles and he has bin treated with the greates respets that could be required. (Moses [Pettigrew Slave], Pettigrew Family Papers, SHC) Washington County

> **Oct. 25, 1861:** Blasingame is **throwed out** of his ofice. he Went out one Sundy and Jump one [= on] A Boy and Beate him Badly so I herd. he was **throwd out** to Day. (Jesse Shipman, Shipman Family Corr., Notre Dame) Henderson County

> **Sept. 14, 1862:** We want to know how much wheat we made and how you all **come on** makeing brandy. it is worth Twenty dollers per gallon here. (James Zimmerman, Zimmerman Papers, Duke) Forsyth County

> **Aug. 7, 1863:** you said th[at] you helped hariet to **lay by** her corn and haul her wheet. I thank your seaing to her. (John L. Putnam, Kendrick Papers, NCSA) Cleveland County

> **Feb. 13, 1863:** I have not Dun a day work at home in about five monts for **taking up** Deserters and Bying corn and haling to the volenteairs wives. (Thomas M. Walker, Vance Papers, NCSA) Granville County

> **Dec. 19, 1863:** we leaveed from tennesse to ashville without having enny thing to fead or eat. that coutry is all **eat out**. (Franklin Setzer, Setzer Corr., UVA) Catawba County

II.5. Adverbs

See also glossary entries for *a most, anymore, directly, ever, hardly, live/leave, middling, nigh, sorter/sorty,* and *thataway.*

II.5.1. *certain (surtain)* and *sure (shore)* meaning "certainly, for certain, for sure" and appearing at the end of a sentence

See glossary entries for additional examples.

> **Feb. 5, 1862:** i want you to com an Sea us **certain**. (Roxy Sandlin, Williams Papers, Duke) Duplin County

> **June 10, 1862:** Brother I have not paid you the five dollars I borrowed of you but I will do that **surtain**. (Ichabod Quinn, Quinn Papers, Duke) Duplin County

> **Feb. 15, 1864:** I cant wear it but I wouldnt take nothing in world for it is a nice little ring **Shore**. (Molly Tesh, Tesh Papers, Duke) Yadkin County

> **Apr. 24, 1864:** there is no fun in fiting **shore**. (G. W. Love, Love Papers, Duke) Henderson County

II.5.2. *awful, mighty (mity), powerful(ly), pretty (purty), right,* and *tolerable/tolerably* as intensifiers and/or qualifiers

> **Dec. 2, 1862:** I have the rumaties and a **powerfull** bad cold and cough. (James Zimmerman, Zimmerman Papers, Duke) Forsyth County

> **May 15, 1863:** we are faring **tolarble** well at this time on our small rations. (A. A. Jackson, Jackson Family Corr., Notre Dame) Moore County

> **June 24, 1863:** he was **right** sick but I hope not dangerous. (Andrew J. Proffit, Proffit Family Letters, SHC) Wilkes County

> **Jan. 1, 1864:** Mr hail is agoing to cum out her and bring all the b[o]xes that the we want to our cumpany and I want you to Send me a **purty** larg box. (Daniel Setzer, Setzer Papers, Duke) Catawba County

> **Dec. 14, 1864:** I can Say to you I am well but **mity** tyred a marching (Alexander Keever, Keever Papers, Duke) Lincoln County

II.5.3. *clean, clear,* and *plum(b)* meaning "completely, all the way"

> **July 12, 1862:** we folard after the yankes thirty mils below richmond **clean** to james river. (J. W. Williams, Williams Papers, Duke) Onslow County

> **Aug. 17, 1862:** other Regiments is leaveing her a round us going down to the valleys About one hundred [miles] or more. if we git down there we Shall be **clear** gon out of hearing near About.

(William Carpenter, Carpenter Family Papers, ECU) Chatham County

Jan. 11, 1863: I Cant rite to day. I hant in the rit fix for riting I wold like to rite you along letter but I am **plum** upside down to day. (John Hartman, Hartman Papers, Duke) Rowan County

II.6. Conjunctions

See also glossary entries for additional examples.

II.6.1. *and*

II.6.1.1. *and* introducing a subordinate clause with a present participle as verb or with an understood verb *be*.

Jan. 24, 1861: the boys left this morning holluring like they was after a fox **and** it Sunday morning but we dont have no Sunday her. (L. W. Griffin, Griffin Papers, NCSA) Rutherford County

II.6.1.2. *and* used in place of *than* or *as*

Mar. 9, 1865: When they taken them they treated us mean **and** our owner ever did. they taken us just like we had been dum beast. (Richard Boyle, *Freedom*, ser. 1, vol. 2, 232) Tyrrell County

II.6.2. *against, again* meaning "before, by the time"

Feb. 5, 1863: I got a small bundle of cloths for you some two week ago, it came in a box with some things of C K. J. G. and Cy and I did not know what to do with them, for the way you wrote before I expected that you was at home **against** they came. (D. R. Hoyle, Kendrick Papers, NCSA) Cleveland County

II.6.3. *till*

II.6.3.1. *till* meaning "before, by the time"

Apr. 21, 1864: I want you to have plenty of good eating **tell** I come Such as eggs and ham and crout and milk and butter and Sallet & Sweat potatoes and So on. (Alexander Keever, Keever Papers, Duke) Lincoln County

II.6.3.2. *till* meaning "so that, in such a manner"

June 22, 1864: I would like we could all be at home a while **till** we could all get to rest a while. (S. E. Love, Love Papers, Duke) Henderson County

II.6.4. *but what* meaning "but that" introducing a subordinate clause following a negative clause

Oct. 23, 1862: we would of sent more but we dont now **but what** we may git some chance to come home. (Robert C. Love, Love Papers, Duke) Henderson County

II.6.5. *to what* meaning "compared to what"

Mar. 24, 1863: I am faring very well **to what** I have ben for I am Getting yust to my fear [= fare]. (Daniel Brown, Brown Collection, NCSA) Duplin County

II.6.6. *without* meaning "unless"

May 25, 1862: it cant be put off much Longer **without** one party or the other withdraws from their presant positions. (Martin Davis, WPA Transcripts, TSLA) Yadkin County

II.6.7. *as* instead of *that,* especailly after the verb *know*

July 22, 1861: I dont know **as** I ever will See you a gain. (Charley Futch, Futch Letters, NCSA) New Hanover County

II.6.8. *nor* following a negative construction without correlative *neither*

Mar. 17, 1864: I cant Rite every week. if I could I would Rite oftiner I cant git paper **nor** invellopes with out money. (F. M. Poteet, Poteet-Dickson Letters, NCSA) McDowell County

II.6.9. *except* meaning "unless"

May 4, 1862: I have some idea of going to Capt Eaves Company at Raleigh **Except** I get some Body to take my place. (G. J. Huntley, Huntley Papers, WCU) Rutherford County

II.6.10. *so as* meaning "so that, in such a manner"

Aug. 14, 1862: I hope the lord wil provid some way for me & you all **so as** we may see one another one more time. (Austin Brown, Brown Family Papers, Duke) Johnston County

II.6.11. *whenever* meaning "as soon as"

Nov. 15, 1864: i will send you that strop an som turnips an som other things **when ever** i get the chance. (Hannah Peterson, Peterson Papers, Duke) Catawba County

II.7. Prepositions

See also glossary entries for *about, amongst, at, athout, betwixt, in, of, only,* and *outen.*

II.7.1. *against, again* meaning "before, by"

Nov. 3, 1863: I think that I will See you **against** Christmast. (F. M. Poteet, Poteet-Dickson Letters, NCSA) McDowell County

II.7.2. *till* meaning "before, by"

Apr. 5, 1863: I onley hope and pray to God I may git home **til** harveist So if thare bee any wheet So I can Save it. (W. F. Wagner, *Confederate Soldier,* 46) Catawba County

II.7.3. *all to* meaning "except for"

Aug. 16, 1863: I can Say to you that I am well **all to** Sore feet and cold. (John Futch, Futch Letters, NCSA) New Hanover County

II.7.4. *owing to* meaning "because of"

Mar. 8, 1863: Me and Nancy intended to go to see you last week but **owing to** so much water we had to give it out. (Betty Thomas, Quinn Papers, Duke) Duplin County

II.7.5. *to* meaning "at"

Mar. 12, 1862: Joseph Williams got back tharsday morning he stade **to** betcy whaleys. (Jane Williams, Williams Papers, Duke) Onslow County

II.8. Syntax

II.8.1. Subject-verb agreement

II.8.1.1. Verb + *s* with a plural, conjoined, or collective noun phrase subject

This is the most common pattern of nonstandard subject-verb agreement in the North Carolina letters with 1,164 examples (including *is*). The pattern is very widespread in the state, but it is especially common in the western half of North Carolina. Atwood reports instances of *oats is* in southern Maine and northern New Hampshire, where it is "fairly common" among older Type IA and IIA informants. In the Middle and South Atlantic states, *is* was used by "about three-fourths" of Type I informants:[4]

Feb. 4, 1862: Solgers sees hardes time. I shore you I have sen hardes time. (J. S. Council, Councill Papers, Duke) Watauga County

Oct. 24, 1862: sum of them has Bin out A long time in the un holy thing. (J. W. Reese, Reese Papers, Duke) Buncombe County

Oct. 27, 1863: the Each and lice keeps mee Rite Bissey. (J. W. Reese, Reese Papers, Duke) Buncombe County

Mar. 11, 1864: the **yankes has** made sum few rads on us This spring with cavelry. (Daniel Abernathy, Abernathy Papers, Duke) Catawba County

Apr. 6, 1864: The **trains is** not running any further down at present the trains is going down to Jonesboro on Monday. (C. A. Walker, Walker Papers, WCU) Cherokee County

II.8.1.2. *is, has,* or verb + *s* with an adjacent pronoun subject

A total of sixty-seven examples of this pattern were found in the North Carolina letter, mostly from the eastern half of the state. Some of the African American writers use it (see the DeRosset, Bizzell, and Jones citations), as do several writers of Highland Scots ancestry from Moore County. The LAMSAS fieldwork recorded four instances of *I works* in Virginia and the Carolinas among Type I informants.[5]

Dec. 19, 1861: Well father I Wish you All Would make peace and you would Stay at home untell I come home but you know best you must let me know wheare **you is.** (W. H. Strickland, Quinn Papers, Duke) Duplin County

Aug. 4, 1862: we wants you here with us & kneeds you too. (Dicy Ann Jackson, Jackson Family Corr., Notre Dame) Moore County

Mar. 25, 1863: I will try & be faithfull to you untill **you Comes** home again. (Jimmy DeRosset, DeRosset Family Papers, SHC) New Hanover County

Apr. 7, 1863: tell all of my kindred that **I sends** my best Respects to them all and Mr Ellingtons family. (J. F. Coghill, Coghill Papers, Duke) Granville County

Apr. 25, 1863: I has to gow down thare evry day with mi squads wrashings to them. we daunt draw but one day at a time sow **we has** to gow evry day. (B. C. Jackson, Jackson Family Corr., Notre Dame) Moore County

June 25, 1863: I was wounded in the Battle of Sharpsburg with a fragment of a Shell. it hit me near my Sholder & loddged near my lungs. it is so deep it cant be extracted. **I has** nearly lost the use of my arm. (Kenneth M. McDonald, Vance Papers, NCSA) Moore County

July 18, 1863: I want you to rite to me how **you is** and where **you is**. whether **you is** in the hospitle or not. (James Broach, Broach Papers, Duke) Person County

July 19, 1863: we get 1 pound of flour a day and and about 1 pound of beef and when I get hingry I can eat it at 1 meal but **I buys** some when I can and gets along some how. (Neill McLeod, McLeod Letters, SHC) Moore County

Dec. 10, 1864: I rites every week and I want you to as long as we can get paper and stamps. (Ann Bowen, Bowen Papers, NCSA) Washington County

II.8.1.3. *is, has,* or verb + *s* with a non-adjacent pronoun subject

There were seventy occurrences of this pattern in the North Carolina letters, and it is widely distributed in the state:

May 23, 1862: I am not well but able to be up and **has** not ben well sence a weeke before I received your letter. (Joseph Cowand, Cowan Papers, Duke) Bertie County

Sept. 21, 1863: the yankes are Still on the other side of the Rapidan River. **they** are in sight and **looks** almost numerous. they are like black birds going in every directions. (J. F. Coghill, Coghill Papers, Duke) Granville County

Mar. 25, 1863: they are very kind to me at the office & **gives** me plenty to Eat. (Jimmy DeRosset, DeRosset Family Papers, SHC) New Hanover County

May 18, 1863: Father the Servis is hard on me but **I** stand it as well as eny of my men & **has** harder duties to perform. (Stephen Whitaker, Whitaker Papers, NCSA) Cherokee County

June 29, 1863: We have Crossed the potomack and **has** passed through Meriland and **is** Now in P A Within 60 miles of harrisburg. (G. J. Huntley, Huntley Papers, WCU) Rutherford County

Mar. 2, 1864: i can Say to you that **we** hav got Sum damd fooles in our Co that **has** reinlisted but i hant nor i will be damd if i do. (Solomon Page, E. Smith Papers, Duke) Stanley County

II.8.1.4. Unmarked third-person singular verb forms

June 10, 1862: ant Juller **Send** hir Love to you and mis Cate wont to see you very Bad in Deed. Dannel **Send** his Love to you. (W. H. Thurber, DeRosset Family Papers, SHC) New Hanover County

Jan. 18, 1863: Rufus n Causey is well at this time. **hee send** his Love to you hee said to tell you to write to him. (A. G. Causey, Hackett Papers,, Duke) Guilford County

II.9. Negation

II.9.1. Negation without *do* support

Verbs other than *be* are typically negated with insertion of auxiliary *do* as in present-day English. The verb *have* is occasionally negated without insertion of *do,* and *need* is very often negated without insertion of *do*:

Nov. 22, 1863: I **havent** no news of interest to write at this time. (Thornton Sexton, Sexton Letters, Duke) Ashe County

Apr. 24, 1864: you **need not** send that book till you can send it by some one coming out. (J. M. Frank, Frank Papers, Duke) Davidson County

II.9.2. Multiple negation

This feature occurs with a wide variety of negative markers and is very common in the North Carolina letters:

July 22, 1861: tell John that he promast to write to me but I have **never** have recived **no** letter from him yet. (Charley Futch, Futch Letters, NCSA) New Hanover County

Sept. 16, 1862: nun of us has **not** got hurt yet but Wilam Hatcher was wonde slitley on the top of his foot. (Bardin Brown, Brown Family Papers, Duke) Johnston County

Oct. 3, 1862: I **dont** think we will **not** fight mabe **no** more this winter. (W. H. Brotherton, Brotherton Papers, Duke) Catawba County

Aug. 14, 1862: we **hant** got **no** money yet. (Austin Brown, Brown Family Papers, Duke) Johnston County

July 14, 1863: this is the first time that I have wrote to you since the 15 of June. tha has **not** Bin **no** male since that time. (J. W. Joyce, Joyce Papers, MHI) Stokes County

Aug. 18, 1863: he has **not** got **nary** letter from his wife sence he left home. (Robert Carpenter, Carpenter Family Papers, ECU) Chatham County

Feb. 12, 1864: if you can git a two horse wagen B[u]y it it **dont** make **no** diferns what it cost. I wod rather have the wagen than the mony. (R. C. Caldwell, Caldwell Collection, ECU) Cabarrus County

II.10. Existential subjects *they* and *it* instead of *there*

See also glossary entries. Existential *they* is very common in the North Carolina letters, occurring a total of 221 times. Existential *it* is uncommon, with only 4 examples in the North Carolina sample:

II.10.1. Existential *they* (also spelled *thay, tha, the*)

Feb. 11, 1862: I dont now whar tha will go but **tha** is som talk of tha going to cantucky. (Samuel Wagoner, Hundley Family Letters, SHC) Stokes County

Apr. 27, 1862: if **they** is any thing the mater any way I want you to tell me of it if you please. (J. S. Councill, Councill Papers, Duke) Watauga County

II.10.2. Existential *it*

Jan. 18, 1863: **it** is no nead of my saying any thing to you about the Fight at Newbern where I was taken for you was then Col of a reg in the same fight. (J. W. Evans, Vance Papers, NCSA) Allegany County

III. Spelling and Pronunciation

Of the three categories of linguistic features, pronunciation offers the greatest challenge for recovering evidence from writing. However phonetic a writer's spelling may be (or appear to be), a writer is still using an alphabet that does not necessarily allow the kind of direct correspondence between sound and symbol that we have with transcriptions using the symbols of the International Phonetic Alphabet (IPA). This is particularly true of vowels, since there are many more vowel sounds in English than there are letters to represent them. English must rely on combinations of vowel letters, which are inconsistently sounded (for example, *head, heal, heart*). We must also consider the conditions under which soldiers often had to write. Letters, even words, were at times accidentally omitted, and on occasion, letters and words were accidentally repeated. Therefore, we are interested in words that have (1) a reasonably clear contrast between standard and nonstandard spelling, which suggests a variant pronunciation, (2) a high degree of consistency in nonstandard spellings among multiple writers, and (3) spellings that can be compared to data contained in *Pronunciation of English in the Atlantic States* (*PEAS*). Readers will very quickly become aware that writers often confuse the many homophones in English: *awl/all, aloud/allowed, close/clothes, deer/dear, flea/flee, for/four/fore, hall/haul, here/hear, hole/whole, hour/our, maid/made, male/mail, meat/meet, no/know, peace/piece, right/write/wright, there/their, to/two/too, sole/soul, way/weigh, weak/week, weather/whether, won/one, wood/would*. While these may sometimes cause confusion for readers and are of interest for a variety of reasons, they have no significance in terms of pronunciation. The same is true of "hypercorrect" spellings that incorporate "silent" letters that writers may remember, imperfectly, from their schooling, especially with an initial *k*: *halve/have, knight/night, Knashville/Nashville, kneedle/needle, knews/news, knot/not, know/now, kneighbors/neighbors, mild/mile, hold/whole, recond/reckon, chicking/chicken, recking/reckon wimming/women, childring/children, waging/wagon, rashing/ration, mutch/much, sutch/such*. Spelling like these certainly or probably have no phonological significance, and even the examples below should be considered possible rather than definite phonological evidence.[6]

III.1. Vowels

III.1.1. The vowel sound in *care*

See *PEAS* map 39. The spelling *cear* (occasionally *kear* or *keer*) is very common in the North Carolina letters (159 occurrences), and some of them may well represent the pronunciation of vowel sounds /i/ or /jɜ/:

> **Oct. 4, 1861:** Direct your letter to Wilmington NC in **Cear** of Col Clingman 25 regiment NC vol. (J. W. Love, Love Papers, Duke) Henderson County

> **Mar. 15, 1863:** take **cear** of your self and do the best you can. (Catherine Ramsey, Futch Letters, NCSA) New Hanover County

III.1.2. The vowel sound in *keg*

See *PEAS* map 64. Variant form *cag* in the NC letters, suggesting the pronunciation of the vowel as /æ/:

> **June 8, 1863:** if you can send that *cag* home we can Send Some molases to you. (Sally Hackett, Hackett Papers, Duke) Guilford County

III.1.3. Word final /i/ in *Marthy, Sary, Barbry*

> **July 27, 1861:** we have a nuther girl Bornd the 9th of may and her name is **sary** Elizabet and is the fine est Child we have. (J. C. Haltom, Frank Papers, Duke) Davidson County

> **Jan. 12, 1864: barbry** took the measels and I Cold not leave her as good as she tended to me when I was sick. (J. E. Keever, Keever Papers, Duke) Lincoln County

III.1.4. Merger of /ɪ/ and /ɛ/ to /ɪ/ in *rigiment, gineral, git*

> **Aug. 7, 1861: gineral** Mcgrooder has tuck 10 thousand men down there And is agoing to attact newport news. (Peter Poteet, Poteet-Dickson Letters, NCSA) McDowell County

> **Nov. 10, 1862:** we hav lost thirteen men out of this **Rigment** Sence we hav Bin hear. (J. W. Reese, Reese Papers, Duke) Buncombe County

> **Oct. 27, 1863:** I want you to **git** A nuf of wheat if you can to sow the ground on the fur Cide of the Branch. (J. W. Reese, Reese Papers,, Duke) Buncombe County

III.1.5. The diphthong /ai/ in *boil, hoist, join, spoil*

See *PEAS* maps 143 and 144. North Carolina, Virginia, West Virginia, Maryland, and New Hampshire.

> **July 16, 1862:** sutch gales [= gals] we have tha will **hist** [= hoist] thar close around thar wast and rube and pull at you and I think lees of them than I dwo of my dog. (Robert Spainhourd, Spainhourd Papers, Duke) Forsythe County

> **Oct. 3, 1862:** I had the worse **Bile** under my left arm I most Ever had. (W. F. Wagner, *Confederate Soldier,* 16) Catawba County

> **Dec. 6, 1863:** Tell Sister Jane not to **spile** Josephus. (James A. Patton, Patton Letters, Emory) Granville County

III.1.6. The vowel /ɛ/ for /ʌ/ in *shut*

See *PEAS* map 90. Common in South Carolina, North Carolina, Virginia, West Virginia, New Hampshire, and Maine. Variant form *shet* in the phrase *get shet of*:

> **Apr. 3, 1862:** I seat my Sef to drop you a few lins to lette you now that I am a getting Able for drill a gain but I ant got **Shet** of the Boul Complaint yet. (Isaac Lefevers, Lefevers Papers, NCSA) Catawba County

III.1.7. The vowel /e/ for /æ/ in *can't, aunt*

> **Dec. 29, 1862:** our men has block aided the river so that the gunboats **caint** get up the river to shell the town & so they **caint** go up to Goldsboro. (T. B. Litten, Fisher Papers, Duke) Catawba County

> **Feb. 20, 1863:** Dear **aints** I take my pen inhand to let yow know that I am fat and Sawccy. (W. H. Brotherton, Brotherton Papers, Duke) Catawba County

III.1.8. The vowel /a/ for /ɪ/ in *learn*

> **Feb. 13, 1863:** tell Bud that he most **larn** his Boock purty tell paw comes home and he will Bring him some little Briches and some candy. (Isaac Lefevers, Lefevers Papers, NCSA) Catawba County

III.1.9. Loss of offglide or monophthong for /ai/ in *hired, fired, Irish*

Examples of the kind in the citations below are extremely uncommon:

Jan. 21, 1862: they ar one Regament hear frome Lusiana and they mostly all **arishmen** and they ar no doing any thing with them. (D. C. Johnson, Jackson Family Corr., Notre Dame) Moore County

July 16, 1862: I suffords a power for somthing to Eat While I Was in the horspital at Richmond I paid 50 cts a quart for some **arish potatoes**. (G. J. Huntley, Huntley Papers, WCU) Rutherford County

Nov. 10, 1862: the yankes reforesed a bout Eight thousan th[e]y said we twok a yanke officer and when we back crosed a Bridge and then set it on **far** and then we run into a caverly an our compinay **fard** on them shot the horse from thy yanke officer and thy all got away. (W. D. Carter, Culberson Papers, Duke) Chatham County

Nov. 4, 1863: we have little John honeycut **hard** [= hired] a month to plow and his month is most out the plowing goes very slow seince you left. (Sarah C. Overcash, Overcash Papers, Duke) Rowan County

III.2. Consonants

III.2.1. Intrusive /r/ in *father, ought, thought, water*

See glossary entries for additional examples. Interestingly, the intrusive *r* in *warsh* does not occur in the North Carolina letters, although *wash* is fairly common:

Feb. 17, 1862: ef you ant mared yet i think that you **ort** to wait tell i com back. (Evin Smith, E. Smith Papers, Duke) Stanley County

Dec. 20, 1862: my dear Partha I want yew and my **farther** to Send me and Daniel abox between yews Send me adram for my crismas. (John Hartman, Hartman Papers, Duke) Rowan County

Dec. 28, 1862: yow said yow thougt of mee a crismas. i **thort** of yow an my little children all that day. (T. F. Baggarly, Baggarly Papers, Duke) Iredell County

Aug. 9, 1863: We are Camped in alarge oake Grov about ahalf mile from kenansville. We hav a splendid Well of **Warter**. (Edgar Smithwick, Smithwick Papers, Duke) Martin County

III.2.2. Final /r/ in *fellow, follow, pillow, widdow, window*

See also glossary entries.

Oct. 26, 1863: i was sory that he got wounded for he was one of the best **felers** we had in our mes. (John H. Robinson, Robinson Papers, Duke) Catawba County

III.2.3. Loss of post-vocalic /r/

This is especially common in *portion* and tolerable and appears occasionally in *first, horse, poor,* and *poorly*. See glossary entries. Loss of the postvocalic /r/ appears to be word-specific and scattered throughout the state:

Dec. 6, 1861: give my best respects to all my freinds receive a **potion** your self. (G. T. Brown, Fisher Papers, Duke) Catawba County

Oct. 4, 1862: I **tolable** well all to a hurtin in my hip and Sholders. (John Ingram, Ingram Papers, Duke) Forsyth County

Aug. 21, 1863: Sally I am very **poly** to day. Sally I did not think that I could of bear what I have but I hope the lord is with me. (J. H. Hundley, Hundley Family Letters, SHC) Stokes County

III.2.4. Metathesis of /r/

This occurs frequently in the adjective, noun, and adverb *pretty* (see glossary entries) and occasionally in the unstressed initial syllables *pre-* and *pro-*. There are sixty-six examples of the spellings *purty, perty,* and *pirty* in the North Carolina letters:

Mar. 1, 1863: there is a great many people that has not got **pervision** to Spar. (Robert Rice, Mar. 1, 1863, Vance Papers, NCSA) Alamance County

Jan. 30, 1864: I hope that you have your hand at Work it is A **purty** time for plowing I hope that you will keep her at work to earn her bord. (Marcus Hefner, Hefner Papers, NCSA) Catawba County

III.2.5. Consonant cluster reduction

III.2.5.1. Final cluster reduction

Reduction of final consonant clusters *-nd, -st, -ld,* and *-zd* is fairly common among all English speakers if the word following the cluster begins with a consonant sound. It is less common if the word following begins with a vowel sound or if the word with the final consonant cluster is at the end of a sentence. Final cluster reduction before vowels and at the end of sentences is very common in the North Carolina letters.

Nov. 10, 1861: I am well at this time except a bad **cole**. (J. S. Beavers, Upchurch Papers, Duke) Chatham County

Aug. 18, 1862: ife i Should be taken as prisioner or Sicken and dye or git **kill** if these things Should tak place and you dont hear from me no more between this and chrismas i want you to Sell my horse if you can git any thing like the worth of him. (William Carpenter, Carpenter Family Papers, ECU) Chatham County

Dec. 1, 1862: We have good **feel** oficers we have no company oficers we expect to hold an election to day or to Marrow. (Marcus Hefner, Hefner Papers, NCSA) Catawba County

Mar. 25, 1863: so mr vance Dow your **bes** an send him home if you can. (M. P. Lytle, Vance Papers, NCSA) Buncombe County

June 28, 1863: i would not be **Surprise** if the yankees was to try to come in to Richmonde before long. (Robert Carpenter, Carpenter Family Papers, ECU) Chatham County

Jan. 19, 1864: we only get a quarter of a **poun** of bacon and one pound of flour a day. (Jesse Hill, Hill Letters, NCSA) Forsyth County

Dec. 8, 1864: no one noes how [= who] will **Stan** or fall in war. (Robert C. Caldwell, Caldwell Collection, ECU) Cabarrus County

III.2.5.2. Medial cluster reduction

Reduction of medial consonant cluster is fairly uncommon in the North Carolina letters but occurs occasionally in words like *candle, children, grumble,* and *tremble.*

Aug. 18, 1862: granmother I must bring my few lines to a Close for I am to weak & **tremly** to write much this time. (James Fisher, Fisher Papers, Duke) Catawba County

Sept. 11, 1862: I think when we get our Stoping place we will fare better. I cant **grumel** yet we will draw loaf and meat to gow to Richmon theas eaving. (W. H. Brotherton, Brotherton Papers, Duke) Catawba County

May 9, 1863: if youe dont make sum rang ments the wim men an **Chilern** wil Sufer hear. (Martha Oakay, Vance Papers, NCSA) Granville County

Feb. 18, 1864: I Dont expect to get home Soon. I want Sum Sap [= soap] hard Soap and coffe and **canels** [= candles]. (R. C. Caldwell, Caldwell Collection, ECU) Cabarrus County

III.2.6. The sound /jɜ/ in *ear*, especially in *roasting ear*

See *PEAS* map 34 (widespread in North Carolina and West Virginia).

Sept. 9, 1862: last monday wee had A splended chicken stew and A plenty of **rosen years**. (J. F. Coghill, Coghill Papers, Duke) Granville County

Sept. 9. 1863: sam fanny and bet was all sick last weake with colds and **year** ache sam and fanny has got well but bet hant well yet. (Molly Tesh, Tesh Papers, Duke) Yadkin County

Aug. 21, 1864: if any body will fetch me any thing I want you to send me sum 5 ore 6 **Rosenyears**. I haint tasted one this year. (F. M. Poteet, Poteet-Dickson Letters, NCSA) McDowell County

III.2.7. Substitution of /d/ for /ð/; alternation of /w/ and /v/, final /t/ and /d/

Several letter writers from Catawba County who are of Pennsylvania German ancestry show traces of their linguistic heritage occasionally through their spelling. Of these writers, William P. Cline is the only one who regularly uses /d/ rather than /ð/ at the beginnings of words. Cline uses the standard spelling *this* 13 times and *dis* 130 times. For *there* and *their* he uses spellings beginning with th- 22 times and the spellings *dir, dire,* and *dare* 49 times. On the other hand, Cline uses *that* 366 times and *dat* only 22 times, and he uses *them* 48 times and *dem* only 3 times. Other examples of initial /d/ in the writing of Cline and others include *day* (they), *dese* (these), *dose* (those), and *den* (then). Several writers have alternation between voiced and voiceless final stops, including *brigate* (brigade), *raste* (raised), *weight* (weighed), *ged* (get), *roberd* (Robert), and *wand* (want), or alternation between /w/ and /v/, including *V* (we), *vinchester* or *veaval* (weevil), *Wixburg* or *wesel* (vessel), *wery* (very), and *dewide* (divide):

Apr. 14, 1862: the boys had rote nasty leter for mey. after **dis** i will rite my one leters i rote **dis**

leter my self. (W. P. Cline, Cline Papers, SHC) Catawba County

Sept. 21, 1862: Dear Wife I can say to you we are in a **brigate** we are in ginerl Wises **Brigate** and they say we have to go to wilmmingsburg to fite or run the yankeys away. (W. F. Wagner, *Confederate Soldier,* 15) Catawba County

Apr. 13, 1864: i think this war wil come to a close before **werry** long. i hope and pray that it wil so that i can get home. (Franklin Setzer, Setzer Corr, UVA) Catawba County

May 31, 1863: they are a fiting at **wixburg** and our men still whiped them so far yet if it is onley Gods will that we can whip them thare for if they git **wixburg** the git half of the confedersy. (W. F. Wagner, *Confederate Soldier,* 52) Catawba County

NOTES

1. For a detailed treatment of grammar, see especially Michael B. Montgomery and Joseph S. Hall, *Dictionary of Smoky Mountain English* (Knoxville: Univ. of Tennessee Press, 2004), xxv–lxv. See also *DARE* 1:xxxvii–xxxix.

2. Most of these verbs are in agreement with the LAMSAS data collected in the 1930s and published in E. Bagby Atwood, *A Survey of Verb Forms in the Eastern United States* (Ann Arbor: Univ. of Michigan Press, 1953), but there are some exceptions. The verb *ask,* with its variant forms, is too uncommon in North Carolina to draw any useful conclusions. The form *hearn* as past tense and past participle and *taken* were much more widespread in the state than Atwood's figure 30 suggests. Past tense *seen* in the North Carolina letters is less widespread than in Atwood's figure 17 and is restricted to the western half of the state.

3. *Shall* occurs with *you* only twenty-one times, and with third-person subjects only twelve times. *I shall* occurs 432 times (11.5%) out of 3,775 possible occurrences. *We shall* occurs 102 times (9.7%) out of 1,048 possible occurrences. *I should like* occurs 51 times (8.5%) compared to 550 occurrences of *I would like. I/we shant* occurs 36 times (19.9%) out of 181 possible occurrences.

4. Atwood, *Survey of Verb Forms,* 30.

5. Atwood, *Survey of Verb Forms,* 26.

6. H. R. Wilson, "From Postulates to Procedures in the Interpretation of Spellings," in *Studies in Linguistics in Honor of Raven I. McDavid, Jr.,* ed. L. M. Davis (University: Univ. of Alabama Press, 1972), 215–228. See also Bell Irvin Wiley, *The Life of Johnny Reb: The Common Soldier of the Confederacy* (Baton Rouge: Louisiana State Univ. Press, 2005), 203–4.

Abbreviations

ADAH = Alabama Department of Archives and History

arch. = archaic

CACWL = Corpus of American Civil War Letters

Coll. = Collection

colloq. = colloquial

Corr. = Correspondence

CS = Confederate States

DARE = *Dictionary of American Regional English*

dial. = dialectal

DSME = *Dictionary of Smoky Mountain English*

Du = Dutch

Duke = Duke University, David M. Rubenstein Rare Book and Manuscript Library

ECU = East Carolina University, Joyner Library Special Collections

EDD = *English Dialect Dictionary*

Emory = Emory University, Manuscript and Rare Book Library

Eng = English

esp. = especially

euphem. = euphemism

exc. = except

fig. = figurative

freq. = frequent

Germ, Ger = German

hist. = historical

intr. = intransitive verb

Ir = Irish

LSU = Louisiana State University, Hill Memorial Library Special Collections

Misc. = Miscellany

MHI = United States Army Military History Institute, Carlisle, Pennsylvania

NCSA = North Carolina State Archives, Raleigh

ND = No date

Notre Dame = University of Notre Dame, Hesburgh Libraries, Rare Books and Manuscript Collections

obs. = obsolete

OED = *Oxford English Dictionary*

PaGer = Pennsylvania German

pron. = pronunciation

Sc. = Scots, Scottish English

SHC = Southern Historical Collection, University of North Carolina, Chapel Hill

SRNB = Stones River National Battlefield, Murfreesboro, Tennessee

sb. = substantive, a noun

trans. = transitive verb

TSLA = Tennessee State Library and Archives, Nashville

UGA = University of Georgia, Hargrett Library Special Collections

UNCA = University of North Carolina, Ashville

usu = usual

UVA = University of Virginia Library Special Collections

vbl aux = auxiliary verb

VPI = Virginia Polytechnic Institute and State University Libraries, Special Collections

WCU = Western Carolina University, Hunter Library Special Collections

Using the Glossary

1. Arrangement within Entries

Entries consist of the following:

1. A headword in bold type
2. The part of speech in italics
3. A brief definition or reason for including the word, for example, "variant form"
4. Additional information from dictionary sources in square brackets
5. A citation or citations, consisting of
   a. the date of the letter (in bold);
   b. an illustrative quote with the example of the entry's headword in bold;
   c. in parenthesis, the name of the letter writer;
   d. identification of the specific collection (citations from published sources include a short title in italics for the book, followed by page numbers); and
   e. identification of the archive
6. After the end parenthesis, the writer's county of residence

Sample Entry

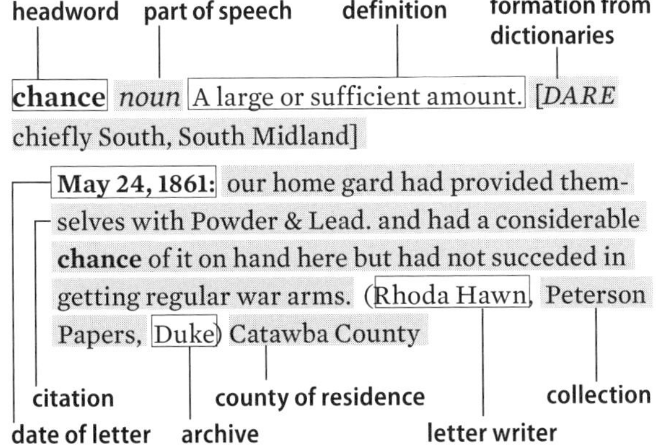

2. Entries with Multiple Grammatical Forms or Senses

In cases in which the headword of an entry has multiple grammatical forms or functions, or multiple senses, these are listed in separate paragraphs under the headword. Definitions begin with a capital letter; identification of variant forms, including grammatical forms, begin with a lowercase letter. A sample entry follows:

tight, tite *adjective*

1. Strict. [*OED* **tight**, adjective, 6. b. *fig.*]

ND: our fear is but ondifearnt and **tite** laws tha will not let a man pass out with out commision ofecr with him. (Charley Futch, Futch Letters, NCSA) New Hanover County

2. Intoxicated, tipsy. [*OED* **tight**, adjective, 7]

June 10, 1861: old Jimy Deaton got **tite** and fell out of the bugy and broke his thy and two ribs and is very bad off. (Joseph Overcash, Overcash Papers, Duke) Rowan County

Feb. 11, 1862: Capt barry is under A rest at the presant for getting **tite** but he is A man I Like as A Captain and I intend to Stick up to him. (J. W. Williams, Williams Papers, Duke) Onslow County

July 9, 1864: J J wevear got A gun A Rifle thas A hed of any thing I Ever saw in the way of A gun in my life it shoots sixteen times with out loding if it was mine I wood not take A thousan dollars for it Weevr was in Charg of of the picket that and after he was Run in he was Reposting his pickets and this yankey was **tite** he Sed he was orderd to advanc his post and he was so drunk he did not no what he was dooing and advanct two fur and Cum throu ouer lins. (J. W. Reese, Reese Papers, Duke) Buncombe County

3. Additional Information from Dictionary Sources

Some entries include additional information from other dictionaries. Information from *DARE* most often identifies the dialect area or areas in which the word or usage most commonly occurs, as in “South, South Midland.” Parts of speech and dialect regions have been spelled out rather than abbreviated. Other information from dictionary sources, including abbreviations, follows the form (for example, punctuation or use of italics) of the original.

4. Cross-Referencing

As much as is practical, variant spellings, especially those not immediately adjacent to the entry, are cross-referenced. This is especially important in the glossary since Civil War letters may contain numerous nonstandard spelling variants.

5. Brackets within Citations

In cases in which a missing word or letter makes understanding the quotation difficult, missing words or letters have been supplied with square brackets, for example, “[h]ours.” In cases in which spelling or grammatical variation makes a word difficult to understand, or in which the meaning of a word is obscure, a gloss has been added within square brackets, for example, “gambadoes [= leggings].” Question marks enclosed by angle brackets—i.e., “<?>”—indicate illegible letters or words.

6. Silent Punctuation

As noted previously, the original letters had little or no punctuation. To aid the modern reader, some punctuation (mostly periods with a few commas) has been silently introduced throughout the glossary entries.

A Gallery of Carolina Letters

The following gallery reproduces six of the Civil War letters from the North Carolina sample. The text of the letters, along with source and biographical background information, is printed opposite each image. Some punctuation has been silently added to the letter transcriptions to aid readability.

William M. Patton to J. L. and Sarah Patton (Page 1)

1861

State of N C Raleigh May th 26

My dear Father and mother,

I take my pen in hand this eavenig to drop you a few lines to let you know that we are well at this time. hoping that you are all enjoying the same blessing. we have all ben enjoying very good health since we left home except the bowel complaint and a few founders there has ben several of us had a light tuch of the bowel complaint but we are all giting better of it. W P Fortune delivered us a letter from you last wednesday morning. We were very glad to heare from you all. Jacob wrote a leter to you last sunday morning at statesville and sent it to the post office and forgot to put a postedge stamp on it and did not know whether it went on or not. We left Statesville last sunday morning and went down as far as saulsbery.

Source: Letter from William M. Patton to J. L. and Sarah Patton, 26 May 1861, in the Patton Family Letters, 1860–1864, #00581z, Southern Historical Collection, Wilson Library, University of North Carolina at Chapel Hill.

Background: Buncombe County, North Carolina, farmer James L. Patton and his wife Sarah had four sons who served in the Confederate army, including William M. Patton (b. ca. 1839), who served in Company F, Fourteenth North Carolina Infantry. He was wounded at the Battle of Chancellorsville sometime between May 1 and 3, 1863, and died of his wounds on May 21.

State of N C Raleigh May 26 1861

My dear Father and mother

I take my pen in hand this evening to drop you a few lines to let you know that we are well at this time hoping that you are all enjoying the same blessing. We have all ben enjoying very good health since we left home except the bowel complaint and a few founders there has ben several of us had a light tuch of the bowel complaint but we are all giting better of it W P Fortune delivered us a letter from you last wednesday morning We were very glad to heare from you all Jacob wrote a leter to you last sunday morning at stateville and sent it to the postoffice and forgot to put a postedge stamp on it and did not know whether it went on or not We left Statesville last sunday morning and went down as far as saulsbery

Charley Futch to John Futch

Acquia Creek

Oct the 16 1861

Dear Brother, I take my pen in hand to let you no that I am well at this time & I hope thase few lines may find you all well. John, I want you to write to me more plainer then you have bin a writing for the letters that capt williams brought to me. I carried them though the 3d regement and they was not a one that could read them so I can not answer them letters and I carried them to the 40th regement and they was not a man that could read the date of the month. John, I want you to send me that Likeness that is in my trunk.

Source: Futch Family Letters, 1861–1863, PC. 507, courtesy of the State Archives of North Carolina.

Background: The Futch family lived in New Hanover County, North Carolina. Brothers Charles and John Futch served as privates in Company K, Third North Carolina Infantry. Charley was mortally wounded at Gettysburg on July 2, 1863, and died the next day. John survived the battle but left his regiment a few weeks later and was shot for desertion in September 1863. Many of the brothers' letters were written for them by others.

Acquia Creek
Oct the 16 1861

Dear Brother I take my pen in hand to let you no that I am well at this time & I hope those few lines may find you all well John I want you to write to me more plainer then you have bin a writing for the letters that Capt williams brought to me I carried them though the 3d regiment and they was not a one that could read them so I can not answer them letters and I carried them to the 40th regiment and they was not a man that could read the date of the month John I want you to send me that Likeness that is in my trunk

Alfred Walsh to Calvin Luther Proffit and Alfred N. Proffit (Page 1)

Richmond V.a. June 12, 1862

MrS [= Misters] C. L. & A. N. Proffit

Dear cousins,

I Seat My Self for the purpose of writing you afew Lines in answer to yours which reached me this Ev. you of corce Love to hear from our army at Every point but I can Not gave you a Strate Account of them only at Somes points. the army is all rite hear and our army in Western V.a. is rite thare. old Stone Wall Jackson has Whiped out the yankees thare and got Lots of prisners. also Lots of Amunition comisaries stores & Munitions of ware camp Equipage &c &c. our forses halv falen back from Corinth. the yankees are reported to halv falen back hear. there fiting going on at Charlstown S.C. this is the News in to days dispach. it is rumerd hear that our reg. is orderd away from hear. I do Not know and I dont care if it is for the Strong Limstone Warter is Not good for No 1. We halv plenty to Eat and Ware but our rashones of whis key is quite Small. we got a dram the other Morning. is the second drop I hav had since I Saw you. only a Little in <?????>

Source: Letter from Alfred Walsh to Calvin Luther Proffit and Alfred N. Proffit, in the Proffit Family Letters, 1860–1865, #03408-z, Southern Historical Collection, Wilson Library, University of North Carolina at Chapel Hill.

Background: The Proffits were a farm family in Wilkes County, North Carolina. William Proffit (b. ca. 1803) and Mary Proffit (b. ca. 1805) were the parents of four sons who served in the Confederate army. Nephew Alfred Walsh served in Company B, First North Carolina Infantry, and was killed at the Battle of Malvern Hill on July 1, 1862.

Richmond Va. June 13, 1862.

Mrs C. S. & A. N. Braffit

Dear cousins

I seat Myself for the purpose of Writing you afew Lines in answer to yours Which reached me this Ev You of corse Love to hear from our army at Every point but I can not give you a Strate Acc ount of them only at Somes points the army is all rite hear and our army in Western Va. is rite there old Stone wall Jackson has Whipe out the yankees there and got Lots of prisners also Lots of Ammunition Comisaries Stores & Munitions of ware camp Equipage &c our forses hav falen back from corinth the yankees are reported to hav falen back hear there fiting going on at Charlstown S.C. this is the News in to days dispach it is rumered hear that our reg. is ordered away from hear I do Not know and I dont care if it is for the Strong Limestone Warter is Not Good for No. 1 We hav plenty to Eat and Ware but our rashones at whis key is quite Small we got a drem the other Morning is the Second drap I hav had since ^only a Little in yellow I saw you

James Fisher to Lavinia Fisher (Page 1)

Richmond V.A.

August 18th 1862

Miss Viney Fisher

Dear cosen, I take the opportunity of answering your kind letter which came to hand to day but did knot find me well. I hav knot bin well for a good while but I hope I will be well in a few weeks. I do knot no what is the matter with me. without it is the fever I am knot Dangerously Sick. I hope thos lines may find you all well. I hav no news to write to you this time only I would like to See you all. I would like to com home & go to Bauls Creek [Balls Creek in Catawba County] Camp meeting with you all. I was glad to hear You had a good Campmeeting at Rock Spring & I hope you will hav a good one at Bauls Creek. I want you all to be good folks to pray for us pore Soldiers out here Suffering So much. So nothing more on that Subject.

Source: Jane Fisher Papers, 1858–1904, letter dated August 18, 1864 (#1806), David M. Rubenstein Rare Book and Manuscript Library, Duke University.

Background: The Fisher family lived in the Sherrill's Ford section of Catawba County, North Carolina. At the time of the 1860 federal census, David Fisher (b. ca. 1803) and Elizabeth Fisher (b. ca. 1819) were living on their Catawba County farm with their four daughters and one son. Most of the letters in this collection were written to two of the daughters, Lavinia "Viney" Fisher (b. ca. 1838) and Elizabeth Amanda "Mandy" Fisher (b. ca. 1843) by a number of relatives and former neighbors serving in the Confederate army. Among these was James Fisher, who served in the Twenty-third North Carolina Infantry and died near Fredericksburg on April 2, 1863 (cause not reported).

Richmond, V.a
August 18th 1862

Miss Viney Fisher

Dear cosen i take
the oppertunity of answering your kind letter which
came to hand to day but did knot find me well
i hav knot bin well for a good while but i hope
i will be well in a few weeks i do knot no what
is the matter with me without it is the fever
I am knot Dangerously Sick i hope thes lines
may find you all well i hav no news to write to
you this time only I would like to See you all
i would like to com home & go to Bauls Creek
Campmeeting with you all i was glad to hear
you had a good Campmeeting at Rock Spring
& i hope you will have a good one at Bauls
creek i want you all to be good folks &
pray for us pore Soldiers out her suffering
So much I nothing more on that Subject

Beady M. Alley to Governor Vance (Page 1)

Franklinton

To the gov of NC

Feb 18th 1863

Dear Sir, I take my pen to rite you a few lines concerning my son that is In the armey. he had bin in servis ever sence last march. he is in the 47 regment in Capt W C lankfords Company and my husband is in the same company and I am left a lone with fore girl children and no person to help me and as my son is a harness maker. I was advised by my friends to rite to you if you pleas to hav him taken out of the armey to work for the government. two or three harness makers has rote for him but he Could not git of from lankford and I thaught I wood try

Source: Governor Zebulon Baird Vance Papers, G.P.160, 161, 162, courtesy of the State Archives of North Carolina.

Background: The Alley family was from near Franklinton in Franklin County. Francis T. Alley (b. ca. 1814) was a cabinetmaker. At time of the 1860 census, he and his wife, Beady (b. ca. 1818), had six children living at home, including Isaiah (age nineteen), a farm laborer. The name "Beady" (spelled "Bedie" in the census) may be a form of "Betty." Francis T. Alley and his son Isaiah D. Alley served as privates in Company F, Forty-seventh North Carolina Infantry.

Franklinton

To the gov of NC Feb 18th 1863

Dear sir I take my pen to rite you
a few lines concerning my son that is
In the armey he has bin in servis
ever sence last march he is in the
47 regment in Capt W C lankfords
Company and my husband is in the
same company and I am left a lone
with fore girl children and no
person to help me and as my son
is a harness maker I was advised
by my friends to rite to you if
you pleas to hav him taken out
of the armey to work for the
goverment two or three harness
makers has rote for him but he
could not git of from lankford
and I thaught I wood try

Peter J. Peterson to John and Hannah Peterson (Page 2)

March 21st 1864

it is very cold here now and geting colder every minit. I saw a man shot last Fryday and I dont want to see ary other one. this morning about too hours before day we saw our courier come rideing as hard as he could and he said we should reinforce our picket post for the yankees was a coming. but it was so cold that they did not and I think wont as long as it stays so cold. so I will close hopeing to here from you soon So no more at onley I remain your affectionate son untill death.

From Peter J Peterson
To John Peterson
Direct as before

Source: John Peterson Papers, 1850 (160-1899) 1927, letter dated March 21, 1864 (#4161), David M. Rubenstein Rare Book and Manuscript Library, Duke University.

Background: John Peterson (b. ca. 1821) was a Catawba County, North Carolina, farmer and gunsmith. At the time of the 1860 census, Peterson and his wife, Hannah (b. ca. 1820), were living in the Hickory Tavern neighborhood of Catawba County with their eight children. Their son Peter J. Peterson (b. ca. 1846) enlisted in the Twenty-eighth North Carolina Infantry on March 1, 1864, and died of wounds on May 20, 1864.

it is very cold here now and geting colder every minit I saw a man shot last Fryday and I dont want to see ary other one. this morning about too hours before day we saw our courier come rideing as hard as he could and he said we should reinforece our picket post for the yankees was a coming but it was so cold that they did not and I think want as long as it stays so cold so I will close hopeing to here from you soon so no more at oaley I remain your afectionate son untell death

From Peter J Peterson

To John Peterson

Direct as before

A Glossary of North Carolina English, 1861–1865

Words, Usages, and Variant Forms Contained in the 2,299 Civil War Letters and Three Diaries of the North Carolina Sample

A

a *indefinite article* instead of *an* before a vowel sound.

Sept. 25, 1862: I will rite a little something in this letter a bout the big Battle that was foght the 17th Day of this month. I can tell you that it was **a** awful fight. the fight was own [= on] yan side of the potomace River own the Mariland side. (Isaac Lefevers, Lefevers Papers, NCSA) Catawba County

Dec. 6, 1862: we have Drawn clothing and I Drawd me **a** over coat and one pr pants and one shirt and pr Drawers and 1 pr shoes and I want you to send me them two shirts and that comfort the First chance you get. (William Tesh, Tesh Papers, Duke) Yadkin County

Dec. 21, 1862: I have wrote it in Several Letters and have never received **A** Answer yet that you have ever got eny of them. (J. F. Coghill, Coghill Papers, Duke) Granville County

a *auxiliary verb* reduced form of *have.* [*DARE* **have**, verb[2], widespread but chiefly South, South Midland]

Oct. 7, 1861: tel Jim that I would **A** liked mity to **a** helpt him **a** Shucked his corn but it was So I couldent. (Harrison Hanes, Hanes Papers, Duke) Davie County

Nov. 16, 1862: i wod **A** rote b fore now but i had no paper. (W. P. Cline, Cline Papers, SHC) Catawba County

Dec. 18, 1862: if the yankes would **a** come out from the River we could **a** kiled nearley all of them I think the way we was fixed. (W. F. Wagner, *Confederate Soldier,* 27) Catawba County

Dec. 23, 1862: it wold only been three or fowr weeks Job an then i wold **a** had to went to my regiment. (T. F. Baggarly, Baggarly Papers, Duke) Iredell County

Jan. 20, 1864: if youe had to stade thar and **a** bin Satsfide and mebby youe cold **a** got to com hom this winter. (Susan Setzer, Setzer Papers, Duke) Catawba County

a *preposition* reduced form of *on,* especially before a day of the week or a holiday (see also **apurpose**). [*DARE* **a**, preposition[1], 2]

Mar. 22, 1862: thay was a party at Gorge Gilekrist **a thursday** Night. thay saye thay was a heape there. (Effie Jane Graham, Jackson Family Corr., Notre Dame) Moore County

Dec. 28, 1862: yow said yow thougt of mee **a crismas.** i thort of yow an my little children all that day. (T. F. Baggarly, Baggarly Papers, Duke) Iredell County

Mar. 29, 1863: dear husban I receved your kind Letters **a fridy.** I receved those and I was glad to hir from you. (Martha Futch, Futch Letters, NCSA) New Hanover County

Dec. 23, 1863: the childarn is agoing to [s]chool now. tha start **a monday** morning. (Susan Setzer, Setzer Papers, Duke) Catawba County

a *preposition* reduced form of *of.*

July 16, 1862: I hope the time is not far of[f] when I can go home for thair is a heep **A** talk of peace here. (J. W. Williams, Williams Papers, Duke) Onslow County

June 5, 1863: I must soon come to a close for I am a getten very tired **a** riten. (Isaac Lefevers, Lefevers Papers, NCSA) Catawba County

Nov. 12, 1863: you neden to bleve all that you hear. if you du you will blev A heap **A** lies. (W. P. Cline, Cline Papers, SHC) Catawba County

a- *prefix* the sound /ə/ prefixed to the present participle of verbs (e.g., *uh-going*), less commonly to past participles and to adjectives. [CACWL data indicate that the *a-* prefix was commonly added to the present participles of verbs throughout the country in the mid-nineteenth century, especially among less-educated speakers]

1. added to the present participle.

Aug. 7, 1861: gineral Mcgrooder has tuck 10 thousand men down there And is **agoing** to attact newport news. (Peter Poteet, Poteet-Dickson Letters, NCSA) Burke County

Mar. 20, 1862: the talk is now they are **A going** to stop the male and if they Do this may be the last letter you will get from me. (J. W. Love, Love Papers, Duke) Henderson County

Mar. 13, 1863: I seat my self this morning to let you no that we are all yet **A living** though very poly [= poorly]. (Sally Bauldin, Hundley Family Letters, SHC) Stokes County

Apr. 20, 1863: the pepel is planting corn hier and the woods is geting green and it makes me want to be at home **aplanting** corn so bad I cant rest. (Daniel Revis, Revis Letters, NCSA) Henderson County

June 12, 1863: I hope thair is aday **acoming** when we may all meet in pece again. (Daniel Revis, Revis Letters, NCSA) Henderson County

Dec. 21, 1863: Dear loveing wife. [I] drempt last knight that I was at home and you had Some good chicken cookt and i was **aeaten** [= a eating] wen I got awake. (Daniel Setzer, Setzer Papers, Duke) Catawba County

June 12, 1864: I want you to taker [= take care] of yor Self and dont hurt yor Self **A huging** the gals. (Julius Myers, Alman Papers, Duke) Cabarrus County

Aug. 17, 1864: tel Z D to right to me how the mule is **a gitting** a long an all of the stock. (A. S. Harrill, Civil War Coll., TSLA) Rutherford County

Oct. 4, 1864: I cant git Along **A walking** like I once could. (F. M. Poteet, Poteet-Dickson Letters, NCSA) McDowell County

2. added to a present participle form of a compound verb or verb phrase.

Jan. 14, 1862: Mr. Clover and Young and Joshua and my self went **a rabbit hunting** and caught one squirl And indeed we saw a heep of fun that day. (B. Y. Malone, *Malone Diary*, 12) Caswell County

Jan. 5, 1864: The Lewtenent went **a Rabbet hunten** but he hant come back yet. I dont Know if he will ketch eny or not. (A. J. Spease, Zimmerman Papers, Duke) Forsyth County

3. added to the past participle of a verb.

July 31, 1862: hit cood ben hop [= helped]. if they had **atride** but they wood not do hit. (L. W. Griffin, Griffin Papers, NCSA) Rutherford County

Nov. 23, 1862: I would love to a went their to a see they place but I think if i had **a went** their i would a staid their. (T. B. Litten, Fisher Papers, Duke) Catawba County

Apr. 7, 1863: i Wold have Goten a furlow if i hadnt **a ben** trans ferd from lynchburgs as sone as i was. (J. H. Hundley, Hundley Family Letters, SHC) Stokes County

Aug. 2, 1863: Me and charley bothe aimed to come home crismas if we both had **a lived** but charley pore feler got kild. (John Futch, Futch Letters, NCSA) New Hanover County

4. prefixed to an adjective.

June 6, 1862: it is all that I can do to get A plenty to eat for I am all the time **A hungry**. (J. W. Williams, Williams Papers, Duke) Onslow County

abed *adverb* In bed, and obliged to stay there due to an illness. [*OED* **abed**, adverb, 2, "Now somewhat *arch*"]

Sept. 17, 1860: the reason I have not Ritten to you Soner I wours [= was] Sick **a bead** when I receve your letter with the agur an fever. (Thomas Harding, Blount Papers, NCSA) Beaufort County

ablege see **obliged**

about *preposition* and *adverb*. [*OED* **about**, A. adverb, II. Expressing position, 7. "In the vicinity, nearby; in some place or various places nearby"; B, preposition[1], I. Expressing position, 3. "In and around, in the vicinity of"]

1. Around, near, in the vicinity of, close to.

Dec. 19, 1861: I am so much upset A Bout the way things that is going on **About** home I dont know what to do. (Isaac J. Strickland, Quinn Papers, Duke) Duplin County

July 20, 1862: I want to see you all **a bot** thare but I dont know when I Shal eve[r] shal see you eney more. (Jesse Brown, Brown Family Papers, Duke) Johnston County

June 4, 1863: Sally you must excuse this paper for it was the Best I could do for there is no paper to Be Had

about Hear. (Elizabeth Wagoner, Hundley Family Letters, SHC) Stokes County

Nov. 23, 1863: this is the levlest contry that I ever Saw. it tis as leval as your garden. tha ant a hill that can be seen **about** hear. (F. M. Poteet, Poteet-Dickson Letters, NCSA) McDowell County

Jan. 2, 1865: I heard Since riting this that general lee has given general grant a whipping over **a bout** Richmond but we can heare any thing heare but the truth. (Henry Bowen, Bowen Papers, NCSA) Washington County

2. On the point of (followed by the present participle of a verb rather than the infinitive). [*DARE* **about**, B, preposition]

May 4, 1862: some times We hear that they are **about** Leaving Fredericksberg and then again in a fiew hours We hear that they are advancing upon Our troops. (G. J. Huntley, Huntley Papers, WCU) Rutherford County

account *noun* Worth, value (usually in negative contexts; often following *any* or *much*). See also **nocount**.

Feb. 18, 1864: there aint corn to do till Harvest and Wheat dont look like it will be any **acount. (**Martha Poteet, Poteet-Dickson Letters, NCSA) McDowell County

Mar. 25, 1864: I will state how much I scent. there were twenty Papers, of snuff and I stated for you to give Francis Sarah and Catharine a paper a peace and the other was for you all. I told Aann Adaline that I would scend some home. I stated too that I did not no whether it was any **account** or not. (J. W. Lineberger, *Gaston Ranger,* 91) Gaston County

Feb. 5, 1865: if you can mak out to pay the taxeses and have money to Spair you had beter pay hit for the money want be eny **acount**. (Wade Hubbard, Hubbard Papers, Duke) Anson County

acks see **ask**

admit, admit of *verb* To allow or permit, usually in a negative context.

Oct. 20, 1855: I want go home at the end of this yeare if life laste and helth will **admite** but it is porley wo[r]th my while to thinke of my people fur none of them thinkes a nuff of me to rite to me but youre Self. (Hugh McGregor, Jackson Family Corr., Notre Dame) Moore County

Oct. 22, 1861: it would have been useless for me to a tried to a got home, for our colonel would not **admit of** that for there would be so many that would want to go that it would not do. (H. J. Davis, WPA Transcripts, TSLA) Yadkin County

Dec.12, 1862: my age and health will not **admit of** me staying out in the defence of my cuntry. (Thomas Griffin, Griffin Papers, NCSA) Rutherford County

July 13, 1863: thare is agrate many things I would like to inform you of but time and space will not **admit of** it now. (John Revis, Revis Letters, NCSA) Henderson County

afeard, afierd *adjective* Afraid. [*DARE* chiefly South, Midland]

Nov. 6, 1862: Dear wife I have Ten Dollars by me at this time & I will send you five of it in this letter and resk it. if I nowed it would Come safe to you I would draw it and send it all to you but I am **afeard** that it might not reach you and then all would be lost. (Isaac Lefevers, Lefevers Papers, NCSA) Catawba County

May 31, 1863: I have not bin well Since the fight and I am **a feard** I never will be a Sound man any more. (James M. Amos, Amos Papers, Duke) Rockingham County

Oct. 12, 1863: I did not leave bee Cause I wais a coward nor bee Cause I wais **afierd** of Servis and I am as willing to pay my best in the Survis as any one in the Confedersy. (Jacob Herring, Vance Papers, NCSA) Columbus County

Dec. 25, 1864: I have Some coffee and Sugar this moring for Breakfast and I exspect that is mor than you can say. so you may gess that I am faring pretty well at the presant But I am **afeard** that it wont hould out loung. (J. W. Joyce, Joyce Papers, MHI) Stokes County

affection *noun* A disease or medical condition. [*OED* **affection**, noun[1], II.7.]

July 1, 1863: I have two Sons in the service in the 56th Regt Compy B. Capt F N Roberts James H aged 17 years John R B Walker aged 21 years. both in feeble health. the Oldest one is suffering from a Pulmonary **affection** and cannot rest day or night from Cough.

(Mary Walker, Vance Papers, NCSA) Cumberland County

July 13, 1863: I have not Been able to make a Support in the last four years, from a fatta [= fatty] tumor on my Right shoulder and a Dropsical **affection** of the Legs, and old age has broken me down. (John Livingston, Vance Papers, NCSA) Henderson County

afore *adverb* and *preposition* Before. [*DARE* now chiefly South, Midland; *OED* **afore**, B. preposition, 3, *"arch. & dial."*]

Dec. 29, 1862: I am as Bad a boy as I ever was And as coning [= cunning] as **afore.** I no you dont no how good I Love you. (Joseph Cowand, Cowand Papers, Duke) Bertie County

Apr. 3, 1863: Direct as you did **afore.** pleas write Soon. (James Keever, Keever Papers, Duke) Lincoln County

Apr. 19, 1863: Giv them all my lov an respects an tell them i will rite to them **a for** long. (T. F. Baggarly, Baggarly Papers, Duke) Iredell County

afterwhile *adverb* Later on (from *after a while*).

Apr. 13, 1862: I will tell you a dream of a soldier. one day he fell a sleepe and his capt tried to wake him upe but he could not and **after while** he woke him self and he told them that he would die next day a bout twelve o clock. (Jonas Bradshaw, Bradshaw Papers, Duke) Alexander County

against (also *again, agane, aganst, agence, agin, aginst*)

1. *preposition* Against; variant forms *again, agin.*

Feb. 23, 1862: they was firing Salouts Over the Great victory they gained at Ronoak. they will call it that but I do not think it is much honor to them to bring fiftee[n] thousand **again** 3 thousan. (James W. Overcash, Overcash Papers, Duke) Rowan County

June 15, 1863: You had better take half of it but I tell You it goes mightly **a gin** the Grain For I think he could better pay it all. (William Tesh, Tesh Papers, Duke) Yadkin County

Oct. 11, 1863: Dear Brother you wanted to know if i was willing for Girken to take up the note that i had **again** him as he wanted to pay it. you can do just as you think best. i want you to doo just like you wold for you self. (Alfred Roberson, Roberson Family Papers, ECU) Martin County

2. *preposition* Before, by.

June 28, 1861: father I am Coming home next Saturday. I want you to hav me a good horse **aganst** then. (Jesse Shipman, Shipman Family Corr., Notre Dame) Henderson County

Nov. 3, 1863: I think that I will See you **against** Christmast. (F. M. Poteet, Poteet-Dickson Letters, NCSA) McDowell County

Sept. 7, 1862: we will gow to Ralleigh and stop their a day or two. I dont exspect we will get to Richman before the last of the week. it may be that we will get their **agence** wesday. (W. H. Brotherton, Brotherton Papers, Duke) Catawba County

3. *conjunction* Before, by the time. [*DARE* chiefly Midland]

Mar. 6, 1862: I have had Some notion of going in for the War. I Will git 50 dollars Bounty By going in fer the War and I think the War Will Be ended **against** my time is out eny how. (G. J. Huntley, Huntley Papers, WCU) Rutherford County

Apr. 13, 1862: I want you to have mee a good mess of eggs **aginst** I Com home. (M. W. Parris, Parris Papers, WCU) Jackson County

Nov. 25, 1863: I want you to have all my clothing redy for me **agane** I get home. (C. F. Mills, Mills Papers, Duke) Iredell County

Aug. 30, 1864: he sed that he would try to save the dried fruit for me till I got well. I told him to sell the potatoes for what he could <get?>. that tha would not bee fit to eat **again** I got well. he dident say any thing about any unions. (F. M. Poteet, Poteet-Dickson Letters, NCSA) McDowell County

Jan. 4, 1865: I want you to put up a Shoat and have it fat **a ginst** I git home I expect to come home Some time this winter if nothing happens to me. (Joseph Wright, Wright Papers, Duke) Alamance County

agur *noun* A high fever; variant of *ague.*

Sept. 17, 1860: the reason I have not Ritten to you Soner I wours [= was] Sick a bead when I receve your letter with the **agur** an fever. (Thomas Harding, Blount Papers, NCSA) Beaufort County

Aug. 25, 1862: I got the **Agur** an fever working on me and I am going to make me some bitters for I think it will help me. (J. W. Williams, Williams Papers, Duke) Onslow County

Sept. 17, 1862: I have ben Down with the fever and **eagor** better than A weeke. (Joseph Cowand, Cowand Papers, Duke) Bertie County

a holt *noun* A grasp (after verbs *get, lay, take*); variant form of *ahold.* See also **holt** *noun.*

Apr. 14, 1863: I want you tell fathernlaw to write. if he dont I will hav to get **a holt** of him som time. (Leonard Alman, Alman Papers, Duke) Cabarrus County

aim, ame *verb* To intend (to do something). [*DARE* now chiefly South, South Midland]

Apr. 8, 1863: Some of my neighbours is **aming** for a tobacco crop, one is [a] Young Single man with a substitute in the army and a gang of Negroes at home who Sed he **aimed** to make 4 or 5 or 8 thousand pounds this year. (Levi Walker, Vance Papers, NCSA) Guilford County

Apr. 26, 1863: this war is atrubblesom one. I **ame** to alter my way of living. I am tired of being bound up wors than a negro. (J. C. Owens, Confederate Papers, SHC) Wilkes County

Aug. 2, 1863: Me and charley bothe **amed** to come home crismas if we both had a lived but charley pore feler got kild. (John Futch, Futch Letters, NCSA) New Hanover County

Sept. 21, 1864: I think thay **ame** at take the danvill rode and holde it when thay git evr thing fixt to ther notion. (Arthur Putnam, Kendrick Papers, NCSA) Cleveland County

aint, ant *linking verb* and *auxiliary verb* contracted form with negative particle *not.*

1. for *am not.*

Nov. 24, 1861: if I **ant** Kill[ed] in the batle I will write to you as soon as it is over. (L. W. Griffin, Griffin Papers, NCSA) Rutherford County

Apr. 8, 1864: i **aint** satisfide here. nelly i tel you there is now [= no] where with mee like home. i hope to here from you Soon. (Silas Stepp, Stepp Letters, UNCA) Buncombe County

2. for *isn't, aren't.*

Feb. 1, 1863: they **aint** satisfied yet with the rebels of the south. (J. W. Lineberger, *Gaston Ranger,* 39) Gaston County

Mar. 2, 1863: I am sorrow to have to frank my letter but I Cant git stamps hear an they **aint** no post office hear for me to pay postage at. (G. H. Hundley, Hundley Family Letters, SHC) Stokes County

May 31, 1863: if we **aint** at the post ofise they wil not folow us. (Daniel Revis, Revis Letters, NCSA) Henderson County

3. for *haven't, hasn't.*

Feb. 4, 1862: I am well at this Time but I **ant** bin well for the last da an nite. (J. S. Councill, Councill Papers, Duke) Watauga County

June 9, 1863: tha wil meet him in any old field and take afight with him and his men but tha **aint** one [= won] it yet nor I dont beleive tha will. (Sarepta Revis, Revis Letters, NCSA) Henderson County

Aug. 4, 1864: let me now wather Thomas Allen attends to you or not. or got Salt or not. if he **aint** go to som Body Elce to by it for you. (Wade Hubbard, Hubbard Papers, Duke) Anson County

all *pronoun*

1. compounded with a personal pronoun. See also **you all**.

June 18, 1862: I dont dout but what you Study as mutch a bout mee as I do about you but you have the the childrean with you and they air a great Sattesfaction to you while I am absent from you zand **them all**. (Isaac Lefevers, Lefevers Papers, NCSA) Catawba County

July 20, 1862: Dear cosin it is with plesure I drop you theas few lines After fast returning from church hear ring the good word of god explain to **us all** for our good. (J. J. Cowand, Cowand Papers, Duke) Bertie County

July 5, 1864: we all conscripes has to start to Ralegh on the 15th of July. (G. W. Lawrence, Joyce Papers, MHI) Stokes County

Oct. 16, 1864: i know you must want to hear from **us all** for it will be quite three weeks before you get this. (Ann Bowen, Bowen Papers, NCSA) Washington County

2. compounded with an interrogative pronoun.

June 19, 1862: I want you to write to mee how times is and how you ar Getting a long and **who al** is working with you. (J. A. Shipman, Shipman Family Corr., Notre Dame) Henderson County

Dec. 25, 1862: he wants butter and onion and litle liquer and Some other things he ditent say **what all**. (W. F. Wagner, *Confederate Soldier,* 30) Catawba County

3. compounded with a noun.

June 2, 1863: I sincerly hope when those lines Come to hand they Will find you all well. Dear Wife you dont get my leters **all**. (Marcus Hefner, Hefner Papers, NCSA) Catawba County

June 15, 1863: I was glad to here from you & to here that you & your children **all** was giten along sou well. (Daniel Thomas, Williams Papers, Duke) Duplin County

4. as a pronoun with the sense of *every one, everybody.*

Oct. 8, 1861: Come as Soon as you can for we all would be glad to See you. John be a good Boy for evry body is inquiring after you and we recived your likeness and **all** Says it is pretty. (F. H. Williams, Williams Papers, Duke) Onslow County

Nov. 2, 1864: all the children Sends you howdy. **all** says that they wish they could see you. I would rather see you than any thing els. (Martha Poteet, Poteet-Dickson Letters, NCSA) McDowell County

allers *adverb* variant form of *always.*

July 19, 1863: I am tired of so much fiting for they is some part of the pertomac army most **allers** afiting. (Neill McLeod, McLeod Letters, SHC) Moore County

all only *preposition* Except for. See also **all to**.

June 15, 1863: he Sed that he was doing as well as could be expeted. he was well **all only** his foot & it was doing as well as could bee. (Daniel Thomas, Williams Papers, Duke) Duplin County

allow *verb* often with deleted first syllable, *lowd, loud.*

1. To assume, think, declare. [*DARE* chiefly South, Midland]

Sept. 4, 1862: Some of J W Banners things was in the Box. we **allowed** you would know them apart. (James Zimmerman, Zimmerman Papers, Duke) Forsyth County

Feb. 19, 1863: Dear wife I read a letter from you a few days ago you rote In that letter that you **loud** mont would leave you. (Isaac Lefevers, Lefevers Papers, NCSA) Catawba County

Nov. 24, 1864: they got three deserters and **loud** they killed Some. (Martha Poteet, Poteet-Dickson Letters, NCSA) McDowell County

2. To plan.

Feb. 16, 1863: Some of our men talk with one of they yankeess. he ask him when they **lowd** to fight us again his Answer was he dint know. he hope nevver again. (W. H. Brotherton, Brotherton Papers, Duke) Catawba County

3. To permit.

May 26, 1862: time will not **low** mee to write any more. (Jesse Shipman, Shipman Family Corr., Notre Dame) Henderson County

all right on the goose *idiomatic expression* Well, safe, getting along; perhaps other senses as well (see the Copeland citation below). [*OED* **goose**, noun, 1.d. in phrases and proverbial sayings, "all right (or sound) on the goose: (*U.S.*) politically orthodox." The citation containing the phrase is from 1856.]

July 20, 1862: tell mam not to be oneasy about me and Brother. **we are all right on the Goose.** (K. W. Coghill, Coghill Papers, Duke) Granville County

Mar. 21, 1863: I was grateley inturestid at what you said a bought Drury hodges saying ly still honey tell make a fire. that is **all right on the goose.** I wish them good luck. (Isaac Copeland, Copeland Letters, NCSA) Surry County

June 13, 1863: these lines leaves us well hopeing you are all well. tell Pap and Mother we are **all rite on the goose.** (Alfred N. Proffit, Proffit Family Letters, SHC) Wilkes County

Apr. 22, 1864: Robert Kirkman arrived last thrusday and by his hand I recived your most welcom letter with a bit of meat and cake and 3 plugs of tobacco. I am **all right on the goose**. you need have no fears about that. (Christopher Hackett, Hackett Papers, Duke) Guilford County

all the *adjective phrase* The only. [*DSME* **all the**, 1; *DARE* **all**, adjective[1], 1]

Nov. 4, 1862: we have a cooper in the twenty sixth regiment that went as a conscript that we cant well do with out. he was **all the** man that followed this Trade anywhere near in this neighborhood. (Cass Marlow, Vance Papers, NCSA) Wilkes County

Aug. 5, 1863: I am a volenteer in the Confedeate Servis and is not abel for the Servis by having a hard Spell of the feaver about 10 monts a go and Just have had a letter from my father and mother. tha ar a faring bad at this time living by ther Selves and my mother is nearly Right blind and has binn unwell all Summer and nobody to take Cear of them a tall. I am **all the** Son my father has got for the want of me at home and I want you to wright to me wheather you can do anything for me or not. (John Hudson, Vance Papers, NCSA) Burke County

Jan. 9, 1865: I have receved three Letters from you since I rote the 31 of December. yours of December the 4 I receved January the 2. yours of December the 15 I receved January the 8. also Decem 25. January the 8th. the one you rote a christmas day is **all the** letter that I have receved while it was aney ways new except that piece that was in georges letter in a long time. (Ann Bowen, Bowen Papers, NCSA) Washington County

Mar. 6, 1865: I wil now tel haret about her riteing. She dus toleable wel. **all the** falt She has She Scatters them a little two much. i want Sophrena to take more panes and rite as plane as She can and dont Slant her Letters quite So much. (Franklin Setzer, Setzer Corr., UVA) Catawba County

all the time *adverb phrase* variant position in the verb phrase, after auxiliary *be* and before the present participle. [see *DSME* **all the time**]

July 8, 1864: us and the yanks is from two to 7 hundred yards apart. We are **all the time** Sharp Shooting and Shelling each other. (S. E. Love, Love Papers, Duke) Henderson County

all to *preposition* Except for. See also **all only**.

Oct. 4, 1862: I [am] tolable well **all to** a hurtin in my hip and Sholders. (John Ingram, Ingram Papers, Duke) Forsyth County

May 29, 1863: I am well **all to** my feet. they have bin swollen up veary bad for a day or two but they are better this morning than they have bin. (J. W. Joyce, Joyce Papers, MHI) Stokes County

Aug. 16, 1863: I can Say to you that I am well **all to** Sore feet and cold. (John Futch, Futch Letters, NCSA) New Hanover County

Nov. 22, 1864: I am about well **al too** misery in my brest and the hard burn [= heartburn]. (J. C. Owens, Confederate Papers, SHC) Wilkes County

all to pieces, all to peaces *adjective phrase* Completely (broken, destroyed, or defeated).

Aug. 9, 1862: I hapened to bad Luck with my bag of pervision. the Chickings was wroten for thair was magets in them. an the pies was sower [= sour] an broke **all to peices** an the sweet cakes was in the same fix. (J. W. Williams, Williams Papers, Duke) Onslow County

Sept. 7, 1862: they men Say that they war will soon end. I had a docter say that we wonint have to fight any atall. he Seiad that the yankees army was cut **all to peaces**. (W. H. Brotherton, Brotherton Papers, Duke) Catawba County

Dec. 20, 1862: I Saw them fightting and I Saw the yankeys run like everything. it looked perty to Se them fighting. our men whiped them **all to peasus**. (John Hartman, Hartman Papers, Duke) Rowan County

Aug. 12, 1863: Brother Daniel is ded. he was wounded at the big fight at Gatysburg in pensilvania on the firste day of July about three hundred miles from her. we all was wonded on the firste day fight. our compinay was cute **all to peaces**. (W. D. Carter, Culberson Papers, Duke) Chatham County

all to smash *adjective phrase* Completely (broken or destroyed); same or similar meaning as *all to pieces*.

July 14, 1863: Francis I got wonded in my left leg and foot. I was wonded with a Bumb Sheel. it Struck me on the leg and cut it to the Bone and a pice Struck in the foot and went half way thugh my foot. my gun was Busted all to peaces. I had a tin cup fasen to my haffer Sack and it got mash **all to Smash**. I was wonded the 2 day of this month. (J. W. Joyce, Joyce Papers, MHI) Stokes County

Feb. 18, 1864: I Dont expect to get home Soon. I want Sum Sap [= soap] hard Soap and coffe and canels [= candles]. my tobacco dus very well. the eggs you Sent me was broke **all to Smash**. (R. C. Caldwell, Caldwell Coll., ECU) Cabarrus County

Apr. 13, 1865: my dear we have but few men hear and I am afraid that our compny will have all the fighting to do and if we do our compny will get cut **all to Smash**. (John Hartman, Hartman Papers, Duke) Rowan County

already see **areddy**

a many (a) (also *a meny, a menny, a meney*) *adjective phrase* Many a. [*DARE* chiefly South, South Midland]

Nov. 24, 1861: when that big batle is over it will stop **ameny** po fellow from coming home at Christmas. (L. W. Griffin, Griffin Papers, NCSA) Rutherford County

July 21, 1862: the 1 of july is the time we was in the Big fight and I hav not got time to tell you A Bout hit. I will tell you they was **A many** one killed there. they lay thick on the grounde. (J. W. Love, Love Papers, Duke) Henderson County

Apr. 7, 1863: I hav thout of my littel sweet **a many a** time sinc I hav bin sick and wanted to be with you. (Daniel Revis, Revis Letters, NCSA) Henderson County

June 8, 1863: we found **a meney** pritty and kind Ladies. they had water all along the streets for the Soldiers to drink. (B. Y. Malone, *Malone Diary,* 34) Caswell County

July 16, 1863: I have bin Sorry **amenny a** time that I dident take you advice and Stay at home (Daniel Setzer, Setzer Papers, Duke) Catawba County

ambrotype *noun* A type of early photograph with a reverse image on a glass plate.

Sept. 7, 1861: Hannah please go over to paps and see my military **ambrotype** and you will say it is one of the best you ever saw. I had it taken in Raleigh and sent it to my mamy. (C. L. Moffitt, Caldwell Coll., Duke) Randolph County

ame see **aim**

a mind *adjective phrase* Disposed, inclined (to do something), often after *be* and before an infinitive. [*DARE* chiefly New England, South]

Mar. 15, 1863: Mr Hardin Sayes he will pay half of that money. if You are **a mine** to You may go and get it. (William Tesh, Tesh Papers, Duke) Yadkin County

July 10, 1864: If you are **a mind** to bee flustrated a bout sutch a beeing as I am but I am proud to tell you that I am all right on the goose. (Alfred N. Proffit, Proffit Family Letters, SHC) Wilkes County

a mind *noun* see **mind**

ammination, aminishion *noun* variant forms of *ammunition*.

Feb. 10, 1865: tell Davy and Josy that they ought to Bin hear to help me to Drink Brandy four I have Bin a Bout half Drunk ever sence I had my Brandy. I think that I have had good luck to goet out of the fight saft. I was in it three Days and I am a feard it is not ovr with yet. they are giving owte **ammination** now. (J. W. Joyce, Joyce Papers, MHI) Stokes County

Jan. 1866: they plundered my house and taken my **aminishion** belonging to my gun that had bin taken. (John Bizzell, *Freedom,* ser. 2: 802) Hertford County

amongst *preposition* Among.

Nov. 25, 1861: I would like to bee in old Catawba to go to the corn shucking to fly around **amongst** the girls. (L. L. Houk, Fisher Papers, Duke) Catawba County

Apr. 5, 1862: I was at a show in Goldsburro last knight wher the slite of hand was performd and **a mongst** his manuvers he made a hundred little flages out of one little flag. (Jonas Bradshaw, Bradshaw Papers, Duke) Alexander County

May 21, 1864: Some of Capt hineses men got **a munst** Some bush whakers and one of his men was kild. (Franklin Setzer, Setzer Corr., UVA) Catawba County

a most (also *most, a moast, a moste*) *adverb* Almost, nearly. [*DARE* chiefly New England, Midland]

Dec. 29, 1861: you need not be surprised at my wanting cabage for **a most** any thing is good down here. (Robert M. Blair, Blair Letters, NCSA) Caldwell County

Jan. 26, 1863: take care of my game chickens for I think I will Soon come home. I think the war is **most** ended. (John Hartman, Hartman Papers, Duke) Rowan County

Mar. 2, 1863: I Was at home last summer but I Was sick **a moast** all the time (G. H. Hundley, Hundley Family Letters, SHC) Stokes County

Mar. 7, 1864: you dont no how bad I want to See you all. I have **most** forgot how you look. (Daniel Setzer, Setzer Papers, Duke) Catawba County

Jan. 2, 1865: I have not receaved a letter from you in **a most** three weeks. (Henry Bowen, Bowen Papers, NCSA) Washington County

anchers, anchious, anchus, ancious see **anxious**

and *conjunction*

1. introducing a subordinate clause with a present participle as verb or with an understood verb *be*. [*OED* **and**, conjunction[1], 9.b., "Now *regional* (chiefly *Irish English*)"; see also *DSME* **and**, 2]

Jan. 24, 1861: the boys left this morning holluring like they was after a fox **and** it Sunday morning but we dont have no Sunday her. (L. W. Griffin, Griffin Papers, NCSA) Rutherford County

June 15, 1863: I think he could better pay it all than For us to have to stay out here at only Eleven Dollars a month and Fight For his property **And** him staying at home a makeing everry thing he can a speculating. (William Tesh, Tesh Papers, Duke) Yadkin County

Jan. 14, 1865: I was afraid to go to the cook house for fear they could come and get in the house **and** I [would be] out. (Ann Bowen, Bowen Papers, NCSA) Washington County

2. used in place of *than* or *as*. [*OED* **and**, conjunction[2]]

June 3, 1862: i Cant rite hafe to you what i have Saw. if i Cood See you i cood tell you more in one day **and** i Can rite to you in A week. (W. P. Cline, Cline Papers, SHC) Catawba County

Feb. 20, 1863: I am enjoying my Self verry well at present I am Stowter **and** ever I was in my life Sister I am abuly [= a bully] lookin man now. I have got abwly Set of musstach and whisker on my chin. (W. H. Brotherton, Brotherton Papers, Duke) Catawba County

Mar. 9, 1865: When they taken them they treated us mean **and** our owner ever did. they taken us just like we had been dum beast. (Richard Boyle, *Freedom*, ser. 1: 232) Tyrrell County

and *preposition* In the phrase *once and a while*. [*DARE* **and**, preposition, "By corr with homophonous *in*"]

Apr. 18, 1862: it is only one mile from here to the yankees camp. it is open fields all the way. we ar Scarde up every night. Some Times tha come out with thare artilray every **wonce and a while** and fire right away and then brake for the woods. (J. F. Gibson, Overcash Papers, Duke) Iredell County

Apr. 29, 1862: Jacob & I are getting a long very well except a chill **once and a while**. (W. H. Patton, Patton Family Letters, SHC) Buncombe County

a-near *preposition* Near, near to.

Feb. 27, 1863: I was sory to hear that the small pox was raging up thare. Nancy I hope you will be cearful and not go in reach of them. tha are a dangers complaint dont go a near them now wheir if Lodemay was to get them I know tha wod kill heir. tell Father to not let Frankling and John nor non of the rest go **a near** them fur tha are easy Caut and dangerous. (Jonas Bradshaw, Bradshaw Papers, Duke) Alexander County

anumail *noun* variant form of *animal;* referrence in the citation is to body lice.

Apr. 4, 1863: Dear I must say to you that you would better wash that shirt rite good for I Expect it had some **anumails** in it. (W. F. Wagner, *Confederate Soldier,* 45) Catawba County

answer *verb* To prove satisfactory, be sufficient.

Dec. 1, 1862: the way cloth is sellin if you have not bot enny Jeane yet you need not by as it is sow high. I can draw pants hear that will **answer** very well. (Isaac Lefevers, Lefevers Papers, NCSA) Catawba County

anxious *adjective* many variant forms, including *anchers, anchus, ancius, anshis, ansious, antious.*

Mar. 26, 1861: you are the only brother that I have living and I am **anchers** to hear from you oftner than I do. (Francis Amos, Amos Papers, Duke) Rockingham County

July 16, 1862: see unkle Deniel About highering some one an I want you to Let me know what he thinks About it an how much he would give for I am **Anchus** to get some body. (J. W. Williams, Williams Papers, Duke) Onslow County

Apr. 7, 1863: i hant Recevd aleter from You since febuary an i am varey **ancius** to heair from hom. (J. H. Hundley, Hundley Family Letters, SHC) Stokes County

May 18, 1863: Dear Father I am **antious** to see the end of the war & an Honerable Peace So that we can all return to our homes. (Stephen Whitaker, Whitaker Papers, NCSA) Cherokee County

Aug. 15, 1864: I Received aletter from home yestarday. they was well but very uneasy about Brother Ben. I am very uneasy about him. I am So **ansious** to hear from him. (T. B. Edmonston, Edmonston-Kelly Family Papers, WCU) Haywood County

Nov. 25, 1864: I hant got any nuse to rit to you as I hant had a letter from home in some time. I am gitting vary **anshis** to hear from home. (W. J. Fisher, Fisher Papers, Duke) Catawba County

anymore *adverb* Again, now. [*DSME* **anymore**, 2]

Aug. 18, 1862: if i wase in thomas and James place i Should Stay [at home] as long as i could before i should turn out **any more**. (Robert Carpenter, Carpenter Family Papers, ECU) Chatham County

Nov. 11, 1863: I dont Suppose it will be long **eny more** til we Setle Some whare for winter and So be reddy. (John Hartman, Hartman Papers, Duke) Rowan County

Sept. 25, 1864: I want you to tell thomas to Rite to me if he is alive yet. I for got to Rite to him. tell him that I pray for him to be spared to live till I can git to see him. I wish that he could git to come to my Company if he has to come back **any more**. I hope and pray to god that he wont have to come back. (F. M. Poteet, Poteet-Dickson Letters, NCSA) McDowell County

any more than *conjunction* Other than.

Apr. 21, 1864: I again take the presant oppotuniety of writing you a few lines to inform you that I am in moderate helth at this time **any more than** I have the rhumatism in my Legs but I am Still about on foot. (Alexander Keever, Keever Papers, Duke) Lincoln County

any odds see **odds**[1]

aplenty

1. *noun* A sufficient or large quantity (of something). [*DARE* chiefly South Atlantic, Midland.]

Sept. 6, 1862: sum times wee git **a plenty** to eat and then wee have to do with out a day or tuo. (Bardin Brown, Brown Family Papers, Duke) Johnston County

Feb. 19, 1863: I want to see you veary bad fore I have **aplenty** of niews to tell you. (Martha Futch, Futch Letters, NCSA) New Hanover County

June 15, 1863: I do truley hope that those few lines will find you well an geting **aplenty** to eat. (J. A. W. Revis, Revis Letters, NCSA) Henderson County

2. *adverb* or *adjective* Enough, in large measure. [*DSME* **a-plenty** B; *OED* **a-plenty**, adjective, "In plenty; in abundance"]

Aug. 15, 1863: Cant never whip the yankes. we Can fit hire tel we are all kild and then the[y] will be yankes **A plenty** yit. (W. P. Cline, Cline Papers, SHC) Catawba County

Feb. 28, 1864: Som of the boyes is gon to the yanks an Sens they went we git meet **aplinty**. they feed yus betr to keep us her. (James Hackett, Hackett Papers, Duke) Guilford County

Mar. 24, 1864: we have Snow **aplenty.** we have snow here now 12 inches deep. (Noah Wagner, *Confederate Soldier,* 88) Catawba County

apple butter *noun* A sweet, thick sauce made from stewed apples. [*DSME* **apple butter**, noun]

Jan. 15, 1863: My Dier Wife. I will giv you A Recpt how to make that **Apple Bwtter**. in the first place you make some sweet cider and pwt it in citle or pot and let it get to boil and the[n] yow hav your apples nicely peild and yow put them in an boil them ontill tha boil soft an then poor in moor an so on till they bee come to Jelly. yow stir them all the time. Just like makin molasses the sweeter the Jwse the beter it is. I seen it makin an hav eat of it. it is ver good. (T. F. Baggarly, Baggarly Papers, Duke) Iredell County

apple jack *noun* Homemade apple brandy.

Feb. 26, 1863: he says he think that you and him will drink some more **appul Jack** to gether a gin be fore long. (Isaac Copeland, Copeland Letters, NCSA) Surry County

apple peeler *noun* Possibly a mechanical apple peeler, but given the early date, most likely a pocket knife.

Aug. 17, 1862: I wrote & sent by John Reid one hundred & fifty also an **apple peeler** of which you have never sayd whether you have recd or not. (A. W. Bell, Bell Papers, Duke) Macon County

apurpose *adverb* Intentionally. [*DARE* chiefly New England, Midland]

July 31, 1861: I am agoing to send you some buter and some pickles as I made **a purpes** for yu. (Letty Long, Long Family Papers, SHC) Alamance County

areddy, a redey *adverb* variant forms of *already*.

July 25, 1862: i got A leter from Calvin Cline and he dont like it **A redey** but he dont now [= know] nothen yit. (W. P. Cline, Cline Papers, SHC) Catawba County

May 31, 1863: whare we are to goo to I cant tell and we may not leave. for we had Such orders before **areddy** and ditent go. (W. F. Wagner, *Confederate Soldier,* 52) Catawba County

arish potato see **Irish potato**

ary, arry *adjective* Any, a single (from *ever a*).

July 24, 1862: I dont think that their Will Be **arry** nother fight hear in some time though I may be rong. (G. J. Huntley, Huntley Papers, WCU) Rutherford County

May 9, 1863: it has Bin So long Since I got **ary** letter from yo. Before I got this I had given out the ider of getting eny more. (J. H. Hundley, Hundley Family Letters, SHC) Stokes County

ary one, er a one *pronoun phrase* Anyone, a single one (from *ever a one*).

Jan. 22, 1863: I dont no whather thar was **ary one** kild or not. I hav not herd from them sins I left them. (J. C. McFee, McFee Letters, SRNB) Buncombe County

June 19, 1863: We are in a bad place fore to get any Letters here I havent got **er a one** from you in Sum time. (John Futch, Futch Letters, NCSA) New Hanover County

Dec. 15, 1864: I receaved one letter fro sister Roda and She did not say that they had got **ary one**. (Henry Bowen, Bowen Papers, NCSA) Washington County

as *conjunction* That; used to introduce subordinate clauses.

July 31, 1861: I am agoing to send you some buter and some pickles **as** I made a purpes for yu. (Letty Long, Long Family Papers, SHC) Alamance County

Dec. 24, 1861: thair is nothing new **as** I know of only thair is A rumer about A battle fought neare Senterville in vergina. (J. W. Williams, Williams Papers, Duke) Onslow County

June 12, 1862: Give my love and respect to Par and family and tell them **as** I am as well and heartty as I ever was. (J. W. Whitfield, Whitfield Papers, Duke) Nash County

Oct. 15, 1863: I have not Done nothing more Since I have Bin at home only I shot some squirls. shot at the malishia But Did not heart no one **as** I Know off [= of]. I Dune this to skeare them. (David West, Vance Papers, NCSA) Gaston County

Dec. 10, 1864: I fear they will get the railroad and if they do I dont knoe **as** thar will be aney chance of hearing from you at all. (Ann Bowen, Bowen Papers, NCSA) Washington County

as good as *adverb phrase* Practically, nearly. [*OED* **good**, adjective, adverb, and noun, VI. idiomatic phrases, 21.b. **as good as**]

Nov. 10, 1862: The health of the Regt is very good considring the Exposure they have to indure. some is **as good as** barefooted and some very near naked. (Dinson Caldwell, Caldwell Coll., ECU) Cabarrus County

May 21, 1864: there was 6 men and one lieutenant detaild to go home after horses. D burnet. A B ward. frank citten. gim wheelon. rile powers. will allison. thare to bea back in 25 days. Some of them **as good as** give there Stock away to go home. (Silas Stepp, Stepp Letters, UNCA) Buncombe County

ash potato see **Irish potato**

ask *verb* variant forms *ax, acks, ast;* see Overview § II.4.1.1.

1. pronounced as *acks.* [*DARE* chiefly South Midland]

Apr. 27, 1855: I want you to **ax** gorry what he has don about that money Malcom Clamont wos due me. (Hugh McGregor, Jackson Family Corr., Notre Dame) Moore County

Mar. 8, 1862: I must rite Something a bout times here. they **acks** Seventy five cts for corn here bacon 12 ½ cts a pound Salt 20 dollars a Sack. (Alfred Wilson, Watson Letters, WCU) Jackson County

Nov. 6, 1864: i most bring mi fu lines to a cloes by **axning** you to writ when this comes to hand. (Gorry Jackson, Jackson Family Corr., Notre Dame) Moore County

2. pronounced as *ast.* [*DARE* chiefly South, Midland]

July 31, 1861: **ast** and yu will receive if yu pray fur it and dont neglect to pray often and the lord will ancer yure prarse. (Letty Long, Long Family Papers, SHC) Alamance County

Feb. 4, 1864: you stated that Bulinger talked very short to you when you **ast** him for my pistol. (Daniel Abernethy, Abernethy Papers, Duke) Catawba County

Mar. 22, 1864: Gen Jackson had me arested for being absent without leave while in N.C. & refused me a trial. I applide to Gen Longstreet & **ast** a trial. he hase granted my request & has ordered Gen Jackso[n] accordingly. (Stephen Whitaker, Whitaker Papers, NCSA) Cherokee County

Nov. 30, 1864: they **ast** him if he had come as a prisner or a deserter. he told them he had come as a distrest conscrip. (Ann Bowen, Bowen Papers, NCSA) Washington County

3. variant form *ackest.*

Aug. 10, 1862: Dear Wife all I **ackest** of you now not to take it so hard for I hope and trust we shall meete a gain. if we dont in this world I hope we will in the next world. (W. F. Wagner, *Confederate Soldier,* 10) Catawba County

association *noun* A regular (sometimes quarterly) gathering of representatives of churches belonging to a single organization within a district.

Oct. 6, 1864: the **Assosiation** has past over. there was 14 or 15 preachers there. your couisen bob Moody was there. he preached on sunday. it rained So Much that they dident hav Much of a **assosiation**. (Martha Poteet, Poteet-Dickson Letters, NCSA) McDowell County

as leave, as live see **leave**

as soon (as) *adverb* As willingly. [*OED* **soon**, adverb, 8.a., **as soon (as)**]

Apr. 28, 1862: i wod **as Sunes** be dire [= there] my Self as to Send my likness. (W. P. Cline, Cline Papers, SHC) Catawba County

ast see **ask**

as thick as hops *idiomatic expression* Too numerous to count, beyond counting. [see *OED* **hop**, noun[1], (usually plural) 1.a. "The ripened cones of the female hop-plant" used in making beer; 3. phrase *as thick as hops* (citations from 1590 and 1630)]

June 20, 1862: the yankees and Our men is throwing Bumshells Right hear close to Our Camp **as thick as hops** and it may End towards Eavening in a general engagement. (G. J. Huntley, Huntley Papers, WCU) Rutherford County

at *preposition*

1. To (especially after *listen*). [*DARE* chiefly South, Midland]

   Aug. 18, 1861: I wish to the Lord I had iv [= had've] been there and herd him for I am particular fond of listning **at** him. (Harrison Hanes, Hanes Papers, Duke) Davie County

   Mar. 30, 1862: the rest of the boyes get Letters but I get nun. when the male comes I stand and lisen **at** the captin call them over but nun fur J N. (Jonas Bradshaw, Bradshaw Papers, Duke) Alexander County

   July 13, 1863: ther was Discharges Rote out for Men and the Col wolddent Give them to the men. Some Men Could Give in the Best Surtificate of Diseases and woulddent Bee listened **at**. (William Martin, Vance Papers, NCSA) Burke County

2. in the phrase *sick at the stomach*.

   Aug. 9, 1862: I have got the direar very bad and am **sick at the stomack** ever now an then. (J. W. Williams, Williams Papers, Duke) Onslow County

at reduced form of relative pronoun *that* see **that**

a talk see **talk**

a tall, atall *adverb* variant form of *at all*. [see *DSME* **at**, B,1]

Apr. 13, 1862: he must of heard more than I hav if he heard eny good nuse **a tall**. (Jonas Bradshaw, Bradshaw Papers, Duke) Alexander County

Aug. 23, 1862: tell mee how the corn is for i Saw bw[t] litle bee tween home an her. i Saw bar fields that wont make nothin **a tol**. (T. F. Baggarly, Baggarly Papers, Duke) Iredell County

Dec. 13, 1862: Brother Burges is well & doing as well as any pirson could do. he is with my Self & Capt Wicker to night in the Hotel. he is fat Sure & doing nothing **atall**. (A. A. Jackson, Jackson Family Corr., Notre Dame) Moore County

Jan. 12, 1863: we dont git but half Rashins of meat and meal and dont git any thing else **A tall** and that is close living. (Jesse Miller, Proffit Family Letters, SHC) Wilkes County

Aug. 7, 1864: The Knight of the 7th A Neagro Sentернel Shot one of our men and kild him for no Cause **at-tall**. (B. Y. Malone, *Malone Diary*, 52) Caswell County

athout *preposition* and *verb particle* reduced form of *without*, especially with verbs *do* and *live*.

May 9, 1863: maby I will git a leter from home this eaving if I dont I will hafter do **athout**. (L. W. Griffin, Griffin Papers, NCSA) Rutherford County

May 9, 1863: Dear Sur i wuill rit youe a fue lines to let youe no that i am neding Sumthing to eat vearry bad. my hus ban is in the army an i Cant live **a thout** Sume. (Martha Oakay, Vance Papers, NCSA) Granville County

July 29, 1863: the Committy doos not abledg [= oblige] them only pay them the Money and then tha have to go and finde it. if tha cant finde it around home tha have to doo **athout** unless some one gose after it for them. (Randall Moore, Vance Papers, NCSA) Johnston County

attack *verb* variant forms *attackt, attact*.

1. infinitive *attackt*.

   Aug. 7, 1861: gineral Mcgrooder has tuck 10 thousand men down there And is agoing to **attact** newport news. (Peter Poteet, Poteet-Dickson Letters, NCSA) McDowell County

   May 25, 1862: whether our Generals intend to **at-tackt** them behind their fortifications or not I cant Say it Seams tha wont **attackt** us. (Martin Davis, WPA Transcripts, TSLA) Yadkin County

2. past tense, past participle *attackted.*

Jan. 17, 1862: some think that Our Coast Will Be **attactted** about Wilmington. others think that the gorgia or Southcarolina Will be **attactted**. (G. J. Huntley, Huntley Papers, WCU) Rutherford County

Sept. 1, 1864: they **attacted** our lines not in our front but close on our rite and broke the line and wee marched round by the rite flanck and **attacted** them on ther left. (Larkin Kendrick, Kendrick Papers, NCSA) Cleveland County

attack *noun* variant forms *attact, atact.*

Sept. 29, 1861: We ar looking for an **a tact** in very short time. (R. P. Crawford, Estes Family Papers, WCU) Jackson County

Aug. 20, 1863: since I last wrote you I have had a vary savear **attact** of disintary which weakened me vary mutch but I am now over it and tolearble Stout. (Alfred N. Proffit, Proffit Family Letters, SHC) Wilkes County

Sept. 21, 1863: if the yankese sould make an **attact** on us here I think they will be vary apt to get awhiping. (William Walsh, Proffit Family Letters, SHC) Wilkes County

Aug. 19, 1864: George Pinkney has had a sevear **atact** of Croup this week but is some better now. (Martha Poteet, Poteet-Dickson Letters, NCSA) McDowell County

attender *noun* An attendant, someone who waits upon, attends to others. [*OED* **attender**, noun, 2]

Dec. 18, 1863: Sir I can in form you your Son Wm. Carpenter went to the Hospittle yestarday he was Rite Sick with his old camplaint of bad cof & misrey in his head & brest & his Bowells Runing off freely. [. . .] Let Elizabeth no a Bout Billey. Sir I Remain your Respictfully James Ennis, **attender**. (James Ennis, Carpenter Family Papers, ECU) Chatham County

away see **thataway**

awful *adverb* Very.

Sept. 9, 1862: I Saw more ded men than I ever Saw before. they Smelt **aufull** bad. the lost of the yankes ware seventeen thousand. (J. F. Coghill, Coghill Papers, Duke) Granville County

Aug. 3, 1863: the old Negroes brought a chicken pie out to camp. they pitched in heavy but when they found out it was a mixture hog chicken & mostly dog. they even had the head of the dog. it was old times. Some of them said it was good but was **awful** tuff. (J. W. Lineberger, *Gaston Ranger,* 61) Gaston County

ax see **ask**

B

baby handkerchief *noun* A diaper.

Aug. 17, 1862: tell Matt that I hunted this town over for gingham, for Bonnets & cotton flannel for **baby handercheifs** & neither was to be had hear. (A. W. Bell, Bell Papers, Duke) Macon County

bach *verb* Usually of an unmarried male: to live alone (from *bachelor*); pronounced as *batch.*

Oct. 2, 1860: H M Hutcheson & E W Townsend is going to **Bach** on A while yet. (J. W. Love, Love Papers, Duke) Henderson County

bachelors hall *noun* A house occupied by unmarried males. [*OED* **hall,** noun[1], 11]

Feb. 15, 1863: I have got all most tird out on fritters. We have had no other bred hardly Sence we hav been keping **bachlors hall**. miller and martin is the Cooks. (John J. Taylor, Taylor Papers, Duke) Orange County

back *verb* To address an envelope or package. [*DARE,* chiefly South, South Midland]

1. infinitive and present tense.

Oct. 16, 1862: fold it up in a Sheat of paper and **Back** it to me and do be Shore and Send it. (Charley Futch, Futch Letters, NCSA) New Hanover County

Nov. 10, 1861: Direct you letter to Beaufort Dist Pocataligo Po 25 regment and if we are gone it will foller us if you will **Backet** to the 25 regment in the cear of Capt Blake. (John B. Lance, Lance Papers, LSU) Henderson County

Nov. 22, 1863: I will right as son as I can an let you no how to right an how to **back** youre Letters. (A. S. Harrill, Civil War Coll., TSLA) Rutherford County

2. past tense and past participle, *backed, bact*.

Apr. 13, 1862: tell the old man that severel of us boyes has mad a box and pact it full of close a blankets and sent it to statesvill. we **bact** it to him. (Jonas Bradshaw, Bradshaw Papers, Duke) Alexander County

Jan. 15, 1863: i have rote 3 or 4 four times since i have been hear but i suppose they hant been **backed** rite or Something. (James Hackett, Hackett Papers, Duke) Guilford County

Sept. 28, 1864: i do not no what is the matter excpt you have **backed** your Letters Rong to me. (Wade Hubbard, Hubbard Papers, Duke) Anson County

backbone *noun* Pork backbones with meat attached.

Dec. 5, 1863: I wish I was at home now to get some **Back bones** and Spar ribs and Cabage. (William Tesh, Tesh Papers, Duke) Yadkin County

Feb. 21, 1864: I want to go to her house & I want her to have some **Back bones** & collards. (Ellis J. Holland, Quinn Papers, Duke) Duplin County

backed *adjective* Of an envelope: addressed.

Oct. 10, 1864: I will enclose a **backed** envelop for you to send a letter in. (James Zimmerman, Zimmerman Papers, Duke) Forsyth County

back of *preposition* Of a place: beyond, behind. [*DSME*, **back of**, preposition]

Jan. 17, 1863: I want that fence fixt **back of** the garden next [to] teters [= name of a neighbor] and up the rode to the house and I want the fence repard from the medow to teters fenc. (R. C. Caldwell, Caldwell Coll., ECU) Cabarrus County

backset *noun* A setback, especially in terms of health. [*DARE*, chiefly South, South Midland]

July 31, 1862: I have <?>ased my brother agin if he gits no **back set**. I hope he wont. (L. W. Griffin, Griffin Papers, NCSA) Rutherford County

Aug. 30, 1864: I was sick and could not Injoy my self as I would if I had of bin well. I am not dangrous if I dont take A **back Set**. (F. M. Poteet, Poteet-Dickson Letters, NCSA) McDowell County

backslider *noun* A person who falls away from religious faith, abandons religious practice. [*OED* **blackslider**, noun]

Aug. 17, 1862: He preached a very good sermon, he urged Christians to take heed and not to become **back sliders**. (C. A. Hege, Hege Papers, MHI) Davidson County

backward *adjective*

1. Hesitant, shy.

Dec. 3, 1861: I have fifteen Dollars thare at home and tell pap if he needs hit I dont Waunt him to be **Backward** about spending it fer I never expect to need it. (G. J. Huntley, Huntley Papers, WCU) Rutherford County

2. Of crops: late maturing.

Sept. 5, 1864: times is very **bacward** in our cuntry for they aint no foder puld yet evry thing appears late hear. corns crops is short on upland. bottom is very good. (Thomas Brotherton, Brotherton Papers, Duke) Catawba County

backward(s) *adverb* variant form *backerds*.

Sept. 17, 1862: looke to the end of this line and that is the head of it. Cosin that is Rote **Backerds** and forwards so it will hold out. (Joseph Cowand, Cowand Papers, Duke) Bertie County

badest *adjective* Worst.

Nov. 19, 1863: I am seeing the **badest** time now I Ever saw in my life. (J. W. Reese, Reese Papers, Duke) Buncombe County

bad chance *noun phrase* A poor prospect. [CACWL data indicate the expression was common throughout the South, South Midland]

May 9, 1863: I hope you will not think hard of me for not writing. I have a mighty **bad chance** to do any thing here. (John Futch, Futch Letters, NCSA) New Hanover County

July 13, 1863: I have to hyar some body to plough for us and I have to Pay them from 2 to 4 dollars a Day when you dont get but about 11 or 15 dollars a mounth. that is **bad chance** I thinck. (John Revis, Revis Letters, NCSA) Henderson County

Aug. 19, 1863: Sally you must Be sure to come down to see us all this fall for you know it is a **Bad chance** for me to come again. (Elizabeth Wagoner, Hundley Family Letters, SHC) Stokes County

bad go *noun phrase* An unpleasant time, unfortunate turn of events. [see *OED* **go**, noun[1], 3]

June 16, 1864: Monroe Howard youngest Child Died this Morning. it had the Scar Lett fever. [. . .] I have to go to Monroe to Set up and I am A fraid that it is A going to Bee A **Bad** old **go** with me. (Nancy Howard, Brotherton Papers, Duke) Lincoln County

bad off *adjective phrase* Very sick, in great need.

Aug. 7, 1861: I have bin Sick for 3 weekes & was very low When I Received your leter & I am **bad of** yet. (Peter Poteet, Poteet-Dickson Letters, NCSA) McDowell County

Feb. 14, 1864: ihav herd that harvy fipps is at our house very **Bad off**. rite to me and let me now how he is. rite to me me and lit me now what complaint it is and if eny more of my pepol has hit. (Thornton Sexton, Sexton Letters, Duke) Ashe County

Nov. 10, 1864: I hav bin very **bad off** with hemrods Sinc I hav bin here and it panes me very much. (F. A. Bleckley, Bleckley Papers, Duke) Catawba County

Dec. 14, 1864: Cornelia Ann has a sore throat Something like the quinsey but she is not **bad off**. (Ann Bowen, Bowen Papers, NCSA) Washington County

bad sick *adjective phrase* Seriously ill. [*DARE* chiefly South, South Midland, but especially Inland South]

Dec. 9, 1863: Sirenus Alexander gut a leter from Dr. Housten Stating that his wife was **bad Sick**. (R. C. Caldwell, Caldwell Coll., ECU) Cabarrus County

bagging *noun* A woven sack.

Feb. 12, 1864: I o[w]e Sandy Mckinley for 3 Bales **Bagin** and hoops. thare was no rops on them. (R. C. Caldwell, Caldwell Coll., ECU) Cabarrus County

bait, bate, bat *noun* An ample or generous portion of food. [*DARE* chiefly South, South Midland]

Aug. 24, 1861: I crave cider an water milion more than any thing in the world. it looks lik I would giv most any thing in the world if I cood get one **bate** of cider an water milions. (G. T. Beavers, Upchurch Papers, Duke) Chatham County

Aug. 18, 1864: I got belley full of dumplins for dinner and they no that they did eat a big **bat** of them. (Gorry Jackson, Jackson Family Corr., Notre Dame) Moore County

Feb. 4, 1865: I got A good **bate** of something To Eat when he got hear of sausag and ham Biscuits Custards &c What he braut With him. (T. C. Wester, Wester Coll., NCSA) Franklin County

Feb. 10, 1865: tell Mother that I Eat the last of hir S[w]eetpotaters last night. I tell you that I had a fine **Bait** of them. I hun[g] on to my ham of meat and all of my Butter. I have got most all of hit in hand yet. (J. W. Joyce, Joyce Papers, MHI) Stokes County

bake oven bread *noun phrase* Bread baked in an indoor or outdoor oven or in a Dutch oven rather than in an open skillet or pan.

Apr. 9, 1863: I want you to Send Some flower over to <S???> Speagle or down to franks and have me Some **Backe oven bread** Backed that wil save the Beast [= best] and it wil not Be as hard own you to Bake over the fire. (Isaac Lefevers, Lefevers Papers, NCSA) Catawba County

ball *noun* The most commonly used term for a bullet, regardless of its shape. See also **minie ball**.

Aug. 13, 1862: I saw a Site yesterday that I never saw before nor I never want to See no more. I saw a man Shot for deserting and trying to go to the yankes.

they Shot 5 **balls** threw him. the werd he sed is this. I am now on the field of execution. you are going to See abrave irishman di. good by gentleme[n]. (Neill McLeod, McLeod Letters, SHC) Moore County

Oct. 26, 1863: mi file leder got shot of[f] ov his horse. i had to stop mi mare to keep from runin over him. the **ball** went threw his head. the boolets and bum Shels flew all round me thick. i thaut mi time had Com but i Com threw safe as good luck wood hav it. (J. H. Robinson, Robinson Papers, Duke) Catawba County

Nov. 20, 1864: John Wad King [= Watkins] was killed the 16 of this month. he live 6 or 8 hours after he was shot. his brains was shot out. the **ball** struck him in the right side of his head and come out on the left side of his forade [= forehead]. it was a dredful looking head. (F. M. Poteet, Poteet-Dickson Letters, NCSA) McDowell County

ballet, song ballet *noun* A ballad, often in the form of a printed or hand-copied song; often applied to any kind of traditional or composed popular song. [*DARE* chiefly South Midland]

Nov. 2, 1861: I hav Not time to right you a long leter this time. I want you to Send me the **Balet** of dixie If you plese. (John Riddle, Jackson Family Corr., Notre Dame) Moore County

Apr. 29, 1863: you sed you was agoing to send me sum shirts but I doant need any more Close now. I doant want you to send me any more Close now by S A Syks. I will send you a himd [= hymn] book an a **song ballet**. (Joseph Wright, Wright Papers, Duke) Alamance County

Sept. 26, 1863: I wonder if Miss Moly king plays the pianer as rapd as ever. if so tell hir to play up the perary flour [= prairie flower]. Miss mary I want you to send me a **ballet** of the Perarey flour. send all the wordes of it. (John C. Smith, McNeill Papers, Duke) Robeson County

balls to the pound *noun phrase* A unit of measure for the inside diameter of a gun barrel, equal to the number of bullets that could be cast from a pound of lead, for example, 75 balls to the pound would be the approximate equivalent of .40 inches or .40 caliber.

Mar. 8, 1858: I want you to get gillcrease to have me a gune put in order. two feet 8 inches long. 75 **Balls to the pound.** percushion Lock. half Stock. Silver mounted and I want you to Bring it out in the fall when you Come and I will pay all Expense. (David Headrick, Frank Papers, Duke) Davidson County

barefooted (also *barfooted, berfooted, bairfooted*) *adjective* variant form of *barefoot.*

Oct. 16, 1862: I wroat to you once that I had got them Shooes and Socks. I got them the night before we went ove[r] in to Maryland. the pair that was for me was too Small for me. I had bin **bair footed** So long That I could Sceacley [= scarcely] wair Shooes at al. (James W. Overcash, Overcash Papers, Duke) Rowan County

Sept. 16, 1862: I have marched About A hundered an fifty mils **bare footed** Across the mountins an rocks. (J. W. Williams, Williams Papers, Duke) Onslow County

Apr. 10, 1863: i am here **berfooted** and Cant do no duty for the lake of shoes and if you will send me home on a fur low i will git my self a pare of shouse. (Benjamin Gurley, Vance Papers, NCSA) Stanley County

Jan. 15, 1864: Well, i receivd them things you sent me. i thank you for it. it done me good to get things from home. i got my close in good time. i was about **barfooted**. (James A. Patton, Patton Letters, Emory) Granville County

barlow knife *noun* A type of strong, inexpensive jack knife originated by Sheffield cutler Obediah Barlow in the late seventeenth century.

Aug. 2, 1864: tell little Marcus I have got a little **Barlow knife** for him if I ever git Back. (John B. Lance, Lance Papers, LSU) Henderson County

barosh *noun* A *barouche,* a type of four-wheeled, horse-drawn carriage.

July 24, 1861: there was a power of me[n] killed But more yanks then Sotherners. we took 96 Cannons from them and killed all of there horses and General Scots **Barosh** and apalets[= epaulets] and all of there amunition. (Levi Festerman, Festerman Papers, Duke) Rowan County

bat, bate see **bait**

be *verb* and *auxiliary verb*

A. VARIANT FORMS.

1. *are* spelled *air*. [*DARE* now chiefly South, South Midland]

Mar. 20, 1862: I hear that thear **air** fiting at neauborn and has bin ever sence satuaday. (Martha Futch, Futch Letters, NCSA) New Hanover County

July 16, 1862: I wood bee glad to he[a]r from you an he[a]r how you all **air** gitting A Long. (Leonard Alman, Alman Papers, Duke) Cabarrus County

Feb. 13, 1863: I want you to try and come and see me if it can be in your power. But as the smallpox **air** still about I will not Insist own you comen tell after their Is a change in them. (Isaac Lefevers, Lefevers Papers, NCSA) Catawba County

Mar. 1, 1863: I Cood Reed your Letters if tha was as long A gain as what tha **air** if tha was A little Better spelt. (J. W. Reese, Reese Papers, Duke) Buncombe County

Nov. 2, 1864: I want you to be in gage in prair while you **air** hier on erth and try to meete in heven. (J. R. Redmond, Military Coll., Civil War, NCSA) Buncombe County

2. *were* spelled *war* or *ware*.

Sept. 9, 1862: I Saw more ded men than I ever saw before. they smelt aufull bad. the lost of the yankes **ware** seventeen thousand. so they acknowledge that number in thare Papers,. our loss I do not know. (J. F. Coghill, Coghill Papers, Duke) Granville County

March 1, 1863: I thou[ght] if you know them poor wiman [. . .] was treated by those facttory men that you would put astop to the way they are treating the people. those facttory men they wont notice the people that goes with their money much more then if they **ware** dogs. (Robert Rice, Vance Papers, NCSA) Alamance County

Mar. 16, 1863: we are veary ancious to get to our on [= own] State and to get in the Same Regment as we have Each one of us a Brother in that Regment as we **ware** Bouth Raised in Henderson county N.C. and oure famalys is Residing in that county. (John Johnson, Vance Papers, NCSA) Henderson County

Apr. 17, 1864: I am transferee from Lees army to the Navy, I have bin on board the Patrick Henry for 4 or 5 days and then we **ware** put on Shore at drurys Bluff. (Isaac Copeland, Copeland Letters, NCSA) Surry County

B. GRAMMAR.

1. *be* in a subordinate clause introduced by *if* or *unless*.

Apr. 23, 1863: if the report **be** true thare will leave next month 300.000 Soildiers from the yankey army. (J. F. Coghill, Coghill Papers, Duke) Granville County

Nov. 6, 1864: they say that we will git of[f] home the 8 of Desember and if that **be** so hit wont be loung be fore we git home. (Gorry Jackson, Jackson Family Corr., Notre Dame) Moore County

Feb. 4, 1865: I have bin thinking A bout trying to get A Transfer to Kittrills Springs but I dont know Whether I can or Not. some say that they are filled up at Kittrills. if that **Be** the case I will try to stay hear as long as possible. (T. C. Wester, Wester Coll., NCSA) Franklin County

2. *am* = *have*.

Feb. 9, 1865: you wanted to [know] how mi feet Was. they air not any bet ter than they was when I left home. I **am** not got Stout yet but I think I will Soon be all rite again. (G. W. Love, Love Papers, Duke) Henderson County

3. *are* with first-person and third-person singular subjects.

June 11, 1862: i **er** Abot ten miles from p r Cline. [I] hearde from him. he was weell. he went thrue that batel safe. (W. P. Cline, Cline Papers, SHC) Catawba County

July 20, 1862: Dear Sister. As Papa **are** going to leave in the Morning I take from my portfolio Some yanke paper to drop you a few lines to inform you all that Iam well as usual and all the rest of the Boys. (K. W. Coghill, Coghill Papers, Duke) Granville County

July 9, 1864: tell Rebecky that I Still **air** trying to Surv my god. (J. W. Reese, Reese Papers, Duke) Buncombe County

4. *is* with an adjacent pronoun subject.

Aug. 7, 1859: we **is** geting tired a wating for that tickit to you and Miss Mays weding. (Isabella Johnson, Jackson Family Corr., Notre Dame) Robeson County

Oct. 1, 1861: I **is** not able to writ you along letter. my hand is So nurves that I cant write I would have writen to you befoure now. (K. W. Coghill, Coghill Papers, Duke) Granville County

Aug. 4, 1862: we **is** ancious to no if B.C. is a wating on you. (Dicy Ann Jackson, Jackson Family Corr., Notre Dame) Moore County

5. *is* with a plural or conjoined noun subject.

Mar. 20, 1862: I and Mathew **is** well and all of my mess is well. (J. W. Love, Love Papers, Duke) Henderson County

Jan. 12, 1863: men up to forty **is** orderd out now forth with. if tha dont come willing tha will be forst. (Jesse Miller, Proffit Family Letters, SHC) Wilkes County

Feb. 24, 1863: my britches **is** giting tolereble bad but I think I can make them do me til I come home. (Daniel Revis, Revis Letters, NCSA) Henderson County

Jan. 7, 1863: the children **is** sick with bad colds and I haint seen a well day since you left. (Martha Poteet, Poteet-Dickson Letters, NCSA) McDowell County

May 1, 1864: let mee no how your cows and yearlings **is** dooing. (J. W. Reese, Reese Papers, Duke) Buncombe County

6. *is* with a non-adjacent pronoun subject.

Oct. 2, 1860: Dear Sister. I take my pen in hand to let you know I and all **is** well. (J. W. Love, Love Papers, Duke) Henderson County

Nov. 22, 1861: I found the camp ground a butiful place and the finest tents I Ever Saw. they Will not leak One drop and **is** vary Warm. (G. J. Huntley, Huntley Papers, WCU) Rutherford County

7. *was* with a plural subject.

Sept. 7, 1862: I have nowthing partictoler to write only this is a wright smart place hear. I have Saw Some yankees hear. I Saw two yankees doctors scienc I come hear. they **was** mighty nice looking men. (W. H. Brotherton, Brotherton Papers, Duke) Catawba County

Aug. 12, 1863: Brother Daniel is ded. he was wounded at the big fight at Gatysburg in pensilvania on the firste day of July about three hundred miles from her. we all **was** wonded on the firste day fight. our compinay was cute all to peaces. (W. D. Carter, Culberson Papers, Duke) Chatham County

8. *were, war, ware* with a first or third-person singular subject.

Oct. 28, 1862: Dear sistor you dont now how glad I **wer** to hear from you and to hear that John had got home. (Jonas Bradshaw, Bradshaw Papers, Duke) Alexander County

Mar. 31, 1863: I Came home from gordens vill and while I **war** at home the Company wear exchanged to go to the Strawbury plains to thomases legon. (Elihu Chambers, Vance Papers, NCSA) Buncombe County

Mar. 28, 1864: wee had to cross on the Railroad bridge which was very high from the ground. so wee fought on the bridge and I **ware** the one to go in front when wee advanced and in the rear when wee retreated. (J. F. Coghill, Coghill Papers, Duke) Granville County

9. negative past tense *weren't, want, warnt* with a singular subject.

Aug. 14, 1862: Bardin is gon to the horsepittle. he **want** verry bad of when he left us. (Austin Brown, Brown Family Papers, Duke) Johnston County

Nov. 12, 1862: i **warnt** fit for servies nor never wold bee a gain. (Samuel J. Guy, Vance Papers, NCSA) Cumberland County

Feb. 19, 1863: captin said that when he come back and you **want** able for feeal [= field] duty that he would trans fur you and send you to the hors pittle. (Martha Futch, Futch Letters, NCSA) New Hanover County

May 31, 1863: he had a sore arm and **want** in the fight and I havent hern from him since. (James M. Amos, Amos Papers, Duke) Rockingham County

Oct. 21, 1863: our Briggade **warnt** in the fight But was in the line of Batle. (Thornton Sexton, Sexton Letters, Duke) Ashe County

10. *is* meaning *has*.

Apr. 18, 1862: my helth **is** been bad for some three weeks tho it is some better at this time. (James W. Overcash, Overcash Papers, Duke) Rowan County

Apr. 24, 1862: Dear Wife I am Sorrow to lette you now that my Boxes **is** not come to hand yet and I dont now whether they will come or not. (Isaac Lefevers, Lefevers Papers, NCSA) Catawba County

June 4, 1863: I Can now State that our runaways **is** Come back. they got taken up. they Come in yesterday. (Marcus Hefner, Hefner Papers, NCSA) Catawba County

Feb. 4, 1864: I can Say to you that the Sweling **is** all left me and I hope that it will s[t]ay away. (Alexander Keever, Keever Papers, Duke) Lincoln County

beal *verb* To be infected, fester, suppurate.

July 12, 1863: Marys head is very sore outside. it has not **Bealed** since you Left. (Amanda Murph, Murph Papers, Duke) Catawba County

beast *noun* A horse. [*DARE* South, South Midland, New England]

Oct. 16, 1862: If you want a **Beast** try and git a trusty one. an ole one woul suit the Best. not too ole neather. (W. F. Wagner, *Confederate Soldier,* 22) Catawba County

Apr. 9, 1863: Dear wife you Rote that Arch was to plow for you and He gets the nag to Tend his [land]. Be Shore and keep the **Beast** at home to feed it and keep the nomber of days he has the **Be[a]st.** I think If you give him the forth out of that at home he oat [= ought] to pay you at least 40 cents a day for the nag and a plow al together. and the feed wil be worth Rite smart. (Isaac Lefevers, Lefevers Papers, NCSA) Catawba County

beat *verb* Of fruit: to crush or pulverize. [*OED* **beat**, verb[1], II, 22.]

Oct. 26, 1864: I have 4 barrels of cider and enough apples **beat** to fill another. (Ann Bowen, Bowen Papers, NCSA) Washington County

(the) beat *noun phrase* Anything comparable (in negative constructions). [*DARE* chiefly New England, Midland]

Sept. 21, 1862: I Seede houses tore down and burnt up and all the fences Burned up and all the corne and wheat destroyed. I never Saw **the Beat** in my life. (W. F. Wagner, *Confederate Soldier,* 15) Catawba County

bedstid *noun* variant form of *bedstead.*

Mar. 30, 1863: I have raised Robert Hall and learnt him his trade. he is Well Skild in the trad. he can make plans [= woodworking planes] hoes axes knives Spinning Wheels reals **Bedstids** cubbords Beauros fine tooth combs Wageons Besides many other things. I hope you will permit him to stay at home and Work for the public as I think he is badly needed. (Benjamin Hall, Vance Papers, NCSA) Wilkes County

bed tick *noun* A mattress covering. See also **tick**.

Sept. 7, 1862: I will tell yow how we faird last night. we slep in the old feild with owt any tents over us. I Spred down my **bed tick** and Spred my blanket over me. I Rested very well. (W. H. Brotherton, Brotherton Papers, Duke) Catawba County

beef *noun* plural forms *beefs, beeves.*

Oct. 27, 1862: So we took Some for or five hunared prisnirs an about 2 hundred nigars of all sises women an children an seven peases of Canon an Some three hundred Larg **beefes** an we burnt the Railrod Brig across Bull Run an so forth. (William Howard, Williams-Womble Papers, NCSA) Chatham County

Dec. 31, 1863: the enimy appears to be quiet at this time except cavelry. they have bin moving about some and they captured eighteen hundred of our **beeves** so we have not bin geting mutch meete for the last week or so. (Daniel Abernathy, Abernathy Papers, Duke) Catawba County

Oct. 16, 1864: i want you to kill All three of them **Beafs** when the wether gits Cold. (Wade Hubbard, Hubbard Papers, Duke) Anson County

beef pudding see **pudding**

bee gum, gum *noun* A beehive fashioned from a hollowed-out section of trunk from a sweet gum tree. [*DARE* chiefly South, South Midland]

July 18, 1863: Some boddy come hear wednesday night and stold a **bee gum**. as good one as we had I recon. (James Broach, Broach Papers, Duke) Person County

Aug. 2, 1863: I was Mity glad that you taken the honey as long as it was sitch a god price. I wish that you had a taken both **gumes**. (John Futch, Futch Letters, NCSA) New Hanover County

Apr. 19, 1864: You know nothing about soldiers unless you could be where they was awhile. every **bee gum** every hog chicken goose duck and every thing to eat is taken. (C. A. Walker, Walker Papers, WCU) Cherokee County

bee stand *noun* A beehive.

Dec. 25, 1858: I can inform you that we have bought one cow and calf for 13 Dolars and another one for 15 Dolars. She has no calf but will have in afew days. we have also bought 15 hed of sheep for 15 Dolars and 2 **bee stands** for three Dolars. (William Boss, Frank Papers, Duke) Davidson County

begin *verb* past tense *begant.*

Feb. 4, 1864: I **beegant** to git out of hart to think that I was not a gont to git a letter. (J. S. Councill, Councill Papers, Duke) Watauga County

bellows *noun* variant form *belloses.* [*DARE* **bellows**, noun; especially South Midland (formerly also New England)]

Jan. 15, 1863: thay [= a band of deserters] ar doing agreat deal of mischief. cuttin **belloses** and carry of[f] tools. taking just what thay want to eat and ware. I fear thay will be a great deal of miscief don between now and spring. (B. B. Marley, Vance Papers, NCSA) Randolph County

be shet of see **shut of**

(the) best in the world *adverb phrase* More than anything. [*DSME* **best in the world**]

Apr. 7, 1863: I would like to See you all **the best in the world** but distanc will not permit. (W. H. Brotherton, Brotherton Papers, Duke) Catawba County

July 20, 1864: Aunt I would like to see you all **the Best in the world**. Bout it is so that I Cant Come home. (J. W. Horton, Councill Papers, Duke) Watauga County

(the) best kind *adverb phrase* Exceedingly, very much, more than anything.

Mar. 20, 1862: i Dont know when I will be at home tho I would like **the Best kind** to be at home A few Days but Do not know when I Will be ther. (J. W. Love, Love Papers, Duke) Henderson County

May 11, 1862: We are geting along **the best kind**. I havent stood gard but twice cince I came from home for We halv No gard around our camp. (Alfred Walsh, Proffit Family Letters, SHC) Wilkes County

Mar. 26, 1863: I Am vary Proud of my Shirt. it tuck the pre<ums?> and my Slips [= men's underpants] in fact All you sent mee. tha fit mee **the Best kind**. Jest like tena fits mee for A wife. (J. W. Reese, Reese Papers, Duke) Buncombe County

(the) best sort *adverb phrase* Very much; same as **best in the world, best kind.**

Nov. 22, 1861: I would like **the best Sort** to go home a christmas but there is no chance for going home now. they ar expecting the Yankees to break in on us every day now and they will not let any one go off now at all. (James W. Overcash, Overcash Papers, Duke) Rowan County

be sun see **by sun**

better of see **of**

betwixt *preposition* Between. [*DARE* chiefly South, South Midland]

Sept. 10, 1862: we haft to drill one [h]our be fore break first [= breakfast] and one our **be tweixt** that and dinner. (Robert C. Love, Love Papers, Duke) Henderson County

Feb. 13, 1864: we have a bout 5lbs of sausage and a bout 8 or 10lbS of Back bones and sparribs and **betwixt** a half a bushel and three pecks of dried fruit. (William Tesh, Tesh Papers, Duke) Yadkin County

Feb. 15, 1864: the boys has got orders to meete the Board in Newton on the 23rd of this month **betwixt** the age of Eighteen and forty-five to be Examined. (J. W. Edwards, Keever Papers, Duke) Catawba County

big bug *noun phrase* A term of contempt for a politician or a member of the social elite; same meaning as **big man.**

June 2, 1863: we may Whip them hear and at Some other point they whip us and afte while we ar ruint for ever. I think if this war Comes to A close and we all get home those **big bugs** would beter hold ther peace while times is good. (Marcus Hefner, Hefner Papers, NCSA) Catawba County

big-headed *adjective* Conceited, vain.

June 7, 1863: tell me what them **big hedded** hardins is at & if tha havent took them yet. (John C. Barnes, Phillips Papers, Duke) Robeson County

big man *noun phrase* A term of contempt for a politician, wealthy planter, speculator, anyone blamed for starting the war or profiting from it.

Mar. 6, 1862: Wm James has Bin trying to git to Come home to make up a Company of volunteers But the Colonel Wont let him. yet he given James Miller leaf to go home to make a company mearly I suppose Because he is a **Big man**. (G. J. Huntley, Huntley Papers, WCU) Rutherford County

Aug. 15, 1863: our **Big men** drawed up a resolution. they Said they [= the] men was a holdeing union meetings in N.C. and this Election was to bring them out in the Arma. Dear I wish they would holde meetings in N.C. to stop the war on some fare terms or a nother. Dear I will tell you how they done. the[y] held a Election and the most of the solegers voted for peese and now they got it published that we had voted to keepe on the war. we never voted that a way. (W. F. Wagner, *Confederate Soldier,* 65) Catawba County

Feb. 2, 1865: old vance says that if they dont Make peace and let the men come home in time to make a crop that starvation will be at evry mans door and if they dont come it will be so. I hate for you to suffer for the **big men**. (Martha Poteet, Poteet-Dickson Letters, NCSA) McDowell County

bigon *pronoun phrase* variant form of *big one.*

Sept. 10, 1861: the girls Wrote me thay were drying fruit to make pies. I told them to fix a pockut in my over coat a **bigon** behind and fill <up?> with aples tarts and I would come after it. (Alfred Walsh, Proffit Family Letters, SHC) Wilkes County

big time *noun phrase* A party, celebration. [*DARE* especially South, South Midland]

Oct. 11, 1862: Some of you boys mus come home Chrismas and we will have a **big old time** of it. (Letitia Kirkpatrick, Long Family Papers, SHC) Alamance County

bile *noun* and *verb* variant form of *boil.* [*DARE* especially South, Midland, New England]

Nov. 22, 1861: I Run doubell quick about one hour or nearly that yesterday. it made the Sweat **Bile**. (G. J. Huntley, Huntley Papers, WCU) Rutherford County

Oct. 3, 1862: I had the worse **Bile** under my left arm I most Ever had. (W. F. Wagner, *Confederate Soldier,* 16) Catawba County

Aug. 18, 1863: dear cousin I Seat my Self to let you now that I am not all well at present. I have a very Sor nee. I have a large **bile** on my knee and I can <hardly?> walk. (Mary E. Gibson, Overcash Papers, Duke) Iredell County

Aug. 29, 1863: I hav had aveary Bad **Bile** on me Since I hav left home, it was fifteen days Bee fore it Broke. (Edgar Smithwick, Smithwick Papers, Duke) Martin County

bilious fever *noun phrase* A term used in the eighteenth and nineteenth centuries to describe a fever accompanied by nausea, vomiting, and diarrhea.

Nov. 22, 1861: the reason that I have not wroat to you Sooner is that I have bin Sick and was not able to writ at all. I have the mumps and Something like the **Billeos feaver**. ther was but 3 or 4 days that I could not be up and about. (J. W. Overcash, Overcash Papers, Duke) Rowan County

Nov. 1, 1864: father has bin very Sick but is Som better at present. he had something like the **bilious fever**. (Ann Bowen, Bowen Papers, NCSA) Washington County

blade *noun* A leaf on a cornstalk.

Apr. 26, 1863: we have very fine weather hear at this time warm and pleasant. there is plums and peaches hear as large as bird eggs now and corn six or eight **blades** high now and the leaves is nearly grown down hear on the trees. it look like summer time down heare now. (Ervin Q. Davis, McNeill Papers, Duke) Robeson County

blazes *noun* A euphemism for *hell.*

Aug. 7, 1862: wee had dry weather all the time onley too days and nites it raind like **blaises** but wee had to grin and bear it. (A. P. Ward, Whitner Papers, Duke) Catawba County

bloody flux see **flux**

blow *verb*

1. past tense *blowed.*

Nov. 10, 1861: Some of the tents **Blowd** down. it tore Some of [the] tents in two But not of our company. (John B. Lance, Lance Papers, LSU) Henderson County

Feb. 25, 1862: the Wind **Blowed** the hardest hier Yesterday I Ever saw. it made the Waves Role on the River. (G. J. Huntley, Huntley Papers, WCU) Rutherford County

Nov. 11, 1864: the yankees come thear and unlocked them logs around her and put a torpeder under her and **blowed** a hole in her. (Ann Bowen, Bowen Papers, NCSA) Washington County

2. past tense *blown.*

Mar. 15, 1863: I taken One of my new Shirts down to the branch to get it washed and the wind blew verry Hard and a Spark **blown** on it and burnt it clean up. (William Tesh, Tesh Papers, Duke) Yadkin County

3. past participle *blowed.*

Feb. 2, 1862: we have bin looking for a fight ever since but it has not come to pass yet and they is not much talk of it at this time. the report is that the storm has **blowed** them back and droned [= drowned] a g[r]eat-many of them. (P. S. Whitner, Whitner Papers, Duke) Catawba County

blow *verb* To brag.

July 25, 1864: this ware wont last fore every and then we can go home an **blow** about wat we have done. (Lewis Moore, Moore Letter, CACWL) Cumberland County

blow up *verb* To destroy with explosives; see Overview § II.4.7.

Mar. 11, 1862: they had a right Smart little battle at Newport News last Saturday evening and Sunday morning the old Merry Mack run the blockade out of James river. I tell you She give it to the Yankees vessels. She Sunk one and **blowed up** one and badily injured Several others. (H. J. Davis, WPA Transcripts, TSLA) Yadkin County

Aug. 6, 1864: I will informe you that the yankees has **Blode up** A Porsion of our Brest works not But A few days ago. (Jesse Hill, Hill Letters, NCSA) Forsyth County

Aug. 9, 1864: We had a hard fight on the 30 th of July. the yankees **Blowed upt** our Brest Work. (Edgar Smithwick, Smithwick Papers, Duke) Martin County

blow up *noun* An explosion; the citation below and two in the previous entry refer to the Battle of the Crater at Petersburg on July 30, 1864. [*OED* **blow-up**, noun, 1.b.]

Aug. 3, 1864: they had a **blow up** and a fight over the other Side of peter burg last Saturday. the yankees Blowed up apart of our Breast works and killed Some of our men. (W. H. Brotherton, Brotherton Papers, Duke) Catawba County

blue beef *noun* Usually salted or brined (pickled) beef, but also apparently used for poor quality beef in general.

Mar. 26, 1863: I tel you we nead something mig-tey Bad from home. we have not Drawd a handful of flower since we left North Carolina. we get the worsed kind of corn meal and some old **Blew Beef** and that is some of it Kiled a weak Before we get it. you can gess how we fair. you have a eye dea [= idea] how Beff is that is kiled this time a year without it is fattend. (Isaac Lefevers, Lefevers Papers, NCSA) Catawba County

bob around *verb* To court. See also **fly around**; see Overview § II.4.7.

Jan. 23, 1862: yow must not go **bobing around** the gals So much. (C. F. Mills, Mills Papers, Duke) Iredell County

body *noun* A person. [*DARE* widespread, but especially Midland]

Jan. 13, 1863: I drawed $50.00 bounty money on Christmas day. I have also drawed $30.00 monthly wages, but it goes very fast, because every thing sells so very high and a **body** will buy before they will go with a hungry belly. (C. A. Hege, Hege Papers, MHI) Davidson County

Aug. 24, 1863: I want to see you as bad as ever a Mother could want to see her son but a **body** would be in adread for fear tha would be punisht or killd or Something else a **body** could not stand. (Molly Tesh, Tesh Papers, Duke) Yadkin County

Dec. 19, 1863: thar is no chance hardly that ever that a **boddy** can Send a box but if Mr troye takes boxes I will Send you on too. (Susan Setzer, Setzer Papers, Duke) Catawba County

body bug *noun* A body louse.

Nov. 6, 1862: send me one Shirt one pair Drawers one pair socks one good thick pair gloves. please sow the seames down close as the pleged **Body bugs** pesters us a good deal. (Isaac Lefevers, Lefevers Papers, NCSA) Catawba County

boil *noun* A secretion of the liver; variant form of *bile*. [see *DARE* **boil**, noun², "Hypercorrection of *bile* the fluid secreted by the liver"]

May 16, 1862: I think that I shall mend now for I throwed up **boil** of[f] my stumak three days. (J. W. Williams, Williams Papers, Duke) Onslow County

bolted *adjective* Of flour or cornmeal: sifted.

Mar. 2, 1864: Provisions is very carce [= scarce] in this country tho we git tolerable rations [of] flower not **bolted.** tho it dose very well neads no sodey. (Stephen Whitaker, Whitaker Papers, NCSA) Cherokee County

bomb, bombshell *noun* variant forms *bum, bumshell.*

Nov. 11, 1861: they yankies is putting up batteries on the other side of the river even with ours. they are throwing **bum shells** across to our batteries and our men returns the same over at theirs. (W. P. Burns, Peterson Papers, Duke) Catawba County

June 20, 1862: the yankees and Our men is throwing **Bumshells** Right hear close to Our Camp as thick as hops and it may End towards Eavening in a general engagement. (G. J. Huntley, Huntley Papers, WCU) Rutherford County

Dec. 24, 1862: he went out in picket and was shot through the leg and bled to death in about 20 mins [= minutes]. cut the arter in his leg and the other man was killed by a **bum**. [it] struck him in the head and killed him dead. (John S. Overcash, Overcash Papers, Duke) Rowan County

July 5, 1864: i hav Com out Safe this fair thank God for i do not no how as meney comes out as dos when the Bullets is as thick as you ever Saw it hail in youre life aind the **Bumes** busting lik thunddr. on[e] **Bum** hirt 6 or 7 of our men at one time. (G. W. Lawrence, Joyce Papers, MHI) Stokes County

bomb *verb* variant form *bum.*

Sept. 28, 1862: they run up in helf mile of the Shore and **bumed** our artillery company that be longed to this regt the bum Shells whis teld round our camp they **bumed** us about three ours. (J. W. Love, Love Papers, Duke) Henderson County

Apr. 17, 1863: I havent much to rite only hard times. we have ben Seven miles b[e]low Washington on tar river at a fort. they **bumed** at thare evry day. (W. H. Brotherton, Brotherton Papers, Duke) Catawba County

boot *noun*

1. In the adverb phrase *to boot:* besides, in addition. [*DARE* widespread, but especially Atlantic States, Mississippi Valley]

Oct. 29, 1860: I have swaped Bald eagle [= name of a horse] this morning and got $1.10 Dollars to **Boot.** (William Amos, Amos Papers, Duke) Rockingham County

Apr. 7, 1863: I was down to See uncil william and uncil john. thay was both well bwt they drill them mighty hard. they can come to our company by giveing 25 Dollars to **boot**. they look tollibol well. (W. H. Brotherton, Brotherton Papers, Duke) Catawba County

May 21, 1864: the last letter i got from you was rote 12. i rote 2 to ben to swap [= change places] for mee if he can. i will give my horse to **boot** if i can get to Stay amoung the mountains. (Silas Stepp, Stepp Letters, UNCA) Buncombe County

2. Anything extra; special favors or treatment (see citation).

Feb. 27, 1863: we are a bel [= able] to bare all he can poot on us. he poot John in the garde house and left others out that was to blame worse than John. this is the way he dose buisness but he can just rip we dont aske him eny **boot** So dont be oneasy a bout us. (Jonas Bradshaw, Bradshaw Papers, Duke) Alexander County

borned *verb* variant past participle of *bear;* in passive constructions often indicating a time or place of birth. See also **newborned**. [*DARE* chiefly South, South Midland]

Oct. 15, 1861: yesterday I was mesured how high. then I was ask whare I was **borned.** how old and what was my occupacion. (J. W. Williams, Williams Papers, Duke) Onslow County

Nov. 7, 1862: I am only 16 yers of age or I was **Borned** 1846 Oct 10. (Jeremiah Glover, Vance Papers, NCSA) Rowan County

Apr. 6, 1863: I was marred in the year 1849 in Halifax County N C where I was **borned** and raised and reside in Said County untell the year 1857. then my Husband moved to Granville County NC. (Sarah Dicken, Vance Papers, NCSA) Halifax County

boss man *noun* A person in authority, commander, supervisor. [*DARE* chiefly South, Southern Appalachians]

Dec. 16, 1863: a Yankey Captain shot his Pistel among our men and wounded 5 of them; sence one has died—he shot them for crowding arond the gate. The captain's name that shot was Sids. Him and Captain Patison and Segt Finegan was the 3 **boss men** of the prisoners camp. (B. Y. Malone, *Malone Diary,* 44) Caswell County

bottom *noun* A low-lying portion of land close to a river or creek. [*DARE* chiefly South, West Midland]

May 2, 1864: It keeps so wet I cant plant the **bottoms.** It rains every day or so. (James Zimmerman, Zimmerman Papers, Duke) Forsyth County

Sept. 5, 1864: corn crops is short on upland. **bottom** is very good. my **bottom** is better than it evry was. my upland is short like the neigh bours is. (Thomas Brotherton, Brotherton Papers, Duke) Catawba County

Mar. 6, 1865: you sed Something about Noah Cloninger wanting to rent some of the **bottom.** what you cant tend let him have it. (Franklin Setzer, Setzer Corr., UVA) Catawba County

bound *adjective* Certain, destined.

July 1862: the enemy was throwing ther grape Shot at us By the Bushel and Thousands Shooting at us with ther mus kets where you would a thought that if a mans hat had a Bin hel up in the air that it was **Bound** to Be Shot to pieces. (P. S. Whitner, Whitner Papers, Duke) Catawba County

Dec. 16, 1863: I thought the first of the week she had the scarlet fever but I am in hopes it is not. Mr H Comptons children has all got it. Dr Woods told me last monday that he thought the baby was **bound** to die. (Alvira Taylor, Taylor Papers, Duke) Orange County

Feb. 4, 1864: me and my children are **bound** to perish. all the honest men is gone and a set of speckalating dogs is left to press the lives out of the poor Women and children while the soldiers is standing as a wall between them and the enemy. (Martha Poteet, Poteet-Dickson Letters, NCSA) McDowell County

bowel complaint *noun phrase* Chronic diarrhea.

Apr. 3, 1862: I Seat my Sef to drop you a few lins to lette you now that I am a getting Able for drill a gain but I ant got Shet of the **Boul Complaint** yet. (Isaac Lefevers, Lefevers Papers, NCSA) Catawba County

Aug. 28, 1862: I am not very Well at p[r]eant. I have got the **Bowel complaint** and Soar throat. (John Ingram, Ingram Papers, Duke) Forsyth County

Oct. 3, 1862: I wasent sick since I left home onely bad cole and caugh and the **Bowel complaint**. that is nothing much in camp for they nearly all git it. (W. F. Wagner, *Confederate Soldier,* 17) Catawba County

bowie knife *noun* A large-bladed knife named after frontiersman James Bowie.

Apr. 12, 1863: I will tell yow what tuck place in Richmon the other day. the women rased a mob and tha armed them selvs with axes and **bowenives** and suoards and they went to work. they went in the comisaryes stoars and all others that they come to. (Daniel Brown, Brown Coll., NCSA) Duplin County

box (from home) *noun* A wooden crate constructed in various sizes and used to send food, clothing, and other sought-after items to soldiers. Sometimes boxes were shipped by express and sometimes they were conveyed to their recipients by neighbors or relatives visiting the troops or by soldiers returning from furloughs.

Aug. 15, 1862: If you send a **box** have it bord full of small auger holes and have every thing cool before put in the **Box**. I would like to have a few good apples if you think they will save tell they get hear. you had better not fix too big a **box.** have it sow one man can handle it. (Isaac Lefevers, Lefevers Papers, NCSA) Catawba County

Nov. 11, 1863: if you send me any thing by Micel have it put in a small **box** nailed up and mark it to me. put the co and reg on it in care of Dr. Peace. send me two pare of socks, some tobacco, potatoes, parched wheat ground, and some butter if you can get it. tell Buck to get me some apples and send also some corn bread what ever you do. Tell sister Ann to send me some potato bisket. I get a plenty to eat such as it is but I cant eat it. (James A. Patton, Patton Letters, Emory) Granville County

Oct. 11, 1864: Dear wife I Can Say to you that I do not get enough to eat and I want you to Send me a **box** of provision out hear if you Can and my Coat and vest and miten. I want 20 lbs of flour, a peck of potatoes of each Sort and Some bacon and peas and a peck of unions and a Corn pone Some Sweat cake, Some biscuits, baked chicken, a half galon of molasses, wry [= rye] Coffea ground, Some Soap. Some dride fruit, one paire of Socks, a little hand towel, a needle and Some thread, one quart of honey, Some pies and 2 or 3 lbs of butter, 2 or 3 dusens of eggs. (Alexander Keever, Keever Papers, Duke) Lincoln County

brain fever, brane fever *noun* A common term in the nineteenth century for encephalitis or meningitis.

Jan. 14, 1862: Russel is better this morning. he has the **Brain fever**. the doctor ses he will get well now if he will take care of him self but our doctors dont now much. he cant set up but what he fants. (Samuel Bell, Bell Papers, Duke) Macon County

July 18, 1862: he died the 16 of this instan [= month] in the camps this side of Kinston. he was taken sick the 13 with the **braine fever**. (Lydia Edmundson, Whitfield Papers, Duke) Wayne County

Nov. 10, 1862: thair is A heep of Sickness hear with the **Brane feaver**. (J. W. Reese, Reese Papers, Duke) Buncombe County

branch *noun* A flowing body of water usually smaller than a creek. [*DARE* chiefly South, South Midland]

June 13, 1862: I never saw such a time in my life. we Run thru **Branchs** and Swamps. it was the wettest Place to fight a battel in that could be found. (James A. May, Military Coll., Civil War, NCSA) Guilford County

Dec. 24, 1862: Send me how fur you have got up the **branch** A cutting and evry thing that you can think of for it revives my feelings when I can here the nuse from Onslow. (J. W. Williams, Williams Papers, Duke) Onslow County

Oct. 27, 1863: I want you to git A nuf of wheat if you can to Sow the ground on the fur Cide of the **Branch**. (J. W. Reese, Reese Papers, Duke) Buncombe County

branch water *noun* Water from a stream rather than from a well or cistern. [*DARE* chiefly South, South Midland]

Sept. 8, 1862: I have bin writ bad but I am on the mand rit Smart. I think of the chiles an fevers. the water is bad. hit is as warm as the **branch water** is a bout hear. (Robert Spainhourd, Spainhourd Papers, Duke) Forsyth County

Apr. 28, 1863: times is hard hear harder than I ever thout that I should se. they give us **Branch water** and gollop for Brexfus dinner and Supper. (Joseph Cowand, Cowand Papers, Duke) Bertie County

brane fever see **brain fever**

brang see **bring**

bread *verb* To keep one furnished with bread.

July 12, 1863: there is a great prospect of corn according to the ground that is Cultivated. I think I will make near enough to **Bread** me next year if nothing hapends. (Amanda Murph, Murph Papers, Duke) Catawba County

bread stuff *noun* Flour and cornmeal, supplies for making bread. [see *OED* **bread-stuff**, noun, "Material for bread; grain, flour"]

Mar. 15, 1863: Tell Elick, Mike and sam that I want them to be smart [= hard working] and raise all the grain they can, because **bread stufts** will soon be verry scarce. (C. A. Hege, Hege Papers, MHI) Davidson County

Sept. 19, 1863: I hav had Six Sunes in this wor and thre is [in] it yeat an the pri[c]es of meete And **bred Stuf** will parish thar famlys to death without giving them moer or bring doun the price of purvishion. (Jesse Coppedge, Vance Papers, NCSA) Nash County

break *verb*

1. past participle *broke*.

Sept. 27, 1863: I hav not got no grond **broke.** it is so dry at this time that ther cant be no ploing don and I hav giv out having eny broke. (Catherine Lefevers, Lefevers Papers, NCSA) Catawba

May 15, 1864: Gen gordon was wounded on friday in his arm and it is said his arm is **broak**. (John A. Smith, J. A. Smith Papers, Duke) Cabarrus County

2. Of the weather: to moderate.

Apr. 27, 1863: it dont looke like wnter will **brake** this year. it snowed hir on the 24th of this Instint. (Wilburn Garren, Vance Papers, NCSA) Henderson County

3. Of school: to end a session. See also **break up**.

Dec. 21, 1860: the Schooll **Broke** last tusday. we hade fin tim at the school hous. ther was a graet meny out ther to hear the scholler make ther speaches and a fine table Sat. (Catherine Strickland, Quinn Papers, Duke) Duplin County

4. Of the war: to end.

May 20, 1863: I want you to tranc fur me to the fifty frth Regment N C trups. my Brothers are thare all of them and I want you to let me go thare if you please to Co A. I am here in wilmington Provost Gard in Capt Andres Co. if you will let me go I will Serve you until the war **brakes**. (Alexander Beck, Vance Papers, NCSA) New Hanover County

break open *verb* Of a letter: to open (sometimes to steal money or other items); see Overview § II.4.7.

May 9, 1863: the Brigade male boy was rested and confined for **braking open** leters. he is to be shot i recken. he belong to the 22 NC Reg. he stole lots of money. (L. W. Griffin, Griffin Papers, NCSA) Rutherford County

June 1, 1863: There was a letter come here for him from Sid. I **broke it open** and red it, he was well and at Franklin Depot on Blackwater. i was sorry to here that your Pap was so poorly and had no one to do work on the farm. (James Zimmerman, Zimmerman Papers, Duke) Forsyth County

Dec. 13, 1863: Dear wife I would rite A grate Many things but it dont Soot at this time. our leters is **broke open** and red. I cant rite to do much good til I get out of this Scrape. (Marcus Hefner, Hefner Papers, NCSA) Catawba County

Feb. 24, 1864: Mother I never have got that dollar Yet You Sent in a letter. I reacon Some Body Must of **Broken it open**. (William Tesh, Tesh Papers, Duke) Yadkin County

break up *verb* See Overview § II.4.7.

1. To plow a field for the first time in the spring.

Oct. 5, 1863: send mee word if you got your rosnears [= roasting ears] planted or not. I think you had better soe your lot down in wheet a gin. if you can get any one to do it you had better hav it **Broke up** first. (T. F. Baggarly, Baggarly Papers, Duke) Iredell County

Oct. 11, 1864: I was Sorrow to heare that lackeys [= their hired hand] had not **broke up** none of the ground yet. I think it will be late Seeding their this yeare tell they get the ground broke. (Alexander Keever, Keever Papers, Duke) Lincoln County

Jan. 6, 1865: tel dock that I want him [to] **brake up** all of his corn groun if the wether is nice and fix for a big corn crope and sow all the oats he can. (Jesse Hill, Hill Letters, NCSA) Forsyth County

2. To cease, come to an end.

Aug. 8, 1861: I want you to write to me as Soon as you can and what Sort of a meetin they had at Bethlehem and when it **broke up** and how long it lasted (Harrison Hanes, Hanes Papers, Duke) Davie County

Jan. 19, 1865: i got a letter from israel the other day. he was wel but lo down in Sperits and geting but little to eat. i dont think we can Stand this thing long. i think it wil **brake up** in the Spring but the lord only nose. our men is d[e]serting and going to the yanky. (Franklin Setzer, Setzer Corr., UVA) Catawba County

3. To discontinue (housekeeping).

Apr. 3, 1863: I think if you cant tend a crop that you had Better **Brake upt** House keeping. (Edgar Smithwick, Smithwick Papers, Duke) Martin County

breast *noun* The chest.

Sept. 22, 1861: I am well except my **brest** it hurts very bad the latter part of the night so that I hardly can sleep. the docter ses I hant got clear of the mesles. (G. T. Beavers, Upchurch Papers, Duke) Chatham County

Nov. 6, 1862: the pain own my **breast** has almost left me and I feal very well at this time. I think I am fleshier at this time then I was when I lefte home. (Isaac Lefevers, Lefevers Papers, NCSA) Catawba County

Sept. 25, 1864: I got wonded in my left arm last mounday. I Did not git the born [= bone] broken. it is a vary bad flash woned. the Ball breshed me across the **brest** and went through my arm. I think my arm is on the mend. (J. W. Joyce, Joyce Papers, MHI) Stokes County

breast complaint *noun* Usually pulmonary tuberculosis.

Nov. 10, 1862: we hav lost thirteen men out of this Rigment Sence we hav Bin hear mils snider is ded. he died yesterday. Send word to his wife if you Can. he died with A **Brest Complant**. (J. W. Reese, Reese Papers, Duke) Buncombe County

bresh *noun* and *verb* variant form of *brush*.

Nov. 10, 1862: we lie onder a **bresh** tent. we heare the caneon plane and I Should Sopos tha is a heve batle on hand. (Robert Spainhourd, Spainhourd Papers, Duke) Forsyth County

Jan. 10, 1863: tena I send you A hair **Bresh** for the galls to keep slick hair and tha must let Brug hav it to **Bresh** his Curls. (J. W. Reese, Reese Papers, Duke) Buncombe County

Sept. 25, 1864: I got wonded in my left arm last mounday. I Did not git the born [= bone] broken. it is a vary bad flash woned. the Ball **breshed** me across the brest and went through my arm. I think my arm is on the mend. (J. W. Joyce, Joyce Papers, MHI) Stokes County

bring *verb* variant forms *brang, brong, brung.*

Aug. 12, 1863: I laid on the battle field with Daniel that Night and outhers of our compinay. he was **brange** to winchester thirty miles this side of pertomack river. I stade with him till he died. he died in Winchester on the 21 of July. (W. D. Carter, Culberson Papers, Duke) Chatham County

Feb. 13, 1863: they **Brung** there arms and thay are all together and is making there threts against mee. (Thomas M. Walker, Vance Papers, NCSA) Polk County

Mar. 18, 1864: iwill Say to you that i Saw a man Shot today. he Belongs to the 7 north carline ridgment in our Briggade. i will Say to you that five of our company runway on the 14 day of March and on the 17. day of March. tha was **brong** Back and put in the gard house. (Thornton Sexton, Sexton Letters, Duke) Ashe County

Aug. 30, 1864: the thing[s] that Pery Walker **brung** I haint never Seen them and I dont expect to See them. (F. M. Poteet, Poteet-Dickson Letters, NCSA) McDowell County

britches *noun* Pants, trousers; variant form of *breeches*. [*DARE* chiefly South, South Midland]

Feb. 13, 1863: tell Bud that he most larn his Boock purty tell paw comes home and he will Bring him some little **Briches** and some candy. (Isaac Lefevers, Lefevers Papers, NCSA) Catawba County

Feb. 24, 1863: my **britches** is giting tolereble bad but I think I can make them do me til I come home if ever i do. (Daniel Revis, Revis Letters, NCSA) Henderson County

Nov. 30, 1864: I hant got but one old pair of ragged **britches** and one old ragged shirt but I hope and trust to god that they is a day a coming when poor privats will be as free as big ritch officers. This Cruel war is a rich mans war and a poor mans fight. (W. H. Horton, Councill Papers, Duke) Watauga County

broke down *adjective* Exhausted, weary, physically spent.

Nov. 23, 1862: I can inform that I never Saw as many **broke down** men in my life there is Some coming in this Morning yet. (Marcus Hefner, Hefner Papers, NCSA) Catawba County

Sept. 21, 1863: I have no news to rite only. our hole bytalion has adischarge from dewty for thirty days. our horses is all **broke down** that we cannot travail and we air at liberty but we must Stay at camp. (John Hartman, Hartman Papers, Duke) Rowan County

Oct. 21, 1864: I can tel I was in another hard fight. the hardest fight tha[t] we ever had yet. I com out safe again. me and Franklin Lashmit is to gether. not hurt but both **broke down**. (Jesse Hill, Hill Letters, NCSA) Forsyth County

Buck *verb* To tie a prisoner's hands together, place him in a squatting position, then insert a stick under his knees and over his arms. This was a common form of military punishment on both sides during the Civil War. [*DARE* **buck,** verb[1], B, 6a]

Dec. 21, 1862: I would like to see you coming back before long if you are abel for tha have bin **bucking** some of our boys down for 6 ouars [= hours] for staying too long. (Philip Shull, Councill Papers, Duke) Watauga County

buck fashion *adjective phrase* See **buck** *verb.*

June 13, 1862: All quiate To day onley our men will Run the Blockad. I git Drunk some times. They will Runn the line. I was Sergant of the gard last night & they under Taken To Runn The line. the Colonal found it out & sent out a Detail gard & Braught them in. 24 of them & put them in the gard house next day put them on the gard line. I think it will brake them. Thare was one man had to tie him down **Buck fashion**. (A. F. Harrington, Hubbard Papers, Duke) Moore County

buffalo *noun* An eastern North Carolina Unionist.

Dec. 2, 1864: a great many **bufalows** familys is comeing back. i expect it will be hard times with them for something to eat. (Ann Bowen, Bowen Papers, NCSA) Washington County

Bull Run trot *noun* A disorderly retreat, a rout.

Feb. 8, 1862: Genl Price of Mosura has had a big fight & whiped the yanks. there was nine hundred yanks left dead on the field. our forces gained a decisive victory. the yanks took the **Bull Run trot** & the field was ours. (A. W. Bell, Bell Papers, Duke) Macon County

bull tongue (plow) *noun* A hillside plow with a narrow plowshare. [*DARE* chiefly South, South Midland]

Dec. 14, 1864: I was glad to heare that you was most done Seeding wheat. I fear you will be too late Seeding your wrye. I want it plowed in with the **bull tong**. Lewis can plow it in if R P Sows it for him. (Alexander Keever, Keever Papers, Duke) Lincoln County

bully *adjective* First-rate, very good, very well. [*OED* **bully**, adjective[1], 2.a., "*U.S.* and *Colonial*"]

June 12, 1862: I had the plasure of seeing our Noble president Some few days ago. I Nead Not try to gave you a discription of him. if you Will Look at a postedg Stamp he is fully pictured thare. also gen Lee & Longstreet gen hill of N.C. homes [= Holmes] & cobb. these generals Make a **booly** apearanc. (Alfred Walsh, Proffit Family Letters, SHC) Wilkes County

Feb. 20, 1863: I am enjoying my self verry well at present. I am stowter and ever I was in my life. Sister I am **abuly** lookin man now. I have got **abwly** set of musstach and whisker on my chin. (W. H. Brotherton, Brotherton Papers, Duke) Catawba County

bum, bumshell see **bomb, bombshell**

bunch *noun* A skein of thread or yarn.

Feb. 2, 1863: evry thing is high. Shoes 10 and 12 dollars per pair. thread from 4 to 7 dollars per **bunch**. there is two waggon loads of us women going to the factory to Morrow after thread. (Mary Driskell, Caldwell Coll., ECU) Cabarrus County

Apr. 19, 1863: I want you to help me As afreind. we cant git one bit of coten yarn. the big men buis it for 6 dolars a**bunch** and Sells it for 12 and we Shall hav to go and take it or beg one. (Fereby Core, Vance Papers, NCSA) Cumberland County

July 11, 1863: my Husband bin in the service two years the 12th of this mo and I have not had but one **bunch** of thread yet and myself and family are very bare indeed for clothes now. (Abetha Crowell, Vance Papers, NCSA) Guilford County

burn *verb* To fire (earthenware or stoneware) in a kiln.

June 14, 1863: Dear wife you Rote to me that Bil had not paid you yet. If Stamy wil not settle it in that way I want you to Be shore and kee[p] what wair [= ware] and clay is their and dont allow him to move it. it may be that some one wil turn it up for you own Shears [= on Shares] and **burn** it. (Isaac Lefevers, Lefevers Papers, NCSA) Catawba County

burst *verb* past tense *bursted*.

Oct. 11, 1861: we went on till a bout three O Clock that night and there the Cars run to gether and **bursted** the boiler and one box car and would of killed our Major and other man if they hadent of jumped off. (J. T. Hamilton, Davison Papers, Duke) Gaston County

burying *noun* A graveside burial service.

Nov. 23, 1862: we could hav sent him to Raleigh but their was no way to get him home fro[m] Raleigh. he will be buryed this evening. we are going to the **burying.** Wyatt is very low with the feaver and William Gunter is very low. I must close letter this Nov. 23rd. Thomas Cotton is dead. (Elbert Carpenter, Carpenter Family Papers, ECU) Chatham County

Jan. 17, 1863: he Rote that John Campbell & Betty an had both died with the small pox. I am very own easy a bout you & the childrean as you Rote in the last letter that I read from you that you Rote that you had bin at the **Buring** when John was Beried. (Isaac Lefevers, Lefevers Papers, NCSA) Catawba County

bushwhack *verb* To attack, harass, ambush.

ND [1864]: he told mee that the yankeys was at marshel and ouer men at the mouth of Big ivey and that tha was **Bush whacking** A Baut Elxanders. (J. W. Reese, Reese Papers, Duke) Buncombe County

bushwhacker, bushwhack *noun* A guerrilla, outlaw, deserter; someone who operates from ambush. In the North Carolina letters *bushwhacker* is often synonymous with *Unionist*. See also **Lincolnite**, **tory**.

Mar. 22, 1863: I hear the yanks have bin thar Sence I left & the last news from thar is that the **Bushwhacks** is on Valley Riv[er]. I thort they will take all I have left including my negro boys. (Stephen Whitaker, Whitaker Papers, NCSA) Cherokee County

May 31, 1863: we had 2 batels with the **bush whackers**. we kiled 3 of them. they wounded 1 of our men but not very bad. we broght afine drove of catel and all so afine lot of hogs that we taken from the. **bush whackers**. (Daniel Revis, Revis Letters, NCSA) Henderson County

Dec. 24, 1863: the **Bushwhackers** & Yankies has Ruind the County. (N. G. Phillips, Cathey Letters, WCU) Cherokee County

May 21, 1864: Some of Capt hineses men got a munst Some **bush whakers** and one of his men was kild. (Franklin Setzer, Setzer Corr., UVA) Catawba County

buss *noun* A kiss. [*DARE* chiefly Midland]

Jan. 19, 1865: tel my baby i have a **bus** for her. (Franklin Setzer, Setzer Corr., UVA) Catawba County

buss *verb* To kiss. [*DARE* chiefly South Midland]

May 17, 1863: margaret has plowed the corne over one time and she hopes that yo will be at home to plow it the next time. ann and sarah has done all the howing [= hoeing] to it. they are smarte litle girls. they think that. papay will be at home some day. they all want to see yo mity bad. they dont care how soon yo come home. they will all hug and **buss** yo when yo com home. (Amanda Murph, Murph Papers, Duke) Catawba County

buster *noun* Something extraordinary, unusually large. [*DARE* especially Midland]

Jan. 8, 1864: I want you to plant them in a good place for they are the Best I ever Saw. the mush melon waid 28 lbs. I think they will make **Busters** certain. (John W. Love, Love Papers, Duke) Henderson County

but what *conjunction* But that; introducing subordinate clauses following a negative clause. [see *OED* **but**, conjunction, 30, **but what** *"dial.* and *colloq."*]

Aug. 8, 1861: tel them to take good car of there selves and not mary to soon for they dont know **but what** there husbens would hav to go to the war. (Harrison Hanes, Hanes Papers, Duke) Davie County

Mar. 25, 1863: he is A giting sow as he can walk A bout wright smart now I daunt think they is any danger **but what** he wil git over it now if he daunt take the relaps A gane. (B. C. Jackson, Jackson Family Corr., Notre Dame) Moore County

Aug. 21, 1864: I wonto no whare you air Staying at and whether you air going to move to my farthers or not. I dont no whare you air Staying nor nothing about you. I dont no **but what** you air camping out in the woods. (John Hartman, Hartman Papers, Duke) Rowan County

Nov. 1, 1864: the yankees sliped up on the iron clad and threw torpeders under her and blew a hole in her. I heard they took [= captured] the men that done it. they dident injer her so **but what** she could of bin mended. (Ann Bowen, Bowen Papers, NCSA) Washington County

butterfly root *noun* The root of the butterfly weed, *Asclepias tuberosa,* a plant once used as a herbal remedy. [see *DARE* **butterfly weed**]

Feb. 10, 1862: I waunt you to send me some kind of sweating medicin. I dont care what kind any kind that Would Be good For the Fever or to sweat. I think the **Butterfly Root** Would Be good or any kind that you think Would Be good. (G. J. Huntley, Huntley Papers, WCU) Rutherford County

by sun, be sun *prepositional phrase* The period after sunrise or before sunset. [*DSME* **by sun**, prepositional phrase; *DARE* **by**, preposition, 4, *by sun*]

May 8, 1863: Francis I tel you that we have bin in a hard place last Wensday. we went in the hardest fight that I hav sead in my life. we went in to it a bot two ours **be sun** an Come out a bot Dark. (J. W. Joyce, Joyce Papers, MHI) Stokes County

July 15, 1863: we still staid at Darksvill untell about a hour **by sun** and marched to the Alagater mountain. (B. Y. Malone, *Malone Diary,* 38) Caswell County

June 3, 1864: the yankees charged us about three or four Oclock in the evening and we ran them back about a half an hour **besun.** they flanked our men on the left and come up in our rear. (John G. Hall, Hall Coll., NCSA) Cumberland County

C

cabin *noun* A temporary shelter used for winter quarters, built of logs, scrap lumber, and canvas. See also **shanty**. [*OED* **cabin**, noun, †1. a., "temporary shelter of slight materials; a tent, booth, temporary hut" and †b. "A soldier's tent or temporary shelter"]

Dec. 9, 1861: we are very comfortable situated in our **cabins**. I hope we will gett to stay here til our time expires. (J. E. Patton, Patton Family Letters, SHC) Buncombe County

Jan. 23, 1862: this day is Cold an ough [= enough] to freeze a muley Bools [= bull's] horns off. we have got moved into our **Cabin** But wee have not got all the Chimneys Bilt. (J. T. Hamilton, Davison Papers, Duke) Gaston County

Dec. 11, 1864: we lefte the valleys last tuesday and we came to this place Fridy night. it snowed the same night that we came to this place But we had vary good little **Cabbins** to go in. we was siting and talking by the fire yestedday. (J. W. Joyce, Joyce Papers, MHI) Stokes County

cag *noun* variant form of *keg.* [see *DARE* **keg,** noun, chiefly Northeast, South Midland, South]

Oct. 16, 1863: I want you to send me some cloths by him. the coat that I wore of before and my boots and one par of pantaloons and some socks and a **cag** of Brandy and some honey. (Isaac Copeland, Copeland Letters, NCSA) Surry County

June 8, 1863: if you can send that **cag** home we can Send Some molases to you. (Sally Hackett, Hackett Papers, Duke) Guilford County

Dec. 6, 1863: as soon as I git my money I am Cuming home and I want my little **Cag** ful of Brandey to work the Cold out of mee. (J. W. Reese, Reese Papers, Duke) Buncombe County

Dec. 19, 1863: you Say you want som brandy. I hante hardly got eneything to put eney in to send to you that holds eney hardley but I will try to git frank Deal to make a **cag** that will [hold] ahalf a galling. (Susan Setzer, Setzer Papers, Duke) Catawba County

cake bread *noun* See citation. [*OED* **cake-bread,** noun, a., "Bread made in flattened cakes; or of the finer and more dainty quality of cake"]

Mar. 19, 1865: the men in richmon sais the Solgers famelys is perishing to death for something to eat and to ware and god only knows how soon it may [be] the case with many others. they say they never sen the time tell now that they couldent get abit of **cake b[r]ead** to eat but havent had eny for 3 months. (F. A. Bleckley, Bleckley Papers, Duke) Catawba County

calculate *verb* To plan.

Feb. 26, 1863: some seemes to think that pees will be mad shortly but i dont **Cal Culate** on gitting to Come home before lincons times is out. (Isaac Copeland, Copeland Letters, NCSA) Surry County

calculation *noun* A plan or plans.

July 5, 1864: my horse is a bout as good as he was when i started. we got a long wel. better the i expected. the peopl treated us mity kind. it dident cost us verry much. we hant had time to make **calculation** yet. (Franklin Setzer, Setzer Corr., UVA) Catawba County

cale *noun* An edible plant of the genus *Brassica;* a variety of cabbage; commonly spelled *kale.* See also **colewort**. [*OED* **kale,** noun, 1.a.]

May 14, 1864: i am in good health but i am get ing verry lean. i nead little things to eat to ceap up my flesh but i cant get them here. i went 5 miles yisterday to get a mes[s] of **cale**. (Silas Stepp, Stepp Letters, UNCA) Buncombe County

calico supper *noun* Probably a courting party at which food is served (see citation); origin uncertain, possibly from *calico* cloth. [*OED* **calico,** noun (from *Calicut,* a city in India) 2.a., "cotton cloth of all kinds imported from the East, 2.c., "in U.S. to printed cotton cloth, coarser than muslin," 3.a., "**calico ball,** a ball where the ladies wear only cotton dresses"; but see also *DARE* **calico,** noun, 1a., "A woman"; *EDD* Scots **callack,** "A young girl" (from Scots Gaelic *caileag*)]

Apr. 1860: I am coming to Sea you some tim be fore long certain and I want you to kill a chicking and churn and hav a **calico supper**. (James Fisher, Fisher Papers, Duke) Catawba County

call *verb* To name (a child). [*OED* **call,** verb, II, "*arch.* and *dial.*"]

June 3, 1862: if you **call** hear By ary wone that I Sent Learn yourselves to **Call** her Enery Emery. (G. J. Huntley, Huntley Papers, WCU) Rutherford County

Jan. 31, 1863: you wrote me to send you a name for him. you can name him to suit yourslf as you are there to **call** it and I am not. (J. H. Hundley, Hundley Family Letters, SHC) Stokes County

call (the mail) over *verb phrase* To deliver mail by calling out the names of addressees. [perhaps related to *DARE* **call,** verb, 11, *call over;* see also *OED* **call,** verb, **call over,** 2]

Mar. 30, 1862: the rest of the boyes get Letters but I get nun. when the male comes I stand and lisen at the captin **call them over** but nun fur J N. (Jonas Bradshaw, Bradshaw Papers, Duke) Alexander County

calomel *noun* Mercurous chloride, once used as a laxative.

June 25, 1863: I took soom **calomel** when I first took sicke. we have no docter here and the put me on duty too soon and it fell into my head and teeth and salivated me a little. I feel a little better today. I think if i dont improve tolerable fast i will go to the hospitle. I have no stomach to eat any thin at all hardly. (Daniel Murph, Murph Papers, Duke) Catawba County

calvary see **cavalry**

camfire *noun* variant form of *camphor*.

Oct. 28, 1864: I want sweet Bread and pyes and cabig heads and all you think nesery and some of that strong stuff. its a little like **camfire** [= camphor]. all it lacks the **camfire** ant in it. But it drinkes all write any way. (George Lenard, Frank Papers, Duke) Davidson County

camps *noun plural* The common Southern designation for a military camp, rather than the singular form.

Dec. 3, 1861: I have taken so mutch cold sense I came into **Camps** that I have Bin vary puny for several days past. But I think that I Will Recver Before long. (G. J. Huntley, Huntley Papers, WCU) Rutherford County

Jan. 17, 1863: Dear Wife I have nothing much more to rite at this time as I have bin Riten often to you for the last two weaks & we have Just got to **camps**. (Isaac Lefevers, Lefevers Papers, NCSA) Catawba County

Mar. 1, 1863: the times is A Bout as tha was when I Rote to you the other day. this is the third letter I hav started sence James W Ray left **Camps**. (J. W. Reese, Reese Papers, Duke) Buncombe County

cane mill *noun* A mill for pressing the juice from sorgum cane. [*DSME* **cane mill**]

Sept. 21, 1864: we have got our **cane mill** done and been fixing the furnace to day to go to making the molasses. (Huldah Hubbard, Hubbard Papers, Duke) Anson County

candy stew *noun* A party at which candy is made; similar to *candy pulling* and *molasses pulling*. [*DARE* Kentucky, North Carolina, Virginia]

Jan. 31, 1862: Frank I would like to See you and tell you about the **Candy Stews** up here, had one at Opp. Allisons last night. Lots at it. I did not go. (R. W. Mills, Mills Papers, Duke) Iredell County

Dec. 28, 1862: Master gave us three days Christmas. I wish you could have been here to enjoy it with me for I did not enjoy myself much because you were not here. I went up to Miss Oek's to a **candy stew** last Friday night, I wish you could have been here to gone with me, I know I would have enjoyed myself So much better. (Fannie Perry, Person Family Papers, Duke) Franklin County

cap box *noun* A stiff leather pouch attached to a belt and used to carry percussion caps.

Dec. 6, 1862: our **cap box** and Catherage [= cartridge] box are here but is not give out to us yet. (J. W. Williams, Williams Papers, Duke) Onslow County

May 17, 1864: i sent you half quir of paper. some envelop. some indigo seed. some butons. abelt and **cap box** with caps init. 2 Papers, of catridg. my gloves and cap. one bottle of pouder. 2 pen pints [= pen points] 10 stamps one hammer. isent them in my dirty hbersack [= haversack]. (Silas Stepp, Stepp Letters, UNCA) Buncombe County

capital *adjective* Excellent, superior, very good.

July 12, 1863: wheat is **Capitol** this year. it is splended now. (Amanda Murph, Murph Papers, Duke) Catawba County

car (also *care, kar*) *noun* A railcar, railroad carriage (usually in the plural form).

June 11, 1862: we left Chickahominy And went to Richmond and taken the **cars** and went to the Junction. (B. Y. Malone, Malone Diary, SHC) Caswell County

Feb. 24, 1863: i wos on the **karse** too night and too days. (W. P. Cline, Cline Papers, SHC) Catawba County

Oct. 10, 1864: I love to ride on the steem **cars** first rate. we have come over rivers and under bridges and traveled day and nite. (Henry Bowen, Bowen Papers, NCSA) Washington County

Oct. 11, 1864: the **cares** run off tuesday betwen greensborough and Danvil and killed and wounded

15 or 20 men. (F. A. Bleckley, Bleckley Papers, Duke) Catawba County

carce see **scarce**

care *verb, noun* variant form *cear.*

Oct. 22, 1862: I want you to take **cear** of yur Self and I wood be glad to see you a cuming home. (Sarepta Revis, Revis Letters, NCSA) Henderson County

Jan. 6, 1863: without [= unless] i can get my Son to come home and take **kear** of mee tha [= there] is all Probabilaty of my sufering. (Elizabeth Nance, Vance Papers, NCSA) Randolph County

Jan. 16, 1863: I Will send you one hundred & ten dollars by Dunkin Tucker & I want you to take **cear** of it & use it as you nead. (Evin Smith, E. Smith Papers, Duke) Stanley County

Apr. 25, 1863: I do not **ceare** what comes. it Seems to Me as I had just as soon Be Dead out of my Troubles as to be heare. (W. R. Best, Quinn Papers, Duke) Duplin County

Sept. 11, 1864: Direct your Letters to Camp Whitin. Near Wilmington in the **Cear** of Capt D Biles. (Wade Hubbard, Hubbard Papers, Duke) Anson County

careful *adjective* variant form *cearful.*

Dec. 1, 1862: be **cearful** and dont get his shorlders hurt with the collar and have good gearing own him sow he dont get spoilt. (Isaac Lefevers, Lefevers Papers, NCSA) Catawba County

Carolina *noun* variant forms including *Carlina, Calina, Caroliner.*

Sept. 24, 1861: Camp **Carlinar.** September the 24. Dear cosen. I seat mi self this moring to ancer your vary kind leter. (J. W. Williams, Williams Papers, Duke) Onslow County

Nov. 13, 1861: thir is Som talk of us a moving back to old North **Calina.** which I hope wee will if wee do maby thir will be som Chance of us Coming home to sea you all. (James Fisher, Fisher Papers, Duke) Catawba County

June 5, 1863: I bee long to the 31. Regt and was at Charlston all the time the Reg was thare until the eighteen of April and I was taken Sick and was Sent to Hos pitel at Charlston and then to Columba South **Carlina** and they Sent me home on a Furlow. (Samuel Garrard, Vance Papers, NCSA) Orange County

Aug. 17, 1863: I want you to right to mee and let mee know how times is agoing on in old **Caroliner**. (O. C. Morgan, Revis Letters, NCSA) Henderson County

carpet bag, carpet sack *noun* A traveling bag typically made from used carpets.

Sept. 11, 1861: John give my love to Sister Cathrine and tell hir that I would Be glad to see hir and I want you to Send me werd if you have got my **Carpet Bag** or not. I sent it home when I was at garys Burg. (Charley Futch, Futch Letters, NCSA) New Hanover County

May 3, 1862: i Wont you to gow to newton and git my **carpit bag**. it is At lawson fry. it has got one <?>wit bed blankit in it one Shurt one pare of slips [= men's underpants]. (W. P. Cline, Cline Papers, SHC) Catawba County

June 1, 1862: Write Whether you get the clothes and money that I sent By Toliver Huse and Whether you got the pair of shoes that I sent By scot hill from Goldsboro. I also Sent my **carpet sack** and Wollen vest. (G. J. Huntley, Huntley Papers, WCU) Rutherford County

carry *verb*

1. To take, escort, convey (a person). [*DARE* **carry**, 1; now chiefly South, South Midland]

Apr. 27, 1862: I tole you beefor I lefet home that if [you] was not sades fide that I would **Cary** you a way. (J. S. Councill, Councill Papers, Duke) Watauga County

Aug. 13, 1862: they want us at gordenville. we can get on the train and go. if they want us about Richmand they can **carry** us the[re] in a short time. (J. W. Whitfield, Whitfield Papers, Duke) Nash County

June 29, 1863: I Cant tell whare old Lee Will **Carry** us tow. (G. J. Huntley, Huntley Papers, WCU) Rutherford County

2. To take, bring (an object or item). [*DARE* **carry**, 2; chiefly South, South Midland]

Sept. 2, 1861: We are fixing youre winter Socks and when Papa comes out there he is to **cary** them and some clothes. (Ann Coghill, Coghill Papers, Duke) Granville County

Mar. 5, 1862: Tom must **carry** his plows to George Best and have them repaired. (Ichabod Quinn, Quinn Papers, Duke) Duplin County

Apr. 13, 1862: Wm tanner is hear this morning. I Will send this Letter by him and I intend to send One pair of shous By him if he Will **Carry** them. (G. J. Huntley, Huntley Papers, WCU) Rutherford County

Feb. 18, 1864: I gave your socks to Mr Macy. he sed he would **carry** them to you. (Molly Tesh, Tesh Papers, Duke) Yadkin County

3. To haul, transport. [*DARE* **carry**, 3; formerly Middle Atlantic, now widespread]

Jan. 14, 1865: the columbia run a ground and I cant tel how long we shal stay heare but they say th[e]y are a going to try to pump her out and **carry** her back in the dry dock again. (Henry Bowen, Bowen Papers, NCSA) Washington County

cartridge see **catridge**

case knife *noun* A kitchen or table knife. [see *OED* **case-knife**, noun; *DARE* **case knife**, noun; especially frequent in Midland]

May 21, 1864: i rote aletter to you by D burnet. i sent Some little things by him to you. i sent my gloves and cap. 1 hammer. 1 bottle of powder. 1 belt and capbox and capts. 2 Papers, of cotridge. Some indigo seede. one **case knife**. half quire of paper and some envalopes. (Silas Stepp, Stepp Letters, UNCA) Buncombe County

cast *verb* To shoot (at someone); past participle *casted.*

Apr. 24, 1862: what Ever is to Be will Be and if I am to Be Killd her it will Be So and if not that will all Be So But I haven thought They have Ever **Casted** a Ball for me yet. (James W. Gibson, Gibson Papers, Duke) Catawba County

catch *verb* See Overview § II.4.1.2.

1. infinitive, present tense, present participle *ketch, cetch, ketching.*

May 3, 1863: I go A fishing evry day or So and **ketch** Some fish. (Green B. Woody, Woody Letters, Confederate Misc., Emory) Yancy County

Dec. 25, 1863: Tell Sam & John to **Ketch** me a rabit and Skin and Dry him For me and to send it to me By the First one that Passes. (William Tesh, Tesh Papers, Duke) Yadkin County

Apr. 2, 1864: I and Erven had a fine time **ketching** Rabbits we caught 12 we had Rashtions a plenty while they lasted. (Stephen H. Phillips, Love Papers, Duke) Henderson County

Nov. 15, 1864: he has caught Some lise [= lice]. it is impossible to keep clare of them heare but thare is not very bad here. I have caught a few off of my self but they cant hurt me much heare for I can look for them and **cetch** them. (Henry Bowen, Bowen Papers, NCSA) Washington County

2. past tense, past participle *cotch, kotch, cetch.*

May 13, 1863: we **cotch** a tory as we came on and kild him and the tories shot at our boys and shot one threw the hat. (Daniel Revis, Revis Letters, NCSA) Henderson County

Aug. 26, 1863: him and Laws Hunsuckers went to steele aples to make money and got **cetch** at it and they poot them Boath in the guard house. (W. F. Wagner, *Confederate Soldier,* 72) Catawba County

Dec. 5, 1863: Sam I wanto know if You and John Ketches anny Rabits these days or not and how many You have **Kotch**. (William Tesh, Tesh Papers, Duke) Yadkin County

3. past tense, past participle *catched, ketched, cetched.*

June 10, 1861: he came throw the woods back of Jack Leazers riding a good gray hors and they thought that he had stole the horse and they followed him down to the left of concord and **cetched** him and fetchd him to trial. (Joseph Overcash, Overcash Papers, Duke) Rowan County

Sept. 8, 1862: I would of liked to a saw you very much: long as you traveld So far: but you could not of **catched** us if you had a tride. (W. M. Patton, Patton Family Letters, SHC) Buncombe County

Oct. 26, 1862: I an manass Herndon & E. Parish has built us a small bunk down side of a larg rock but

Sence I hav comenced writing the leves an dirt has becom wet an the fork Split but as it hapend the fork **ketched** the cross pece a[nd] held it till I got a fork an placed it in the place of the other. (G. T. Beavers, Upchurch Papers, Duke) Chatham County

catch up *verb* To take, apprehend, arrest. See also **take up**.

Aug. 15, 1863: some of the malitia started out to **ketch up** conscrips and they stopt us hier and wont let us go any further. (Daniel Revis, Revis Letters, NCSA) Henderson County

catridge (also *catrige, cotterage, catherage*) *noun* variant forms of *cartridge*.

Dec. 6, 1862: our cap box and **Catherage** box are here but is not give out to us yet. (J. W. Williams, Williams Papers, Duke) Onslow County

Jan. 25, 1863: wee ware orded to cook up our rations and be ready to leave at any moment and wee had to have 60 rounds of **catriges**. (J. F. Coghill, Coghill Letters, SHC) Granville County

Mar. 16, 1863: I ad vis you to join the calvary for I tel you that this marching a foot and carying a gun and **cotterrage** box and bayonete and nap sack and haver sack and a blankeit thats a nuf to brake doun aney man. (Noah Wike, Setzer Papers, Duke) Catawba County

July 9, 1863: I shot every one of my **Catridges** away witch was 40 rounds and you may know that was A hot place. (J. F. Coghill, Coghill Papers, Duke) Granville County

May 21, 1864: i rote aletter to you by D burnet. i sent Some little things by him to you. i sent my gloves and cap. 1 hammer. 1 bottle of powder. 1 belt and capbox and capts. 2 Papers, of **cotridge**. Some indigo seede. one case knife. half quire of paper and some envalopes. (Silas Stepp, Stepp Letters, UNCA) Buncombe County

caution *noun* An unusual, humorous, or remarkable person or occurrence.

July 31, 1863: the way we make the chickens and ducks walk is a **caution** to what is left be hinde. (John Futch, Futch Letters, NCSA) New Hanover County

cavalry *noun*

1. variant form *calvary* with metathesis or reversal of *v* and *l*.

May 2, 1862: the Yankees **Calvery** overtaken ours clost to Williamsburg and we had a little brush. (B. Y. Malone, *Malone Diary,* 19) Caswell County

Sept. 25, 1863: I Seede mor **calverrey** men then I ever Saw in mi life. (Daniel Setzer, Setzer Papers, Duke) Catawba County

Mar. 6, 1864: he was kild out there some Where in a fite. they **Calvary** had a fite beteene richmond and orn [= Orange] Court house. (Caroline Setzer, Setzer Corr., UVA) Catawba County

Nov. 30, 1864: they havent got no force yet only the boats and a few **calvry**. (Ann Bowen, Bowen Papers, NCSA) Washington County

2. variant form *caverly* with metathesis or reversal of *r* and *l*.

Oct. 26, 1863: we drove them Some 25 or 30 Miles. we was with in 4 Miles of Manassis and then we tore up they Rail Road and Burned they timber and Iron But Some **Caverly** followed us. (W. F. Wagner, *Confederate Soldier,* 77) Catawba County

Nov. 24, 1864: Sum of ourer Squad is gone to peters burg and soum of them gone home to get horses to go to the **caverly**. (F. A. Bleckley, Bleckley Papers, Duke) Catawba County

3. variant forms *caveldry, caveraldry* with intrusive *d*.

Feb. 9, 1862: they was Some **caveldry** men on picket close to Beaufort and the cused yankes com A cross the river one night and Shot 2 of them. (John W. Love, Love Papers, Duke) Henderson County

Sept. 28, 1862: I went out the other day on the turnpike roade & I saw soldiers for five miles. artil-erry **cavedritly** & infatry. (James A. Patton, Patton Letters, Emory) Granville County

July 13, 1863: if we can get the chance I want to Join the **caveraldry.** that is the notion of us. (J. M. Revis, Revis Letters, NCSA) Henderson County

cear see **care**

cecesh see **secesh**

certain (also *sirten, surtain*) *adverb* For certain, certainly (occurs after the verb and usually at the end of a sentence).

Oct. 15, 1861: please meet me on the way if you can. I shall come **surtain.** (J. W. Williams, Williams Papers, Duke) Onslow County

Jan. 5, 1862: the 35 Rigmint Leaves next Weak or the Weak after **Certain.** (G. J. Huntley, Huntley Papers, WCU) Rutherford County

Jan. 12, 1862: we are all glat to get away from this plas for we are tired **sirten.** (James Keever, Keever Papers, Duke) Lincoln County

Jan. 8, 1864: I want you to plant them in a good place for they are the Best I ever Saw. the mush melon waid 28 lbs. I think they will make Busters **certain.** (John W. Love, Love Papers, Duke) Henderson County

cesesh see **secesh**

chair see **cher**

chamber mug *noun* A chamber pot.

May 30, 1863: I can stand making ware beter then marching. for instans for **chamber Mugs** for Hospital use also galon pitchers and too gallon pitchers would be Necessary for Hosptial use. (Joseph Richey, Vance Papers, NCSA) Lincoln County

chance *noun* A large or sufficient amount. [*DARE* chiefly South, South Midland]

May 24, 1861: our home gard had provided themselves with Powder & Lead. and had a considerable **chance** of it on hand here but had not succeded in getting regular war arms. (Rhoda Hawn, Peterson Papers, Duke) Catawba County

Aug. 24, 1863: I have nice potatoes and some onions to and if it rains some I shall have a fine **chance** of cabage. (Molly Tesh, Tesh Papers, Duke) Yadkin County

Dec. 2, 1864: Cornelia Ann and Olivia helped us get in the potatoes and peas. we had a nice **chance** of potatoes. (Ann Bowen, Bowen Papers, NCSA) Washington County

chap *noun* A young child.

Mar. 5, 1865: I am well and harty at presant hoping this few lins may find you and your little **Chaps** all well. that is good nuse for me to hear. (J. W. Joyce, Joyce Papers, MHI) Stokes County

chat *noun* Idle talk, chatter, rumors, lies. [see *OED* **chat**, noun[1], sense †1. *obs.*]

Oct. 7, 1863: there was some **chat** that they wer going to pay us off Today but I cannot put any confidence in camp news any more. (James Zimmerman, Zimmerman Papers, Duke) Forsyth County

Mar. 20, 1864: My dear wife you Sead that Riggs told a ly on you. well now my dear you must not think hard of me for teling you what I heard him Say for it made me mad to hear Sutch **chat** and wold make eny man mad to hear Sutch as that about his wife. (John Hartman, Hartman Papers, Duke) Rowan County

Mar. 17, 1865: I should like to Come hom But I am afeard to runway. when they sent after them that had left I tell you that it sceard me in to my ground hole and I am a feard to come oute. so you may gess that I am a feard to runway. so I will stop my foolish **chat** for to Day. (J. W. Joyce, Joyce Papers, MHI) Stokes County

chaw *noun* A small portion of chewing tobacco cut from a plug; variant of *chew.*

May 17, 1863: I would send yo some money if I node that yo would get it and I will send yo another **chaw** of to baco in this leter. (Amanda Murph, Murph Papers, Duke) Catawba County

chaw *verb* variant of *chew.*

Feb. 9, 1863: I fell like I am at home only I cant qite turn my cher Round as qick as yow might Serspose fur that dont differ. I can Set crosslegged and **chaw** my tobacco. (W. H. Brotherton, Brotherton Papers, Duke) Catawba County

check line *noun* A check rein, a leather line used to guide a horse.

June 8, 1863: the deserters had come to hir House one night prised off one corner of the roof of the Smoke House went in drawn as much hard Sider as they wanted taken 16 or 18 of the largest peaces of

Bacon they could pick out went to my corn crib taken as much corn as they wanted went in my Barn taken my **check lines** and taken a new Iron off of one of my Plows. (James Tyson, Vance Papers, NCSA) Randolph County

cher *noun* variant form of *chair*.

Apr. 1860: I this day Seat my self as in a **cher** torite you a feu to let you now that I am well at presant. (James Fisher, Fisher Papers, Duke) Catawba County

Feb. 9, 1863: I fell like I am at home only I cant qite turn my **cher** Round as qick as yow might Serspose fur that dont differ. I can Set crosslegged and chaw my tobacco. (W. H. Brotherton , Brotherton Papers, Duke) Catawba County

chew see **chaw**

chicking *noun* variant form of *chicken*.

Apr. 1860: I am coming to Sea you Some tim be fore long certain and I want you to kill a **chicking** and churn and hav a calico supper. (James Fisher, Fisher Papers, Duke) Catawba County

Aug. 9, 1862: I hapened to bad Luck with my bag of pervision. the **Chickings** was wroten. (J. W. Williams, Williams Papers, Duke) Onslow County

June 29, 1863: we just got eny thing that we wanted. Milke and Butter **chickings** and eggs eny thing that we wanted. (Leonard Alman, Alman Papers, Duke) Cabarrus County

Dec. 4, 1863: he Brok it open an brought mee a pair of socks an som pork an **chicking** an one Sweet cake. (T. F. Baggarly, Baggarly Papers, Duke) Iredell County

children *noun plural*

1. variant forms with *r* metathesis, including *childern, childearn, chilern*. [*DARE* chiefly South, South Midland]

May 9, 1863: if youe dont make Sum rang ments [= arrangements] the wim men an **Chilern** wil Sufer hear. (Martha Oakay, Vance Papers, NCSA) Granville County

June 29, 1863: A few linds to my little **Childearn**. tel Bude and Sis to Be gode **childearn** and tel them houdy for me. (Leonard Alman, Alman Papers, Duke) Cabarrus County

Dec. 23, 1863: the **childarn** is agoing to [s]chool now. tha Start a monday morning. (Susan Setzer, Setzer Papers, Duke) Catawba County

Sept. 11, 1864: the time will soon Come wen i can Come home and Be with my Dear wiefe and **childern** once more in this woorld and eat some of your good vittles. (Wade Hubbard, Hubbard Papers, Duke) Anson County

2. variant forms *childring, childing*.

Oct. 2, 1862: if we get back what glad men we will be. we get to sea our dear wives an our **childing** our hom our frends. (Henry Baker, Henry Baker Papers, Duke) Catawba County

Nov. 18, 1862: I want you to give Uncle And Ant and all of the **childring** My love and best respecks an also Ant celia and ant pat and the **childring**. (Joseph Cowand, Cowand Papers, Duke) Bertie County

May 5, 1863: I have grate troble Rasing my **childing.** thare father dide When they War babes & I think it is hard to take my child from mee. (Dista Swindell, Vance Papers, NCSA) Hyde County

3. variant forms *childen, childon, childer*.

July 5, 1863: I never want it sed that I ever dide a deser[t]or for it will be a disgrace to me as long as I live an to my pore little **childon** after I am ded. I had ote [= ought] to a rote be fore now but I was a frade. (John Averett, Vance Papers, NCSA) Pitt County

July 20, 1863: I hav a vary larg famly. a 11 and the most Smal **childer** and my ag is 41 one yers and the malish[a] offers [= officers] has in rold my nam with the concripes thru a mistak. (William Richardson, Vance Papers, NCSA) Ashe County

Sept. 9, 1863: I have two **childen** and I am very unhelth and I serttinly can not get along this winter without help. (Roseann Phillips, Vance Papers, NCSA) Lenoir County

chimley *noun* variant form of *chimney*. [*DARE* chiefly South, Midland, occasionally New England]

Feb. 9, 1862: we hav our tents fix up **chimleys** to them so we can keep Dry as A pouder house. (John W. Love, Love Papers, Duke) Henderson County

Jan. 11, 1863: I have nothing of importance to rite but I have a **chimly** to my tent and it is as warm as in ahouse. (John Hartman, Hartman Papers, Duke) Rowan County

Jan. 15, 1863: I hant got mutch time to Right for I am engage in bilding a Shanty. I have got it all done bwt the **chimly**. we are all bilding winter qwarter. (W. H. Brotherton, Brotherton Papers, Duke) Catawba County

chinquapin *noun* A kind of nut and small tree or shrub, *Castanea pumila,* related to the American chestnut. [*DARE* chiefly South, South Midland]

Mar. 25, 1863: I want you to gether all the **chinkepins** and chestnuts you can and send me a few if you can. (C. A. Hege, Hege Papers, MHI) Davidson County

Oct. 2, 1863: I found some apples & graps and muskadines and **chickapines** though I walked a good peace for to get them. (J. W. Lineberger, *Gaston Ranger,* 68) Gaston County

Aug. 11, 1864: I woud be mitty glad if I waus ther to help them find **Chinkpen**. (Gorry Jackson, Jackson Family Corr., Notre Dame) Moore County

chip *noun plural* A small piece of wood used to kindle a fire.

Feb. 7, 1863: a few lines for sissey & Buddy. you must be purty children for maw. you most toat **chips** and water for maw and you most not fite nor hurt the sweat little Baby and mind it good for maw. (Isaac Lefevers, Lefevers Papers, NCSA) Catawba County

chist *noun* variant form of *chest.*

May 12, 1863: I want want you to send me a few little things by him if he can bring them sutch as butter and honey or any thing els that will do to eat. I Sent my coat and **chist** and a few more litle things by bill Ruth. (R. C. Love, Love Papers, Duke) Henderson County

chop *verb* To hoe, clear weeds, cultivate. [*DARE* chiefly South, Midland]

June 13 1852: I am behind in my cotton crop. I have **choped** out 13 acors and have 8 or the rise to **chope** I have cotton nea hie and full of formes [= buds?] nearly ready to blosom. (Neill McGregor, Jackson Family Corr., Notre Dame) Moore County

Feb. 18, 1865: tell Eldrig I dont [know] whether I can help her **chop** or not unless she can put it off awhile. (F. A. Bleckley, Bleckley Papers, Duke) Catawba County

chopping see **corn chopping**

Christmas devil *noun* A kind of firework; see citation.

Mar. 9, 1865: the next is Concerning of our White Soldiers. they Come to our Church and we treat them with all the Politeness that we can and Some of them treats us as though we were beast and we cant help our Selves. Some of them brings Pop Crackers and **Christmas devils** and throws a mong the woman and if we Say any thing to them they will talk about mobin us. (Richard Boyle, *Freedom,* ser. 1, vol. 2: 233) Tyrrell County

Christmas gift *interjection* A Christmas greeting; originally the first person to say this was owed a token gift by the person addressed. [*DSME* **Christmas gift, Christmas give** *interjection; DARE* chiefly South, South Midland]

Dec. 1861: Dear Sisters a few lins to you as brother has Claim A **Christmas gifte.** I think I might have one to. I Claim one from gorge and from Joseph. you Can tell them to have it for me when I come home If I live. (L. W. Griffin, Griffin Papers, NCSA) Rutherford County

Dec. 22, 1861: I want you to give Miss N.H. and Miss Hariet G. my very Best Respects if you pleas and tell them I Claim a **Christmass Gift** off of Boath of them. I Cant See them my self But you must get it off of them for me. (James W. Gibson, Gibson Papers, Duke) Catawba County

cider see **hard cider, sweet cider**

circuit preacher *noun* A circuit rider, a minister serving several rural congregations that are often located some distance from each other and that he can only tend by visiting on a periodic basis (e.g., weekly or monthly).

Aug. 24, 1863: William I must tell you about the two days meeting we had up at union last Thursday and Friday the **Sircuit preacher** had. his name is whilsington he is the best Methodist preacher I nearly ever heard. (Molly Tesh, Tesh Papers, Duke) Yadkin County

citle, cittle see **kettle**

civer, kiver *verb* and *noun* variant forms of *cover*. [*DARE* South, Midland, occasionally New England]

May 20, 1862: I Suppose that you get Along plowing very well you must try an run close to the corn to **civer** up the grass but dont Leave the corn coverd up. (J. W. Williams, Williams Papers, Duke) Onslow County

Sept. 14, 1862: the Barn needs a Roof bad I know it does need one bad try and git some person to poot a roof on it maby you could git Langdon Hoffman to doo it. git plaits and raftters and **kiver** it. (W. F. Wagner, *Confederate Soldier,* 14) Catawba County

Jan. 11, 1863: i hav a very good bed an plenty of **civer.** 4 blanket an 2 Sheets. (T. F. Baggarly, Baggarly Papers, Duke) Iredell County

claboard *noun* A board used as siding for a house; variant form of *clapboard*. [*DARE* scattered, but chiefly Northeast]

Jan. 3, 1864: I made a house out of **Clabords** Since here. I have bin the colds [= coldest] work I ever dun. Sum put up tents but the [wind] tore them all to peces. (R. C. Caldwell, Caldwell Coll., ECU) Cabarrus County

claybank *adjective* Of a horse: tan in color.

Jan. 26, 1863: take care of my game chickens for I think I will Soon come home. I think the war is most ended. I have two perty **clabank** horses. (John Hartman, Hartman Papers, Duke) Rowan County

clean *adverb* Completely, all the way.

July 12, 1862: we are all broke down an wared to death for we folard after the yankes thirty mil below richmond **clean** to James river. (J. W. Williams, Williams Papers, Duke) Onslow County

Mar. 15, 1863: I taken One of my new shirts down to the branch to get it washed and the wind blew verry Hard and a Spark blown on it and burnt it **clean** up. (William Tesh, Tesh Papers, Duke) Yadkin County

Aug. 5, 1864: we had a race with Hunter to Linchburg beet him thar whipt him & run him past Salum **Clean** off out of the Cuntry. (Stephen Whitaker, Whitaker Papers, NCSA) Cherokee County

clear

1. *verb* To exempt or excuse from military service. See also **come clear**.

July 12, 1862: they Aught to be Some one that will **clare** me for the war. (J. W. Williams, Williams Papers, Duke) Onslow County

May 1863: I Waunt you to tell Pap that I Waunt him to Git into some kind of Bussiness that Will **Clear** him from thise War. (G. J. Huntley, Huntley Papers, WCU) Rutherford County

2. *adjective* Excused or exempt from military service.

Dec. 7, 1862: grant me Twelve men **clear** of conscription together withe my three Lieutenanc for the purpose of taking up Deserters. (William N. Pierce, Vance Papers, NCSA) Wilkes County

June 24, 1863: I have two sons in the army. my oldest 22 and the other 17 years of age and as my situation is very distressing in the extreme I appeal to you say and get my youngest son **clear** and discharge him for I need him very much at home. (Hester Bowden, Vance Papers, NCSA) New Hanover County

3. *adjective* Innocent of a crime.

Nov. 30, 1864: they ast him Several other questions and told him if he could prove himself **clear** of carting furniture out of town he was **clear**. so he got a parsel of wimen and proved him **clear.** so they dident do aney thing more with him. (Ann Bowen, Bowen Papers, NCSA) Washington County

clear *adverb* Completely, all the way.

June 6, 1862: if he leaves it at Lincolton he Will let you know Whare it is and you can send for it and you can pay him for his trouble Out of my money. he may carry it **clear** home. (G. J. Huntley, Huntley Papers, WCU) Rutherford County

Aug. 17, 1862: other Regiments is leaveing her a round us going down to the valleys About one hundred or more. if we git down there we Shall be **clear** gon out of hearing near About. i want to leave this place but i want to come to old north caroliner if i could. (William Carpenter, Carpenter Family Papers, ECU) Chatham County

Sept. 1, 1864: thay ways [= was] fight going on hear afew days a go but our Brigade was not in it this time. it begaind to Rain vary hard and the fighting Stopt. I have not heard of the yankeys since. I hope thay are **clar** gon whare we will never ce them a gain. (J. W. Joyce, Joyce Papers, MHI) Stokes County

clever *adjective* Various positive senses used to describe people. [*DARE* formerly New England, now chiefly South, South Midland]

1. Kind, generous, hospitable.

Jan. 22, 1862: I Beleave it is the nisest place I Ever saw and the peopell is vary **clever** and patriotick. (G. J. Huntley, Huntley Papers, WCU) Rutherford County

June 19, 1863: The citizens seemed very kind and **clever** in some parts of the country. (J. H. Hundley, Hundley Family Letters, SHC) Stokes County

Feb. 29, 1864: Benson was the Doctor that gave me my furlough and I always will respect him for it he was a **cleaver** man and had come out as a private in the armey and he has some Respect for a pore Soldier. (Isaac Lefevers, Lefevers Papers, NCSA) Catawba County

Mar. 17, 1864: I want you to Rite whether Johnthan Walker is at home are [= or] not. he has acted very **cleaver** with you. tell him that I hope that god will bless him. (F. M. Poteet, Poteet-Dickson Letters, NCSA) McDowell

2. Pleasant, agreeable, attractive in appearance or manner.

Mar. 2, 1859: I was at a frolic yesterday where there were some **clever** looking young ladies. but ah, I saw one done [= down] the country that took the Shine off of them. (John McGregor, Jackson Family Corr., Notre Dame) Moore County

Sept. 16, 1862: thare are one girl her gust like Mathy Farmer and as **clever** as She can be. (R. P. Kelly, Edmonston-Kelly Family Papers, WCU) Haywood County

clost, closter *adjective* variant forms of *close, closer.*

Oct. 24, 1862: the hospittle is at garysburg right **clost** to the railroad. (T. B. Litton, Fisher Papers, Duke) Catawba County

Nov. 1, 1862: I will try an git tranceferd to Danvill wher I will be **closter** to home. (J. H. Hundley, Hundley Family Letters, SHC) Stokes County

June 8, 1863: I exspect the next time you hear from me we will be in maryland. we air **clost** after the yankeys now and we air gointo drive them clare out of virginia. (John Hartman, Hartman Papers, Duke) Rowan County

June 12, 1864: we ar l[y]ing in lin of batle yet. our line an the yankey line is **clost** together. (Julius Myers, Alman Papers, Duke) Cabarrus County

clost door neighbors *noun phrase* Families living in the immediate vicinity.

Sept. 4, 1863: thare is three famles write [right] **Clost dore nabors**. the husbans volentared an left thare wives. i have to waite apun them. (James Hemby, Vance Papers, NCSA) Greene County

cloth shoe *noun* A type of shoe made with canvas uppers, a leather sole, and sometimes a heel made of wood; because of chronic shortages, cloth shoes were sometimes issued to soldiers in place of leather shoes. R. C. Caldwell sent his home with instructions to replace the canvas uppers with leather.

Feb. 12, 1864: you never told me wether you got that hay or no. my **cloth Shous** no word. I have asqued you about Sum of the neighbors and no Satsfactory answer. (R. C. Caldwell, Caldwell Coll., ECU) Cabarrus County

colewort *noun* A type of cabbage that does not form a head, e.g., kale, collard greens. See also **cale**. [*OED* **colewort**, noun, 1.a. and 2.a.]

June 11, 1862: you wrote my hogs were about to dy. please dont let them perish. let them go in the <ivy?>

patch. make a gap [in the fence] and let them go in and out give them **colwort** leaves and all the slops. (Ichabod Quinn, Quinn Papers, Duke) Duplin County

come *verb*

1. past tense *come*.

Feb. 25, 1863: they was too steamers run the blockade and **come** in last night. (J. W. Lineberger, *Gaston Ranger,* 41) Gaston County

Feb. 27, 1863: he aught to have given the rest of us furlows and let him a wated untill his turn **come**. (Jonas Bradshaw, Bradshaw Papers, Duke) Alexander County

July 26, 1863: The 26th we past threw Hawkenstown and 3 miles from ther we **come** to Mount Jackson. (B. Y. Malone, *Malone Diary,* 39) Caswell County

May 1, 1864: your let ter was dated April the 21 and maild April 25 and I got it 29. it **come** to mee in fore days from the time it was maild. (J. W. Reese, Reese Papers, Duke) Buncombe County

2. past participle *came*.

Dec. 21, 1862: the news has just **came** this morning that James Overton is dead. he died with the Typhoyd fever. (J. F. Coghill, Coghill Papers, Duke) Granville County

3. In the phrase *how come* (something), how did (it/something) happen; often with a personal pronoun in the objective case.

Dec. 17, 1862: Then our Colonel told the pickets to advance. They did so. they went to the river and they took very neare 100 yankes whare they had left. one of our men took 6 yankes with thare guns in thare hands. when they come up wee asked them **how comes** them over this Side and all the rest gone. (J. F. Coghill, Coghill Papers, Duke) Granville County

come clear *verb* See Overview § II.4.7.

1. To be acquitted of a crime.

Oct. 29, 1861: S I Calhoun **came clare** of killing crane. (Elizabeth Watson, Watson Letters, WCU) Jackson County

June 2, 1863: I heard that I was Sentenans to Be Shot and I Broke thru the gard & com home & after I come home I heard that I **come Clear** & if I had new that I had **come clear** I would not ov left ther By no means whatever. (A. R. Harris, Vance Papers, NCSA) Iredell County

Nov. 13, 1863: tell him not to come under gard for if he does he will be Shot and if he will come rite on he will **come clear** for bad Robert Mccarmick has come and has **come clear** and is out of the guard House. (Thornton Sexton, Sexton Letters, Duke) Ashe County

2. To avoid being wounded or killed in battle.

May 17, 1863: Dave B was wounded in the face with a bum shel. leevie hicks and leevie ingle **come cleare**. I have never heard from fisher Since the fight. I donte no whether he was in the fight or not. (Amanda Murph, Murph Papers, Duke) Catawba County

come it *verb* To succeed. [*DARE* **come**, verb, 5]

Mar. 15, 1864: please Rite and lette me no how Sol is getten a long with the work and whether you have got the Logs to geather on the new grownd. I should like to fill up the this Sheat with Something But I cant Quiet [= quite] **come it** this time. (Isaac Lefevers, Lefevers Papers, NCSA) Catawba County

come off *verb* To happen, take place; see Overview § II.4.7.

July 16, 1861: We ar expecting A fearful Battle at this place every day and When it dose **Come off** it Will be one that Will be long remembered By them that escapes. (Peter Poteet, Poteet-Dickson Letters, NCSA) McDowell County

Apr. 24, 1862: we have Been her at yorktown for Some time and have Been Exspecting a Battle Every Day cince we landed But it has not **Come off** yet but the prospects is very faverable for a heavy Battle. (James W. Gibson, Gibson Papers, Duke) Catawba County

July 24, 1864: there will be a big examination at Waynesvill the last of this weake. I will go there surtain if Nothing happens. All the girls is going on the River and I cant help but hav a fin time. I will write you when it **comes off** and give you all the news. (T. B. Edmonston, Edmonston-Kelly Family Papers, WCU) Haywood County

come off *noun* An outcome, result. [*DARE* South, South Midland]

Mar. 13, 1864: yow sad yow hed not seen Olevia and the Children since Christmast. I think it apoor **come off** that you cannot see them oftener. (W. L. Bleckley, Bleckley Papers, Duke) Catawba County

come on *verb* In a phrase following *how:* to get along, fare; see Overview § II.4.7. [*DARE* **come on**, verb phrase, 3; chiefly South Midland]

Sept. 14, 1862: We want to know how much wheat we made and how you all **come on** makeing brandy. it is worth Twenty dollers per gallon here. (James Zimmerman, Zimmerman Papers, Duke) Forsyth County

May 19, 1863: I want you to rite and tell Me all the news and tell me how your old Mother is **Comeing on** And how my Mother is **Coming on** and how they ar all getting A long. I do love to hear from home and from all. (Marcus Hefner, Hefner Papers, NCSA) Catawba County

July 16, 1863: I want you to write to me how you are giten along with your wheat and how corn looks and how oats is if you hav any and how the stock is giten along I want to k[n]ow how all the things is **coming on** at hom. (T. B. Edmonston, Edmonston-Kelly Family Papers, WCU) Haywood County

come up *verb* Of weather: to arise, develop into; see Overview § II.4.7.

June 1, 1862: you must Excuse my Bad Writing for I am nervious and hant taken any pains. you can tell that By my Writing. Writ soon. I must quit for there is **coming up** a heavy thunder Storm. (G. J. Huntley, Huntley Papers, WCU) Rutherford County

comfort *noun* A comforter, quilt, bedspread. [*DARE* chiefly South, Midland]

Dec. 1, 1862: you Stated in your leter that you would Send me A neclas [= scarf] and A **comfert.** I dont want you to Send them. I can make it at this time. I have good Clothing at this time and I drawd A blanket. (Marcus Hefner, Hefner Papers, NCSA) Catawba County

Dec. 6, 1862: I want you to send me them two shirts and that **comfort** the First chance you get and tell miss Beca to send the price of the **comfort** and I will send her the money. (William Tesh, Tesh Papers, Duke) Yadkin County

Dec. 17, 1862: I want A coat and two pair of socks and A pair of Gambadoes [= leggings] and pair of shoes and my **comfort**. (J. F. Coghill, Coghill Papers, Duke) Granville County

commence *verb* To begin, start.

1. infinitive.

Feb. 8, 1863: oats tha haint Sowd very much yet tho tha are going to **Comence** next weake if the weather is good. (Molly Tesh, Tesh Papers, Duke) Yadkin County

2. past tense *commenced, commenct.*

July 3, 1862: Som of our brave boys has got kild and Severl wounded in the great battle at richmond which **Commenct** last wensday and is Still fiting yet. (M. W. Parris, Parris Papers, WCU) Jackson County

Oct. 7, 1864: We have saved all the fodder in and we have got that hay saved and we **commencd** on our cane day before yesterday. (Huldah Hubbard, Hubbard Papers, Duke) Anson County

Oct. 18, 1864: this Cruel war **Commenced** with lies and it will end with lies if it ever ends. (William H. Horton, Councill Papers, Duke) Watauga County

3. past participle *comenst, commence.*

Feb. 8, 1863: I can say to you that Bils [= Bill's family] is awl well agan. he has not **comenst** work yet. ther has no one taken the pox yet and I do not think that tha wil take them eny more. (Catherine Lefevers, Lefevers Papers, NCSA) Catawba County

June 9, 1863: I have bad news to rite to you at this time for the war has **commence** hear at last. (Sarepta Revis, Revis Letters, NCSA) Henderson County

common *adjective* Of health: average, fair, usual. See also **well as common**.

Aug. 21, 1864: I Seat my self this morning to Rite you afew lines to let you now that I am only in **Comon** health at this time but I doo hope that these few lines may Reach your kind hands and find you all in good health. (F. M. Poteet, Poteet-Dickson Letters, NCSA) McDowell County

commutation money *noun* A cash payment for rations or clothing not issued. [*OED* **commutation**, noun, 4.a. and 4.c.]

Nov. 19, 1863: tha air owing mee 77 dollars for wagers and A Baut 60 dollars of **Comppotishing money** that was A lowed for my Clothing that I never tuck up in All making one hundred and thirty Seven dollars. (J. W. Reese, Reese Papers, Duke) Buncombe County

Nov. 25, 1863: he cut me out getting my **comuitushion money** on last years clothing. (C. F. Mills, Mills Papers, Duke) Iredell County

complected *adjective* Complexioned.

Mar. 18, 1863: tell pap that I Went into Holdens office to day and staid some time and Converesed he Was dresed quite Onery [= ordinary] vary Large pants short Coat and is dark **Complected**. (G. J. Huntley, Huntley Papers, WCU) Rutherford County

concern *noun* An article of some kind; in this case a knitted scarf. [*EDD* **concern**, *sb.* 3. "Article, thing; a contrivance"; *OED* **concern**, noun, 11. "A material contrivance or object"]

Sept. 1862: I want you to get me a nit [= knitted] **concern** to were around my neck any where you can. I rote to mary to nit me apair of Gloves. (David Sherrill, Robinson Papers, Duke) Catawba County

concript, concrip, concrit *noun* and *verb* variant forms of *conscript*.

Feb. 6, 1863: I want yow to Right and give me all the news what theas old **concrips** is gowing to do. I think if they have to come owt they had better come to this compay. (W. H. Brotherton, Brotherton Papers, Duke) Catawba County

Mar. 25, 1863: I am to remain at Coco Creek a while yet to ceth [= catch] deserters & **concrits** & to pevent catel from being drive from this state. (Stephen Whitaker Whitaker Papers, NCSA) Cherokee County

Apr. 23, 1863: Der sir I was **concripted** Last sumer the 8 of August and was mustard in to searvies. I was transferde to the 5th N C Regiment at camp Hill. I wanted to go to the 42 or 52 Regiment Bute they woulden Let me go. (Daniel Ridenhour, Vance Papers, NCSA) Stanley County

June 14, 1863: they sent him off as a **Concript.** he started the 2 of October. he is now a **Concript** in the 50 regt in Care of Captin Ford whare he hant got no Conection nor a quaintence and where I cant send him no Clothes. (Intha McCraw, Vance Papers, NCSA) Polk County

July 20, 1863: I thot I was over the ag of **con cripes** and men is nerly all gon from her and hites [= it] Lokes Like if Some body Dont stay her that wimmen will bea Bound to starv and childern too. (William Richardson, Vance Papers, NCSA) Ashe County

connection *noun* Relative(s); usually treated as a collective noun. [*OED* **connection**, noun, 6.a. and 6.b.]

Mar. 3, 1859: this leaves us all well hoping that it may find you all in the same state of halth and hoping that grand Ma and Aunt an Cousin Flora and all the **connection** is well. (Isabella Johnson, Jackson Family Corr., Notre Dame) Robeson County

Feb. 24, 1863: Write how all the **connection** are coming on also the friends. (Marion Sexton, Sexton Letters, Duke) Ashe County

Mar. 25, 1863: your uncle James Family is well an all your **connection** So fair as I know. (Lucinda Ingram, Ingram Papers, Duke) Forsyth County

May 21, 1864: tel me if enny of our **connection** was kild at Richmond or not. (Franklin Setzer, Setzer Corr., UVA) Catawba County

considerable *adjective* Great, large, persistent.

June 2, 1863: We have a **considerabal** Drouth her we havant had scarsly any rain. (John Futch, Futch Letters, NCSA) New Hanover County

considerable *noun* A large amount.

Sept. 17, 1860: ther has bin a **considerable** of Sickness hear but they ar all on the mend except little clarissa. (Thomas Harding, Blount Papers, NCSA) Beaufort County

consumption *noun* An older term for tuberculosis or other wasting diseases. [*OED* **consumption**, noun, 2.a., "Now chiefly *hist.*"]

Mar. 29, 1860: we had two death in our neighborhood. one of them was Miss Cattie Mc Leain. she was a yong girl the daughter of Daniel .H. McLeain a rich old farmer. she had thc **consumption** and has bin lingering for the last six months but was not confined to her bed untill the day before she died she was I believe one of gods people. her parents takes her death very hard. (Isabella Johnson, Jackson Family Corr., Notre Dame) Robeson County

June 18, 1863: i am not fit for camp lif let alon the duty of the man for i hav Bin gevin to hart pluricey and the **consuption** and i am fity By Spells 4 or 5 tims in a weeck. (Bluford Lucas, Vance Papers, NCSA) Harnett County

July 21, 1863: i am in a bad s[t]ate of health. i am swellde So that i cannot bare my cloths tight on me And i feare that i have got the **consumtion**. the Doctor that atteaned to me said that i was unfit For duty and never wolde be agane. (John Roberts, Vance Papers, NCSA) Onslow County

contrary *adjective* Stubborn, obstinate, uncooperative.

May 9, 1863: i want youe to Send mee ward whith [= which] County i mus Draugh from. the men is vearry **Contrary** a bout it. (Martha Oakay, Vance Papers, NCSA) Granville County

Oct. 21, 1864: they put in our mule and she got **contrary** and wouldent pull. (Ann Bowen, Bowen Papers, NCSA) Washington County

contrary *verb* To oppose, annoy, anger. [*DARE* chiefly South Midland]

Feb. 4, 1862: the officers like me vary well so far as I now. I like them so far as I have had them. they all seem vary kind to ward me an I will try to please them Just as long as I can. I ant a gont **to Contrary** to them. (J. S. Council, Councill Papers, Duke) Watauga County

contrive *verb*

1. To convey or cause to be conveyed. [*DARE* **contrive**, verb, "*old- fash*"]

Nov. 25, 1861: I will Send uncle Enos a few lines and send it in this envelop and you must **contrive** it to him as soon as you can. (Harrison Hanes, Hanes Papers, Duke) Davie County

June 17, 1864: Mrs. Nancy Roberts I will write you a few lines to let you know that I havent for g[e]t you. we recieve your letter in good time and was glad to heare from you and heare that you was well. I send this in your cear and I wante you to **contrive** it to my children as soon as you can and I will bee under many obligations to you. (George Williams, Williams-Womble Papers, NCSA) Orange County

2. To plan, manage, arrange. [*OED* **contrive**, verb[1], 6, "To succeed in bringing to pass; to 'manage,' to effect (a purpose)"]

June 1, 1863: I hope you will not expose or overdo yourself in trying to save two much. I am not willing that Should be done but you can save a great deel by **contriveing** the right way and seeing to thing in good time. this you know very well and must be your own judge. (James Zimmerman, Zimmerman Papers, Duke) Forsyth County

Nov. 15, 1864: I cant **contrive** for you now for I dont no the conditions of the times. (Henry Bowen, Bowen Papers, NCSA) Washington County

cook yard *noun* An area in camp where cooking was done and provisions stored.

Oct. 30, 1864: I will Say to you that B F & P d Hedrick are well. we keep our Boxes at the **cook yard**. (J. M. Frank, Frank Papers, Duke) Davidson County

Nov. 10, 1864: there has bin a great many of our old Company taken prisoners Since I wrote to you last but I Supose that you have heard all about that before this time. more than I can tell you. I was not in the fight my Self. I dont do any duty now my Self. I Stay out at the **cook yard** & So I dont know what to Say to you this morning. there is no news a tall that is worth your attention. (Joseph Wright, Wright Papers, Duke) Alamance County

coon's age *idiomatic expression* A long period of time.

July 21, 1862: Well Betsy you and george must tell the girls that I am alive yet for I hav not [written] to one in a **coons age** But I Do not know but what I might yet. (John W. Love, Love Papers, Duke) Henderson County

coopering *noun* The making of barrels, casks, tubs, and other wooden vessels constructed of staves and hoops.

Nov. 1, 1861: I want you to let me know if you ever have got pay for the **coopering** that we done. (Charley Futch, Futch Letters, NCSA) New Hanover County

copperhead *noun* An antiwar Northern Democrat, a Northerner sympathetic to the South.

May–June 1865: Mr Steeter the Asst Sipt [= superindendent] of Negro aff's at Roanoke Island is a througher **Cooper head** a man who Says that he is no part of a Abolitionist. (Richard Etheredge, *Freedom*, ser. 2: 729–30) Tyrrell County

cordial *noun* An aromatic, sweetened beverage containing alcohol and believed to have medicinal qualities. [*OED* **cordial**, B. noun, a.]

Dec. 21, 1862: I want you also to send me some Dysentery **Cordial**, some Blackbury **Cordial** and some more No 6. (Constantine Hege, Hege Papers, Lewis-Leigh Coll., MHI) Davidson County

corn cake *noun* A flat cake of fried cornbread. [*DARE* chiefly South, Midland]

Dec. 23, 1862: Mag i Will tell some thing abowt the prices of things her. aples $3 per bw [= bushel]. swete tatos do. [= ditto] polk 50 ct per lb small onions .2. 10cts what tha call snacks as mwch as Sis can eat .50. cts beef 30 an 20 lb. licker $4 qt. eggs $.100. [= $1.00] doz. bwtter $125 [= $1.25]. not fit to eat. chickens larg enwf to fry 75 cts. grown hens $.100. Spice $100 lb. red peper abowt 30 pods $100. small pies from 25 to 50 cts a piece no fruit in them. thin crwst. one litle bisket 5 cts. **corn cake** broad as yowr hand 15cts apiece. (T. F. Baggarly, Baggarly Papers, Duke) Iredell County

corn chopping *noun* Coarsely ground cornmeal. [*DARE* **chop**, noun[1], 1]

Feb. 2, 1863: Our fare is rough. we draw **Corn chopin** and pork and not very much of that. (C. A. Hege, Hege Papers, MHI) Davidson County

Mar. 16, 1864: we get tolerble plenty now Such as it is. it is **corn choping** the roughest Sort and fat mete a third of a pound to the man for a day. (Jesse Hill, Hill Letters, NCSA) Forsyth County

corn ground *noun* A field used for raising a crop of corn.

Jan. 26, 1864: we have very nice weather now our folks has begun to break up there **corn ground**. (Molly Tesh, Tesh Papers, Duke) Yadkin County

Jan. 6, 1865: tel dock that I want him brake up all of his **corn groun** if the wether is nice and fix for a big corn crope and sow all the oats he can. (Jesse Hill, Hill Letters, NCSA) Forsyth County

corn house *noun* A corncrib. [*DARE* chiefly New England, Middle Atlantic]

Feb. 27, 1865: if you cant keep things Safe in the **corn houses** you would better move it in the house. if you get too Scarce of corn the mule must doe with out corn and all the other Stock. (John Peterson, Peterson Papers, Duke) Catawba County

corn pone *noun* A flat cake of corn bread fried or baked in a skillet. See also **pone (of bread)**.

Oct. 11, 1864: I want 20 lbs of flour a peck of potatoes of each Sort and Some bacon and peas and a peck of unions and a **Corn pone**. (Alexander Keever, Keever Papers, Duke) Lincoln County

corn shucking see **shucking**

cost *verb* variant past tense *costed.*

May 22, 1862: I draud too big bay horses. the finest horses I ever Saw in my life. they air as fat and as slick as moles. they **costed** the goverment too thousand dollars and if I had them at home I wold not take five thousand. (John Hartman, Hartman Papers, Duke) Rowan County

cotch see **catch**

count see **nocount**

covalid *noun* variant form of *coverlet.*

Feb. 4, 1862: I wosch [= wish] I had my **Covalid** at home fore I have got as mutch as I can tote. (J. S. Councill, Councill Papers, Duke) Watauga County

cover see **civer**

cowcumber *noun* A cucumber. [*EDD* **cowcumber**, *sb.* "In *gen.* dial. use in Sc. Ire., and Eng."; citations for *cowcumber* in the *OED* as early as the sixteenth century]

June 12, 1862: Dear Catharine I can say to you that I want you to plant a heap of late **cowcombers**. (Isaac Lefevers, Lefevers Papers, NCSA) Catawba County

Aug. 9, 1862: I Saved nothing but the apples **cowcumbers** an the corn meal an ham of meet. (J. W. Williams, Williams Papers, Duke) Onslow County

cow hide *noun* A coarse whip made of braided leather.

Sept. 28, 1860: ther is Sverl [= several] of your negres laid up Sick or Pretending to be so I have de turmd [= determined] to Stop ther meat this weeak an applay the **cow hide** next. four I think that will dwo mour good than Dr king. (Thomas Harding, Blount Papers, NCSA) Beaufort County

crach (of a pen) see **scratch of a pen**

crackling bread *noun* Bread, usually corn bread, made with crisp pieces of fried pork skin left after the fat has been rendered.

Dec. 8, 1862: I Wold like to be at home to eat Som God **crackling bred** and Wold like to take crismas With you all but I See tha is no chance for hit. (Robert Spainhourd, Spainhourd Papers, Duke) Forsyth County

cradle *noun* A cradle scythe, a mowing scythe with a forklike wooden frame attached to catch the wheat or other grain stalks as they are harvested.

June 3, 1863: O how I wish that I could be at home with you now to help mow the grass and to swing my new **cradle** in the golden harvest. (C. A. Hege, Hege Papers, MHI) Davidson County

July 13, 1863: the pore labering Man that helps the pore Women all he can and work his Self Down he has to Goe and ther will Bee no Chance for them. ther is Woman in this Settle Ment that had to take the **cr[a]dle** and cut ther wheat. (William Martin, Vance Papers, NCSA) Burke County

cradle *verb* To harvest wheat or other small grain with a cradle scythe.

June 12, 1862: Iwant you to lette me now how the wheat is doing till this time and lette me now [w]hether it is Amost ripe or not and whether you have got enny one to help you off with it or not. if Abs Rudesal cant **cradle** for you maby maniel will **cradle** it off for you and you mos get some bodey to binde for you. (Isaac Lefevers, Lefevers Papers, NCSA) Catawba County

cramp colic *noun* Abdominal spasms. [*DARE* **cramp-colic**, noun; scattered South, South Midland]

ND [Mar. 1863]: Solomon Tesh is in tolerably good health now but he had a verry severe attact of the **cramp collick** last saturday night. (C. A. Hege, Hege Papers, MHI) Davidson County

cratch see **scratch**

craut see **kraut**

crick *noun* variant form of *creek*.

July 18, 1862: I can informe you that we take a march to the **Crick** once a day to wash and drill. (Marcus Hefner, Hefner Papers, NCSA) Catawba County

crips *noun* metathesized form of *crisp*.

May 20, 1864: Dear wife I will close on this for the present. I most tel you that I have neaver saw such a site in no Battle as I have in this. I have saw lots of Dead bodes Burnt in to a **crips** and I have no Eyedea but what some of the wonded was burnt of both sides. but the most that I saw was of the enemy. I saw one man that was burnt that had the picture I Suppose of his little Daughter in his pocket. it was all burnt only the glass. it loocked to be the Sise of Ida. a very sick little girl. I neaver saw enny thing that made me feel more sorrow. (Isaac Lefevers, Lefevers Papers, NCSA) Catawba County

crossway *noun* A crossing or causeway over a stream.

Jan. 3, 1861: as to cutting in the Branch we have not got half way up to the **crossway**. (F. H. Williams, Williams Papers, Duke) Onslow County

crossways *adjective* Cross, irritated. [*DARE* chiefly South, South Midland]

Feb. 22, 1863: We got behind time at Weldon and Petersburg. We reported to our Colonel. he was a little **crossways**: but we told him of the accidents on the road and it was all right: He Said we orto of brought a Surtifficat to Show that it was so: but he said he would take our word as quick as any boddys. (W. M. Patton, Patton Family Letters, SHC) Buncombe County

crout see **kraut**

crust *noun* A meal. [see *DARE* **crust**, noun, 3]

Feb. 17, 1862: ef you ant mared yet i think that you ort to wait tell i com back for i want to eat sum of the **crust**. (Evin Smith, E. Smith Papers, Duke) Stanley County

crustard *noun* A pie made with eggs; a custard. [*OED* **crustade**, noun]

Dec. 16, 1863: Mother I Still remember you. Send me a tater **crustard.** So adew. (J. M. Frank, Frank Papers, Duke) Davidson County

cussed *adjective* variant form of *cursed* (*cussed* possibly pronounced with two syllables).

Feb. 9, 1862: they was Some caveldry men on picket close to Beaufort and the **cused** yankes com A cross the river one night and Shot 2 of them and killed them and then run Back on the other. (J. W. Love, Love Papers, Duke) Henderson County

Jan. 11, 1865: I think this **cussed** ware will end soon and in the way I have thought all the time. (James W. Parlier, Military Coll., Civil War, NCSA) Wilkes County

cut *noun* A portion of cultivated land. [*DARE* **cut** noun, 2, chiefly South, South Midland]

Jan. 14, 1865: you can tend the house **cut** and the upper **cut.** they beter brake it up in rowes as soon as you can and run a furrow on top of the beds to plant the corn in. (Henry Bowen, Bowen Papers, NCSA) Washington County

cut the blood (out of) *verb phrase* To whip severely.

Jan. 24, 1863: I Saw five men striped and Each one Received 37 lashes own their Bair Back. I was Detailed to whip two of them my self. I can tell you that I hated to do the like But I could not help my self. I was Detailed By the colon[el]. they was whipe for Running a way. Some of them was gon ever since we left Camp Mangum. **the Blud was cut out of** some of them. (Isaac Lefevers, Lefevers Papers, NCSA) Catawba County

cymling see **simblin**

D

dad *noun* Father; see Overview § I.1.1. [*Dad* is the least common term for father found in the North Carolina letters.]

Feb. 13, 1863: please lette me now how **Dad** is agetten along and how his health is. tell him I send him I send my love and howdy to him. (Isaac Lefevers, Lefevers Papers, NCSA) Catawba County

daddy *noun* Father; see Overview § I.1.1. [*DARE* widespread, but somewhat more frequent South, South Midland; CACWL data indicate the term is much less common in the South and Midland than *pap*.]

June 22, 1861: tell your mamy and **dady** that I am well and that I would like to harvest for them. (Harrison Hanes, Hanes Papers, Duke) Davie County

Dec. 3, 1861: I will Send these Letters with Noah yount. him and his **daddy** and daniel Litle are here at this time. (T. J. Wagner, *Confederate Soldier,* 86) Catawba County

Dec. 3, 1862: I recived a letter from you dated the 10 of Nov. and I was glad to hear from you all. Livingston got one from **daddy** the Same date and one from davy dated the 16. tell **dady** that I am a cuming home a bout crismous to kill his big hog and eate some of it too. (J. W. Joyce, Joyce Papers, MHI) Stokes County

daguerreotype *noun* The earliest type of photograph, an image made on silver-coated copper plate (named after L. J. M. Daguerre); numerous variants.

Mar. 10, 1862: I want to bring you my **Degroue-type** & some sugar & some soap [and] calacodreses. (James A. Patton, Patton Letters, Emory) Granville County

May 29, 1862: I had my **degaratype** taken yesterday and I send it with Mr. R. Falls. (J. W. Lineberger, *Gaston Ranger,* 10) Gaston County

Apr. 12, 1864: I want [= wasn't] caring for the knapsack. all I hate about it is loosing Sophys **Garotipe**. (B. Y. Malone, *Malone Diary,* 48) Caswell County

dangerous (also *dangers, daingerous, dangrous*) *adjective* Of a person: seriously ill or injured. [*OED* "now *dial.* and *U.S. colloq.*"]

Aug. 9, 1862: T G Freman is Ded and they is Several mor that is **Dangerous** with the feever. (J. W. Love, Love Papers, Duke) Henderson County

Aug. 20, 1862: Mother I am not **dangerous** as I know of but I am so week that I am fit for nothing. (J. W. Williams, Williams Papers, Duke) Onslow County

May 7, 1864: I have bin in the hardest fite that has bin Sence the war begun. I am wounded in the thi but not **dangers**. (Daniel Setzer, Setzer Papers, Duke) Catawba County

Aug. 30, 1864: I was sick and could not Injoy my self as I would if I had of bin well. I am not **dangrous** if I dont take A back set (F. M. Poteet, Poteet-Dickson Letters, NCSA) McDowell

Nov. 8, 1864: iam about like i was when i wrote you before. idoo not think i am any ways **daingerous.** i hope i wil get well after a while. (J. H. Baker, *J. H. Baker Papers,* Duke) Rockingham County

dangerously *adverb* Extremely (ill), badly (wounded).

Aug. 14, 1861: we are as well as common all except yancy and I am sorry to say that he is **dangerously** sick. (J. N. Coghill, Coghill Papers, Duke) Granville County

Aug. 18, 1862: I hav knot bin well for a good while but I hope I will be well in a few weeks. I do knot no what is the matter with me without it is the fever. I am knot **Dangerously** sick. (James Fisher, Fisher Papers, Duke) Catawba County

Oct. 14, 1863: Dear wife I cant Rite half what I would like to rite at this time as we air orderd to coock Rations. I will yet tell you that we had our genel Coock [= Cooke] wonded but not **Daingerously**. (Isaac Lefevers, Lefevers Papers, NCSA) Catawba County

dead *adjective* Lost? (meaning uncertain; see citation).

Mar. 9, 1865: Capt James Came on the Island Jan. 1864 and told they men that he had made all the matters wright a bout they back pay and now says he I want all of you men that has due bills to carry them to Mr Bonnell at head quarters and all them has not got no paper to show for they work I will make them Swear and kiss the Bibel. and the men done just as he told them and he told us that he had made out the rolls and sent them up to Washington City and now he Says that money is all **dead**. (Richard Boyle, *Freedom,* ser. 1, vol. 2: 234) Tyrrell County

dead house *noun* A mortuary.

June 28, 1863: as to the way he was put a way I no nothing for as soon as a man dies here he is taken out to what they call the **ded house** and no boddy seas how they are put a way. (John Bachelor, Brown Coll., NCSA) Duplin County

debar *verb* To prevent or prohibit. [*OED* **debar**, verb, 2]

Oct. 29, 1861: thir is good crops made in our county. I think corn can bea bought at 50 cts all through the winter and now the people is **debard** of halling off thir meat. I dont now how wee will git our nessaryes for money is scerce here. (Elizabeth Watson, Watson Letters, WCU) Jackson County

declare *verb* To swear (usually in the phrase *I declare*). [*DARE* especially frequent South, South Midland]

Mar. 20, 1862: you Sed that Ervin and Robert had volunteer in Lanes company. I **Declare** I Dont know what to say to them for the best. (J. W. Love, Love Papers, Duke) Henderson County

delft *noun* A kind of blue and white glazed dinnerware (after *Delft,* a town in the Netherlands).

July 24, 1864: they Just tore up every thing that was in their House & broke all the fine furniture & **Delf** at was in they houses. (Thomas B. Litten, Robinson Papers, Duke) Catawba County

depend *verb* To impend, be imminent. [*OED* **depend**, verb, †8. *Obs.*]

Apr. 24, 1862: there is a heavy Battle **Depending.** there is a great number of us that have never herd Bomb shells fly till we Come heir But we have herd them frequentley cince we landed at this point. (James W. Gibson, Gibson Papers, Duke) Catawba County

deranged *adjective* Disordered, out of order. [*OED* **deranged**, adjective, 1]

May 22, 1864: I have a risen [a rising] on my neck rite in frunt. I cant buten my Shirt color and my Bow[e]ls is **Deranged** So I feel like I am aflicted this morning. (R. C. Caldwell, Caldwell Coll., ECU) Cabarrus County

description list, descriptive list *noun* A record kept by an officer or orderly sergeant in each company, including the name and a physical description of each recruit at time of enlistment, along with his home county, age, and sometimes occupation.

Feb. 22, 1863: I forgot our **descriptive list.** I left it in the beaurow draw. I want you to send it with lieutenant Johnston or the first chance. (W. M. Patton, Patton Family Letters, SHC) Buncombe County

Aug. 7, 1864: i dident have but little time to talk with him for he couldent stop long a bout my **discription list**. (Franklin Setzer, Setzer Corr., UVA) Catawba County

detail, detale *noun* A member of a military unit authorized or ordered to arrest deserters; the reference is to individuals belonging to the unit (usually in the plural) rather than the unit as a whole.

Oct. 16, 1863: the **details** com on them and took them and handcuffed them and Started with them to they army. he was like the mos of men. he was determed not to go in chains and he Succeeded in geting a way. (Pattie Vernon, Vance Papers, NCSA) Rockingham County

Oct. 17, 1863: I have been Damage this weeke By the **Detales** Sente from the 42 Rigment of North-carolina to hunt Deserters and twelve of them come to my house and stayed all night. I fede them night and mor[n]ing. thay dident paye me Any thing for it But When thay Went to Leave thay Plundder my house and taken sume of my Clothing and some of my harness and sume stocking and taken them of[f] with them and payd me nothing for Any thing thay don. (Jesse Kinley, Vance Papers, NCSA) Davidson County

July 24, 1864: we are all down hear in one little hole with all the cesech a round us. <Drey?> is gone home and [he] dont ask the **details** no ods. he is as black is ever. he says he had rather see you than any body in this world. (Cassie Davenport, Hundley Family Letters, SHC) Stokes County

devil *verb* To harass, annoy, torment.

Apr. 28, 1861: you no a man can bee **deviled** out of his life by a foole. (Charles Lance, Lance Papers, LSU) Henderson County

devilment *noun* Mischief.

Aug. 28, 1861: i got hear saf and sound. i am well pleased with the Company. i tell you wee have a heap of fun and All Cinds of **Devilment**. (J. T. Hamilton, Davison Papers, Duke) Gaston County

differ *verb* To matter, make a difference.

Feb. 9, 1863: I fell like I am at home only I cant qite turn my cher Round as qick as yow might Serspose fur that dont **differ.** I can Set crosslegged and chaw my tobacco. (W. H. Brotherton, Brotherton Papers, Duke) Catawba County

dip *verb* To baptize with full immersion.

July 26, 1863: we had too sermons preached today. Rev. P. Nicolson he is our Ch[a]plin. he is a baptist. they be [= there will be] Some **diped** to morrow. (J. W. Linberger, *Gaston Ranger,* 58) Gaston County

directly (also *toreckly, the reckly*) *adverb* Before long, soon. [*DARE* chiefly South, South Midland]

Apr. 3, 1862: Dear Wife have not mutch to rite to you now for we will haf to gow to drill **the Reckley**. (Isaac Lefervers, Lefevers Papers, NCSA) Catawba County

Apr. 28, 1863: the man come back and sais Boys we will have a fight hear **to reckly** and I comenced geting up. (B. Y. Malone, *Malone Diary,* 32) Caswell County

Apr. 26, 1864: This morning the Yanks commenced firing at us. we returned the fire and about 10 oclock the Yanks from our front they also fortified during the night. next morning we would stick up our hats and they would fire at us and **directly** the[y] begin to leave their brest works and we poured it into them. (C. A. Walker, Walker Papers, WCU) Cherokee County

disabled *adjective* superlative form *disablest.*

July 13, 1863: this is to inform you Dear Sir how the Surgent Doctor acted when the militia was cald oup to forty five. he Discharged the Men Seems like that was his friends and the **Disablest** Bodyed Men that wasent he Dident. So I pray your Sincear attention and Scend aboard of Strang [= not local] Doctors and Give us a fair Chance. (William Martin, Vance Papers, NCSA) Burke County

disfurnish *verb* To deprive of belongings or provisions, to render destitute. [see *OED* **disfurnish**, verb]

Feb. 15, 1864: Mother if you have any Potatoes and you can see anay chance to send me any I would like to have them but dont put your self to any trubel a bout it for I get a plenty and I had Rathe you would not **disfurnish** your self. (D. R. Barnhill, Military Coll., Civil War, NCSA) Bladen County

do verb, auxiliary verb

A. FORMS.

1. past tense *done* (also *don, dun, dwon*).

Nov. 1, 1861: I want you to let me know if you ever have got pay for the coopering that we **done**. (Charley Futch, Futch Letters, NCSA) New Hanover County

Oct. 8, 1863: Capt we **don** a great deal harder fighting at chickamaga than Murfreesburr. (William Tippett, Bell Papers, Duke) Macon County

Nov. 8, 1863: i want you to tel me wat they **dun** with Brother Daniel and the rest of the boys. (Franklin Setzer, Setzer Corr., UVA) Catawba County

Sept. 25, 1864: it Seems like that it **done** me more good when I heard that Elizabeth and Thomas had Joined the church. (F. M. Poteet, Poteet-Dickson Letters, NCSA) McDowell County

2. *done* as auxiliary with past participle: already.

Oct. 17, 1862: you awl may not think heard [= hard] of mi not coming hom when mos [= Moses] Dye com. I am in for the waur. I hav **dwon** receiv mi Bounty I weigh one hundred and nintey nine pounes. (Louis Wright, Wright Papers, Duke) Alamance County

Nov. 8, 1862: you Rote to me that you had **done** broke one of you <???> teath and mary Eetter had fell dow[n] broke out some of hern. you and hear must take care of you teath better than that. (J. W. Joyce, Joyce Papers, MHI) Stokes County

3. *done* as auxiliary followed by a present participle: finished.

Oct. 10, 1862: the troops is **don** cuming hear now. thar is about 50 or 60 thausand hear and thare is a talk of our mooving back a peace to Ward old NC in afew das. (J. E. McFee, McFee Letters, SRNB) Buncombe County

Dec. 27, 1862: Dear Sister I want yow you to Right to me weather yow got **done** shuckin or not. (W. H. Brotherton, Brotherton Papers, Duke) Catawba County

Jan. 25, 1863: it raind all night and day and wee came back and have ben working ever cince very near but I am in hopes that wee are **dun** working very near. (J. F. Coghill, Coghill Letters, SHC) Granville County

May 19, 1863: Dear wife you Stated in your Leter that you was **done** planting and I am sory to hear that you have your work to do and mine to. (Marcus Hefner, Hefner Papers, NCSA) Catawba County

4. third-person, present singular *don't*.

Mar. 25, 1863: he is A giting sow as he can walk A bout wright smart now. I daunt think they is any danger but what he wil git over it now if he **daunt** take the relaps A gane. (B. C. Jackson, Jackson Family Corr., Notre Dame) Moore County

Apr. 14, 1863: I want you tell fathernlaw to write. if he **dont** I will hav to get a holt of him som time. (Leonard Alman, Alman Papers, Duke) Cabarrus County

July 9, 1863: it **dont** seem to mee that I can stay away from my little sweet much longer. (Daniel Revis, Revis Letters, NCSA) Henderson County

May 31, 1864: if my leg **dont** git well by the time this fit [= fight] cums off I will git a fur low and cum home. (J. W. Reese, Reese Papers, Duke) Buncombe County

B. SENSES.

1. To suffice, be sufficent for.

Feb. 4, 1862: we have plenty to eat. I drad ennuf to **do** us seven days to day. Pork an rise an sugur an Pees an molases an soap. (J. S. Councill, Councill Papers, Duke) Watauga County

Aug. 11, 1862: I will Send 50 fifty Dollars more in this letter with Jarrette & I want you to lette Henry pay it to Jas, Stamy own my note pervided you kep a nuff to **do** you out of the other I sent you. (Isaac Lefevers, Lefevers Papers, NCSA) Catawba County

June 1, 1863: I went to mr Joseph Hacet to By grain to **do** me tell my Harves cum in. he said he could Let me have none but advised me to go to the Agent for I had as good a right to my share as any one els. (Mariah Eller, Vance Papers, NCSA) Wilkes County

2. To be acceptable, suitable.

May 12, 1863: I want want you to send me a few little things by him if he can bring them sutch as butter and honey or any thing els that will **do** to eat. (R. C. Love, Love Papers, Duke) Henderson County

3. To treat unfairly or with malice.

Aug. 3, 1863: I Send you a fiew Lines by My wife to Let you no how Mr G W Thompson is a **dooing** My wife. he Dont find hir half anuf to Eat and She complains to me. I am here a dooing govme[nt] work and She and the children at home a Suffering for Somthing to Eat. (J. Sykes, Vance Papers, NCSA)

dock *noun* A wild edible green of the sorrel family.

Apr. 5, 1863: we are Going in the plantations Getting weeds for Salett. we are Getting creeses [= cress]. they are like turnups and we are Getting a wede like ole Gueading [= garden?] **dock**. (Daniel Brown, Brown Coll., NCSA) Duplin County

doctor (up) *verb* To receive medical treatment; to treat (an illness or injury), especially with home remedies. [*DSME* **doctor**, verb; *DARE* chiefly South, South Midland, New England]

Aug. 16, 1863: Doctor A.A. Scroggs ses he can help the dropsy but cant help my eys. I have had it all winter and spring in my Legs and their and now it is up in my boddy. I want you to let me stay at home awhile and be **doctord up** and without being int-erupted if you pleas and then I will be willing to go Back. (M. D. Laney, Vance Papers, NCSA) Cald-well County

Dec. 4, 1864: the doctor is a **doctering** my head and I will rite to you when I rite a gain how it is ondley bin **doctoring** it two or three days. (Henry Bowen, Bowen Papers, NCSA) Washington County

Mar. 12, 1865: I am tolable well at this time all but the Each. tell Davy and Josy that I have got the old Each the wo[r]st sort. tell thim they must bring Down me a pot full of poke root for I think I Shal haft to be gin **to Docter** for it. (J. W. Joyce, Joyce Papers, MHI) Stokes County

dodge *verb* To avoid arrest or conscription. [*DARE* chiefly South]

Feb. 26, 1863: I will Cum home any how if you think we can meck out By my **doging** A Baut to ceep out of the way. (J. W. Reese, Reese Papers, Duke) Buncombe County

Mar. 16, 1863: I inqurd of thes mens authority when I was in Knox ville the other day and they are not known By the goverment. they are conscripts from East Tenn that are trading Back wards and fort[h] to **dodg**. (James Wiseman, Vance Papers, NCSA) Mitchell County

dodger, corn dodger *noun* A small cake of cornbread.

Feb. 2, 1863: now I must quit and fix to go to the factory. I have just got word to Start this evening s[o] I must bake My **doger** and go. (Mary Driskell, Caldwell Coll., ECU) Cabarrus County

dog haul *verb* Of a prisoner: to be treated roughly, without dignity; see Overview § II.4.7.

July 26, 1863: I dont want you to Come home unless you get a furlough for I could not se you **dog hauld** about Like some here. (Amanda Murph, Murph Papers, Duke) Catawba County

dog pelter *noun* A term of contempt; the lowest kind of elected officer. [see *DSME* **dog pelter**; *DARE* "By analogy with *dogcatcher*" chiefly South Midland]

Oct. 29, 1862: I dont like to taulk About my offficers But I hav hearn lots of our men say that the Colonel Cood not Re Elected fur **dog Pilter**. (J. W. Reese, Reese Papers, Duke) Buncombe County

doings *noun plural* Activities.

May 25, 1863: there are a number of deserters Lerking about in this County and the malitia are making no effort to arrest them and they are a doing agreat deal of mischief Robing meat houses and Breaking open mills and Stealing meal and flower and I have bean told that along this mountain they have Broke and carried off all the farming tools wash pots and kettles. Besides they are adoing a great dea[l] of mischif. ther fore I take this me[th]od of informing your oner of their **doings** hoping you will devise means to arrest this. (G. W. Dobson, Vance Papers, NCSA) McDowell County

double-quick

1. *adverb* An increased pace in marching. [*OED* **double-quick,** adverb, "double-quick time consisted of 165 steps of 33 inches (= 453 3/4 ft.) to the minute"]

Nov. 22, 1861: I Run **doubell quick** about one hour or nearly that yesterday. it made the Sweat Bile. (G. J. Huntley, Huntley Papers, WCU) Rutherford County

2. *verb* To march at double quick time.

July 21, 1862: we marcht on a peice and then we **Double quick** a pease and formed our line and marcht up A little closer. (J. W. Love, Love Papers, Duke) Henderson County

Nov. 7, 1863: we was **doubbelquicked** down to the river [. . .] and crost and formed a line of battel. (B. Y. Malone, *Malone Diary,* 43) Caswell County

down on *adverb phrase* In opposition to. [*OED* **down**, adverb, 23 c., "Chiefly *U.S.*"]

Dec. 2, 1864: Thomas come home on saturday and come to see me on monday and left his granfathers on thursday and went rite to the yankees. [I] hered [= heard] when he come he had 30 days furlow. he has rote to gamery [= grandma] that he is at Newbern and is agent on the rail road getting 40 dolars a month. I tel you farther is **down on** him. I am sorry he done it. (Ann Bowen, Bowen Papers, NCSA) Washington County

down sick *adjective phrase* Ill, bedridden.

July 16, 1862: it Seems to me that more than half the Regiment is **down sick** and they are all vary mutch Depressed in spirits and Out of hart. (G. J. Huntley, Huntley Papers, WCU) Rutherford County

down the country *prepositional phrase* In the country; also used variously to indicate a direction or a lower elevation. [see *DARE* **down**, B adverb, 1, and C preposition]

Mar. 2, 1859: I was at a frolic yesterday where there were some clever looking young ladies. but ah, I saw one **done the country** that took the Shine off of them. (John McGregor, Jackson Family Corr., Notre Dame) Moore County

dragoon bit *noun* A special bit (the mouthpiece of a bridle) favored by the cavalry.

Jan. 22, 1865: I sent home a new bridel withe too good **Drigoons bitts** to it and I want you to see some of paps folks and tell them to get it and take good cere as the bridel and one of the bitts a put on that mules bridel. (W. D. Smith, W. D. Smith Papers, Duke) Davie County

dram *noun* A single drink or a small measure of whiskey or brandy. [*OED* **dram**[1], 3.b., "A small draught of cordial, stimulant, or spirituous liquor"; *DARE* chiefly South Midland]

June 12, 1862: We halv plenty to Eat and Ware but our rashones of whiskey is quite Small. we got a **dram** the other Morning. [it] is the second drop I hav had since I Saw you. (Alfred Walsh, Proffit Family Letters, SHC) Wilkes County

Dec. 6, 1862: I would give Fifty Dollars For a Furlow For thirty days just to be home a Christmas to get something good to Eat and get a **Dram**. (William Tesh, Tesh Papers, Duke) Yadkin County

Dec. 20, 1862: my dear Partha I want yew and my farther to Send me and Daniel abox between yews. Send me a **dram** for my crismas. (John Hartman, Hartman Papers, Duke) Rowan County

Dec. 21, 1863: it is geting nere crisamas and I wish I could be at home and get a big potatoe and a **dram**. (Neill McLeod, McLeod Letters, SHC) Moore County

draw *verb* To receive; to be issued (by the military or government, items including rations, pay, arms, horses, and uniforms); see Overview § II.4.1.3.

1. past tense *drawed*.

Sept. 29, 1861: We **Drawd** our guns to Day. (R. P. Crawford, Estes Family Papers, WCU) Jackson County

Feb. 4, 1862: I **drad** ennuf to do us seven days to day Pork an rise an sugur an Pees an molases an soap. (J. S. Councill, Councill Papers, Duke) Watauga County

May 4, 1864: I must tell you what we **drawed** to eat. (J. W. Lineberger, *Gaston Ranger,* 99) Gaston County

2. past tense *drawn*.

Mar. 20, 1863: wee **drawn** clothing yester day. I **drawn** 2 shirts an 2 par of slips [men's underpants] an one military coat an pants. (T. F. Baggarly, Baggarly Papers, Duke) Iredell County

June 2, 1863: I **drawn** Cloths Cence I writting to you before. (John Futch, Futch Letters, NCSA) New Hanover County

3. past participle *drawed.*

Feb. 6, 1862: we have not **drawd** any mor money yet and I dont now when we will. (M. W. Parris, Parris Papers, WCU) Jackson County

Dec. 8, 1862: I have never **drawed** any money yet nor no close unly what I drew at rolly as I came on. (J. H. Hundley, Hundley Family Letters, SHC) Stokes County

June 1, 1863: we have not **drawed** any money yet nor I dont know when we will. (Christopher Hackett, Hackett Papers, Duke) Guilford County

4. past participle *drew.*

July 12, 1864: we hav never **Drew** any Money yet Since I left But we will Draw in a day or too. (J. W. Love, Love Papers, Duke) Henderson County

Aug. 21, 1864: I haint **drew** no money yet and I dont now when I will. I have borrowed 10 are [= or] 15 Dollars to get me sumthing to eat but the time is now when we cant borrow. (F. M. Poteet, Poteet-Dickson Letters, NCSA) McDowell

Jan. 20, 1865: I have not **drew** eny money yet neither do I expect to draw eny. (F. A. Bleckley, Bleckley Papers, Duke) Catawba County

draw *noun* The act of (or occasion for) issuing pay, rations, or other items. [see *DARE* **draw** noun, 4; see also **draw day**]

Sept. 28, 1862: I would of sent you somting by John Parker but we had not drawed our money then. they say we will mak a nother **draw** next weeake. (James A. Patton, Patton Letters, Emory) Granville County

draw *noun* variant form of *drawer.*

Feb. 22, 1863: I forgot our descriptive list. I left it in the beaurow **draw**. I want you to send it with lieutenant Johnston or the first chance. (W. M. Patton, Patton Family Letters, SHC) Buncombe County

draws *noun plural* Underpants; variant form of *drawers*. [*DARE* especially South Midland]

Aug. 26, 1862: we drawed some cloathing we drawed warmises [= jackets] and pants and **draws** and shirts and caps each of us a soot all but shoose and sock. (W. F. Wagner, *Confederate Soldier,* 11) Catawba County

May 18, 1863: I wrote to sister Ann some days ago & sent by her James Mitchel some more of my cloathing two shirts two par of **draws** two par of socacks [= socks] & one par of pants & one pound of shugar. (James A. Patton, Patton Letters, Emory) Granville County

dread *noun* A state of intense fear or anxiety. [see *DARE* **dread**, noun]

Aug. 24, 1863: I want to see you as bad as ever a Mother could want to see her son but a body. would be in a**dread** for fear tha would be punisht or killd or Something else a body could not stand. (Molly Tesh, Tesh Papers, Duke) Yadkin County

dremp, drempt *verb* variant past tense forms of *dream*.

Apr. 19, 1863: I **drempt** last night of being at home to stay and I hope that time will soon come when peace will be made. (C. A. Hege, Hege Papers, MHI) Davidson County

Dec. 3, 1864: I **Dremp** last night that I saw you and I **Dremp** that I got wounded in the hip and in the sholder. I hope and pray to god that I never will git wounded as long as I live. (F. M. Poteet, Poteet-Dickson Letters, NCSA) McDowell County

drigoon see **dragoon**

drink *verb*

1. To be suitable for drinking.

Oct. 28, 1864: I want sweet Bread and pyes and cabig heads and all you think nesery and some of that strong stuff. its a little like camfire [= camphor]. all it lacks the camfire ant in it. But it **drinkes** all write any way. (George Lenard, Frank Papers, Duke) Davidson County

2. past tense *drunk*.

Aug. 21, 1861: water that was thick with mud but we come to an old branch whair we just broke out of ranks and got some water that was thick with mud but we **drunk** of it like it was good. (James W. Overcash, Overcash Papers, Duke) Rowan County

drive verb

1. past tense *druv*.

Oct. 30, 1864: the Yankys trid to git to the south sid rale rod but they diden nt git thar. we **druv** theme back. (Gorry Jackson, Jackson Family Corr., Notre Dame) Moore County

2. past participle *drove, druv*.

July 3, 1862: our men has whipt them evry fite and has **drove** them Severl miles. (M. W. Parris, Parris Papers, WCU) Jackson County

Dec. 27, 1862: the yankeys has **druv** our troops Back seven mils. (J. W. Reese, Reese Papers, Duke) Buncombe County

June 19, 1864: the yankees has took our breast works at peters burg and we have **drovee** them back with heavey loss on both sides. (J. H. Baker, J. H. Baker Papers, Duke) Rockingham County

drown *verb* past tense, past participle *drownded*.

June 9, 1862: Mother I want to know if any of your corn is **drounded** with the wet wether. (J. W. Williams, Williams Papers, Duke) Onslow County

Aug. 2, 1863: there was lots of our men **Drounded** in the river comeing a cross. (W. F. Wagner, *Confederate Soldier,* 62) Catawba County

druther *adverb* Rather; from *(woul)d rather* or *(ha)d rather*.

July 23, 1861: I am goin to write you another leter which will caus. you to see a great deal of trouble but I had much **drother** it woulden. (Harrison Hanes, Hanes Papers, Duke) Davie County

Sept. 6, 1862: I had ten thousant time **drother** be at home but I dont now whether I ever shal or not. (Bardin Brown, Brown Family Papers, Duke) Johnston County

Feb. 5, 1865: i had **drother** pay All that i have got in the World then to S[t]ay hear. (Wade Hubbard, Hubbard Papers, Duke) Anson County

duncy *noun* A sweetheart. [The form *duncy* is perhaps results from conflation of the adjective *donsie* (having a wide variety of meanings, mostly negative) and the noun *doney:* sweetheart, girlfriend]

May 31, 1863: I have Recieved to of the sweetest Letters from my old **duncy** you ever Red in your life. I can dip them in my tee and it will make it Right Sweete. (Joseph Cowand, Cowand Papers, Duke) Bertie County

Dunkard *noun* A member of a sect of German-American Baptists; variant of *Dunker; DARE* chiefly North Midland]

Apr. 2, 1864: There was one old **Dunkard** preached near here the other day and give out his text <12th?> Chapter and 5th verse of the Revelations of St. John the Divine. (C. A. Walker, Walker Papers, WCU) Cherokee County

June 28, 1864: I gathered all the information I could till Sunset yesterday & then repaired to look at Brothers grave. it was well marked. He was buried between a Tenn & a Va Soldier in the **Dunkard** Church yard. (Robert T. Conley, CW Soldier's Letters, ADAH) Jackson County

Dutch *adjective* German (from a misunderstanding of *Deutsch*); parts of the western Piedmont of North Carolina were heavily populated by people of Pennsylvania German ancestry. [*OED* **Dutch**, adjective, †1. "Of or relating to the people of Germany; German. *Obs.* exc. as a historical archaism, and in some parts of U.S."; *DARE* scattered but less frequent South, Northeast]

Oct. 18, 1864: this Cruel war Commenced with lies and it will end with lies if it ever ends and I am in hops that it will end before long for I want to go home to live with my **dutch** gal for I am a getting mity tiard of living the way we haft to live hear. (W. H. Horton, Councill Papers, Duke) Watauga County

E

each *noun* variant form of *itch.* [*DARE* scattered, but chiefly South, South Midland]

Oct. 8, 1861: The mumps and hooping cough is in our company and the **each** is in the Reg. (James W. Overcash, Overcash Papers, Duke) Rowan County

Aug. 27, 1862: your kind letter reached me evening before last and found me unwell. I have the **each** very bad and A verry sore mouth. (Joseph F. Maides, Maides Papers, Duke) Jones County

Feb. 1, 1863: My dear Partha the **each** is in our compny. Calvan Brown and John brinkle and Elec Holshouser but dont tell hoo told it for they will get mad at me. (John Hartman, Hartman Papers, Duke) Rowan County

Mar. 12, 1865: I am tolable well at this time all but the **Each**. tell Davy and Josy that I have got the old **Each** the wost sort. tell thim they must bring Down me a pot full of poke root for I think I Shal haft to be gin to Docter for it. (J. W. Joyce, Joyce Papers, MHI) Stokes County

each *verb* variant form of *itch.*

Aug. 4, 1862: all our nose has bin **eaching** so much we think Archy is a coming home. (Dicy Ann Jackson, Jackson Family Corr., Notre Dame) Moore County

eagor see **agur**

ear see **year**

earn see **yearn**

east *noun* variant form of *yeast.* [*DARE* **east**, noun[2], chiefly South, South Midland]

Nov. 1, 1863: I will send you a peice of doe which I will describe to you as **east** to go in bread. it will do you A great deal of good if you use it in the proper manner. if it be dry or soft desolve it in warm watter. do not put much watter nor flower in this untill you gets A supply. stur in the flour untill it becomes as thick or thicker as batter doe. then set it by the fire untill it rises and then make up your doe. [. . .] I will send you A buiscuit so you may see the good of this **east**. (J. F. Coghill, Coghill Letters, SHC) Granville County

easy *adverb* Easily.

Feb. 27, 1863: I was sory to hear that the small pox was raging up thare. Nancy I hope you will be cearful and not go in reach of them. tha are a dangers complaint. dont go a near them now wheir. if Lodemay was to get them I know tha wod kill heir. tell Father to not let Frankling and John nor non of the rest go a near them fur tha are **easy** Caut and dangerous. (Jonas Bradshaw, Bradshaw Papers, Duke) Alexander County

eat *verb* See Overview § II.4.1.4.

1. past tense *eat, et.*

Jan. 12, 1862: me and Young **eat** our big oposam today for dinner and indeed it was sum good. (B. Y. Malone, *Malone Diary,* 12) Caswell County

Feb. 27, 1863: so der wife fare well. here is a ring. I **ett** the meet off the bone and made a ring of it. poot it on your finger. (Jonas Bradshaw, Bradshaw Papers, Duke) Alexander County

Aug. 24, 1863: I paid a half a dollar for a quart of milk last evning and **eat** it for my breakfast this morning too [= with] some warm corne bread. (W. F. Wagner, *Confederate Soldier,* 70) Catawba County

Mar. 1864: I **eat** a good Breakfast this morning. (C. A. Walker, Walker Papers, WCU) Cherokee County

2. past participle *eat, et.*

Oct. 5, 1861: Ther was aman droned [= drowned] time of the Storm. a boat up Set with him and when thay found him his erse and fase was **eat** of[f] by the watter animals. (C. F. Mills, Mills Papers, Duke) Iredell County

Apr. 5, 1862: I must stop and go and drill. I have now returned from the field and **et** my dinner. I will now pro sead to write you a few more lines. (Jonas Bradshaw, Bradshaw Papers, Duke) Alexander County

Jan. 26, 1864: i got mi pants and apels and the[y] was all good. the was the first that i have **eat** dis [= this] winter. (W. P. Cline, Cline Papers, SHC) Catawba County

Dec. 15, 1864: I have Just **eat** dinner and had fresh pork and potatoes for dinner and a plenty of it. (Henry Bowen, Bowen Papers, NCSA) Washington County

3. To be suitable for consumption. [*DARE* **eat** verb, 3, intransitive]

Mar. 3, 1865: we draw as much meal and meet as we eat but Some flower bred [= flour bread] wold **eat** Some better. (James A. Smith, J. A. Smith Papers, Duke) Cabarrus County

eatables *noun plural* Food, provisions.

Jan. 6, 1863: let me know how you are making out for clothes and Shoes and also let me know how you are making out for **eatables**. (Jesse Smith, Vance Papers, NCSA) Alexander County

Apr. 28, 1863: eatables are Scarse an dear [= expensive]. peas Sell here for one dollar a quart. bacon one dolar a pound. tobacco two an a half dollars per plug. (James Keever, Keever Papers, Duke) Lincoln County

July 27, 1863: I receved the **eatables** which you sent with Mr Livengood last saturday and I am verry thankfull to you for them. (C. A. Hege, Hege Papers, MHI) Davidson County

eating, eatings *noun* Food; a meal; the action of taking food. [*OED* **eating**, noun, especially 1.c., "good, etc., eating: said of an article of food"]

Mar. 19, 1863: I would like to be with you to get some of your good **eatings**. (John Futch, Futch Letters, NCSA) New Hanover County

July 26, 1863: I would like to come home to get somthing good to eat such as fruit and water melons. peches is worth fifty cents a peace and you now that is dear [= expensive] **eating**. (J. W. Lineberger, *Gaston Ranger,* 58) Gaston County

Apr. 21, 1864: I want you to have plenty of good **eating** tell [= by the time] I come Such as eggs and ham and crout and milk and butter and Sallet & Sweat potatoes and So on. (Alexander Keever, Keever Papers, Duke) Lincoln County

June 27, 1864: I got me a chicking last night and I eat it this moring. I have had milk and Butter aplenty for two or three Days. I have eat so mutch it made me a little Sick. I have got coffee a nuf to last me a weak and I have some light Bread on hand at this time. So you may gess that I have prety good **Eetting**. (J. W. Joyce, Joyce Papers, MHI) Stokes County

eat out *verb* Of a place: to be stripped of food, provisions, livestock feed; variant past participle *eat out;* see Overview § II.4.7.

Dec. 19, 1863: we leaveed from tennesse to ashville without having enny thing to fead or eat. that coutry is all **eat out**. (Franklin Setzer, Setzer Corr., UVA) Catawba County

Dec. 22, 1863: I tel you courne is scirce here. the people will suffer in this country an I think Rutherford will bee **eat out** this winter. (A. S. Harrill, Civil War Coll., TSLA) Rutherford County

elum *noun* variant form of *elm;* one of several species belonging to the genus *Ulmus*. [*DARE* widespread but somewhat more frequent South, South Midland]

Dec. 25, 1858: as you requested to know what kind of timber we have in this country. thare is white oke. black oke. red oake. Spanish oake and hickrey black white and scaly barke. black walnut white walnut. mulbery. cotton wood. wile chery. **elum** and lin wood. shugar trees. sicamore and buckei. buroake. severl other kinds too tedous to mention. the under groth is mostley hasle and shumake. (William Boss, Frank Papers, Duke) Davidson County

enlist *verb* variant form *list* without the initial syllable.

Feb. 20, 1863: She Rang her lilly white hands. So mowrnful She did cry. yow **listed** as a Soldier. And in the war yow shal die. (W. H. Brotherton, Brotherton Papers, Duke) Catawba County

envelope *noun* variant form *invelip.*

Nov. 23, 1863: it seems like it will take all that I can make hear to git sumthing to Eat and to git paper and tobacco and **invelips**. (F. M. Poteet, Poteet-Dickson Letters, NCSA) McDowell County

ever *adjective* Every. [*DARE* widespread, but chiefly South, South Midland, especially TX]

Feb. 2, 1863: when I git A letter **ever** week from you the time Rols off A heep faster to mee. (J. W. Reese, Reese Papers, Duke) Buncombe County

Apr. 9, 1863: provishions is very high up here. Tobacco is 5 dollars a pound and meal is $1 & 25 Cts a gallon. fresh meat is $1.50 cts Coffee is $5 a pound and **ever** thing is high. (John Futch, Futch Letters, NCSA) New Hanover County

Oct. 1, 1863: we draw flower **ever** day now and fresh beef and sugar and rice. (Daniel Setzer, Setzer Papers, Duke) Catawba County

Nov. 3, 1863: I would give **Ever** thing that I am worth to be with you. (F. M. Poteet, Poteet-Dickson Letters, NCSA) McDowell County

ever *adverb*

1. variant syntax, precedes subject. [*DARE* chiefly South, South Midland, occasionally New England]

Mar. 25, 1862: Bill told him that she was the prettyest girl that **ever** he saw. (Harrison Hanes, Hanes Papers, Duke) Davie County

Aug. 3, 1863: My dear wife I will send you Some cherry Seed. Some of the best cherrys **ever** I eat in my life. thear as big as big plums and the trees air as big as them big chesnutts trees at your farthers. (John Hartman, Hartman Papers, Duke) Rowan County

Aug. 24, 1863: I want to see you as bad as **ever** a Mother could want to see her son. (Molly Tesh, Tesh Papers, Duke) Yadkin County

Oct. 23, 1864: it would bee more satisfaction to me to see you all than any thing that **ever** I saw. (F. M. Poteet, Poteet-Dickson Letters, NCSA) McDowell County

2. with the sense of *always*. [*DARE* chiefly South, South Midland]

Aug. 19, 1864: we are all well at this time **ever** hoping this will Reach your kind hands and find you in good health. (Martha Poteet, Poteet-Dickson Letters, NCSA) McDowell County

everhow *adverb* In every manner, by every means.

May 7, 1863: I tell yow father it is A Sight to See they wounded men at the hospittle. they are shot ever way and **ever how**. (W. H. Brotherton, Brotherton Papers, Duke) Catawba County

evernear *adverb* Nearly, about.

Jan. 25, 1863: it is A hard <???> to set down to write A letter and hardly ever get one once A month is **ever near** as often as I get one and you say that you write every weeak. (J. F. Coghill, Coghill Letters, SHC) Granville County

every *adverb* Ever.

Nov. 24, 1861: thare will be the hardest fight that has **every** ben. (L. W. Griffin, Griffin Papers, NCSA) Rutherford County

Sept. 8, 1861: all of your friends are Well in camp Except a few cases of the Messels. all of our boys that hav them are giting Well. W. H. and Wm are as fate as a bar. thay Look better than i **evry** saw them. (Alfred Walsh, Proffit Family Letters, SHC) Wilkes County

Jan. 15, 1863: I have herd Sed that you was as good a man as **every** lived or died. (Catherine Hunt Vance Papers, NCSA) Randolph County

Feb. 15, 1863: if **every** he crosses the river he will find out who is here in time to get his hook broke he will get a wors thrasen than Gen Burinsids got. (James Zimmerman, Zimmerman Papers, Duke) Forsyth County

except *conjunction* Unless, if. [*DARE* South, South Midland]

May 4, 1862: I have some idea of going to Capt Eaves Company at Raleigh **Except** I get some Body to take my place. (G. J. Huntley, Huntley Papers, WCU) Rutherford County

Mar. 9, 1865: in the first place his Proclamation was that no able boded man was to draw any rations **except** he was at work for the Government. (Richard Boyle, *Freedom,* ser. 1: 231) Tyrrell County

excepting *prepostion* Except for.

Nov. 24, 1864: I Seat My self this eavning to write you a few lines to let you know that we are still in the land of the living. I aint very well. the children is well **excepting** bad colds. (Martha Poteet, Poteet-Dickson Letters, NCSA) McDowell

extry *adjective* variant form of *extra.*

Apr. 27, 1862: Mother I think that you are doing **extry** to be so forward in your farm. (J. W. Williams, Williams Papers, Duke) Onslow County

Aug. 13, 1862: they hav never had us in the gard house yet nor on **extry** duty. (R. C. Love, Love Papers, Duke) Henderson County

Feb. 15, 1863: it wont take long to amount to two hundred dollars and no **extry** work at that. (James Zimmerman, Zimmerman Papers, Duke) Forsyth County

F

fair *adjective* comparative form *fairieder.*

Sept. 17, 1860: your cotton is **farrieder** than it wours [= was] last year but I dont think it is So ful of boles. (Thomas Harding, Blount Papers, NCSA) Beaufort County

fair play *noun* Good or equal treatment.

Nov. 24, 1864: See that the mule has **fare play** and other Stock but be as Saveing with corn as you can. (John Peterson, Peterson Papers, Duke) Catawba County

fall *verb*

1. past participle *fell.*

Mar. 25, 1862: Bill told him that she was the prettyest girl that ever he saw and that he had **fel** in love with her. (Harrison Hanes, Hanes Papers, Duke) Davie County

May 4, 1862: thare is a Rumor in Our Camp today that Our troops has Burned yorketown and **fell** Back from that place But I dont put mutch Confidence in the Report. (G. J. Huntley, Huntley Papers, WCU) Rutherford County

Aug. 24, 1863: Dear I thaut one time we would git to go to N.C. but it is all **fell** through. (W. F. Wagner, *Confederate Soldier,* 70) Catawba County

2. Of a fever: to settle in the lower extremities.

Oct. 8, 1863: the fever **fell** in my feet & Legs so that I could not walk nor get off of my bed for sometime. (Andrew J. Proffit, Proffit Family Letters, SHC) Wilkes County

fall dead *verb phrase* To drop down dead. [see *OED* **fall**, verb, 23.a.]

June 24, 1863: I can say to you that A. N. give out. I was sent back to Culpepper. he was right sick but I hope not dangerous. It was said that many marched until they **fell dead** on this march. (Andrew J. Proffit, Proffit Family Letters, SHC) Wilkes County

fall off *verb* To lose weight, become emaciated; see Overview § II.4.7. [*OED* **fall**, verb, **to fall off** 7; *DARE* chiefly South, South Midland]

Aug. 14, 1861: he has got a good cot to lay upon and is verry well fixed but he has **fallen off** So much and weakened by the Daeirhoea that we dont think he will ever get well. (J. N. Coghill, Coghill Papers, Duke) Granville County

July 16, 1862: Mother I have **fell of[f]** the most you ever saw A person to not be sick. (J. W. Williams, Williams Papers, Duke) Onslow County

(in a/the) family way *adjective phrase* A euphemism for *pregnant.*

Feb. 25, 1864: I told you that I thot you had beter hire that gurl of Staffords if She is not in a **famly way**. (R. C. Caldwell, Caldwell Coll., ECU) Cabarrus County

Mar. 9, 1864: It has Bin reported here in Camp that Sophia was in the **family way**, And I want to know if it is So or not, But dont say any thing to here a Bout it, And it [is] reported that Joel is the Farther of it. (Edgar Smithwick, Smithwick Papers, Duke) Martin County

famish *verb* To starve.

Mar. 6, 1863: I hav 7 grand Sons in Wor Survis. one of them I have Raised and it appears if he Dont nor Cant Be releast nor Spaird Back home we must **famish** and di. (Margaret Phelps, Vance Papers, NCSA) Brunswick County

farther *noun* variant form of *father.*

Dec. 5 1858: you Say that the Land that **farther** intended to give me is not worth more than Seventy five Dollars. (Francis Amos, Amos Papers, Duke) Rockingham County

Mar. 21, 1862: he dyed happy and is now happy in heven I hope. he sead he was going to heven to see his dear old **farther**. (James Keever, Keever Papers, Duke) Lincoln County

July 18, 1863: farther and Mother is up and about as common and the rest is all well. (James Broach, Broach Papers, Duke) Person County

Jan. 20, 1865: Dear **farther** I want you to dou the best you Can. my time will bee up the 10 of augus. (James Cowand, Cowand Papers, Duke) Bertie County

fat *verb* To fatten, gain weight.

Dec. 27, 1862: I want to know how your corn turn owt and how your hog is **fating** and how mutch wheat you soad. (W. H. Brotherton, Brotherton Papers, Duke) Catawba County

Apr. 30, 1864: Francis I waide this moring one 126 lb. So you may know that I am a **fating** vary fast since I come to the army. (J. W. Joyce, Joyce Papers, MHI) Stokes County

fat and sassy *adjective phrase* Healthy, in good spirits.

Oct. 7, 1861: Wee are all doing finly all **fat and Sassy**. I way one hundred and forty eight ponds. I am giting as fat as I was when I got well. (James Fisher, Fisher Papers, Duke) Catawba County

Dec. 3, 1862: My dear Partha I now Seat my Self to drop yew afew lines to inform yew that I am **fat and sasey** at the present. (John Hartman, Hartman Papers, Duke) Rowan County

Apr. 13, 1863: you rote that the boys was **fat and Sassy**. I am glad to hear that. I would like to see you all the best in this world. (Marcus Hefner, Hefner Papers, NCSA) Catawba County

favor *verb* To resemble, have a family resemblance to. [*DARE* widespread, but chiefly South, South Midland]

Feb. 20, 1864: I hard that an [= Ann] Bost had afine yong Son and I want you to tel me whoo it **favers**. (Daniel Setzer, Setzer Papers, Duke) Catawba County

feard see **afeard**

feather *verb* Of trees and shrubs: to leaf out in the spring.

Mar. 26, 1863: tha hav bin shoo[t]ing severil hear latley for Runing A way But I think when the woods **fethers** thair will Be A many A man go home. (J. W. Reese, Reese Papers, Duke) Buncombe County

Fed *noun* A Union soldier, short form of *Federal*.

Feb. 12, 1863: ther was only five thousan of our men and thirty five thousan **feds.** we killed and wound about won thousan of them and they kiled and wound won hundred of our men. (James W. Hall, Hall Coll., NCSA) Cumberland County

Apr. 23, 1863: the **feds** is advancing on us. tha Capturd A trane of Cars from us nite Be fore last and has taken mcmin vill Just 30 mils from hear. (J. W. Reese, Reese Papers, Duke) Buncombe County

feel to *verb* To want to, desire to; see Overview § II.4.7.

June 4, 1863: Well father as this is the 4th of June I suppose that you are 60 years old to day. I **feel to** hope that you are stout and harty. you and mother has lived & been highly blessed for a number of years although the days of trouble are now on us. (Andrew J. Proffit, Proffit Family Letters, SHC) Wilkes County

feller *noun* variant form of *fellow*.

Feb. 10, 1863: he looked so bad in so short a time. poor **feller** has gon as many will have to go before this ware ends. (James Zimmerman, Zimmerman Papers, Duke) Forsyth County

Apr. 28, 1863: I think [from] what you sead in your letter you **felers** have to pay for what bacon and flour you eat. (James Keever, Keever Papers, Duke) Lincoln County

May 7, 1863: we have had har hard times for the last nine day And lost many A frend. I Can inform that I got throu Safe. I can Inform that there is A many A poor **feler** A sufering at this time. (Marcus Hefner, Hefner Papers, NCSA) Catawba County

felon, fellen *noun* An inflamation of a bone, usually of the hands or feet.

June 20, 1864: I am Sorry that you have the **fellen** own your hand for I now that is bad. (Noah Wagner, *Confederate Soldier,* 91) Catawba County

fer see **for**

fester *noun* A suppurating sore. [*DARE* scattered, but especially North, North Midland]

Dec. 10, 1864: the baby is not rite well. she has the thrash and her chin broke out in **festers** which makes her more fretful than she ever was. (Ann Bowen, Bowen Papers, NCSA) Washington County

fetch *verb*

1. past tense and past participle *fetch, fetched, fetcht, fotch.*

   Aug. 21, 1862: John fletcher **fetch** a leter an I was glad to hear from you all. (S. E. Love, Love Papers, Duke) Henderson County

   Nov. 3, 1862: tha have **fetcht** his horse home and i d[o]nt now [= know] when hee will go back. (Sarepta Revis, Revis Letters, NCSA) Henderson County

   Jan. 15, 1863: Mr Coble **fetched** me mi Shoes flower & some other things. (James Hackett, Hackett Papers, Duke) Guilford County

   Mar. 6, 1863: i resevd too leters from you one that hass **fot[c]h** and one that routh brout. (W. P. Cline, Cline Papers, SHC) Catawba County

2. To bring, take, carry; to convey.

   Mar. 1, 1863: Francis I Sead a man Shot yester day for runing way. he had run away three time in the time of fighting. the hole brigade was muster out and then tha **fetch** him out with his coffin and tha tide a white honkercheif over his eyes and tuelve men shot him. (J. W. Joyce, Joyce Papers, MHI) Stokes County

   May 25, 1863: I wish I had **fetched** my short coat and left my brown one for I had to pay 12 1/2 for one. (Neill McLeod, McLeod Letters, SHC) Moore County

Nov. 5, 1863: i want you to **fetch** me onion and Som dride fruit and Some Buter and Some gren fruit and molases. (Thornton Sexton, Sexton Letters, Duke) Ashe County

3. To conclude, finish.

June 28, 1861: I must **fettch** my leter to a close. (Jesse Shipman, Shipman Family Corr., Notre Dame) Henderson County

Mar. 20, 1864: i only see one Chance for peas [= peace] and that is to lect [= elect] W W holden for our guvarn and i think that he will **fetch** the ware to A Close. (W. P. Cline, Cline Papers, SHC) Catawba County

4. To draw, bring forth.

Mar. 16, 1862: one ball grased my hand & berly **fetc[h]ed** the blood. (C. F. Mills, Mills Papers, Duke) Iredell County

fight *noun* A common term for a military engagement regardless of size.

July 1862: cousin we have Saw Some very hard times since I have heard from you. we have Bin in three **fights** since. Two Small skermish **fights** and Tuesday the 1St day of July we had to go into a regular hard **fight**. we was rushed into a place where the enemy was throwing ther grape Shot at us By the Bushel. (P. S. Whitner, Whitner Papers, Duke) Catawba County

fight *verb* past tense *fit*.

Aug. 7, 1861: they had apourful Battle there. they **fit** one hole day. they only kiled about 5 hundred of our men. (Peter Poteet, Poteet-Dickson Letters, NCSA) McDowell

July 14, 1863: we cros the potomac River the 22 day of June and went thugh mariland and in to pencilvia. thar we met with the yankes By thausans. thay **fit** four day and nights. Francis it has Bin 12 day seance I got hurt. I am men[d]ing vary fast. I can walk with a stick Right smart. (J. W. Joyce, Joyce Papers, MHI) Stokes County

May 7, 1864: wee flank[ed] round. dis mountid and fired occasonly. wee got the fort surrounded. our company and gashes com[pany] advance[d] on them. wee **fit** some time and our men. demanded surrender. they surrender[ed] on condition that was if wee cold let them keap there money and close. (Silas Stepp, Stepp Letters, UNCA) Buncombe County

find *verb*

1. To supply with provisions. [*DARE* chiefly Northeast, South Atlantic]

Aug. 11, 1861: the is atalk of Va not **finden** us no longer th[a]n the 20 of Aug an if that bee so we well return to NC wonst more. (Pleasant Ray, Amos Papers, Duke) Stokes County

May 22, 1863: I resived yore letter an was glad to resev it. i Carred it to the Com mitty an thay Wodent **fine** mee nuthen. thay Sed if i wase in ther Destrck thay wod **fine** mee but i had to muve whar i Cod get a house to liv in. (Martha Oakay, Vance Papers, NCSA) Granville County

Aug. 3, 1863: I Send you a fiew Lines by My wife to Let you no how Mr G W Thompson is a dooing My wife. he Dont **find** hir half anuf to Eat and She complains to me. I am here a dooing govme[nt] work and She and the children at home a Suffering for Somthing to Eat. (J. Sykes, Vance Papers, NCSA)

2. To provide (something; in the case of the citations below, seed in exchange for work).

Sept. 27, 1863: manuel Spegle wanted me to **find** the wheat and let him so it and go havers [= half shares] but I will hav it sode mi self. Arch will so this at home if I **find** him sead to so his at home and I expect I had beter do it. (Catherine Lefevers, Lefevers Papers, NCSA) Lincoln County

Aug. 30, 1864: try and get lackes to Sowe it and you **find** the Seed and the plows to breake the ground and Lewis can Sprout it. (Alexander Keever, Keever Papers, Duke) Lincoln County

finely *adjective* Fine.

Oct. 8, 1863: we have been cooking three days rations to day in order for a march but to what place I am unable to say as news is Scarce & my hand is quite nervious. I will soon close. A.N. is quite stout & look **finely**. (A. J. Proffit, Proffit Family Letters, SHC) Wilkes County

Mar. 27, 1864: we hav had a **finly** time sinc the snow fell But when it al gits off I exspect we will have it to try in a different maner. (Isaac Copeland, Copeland Letters, NCSA) Surry County

finely *adverb* Well.

Oct. 7, 1861: Wee are all doing **finly** all fat and Sassy. I way one hundred and forty eight ponds. I am giting as fat as I was when I got well. (James Fisher, Fisher Papers, Duke) Catawba County

Nov. 26, 1861: it will be good for the boys if they are kep under a while. I think it will make men out of them. Some of them complains rite smart sometimes but for my part I take it very easy and am enjoying myself **finely**. (P. S. Whitner, Whitner Papers, Duke) Catawba County

May 17, 1864: mi cow does verry well. to of mi hens has got chickens. i turned out mi pig and it is doing verry well now. your hog is growing **finely**. (Sarah Wester, Wester Coll., NCSA) Franklin County

fired *adjective* Of crops: turning yellow because of dry weather or drought.

Aug. 2, 1856: I am Sorrow to inform master of such a drouth in the lands. the corn on Belgrade is **fired** veary bad. unless we have A good eal of rain the corn will be veary much damage. (Moses [Pettigrew slave], Pettigrew Family Papers, SHC) Washington County

July 19, 1860: we had a good Shower of rain tus day witch makes your crop look a grateel better. the weat[h]er has bin so dry an hot that the corn is **fired.** tho not so mutch but what if we can have Rain in time it cum out. (Thomas Harding, Blount Papers, NCSA) Beaufort County

first see **fust**

fisherman's luck *noun* Bad luck in fishing. [*DARE* scattered, but more frequent South, Midland]

Apr. 2, 1864: We fish a good part of our time. that is a vary good traid mutch like whare you live. we jeneraly have **fishermans luck**. a wet ass and hungry gut. (Alfred N. Proffit, Proffit Family Letters, SHC) Wilkes County

(the) first one *noun phrase* None, not one, nothing (following a negated verb).

Nov. 10, 1861: I would write you a long letter But I hav wrote you 6 Letters and I hav never receivd **the first one** yet. I would suppose mine have never reacht your hand. (J. W. Love, Love Papers, Duke) Henderson County

fit see **fight**

fit *adverb* Ready, expecting (followed by an infinitive, often expressing an extreme state). [*DSME* **fit**[2]]

June 3, 1864: I tell you it [is] hard times about here now. bread cant be got. people is **fit** to starve it seems like. (Betsy Phillips, Phillips Papers, Duke) Robeson County

fitten *adjective* Fit, appropriate (usually in the negative sense). [*DARE* "Engl dial; pronc varr of *fitting*"; chiefly South, South Midland]

May 19, 1862: we air treted verry bad. we dont get enny thing to eat more then one half of our time and when we do get it it aint **fitten** to eat. (John Hartman, Hartman Papers, Duke) Rowan County

Feb. 19, 1863: I asked the captin a bout comen back with him to see you and he seas that I could come with him but tha was no **fiten** plase hear fore me. (Martha Futch, Futch Letters, NCSA) New Hanover County

fittified *adjective* Subject to fits, convulsions, or epileptic seizures.

Sept. 4, 1863: ihav an aflected wife an 4 Children. one of my letle sones has bin **fitey fide** ever sence he Cud Crale [= crawl]. (James Hemby, Vance Papers, NCSA) Greene County

fitty *adjective* Subject to fits; same as *fittified*.

June 18, 1863: i am not fit for camp lif let alon the duty of the man for i hav Bin gevin to hart pluricey and the consuption and i am **fity** By Spells 4 or 5 tims in a weeck. this i have haid for the last 8 or 10 years now. you now that a man that is so plegued is not fit for sirves. (Bluford Lucas, Vance Papers, NCSA) Harnett County

fix *verb*

1. To put in order, prepare (something); also with *up*.

Aug. 23, 1862: We are all **fixing up** our things to leave here a monday next. (James Zimmerman, Zimmerman Papers, Duke) Forsyth County

Aug. 6, 1863: Father is A fixing to start in the morning and Mother is **A fixing** vitles to send to him. (Sally Bauldin, Hundley Family Letters, SHC) Stokes County

Sept. 21, 1864: we have got our cane mill done and been **fixing** the furnace to day to go to making the molasses. (Huldah Hubbard, Hubbard Papers, Duke) Anson County

Nov. 24, 1864: I sent you a box of provision. I recon it wasent good. you wrote to your Mother and mima to send you a box of provision. I hope they will send you somthing good and plenty of it. I sent as good as I could get and the baby died in the time I was **fixing** it. (Martha Poteet, Poteet-Dickson Letters, NCSA) McDowell County

2. To make preparations, get ready; with *for*.

Dec. 17, 1861: I dont think we will stay hear more that 2 or 3 weeks. we are not **fixing for** winter yet an I dont think we will hear. (Reuben Overcash, Overcash Papers, Duke) Rowan County

Jan. 6, 1865: tel dock that I want him brake up all of his corn groun if the wether is nice and **fix for** a big corn crope and sow all the oats he can. (Jesse Hill, Hill Letters, NCSA) Forsyth County

3. To arrange, contrive, attend to.

July 3, 1863: I want you to discharge My sone Joseph G. Godward for two or three Months to get my stock and **fix** my business so I can attend to it. (Eliza Godward, Vance Papers, NCSA) Martin County

July 5, 1863: I wa[n]t to go back an if you will **fix** for me to git back I will be more then a blige to you an God dos know my hart I never will leave my comorne [= command] no more for I had rather dye on battle feal then to dye a deser[t]or. (John Averett, Vance Papers, NCSA) Pitt County

Oct. 20, 1863: I left the army after we come out of Maryland and if you can **fix** any way and send me instrument of riting that i can git back and not be hurt i will go and i will git all i can to go. they are severl ses that they will go back if they nowed that they would not be shot. (L. F. Holder, Vance Papers, NCSA) Randolph County

4. To prepare (a written order or other official document); also with *out*.

Dec. 30, 1861: the oficers are **fixing out** the pay roles expecting to receive our money to morrow. (J. W. Williams, Williams Papers, Duke) Onslow County

Jan. 4, 1865: I ex pect to come home some time this winter if nothing happens to me. thay are **fixing** 8 furlows to evry hundard men for duty. (Joseph Wright, Wright Papers, Duke) Alamance County

5. To prepare, get ready; followed by an infinitive.

June 18, 1862: I most now **fix** to come to a close by asken you to rite as soon as you can find out wheir the company is and lette me now how you and the childrean is geten a longue. (Isaac Lefevers, Lefevers Papers, NCSA) Catawba County

June 28, 1863: I have not time to write more as I have **to fix** to go to Knoxvill. (Stephen Whitaker, Whitaker Papers, NCSA) Cherokee County

6. To intend, get ready; present participle followed by an infinitive. [see *DSME* **fix**, B2]

Mar. 3, 1862: we ar **fixing** to plant our artilery & to entrench to be in rediness to meet the yankes. (Larkin Kendrick, Kendrick Papers, NCSA) Cleveland County

Sept. 29, 1863: the yankies is with in a Bout five mils of us now and we ar a **fixin** to meet them and I think that we will give them a nise little whippin if tha Dar com any farther. (John H. Brann, Tesh Papers, Duke) Yadkin County

Jan. 12, 1864: we have not drild eny in 8 days. we have be[en] **fixen** to move. I wold like to have Come to saw [you] while I was at home but Cold not get started. barbry took the measels and I Cold not leave her as good as she tended to me when I was sick. (James Keever, Keever Papers, Duke) Lincoln County

Apr. 26, 1864: we are in camp yet but are **fixing** for to leave at any time. life is so un certain and deth is shure. (J. M. Frank, Frank Papers, Duke) Davidson County

fix *noun*

1. A predicament, condition, situation, state. [*DARE* **fix**, noun, 1]

Apr. 16, 1863: I hardly no what to do in my **fix** but I dont see any chance to better my condishion atall. (C. F. Mills, Mills Papers, Duke) Iredell County

June 26, 1863: I will close for I am in no **fix** for writing today. (C. L. Proffit, Proffit Family Letters, SHC) Wilkes County

Mar. 20, 1864: you sed in youer leter that h p summit was not sedfid [= satisfied] sence he was at home. i can tel you that thear is a heap in that **fix** but that dont seme to doo much good. (W. P. Cline, Cline Papers, SHC) Catawba County

2. A state of repair or health (good or bad). [*DARE* **fix**, noun, 2]

May 1, 1863: I was offerd 8 hundred dollar and he [= his horse] was then in very bad **fix**. (Jesse Shipman, Shipman Family Corr., Notre Dame) Henderson County

Nov. 18, 1864: we want some good tow to wipe our guns as we have to keep them in good **fix**. (John Peterson, Peterson Papers, Duke) Catawba County

3. In the phrase *out of fix:* out of sorts, upset, dissatisfied, in a troubled state of mind.

Apr. 9, 1862: The most that ails me is my stomach **out of fix** or a weak stomach. The medicine that I am taking is to strengthen my stomach. (S. A. Patton, Patton Family Letters, SHC) Buncombe County

Aug. 21, 1863: Dear Belovid I can informe you that the solegers is verry much **out of fix** at this time and I am one of them that is **out of fix** they way every thing gose. to be out hear and fite and what little money we git we have to pay it all if we want a little some thing [to eat]. if we all had yankee money we could buy as much with one dollar as we could with 7 dollars of confederate mone[y]. (W. F. Wagner, *Confederate Soldier,* 68) Catawba County

fixed *adjective* Prepared, equipped, situated (from the past participle of *fix*).

July 18, 1861: we had to go about to mils to camp and it was about 12.O.clock when we got **fixed.** so we arose up this Morning in the beautiful City of Richmon. (J. W. Coghill, Coghill Papers, Duke) Granville County

Aug. 14, 1861: he has got a good cot to lay upon and is verry well **fixed** but he has fallen off so much and weakened by the Daeirhoea that we dont think he will ever get well. (J. N. Coghill, Coghill Papers, Duke) Granville County

Dec. 18, 1862: if the yankes would a come out from the River we could a kiled nearley all of them I think the way we was **fixed**. (W. F. Wagner, *Confederate Soldier,* 27) Catawba County

Sept. 21, 1864: I think thay ame at take the danvill rode and holde it when thay git evr thing **fixt** to ther notion. (Arthur Putnam, Kendrick Papers, NCSA) Cleveland County

fixments *noun* Household furniture, accommodations. [*EDD* **fixment**, "The furniture of a house"]

Mar. 9, 1862: I Shal com down thare and See you all and Stay with you all two or three days and look at the **fixments**. (Austin Brown, Confederate Papers, SHC) Johnston County

flannen *noun* Flannel. [*DARE* **flannen**, noun, "Scots, Engl dial varr of flannel"]

Nov. 24, 1861: if they ar coten [= cotton] shirts we wont want them for we have got mor now then we can tote. we want some **flanin** shirts. (L. W. Griffin, Griffin Papers, NCSA) Rutherford County

Apr. 23, 1863: tena I will send my **flanen** shirt and drawers Back home the first good Chance I have. (J. W. Reese, Reese Papers, Duke) Buncombe County

flashy see **fleshy**

flat *noun* A railroad flatcar.

June 3, 1862: we had a pleasant trip from Goldsboro. we had a wood **flat** to ride on. the road comes strait north. there is a great deal of swampy land. I suppose we are about three hundred miles from home. (G. W. Frank, Frank Papers, Duke) Davison County

fleshy, flashy *adjective* Well fed, healthy.

Mar. 29, 1861: if you wast to sea me you wood not no me hardly for I hav got So fat an **fleshy.** (James Fisher, Fisher Papers, Duke) Catawba County

Jan. 19, 1862: Is[h]am tell pappy and famely that I am well as ever. tell him Ship [= his brother, Winship] is not verry. he is not as **flashy** as he was when he come from home. (Williford Upchurch, Upchurch Papers, Duke) Chatham County

Nov. 6, 1862: the pain own my breast has almost left me and I feal very well at this time. I think I am **fleshier** at this time then I was when I lefte home. (Isaac Lefevers, Lefevers Papers, NCSA) Catawba County

Feb. 2, 1863: Gen Price is the best looking man of his age I ever saw, a fat **fleshey** harty fellow a bout 200 lbs. (R. P. Kelly, Edmonston-Kelly Family Papers, WCU) Haywood County

flour bread *noun* Bread made with wheat flour. [*DARE* "Scots dial," now chiefly South]

Sept. 29, 1862: if I had something to eat as my appetite would take I should mend Rite smart but we dont get any thing but fresh beef and not much salt to go with hite and **flour bread** & I can skecly [= scarcely] eat enough to live on. (Austen Brown, Brown Family Papers, Duke) Johnston County

May 14, 1863: you could not of sent it in a better time. it is the first **flour bread** that I have eat in a long time. (James A. Patton, Patton Letters, Emory) Granville County

Mar. 3, 1865: we draw as much meal and meet as we eat but Some **flower bred** wold eat Some better. (James A. Smith, J. A. Smith Papers, Duke) Cabarrus County

flush *adjective* Of money: plentiful. [*OED* **flush**, adjective[1], 3.a.]

July 13, 1863: There is one thing, I wish you to have done, in the Call Session of the Legislator, and that is all entrys made from the Beginning of 1850 to Stand good till the 1 day January 1865 So that all Soldiers wives and widows and all Concerned Can Get Rights for Land while money is **flush**, and women have Bad Chances to Get Land Run out, the Ladies will thank you, and hollow hurrah for Vance. (John Livingston, Vance Papers, NCSA) Henderson County

flustrated *adjectve* Frustrated, confused, in turmoil.

Apr. 5, 1864: it did him so much good to kiss her that he Fainted and she become **flusterated** and frisking around poaring spices and every thing elce to stimulat him. (A. A. Jackson, Jackson Family Corr., Notre Dame) Moore County

July 10, 1864: I suppose you have been vary uneasy about me. If you are a mind to bee **flustrated** a bout sutch a beeing as I am but I am proud to tell you that I am all right on the goose. (Alfred N. Proffit, Proffit Family Letters, SHC) Wilkes County

flux, bloody flux *noun* Acute diarrhea or dysentery. [*DARE* chiefly Southern Appalachians, Lower Mississippi Valley]

June 1, 1862: Dear wife i now [= know] you will want to now what is the matter with mee. I first taken the Boulcomplaint and then it turned to the **Flux** and then I taken the mumps and cold. (Isaac Lefevers, Lefevers Papers, NCSA) Catawba County

Aug. 22, 1863: E W Blair has bin sick and poke [= Polk] has bin sick and I thought tha wood die. tha had the **bludey flux** but thay ar on the mend. (Francis Blair, J. H. Baker Papers, Duke) Rockingham County

Oct. 29, 1863: I have bin in bad health for ten days with my bowels. sumthing like **flux** and fevar. I am sum beter now but not well yet. (R. C. Caldwell, Caldwell Coll., ECU) Cabarrus County

Oct. 6, 1864: tell them that your family is down with the Measels and **flux** and there aint nobody to gather the corn. (Martha Poteet, Poteet-Dixon Letters, NCSA) McDowell County

fly around *verb* See Overview § II.4.7.

1. To court, flirt, gallivant. [*DARE* **fly around**, verb phrase, 2]

Sept. 19, 1861: write where the boys are **flying a round** at and how they are getin along with the girls. (Harrison Hanes, Hanes Papers, Duke) Davie County

Nov. 25, 1861: I would like to bee in old Catawba to go to the corn shucking to **fly around** amongst the girls. (L. L. Houk, Fisher Papers, Duke) Catawba County

Feb. 8, 1863: Jane says she wishes you had bin here to seen that fellow **fly around**. (Molly Tesh, Tesh Papers, Duke) Yadkin County

2. To hurry, make haste. [*DARE* **fly around**, verb phrase, 1]

May 20, 1863: I Waunt You to send me tow pair of Drawers Tow nice striped shirts With Pockets on the Outside of Both of them. a Good Pocket Handkerchief. I Waunt them tow marrow on review so **fly round** if You please. I Waunt them all soon. (G. J. Huntley, Huntley Papers, WCU) Rutherford County

fly around *noun phrase* A courting party.

Oct. 8, 1861: I would like very much to be with you to take a **fly around**. but Circumstances will not admt of it. (J. T. Groves, Davison Papers, Duke) Gaston County

May 23, 1862: we are agoing to come home after a while and have a big dinner and a **fly around**. (Christopher Sherrill, CS Army Misc., Duke) Catawba County

Apr. 25, 1863: you sed you and Shove had A **fly round** with the girls the day be fore. I think hear is the place for Shove to fly around my self. (James M. Amos, Amos Papers, Duke) Rockingham County

flying news *noun* A rumor, recent report; probably the same as **flying report**.

Feb. 22, 1865: you must write wether Buck and john is at home yet or not. you said that you heard that Mace had got home. I wrote to you in som of my outhe[r] Letters that I had heard som **flying nuse** from him. (J. W. Joyce, Joyce Papers, MHI) Stokes County

flying report *noun* A rumor or unconfirmed story. [see *OED* **flying**, adjective, 5.a. (earliest citation is from 1630)]

Apr. 22, 1864: it is a **flying report** that we captured some three thousand of their men though you will see it in the Papers, before you get this letter. (J. W. Lineberger, *Gaston Ranger,* 96) Gaston County

Jan. 21, 1865: I heard to day that the yankees had got willmington. it is the yankeey news also that the southerners had newbern. it is **flying report**. I dont no as it is so. they have bin shooting that way last sunday and thursday. I dont think it is so for Rodah was at the lines yesterday and heard notthing of it. (Ann Bowen, Bowen Papers, NCSA) Washington County

fodder pulling time *noun* The time to strip and gather nearly dry leaves from standing corn stalks. [see *DARE* **fodder time**, chiefly South, South Midland; see also *DSME* **foddering time**]

Aug. 24, 1862: if my health was rite good I would not offer Such a price as I have don but I can not get a hand in for a month or two and if he will come Iwant him him to come Sow I can get home tell **fodder pullen time**. (Isaac Lefevers, Lefevers Papers, NCSA) Catawba County

folks *noun*

1. Parents, family.

Nov. 11, 1861: if you see any of my **folks** tell them I am well and doing as well as could be exspected at this time. (W. P. Burns, Peterson Papers, Duke) Catawba County

Jan. 5, 1862: you can tell Dobbins **folks** that Calloway is Well. me and him and tolliver had a pretty smart singing Last night. (G. J. Huntley, Huntley Papers, WCU) Rutherford County

Apr. 18, 1863: I have let my men all go home but about 20 to git thar close & see thar **folks** before they leave for good. (Stephen Whitaker, Whitaker Papers, NCSA) Cherokee County

Apr. 28, 1863: I want you to ask my **folks** why they wont Right. I have not heard from them cence I left home. (Joseph Cowand, Cowand Papers, Duke) Bertie County

2. People, human beings.

Sept. 25, 1862: the time is drawing near that we will soon have to take up winter qarters and then their will bee nothing don tell Spring now more and I think the most of the fighten is over or at least that is the oppineon of the most of **folks** in the army. (Isaac Lefevers, Lefevers Papers, NCSA) Catawba County

Jan. 25, 1863: wee live know [= now] like **folks** and before wee lived like hogs. we have A plenty to eat. me and Rial make pies and eat just when wee get ready. (J. F. Coghill, Coghill Letters, SHC) Granville County

May 3, 1863: I Can inform you that the **folks** is A Dieing Pouerfull A bout her. thare was too wennon [= women] Buried this week that thare men was in the army. (Keziah Hefner, Hefner Papers, NCSA) Catawba County

follow, foller *verb*

1. variant forms *foller, foler.*

Nov. 10, 1861: Direct you letter to Beaufort Dist Pocataligo Po. 25 regment and if we are gone it will **foller** us if you will Backet to the 25 regment in the cear of Capt Blake. (John B. Lance, Lance Papers, LSU) Henderson County

July 12, 1862: we are all broke down an wared to death for we **folard** after the yankes thirty milsbe-low richmond clean to James river. (J. W. Williams, Williams Papers, Duke) Onslow County

June 15, 1863: the report is nou tha have left & I am Sory of it foure we will have to **follere** them. (Daniel Thomas, Williams Papers, Duke) Duplin County

2. To engage in a particular occupation. [*DARE* **follow**, verb, 1, chiefly South Midland]

Nov. 4, 1862: we have a cooper in the twenty sixth regiment that went as a conscript that we cant well do with out. he was all the man that **followed** this Trade anywhere near in this neighborhood. people depended on him for all kinds of vessels in our coun-try. he **followed** this for his Trade mostly for the last Six or seven years in particular. people come from fifteen to twenty miles for his work. (Cass Marlow, Vance Papers, NCSA) Wilkes County

Nov. 6, 1862: i Can put up as good Shoes and Boots as any man, So i have **folerd** the trade Before i went off. (Archibald Curlee, Vance Papers, NCSA) Union County

May 23, 1863: if the yankees kills me tha will haft to shoot a gain tho it dont take them long to do that for that is the bisness tha **foler** at this time and tha have lernt the trade very well Shore. (Lee Hendrix, *Hendrix Corr.*, VPI) Forsyth County

fool with *verb* To provoke or meddle with (some-thing potentially dangerous); see Overview § II.4.7. [*DSME* **fool with**; see also *OED* **fool**, verb, 2]

Mar. 11, 1862: sunday morning the old Merry Mack run the blockade out of James river. I tell you she give it to the Yankees vessels, she sunk one and blowed up one and badily injured several others and runn the rest. I tell you the roaring of cannons was rapid we could hear them distictly and from prairs battery they could see them fighting sunday morning. it was a glorious victory. I tell you the old Merry Mack is not to be **fooled with**. (H. J. Davis, WPA Transcripts, TSLA) Yadkin County

footing *noun* A condition, arrangement, state of affairs. [see *OED* **footing**, noun, 8.a.]

Apr. 27, 1863: if things dont change hir our famileys must sufer. how can a man injoy himself whene he knows his family is sufring. It is a harde trial for us to leve homes on thes **footings**. (Wilburn Garren, Vance Papers, NCSA) Henderson County

foot it *verb* To walk, go on foot. [*DSME* **foot it**, verb]

June 1, 1863: We left Kinston the 20th ult.[= day of the previous month] and come as far as Richmond on the cars and from there here. we had **to foot it**. (Christopher Hackett, Hackett Papers, Duke) Guilford County

fop *noun* A fool. [see *OED* **fop**, noun, 1.a. and 2]

Mar. 6, 1862: try to get the peopell in the notion of putting **fops** and drunkards out of power and put in men in all publick matters that Will discharge their duty and go for the interest of Our Country. (G. J. Huntley, Huntley Papers, WCU) Rutherford County

for *conjunction* and *preposition* variant forms *fer, fur.*

Oct. 20, 1855: I want go home at the end of this yeare if life laste and helth will admite but it is porley wo[r]th my while to thinke of my people **fur** none of them thinkes a nuff of me to rite to me but youre Self. (Hugh McGregor, Jackson Family Corr., Notre Dame) Moore County

Nov. 19, 1862: mi Legs hav bin paning me writ Smart **fur** the last few dase but it is owing to the weather. (B. C. Jackson, Jackson Family Corr., Notre Dame) Moore County

Oct. 28, 1862: tell John and Mary to not hug to hard **fur** I think he will git a discharge when he comes back and then he can have his time **fur** huging. (Jonas Bradshaw, Bradshaw Papers, Duke) Alexander County

Feb. 8, 1863: I wish that I could ove ben thare just to have taken A stick and have worn it out on thare heads. if that wouldnt do I give them some lead and I want you and Ma if they ever come thare again to do your best in trying to kill them **fer** they are worse than A yankey. (J. F. Coghill, Coghill Papers, Duke) Granville County

Apr. 26, 1863: you wanted to Know whether any Boday had helped me about plant my corn. H F procter Laid off the old feild **fer** me. (Amanda Murph, Murph Papers, Duke) Catawba County

for a song *idiomiomatic expression* Cheaply, at a low price.

Apr. 3, 1863: if you sell any of your pigs I would not sell them **for a song**. (Edgar Smithwick, Smithwick Papers, Duke) Martin County

forenoon *noun* Late morning. [*DARE* especially North]

Aug. 13, 1862: we have to drill 4 times a day, twise in the **forenoon** and twise in the afternoon. (C. A. Hege, Hege Papers, MHI) Davidson County

Nov. 5, 1864: we got here last evening. this **forenoon** we bilt our Selves a tent and So I now have time to rite a few lines. (John Peterson, Peterson Papers, Duke) Catawba County

forepart *noun* The first or front part (of something). [*OED* **fore-part, forepart**, noun, 1.a.]

Apr. 18, 1864: I can inform you that you need not tell that lady what I Sead you Shold in the **fore part** of my letter for Daniel will Send her one in this letter. tel her aring and if he ever gets home he intends to have asweat kiss for the ring. (John Hartman, Hartman Papers, Duke) Rowan County

forget *verb* past participle *forgot*.

Aug. 14, 1862: tel Fanny to do the best She can for you all & if I ever come back I hope it wont be **forgot**. (Austin Brown, Brown Family Papers, Duke) Johnston County

fork over *verb* To give, repay (often unwillingly); see Overview § II.4.7.

Apr. 8, 1862: we detailed 20 men and went in town and told the quarter master if he would not give in to us we would take it and [he] **forked** it **over**. (Ichabod Quinn, Quinn Papers, Duke) Duplin County

(in) for the war *prepositional phrase* Of the length of an enlistment: for the duration of the war rather than a fixed period of time (e.g., six months, two years).

Feb. 11, 1862: thei wont gave a furlow without we inlist **fur the ware** and I dont intend to dooit. (Thornton Sexton, Sexton Letters, Duke) Ashe County

Mar. 6, 1862: I have had Some notion of going **in for the War**. I Will git 50 dollars Bounty By going **in fer the War** and I think the War Will Be ended against my time is out eny how. (G. J. Huntley, Huntley Papers, WCU) Rutherford County

Apr. 26, 1862: I Suppose that you hav heard that all from 18 to 35 is prest **in for the war** and you know it is A bad Lick on me. (J. W. Williams, Williams Papers, Duke) Onslow County

Oct. 17, 1862: you awl may not think heard of mi not coming hom when mos [= Moses] Dye com. I am **in for the waur**. I hav dwon receiv mi Bounty. I weigh one hundred and nintey nine pounes. (Louis Wright, Wright Papers, Duke) Alamance County

for to *infinitive phrase* To. [*DARE* **for**, grammatical functions, B 1; see also *OED* **for**, preposition, 11.a.]

Sept. 24, 1861: you Said that if anderso tow Rote to me A Bout the Contract Between you and him **for to** not Answer him. (Jesse Shipman, Shipman Family Corr., Notre Dame) Henderson County

July 11, 1862: we drove them some ten miles father where they taken shelter under their gunboats **for to** keep from being killed and and taken prisoners. (L. L. Houk, Fisher Papers, Duke) Catawba County

Jan. 12, 1863: I no you have A hard time to git along for thar is no chance **for to** hire any help and times will git worse. (Jesse Miller, Proffit Family Letters, SHC) Wilkes County

Apr. 6, 1864: it was an agreement between Lieut Genl Longstreet and Gen Sherman to both Armies **for to** evacuate East Tennessee and leave what Provisions there is here to feed the Citizens on. (C. A. Walker, Walker Papers, WCU) Cherokee County

Apr. 24, 1864: he told the old man that he had Run over him as long as he intended **for to** do it. so he pick up A verry large Stick And Strwck the old man By the Side of they head. (W. H. Brotherton, Brotherton Papers, Duke) Catawba County

forward *adjective* Of a crop: ahead, advanced in growth. [*DARE* **forward**, B, as adjective, b]

Apr. 27, 1862: I am proud to here that you are getting Along so well About farmin. I think that you all get Along very well by what I am Learn[ing]. you said that the crows was poling [= pulling] up your corn. try and hang something white up in the feild and probly it may do some good. Mother I think that you are doing extry to be So **forward** in your farm. (John W. Williams, Williams Papers, Duke) Onslow County

founder *noun* A cold. [*EDD* **founder**, 4. "A catarrh, cold; an illness"]

May 26, 1861: we have all ben enjoying very good health since we left home except the bowel complaint and a few **founders**. there has ben several of us had a light tuch of the bowel complaint but we are all giting better of it. (W. M. Patton, Patton Family Letters, SHC) Buncombe County

fox squirrel *noun* A species of squirrel, *Sciurus niger,* somewhat larger than a gray squirrel and often reddish brown in color.

May 17, 1858: you are anctious to git ware thare is game to kill. Come out hear. thare is game plenty hear. Deer Turkeys **fox Squerrels** Rabits but few gray Squerrels. we have kild lots of Turkeys & Red Squrrels. (John Frank, Frank Papers, Duke) Davidson County

fracas *noun* A noisy uproar or quarrel; a fight or skirmish.

Oct. 28, 1861: I will tell you Something about Times hier. Some too or three weeks ago they they had a little **fracus** with the yankeys every morning but they have not bin doing any thing at it for Several days. (James W. Overcash, Overcash Papers, Duke) Rowan County

frank *verb* To sign an envelope instead of applying a postage stamp, so that it will be delivered postage due. [*OED* **frank**, verb², 1.a.]

Feb. 9, 1863: I am bound to **frank.** I cant get any Stamps hear. (W. H. Brotherton, Brotherton Papers, Duke) Catawba County

Mar. 2, 1863: I am sorrow to have to **frank** my letter but I Cant git stamps hear an they aint no post office hear for me to pay postage at. (G. H. Hundley, Hundley Family Letters, SHC) Stokes County

Aug. 26, 1863: I jest **franked** it. that is poot my name on the back of it and then you would pay for it in Newton. (W. F. Wagner, *Confederate Soldier,* 71) Catawba County

freestone water *noun phrase* "Soft" water, relatively mineral free. [*DARE* chiefly South Midland]

Sept. 1, 1862: I like the lime Stone water just as good as the **free Stone**. (R. P. Kelly, Edmonston-Kelly Family Papers, WCU) Haywood County

freeze *verb* variant past tense forms *freezed, frozed.*

Jan. 15, 1862: The 15 day was a very bad day. it raind all day and **freezed** as it fell. (B. Y. Malone, *Malone Diary,* 12) Caswell County

Feb. 5, 1865: we even marched to foart fisher twoo before the fight and had to Ly in the intrenshments for 18 days and nights and nearly **frozed** to Death. (Wade Hubbard, Hubbard Papers, Duke) Anson County

fresh *noun* A freshet, a flash flood.

Sept. 8, 1862: I am sory to hear that there was A **fresh** on the crick for I no that it has ingerd yore crop. (Marcus Hefner, Hefner Papers, NCSA) Catawba County

fresh ground *noun phrase* Perhaps the same as *newground.*

June 8, 1863: tha are a plowing the **fresh ground** corn the second time. it looks very well. (Sally Hackett, Hackett Papers, Duke) Guilford County

fret *verb* To bother, worry. [*DARE* chiefly South]

Mar. 7, 1863: I want you if you pleas to find out what day he will start back. send me a little snack to eat by him. you kneed not **fret** yourself to much trubel about it. just some little thing so it comes frome home. (James A. Patton, Patton Letters, Emory) Granville County

June 5, 1863: we will have to go to virginia I expect but mi darling wife I dont want you to **fret** after me for I dont no when I will git to cum home but I want you to do the best you can tel I cum. (Daniel Setzer, Setzer Papers, Duke) Catawba County

Feb. 27, 1865: you must not be on easy or **fret** for me. I am doing verry well and will doe the best I can. (John Peterson, Peterson Papers, Duke) Catawba County

fritter *noun* Fried bread made from a batter and either deep-fried or fried in a skillet (like a griddle cake or pancake).

Feb. 15, 1863: I have got all most tird out on **fritters.** We have had no other bred hardly sence we hav been keping bachlors hall. miller and martin is the Cooks. (John J. Taylor, Taylor Papers, Duke) Orange County

frocktail (coat) *noun* An type of overcoat. [see *OED* **frock-coat**, noun; see also *DARE* **frock**, noun, "A men's outer garment, esp a work jacket, often made of denim"]

Dec. 2, 1862: I like A coat if you can getit and one or two pare of Socks if you can get the coat make it A **frocktail** with the pockets in the side. (J. F. Coghill, *Coghill Papers* Duke) Granville County

frolic *noun*

1. A lively party with dancing, music, and sometimes drinking; also used figuratively. [*DARE* chiefly South Midland]

Mar. 2, 1859: I was at a **frolic** yesterday where there were some clever looking young ladies. but ah, I saw one done the country that that took the shine off of them. (John McGregor, Jackson Family Corr., Notre Dame) Moore County

Dec. 24, 1862: you may send me a shirt or two if you can so[o]n. [with] the seems sown so that the lice dont h[a]ve a god chanch. we have a great many of them at this time. I think that I will have a Christmas **frolick.** kiling the lice in plase of hunting rabbits. (John S. Overcash, Overcash Papers, Duke) Rowan County

Feb. 10, 1863: Jinny sed that she was loking for a **frolic** ever day and night and I must come home and play the fiddle. you must tell hear that I have quite gwine to **frolics** and I have quite gitting drunk and and have quit all such bad tricks though I would bin glad to ov bin at your **frollick** but it was out of my power. (J. W. Joyce, Joyce Papers, MHI) Stokes County

2. A state of intense excitment, merriment.

Dec. 29, 1861: We left Lincolnton on Wednesday morning and Reached Charlott about one a clock. it Was a powerful Time in charlott all day. hundreds of peopell and all in a **frollick.** (G. J. Huntley, Huntley Papers, WCU) Rutherford County

frolic *verb* To play, to have a party.

Jan. 21, 1862: you fellows in N C ar only a **frolickin** to that we heave to do hear. they ar not and hour in the day but what one can hear canon. (D. C. Johnson, Jackson Family Corr., Notre Dame) Moore County

Jan. 26, 1864: Branns has been a **frolicing** ever since Chrismas. (Molly Tesh, Tesh Papers, Duke) Yadkin County

frozed see **freeze**

fry *noun* An amount or portion of meat suitable for frying at one time.

Dec. 24, 1861: Mother I received thoes Sorcerges you Sent to me thankfuly and has got one more **fry** yet. (J. W. Williams, Williams Papers, Duke) Onslow County

fun at *verb* To tease, make fun of; see Overview § II.4.7.

Nov. 25, 1863: my dear you Sead Something about the Solders making fun of wimen coming to camp. my dear I can inform you that our compny has never made no fun of eny woman yet but this is the thing you air not oblidge to come to camp. I exspect to have ahouse for you to Stay at and you need not go to camp atall if you dont want to. I will be all the Soldier that will make fun at you and that we will make after night. you need not be afeard of beng **fund at** for ramsy wont allow it. I will be all the man that will fun with you. that will be Secret fun. (John Hartman, Hartman Papers, Duke) Rowan County

fur see **for**

furder, fudder *adverb* Farther, further. [*DARE* chiefly South, South Midland]

June 25, 1862: V [= We] darto leve the Camp no **fuder** then to gow to the Spring. (W. P. Cline, Cline Papers, SHC) Catawba County

Aug. 24, 1862: we left our old camp last wedens-day morning. we air now a bout three miles from Richmond whear we will Stay till **fudder** orders. there is now yankes Close hear now. (Isaac Lefevers, Lefevers Papers, NCSA) Catawba County

Sept. 21, 1862: Dear Wife we are **furder** a part then I ever expectted to that we would be and stil Expect to go **fudder**. (W. F. Wagner, *Confederate Soldier,* 14) Catawba County

Mar. 15, 1863: dear husban i hear that you are moved **furder** and I am sorrow to hir it. (Martha Futch, Futch Letters, NCSA) New Hanover County

fuss *noun* An argument, dispute, quarrel; excite-ment, commotion; figuratively: the war. [*DARE* scattered, but chiefly South, Midland]

Oct. 2, 1860: tell Father & Mother that they k[n]eed not Be uneasy A Bout mee for I hav got A long very well. I hav had no **fuses**. (J. W. Love, Love Papers, Duke) Henderson County

Jan. 11, 1862: I dont want you to expose this leter for it may rase a **fus** an I dont want you to let every body know hoo rote it to you. (G. T. Beavers, Upchurch Papers, Duke) Chatham County

Mar. 27, 1864: my notion is that this **Fuss** will end by the first of next Septtember But the most of us may be kild by that time and it never will doo us aney good. (Isaac Copeland, Copeland Letters, NCSA) Surry County

Oct. 25, 1864: my health is very at present. I hant bin Sick Since last I Saw you. well M J there is a great **fus** here a bout a fight cuming of[f] Sum of those days [= one of these days]. (R. C. Caldwell, Caldwell Coll., ECU) Cabarrus County

fuss *verb* To argue, quarrel.

May 24, 1861: they got to **fussing** and the Sherriff was called to make arrests. one of the republicans shot at the Sherriff four times but happend not to hit him. the Sherriff drew his revolver & was only prevented shooting by a crowd getting between them. (Rhoda Hawn, Peterson Papers, Duke) Catawba County

fust *adjective, adverb* variant form of *first.*

Apr. 17, 1859: I will inform you at **fust** that I am well at presant. (Enoch Garner, Jackson Family Corr., Notre Dame) Davidson County

Nov. 3, 1861: I want to come home by the **fust** of march. (A. V. Broach, Broach Papers, Duke) Person County

G

gab *verb* To talk, converse.

ND [1864]: tell John to learn gard to tree Rabbits and Squirls Susan and Ruprt to Rais all the Chickens tha Can and mar grett the tobacco and mee and hur will smok and spit and **gab**. (J. W. Reese, Reese Papers, Duke) Buncombe County

gal *noun* A girl; a young, unmarried female.

June 16, 1862: tell alford I want him to bhave him self and let the **gals** alone. (Joseph Cowand, Cowand Papers, Duke) Bertie County

Oct. 4, 1862: I want to know Wether my little **gal** has got her Shous [= shoes] yet or not. (John Ingram, Ingram Papers, Duke) Forsyth County

Jan. 10, 1863: I send you A hair Bresh for the **galls** to keep slick hair. (J. W. Reese, Reese Papers, Duke) Buncombe County

June 12, 1864: I want you to tell all the **Gals** ho[w]dy for me. tell them to not forgit me. (Julius Myers, Alman Papers, Duke) Cabarrus County

Oct. 18, 1864: I want to go home to live with my dutch **gal**. (William H. Horton, Councill Papers, Duke) Watauga County

galey *adjective* In good health, well; variant of *gaily*. [*DARE* **gaily**, 2, as adverb]

Oct. 28, 1862: tell Mary howdy fur me. tell Father and Mother that I am well and **galey** and would be glad to see them. (Jonas Bradshaw, Bradshaw Papers, Duke) Alexander County

gallisses, galises, gallowes *noun plural* Suspenders; variant forms of *galluses*.

Sept. 29, 1862: if you Can Send mee an thing doo it. I need A pair of **Gallisses** and Socks. (J. W. Reese, Reese Papers, Duke) Buncombe County

Oct. 13, 1862: if Monrow Miller comes once please send me Some **galises.** mine is a bout wore out. that is suspenders. (W. F. Wagner, *Confederate Soldier,* 21) Catawba County

Jan. 26, 1864: I sent you a pair of **gallowes** in that Box to wear with your new pants. (Molly Tesh, Tesh Papers, Duke) Yadkin County

gambadoes *noun plural* Leather leggings. [*OED* **gambado**, noun[1] (from Italian *gamba,* "leg")]

Dec. 17, 1862: I want A coat and two pair of socks and A pair of **Gambadoes** and pair of shoes and my comfort. (J. F. Coghill, Coghill Papers, Duke) Granville County

game chicken *noun* A game or fighting cock.

Jan. 26, 1863: take care of my **game chickens** for I think I will Soon come home. I think the war is most ended. (John Hartman, Hartman Papers, Duke) Rowan County

gamery *noun* Grandmother. [see *OED* **gammer**, noun]

Dec. 2, 1864: Thomas come home on saturday and come to see me on monday and left his granfathers on thursday and went rite to the yankees [I] hered [= heard] when he come he had 30 days furlow. he has rote to **gamery** that he is at Newbern and is agent on the rail road getting 40 dolars a month. I tel you farther is down on him. I am sorry he done it. (Ann Bowen, Bowen Papers, NCSA) Washington County

ganders see **janders**

gang *noun* A large number, a bunch (of people). [*DARE* **gang**, noun, 2]

Apr. 9, 1863: I wish to informe you that some of my neighbours is aming for a tobacco crop, one is Young Single man with a Substitute in the army and a **gang** of Negroes at home who Sed he aimed to make 4 or 5 or 8 thousand pounds this year, I think all tobacco groers aught to be Sent to the army. (Levi Walker, Vance Papers, NCSA) Guilford County

May 14, 1864: itel you my dear iam tired of Staying here and living the way wee doo. i am tired of sleeping among a **gang** of men on the ground like hogs. (Silas Stepp, Stepp Letters, UNCA) Buncombe County

gant, gants see **in the gants**

gap *noun*

1. In place names: a pass or opening in a mountain range or ridge. [*DARE* widespread but especially Appalachians]

Oct. 26, 1862: Tusday the 26 we star ted agane very erley an Continuad our Corse on past through salem an a nother Litle town Cald orleans an hay market and we past through the **manassas gap** an went on close by Bull Run wher the old battle was fort [= fought] an we crost Bull run about 10 oclock in the night. (W. B. Howard, Williams-Womble Papers, NCSA) Chatham County

Mar. 1, 1863: the yankeys has has taken huntsvill in Alabam and Reports say that thirty thousan has Crost at the **Cumberlen gap** in to East tennessee. (J. W. Reese, Reese Papers, Duke) Buncombe County

Mar. 22, 1864: Gen Longstreat is her. his hedquarters is her. he has a large army her & at **Bulls gap** the yanks advanced the other day above Moristown but got scard & fell back. (Stephen Whitaker, Whitaker Papers, NCSA) Cherokee County

2. An opening in a fence. [*DARE* chiefly South Midland, South]

June 11, 1862: you wrote my hogs were about to dy. please dont let them perish. let them go in the <ivy?> patch. make a **gap** and let them go in and out give them colwort leaves and all the slops. (Ichabod Quinn, Quinn Papers, Duke) Duplin County

Jan. 17, 1864: I want hen [= Henry] to make rails cut his timber along Side of the nuground **Gap**. cut them big trees where the wood was piled. cut his limbs along both ways from the **gap**. make 5 hundred [fence rails] along there and cut the tops for wood. (R. C. Caldwell, Caldwell Coll., ECU) Cabarrus County

gearing *noun* A harness. [*DARE* **gearing**, noun, "Engl dial"; *OED* **gearing**, noun,1, *dial.*]

Dec. 1, 1862: I was very glad to hear that mike [= a young horse] worked verry well but you most not have him strained. he is too younge to do much yet and be cearful and dont get him spoilt now as he is younge yet and if he gets spoilt now he will never get over it. be cearful and dont get his shorlders hurt with the collar and have good **gearing** own [= on] him sow he dont get spoilt. (Isaac Lefevers, Lefevers Papers, NCSA) Catawba County

get about *verb* To walk or go about, after being ill or injured; see Overview § II.4.7.

July 13, 1863: we are all in common Health but Davis. he is not weell. he has to **get about** with his crutches and you no that is sloe **geting about**. (John Revis, Revis Letters, NCSA) Henderson County

Apr. 16, 1864: Mother says she wants to see you and your Dear little childrin Worse than any one she ever aw But she is A fraid that she never Will see you all A gain for she is very Weak and feble so that she can hardly **get A Bout**. (Sally Bauldin, Hundley Family Letters, SHC) Stokes County

July 8, 1864: I was wounded in three places in the face and leg and ankle. I am geting tolerable well though I can not **get about** any yet. my ankle is not healed up yet. (J. E. Patton, Patton Family Letters, SHC) Buncombe County

get awake *verb* To wake up; see Overview § II.4.7. [*DARE* **get awake**, verb phrase, "Cf Ger *wach werden* to wake up, to become, get awake"; chiefly Pennsylvania]

Apr. 18, 1862: excuse my bad writing and spelling for I have to write on my nee and I was on post last night and I will write as soon as I **get awake**. (James Lineberger, *Gaston Ranger,* 6) Gaston County

Dec. 21, 1863: Dear loveing wife drempt last knight that I was at home and you had some good chicken. cookt and i was aeaten [= a eating] wen I **got awake**. (Daniel Setzer, Setzer Papers, Duke) Catawba County

get better of see **of**

get clear *verb phrase*

1. To avoid military service through exemption or discharge.

Mar. 4, 1863: I want you to write me if Buck has **got cleare** of [the] ware. (James A. Patton, Patton Letters, Emory) Granville County

June 4, 1863: I havent mutch to write about ware & I have bin in the ware and Saw the ware and heard tell of the ware till I have got tired of it. if I Could **get clear** of this ware I neve want to Read of A nother. (Joel Howard, Brotherton Papers, Duke) Lincoln County

Dec. 26, 1864: some say he **got clear** on acount of his toe and some say the company was disbanded. (Ann Bowen, Bowen Papers, NCSA) Washington County

2. To recover, be free from an illness.

Sept. 22, 1861: I am well except my brest. it hurts very bad the latter part of the night so that I hardly can sleep. the docter ses I hant **got clear** of the mesles. (G. T. Beavers, Upchurch Papers, Duke) Chatham County

gether *verb* variant form of *gather.*

Sept. 25, 1862: you had better have [the] new ground sowe as quick as you can before the corn is **getherd.** sow it with new wheat if you think it will do as well as the old. (Isaac Lefevers, Lefevers Papers, NCSA) Catawba County

Oct. 26, 1862: you Stated in your leter that you had hierd Riley bendfeel A haf A month for six dolers. I think that it is low A nuff but try and pay him in money and try to hier him A hole month. I tel you til he **gethers** the corne and wheat. [has] Seeded the wheat and gets wood to do you this winter. (Marcus Hefner, Hefner Papers, NCSA) Catawba

Nov. 4, 1863: we are shucking corn. we have all of our corn **getherd** but that down about the meadow we have not **getherd** any of that. (Sarah Overcash, Overcash Papers, Duke) Rowan County

get religion *verb phrase* To experience a religious conversion, profess one's religious faith.

June 22, 1861: tell Jonathan dunkin that I dont want him to for get me and tell him that I want him to be a good boy and try and **get religion** and tell [him] all so to write to me and tell me all of the good fun that he has had since I left there. (J. N. Cunningham, Cunningham Letters, NCSA) Haywood County

get shet of see **shet of**

get the praise see **the praise**

get to *verb* To start, begin, commence (usually followed by a present participle verb); see Overview § II.4.7.

1. present tense.

Apr. 3, 1862: you need not send them three Garments tell I Write for them for I dont need them now and it may Be tow months Before I need them. I Will Write When I **git to** needing them. (G. J. Huntley, Huntley Papers, WCU) Rutherford County

Jan. 15, 1863: make some sweet cider and pwt it in citle [= kettle] or pot and let it **get to** boil. (T. F. Baggarly, Baggarly Papers, Duke) Iredell County

Feb. 6, 1863: when they **get to** fighting wee fall back to the rear and take up the Straglars. (J. F. Coghill, Coghill Papers, Duke) Granville County

Jan. 21, 1865: I no you think of me when you have oysters. I expect you will **get to** loving them. (Ann Bowen, Bowen Papers, NCSA) Washington County

2. past tense.

May 24, 1861: they **got to** fussing and the Sherriff was called to make arrests. one of the republicans shot at the Sherriff four times but happend not to hit him the Sherriff drew his revolver & was only prevented shooting by a crowd getting between them. (Rhoda Hawn, Peterson Papers, Duke) Catawba County

Sept. 24, 1861: hall and Brown **got to** Drinking and hall kicked Brown and hurt him tolerabile Bad. (Jesse Shipman, Shipman Family Corr., Notre Dame) Henderson County

3. past participle.

May 13, 1863: We have Some vary warm wether her at last and the trees has **got to** putting out vary fast. (Hardy Matthews, McLeod Letters, SHC) Moore County

June 15, 1863: the folks is as well as comon as far as I know but gimey. he has **got to** taking fits he toock one the other day. (J. A.W. Revis, Revis Letters, NCSA) Henderson County

Jan. 5, 1864: tell margrett to rais us sum to bacco for I hav **got to** Smoking Reglear. (J. W. Reese, Reese Papers, Duke) Buncombe County

get well of see **of**

gill *noun* A liquid measure (usually of distilled alcohol) equal to one-half cup or one-quarter pint. [*OED* **gill,** noun[3]]

Aug. 25, 1862: I stoped over to Richmon the other day to get one d dram & I did not get but little over a **gill** & had to pay one dollar for it. (Elijah Gatewood, Amos Papers, Duke) Rockingham County

Oct. 4, 1862: I want olde uncle Mosey to Save mee Ten gallons of His brandyd but I hope he will not charge mee what it is sellen at. their ant one **gill** to bee had hear and I want him to bee shore and save it for me. (Isaac Lefevers, Lefevers Papers, NCSA) Catawba County

Nov. 10, 1864: there is a great deal of grumbling about the Rations we get one third of a pound of <bacon?> a day Some times get beeff. Some times get molases. get 3 **gills** for a day to a Man but dont get meet when we get molases. (Joseph Wright, Wright Papers, Duke) Alamance County

ginger cake *noun* A sweet cake flavored with ginger. [*DARE* especially South, South Midland]

Sept. 14, 1862: peaches is worth 25 cents a dozen. you can tell from that how muney goes. if we buy **ginger**

cake 25 cents a pisce half as big as this paper. (James Zimmerman, Zimmerman Papers, Duke) Forsyth

Feb. 4, 1864: I sent you somthing to eat by Marion Higins. five pies and five **ginger Cakes**, one doz unions, two custerds, 1 ham of Meat, and three twists of tobaco. (Martha Poteet, Poteet-Dickson Letters, NCSA) McDowell County

Mar. 16, 1864: you thaught I was joking last spring whe[n] I told about the Boys steeling the sweetning out of a **ginger cake**. (J. W. Love, Love Papers, Duke) Henderson County

give *verb*

1. past tense *give*.

Feb. 11, 1862: Sunday morning the old Merry Mack run the blockade out of James river. I tell you she **give** it to the Yankees vessels. (H. J. Davis, WPA Transcripts, NCSA) Yadkin County

July 3, 1862: the last leter I received was dated June the 7. it **give** mee great Sattis faction to hear from you that you was well. (M. W. Parris, Parris Papers, WCU) Jackson County

May 1, 1863: they **give** them a thrashing at gum swamp. (J. W. Lineberger, *Gaston Ranger,* 47) Gaston County

2. past tense *given*.

Mar. 6, 1862: Wm James has Bin trying to git to Come home to make up a Company of volunteers But the Colonel Wont let him yet he **given** James Miller leaf to go home to make a company mearly I suppose Because he is a Big man. (G. J. Huntley, Huntley Papers, WCU) Rutherford County

3. past participle *give*.

Nov. 4, 1862: god has **give** his only begoten son that the whole world might live. (Cass A. Marlow, Vance Papers, NCSA) Wilkes County

Mar. 6, 1864: i have **give** all hope up of evry living with you a gin. (Caroline Setzer, Setzer Corr., UVA) Catawba County

4. past participle *gave*.

Jan. 21, 1862: I heave **gave** you all that is worth riting so will come to a close. (D. C. Johnson, Jackson Family Corr., Notre Dame) Moore County

give in *verb* To submit a certificate, account, or other document to someone in a position of authority; see Overview § II.4.7 . [*DARE* especially South Atlantic]

July 13, 1863: ther was Discharges Rote out for Men and the Col wolddent Give them to the men Some Men Could **Give in** the Best Surtificate of Diseases and woulddent Bee listened at. (William Martin, Vance Papers, NCSA) Burke County

given to *adjective phrase* Affected by (a medical condition); afflicted with (an illness).

June 18, 1863: i am not fit for camp lif let alon the duty of the man for i hav Bin **gevin to** hart pluricey and the consuption and i am fity By Spells 4 or 5 tims in a weeck. this i have haid for the last 8 or 10 years now. you now that a man that is so plegued is not fit for sirves. (Bluford Lucas, Vance Papers, NCSA) Harnett County

Sept. 4, 1863: 18 munthes a go i volentard. i had one sun. he wasant 17 yeares of age. he tuck my place. he has never had afurlow yet. i am **given to** the Rumetism ithink buy my having that boy [gone] so long. thare is no orther man in the nabor hood to asist the solgers wives but me. (James Hemby, Vance Papers, NCSA) Greene County

give out *verb* past tense *give out,* past participle *gave out, give out;* see Overview § II.4.7.

1. Of a person: to fail from exhaustion; of clothing or shoes: to be worn out. [see *DSME* **give out**]

Mar. 16, 1862: I had been Sick a day or two before the battle I had to run So much ther I **gave out**. (C. F. Mills, Mills Papers, Duke) Iredell County

ND [1862]: if bet['s] shoes is **give out** I want you to get her a pare if you please for if She has wove as mutch Cloth as She says she has I think that she has yernt [= earned] one pare. (W. D. Smith, W. D. Smith Papers, Duke) Davie County

June 24, 1863: we have had another hard march from Fredericks bur to ward Winchester. the march was so hard and the weather so hot that hundreds **give out**. (Andrew J. Proffit, Proffit Family Letters, SHC) Wilkes County

2. To give up, discontinue, quit, postpone.

Mar. 8, 1863: Me and Nancy intended to go to see you last week but owing to so much water we had to **give** it **out**. (Betty Thomas, Quinn Papers, Duke) Duplin County

Aug. 29, 1863: Mother I Began to think that you had **give out** Writing to me at all. (Edgar Smithwick, Smithwick Papers, Duke) Martin County

July 24, 1864: I hav **give out** the Idie of coming to your Regt for awhile. I think I can git a nice position in the Regt if it is exchanged. (T. B. Edmonston, Edmonston-Kelly Family Papers, WCU) Haywood County

Dec. 4, 1864: i told you in that letter that i sent one 100 dollars in it but i **give out** the notion to send enny [in] that letter. (Franklin Setzer, Setzer Corr., UVA) Catawba County

3. To announce (a religious text).

Apr. 2, 1864: There was one old Dunkard preached near here the other day and **give out** his text <12th?> Chapter and 5th verse of the Revelations of St. John the Divine. (C. A. Walker, Walker Papers, WCU) Cherokee County

give over *verb* To pronounce incurable; see Overview § II.4.7. [*OED* **give**, verb, **to give over**, 5]

Oct. 28, 1862: i Send you this Letter to Let you knoo that wellington is at the pint of Death. the Doc tor **give** him **over** on yestidy But he has not Bin to see him yet on to Day. (William H. Thurber, DeRosset Family Papers, SHC) New Hanover County

give up *verb* To acknowledge, concede, admit; see Overview § II.4.7. [*DARE* chiefly South Midland]

Dec. 24, 1861: it is **given up** that our Company is the best drilled Company in the rigment. (J. W. Williams, Williams Papers, Duke) Onslow County

May 20, 1862: it is pretty mutch **given up** By all men about hear that the yankies Will take Richmond in a fiew days But I have No dout Buwhat they Will have a Bluddy time yet Before they get Richmond. (G. J. Huntley, Huntley Papers, WCU) Rutherford County

June 13, 1862: we see hard times & good times But that is the way to git a long. Co H is **givin up** to be the best Company in the Regiment But some Rascal thare too We hav a good set of officers Sence Swann left. he was turned out & I was glad. (A. F. Harrington, Hubbard Papers, Duke) Moore County

give way *verb* To fall back; variant past participle *give way;* see Overview § II.4.7.

Dec. 6, 1863: we helt the top of the Ridg tell ouer men had **giv way** on Boath Cides. (J. W. Reese, Reese Papers, Duke) Buncombe County

glad of see **of**

glant *verb* To court or flirt; from *gallant.* [*OED* **gallant**, verb, II. 3; *DARE* chiefly South, South Midland]

Jan. 29, 1862: we are a fraid that we will forget how to **glant** with the gentle men before they get back but i recon thay will not want to **glant** with us tho we nead not scear our selvs. (Phebe Gaultney, Baggarly Papers, Duke) Alexander County

go *verb*

A. GRAMMAR.

1. past tense *gone.*

July 21, 1862: the yankeys fired in to us thining our ranks sum but we returnd the fire and I guess we thind them some two and we had it then for 12 or 15 rouns and the yanks **gone** Back and in A few minets we went over to where they was. (J. W. Love, Love Papers, Duke) Henderson County

Aug. 14, 1862: we fought a bout 3 hours or more last saturday evning & **gon** back a little after sunset. (Austin Brown, Brown Papers, Duke) Johnston County

2. past participle *went.*

Feb. 8, 1863: you heard we had **went** to goles Burrow. it is a mistake. (W. F. Wagner, *Confederate Soldier,* 36) Catawba County

Nov. 23, 1863: we had preachen hear twist Sunday But I would of been mutch glader to of bin at home to of **went** to [preaching] with you. (F. M. Poteet, Poteet-Dickson Letters, NCSA) McDowell County

3. present participle followed by infinitive, variants include *gont, gonter, a gont.*

Feb. 4, 1862: I beegant to git out of hart to think that I was not **a gont** to git a letter. (J. S. Councill, Councill Papers, Duke) Watauga County

July 12, 1862: i wont to now if you have Setel with John bumgander er not. i wont you to Setel with all of them an try to git the money for the times is **A gonte** be harde. (W. P. Cline, Cline Papers, SHC) Catawba County

Apr. 20, 1863: he is **gonter** tri to git er change an come to my rigment. (Henry Keever, Keever Papers, Duke) Lincoln County

Feb. 1, 1865: we was **a goent** to get Some man to fech them. (Franklin Setzer, Setzer Corr., UVA) Catawba County

4. present participle *gwine, agwine*. [*DARE* chiefly South, South Midland]

July 11, 1862: I daunt know what is **agwine** on in camp onely right wher I can see it. (Neill McLeod, McLeod Letters, SHC) Moore County

Feb. 10, 1863: Jinny sed that she was loking for a frolic ever day and night and I must come home and play the fiddle. you must tell hear that I have quite **gwine** to frolics and I have quite gitting drunk and and have quit all such bad tricks though I would bin glad to ov bin at your frollick but it was out of my power. (J. W. Joyce, Joyce Papers, MHI) Stokes County

B. SENSES.

1. To be digestible, savory, good to eat.

Nov. 14, 1863: I got to camp without Tetching My butter or molasses. I tell You it **goes** splendid now and it was a sight to see me eat it and Think who cooked it and how good it was. (William Tesh, Tesh Papers, Duke) Yadkin County

2. To "stomach," endure (something).

Jan. 17, 1864: we dont get bread anuf. we draw bread loof So mucha day. wee get half a pound of meet a day it is So Stinkin I cant **go** it. (R. C. Caldwell, Caldwell Coll., ECU) Cabarrus County

3. To cosign or guarantee a loan or bond.

Aug. 30, 1864: I would like to know what you baught at the Sale and what it Caust you and who **went** your Securiety for what you baught. (Alexander Keever, Keever Papers, Duke) Lincoln County

4. To walk, be able to get about.

Nov. 22, 1863: I hav bin so in my hips that I hardly could **go**. I went to the doctor to git excused but he would not excuse me and I said that I never would go to him any more that I would **go** as long as I can and when I cant go no longer I will lay down any plase. (F. M. Poteet, Poteet-Dickson Letters, NCSA) McDowell County

5. Of news: to be in circulation, going around.

Oct. 5, 1862: I want you to rite to me soon and tell me all the newses there is **going**. (Isaac Copeland, Copeland Letters, NCSA) Surry County

6. In the phrase *go it:* to pursue one's course of action vigorously, to go ahead regardless of the consequences. [see *OED* **go**, verb, 46.c.]

May 17, 1863: I Recon you hav hear that Janerel Stone wall Jackson died from feaver and Janeril vandorn giting shot throu the head for sleeping with A doctors wife. I wood hav dun Just as the doctor dun. **go it** doctor. if All Reports is true that doctor ort to hav A grate practice in Buncomb. (J. W. Reese, Reese Papers, Duke) Buncombe County

go for *verb* To vote for, support politically; see Overview § II.4.7.

Apr. 3, 1864: I think Govenor Vance is the man and I want every man to **go for** him for he has dun more for the solderes than anny body elts would. (William Tesh, Tesh Papers, Duke) Yadkin County

gollop *noun* Food swallowed in haste. [*DARE* **gollop** noun; *OED* **gollop**, noun, "A greedy or hasty gulp"; see also *EDD* **gollop**]

Apr. 28, 1863: times is hard hear harder than I ever thout that I should se. they give us Branch water and **gollop** for Brexfus dinner and supper. (Joseph Cowand, Cowand Papers, Duke) Bertie County

gone case *noun phrase* A lost cause, hopeless case.

Feb. 15, 1863: it lucks like a **Gone Case** with us enny way that we can fix it for it lucks like the men is all a going to Dye and Get killd up. (Samuel C. Phillips, Woody Letters, Confederate Misc., Emory) Mitchell County

gonter, gont see **go**, A. 4.

gone up see **go up (the spout)**

goober *noun* A peanut. [*DARE* of African origin; widespread, but chiefly Southeast, Lower Mississippi Valley, Southwest]

Oct. 20, 1861: I have not seen any thing a growing here but **goobers** and yam potatoes. (William Featherston, Love Papers, Duke) Henderson County

Dec. 18, 1863: I think it uncertain a bout our Staying hear Long as we are two fare from the Rail Road & Every thing high. meal 1.00 Dol a qt. **gubers** 1.00 qt. Apples 2 to 4.00 Dol Doz. Paper 3 to 5.00 Dollars pr quire & Every thing Els high &c. (James Ennis, Carpenter Family Papers, ECU) Wake County

goober pea *noun* A peanut. [*DARE* chiefly South Midland]

Feb. 26, 1863: me and B H Wood has Concluded to Stay durin the ware and after the war is over then marry a rich widow [in] South Carelina Whar we Can mak Cotton and S[w]eet patatoes and **guber pees**. (Isaac Copeland, Copeland Letters, NCSA) Surry County

June 15, 1863: there is 5 or 6 suttler Stores in Sight of where we are and we can get 5 onions to the Dollar and we can By cake and cider and **Goober peas**. (William Tesh, Tesh Papers, Duke) Yadkin County

good eal, goodeel *noun phrase* A considerable amount; variant forms of *good deal;* see also **great eal**.

July 28, 1862: tha is a **good eal** sickness hear at this time. (Larkin Kendrick, Kendrick Papers, NCSA) Cleveland County

Sept. 14, 1862: there is a **goodeel** of Money counterfit. you all must be porticu[lar] in what sort of money you take. (James Zimmerman, Zimmerman Papers, Duke) Forsyth County

Nov. 6, 1862: if you Can or will Git me out of the army and let me go to making Shoes i should do **good eal** more Good and be more Benefit to the Confederacy. (Archibald Curlee, Vance Papers, NCSA) Union County

May 13, 1863: This is yankey paper I am writing on. we capterd A **good eal** of yankey paper. (Hardy Matthews, McLeod Letters, SHC) Moore County

go to *verb* To start to, begin, undertake; see Overview § II.4.7. [see *DSME* **go to**; see also *DARE* **go** verb, 2; scattered, but especially South, South Midland]

1. infinitive followed by a present participle.

July 31, 1862: I wish they wood **go to** fiting and fight evry Day tell the[y] was all Killed on one side or other. (L. W. Griffin, Griffin Papers, NCSA) Rutherford County

Dec. 6, 1863: my Socks has got holes in them. I wil have to **go to** nitting. (R. C. Caldwell, Caldwell Coll., ECU) Cabarrus County

Sept. 21, 1864: we have got our cane mill done and been fixing the furnace to day to **go to** making the molasses. (Huldah Hubbard, Hubbard Papers, Duke) Anson County

2. past tense followed by a present participle.

Feb. 6, 1863: the twelth Regt came up to our Regt in A line of battle. wee formed our Regt and **went to** fighting with snow balls. (J. F. Coghill, Coghill Papers, Duke) Granville County

Nov. 30, 1864: they **went to** plundering the house so aunt Betsy had her specia in a matteras. (Ann Bowen, Bowen Papers, NCSA) Washington County

3. with an infinitive.

Dec. 29, 1861: every time I **go to** draw a long breath I can hear them tear So if you are very plenty of cloth you may make me another pair and Send to me but make them larger round, they are long anough. (Robert M. Blair, Blair Letters, NCSA) Caldwell County

Mar. 19, 1863: I hope you will remember me when you **go to** eat. (John Futch, Futch Letters, NCSA) New Hanover County

May 1, 1863: Pap if you and Elyzabeth **goes to** git maried you must Let me no it in time to giv you an ansuer. (Jesse Shipman, Shipman Family Corr., Notre Dame) Henderson County

go to the army *verb phrase* To enlist; to be conscripted.

Mar. 16, 1863: I do hope and trust to god that you wont hafte **go to the armey** for I dont want aney more of my friends and relashen to go aney more. (Noah Wike, Setzer Papers, Duke) Catawba County

Oct. 16, 1863: the latter part of last Septeber my husband was conscripted. he **went to the army** with out a murmer leving me and 5 small Children and my widowed sister with 5 and two of my other Sisters one with 5 and the other 1 and my brothers wife with 7 and his brothers wife 6. his mother and two sisters thier husbans had volenteered and he was all the dependence tell he was conscripted. (Pattie Vernon, Vance Papers, NCSA) Rockingham County

Nov. 13, 1864: let me now how you are coming on since pap has **gone to the army**. rite me all of the news in the kneighbor hood. (J. H. Baker, J. H. Baker Letters, Duke) Rockingham County

Dec. 8, 1864: I would like to here from all the neighbors whoe all has to **go to the army** yet &c &c. and what the People say about this war. by now here in the army the most of the soldiers say tha wont fight an other compaign. (John Peterson, Peterson Papers, Duke) Catawba County

go to the war *verb phrase* To enlist; to be conscripted.

Aug. 8, 1863: I want you rite to me and tel me whoo all has to **go to the war**. I hard frank deel had to go and I hard that non wouldent go. tha would di at home before tha would go and that is the way that I would doo if I was back agane. I never would leave mi home no more to go to such a war like this whar thar is no justus in nothing her. (Daniel Setzer, Setzer Papers, Duke) Catawba County

May 4, 1864: I think you dun righ not cinon [= Signing] Mcgines paper. let him **go to the war**. thats is where he ot [= ought] to be. (R. C. Caldwell, Caldwell Coll., ECU) Cabarrus County

go to the yankees *verb phrase* Of a Confederate soldier: to desert to the enemy.

Aug. 13, 1862: I saw a Site yesterday that I never saw before nor I never want to see no more. I saw a man Shot for deserting and trying to **go to the yankes.** they Shot 5 balls threw him. the werd he sed is this. I am now on the field of execution. you are going to see abrave irishman di. good by gentleme[n]. (Neill McLeod, McLeod Letters, SHC) Moore County

Jan. 24, 1864: there was five from Co. A and one of Co. C. Deserted last monday night and I sopose **went to the yankees**. (J. A. Smith, J. A. Smith Papers, Duke) Cabarrus County

Dec. 8, 1864: the Soldiers purty much all begin to think its all a useless Job some Swar tha wont fight no more. there is a good many **going to the yankies** every night when the are on picket. (John Peterson, Peterson Papers, Duke) Catawba County

Mar. 20, 1865: Dear Mother this is a hard world to live in. I cant live this way any longer. Dear Mother I am **agoing [to] the yankees.** this is the last leter that I will rite home meby forever. (Carr Setzer, Setzer Papers, Duke) Catawba County

go up *verb* To be ruined or lost; to be defeated; see Overview § II.4.7.

July 16, 1863: we under Stood that vicks Burg had **went up** and we got orders to Return Back to Jackson. (J. W. Reese, Reese Papers, Duke) Buncombe County

Aug. 27, 1863: it is thout by Some that E Tenn is to be given up to the yanks. if this is So or they take it western N.C. is gon allso Charleston SC. has or will **go up** & I supose it is to be burnd. (Stephen Whitaker, Whitaker Papers, NCSA) Cherokee County

Jan. 19, 1865: I think the Confedercy is about **gon up**. I think thee yank Will make us say it yet. if they air a going to Wip us I dont cair how quick for I think Wee hav had War a nough. (G. W. Love, Love Papers, Duke) Henderson County

Feb. 26, 1865: it looks like the confedercy is **gone up** to evry bodey in the armey at this time. (Henry Bowen, Bowen Papers, NCSA) Washington County

go up the spout *idiomatic expression* To die, perish, be ruined, lost. [compare with *DARE* **gone up**, adjective phrase; **flue, go up the** and **flume, go up the**]

Mar. 22, 1864: thay Will all doo aney thing that Old Jeff Davis wants them to doo But I fear that the confedercy will **go up the Spout** this Summer. (Isaac Copeland, Copeland Papers, NCSA. Surry County

July 24, 1864: Jim i have bin on every raid at the yankees has maid this summer but I tell you I come dam nigh **going up the spout**. it has bin the heardest campaign i ever hav bin in. (T. B. Litten, Robinson Papers, Duke) Catawba County

Oct. 18, 1864: if he dont bring me something iwill be **gon up the Spout** for they ar giving ous lofe bread & not half anuff. (L. W. Griffin, Griffin Papers, NCSA) Rutherford County

ND [1865]: here the[y] have one Dollar for washing one Shirt or one pair of Drawers, that look like this confederacy is **a going up the spout**. money is hard to get holt of and after a man gets it he cant by nothing with it, this ware canot last longer than till Spring I Dont think. (W. D. Smith, W. D. Smith Papers, Duke) Davie County

go with *verb* To happen to, become of; in interrogative clauses following *what;* see Overview § II.4.7.

Sept. 21, 1863: I heard the gard had taken up Jesse J Bull. I wonder what they will do with him. What has **gone with** Hump Noris. has the gard got him to[o] I reckon Noah Brookshir has taken to the brush again. (William Walsh, Proffit Family Letters, SHC) Wilkes County

Jan. 5, 1864: you wanted to know a bout James Clothing what he left in camp. I cwooden [= couldn't] find out what **wente with** them. (A. J. Spease, Zimmerman Papers, Duke) Forsyth County

graft *verb* To dig; to hoe or cultivate. [*EDD* **graft** verb[2], *OED* **graft** verb[2]]

July 9, 1861: You said you wanted [me] to be with you to **graft** corn. I am goin to **graft** Old Abe befoor I take my station at hom. (G. T. Beavers, Upchurch Papers, Duke) Chatham County

grain *noun* A very small amount, a bit (perhaps from the unit of measure *grain,* traditionally the smallest unit of weight). [see *OED* **grain**, noun[1], 8 and 9]

Feb. 10, 1865: milt phillips is back and well and all rite. they nevr punished him one **grain**. (R. C. Love, Love Papers, Duke) Henderson County

grancer see **grandsire**

granddaddy *noun* Grandfather; see Overview § I.1.1.

Feb. 6, 1862: Jackson Stapp sends his best Respects and he wants you to tell **grandady** and Grany howdy for mee and all the rest of his friends. (J. A. Shipman, Shipman Family Corr., Notre Dame) Henderson County

grandma, grandmar *noun* Grandmother; see Overview § I.1.1.

Apr. 21, 1864: Ma sends you & Aunt hanner & all her Best Love & Ma Said give her Love to our good old **grandma** & Pa. (Elias Peterson, Peterson Papers, Duke) Burke County

July 24, 1864: give my love to **Grand Mar** and all the family and except a potion for you self give Aunt Sallie and all of her little children my love. (Cassie Davenport, Hundley Family Letters, SHC) Stokes County

grandpa, grandpar *noun* Grandfather; see Overview § I.1.1.

Apr. 21, 1864: give my Love to grandm[a] & **grandpa.** tell them I often think of them. (Elias Peterson, Peterson Papers, Duke) Burke County

July 24, 1864: Aunt Sue as I have bin writing to **Grand Par** I thought I would write you afew lines. Aunt Sue I want you to come down hear and stay with me a month. (Cassie Davenport, Hundley Family Letters, SHC) Stokes County

grandpap *noun* Grandfather; see Overview § I.1.1.

Nov. 24, 1864: you can keep the wagon in repare. there is a little ring off of one of the axel Spindels. get **gran pap** to put one on and new linch pins. you must tend to the greasing it. (John Peterson, Peterson Papers, Duke) Catawba County

grandpappy *noun* Grandfather; see Overview § I.1.1.

May 23, 1862: I drop you theas few lines to inform you that I am not well and has not bn for Severl weeks hoping theas few lines m[a]y find you and **granpappy** Well. (Joseph Cowand, Cowand Papers, Duke) Bertie County

grandsire *noun* Grandfather. [*DARE* chiefly New England, South Midland]

Jan. 12, 1862: I want you to take my Sone down to his **grancers** and let him Sea him. (Evin Smith, E. Smith Papers, Duke) Stanley County

granny *noun*

1. Grandmother; see Overview § I.1.1.

Sept. 7, 1862: well **grany** I Seat my self down to drop you afew lines to let yow now that I am well at present hoping when theas few lines comes to hand they find you enjoying the Same Kind blessing. (W. H. Brotherton, Brotherton Papers, Duke) Catawba County

May 3, 1864: Dear wife I Recd a letter from Rockett also last Night. they sent me alittle somthing to eat. it come very good for we got but Short Rations hear. give them my thankes for it. I will Say to you that Sister Sarah and old **granny** Barges Sent me a haversack of Something to eat Some time a go. (Isaac Lefevers, Lefevers Papers, NCSA) Catawba County

2. A midwife. [*DARE* chiefly South, South Midland]

May 3, 1863: I Can inform you that Conne Miller has got A nother big son an he was the **graney** him self. (Keziah Hefner, Hefner Papers, NCSA) Catawba County

grape *noun* An artillery projectile consisting of small, strongly connected iron balls; short form of *grapeshot*.

Jan. 11, 1863: I had 50 men & my self & Lt. Anderson. all of my boys with but little exception acted bravely. I must confess that I am not as brave as I thought I was. I never wanted out of a place as bad in my life. the balles hailed the shells sung & the **grape** rattled. I want in nomore Battles. the last day of 1862 will long be remembered by many of us. (A. W. Bell, Bell Papers, Duke) Macon County

July 5, 1863: the yank **throud** grape and canister at us. (J. W. Lineberger, *Gaston Ranger,* 55) Gaston County

grassnut *noun* An edible tuber native to North America. [*DARE* **grassnut**, noun; South, South Midland; see also *OED* **nut grass**, noun]

Dec. 8, 1862: I would be very glad if you could bring me some molases or honey, some butter, some good old ham, a little salt, and some Sweet cakes for christmas and some ground peas, **grassnuts**, chestnuts &c. (C. A. Hege, Hege Papers, MHI) Davidson County

grass widow *noun* An unmarried mother; a divorced woman. [see *DARE* **grass widow**, noun, 1, "A woman Separated from her husband, either permanently or temporarily, for some reason other than death. *Somewhat old-fash,*" and 2, "An unmarried mother"]

Mar. 2, 1859: I hope you will not unite in wedlock to the **grass widow** without letting me know it. (John W. McGregor, Jackson Family Corr., Notre Dame) Moore County

gravel *noun* An abscess on a horse's hoof. [*OED* **gravel**, verb, 5; **gravelling**, noun, 2]

Oct. 24, 1864: I dont know what is the matter with him unless it is the **gravil**. (Huldah Hubbard, Hubbard Papers, Duke) Anson County

great eal, gradeal, grateel *noun phrase* A large amount; variant forms of *great deal*. See also **good eal**. [see *OED* **deal,** noun[1], 3]

Feb. 14, 1862: we hav had a bad time of hit. ther was a **gradeal** of the yankes kild and a bout too hundred of ou[r] men. (E. M. Phillips, Phillips Papers, Duke) Robeson County

Nov. 4, 1862: he has had his back nearly brok by a fall and that injures him a **great eal** at times. (Cass A. Marlow, Vance Papers, NCSA) Wilkes County

June 2, 1864: you wood try to do the best you could an recommended me to doo the best I could fore my scelf. that hope [= helped] my feleing a **grateel**. (A. S. Harrill, Civil War Coll., TSLA) Rutherford County

Nov. 15, 1864: I no you See a **great eal** of troble a bout the yankes takeen plymouth. (Henry Bowen, Bowen Papers, NCSA) Washington County

green *adjective*

1. Of people: inexperienced, lacking knowledge. [*OED* **green**, adjective, 8.c.]

   Nov. 6, 1862: i am young and **green** about the law in these Criticle times. (Archibald Curlee, Vance Papers, NCSA) Union County

2. Of hides: uncured, not tanned. [*OED* **green**, adjective, 6.b.]

   Feb. 12, 1864: wash o[w]ed me for two hids I took there when he was drunk and tha wasent charge on his Books. him and MC colby was both dronk and he ode me fore 12 Bushels of cotin Seeds. the hides and Seeds was worth 8 or ten dolars. the hides wold [have] waid about 65 pounds **green**. (R. C. Caldwell, Caldwell Coll., ECU) Cabarrus County

greenback *noun* A piece of paper currency issued by the U.S. Treasury, not Confederate currency or currency issued by states or by banks; typically in the singular form regardless of amount.

Oct. 21, 1864: I will tel you what I capturd. I got a pocket book with 44 dollars of **green back** and a nap sack and a blanket and a good oil chloth and pare of boots and severl other little tricks and little pocket knife. (Jesse Hill, Hill Letters, NCSA) Forsyth

Nov. 18, 1864: I will enclose one dollar in **green Back** to you. it will help you a little to pay poastage. (Adaline Zimmerman, Zimmerman Papers, Duke) Forsyth County

green bean *noun* Any of several varieties of cultivated bean eaten in the pod; formerly a Midland term in contrast with Northern *string bean* and Southern *snap bean*. [*DARE* widespread, but less frequent New England, South]

May 31, 1863: I saw corn in silk and Tasels and I saw lots of wheat cut and in shocks and som stacked and as we com on the steam boat. I eat my diner on the Boat and I had **green Beens** fish Boild ham soop &c. I only paid two Dollars for it. (W. B. Lance, Lance Papers, LSU) Henderson County

June 7, 1863: it is as hot hear now as I Ever Saw it in Bun comb in August. thair is **green Beenes**. pees is A Baut dun Bairing and Cuw Cumbers and Corne is silking and tasling. (J. W. Reese, Reese Papers, Duke) Buncombe County

grits *noun* Cereal made with corn meal. [*DARE* chiefly South, South Midland, especially South Atlantic, Gulf States]

Mar. 26, 1863: ouer meal is so coarse that we make **grits** out of A part of ouer Rashings. (J. W. Reese, Reese Papers, Duke) Buncombe County

ground pea *noun* A peanut. [*DARE* chiefly South Atlantic]

Oct. 7, 1862: I want you to dig my **ground peas** and grass nuts and send me a few of them. (C. A. Hege, Hege Papers, MHI) Davidson County

grow *verb* past participle and adjective *growed, groad, grode*.

June 22, 1863: I did not now of her haven enny small children with hur. she has one girl that is a bout **growed** that she had By hur husband. (Isaac Lefevers, Lefevers Papers, NCSA) Catawba County

Aug. 11, 1863: the baby has not **groad** much since yow have bin gon. it has bin mity puney this summar and is yet. (Mary Kinsland, Kinsland Letter, UGA) Haywood County

Jan. 20, 1864: Dare love yore little sweete babe has **grode** So much youe Woldent no hir. (Susan Setzer, Setzer Papers, Duke) Catawba County

Aug. 7, 1864: tell Letty francis she must send word if she has **groad** any cince I left home. I am agoing to send Mary Etter [and] Letty a pretty flower a peace in this leter. tell Letty she must take Care of hern un till I come home. (J. W. Joyce, Joyce Papers, MHI) Stokes County

grub up *verb* To dig with a heavy hoe (*grub hoe*) in order to clear roots from *newground* or to harvest potatoes; see Overview § II.4.7. [see *DSME* **grub, grub off, grub out, grub up** verb, verb phrase]

April 4, 1864: I would like to be there and see you and plant corn and patatoes. I want you to plant patoes plenty. for I think I will be <there in?> time to **grubb** them **up**. (J. W. Love, Love Papers, Duke) Henderson County

gum see **bee gum**

gun lock *noun* A part of the firing mechanism for a flintlock or percussion lock firearm, consisting of a steel sideplate, the hammer, and a spring and catch mechanism, which releases the hammer when the trigger is pulled.

Nov. 29, 1862: I sent a Cartrige box, cap box, **Gun lock** and several other little things that I brought from the Maryland battle ground that I hope you will keep untill I come home. (C. A. Hege, Hege Papers, MHI) Davidson County

guinea *noun* A type of domestic fowl with speckled plumage, *Numida meleagris*.

May 18, 1863: Tell Mary & Julius to write all about affairs at home whether they go to sunday school yet or not and how many little ducks, chickens and **guinies** you have. (C. A. Hege, Hege Papers, MHI) Davidson County

H

habersack *noun* A canvas bag with a strap, worn over the shoulder and used for carrying rations and personal items; variant form of *haversack*. [*OED* **haversack**, noun, a. (from French *havresac*, which is from German *habersack*)]

May 26, 1862: wee dismounted 2 of our cavaldry Cos. and fierd on them and they evacuated a little town 12 miles this side of Neuborn and wee went next day and found Kanteens Belts **habersacks** and other thing too numerous to menchon. (J. A. Shipman, Shipman Family Corr., Notre Dame) Henderson County

May 21, 1864: i rote aletter to you by D burnet. i sent Some little things by him to you. i sent my gloves and cap. 1 hammer. 1 bottle of powder. 1 belt and capbox and capts 2 Papers, of cotridge. Some indigo seede. one case knife. half quire of paper and some envalopes and Some ons but one dollars worth of stamps. 2 pen points. i sode them up in my **habber sack**. (Silas Stepp, Stepp Letters, UNCA) Buncombe County

hack *noun* A carriage for hire; short form of *hackney*. [*OED* **hack**, noun[3], 2]

Jan. 12, 1862: I write you a few lines as I am here to night on my way to Raleigh. Will take the **Hack** at 5 Oclock in the morning & will be gone a week or 10 day. (A. W. Bell, Bell Papers, Duke) Macon County

hafter *auxiliary verb* variant form of *have to*.

Mar. 16, 1863: if you do **hafter** go I ad vis you to join the calvary. (Noah Wike, Setzer Papers, Duke) Catawba County

Apr. 20, 1863: dear brother if you **hafter** come to the army i want you to come to my company. dear brother our rashens is Short an the meat we **hafter** eat is old an rotten at that. (Henry Keever, Keever Papers, Duke) Lincoln County

Mar. 7, 1864: mi foot is Sweld So much that I cant git mi Shoo on. I hant had mi Shoo on in too weeks. I made me a shoo out of cloth that I ware. I think it will **hafter** bee opend at mi ankel. (Daniel Setzer, Setzer Papers, Duke) Catawba County

haint, hant *verb* negative contraction of forms of *have* and *be*.

1. *haven't, hasn't*. [CACWL data indicate this form was very widespread in the mid-nineteenth century; *DARE* chiefly Northeast, South, South Midland, especially Appalachians]

July 16, 1861: We **haint** lost many men out of our Company yet and I hope that We will all live to git home again. (Peter Poteet, Poteet-Dickson Letters, NCSA) Burke County

Nov. 3, 1862: toliver nor clinton nor nun of them **hant** gote mee astick of wood sense you left home. (Sarepta Revis, Revis Letters, NCSA) Henderson County

Oct. 27, 1863: I am nearley Bar footted and my old Britches is to the patch and **hant** Bin washt sence I left home. (J. W. Reese, Reese Papers, Duke) Buncombe County

Jan. 7, 1864: the children is sick with bad colds and I **haint** seen a well day since you left. (Martha Poteet, Poteet-Dickson Letters, NCSA) McDowell County

2. am not.

Jan. 11, 1863: I Cant rite to day. I **hant** in the rit fix for riting. I wold like to rite you along letter but I am plum upside down to day. (John Hartman, Hartman Papers, Duke) Rowan County

3. isn't, aren't.

Oct. 13, 1862: their **haint** no chance to get a Furlow now unless a man be sick. (William Tesh, Tesh Papers, Duke) Yadkin County

July 25, 1864: thare **hant** no youse in giting out of hart. all we haf to do is think this ware wont last fore every. (Lewis Moore, Moore Letter, CACWL) Cumberland County

Oct. 6, 1864: dont greave your self no more then you can help for all dangers **hant** death. (Henry Bowen, Bowen Papers, NCSA) Washington County

halvers *noun plural* Half shares (see citation). [*DARE* scattered but especially South, South Midland]

Sept. 27, 1863: Dear husband I will hav the stalk [= stock] grond Soad in wheat an will gether the corn as sone as it will bear gethern and hav the grond soad in wheat. manuel Spegle wanted me to find [= supply] the wheat and let him So [= sow] it and go **havers** but I will hav it sode mi self. (Catherine Lefevers, Lefevers Papers, NCSA) Catawba County

ham of meat *noun phrase* A cured (i.e., salted or smoked) ham.

ND [1862]: I have wrote home what I wanted but I will [do] it agane. I want 2 or 3 galens of brandy and 15 or 20 pound of butter and a bout 2 galens of molases and about 2 **hames of meat.** some drid fruit and drid beanes gren aples. some unions and Some Sweet bred and if Paw has Kiled his hoges they have any saseges I want a mess or 2. (J. S. Councill, Councill Papers, Duke) Watauga County

Aug. 9, 1862: I Saved nothing but the apples cow-cumbers an the corn meal an **ham of meet**. (J. W. Williams, Williams Papers, Duke) Onslow County

Nov. 4, 1863: I wont some more honey comb and butter irish and sweet potatoes. a few cakes. a small sack flour. B F sends for meal and molasses. you please send a **ham of meat** for us 3. (J. M. Frank, Frank Papers, Duke) Davidson County

Feb. 4, 1864: I sent you somthing to eat by Marion Higins five pies and five ginger Cakes one doz unions two custerds 1 **ham of Meat** and three twists of tobaco. (Martha Poteet, Poteet-Dickson Letters, NCSA) McDowell County

hand *noun* A laborer, farm worker; a slave.

July 5, 1856: I got through towo hundred an 10 acres before harvest then spared all the **hands** to Moses at Belgrade. (Henry [Pettigrew slave], Pettigrew Family Papers, SHC) Washington County

Feb. 26, 1862: If you cant come now you will never have a better chance this year and If you will come and you can get a **hand** to plow for you while you air comen. I will pay the time you loose own the road. (Isaac Lefevers, Lefevers Papers, NCSA) Catawba County

Apr. 27, 1863: I have got Receipts how to make Soap of all Sorts I can make one Barrel of Soft Soap Every day and with Some **hands** I can make Eny amount required. (J. Caddell, Vance Papers, NCSA) Robeson County

Jan. 30, 1864: I hope that you have your **hand** at Work. it is A purty time for plowing I hope that you will keep her at work to earn her bord. (Marcus Hefner, Hefner Papers, NCSA) Catawba County

handsome *adjective* superlative form *han(d)somist.*

Aug. 10, 1861: we are at Camp wigfall one mile from manassa in a most **Hansomist** place you Ever saw sur rounded by mountains large Clover fields And Bact by a Great number of Southern Soldiers Large stout & well Drilled men. (W. R. D. Bost, Gibson Papers, Duke) Catawba County

hand's turn *noun* A helping hand, assistance; perhaps also a quantity of cornmeal or other commodity (see citation). [*DARE* **hand's turn** noun, 1; see also *DSME* **turn** noun, 2]

July 13, 1863: there is Men plenty in the Cuntry that is Surrounded with Ever thing plenty and wont help apore woman to one **hands turn**. (William Martin, Vance Papers, NCSA) Burke County

hankering *noun* A desire or craving.

Nov. 10, 1862: send me somting good Eat for I have a power full **hankern** aftera Change of food if you want to send me a small Box send it by Express to weldon NC. (Dinson Caldwell, Caldwell Coll., ECU) Cabarrus County

hankering *adjective* Desirous, wishful.

Apr. 17, 1859: I am a giting affrad that I will Merry for I have taken a sort of **hankering** notion after the girls for thare has been somany Weedings in this Neighborhood laterley. (Enoch Garner, Jackson Family Corr., Notre Dame) Davidson County

hant see **haint**

happen to *verb* To encounter, meet with, chance to; see Overview § II.4.7. [*EDD* **happen** verb[1], 2; *DARE* chiefly South Midland]

Nov. 16, 1856: I **hapend to** A little of good luck one tim in my life. in the time of the Indaan ware I was in the sirves about 20 years ago and I have Jest reseived my land warnt [= warrant] for my sirveses. (Stephen Phillips, Phillips Papers, Duke) Robeson County

Aug. 9, 1862: I **hapened to** bad Luck with my bag of pervision. the Chickings was wroten for thair was magets in them. an the pies was sower an broke all to peices an the sweet cakes was in the same fix. (J. W. Williams, Williams Papers, Duke) Onslow County

hard cider *noun* Apple cider that has been allowed to ferment so that it has alcoholic content, as opposed to non-alcoholic cider **sweet cider**. [*OED* **hard**, adjective, 14.c., "Intoxicating, spirituous, 'strong,' *colloq.* orig. *U.S.*"]

June 8, 1863: I received a letter from my wife last week Stating that the deserters had come to hir House one night prised off one corner of the roof of the Smoke House went in drawn as much **hard Sider** as they wanted. taken 16 or 18 of the largest peaces of Bacon they could pick out. (James Tyson, Vance Papers, NCSA) Randolph County

hardly *adverb* used with redundant negative, often following the verb. [*DARE* chiefly South, South Midland]

Jan. 15, 1863: I had A verry hard spell of Tyfoid Fever last Winter spring and summer. I got no corn planted **hardly**. (B. B. Marley, Vance Papers, NCSA) Randolph County

Feb. 15, 1863: he has to by Some provision for they dont get any thing to eat **hardly** down there. (Mary H. Williams, Vance Papers, NCSA) Wake County

Feb. 15, 1863: thare is famileys that cant git bread to Eat **hardley**. (E. D. Hawkins, Vance Papers, NCSA) Rutherford County

hard road to travel *noun phrase* Figuratively: a very difficult task. [from the popular minstrel song "Jordan Is a Hard Road to Travel" and the Confederate version "Richmond Is a Hard Road to Travel"]

Mar. 1864: the yankees is said to be leaving E Tennessee and going around to try and take Richmond but I think Richmond will be a **hard road to travel**. (C. A. Walker, Walker Papers, WCU) Cherokee County

June 18, 1864: the yankes wold a taken the Sity of lynch birg but I think thay will have a **hard rode to travil** the balance of the way though thay may get thair yet. (J. W. Joyce, Joyce Papers, MHI) Stokes County

hard run *adjective phrase* Hard pressed, lacking in (necessities).

May 6, 1864: we have more men & beter armes than we have ever had since the war began. I know Provisions is [s]carce & we will be **hard run** for Rations but we can live on one fourth of what we have bin uset to eating. (Stephen Whitaker, Whitaker Papers, NCSA) Cherokee County

hard-sided *adjective* Conservative, unyielding in religious beliefs; variant form of *hard-shell (Baptist)*. [see *DARE* **hard-shell**, adjective, 2]

Jan. 21, 1865: you know how **hardsided** she is and you know it is a dangers belief. she cant live many years longer at most and sight her to god who is able to save and make her piece with god to meet her children. (Ann Bowen, Bowen Papers, NCSA) Washington County

harn see **hear**

hash *noun* A mixture of spices and pieces of meat from a hog's head. [*DARE* South, South Midland]

Dec. 22, 1861: this is Sunday and I suppose you are in Salsbury today. bring sage and onions So we Can make **hash**. (James W. Gibson, Gibson Papers, Duke) Catawba County

Jan. 17, 1863: If Henry comes I want him to fetch me a Box of provision. I want sosedg inpoticlar & some good sower [= sour] souse. I Recken you will have now [= no] **hash** to send. you nead not send much Pork for fear it may be that we will have to move & then I could not take it. (Isaac Lefevers, Lefevers Papers, NCSA) Catawba County

hate *verb* To regret, be sorry that. [*DARE* Kentucky, Tennessee, Ozarks]

Mar. 16, 1864: tel dock to take good cear of his little dog and all the rest of his Stock. I **hated** the little sheep all dide. I was in hopes we would hav a good Stock. (Jesse Hill, Hill Letters, NCSA) Forsyth County

have *verb* and *auxiliary verb*

1. *has* with a plural or conjoined noun subject.

Apr. 13, 1862: severel of us boyes **has** mad a box and pact it full of close a blankets and sent it to states vill. (Jonas Bradshaw, Bradshaw Papers, Duke) Alexander County

Aug. 14, 1862: there is so many that wants to come home before they leave and a good many that **has** not been at home atall saince they have been down here. (James Zimmerman, Zimmerman Papers, Duke) Forsyth County

Dec. 27, 1862: the news was yester day that the yankeys **has** druv our troops Back seven mils. (J. W. Reese, Reese Papers, Duke) Buncombe County

June 4, 1863: you and mother **has** lived & been highly blessed for a number of years although the days of trouble are now on us. (A. J. Proffit, Proffit Family Letters, SHC) Wilkes County

Apr. 16, 1864: I can say to you that the ded **has** come to life for my Dear Nat has come Home. (Sally Bauldin, Hundley Family Letters, SHC) Stokes County

2. *has* with a non-adjacent pronoun subject.

Feb. 6, 1863: they are still on the other side and **has** made and attemped to cross but made A failure and the next time I expect it will be the same case. (J. F. Coghill, Coghill Papers, Duke) Granville County

May 13, 1863: we have had a hard march to get heer and **has** had more rivers to waid than i ever saw. (Daniel Revis, Revis Letters, NCSA) Henderson County

3. *has* with an adjacent pronoun subject.

Apr. 25, 1863: I **has** to gow down thare evry day with mi squads wrashings [= rations] to them. we daunt draw but one day at a time sow we **has** to gow evry day. (B. C. Jackson, Jackson Family Corr., Notre Dame) Moore County

June 25, 1863: I was wounded in the Battle of Sharpsburg with a fragment of a Shell. it hit me near my Sholder & loddged near my lungs. it is so deep it cant be extracted. I **has** nearly lost the use of my arm. (Kenneth McDonald, Vance Papers, NCSA) Moore County

Jan. 1866: in a time of the great Rebelion we Ether had to be puled in this or escape for our lives. we then inlisted at Plymout NC nerly 2 years ago. we **has** bin doing duty a round Newburn and a very short time ago we was all regler discarge. (John Bizzell, *Freedom,* ser. 2: 801) Hertford County

Dec. 1870: Sir I was a volentery Sirlder in 1862. [I] inlested under Capt Crass incruting oficer in Newbren NC Craveing Co an I never **has** Rece[ved] Eny Bounty yeat. Nether eny Back pay Sir all tho I had the promoust of bounty an all so back pay. (Charles Jones, *Freedom,* ser. 2: 798) Craven County

4. *have* with a third-person singular subject.

Dec. 15, 1864: Mistress your Letter are all very hard to Read by any Person exept Mr Burr or Dr John Swann. any Person that **have** been acquainted with you can Read it. as for me I Cant make out but very few Words of it and it very often Puzzils Mr Burr. (Anderson Henderson, Henderson Papers, SHC) Rowan County

5. *haves* with a first-person singular subject.

Dec. 15, 1864: Mistres I **haves** an oppartinity of sending your Flannel and I thought I Would doe so as you might Wish to make it up before Christmas. (Anderson Henderson, Henderson Papers, SHC) Rowan County

havers see **halvers**

haversack see **habersack**

have to see **hafter**

head see **on one's head**

heap *noun* A great deal, a large number. [*DARE* chiefly South, South Midland]

Oct. 29, 1861: I wish I could see you. Wee could have a **heep** of good fun. (Elizabeth Watson, Watson Letters, WCU) Jackson County

June 24, 1863: I Have Seen a **Heap** of trouble in my life But never Had nothing to Hurt me as Bad in my life. (Sally Bauldin, Hundley Family Letters, SHC) Stokes County

Aug. 2, 1863: i want to come home to sea you Mity bad. i have got a **heap** of talk for you if you i cod sea you. (John Futch, Futch Letters, NCSA) New Hanover County

May 31, 1864: we hav lost a **heep** of men and kild a **heep** of yankeys. (J. W. Reese, Reese Papers, Duke) Buncombe County

Nov. 1864: they knock down men & take ther Box & money from them they kill a **heap** of them. thar is a **heap** of danger in passing thro the town. (L. W. Griffin, Griffin Papers, NCSA) Rutherford County

heap *adverb* Very much, a great deal.

July 31, 1862: very hot her in at this time. I think **heape** hoter then thar. (L. W. Griffin, Griffin Papers, NCSA) Rutherford County

Nov. 29, 1862: my throat has not got well yet but it is a **heap** better that it has bin. (J. T. Revis, Revis Letters, NCSA) Henderson County

hearn (also *hern, hirn, harn*) *verb* variant past tense, past participle of *hear*. [*DARE* chiefly South, South Midland]

Aug. 14, 1862: we had orders to march and he coulten kep up and so the Capt sent him & I hante **hern** from him sense. (Austin Brown, Brown Family Papers, Duke) Johnston County

Sept. 29, 1862: O how glad was I and how I felt when I **hearn** houdey from my littel Children. God Bless them. (J. W. Reese, Reese Papers, Duke) Buncombe County

Mar. 26, 1863: I have **hirn** from the 59 regiment. tha had not got back to camp but none of my brothers did not go. (Martha Futch, Futch Letters, NCSA) New Hanover County

July 25, 1863: I hope you will allow me one other white man to assist me at my Mills as the Negroes are ofting going off to yankees. there is no dependence to put in them for one that hope [= helped] attend to the Mills last year left and I have not **hearn** from him since. (Jesse Brown, Vance Papers, NCSA) Edgecombe County

Nov. 27, 1864: if you have **harn** from langley wright to us. we have knot **harn** from him si[n]ce he levt home. (Rhoda Bateman, Bowen Papers, NCSA) Washington County

hear say *verb* To hear, learn by word of mouth; see Overview § II.4.7. [*OED* **hear**, verb, 3.b.]

Jan. 15, 1863: I have **herd Sed** that you was as good a man as every lived or died. (Catherine Hunt, Vance Papers, NCSA) Randolph County

hear tell of *verb* To hear about, learn of, learn by word of mouth; see Overview § II.4.7. [*DARE* chiefly South, South Midland]

Mar. 23 1858: I can in form you that I have not saw a sick purson ner **herd tel of** any won a bean [= being] sick sence I hav ben in Missouri. (David Headrick, Frank Papers, Duke) Davidson County

Feb. 2, 1862: I shod like to **heare tell of** pease bean [= being] maid but still I wod drother bea a Solger than to live under old Abe Lincoln administration. (L. L. Kale, Fisher Papers, Duke) Catawba County

July 12, 1862: I have been in A battle sence I wrote to you it was the hardest fight that I ever **heard tell of**. (J. W. Williams, Williams Papers, Duke) Onslow County

June 4, 1863: I havent mutch to write about ware & I have bin in the ware and Saw the ware and **heard tell of** the ware till I have got tired of it. if I Could get clear of this ware I neve[r] want to Read of A nother. (Joel Howard, Brotherton Papers, Duke) Lincoln County

heart pleurisy *noun* A medical condition caused by inflammation of the pleura, the lining surrounding the lungs; symptoms include stabbing chest pains, especially when coughing.

June 18, 1863: i am not fit for camp lif let alon the duty of the man for i hav Bin gevin to **hart pluricey** and the consuption and i am fity [= subject to fits] By Spells 4 or 5 tims in a weeck. this i have haid for the last 8 or 10 years now. you now that a man that is so plegued is not fit for sirves. (Bluford Lucas, Vance Papers, NCSA) Harnett County

heel irons *noun plural* Flat, horseshoe-shaped iron plates attached to the bottom of shoe heels for reinforcement and to help keep them from wearing out.

Nov. 3, 1862: I want you to have me a large strong and able pair of shoes made and have Rapers Michal to put **irons** on the **heels**. (C. A. Hege, Hege Papers, MHI) Davidson County

help *verb* See Overview § II.4.1.5.

1. variant infinitive and present tense form *hep.* [*DARE* chiefly South, South Midland]

Apr. 14, 1862: i will rite my one [= own] leters my self after this i dont now What the put in my leter if you get mad fore that i cannot **hep** that. (W. P. Cline, Cline Papers, SHC) Catawba County

Aug. 25, 1863: I think I see a harder time a hed than eny of us has yet Saw. I fer I Shall be too far off to **hep** you as I would wish to do in your old age. in fact the chances is as two to one that I will nevr see you again. (Stephen Whitaker, Whitaker Papers, NCSA) Cherokee County

2. past tense *hope.* [variant past tense and past participle form *hope,* from earlier English irregular past tense and past participle forms *holp, holpen;* see *OED* **help**, verb; *DARE* chiefly South, South Midland]

Mar. 10, 1862: I have gust closed our prare meeting. we had A good time of it for severl of the boys **hope** us to sing. (J. W. Williams, Williams Papers, Duke) Onslow County

Dec. 18, 1862: Miles Drum was Shot in his head above his tempel and lodged against the skin on tother side and I **hope** to bery him. (Marcus Hefner, Hefner Papers, NCSA) Catawba County

Apr. 23, 1864: I Staid at Mrs. Meeks last night and got Something good to eat and that **hope** me lots and this morning when I left Mrs. Meeks She give me Some flower and meat anough to last me and Daniel too days. (John Hartman, Hartman Papers, Duke) Rowan County

3. past participle *hope.*

June 12, 1862: If ever you can get the chance to ever send me a box I would you to put mee half or a galon of Whiskey in it. if I had a had a little this long march it would a **hope** mee a great deal. (Isaac Lefevers, Lefevers Papers, NCSA) Catawba County

July 31, 1862: I hate the name of secession for hit has ca[u]sed so meny to see truble when hit cood ben **hope** if they had atride. (L. W. Griffin, Griffin Papers, NCSA) Rutherford County

Feb. 23, 1863: I have Bin sorrow a menney a time that I did not take your advise a Bout comen out to the war But I was serten at the time I come out that I would Be Bound to come out But sow it is it cant Be **hope** now. (Isaac Lefevers, Lefevers Papers, NCSA) Catawba County

Oct. 30, 1864: i waus sorry to heer that Mr Mc Iver had to go to the armey but hit cant be **hope**. (Gorry Jackson, Jackson Family Corr., Notre Dame) Moore County

help *noun* variant form *hep.*

Oct. 7, 1861: tel Mart that I like to a hope him a Shuced his corn but I much drother a hope [= helped] the girls a cooked as you Say my **hep** would hav been very excepteable. (Harrison Hanes, Hanes Papers, Duke) Davie County

helpless *adjective* superlative form *helplessest.*

May 24, 1863: I want you to have a petetion drawn ~~that~~ stateing the necesisity of me at home and the helpliness of my family stateing that the are all girls and cant do any toward work or making a living any way. that I have the **helplessest** family of any one in the service. that my children are all small. (Daniel Murph, Murph Papers, Duke) Catawba County

Jan. 9, 1865: she would have slight chills and some times high fevers and ache so bad she couldent ly but a little while. she dident have pain but ache and sore. she was the **helplessest** person I ever saw. (Ann Bowen, Bowen Papers, NCSA) Washington County

helt *verb* variant past tense of *hold*. [*DARE* South, South Midland]

Aug. 14, 1862: we **helt** the battle field 2 days & then we Re treted back 15 miles. (Austin Brown, Brown Family Papers, Duke) Johnston County

Dec. 6, 1863: we **helt** the top of the Ridg tell ouer men had giv way on Boath Cides. (J. W. Reese, Reese Papers, Duke) Buncombe County

helt out see **hold out**

hern see **hearn**

hern *possessive pronoun* Hers. [*DARE* chiefly South, South Midland, New England]

Aug. 7, 1864: tell Letty francis she must send word if she has groad any cince I left home. I am agoing to send Mary Etter [and] Letty a pretty flower a peace in this leter. tell Letty she must take Care of **hern** un till I come home. (J. W. Joyce, Joyce Papers, MHI) Stokes County

Mar. 29, 1863: martha is wevin. she can weve three and fore yards a day. I think it is purty smart fore the first but she has got **hirn** out and wevin on a nother pece. (Catherine Ramsey, Futch Letters, NCSA) New Hanover County

hickory *noun* A switch or stick made from hickory or some other strong, pliable wood. [*DARE* **hickory** noun, B 2a; chiefly South, South Midland]

Sept. 29, 1862: two of them was taken up and fetcht back this morning. they formed a line of all the men here in camp and ran them threw and every man had a **hickory** and had to hit each of them one lick. (John Ingram, Ingram Papers, Duke) Forsyth County

hide-and-hoop *noun* A children's game similar to hide-and-seek; also called *hide-and-whoop*.

May 24, 1861: they was not prepared to fight & their only chance was in the activity of their Legs and the cunning art of playing **hide but not hoop**. (Rhoda Hawn, Peterson Papers, Duke) Catawba County

high *adjective* Tall.

Oct. 15, 1861: yesterday I was mesured how **high** then I was ask whare I was borned. how old and what was my occupacion. (J. W. Williams, Williams Papers, Duke) Onslow County

Dec. 15, 1864: our first lutenant is named Berry and he is a very fine man. he is six feet and a half **high**. he is a big man. (Henry Bowen, Bowen Papers, NCSA) Washington County

high *adverb* Heavily, richly. [perhaps *OED* **high**, adverb, 2.c.]

Dec. 2, 1864: the whiteaker heffer has a calf. she has a very nice larg bag. the red one two has a calf. I think if they were fed **high** they would be very good for milk. (Ann Bowen, Bowen Papers, NCSA) Washington County

high as *adjective phrase* Much as, many as. [*DSME* **high as**, adjective phrase]

Apr. 24, 1862: there is some companys that come hear after we did and have buried as **high as** 3 and 4 a Day. (Isaac Lefevers, Lefevers Papers, NCSA) Catawba County

Jan. 20, 1865: they ware Some men in richmond to day offord to bet as **high as** ahundred thusand dollers that the war wold be ended in fifteen days and I think theas men knows. Something about the matter. (John Hartman, Hartman Papers, Duke) Rowan County

highlow see take a **highlow**

hill *noun* A mound of earth in which seeds are planted. [*DARE* chiefly South]

June 1, 1864: i think you had had better have the barn field corn thind out to one grain in a**hill** and all the rest in the porest spots. it will year [= ear] better. (Silas Stepp, Stepp Letters, UNCA) Buncombe County

him *reflexive pronoun* Himself (as indirect object). [*DARE* chiefly South, South Midland]

Sept. 25, 1861: tell john hill when we boys comes the girls will not talk to him for thay think so much more of it solger then thay do of him that he will never get **him** A wife. (J. W. Williams, Williams Papers, Duke) Onslow County

hippen *noun* A baby's diaper. [*EDD* Scottish and northern dialect; *DARE* chiefly South, South Midland]

Apr. 2, 1865: he said the first thing when he got home Selena put him nurSing and wonderd what She would put him at the next time he went off and Staid awhile & come home. I wrote to him I dident know what unless She put him to washing **hipens**. (F. A. Bleckley, Bleckley Papers, Duke) Catawba County

hippo *verb* To be preoccupied with imaginary illness or unfounded fears; past participle and adjective *hippoed*. [see *DSME* **hippo**, verb]

Feb. 2, 1862: It apears that I dont write offtimes to you My Mollie. my dear girl I write you nearly by evry maile. I wrote you just as I was starting fore Raleigh. I wrote you from Raleigh. I got here Thursday night 6 miles below town & the maile started Friday morning. So I could not write & git to the office. I wrote you Sunday by Woot. I wrote you by last fridays maile. againe & now againe. I fear you are **hipoed.** you ought to know me well enough to know that I would write you offtimes. (A. W. Bell, Bell Papers, Duke) Macon County

hire *verb*

1. To find employment. [*DARE* **hire**, verb, 2a]

   Aug. 9, 1862: they was A man shot at Drurys Bluff yesterday for Deserting. he **hi[r]ed** as a Substitute and then ran off. (J. W. Love, Love Papers, Duke) Henderson County

2. In the phrase *hire (something) done,* to pay someone to perform a task, complete a job. [*DARE* **hire**, verb, 3]

   Feb. 2, 1863: it is no use to try to **hire any thing done** for there is no Men to hire not even to cut fire wood the women that can Chop has A fire and them that cant has to do without. (Mary Driskell, Caldwell Coll., ECU) Cabarrus County

hisn *possessive pronoun* His. [*DARE* chiefly South, Midland, New England]

Mar. 24, 1864: they stop giving furlows then for a while. they said I daunt now whether **hisen** will ever come or not. (Noah Wagner, *Confederate Soldier,* 88) Catawba County

hisself *reflexive pronoun* Himself. [*DARE* chiefly South, Midland]

Aug. 21, 1862: we got a leter from math last night an he was only tolerbuley **his self** but wes was well. (S. E. Love, Love Papers, Duke) Henderson County

Jan. 15, 1863: he is not caperable of taken care of **his self** as Som is. (Catherine Hunt, Vance Papers, NCSA) Randolph County

June 15, 1863: he has got to taking fits he toock one the other day. he was by **his self**. nobody knse [= knows] how long hit lasted. (J. A. W. Revis, Revis Letters, NCSA) Henderson County

July 13, 1863: the pore labering Man that helps the pore Women all he can and work **his Self** Down he has to Goe and ther will Bee no Chance for them. (William Martin, Vance Papers, NCSA) Burke County

Oct. 8, 1863: he said he was sorey he had ronged the men so. the nabors nose quin and tha Say he will do eny thing to Clar **his Self**. i dont want you to tak my word for it. you can rite for siners [= signers] and you can get as meny as you want. (Nancy Caldwell, Vance Papers, NCSA) Catawba County

hist *verb* variant form of *hoist.*

July 16, 1862: the carse [= train cars] runs bey heare and I must lwok [= look] and sutch gales [= gals] we have tha will **hist** thar close around thar wast and rube and pull at you and I think lees of them than I dwo of my dog. (Robert Spainhourd, Spainhourd Papers, Duke) Forsyth County

Sept. 14, 1862: we had artillery on three sides an oben [= opened] on them very se fearse [= severe] an it was so hot that they sun [= soon] **histed** a whit flag an surrender an our men marched in harpers ferry about

8 ½ A.M an took posision of the town an everything. (W. B. Howard, Williams-Womble Papers, NCSA) Chatham County

hit *pronoun* see **it**

hog fashioned *adverb phrase* Figuratively: without material comforts, adequate shelter, clean clothing, or other necessities associated with normal life.

Jan. 15, 1863: you Said if i needed any thing to rite for it. i can make out very well i Suppose for we live sorty **hog fashion** Any how. (James Hackett, Hackett Papers, Duke) Guilford County

hog shelter *noun* A crude, temporary shelter fashioned from tree branches, boughs, and leaves.

Jan. 28, 1863: We have but very few tents yet. not one fifth enough, but we are in the long leaf pine woods where we can build complete **hogshelter** and cover them with long leaf pine leaves because there are a plenty leaves here. (Constantine Hege, Hege Papers, Lewis-Leigh Coll., MHI) Davidson County

hoist see **hist**

hold out, holt out *verb* To keep, keep on, remain, continue; to last; variant past tense and past participle form *helt out;* see Overview § II.4.7.

July 5, 1856: the people has bin faithful an dutiful to mee an to thare work and all have agreed togather Sence master left home. I am glad that tha have **helt out** So well in thare health all Saving oncle charles and he has bin treated with the greates respets that could be required. (Moses [Pettigrew slave], Pettigrew Family Papers, SHC) Washington County

Aug. 24, 1863: tha all joind the church but bug and jane. bug says she will Join the next Meeting tha have up there. I recon Jane will join the Badtist the first chance she gets. I hope tha will all **hold out** faith full. if tha do it will be a good thing. (Molly Tesh, Tesh Papers, Duke) Yadkin County

Aug. 27, 1863: I dont think it will be lon[g] tell I will get home I think if they **hold owt** Desertin they wont be many men in they feild By Chrismas. (W. H. Brotherton, Brotherton Papers, Duke) Catawba County

May 23, 1864: tena Be in good hart as you Can. I will Be at home Befor vary mutch longer this is so tell Beckey to **hold out** faith ful. (J. W. Reese, Reese Papers, Duke) Buncombe County

Feb. 5, 1865: you Wanted to no how my Provisions **helt out**. i Left my Box with miss harris when wee went to foart fisher. (Wade Hubbard, Hubbard Papers, Duke) Anson County

hold up *verb* Of a rifle or rifled musket: to be accurate at, have an effective range of (a specified distance); see Overview § II.4.7.

Mar. 8, 1858: I want you to get gillcrease to have me a gune put in order. two feet 8 inches long 75 Balls to the pound. percushion Lock. half Stock. Silver mounted. and I want you to Bring it out in the fall when you Come and I will pay all Expense. Make him inshore it to **hold up** 200 yards. (David Headrick, Frank Papers, Duke) Davidson County

Sept. 8, 1862: tewl [tell] them to all to come hear if tha ont to Join a god regement but not dissaisfy them self. we have drod rifel gones. tha will **hold up** from three to five hundreth yeards. (Robert Spainhourd, Spainhourd Papers, Duke) Forsyth County

holler *verb* To shout, yell. [*DARE* chiefly South, South Midland]

July 4, 1862: Tell george Brann I said he better come and help us Whip them and hear us **holler** when we charge on their Batteries. (William Tesh, Tesh Papers, Duke) Yadkin County

holler *adjective* variant form of *hollow*. [see also *DARE* **hollow horn**, **hollow tail**]

Feb. 20, 1865: dont let your Cows get So pour [= poor] then they will die. try and get thear horns opened and Serch thear tails and See if they aint **holler** and try to do the best you Can till I Come home. (Alexander Keever, Keever Papers, Duke) Lincoln County

holt *noun* A grasp (after verbs *get, lay, take*); variant form of *ahold, aholt*. See also **a holt**.

June 1, 1863: I was heaping bresh I got **holt** of one that lay in the road during muddy weather and the wagons had run over it and burried the big end in the mud. (James Zimmerman, Zimmerman Papers, Duke) Forsyth County

May 20, 1864: I think our Armey has lade **holte** on that Determenation that they will lead a better life then what they have hear to fore. their was a great Revival in the armey before we left camps. their was menny that joyned the church of Different Denominations that neaver had made this great obligation to serve their lord before. (Isaac Lefevers, Lefevers Papers, NCSA) Catawba County

ND [1865]: here the[y] have one Dollar for washing one Shirt or one pair of Drawers, that look like this confederacy is a going up the spout. money is hard to get **holt** of and after a man gets it he cant by nothing with it, this ware canot last longer than till Spring I Dont think. (W. D. Smith, W. D. Smith Papers, Duke) Davie County

home guard *noun* A local militia detachment, detailed to patrol an area and often to arrest deserters.

Dec. 25, 1863: I want You to write when You think the **Home Guard** will have to go in camp a gain and if their is anny talk of takeing them out and all the nuse that is a stiring through the settlement. (William Tesh, Tesh Papers, Duke) Yadkin County

Apr. 2, 1864: Wright mee what they have done with the **home guards**. I have understood they have Been sent to the army. (Isaac Copeland, Copeland Letters, NCSA) Surry County

Jan. 8, 1865: I seene som off the **home gards** a goin home last weake and I hope you come home too bea fore long. (Flora Ann Campbell, Campbell Papers, Duke) Moore County

hongry *adjective* variant form of *hungry*. [*DARE* especially South, South Midland]

July 5, 1863: I had bin on a long march an was mity **hongry** an all most naked an I march close by home an left my comarne [= company? command?] an went home to get som thin to ete an som close. (John Averett, Vance Papers, NCSA) Pitt County

hook see **on one's own hook**

hooker house *noun* A house of prostitution. [*OED* **hooker**, noun[1], 4; Eliason, *Tarheel Talk,* has a North Carolina citation from 1845]

June 3, 1862: i heard that markis huit Sade that i went in tell [= into] the **hucker ho[u]ses** and if he sade that he is A lier. (W. P. Cline, Cline Papers, SHC) Catawba County

hope see **help**

hops see **as thick as hops**

horse see **hoss**

horsler One who attends horses, a groom; variant form of *hostler.*

June 7, 1863: I am still **horsler** for Capton Ray. I dont think tena that I will hav to go in to A fite with A gun I may hav to attend to them in time of A fite. he has A fine animel and as fine as fiddle. I hav Bin telling him that Sh[e] is to fine to wair out in this wair [= war] that he had Better send mee home with hur. (J. W. Reese, Reese Papers, Duke) Buncombe County

horspitle, horse pitle, horse pital *noun* variant forms of *hospital.*

Nov. 10, 1861: we left T. M. Lance in the **horse pital** at wilming ton. I do not what will Become of him. (John B. Lance, Lance Papers, LSU) Henderson County

Jan. 31, 1862: you com Doun the Charles sity Road you will find ous. A P Hills Division **Hors pitle**. (L. W. Griffin, Griffin Papers, NCSA) Rutherford County

June 12, 1862: I can inform you that port welch is dead. he dide at the **horse pitle** at richmon. (Thornton Sexton, Sexton Letters, Duke) Ashe County

June 6, 1863: the boys is all tolerable well except captin bening field. he is gon to the **horspitel**. (Daniel Revis, Revis Letters, NCSA) Henderson County

Oct. 7, 1863: Some four or five has come in to this company from the **Horspitles**. (James Zimmerman, Zimmerman Papers, Duke) Forsyth County

horspitable *adjective* variant form of *hospitable.*

Apr. 28, 1861: after Prusing through your leter and finding your kinde **horspitibel** offers maken me wel com at your house. (Charles H. Lance, Lance Papers, LSU) Henderson County

hoss *noun* variant form of *horse.*

Oct. 29, 1862: they mad Another sever charg but Our Boeys stood ther ground An drove them Back agane An the yankes trid it agane But was repu[l]sed agane with hevy lost. so this ended the Battle for this day. so this was a great sight to behol. men an **hosses** lying ded an cripled all over the battlefield. (William Howard, Williams-Womble Papers, NCSA) Chatham County

Nov. 10, 1862: our horses look very well notwith [standing?] the Distemper and hard riding that they have done. Roben is the **hose** among **hoses**, we get plenty of forage and I use it frealey. (Dinson Caldwell, Caldwell Coll., ECU) Cabarrus County

Feb. 26, 1863: their is one thing that I want that I did note Rite for and that is a half galon Jug of Sower Vinegar & **hos** reddich. (Isaac Lefevers, Lefevers Papers, NCSA) Catawba County

hostler see **horsler** *noun*

how come see **come**

howdy *interjection, noun* A greeting; from *how-do-ye?;* often with a noun function as object of the verbs, *send, tell, give.* [CACWL data indicate this form was widespread through the South and South Midland, but particularly common in western North Carolina; see *OED* **how-do-ye, how-d'ye, howdy,** phrase and noun, "Now *obs.* or *dial.* Freq. in colloq. phr. *to tell* (a person) *howdy*"; *DARE* chiefly South, Midland]

1. following *tell,* especially in the phrase *tell* (someone) *howdy for me.*

July 16, 1861: tell my Pore old mother **howdy** for me. (Peter Poteet, Poteet-Dickson Letters, NCSA) Burke County

Mar. 20, 1862: tell the 2 maryes **howdy** for me and give them my best respects and tell all the girls **howdy** for me. (J. W. Love, Love Papers, Duke) Henderson County

June 6, 1863: Sereptia I want you to take good cear of your self tell all the folks **howdey** for mee. (Daniel Revis, Revis Letters, NCSA) Henderson County

June 16, 1864: your Mother says tell you **howdy** for her and the children sends you howdy. (Martha Poteet, Poteet-Dickson Letters, NCSA) McDowell County

2. following *send, give.*

Aug. 7, 1861: I want you to give John hemphill **houdy** for me. tell him that I would be glad To Se him. (Peter Poteet, Poteet-Dickson Letters, NCSA) Burke County

Oct. 29, 1861: ant fany sed to send you **howdy** for her. (Elizabeth Watson, Watson Letters, WCU) Jackson County

Nov. 26, 1863: i hope we wil meet agane so i give **howdy** to all both black and white. (Franklin Setzer, Setzer Corr., UVA) Catawba County

Oct. 7, 1864: Billy & Eliza sends **howdy** to you & wants to see you very bad. (Huldah Hubbard, Hubbard Papers, Duke) Anson County

3. following *say.*

July 18, 1863: I will come to aclose by saying **howdy** and good by and wishing you well. (James Broach, Broach Papers, Duke) Person County

how do *interjection* Probably the same origin and function as **howdy** above. [*DARE* especially South, South Midland]

Jan. 9, 1865: Marion Bayner ses **how do** for her. she hopes you will get home again [. . .] dan ses **how do** for him. he wants to see you. Olivia ses **how do** pa. make her a ring and put her name on it. (Ann Bowen, Bowen Papers, NCSA) Washington County

hucker see **hooker**

huckleberry *noun* A variety of blueberry.

July 5, 1863: we sometimes gather a mess of poalk [= pokeweed] for greens and sometimes gat[h]er blackberies and stue them. I have just been a taking averry good mess of **huckleburies**. (C. A. Hege, Hege Papers, MHI) Davidson County

hug *verb* Apparently sometimes used as a euphemism for having sexual intercourse. [perhaps related to *OED* **hug**, verb, 3.b., "To lie close, cuddle"]

Oct. 28, 1862: tell John and Mary to not **hug** to hard fur I think he will git a discharge when he comes back and then he can have his time fur **huging**. (Jonas Bradshaw, Bradshaw Papers, Duke) Alexander County

July 8, 1863: two or 3 of my nabors have concluded to brake me up. A J loftes that robed the mail and was sened to leav the state. john Robb that **hugs** his one [= own] Daughter. mcguess that runaway from SC for forging noats and steelinng. these are the gentle men that took my stills. (Charles Cison, Vance Papers, NCSA) Transylvania County

hug your neck *verb phrase* To give an affectionate embrace to family members.

Oct. 22, 1862: I wood be glad to sed you a cuming home and I will **hug your nack** good for you and giv you one good kiss. so I have nothing moer at presant. so I will bring my remarks to aclose. (Sarepta Revis, Revis Letters, NCSA) Henderson County

hundred *numeral* variant forms *hunderd, hundard, hunard.*

June 13, 1862: we Can not give no true s[t]atement yet what is our loss. we do not Know yet but we whiped the yankee and the Loss was hevey on boath sides. we took a bout 800 **hundard** Prisners and a good meney of artilry Peaces. (James A. May, Military Coll., Civil War, NCSA) Guilford County

Sept. 12, 1862: If this war dont cease it is shure to Be hard times for Purvisiones can be had whare the armies have Been. they have pulled all the green corn for Miles wide and **hunderds** of Miles long. (John Ingram, Ingram Papers, Duke) Forsyth County

Aug. 9, 1863: We hav lost about one **hunard** Men from our Brigad. (Edgar Smithwick, Smithwick Papers, Duke) Martin County

hungry see **hongry**

hunkers *noun plural* Haunches; in the phrase *on one's hunkers* (= in a squatting position). [see *EDD* **hunkers**; *DARE* **hunker**, noun; chiefly Midland, South]

Jan. 10, 1864: we have got in the garison out of the rain at last this is wet day but not So cold I am Sitting on my **hunkers** writing on my ne. (R. C. Caldwell, Caldwell Coll., ECU) Cabarrus County

hurrah *noun* A ruckus; a skirmish. [see *DARE* **hurrah**, B, 1]

June 28, 1863: thar is a fight goin on at Taliahomer. troops goin thar every trane. this litel **Hurra** at the planes [= Stawberry Plains] is nothing. (Stephen Whitaker, Whitaker Papers, NCSA) Cherokee County

hurting *noun* A pain. [*DARE* chiefly South South Midland]

Feb. 4, 1862: I am well at this Time but I ant bin well for the last da an nite. I stode gard nite beefore last an it give me a **hurten** in my brest an my head an I coft all day an nite. (J. S. Councill, Councill Papers, Duke) Watauga County

I

idey (also *idy, eydie, ider*) *noun* variant forms of *idea*. [*DARE* chiefly South, South Midland; also New England]

Feb. 27, 1863: tena you dont no how Bad I want to see you and the Children. you may think you doo But poor thing you dont. you hav no **idey**. (J. W. Reese, Reese Papers, Duke) Buncombe County

May 9, 1863: it has Bin So long Since I got ary letter from yo. Before I got this I had given out the **ider** of getting eny more. (J. H. Hundley, Hundley Family Letters, SHC) Stokes County

May 14, 1863: I cant giv any **eydies** myself when or where we will go. (John Futch, Futch Letters, NCSA) New Hanover County

Mar. 11, 1864: I dont have any **idy** of coming home this spring to see you and my family. (Daniel Abernethy, Abernethy Papers, Duke) Catawba County

in *preposition* Within, at a distance of; followed by a specific number. [*DARE* **in**, preposition, 4]

Aug. 3, 1861: the yankies is coming on. they ar **in** twelve mils of our camp. (L. W. Griffin, Griffin Papers, NCSA) Rutherford County

July 14, 1862: John tomas Mackingtire got kild the Second Fight **in** twenty steps of me. (Charley Futch, Futch Letters, NCSA) New Hanover County

July 19, 1863: we went in Marland and threw thare and into Pencilvany and marched **in** 18 miles of the captil of Pencilvany. (Neill McLeod, McLeod Letters, SHC) Moore County

July 4, 1864: I am takeing kear of him. we ar **in** one mile of dinwidde court house. (John Black, Black Letters, UVA) Yadkin County

in., inst. see **instant**

in about *prepostion* Near, in the vicinity of.

Dec. 6, 1862: our hole army is Falling back to Take up Winter quarters Some Wher **in a bout** Culppeper Cort House or Gordonsville. (William Tesh, Tesh Papers, Duke) Yadkin County

indigo *noun* The indigo plant (genus *Indigofera*), a common source of dye.

May 21, 1864: i rote aletter to you by D burnet. i sent Some little things by him to you. i sent my gloves and cap. 1 hammer. 1 bottle of powder. 1 belt and capbox and capts. 2 Papers, of cotridge. Some **indigo** seede. one case knife. half quire of paper and some envalopes. (Silas Stepp, Stepp Letters, UNCA) Buncombe County

infare *noun* A dinner and party following a wedding. [*DARE* chiefly South, South Midland]

Apr. 17, 1859: I can inform you that I was at an **infare** of the Rev James Gatlin on the thirteenth of this instant. Wee had a tall time of it thare was a bout Seventy persons at it. (Enoch Garner, Jackson Family Corr., Notre Dame) Davidson County

Feb. 6, 1862: Jesse Case say tell his friends that he is in the land of the living and would like to bee at one more **infare** and espeshly a frolic. (Jesse Shipman, Shipman Family Corr., Notre Dame) Henderson County

in for the war see **for the war**

in (one's) right mind *prepositional phrase* Of person at the point of death: in a state of consciousness, with a rational mind, not delirious. [*OED* **right**, adjective, 8.a.]

June 25, 1862: Bob is ded. he died at the houspotle at Raleigh. he was not in his **right mind** but two days after Got in camp before he got sick when they cared him of to Raleigh he was getin better. he said that if he died he wanted his Brother to hav his mony. (Phillip James, Spainhourd Papers, Duke) Forsyth County

Sept. 29, 1862: your beloved son Thomas is gon from time to eturnity. he Died the 26th of instant in the horspittle. I was with him when he died. I & wm. was sent to the horspittle that day & then I Wm went that nite got there about sun set & he died about one O clocke. he died verry easy & was in his **rite mind** untel the last. (Austen Brown, Brown Family Papers, Duke) Johnston County

June 28, 1863: I think he was in his **right mind** to the last. a bout two hours I recon it was be fore he died he called me to him and said he wanted me to stay with him for he should die but I tried to encourage him. (John Bachelor, Brown Coll., NCSA) Duplin County

July 9, 1863: the ball went in one Side and came out the other. he lived some 4 or 5 hours after he was struck. he was in his **right mind** untill he died. some of our boys staid with him untill he died. (J. F. Coghill, Coghill Papers, Duke) Granville County

instant, inst., in. *noun*

1. The current calendar month. [see *OED* **instant**, adjective, II.2.b.]

Aug. 15, 1862: I received a letter from Jacob the 13th of this **inst.** he had left lynchburg an gon to Liberty va. (W. M. Patton, Patton Family Letters, Duke) Buncombe County

Dec. 21, 1862: Cousin I can say to you that wee have had anoth vary hard batel but have bin suchsesful to drive the Yankes back with a loss of 800 hundred kild Woundid and and misin and a mong the kild I am sory to state the names of som of our brave boyes how [= who] fell on grat and bludy batel field the 13 of this **instant**. (Phillip Shull, Councill Papers, Duke) Watauga County

Apr. 27, 1863: it dont looke like wnter will brake this year. it snowed hir on the 24th of this **Instint**. (Wilburn Garren, Vance Papers, NCSA) Henderson County

Oct. 27, 1863: I want to work to try to do Something for my family. I was arrested on the 18th of this **Inst** at home in caldwell County. (W. R. Raby, Vance Papers, NCSA) Caldwell County

2. A specific day of the month.

May 30, 1862: I Seat my Self for the purpose of droping you afew Lines in answer to Yours which I resived the 17th **ins**. I found 50 cts inclosed in direction What to do With it. I Sent to Golllesboro to day for Stamps which Ill resiev in a Short time. (Alfred Walsh, Proffit Family Letters, SHC) Wilkes County

Dec. 6, 1863: I recved yours and Amzys leters the 5 **in.** lettrs always finds me wating for them. tha never git here too Soon. (R. C. Caldwell, Caldwell Coll., ECU) Cabarrus County

Intell *preposition* Into. [*OED* **intill**, preposition, "*Sc.* and *north. dial.*"]

June 3, 1862: i heard that markis huit sade that i went **in tell** the hucker hoses and if he sade that he is A lier. (W. P. Cline, Cline Papers, SHC) Catawba County

in the bushes *prepositional phrase* Hiding out, avoiding conscription or arrest.

Mar. 16, 1864: I hav not drawd one cent and but mity little of any thing and I hant a going to Stay at no Such a dam plase because I can make more at home **in the bushes** amakeing brooms than I can here in this tornel war. (Jesse Hill, Hill Letters, NCSA) Forsyth County

Apr. 11, 1864: Ervan Dull got away From them right straite and he is **in the Bushes** yet. (Jane Tesh, Tesh Papers, Duke) Yadkin County

in the gants *prepositional phrase* Unwell, tired, thin, undernourished; *gant* from *gaunt*. [see *DARE* **gant**]

Aug. 14, 1862: we are all well at this time except mary. she is a litle **in the gants** tho she is beter this morning. (F. A. Bleckley, Bleckley Papers, Duke) Catawba County

in the notion see **notion**

in the room (of) *prepositional phrase* In the place, instead (of something). [*DARE* **room**, B1]

Jan. 24, 1863: you nead not send me them Sweat potatoes as we air in a countery wheir their is a heap of potatoes Raised & we can get them as low hear as you can up their. they air a thing that is heavey and will take up a heap of Room in a box but you may send me some onions **in the Room of** the potatoes. (Isaac Lefevers, Lefevers Papers, NCSA) Catawba County

in the woods *prepositional phrase* Hiding out; same meaning as **in the bushes**.

June 11, 1863: they threatened shooting me. and said it was all they could do to keep from shooting me comeing up from feeding my Horses Because I have a son **in the woods** that is 23 years of age. I have no controle of him. he certainly is his oun man and will follow his oun mind. (Mark Nelson, Vance Papers, NCSA) Randolph County

Oct. 16, 1863: he had two brothers had bin at work on the railroad and thay got after them to carry them to the army and thay left and com home and went **in the woods**. (Pattie Vernon, Vance Papers, NCSA) Rockingham County

invelip see **envelope**

Irish potato, Irish tater *noun*

1. A white potato in contrast to a sweet potato. [*DARE* scattered, but more frequent South Midland]

July 30, 1863: I can also tell you that I had a good mess of **Irish taters** thare and a couple of nites before that I baked me two Blackberry pies. (W. F. Wagner, *Confederate Soldier*, 59) Catawba County

July 31, 1863: I bout a coupel aquarts of **irish taters** Sence I have bin Sick. I pade one dollar a quart for them. (Daniel Setzer, Setzer Papers, Duke) Catawba County

June 16, 1864: the sweet potatoes is very prety and the **irish potatoes** is the pretyest I ever seen. I hav a mess today. I wish you was hear to eat some with me. (Martha Poteet, Poteet-Dickson Letters, NCSA) McDowell County

Nov. 20, 1864: you can send me sum more **irish potatoes.** tha are what is good. (F. M. Poteet, Poteet-Dickson Letters, NCSA) McDowell County

2. variant forms of the first syllable.

June 1862: I want you to sind me a few **Ashpotatoes** when Alex come back if you have them. (J. W. Whitfield, Whitfield Papers, Duke) Nash County

July 16, 1862: I sufford a power for somthing to Eat While I Was in the horspital at Richmond. I paid 50 cts a quart for Some **arish potatoes**. (G. J. Huntley, Huntley Papers, WCU) Rutherford County

Aug. 9, 1862: thair was thirteen apples four cowcumbers and nineteen **iserspotatoes**. (J. W. Williams, Williams Papers, Duke) Onslow County

Oct. 2, 1862: i wod like to now if you got yores **ishe potatos** dug an put a way. how is yos s[w]eet potatoes an how is the hoges. (Henry Baker, Henry Baker Papers, Duke) Catawba County

irons see **heel irons**

it *existential subject* There. [this form is much less common in the North Carolina sample than existential *they; DARE* scattered, but chiefly South, South Midland]

Apr. 7, 1862: I hope you will rite to as often as you can for **it** is not a hour in the Day but what i think of you and our Dear little childrean. (Isaac Lefevers, Lefevers Papers, NCSA) Catawba County

Jan. 18, 1863: it is no nead of my saying any thing to you about the Fight at Newbern where I was taken for you was then Col of a reg in the same fight. (J. W. Evans, Vance Papers, NCSA) Alleghany County

Apr. 18, 1863: Aaron Speagle Volunteerd in Hainess Co[mpany]. Rockett and Wm Brendel is over the age yet. they are at home But it took a good many of the men. **it** is but few left here now. (HenryRhodes, Lefevers Papers, NCSA) Catawba County

it *personal pronoun*

1. variant form *hit.* [see *OED* **it**, pronoun; from Old and Middle English pronoun *hit;* CACWL data indicate this form was widespread through the South and Midland]

July 16, 1861: you said somthing about our battle being at harpers ferry. **hit** was 15 miles below here At aplace cald bethel Church. (Peter Poteet, Poteet-Dickson Letters, NCSA) Burke County

July 28, 1862: hit is a inglish blanket. one side black and the other read. **hit** wars taken off the battle field. (Larkin Kendrick, Kendrick Papers, NCSA) Cleveland County

June 15, 1863: ther had like to bin alitlet batel her the other day with the boys that runaway an the melishey. but tha got **hit** sorter seteld. (J. A. W. Revis, Revis Letters, NCSA) Henderson County

Feb. 14, 1864: ihav herd that harvy fipps is at our house very Bad off rite to me and let me now how he is rite to me me and lit me now what complaint it is and if eny more of my pepol has **hit**. (Thornton Sexton, Sexton Letters, Duke) Ashe County

2. An infant or very young child. [see *OED* **it**, pronoun, I.1. a.]

Mar. 16, 1862: may god bless my little Peanutt Lodema Jane fur I never expect to see **it** a gain onley through the kind proverdence of kine heavin my God bless you all. (Jonas Bradshaw, Bradshaw Papers, Duke) Alexander County

Dec. 16, 1863: his baby got burned very bad a few days ago. they dont think **it** wil get wel wel. (Alvira Taylor, Taylor Papers, Duke) Orange County

Oct. 4, 1864: Dear wife you dont now how mutch I Study about you and my littel Children. I would love to kiss that littel one that I haint never seen. you Rote that **it** had taken astart to grow and **it** was very purty and smart god bless **it** and speare its life and mine to both till I can git to see **it**. (F. M. Poteet, Poteet-Dickson Letters, NCSA) McDowell County

itch see **each**

J

jack *noun* A male donkey, jackass. [*DARE* **jack**, noun[1], 19]

Feb. 16, 1863: Farther I to know how you are getting along with your farm and if can tend all your land or not. tell Mr Lockman Dock is well. he is a sp[l]ended fellow. I want yow to put my mare to Some **Jack** this Spring. (W. H. Brotherton, Brotherton Papers, Duke) Catawba County

Apr. 7, 1863: Dear friend I want you to do me a favor if you can and please If their is a good horse or **Jack** a bout their I want you to have fan [= Fanny, the mare] taken two him. I want a colt Raised from hur If it can Be sow. please tend to this for me as horses wil Be scearse If this war lasts much longer. (Isaac Lefevers, Lefevers Papers, NCSA) Catawba County

jacknet *noun* A woman's outergarment, a jacket. [see *OED* **jacket**, noun, 1.c.]

Oct. 28, 1863: I could not get the **jacknett** and I have got you a dress if you will except of it. (J. W. Lineberger, *Gaston Ranger*, 73) Gaston County

Jackson War *noun* The War of 1812, including Andrew Jackson's campaign against the Creeks and/or the Battle of New Orleans.

Apr. 13, 1863: they come to my house and take en my son saddle after thay hade killed him and takein one of my best horses i hade and Bridle and and kep them som five weakes and damage worth more then half what thay was when thay was takeen from my house. then thay come and taken me and put me in Jale and kep me thare twenty four days and then thay turnd me out and made me pay for my Board and i am aman About Eighty Eight years old and i was A Soldier in the **Jac son ware** and i want to Know wheder you approve of the Like of that or not. (Isaac Miller, Vance Papers, NCSA) Davidson County

janders, ganders *noun* variant forms of *jaundice*. See also **yellow janders**. [*DARE* especially South, South Midland]

Nov. 10, 1861: I am well at this time except a bad cole. Tom is nearly well of the **Janders**. (J. S. Beavers, Upchurch Papers, Duke) Chatham County

Dec. 25, 1862: There is a great deal of sikness here now in camp such as Pneumonia, **janders** and various other diseases. (C. A. Hege, Hege Papers, MHI) Davidson County

Oct. 16, 1864: i was truly glad to here from you and here you was all well. i aint verry well. i am about. i am better then i have bin. i had the **ganders**. (Silas Stepp, Stepp Letters, UNCA) Buncombe County

janes see **jeans**

jaw *verb* To talk back, quarrel. [see *DSME* **jaw**, verb 1 and **jawback**; *DARE* **jaw back**, verb phrase, "to retort, talk back"]

Mar. 20, 1864: a Yankey Sergt: named Young shot one of our Officers for **jawing** him. (B. Y. Malone, *Malone Diary*, 47) Caswell County

jeans, janes, janes cloth *noun* A coarse, durable cotton fabric; the common older spelling is *janes*. [*OED* **jean**, noun, 2.a.]

Nov. 22, 1861: I Waunt you to have me a lincy [= linen] shirt mad and Send it By mr Jones. you can git some Coat Lining at phillip Davises that Will answer or if you can git some thin Lincy Wolen cloth it Will do vary Well. dont make it o[u]t of **Jeans** for it Will Be to thick. (G. J. Huntley, Huntley Papers, WCU) Rutherford County

Nov. 6, 1862: I am Requested By our Col to ask you By Letter what to Give for **Janes** and Lincy cloth and socks & Blankets. **Janes** has gone up in this part of the country to $5.00 pr yard. (G. Webb, Vance Papers, NCSA) Rutherford County

June 28, 1863: I want you to make me a nice Soot of **Janes** cote & pants as Soon as you can. (Stephen Whitaker, Whitaker Papers, NCSA) Cherokee County

Dec. 16, 1863: if you get sick I want you to let me know. I wil come to see you. I have as much sowing and weaving as I can do. I get 8 dollars for making a coat and a dollar ayard for weaving **jeans**. I am savinng all to come and see you. (Alvira Taylor, Taylor Papers, Duke) Orange County

jest *adverb* variant form of *just*.

Apr. 12, 1863: Dear wife the reason I hant ancerd yours letter yett I had **Jest** started one that same day I Got yourn. (Daniel Brown, Brown Coll., NCSA) Duplin County

Apr. 26, 1863: I can tell you the men is arunning a way from our rig ment rite on. I think it will be all the way the army will be brok we had **Jes** as wel go back to the union for the yankes say that we shant have no confedersy. they say they will fite 20 year longer and if they fite that long we are whiped. (J. C. Owens, Confederate Papers, SHC) Wilkes County

June 18, 1864: I tell you that thay was vary glad to See us a coming and I think it was a nuf to make them glad for the trafling yankes **Jest** tars up evry thing whare thay go. thay Destroy all the propety thay can find. thay eaving to[t]e oute people fethers beads and tare them all to peaces. I Do wish that thay go back and let us a lone. (J. W. Joyce, Joyce Papers, MHI) Stokes County

jewlarker see **jularky**

jine *verb* variant form of *join*.

Aug. 15, 1863: i heard that the[y] was maken A Compney in A bout the mounten A stay at home and i heard that goodmond had **jin** it. (W. P. Cline, Cline Papers, SHC) Catawba County

Sept. 1, 1863: I am well and harty at the presenttime and I am also happy to State to you that I have profest of my Sins and I am going to **Jine** the church and be baptised. (John Hartman, Hartman Papers, Duke) Rowan County

job of work *noun phrase* A specific task with a limited completion time, temporary employment. [*DSME* **job of work**]

Jan. 21, 1862: We have just got through a heard [= hard] **job of Work**. We finisht our Cookhouse (Abraham Maxwell, Love Papers, Duke) Henderson County

join see **jine**

josie *noun* A woman's jacket, probably from *jersey*. [*DARE* chiefly South, South Midland]

Jan. 19, 1865: let me no what you hav don with the money and you ware them shous and you can ware that coat in the plase of a **Josy** if you want it and if you want to ware it you may keep it or do with it what you plese. (Jesse Hill, Hill Letters, NCSA) Forsyth County

jularky *noun* A sweetheart. [see *DARE* **jewlarker**; South, South Midland]

Apr. 3, 1863: my little **Jwlarkey** is as pretty as a pink and as a Rose. oh how I wold like to see her smille it would be the greatis of pleasur. (James Keever, Keever Papers, Duke) Lincoln County

Aug. 20, 1863: there is won thing I now an that is this if you wont to get marid as bad as theas boys wants to get out of virginia you will bee marid long before I get home for we want to com home worse than you ever wanted to see your **Jularkey** in your life. (Ralph D. Myers, Cowand Papers, Duke) Bertie County

Apr. 3, 1864: give my love to all of the girles an tell my **Jularkey** that I love her Just as good as ever. (Alfred Cowand, Cowand Papers, Duke) Bertie County

jump the broom *idiomatic expression* To get married. [*DARE* scattered, but chiefly South, South Midland, Texas]

Aug. 10, 1862: you sade that Jane and leme did **jump the brume**. he wod beter be in the armey for all the good he is dewing dire [= there]. (W. P. Cline, Cline Papers, SHC) Catawba County

june apple *noun* An apple that ripens in the early or midsummer rather than the fall. [*DARE* chiefly South Midland, especially Kentucky]

July 24, 1864: I had afin time Saturday at Hartgroveses with Sallie C and Nan C you ever saw eating **June appels.** the girls is all as lively as tadpoles. (T. B. Edmonston, Edmonston-Kelly Family Papers, WCU) Haywood County

Aug. 21, 1864: I had lefe the horspitel the day bee fore Mrs Dickson come down to See grason. She sent me one union and 4 **June apels**. I eat them but I dont now hoo sent them to me. I thank them to doo so again if tha please. I got 2 thirds of aplug of tobaco with this letter. (F. M. Poteet, Poteet-Dickson Letters, NCSA) McDowell County

just see **jest**

K

kale see **cale**

keep *verb* To stay, remain, continue.

July 18, 1863: my tobacco it is drowned out mitly and dont grow atall hardly it **keeps** so wet. (James Broach, Broach Papers, Duke) Person County

May 2, 1864: I have planted about twenty acres in corn and am not quite done yet. It **keeps** so wet. I cant plant the bottoms. It rains every day or so. (James Zimmerman, Zimmerman Papers, Duke) Forsyth County

Dec. 20, 1864: tell little James that he must not **keep** so fat for when hot wether Comes he will be two lazy to walk. (J. W. Joyce, Joyce Papers, MHI) Stokes County

keep a skinned eye *idiomatic expression* To keep a sharp lookout. [*OED* **skinned**, adjective, phrases, "colloq. (orig. *U.S.*) to keep one's eyes skinned and variants"]

Aug. 21, 1862: tel the girls to hied out for I am coming home. tel all of the girls to writ. tel [name scratched out] to **keep a Skind eye**. (S. E. Love, Love Papers, Duke) Henderson County

keep clear *verb* To avoid, be free from; see Overview § II.4.7.

Nov. 15, 1864: he has caught some lise [= lice]. it is impossible to **keep clare** of them heare. (Henry Bowen, Bowen Papers, NCSA) Washington County

keg see **cag**

Kentucky *noun* variant forms *Kaintucky, Caintucky, Cantucky, Cantuck, caintuck.* [CACWL data indicate these forms were most common in western parts of North Carolina]

Feb. 4, 1862: I think that we will stay here till spring an then we will leave here an goe to **Cantuck** or tenisee. (J. S. Councill, Councill Papers, Duke) Watauga County

Feb. 11, 1862: I dont now whar tha will go but tha is Som talk of tha going to **cantucky**. (Samuel Wagoner, Hundley Family Letters, SHC) Stokes County

Dec. 8, 1862: I Want to no of you Whether I can git A passport from Northcarolina to **Kaintucky** or not. (Lucinda Tweed, Vance Papers, NCSA) Madison County

Mar. 1, 1863: the feds has fixt up the Rail Rode that run from luivill **Cantuckey** to nashvill. (J. W. Reese, Reese Papers, Duke) Buncombe County

May 31, 1863: we hav bin atrip to **cain tuck** and hav Just got back to clinton. (Daniel Revis, Revis Letters, NCSA) Henderson County

Kentuckians *noun* variant form *cane tuckens.*

Oct. 24, 1862: thair is All sorts of folks But the Rite sort hear and the warst locking folks you ever saw in your life. sum of them has Bin out A long time in the un holy thing. thair is lots of **Cane tuckens** hear. (J. W. Reese, Reese Papers, Duke) Buncombe County

ketch, kotch see **catch**

kettle see **kitle**

kill dead *verb phrase* To kill instantly or quickly (especially on the battlefield); frequently as past participle in passive constructions. [*DARE* especially South, South Midland]

June 17, 1862: we went in the field with A bout 65 men and we lost 28 killed and woounded. 9 was **killed ded** on the field. (H. F. Rudasil, Confederate Misc., Emory) Davie County

Dec. 18, 1862: Miles Drum was **kiled dead** on the field. Cain Cline was wounded in the thy. (W. F. Wagner, *Confederate Soldier,* 26) Catawba County

Dec. 24, 1862: he went out in picket and was shot through the leg and bled to death in about 20 mins cut the arter in his leg. and the other man was killed by a bum. [it] struck him in the head and **killed** him **dead**. (John S. Overcash, Overcash Papers, Duke) Rowan County

July 25, 1863: William Andersen was hear this mor-ing and he Said fate Joyce and abe knowlling was wonde. he Said Dock cullum was **killed Dead** on the field. (J. W. Joyce, Joyce Papers, MHI) Stokes County

kill up *verb* To kill, wipe out, destroy; see Overview § II.4.7. [*DARE* chiefly South, South Midland]

Feb. 15, 1863: it lucks like a Gone Case with us enny way that we can fix it for it lucks like the men is all a going to Dye and Get **killd up**. (Samuel C. Phillips, Woody Letters, Confederate Misc., Emory) Mitchell County

June 5, 1863: I will have to try and tuf it out If the good lord Spairs my life to see this Dreadul War end. But it is only nowen to him ho[w] and when it shal End. it appears that it wont End untel finely one Side or the other is **Kiled up**. (Isaac Lefevers, Lefevers Papers, NCSA) Catawba County

Jan. 6, 1865: I do hope tha will hav to quit be fore we hav to fight any more for it is of no use to hav the men **kild up** and destroyed for nothing. (Jesse Hill, Hill Letters, NCSA) Forsyth County

killed up *adjective* Disabled? See citation.

Apr. 16, 1864: oh I wish that tha would come to some conclusion and let the poor **killed up** men stay at home with ther famelys. (Sally Bauldin, Hundley Family Letters, SHC) Stokes County

kin *noun* A relation, relative (sometimes collectively = relatives); a relationship. [*DARE* chiefly South, South Midland]

Oct. 13, 1862: I am sorry to inform you that uncle John Mock is dead. he died the 11th of august at Richmond at the horse pittle. I tell you I was mighty sorry to hear it now I havent got no body of my **Kin** in the army. (William Tesh, Tesh Papers, Duke) Yadkin County

Feb. 18, 1864: Joseph Landis was Married last Saturday Night to Jeanna Coopper a daughter of Bill Coopper. what **kin** is he to Susy Coopper. (Martha Poteet, Poteet-Dickson Letters, NCSA) McDowell County

kinfolk *noun* Relatives. [*DARE* widespread, but chiefly South, South Midland, Central, Texas]

Apr. 27, 1862: you rote to me to no if I was not willin for you to go an see your **kinfolks**. (J. S. Councill, Councill Papers, Duke) Watauga County

kitle, citle *noun* variant forms of *kettle*. [*DARE* chiefly South Midland, also Northeast]

Sept. 25, 1861: we have to pans and one camp **kitle** to cook in. (J. W. Williams, Williams Papers, Duke) Onslow County

Jan. 15, 1863: make some sweet cider and pwt it in **citle** or pot and let it get to boil. (T. F. Baggarly, Baggarly Papers, Duke) Iredell County

kiver see **cover**

knickknack see **nicknack**

knock about *verb* To move about, wander around; see Overview § II.4.7. [*OED* **knock**,verb, **to knock about**, 2.]

Aug. 13, 1862: he is not well nor h[ai]nt bin ever sence we moved but is **a nocking about**. (R. C. Love, Love Papers, Duke) Henderson County

knock along *verb* To get by; see Overview § II.4.7.

Aug. 20, 1862: we Sick ones was Left here **to knock Along** as we can. (J. W. Williams, Williams Papers, Duke) Onslow County

Jan. 9, 1865: cousin Nancy Respess sends her love to you and tel you she is **nocking along** rite smart and hopes you will get home again. (Ann Bowen, Bowen Papers, NCSA) Washington County

knock around *verb* To move around, wander, roam (same as **knock about**); see Overview § II.4.7.

Aug. 7, 1860: tell andy McKever that I am well and am **nocking around** a mung the girls. (James Sherrill, Robinson Papers, Duke) Catawba County

know *verb* See Overview § II.4.1.6.

1. past tense *knowed, nowd, node*. [*DARE* scattered, but chiefly South, South Midland]

   Sept. 21, 1862: the waggon that took them was a bout to leave before I **knowed** they was a going. (W. F. Wagner, *Confederate Soldier,* 15) Catawba County

   Feb. 27, 1863: if you **node** how mutch good it dus mee to git A letter from old Buncomb you wood keep one on the Rode to mee. (J. W. Reese, Reese Papers, Duke) Buncombe County

   Aug. 27, 1863: Jack Says he **nowd** that man that stayd with Albert till he died. (J. K. P. Shipman, Shipman Family Corr., Notre Dame) Buncombe County

   Nov. 20, 1864: Mr. and Mrs Landis wanted to [k] now whether I **node** any thing about John Landis are not. (F. M. Poteet, Poteet-Dickson Letters, NCSA) McDowell County

2. past participle *knowd, node*.

   Aug. 7, 1861: I supose the like never was **knowd** in the world. our men got about 70 peaces of Canon & 20 thousand stand of armes And 500 wagons & teames besides thousands of other things. (Peter Poteet, Poteet-Dickson Letters, NCSA) Burke County

   June 18, 1862: Dear wife If I had a **node** that I would astaid hear this longue I would a had you to a Rote me another letter to this place but sow it tis. (Isaac Lefevers, Lefevers Papers, NCSA) Catawba County

3. past participle *(k)new*.

   June 2, 1863: I heard that I was Sentenans to Be Shot and I Broke thru the gard & com home & after I come home I heard that I come Clear & if I had **new** that I had come clear I would not ov left ther By no means whatever. (A. R. Harris, Vance Papers, NDCA) Iredell County

knowing *noun* Knowledge. [*DARE* chiefly Southern Appalachians, Ozarks]

Mar. 3, 1863: I heard him swar to one ly and hear of him swaring to anther. he has bin run from Columbus County for hogs steeling and from S.C. to brunswick County for steeling and the[y] ant no biger lyre in my **knowing** than he is. (G. Formyduval, Vance Papers, NCSA) Columbus County

kraut, craut, crout *noun* Sauerkraut. [*DARE* chiefly Midland]

Apr. 2, 1863: Captan Ward that Belongs to to this Regmant that lives in polk County N C. he has Bin home on fur low and got Back the othe day and Braut with him A Barrell of **Crout** to sell. it went off like hot cakes at fiftey Cents pur pound and he Cood hav got A dollar as Eassey. (J. W. Reese, Reese Papers, Duke) Buncombe County

Apr. 11, 1863: we got our Box and **crout** last night. the bread and cakes was all Spoilt except two the Sweet potatoes was nearley all Spoilt, the butter was also damag some. (James W. Overcash, Overcash Papers, Duke) Rowan County

Aug. 24, 1863: if live I intend to make a fine tub of **craut** and I think shorly you will get to come some time this fall or winter. then you can have some. (Molly Tesh, Tesh Papers, Duke) Yadkin County

Apr. 21, 1864: I want you to have plenty of good eating tell I come Such as eggs and ham and **crout** and milk and butter and Sallet & Sweat potatoes and So on. (Alexander Keever, Keever Papers, Duke) Lincoln County

L

lack see **like**

lagons *noun plural* variant form of *leggings*.

Nov. 10, 1862: you would bestoe a grate favor on me if you would make me a pr of **lagons** of some substantial cloth to keep my Legs warm. (Dinson Caldwell, Caldwell Coll., ECU) Cabarrus County

laid up *adjective* Sick in bed, incapacitated. [perhaps from *OED* **lie**, verb[1], **to lie up**, 2, "to take to one's bed or keep one's room as an invalid"]

Oct. 28, 1862: i send you A fuw Lines to in form you that i am noo [now] Better and goorn out to wurk. i hav Bin **Laid up** all mos five weeks But the Lord has spar my Life in mis of Death a But i hav Bin very Bad of[f]. (William H. Thurber, DeRosset Family Papers, SHC) New Hanover County

land *verb* To arrive at a place, reach a stage in a journey. [*OED* **land**, verb, II, intransitive, 8.a.]

Dec. 20, 1861: I **landed** to this place last thurs day morning. We are located fore & half miles from Rahley. (Larkin Kendrick, Kendrick Papers, NCSA) Cleveland County

Sept. 8, 1862: When We left Statsville We was ordered to go to the 18 rigment and We **landed** hear to day and ar veary tired. (G. C. Dickson, Poteet-Dickson Letters, NCSA) McDowell County

Dec. 24, 1862: I can tell you that Wm Raby **landed** yesterday and I can tell you what he Brought for me. (W. F. Wagner, *Confederate Soldier,* 29) Catawba County

June 22, 1863: we past threw Shepardstown and ther waded the Potomac and **landed** in Maryland about 8 oclock. (B. Y. Malone, *Malone Diary,* 36) Caswell County

larn see **learn**

lasses see **molasses**

last *noun* A cast-iron shoe-making implement shaped like the sole of a shoe; made in various sizes.

Nov. 27, 1863: Saly tell tom that Nancy wants him to Make her a **last** by this mesure and she will pay him promptly for it. (Betty Thomas, Quinn Papers, Duke) Duplin County

last *adjective* Following a day of the previous week, for example, *Thursday last* instead of *last Thursday.* [*OED* **last**, adjective, 3.b.]

May 15, 1864: Gen Stuard was wounded on t[h]urday **last** and died on friday night. (John A. Smith, J. A. Smith Papers, Duke) Cabarrus County

lay[1] *verb* To blame, attribute. [see *OED* **lay**, verb[1], 27.a.]

Mar. 17, 1862: I Cannot say for Certain what ails me. I suppose it is Being Exposed so mutch and using Bad Water. I **Lay** it more to the Water than to eny thing Else. (G. J. Huntley, Huntley Papers, WCU) Rutherford County

lay[2] *verb* To weld additional metal to the blade of a plow or other implement that has become worn down from use. [see *DARE* **lay**, verb, 4; *OED* **lay**, verb[1], 36. "To re-steel (a cutting instrument). *dial.*"]

Apr. 14, 1862: dere farerlaw [= father-in-law] i take my pen in my hand to let you noy that i am well i hope that these fue linds may find you in the same helth i wood as sune be at home **laing** plows but i dont now when i Will doo dat [= that] A gane. (W. P. Cline, *Cline Papers* SHC) Catawba County

Mar. 22, 1863: J B Brysons Wife of Macon Caroline has a large farm an but 2 very short plows to make her crop with. I went to Franklin 2 to get iron to **la** her plows but coul not get a poun. they woul be glad you would send them some Iron at any price. (A. W. Zachery, Vance Papers, NCSA) Jackson County

July 13, 1863: My Son not quite Eighteen years old has been working at the Black Smith trade for himself and a few of his neighbors Some three or four years, opened his Shop in June last by Advertisement and Gone to work for the Hoopercreek Company and Surrounding Country, at low prices, 10 cts for Sharpening and one Dollar for finding Iron and **laying** a plow only half price of other Shops here. (John Livingston, Vance Papers, NCSA) Henderson County

lay by *verb* To leave a crop to mature before harvest; see Overview § II.4.7. [*DARE* chiefly South, South Midland]

July 5, 1856: Dear master I commenced **laying by** the corn the 7 of June an got two hundred and Seventy acres don before harvest. (Moses [Pettigrew slave], Pettigrew Family Papers, SHC) Washington County

July 19, 1860: I went down ther to day an found mr Jones ther attending to his buseness. they ar go ing on **lay ing by** the corn. they had 50 acurs to **lay by** this morning. (Thomas Harding, Blount Papers, NCSA) Beaufort County

June 18, 1862: you rote to mee that it was sow mutch wet that you could hardly get the chance to work the corn. if you get behinde with it by the wet wether you most try and get some one to help plant and ketch up again. I think when it comes to **laying by** you had maby better **lay buy** the new ground first as it is sow Ruty [= so rooty]. (Isaac Lefevers, Lefevers Papers, NCSA) Catawba County

Aug. 7, 1863: you said th[at] you helped hariet to **lay by** her corn and haul her wheet. I thank your seaing to her. (John L. Putnam, Kendrick Papers, NCSA) Cleveland County

July 28, 1863: I aint **laid by** no corn yet but a bout three days plowing and it is raining now and evry thing wants work. (James Broach, Broach Papers, Duke) Person County

lay off *verb* To prepare or mark a field for plowing; see Overview § II.4.7. [*DARE* South, South Midland]

Apr. 26, 1863: you wanted to Know whether any Boday had helped me about plant my corn. H F procter **Laid off** the old feild fer me. (Amanda Murph, Murph Papers, Duke) Catawba County

lay out see **lie out**

lay up *verb* To save, store, keep for later; see Overview § II.4.7. [*OED* **lay**, verb[1], **to lay up**, 3]

June 22, 1864: I will dwo the best I can but I wold rather you was hear. the children has **laid up** a heap of apples & things for John when he comes. I hope you will come home. (Jane Culberson, Culberson Papers, Duke) Chatham County

leaf, leve *noun* Permission. [*OED* **leave**, noun[1], 1.a. and 1.e. (from Old English *léaf*)]

Mar. 6, 1862: Wm James has Bin trying to git to Come home to make up a Company of volunteers But the Colonel Wont let him. yet he given James Miller **leaf** to go home to make a company mearly I suppose Because he is a Big man. (G. J. Huntley, Huntley Papers, WCU) Rutherford County

Sept. 22, 1863: I left my company on the 22 ond of July without **leaf** which I hated to do t[h]ough I cant stand my officers. I want too go back perviding I can go to some other compay for I shant never go Back to the Same compay any more if I can help it. (John Blackburn, Vance Papers, NCSA) Robeson County

May 1, 1864: we have battalion drill twice a day here now and have to go on drill every time except we get **leve** from the captain. (P. J. Peterson, Peterson Papers, Duke) Catawba County

learn *verb*

1. variant form *larn.*

Nov. 3, 1861: I git A little home Sick wunst and A while but I will hafto **larn** to become of that. yet I expect to befor I dy with old age. (W. P. Burns, Peterson Papers, Duke) Catawba County

Feb. 10, 1862: you mus **larne** to read and then I will send you some money to get you a book or get you a book and send it to you if I can. (J. W. Overcash, Overcash Papers, Duke) Rowan County

Feb. 13, 1863: tell Bud that he most **larn** his Boock purty tell paw comes home and he will Bring him Some little Briches and Some candy. (Isaac Lefevers, Lefevers Papers, NCSA) Catawba County

Dec. 19, 1863: i want you to be a good girl and remember me and try to **larn** all you can. i want you to send me some of you riteing. (Franklin Setzer, Setzer Corr., UVA) Catawba County

2. To teach; to inform.

Mar. 30, 1863: I can certify that I have raised Robert Hall and **learnt** him his trade. he is Well skild in the trad. (Benjamin Hall, Vance Papers, NCSA) Wilkes County

May 27, 1863: I will Send you a few lines By Polk Which will **Learn** you that I am well. (Jesse Shipman, Shipman Family Corr., Notre Dame) Henderson County

Sept. 11, 1863: he gives them choice to study all branches from the alphabet up. he laid in spelling-books grammer & paper. he says he thinks he can do some good and can **learn** them to read & write. (J. W. Lineberger, *Gaston Ranger,* 67) Gaston County

Jan. 6, 1865: tel dock he must **lern** his dog to tree possoms and Squirles So that me and him can go hunting when I get home. (Jesse Hill, Hill Letters, NCSA) Forsyth County

least *adjective* Smallest in size.

Dec. 24, 1862: I can tell you I am spending lots of money I spend nearley or quite 20 Dollars since we left our camp at Richmond aples sells at a Dollar and a Dollar and 25 cents a Dosen the **least** little things and swet cakes litle biger than my hand at 35 cents. (W. F. Wagner, *Confederate Soldier,* 29) Catawba County

Nov. 18, 1864: Send that **least** pot. we need it to cook turnups and other truck. Send a small pan and lid to bake corn bread in. (John Peterson, Peterson Papers, Duke) Catawba County

leave *adverb* see **live**

letter sharers *noun* The collective audience for a letter from a soldier; extended family, in-laws, neighbors.

Feb. 22, 1865: Dear wife I take the oppoituny of writing you afew lins to in form you that I am well at this time and I hope this Letter May find you and your **Letter Sharers** all well. (John W. Joyce, Joyce Papers, MHI) Stokes County

lick *noun*

1. The smallest amount (usually in negative contexts).

July 28, 1863: there is a caul for more men which Reaches my age and if I hav to leav my crop wil Be lost as I hav no one to do a **lick** of work But my Self and my wife not wel able to Sea to hir childern. (Alexander Bracy, Vance Papers, NCSA) Robeson County

2. A sharp hit or blow.

Sept. 29, 1862: two of them was taken up and fetcht back this morning they formed a line of all the men here in camp and ran them threw and every man had a hickory and had to hit each of them one **lick**. (John Ingram, Ingram Papers, Duke) Forsyth County

Feb. 6, 1863: I wish that I could ove ben thare to ove whiped him on the spot. it made me mad when I heard it. So I am affraid that they will hurt him yet but if he hit you try your best to knock him down the next **lick** and give him A good whipping. (J. F. Coghill, Coghill Papers, Duke) Granville County

3. A setback, disappointment, defeat.

Apr. 26, 1862: I suppose that you hav heard that all from 18 to 35 is prest in for the war and you know it is A bad **Lick** on me. (J. W. Williams, Williams Papers, Duke) Onslow County

Aug. 2, 1863: the vixburg Prisoners is giting home daly. they had a hard time they dont blame Pemberton for the Surender & Say Gen Johnson did all he could to relieve them but was not abel to do So. we lost 27000 Prisoners. this is the worst **lick** of the war. (Stephen Whitaker, Whitaker Papers, NCSA) Cherokee County

lie *verb* Of food in the stomach: to be felt; to be digestible (sometimes in a negative context). [*DARE* **lie**, verb[1], 3]

Jan. 14, 1862: M N Russel is verry sick but dont tell his wife i dont think that he can live if he dont get better and that verry soon. nothing wont **lie** on his stomache. (Samuel Bell, Bell Papers, Duke) Macon County

lie out *verb* To hide out, fail to return to one's unit, avoid conscription or arrest; see Overview § II.4.7. [see *DARE,* **lie out**, verb phrase, 1c, 2]

Mar. 3, 1863: I no if he come back the poor women will fair bad for he will steel anny thing he can git holt of and if he git chance to come home he will **ly out** in the green s[w]amp. (G. Formyduval, Vance Papers, NCSA) Columbus County

Mar. 9, 1863: Dear wife tell me in your next letter wheather Thomas litle auctiley **lay out** or not or wheather it onley was a talk. (W. F. Wagner, *Confederate Soldier,* 40) Catawba County

Oct. 12, 1863: I will assure you that I will bee as faith full a Soldier thare is in the Con fedrsay. I no that I owe my Servisis and I am willing to pay them please Govener answer this for I am tirerde of **lying out**. (Jacob Herring, Vance Papers, NCSA) Columbus County

lift (a note) *verb* To take up or collect (rents or money due). [*OED* **lift,** verb, 7, "now *dial.*"; see also *DARE* **lift**, verb, 2]

Apr. 18, 1862: if Fetherton hasent **lifted** that note and if you see hime tell him that Huffstetler owes me five dollars. (J. W. Lineberger, *Gaston Ranger,* 5) Gaston County

June 2, 1863: I sent jonas A leter for him to setel with you and I want you to **lift** that note and I want you to rite how Much o[w]es back yet. I pade him the principel. the amount was the intrust. (Marcus Hefner, Hefner Papers, NCSA) Catawba County

light bread *noun* Loaf bread made with yeast. [*DARE* chiefly South, South Midland, Oklahoma, Texas]

Dec. 6, 1861: we get bacon beef flour corn bread and **Lite bread** A plenty. (J. W. Williams, Williams Papers, Duke) Onslow County

May 14, 1863: I have just receaved the letter you sent by Mr Harris & the chicken & **light bread** you sent me. (James A. Patton, Patton Letters, Emory) Granville County

Apr. 21, 1864: when you send after us you wil have to send us somethin to eat going home. if John gets to go you will have to backe some nice **light bread** for him to eat. he is still rite sick. (Alvira Taylor, Taylor Papers, Duke) Orange County

June 27, 1864: Francis I went to a house the other night and got Supper. I will tell you what I had for Supper. I had Some **light Bread** and Butter. meat and huney and cheas. I tell you that I Eat harty. (J. W. Joyce, Joyce Papers, MHI) Stokes County

lightred, litred *noun* Kindling; variant form of *lightwood.* [*DSME* **lightwood**, variant form *litered; DARE* chiefly South, especially South Atlantic]

Mar. 9, 1862: we got Hawkins [= a woman's name] Some wood and **litred** and I Shal See to here [= her] as well as I can. (Austin Brown, Confederate Papers, SHC) Johnston County

light with *verb* To get, meet with; see Overview § II.4.7. [*OED* **light,** verb[1], b]

Sept. 16, 1862: I would be verry glad to come home and see you all one more time but I dont know when I will **light with** that opportunity. (J. H. Hundley, Hundley Family Letters, SHC) Stokes County

like *noun* see **the like**

like *verb* variant form of *lack.* [*DARE* especially South, South Midland]

Oct. 1, 1861: Pappy we have not recieve our Money and it will be a long time befour we are [= ever] do. I think, if we **like** eny I will write to you for some. (K. W. Coghill, Coghill Papers, Duke) Granville County

Dec. 2, 1862: I **like** A coat if you can getit and one or two pare of Socks. if you can get the coat make it A frocktail with the pockets in the side. (J. F. Coghill, Coghill Papers, Duke) Granville County

likeness *noun* A photograph; in earlier English *likeness* referred to an image or a portrait in any kind of medium. [*OED* **likeness**, noun, 3.a. (from Old English *licnes*)]

Aug. 25, 1861: I receift yore **likness** and it looks v[e]ry Mutch like you. (John A. Long, Long Family Papers, SHC) Alamance County

Apr. 28, 1862: i wod as Sunes be dire [= there] my self as to send my **likness.** (W. P. Cline, Cline Papers, SHC) Catawba County

Aug. 4, 1862: Archy they hav bin the prettest red color in your **likeness** face ever since you hav bin sick. it is shocken pretty know [now]. (Dicy Ann Jackson, Jackson Family Corr., Notre Dame) Moore County

Mar. 3, 1863: i an affe got an order an went to hamelton crossen yesterday an had our **likness** taken an it is exactly like mee they all say. (T. F. Baggarly, Baggarly Papers, Duke) Iredell County

June 1, 1863: tell Delia I wroat her a letter last Saturday week, with a yankee **likeness** in it. (Isham Upchurch, Upchurch Papers, Duke) Chatham County

like that see **that**

liked to, like to *adverb phrase* Nearly, almost; historically the full form is *had like(d) to have,* followed by a past participle (e.g., *I had liked to have died*); *had* is sometimes deleted; *have* following *like(d) to* is often reduced to *a* or deleted. As can be seen in the citations below, there is a considerable amount of variation in this particular structure (often referred to as *liketa*).

[see *DSME* **liked to, like to**; *DARE* **like** verb[1], E, 1 and 2; chiefly South, South Midland]

1. with *had* before and *have* following *liked to, like to.*

Nov. 10, 1861: I had **liked to** have Shot a fisherman while Standing at the mouth of mitchael Sound. (John B. Lance, Lance Papers, LSU) Henderson County

June 12, 1862: I had **Like to** halv forgoten to ask you if you got them postedg stamps I sent you or Not. (Alfred Walsh, Proffit Family Letters, SHC) Wilkes County

2. with *had* deleted before *liked to, like to.*

Aug. 17, 1859: oh I **like to** have forgoten to tell you how Cousin Hugh flew round Miss Lizza when he was down here. (Isabella Johnson, Jackson Family Corr., Notre Dame) Robeson County

Dec. 6, 1863: I will tell you we had a time of it in the cold. we **like to** a froze. (A. J. Spease, Zimmerman Papers, Duke) Forsyth County

3. with *have* reduced or deleted after *liked to, like to.*

June 15, 1863: ther had **like to** bin alittel batel her the other day with the boys that runaway an the melishey but tha got hit sorter seteld. (J. A. W. Revis, Revis Letters, NCSA) Henderson County

Dec. 21, 1863: I had **like to** forgot to tell you I was mite glad to git them Stamps. (Neill McLeod, McLeod Letters, SHC) Moore County

Feb. 10, 1865: we fel Back at night and the yankeys they fel Back two. I think Boath sids was giting tired of it and if evry Body got as coald as I Did they wold a stop be fore they did. the yankeys had **like to** a got our Camp. (J. W. Joyce, Joyce Papers, MHI) Stokes County

Feb. 12, 1865: hit has bin so very cold thear on the warf that wee had **Licked to** frozed to Death. (Wade Hubbard, Hubbard Papers, Duke) Anson County

4. with both *had* and *have* deleted.

Dec. 23, 1862: one thing i **like to** for got. what will bill moor do if he has to go off. i reckin tha ar takin on abowt him. (T. F. Baggarly, Baggarly Papers, Duke) Iredell County

5. with *liken to;* functionally this form appears to be indistinguishable from *liked to, like to.* [see *DARE* **liken**, vbl aux]

Jan. 11, 1863: Dear I was in one fite and never want to git in a nother one. I **liken to** got wounded. thar was a peas of bum shell hit me on the Back. (W. F. Wagner, *Confederate Soldier,* 31) Catawba County

likely *adjective* Promising, having a hopeful appearance.

July 5, 1856: the weat crop is only comon. the corn crop is very **likely** with good seasons an the help of god. it is the best we have had for many years. (Moses [Pettigrew slave], Pettigrew Family Papers, SHC) Washington County

limestone water *noun phrase* Hard water, water containing dissolved minerals.

Sept. 1, 1862: I like the **lime Stone water** just as good as the free Stone. (R. P. Kelly, Edmonston-Kelly Family Papers, WCU) Haywood County

June 12, 1862: it is rumerd hear that our reg. is orderd away from hear. I do Not know and I dont care if it is for the Strong **Limstone Warter** is Not good for No 1 [= no one]. (Alfred Walsh, Proffit Family Letters, SHC) Wilkes County

Apr. 13, 1864: The water here agrees with me very well to be **Limestone Water**. (C. A. Walker, Walker Papers, WCU) Cherokee County

Lincolnite *noun* A Unionist in a Southern or border state. See also **tory**.

Dec. 9, 1861: the health of the regiment is much better than it was some time back. if the **lincolnites** should come I think we will be able to give them a fare showing. (J. E. Patton, Patton Family Letters, Duke) Buncombe County

June 24, 1863: I am an acting Justic of the peace for th[e] County of Chatham an living in the South west corner of Said Conty near Moore and Randolph Countys whar ther is a grate many **linconits** deserters an Conscripts. (Wesley Jones, Vance Papers, NCSA) Chatham County

Aug. 27, 1863: the news is now that the yankeys is above her beyond Bristol this cuts us off intiraly & we are lookin to be attacted every day. we are in the mids [= midst] of **Lincoleites** & Surounded by yankeys. (Stephen Whitaker, Whitaker Papers, NCSA) Cherokee County

lincy *noun* Fabric that is a combination of linen and wool (*linsey-woolsey*) or wool and cotton; variant form of *linsey*. [*DSME* **linsey, linsey cloth, linsey-woolsey**, noun]

Nov. 22, 1861: I Waunt you to have me a **lincy** shirt mad and send it By mr Jones. you can git some Coat Lining at phillip Davises that Will answer or if you can git some thin **Lincy** Wolen cloth. it Will do vary Well. dont make it ot of Jeans for it Will Be to thick. (G. J. Huntley, Huntley Papers, WCU) Rutherford County

Sept. 28, 1862: I rote last Sunday for you to send me a box of appels and a **lincy** Shirt if you had anychance. (R. C. Love, Love Papers, Duke) Henderson County

Nov. 6, 1862: I am Requested By our Col to ask you By Letter what to Give for Janes and **Lincy** cloth and socks & Blankets. (G. M. Webb, Vance Papers, NCSA) Rutherford County

line see **loin**

linnwood *noun* The basswood or linden tree, *Tilia americana*.

Dec. 25, 1858: as you requested to know what kind of timber we have in this country. thare is white oke. black oke. red oake. Spanish oake and hickrey black white and scaly barke. black walnut white walnut. mulbery. cotton wood. wile chery. elum and **lin wood**. shugar trees. sicamore and buckei. buroake. severl other kinds too tedous to mention. the under groth is mostley hasle and shumake. (William Boss, Frank Papers, Duke) Davidson County

linsey see **lincy**

listed see **enlist**

listen at see **at**

litred see **lightred**

live, leave *adverb* Willingly (following *as* or *just as*); variant forms of *lief*. [*DARE* chiefly Northeast, Midland]

May 4, 1862: I am sick and tired of this War and Camp life But I had as **Live** Be On the Battellfield as to go home. (G. J. Huntley, Huntley Papers, WCU) Rutherford County

Apr. 26, 1863: it seames like i never git to come home to see you and Wm. I had as **live** be ded as to never git to see my famly. (J. C. Owens, Confederate Papers, SHC) Wilkes County

Jan. 14, 1864: I had as **liv** stay here as to Stay in North Caralina. Without I could Stay in Martin County. (Edgar Smithwick, Smithwick Papers, Duke) Martin County

Apr. 22, 1864: It put a kind of queer feeling on me but Still I was not frightened at all After the firing commenced. I would just as **leave** been in there as any where. (C. A. Walker, Walker Papers, WCU) Cherokee County

liver complaint *noun* A disease or disorder of the liver.

Jan. 14, 1862: Pat Rone is verry sick now. he has the mumps and the **liver complaint** but not daingeroust i dont think. he caint set up but what it makes him sick. he is in my mess and i am detailed to wait on him. (Samuel Bell, Bell Papers, Duke) Macon County

Oct. 24, 1862: i have bin sick for two week and i haint mutch better yet ~~yo~~ i have got the yallerjanders and the **liver complaint**. (T. B. Litton, Fisher Papers, Duke) Catawba County

loaf bread *noun* Wheat bread leavened with yeast. See also **light bread, flour bread**. [*DARE* "Scots, Engl dial"; chiefly South, South Midland]

Mar. 25, 1863: we have good quarters here and good old Bacon three years old I Exspect from the look and tast of it and plenty of **loaf Bread**. So we will try to be Satisfied with our condition. (W. L. Caldwell, Caldwell Coll., ECU) Cabarrus County

Oct. 18, 1864: if he dont bring me something iwill be gon up the spout for they ar giving ous **lofe bread** & not half anuff. (L. W. Griffin, Griffin Papers, NCSA) Rutherford County

Nov. 10, 1864: I know that you would like to know what sort [of] rations We get. well we dont get any to much to ate. we get **loaf bread**. one loaf for two days. (Joseph Wright, Wright Papers, Duke) Alamance County

lobelia *noun* Any of several wild flowering plants belonging to the genus *Lobelia;* it was once widely believed to have medicinal qualities, especially for the treatment of respiratory illnesses, including pneumonia.

Dec. 29, 1861: I would like to have some Black powders & some **Lobelia** seeds if you can git any chance to send them. (G. J. Huntley, Huntley Papers, WCU) Rutherford County

loden *verb* variant past participle of *load.* [*OED* **load**, verb, 1.a.]

Sept. 27, 1862: some of our men saw heaps of melted lead where they burned wagons **loden** with it. (James Zimmerman, Zimmerman Papers, Duke) Forsyth County

loft *noun* A second story or attic of a house used for storage and as sleeping quarters. [*DARE* **loft** noun, 2; scattered, but chiefly South Midland, South]

Nov. 2, 1864: when it got so that it couldent talk it would point its little finger for what it wanted and the day before it died it would look at me and then point with its little finger towards the **loft.** I think it saw the Angels that come to take it to heaven. it tried to show it to me but I couldent see nothing. (Martha Poteet, Poteet-Dickson Letters, NCSA) McDowell County

log rolling *noun* A community gathering in which land is cleared of trees and the downed timber removed and usually burned; typically followed by a meal or a party.

Mar. 21, 1858: Lemiel has made his house logs. he is a makeing shinggles now but I dont know when he is agoing to rase it but I dont think till fall. he wants to have a **log roleing** nex Friday. (W. F. Wagner, *Confederate Soldier,* 3) Catawba County

Feb. 21, 1864: tell Rebeca Rivenbank that H J Johnson is going to have a **log roling** at his new place on the creek & speeks of askin me. (Willis J. Holland, Quinn Papers, Duke) Duplin County

loin *noun* variant form of *line.*

July 5, 1856: I looked A long time to hear from master an was happy to receve the **loins** master sent. hope that master is in the same good health an remain so. (Moses [Pettigrew slave], Pettigrew Family Papers, SHC) Washington County

May 22, 1863: Dear wife I take the pleasure of wrighting you a few **loines** in ancer to yours Cind letter that come to hand on the 19. (Daniel Brown, Brown Coll., NCSA) Duplin County

Aug. 17, 1863: I seat my selfe this eavning to drop you afiew **loines** to let you know that I am well at presant hoping when thease fiew **loines** reache you they may find you all injoying the same like blessing. (O. C. Morgan, Revis Letters, NCSA) Henderson County

June 15, 1864: I take mi pen in hand to drop you A few **loins** to let you no I am well and truly hope when theas few **loins** cume to hand ma find you well and doing well. (John H. Black, Black Letters, UVA) Yadkin County

lonesome *adjective* superlative form *lonesomest.*

Aug. 20, 1863: Sis I am the **loansomest** chicken you ever saw. no pirson to stay with or talk with of my acquaints. (Alfred N. Proffit, Proffit Family Letters, SHC) Wilkes County

long home *noun phrase* Figuratively: a grave. [*long home* has an extended history, going back to Old English *langne ham;* see *OED* **home**, noun[1], 3]

Apr. 22, 1864: our boat sunk one of thern & they was one hundred and fifty went down with it to their **long homes**. (J. W. Lineberger, *Gaston Ranger,* 96) Gaston County

July 28, 1864: I know there has been a great many boys carried off from this county poor things many of them have gone to there **long home**. (Hannah Smithwick, Smithwick Papers, Duke) Martin County

longleaf pine *noun* A species of pine, *Pinus palustris,* native to the southeastern states; also known as *fat pine, pitch pine,* and *yellow pine.*

Jan. 24, 1863: We are now in the Swampy **long leaf pine** country in the eastern part of N.C about 2 ½ miles from south Washington. (C. A. Hege, Hege Papers, MHI) Davidson County

long mouthed *adjective phrase* Gossipy, "big-mouthed."

Mar. 26, 1863: I want you to not let **long mouth** folks no ever thing. (J. W. Reese, Reese Papers, Duke) Buncombe County

Long Tom *noun* A nickname sometimes given to heavy, long-range artillery pieces, including at least one used for coastal defense in North Carolina.

Sept. 22, 1861: I hird the other day that som men was triing old **long tom** 3 miles at an old ship an sed [they] pluged a hole evey time for 4 times. (G. T. Beavers, Upchurch Papers, Duke) Chatham County

Sept. 28, 1862: we sent down to fort fisher and got old **long tom** and brough him up and give themthree rounds and they run back out of our way. it is supposed that two of the shots hit the vessel. (R. C. Love, Love Papers, Duke) Henderson County

look *verb* To expect, anticipate (followed by an infinitive). [*DARE,* **look**, verb, 4; chiefly South, South Midland]

Jan. 26, 1863: We have been **looking** to go back to N. C. (C. F. Mills, *Mills Papers* Duke) Iredell County

look for *verb* To expect, anticipate; usually as present participle; see Overview § II.4.7. [*DARE,* verb, **look**, 5]

Feb. 6, 1862: We ar **looking for** an a tact in very short time. (R. P. Crawford Feb. 6, 1862:, Estes Family Papers, WCU) Jackson County

Feb. 6, 1862: we have one in the hospitel and we are **looking for** him in Camp. (M. W. Parris, Parris Papers, WCU) Jackson County

Jan. 19, 1863: I am anchieous to hear from you I have ben **looking fur** a letter from you but I have not reseved one sence I saw you last. (Jonas Bradshaw, Bradshaw Papers, Duke) Alexander County

July 25, 1864: you must not **loock fore** me to write you along latter this time fore I Cant think of anything to write. (Lewis Moore, Moore Letter, CACWL) Cumberland County

look out for *verb* To expect, anticipate; see Overview § II.4.7.

July 30, 1861: after we got there the people wer **looking out for** another attack every turn for old Scott said he would have th[i]s place. (J. N. Coghill, Coghill Papers, Duke) Granville County

look over *verb* To overlook, disregard, excuse; see Overview § II.4.7. [*DARE* chiefly South, South Midland]

May 26, 1862: I fear you cannot read this letter. it is don in a hurry. pleas **look over** it this time. (Jesse Shipman, Shipman Family Corr., Notre Dame) Henderson County

lose *verb* past tense form *losten*. [*DARE* **lose**, verb, A 2 "past, past pple. ppl adj: usu *lost;* also *lose(d), loss, losted, losten*"]

Nov. 10, 1862: thy may be a big fight in a few days. I cannot tell. thy are reforsing heavly on both Sides. our campiny **losten** very Near all thy had in the fight. (W. D. Carter, Culberson Papers, Duke) Chatham County

loud see **allow**

low *adjective* Sick, in poor health, weak. [*OED* **low**, adjective, II.8.a.]

Aug. 7, 1861: I have bin sick for 3 weekes & was very **low** When I Received your leter & I am bad of[f] yet. (Peter Poteet, Poteet-Dickson Letters, NCSA) Burke County

Aug. 17, 1861: Neell Wingate is laying very **low** with fever now. (David N. McCorkle, Military Coll., Civil War, NCSA) Catawba County

Aug. 9, 1862: lieutenant Cooper is very **lo**. they hav Been 11 Died with the fever in co A since we left kinston. (J. W. Love, Love Papers, Duke) Henderson County

Nov. 18, 1862: I found Rufus Mitchell with little exspectation Lying vary **low** and you may be Well assure it put a sad feeling on me and when I spoke to him he Bursted out crying. (Joseph Cowand, Cowand Papers, Duke) Bertie County

lowdown *adjective* Mean, corrupt, contemptible, of low moral character. [*DARE* formerly chiefly South, South Midland; now more widespread]

May 7, 1863: there are wealthy people here that furnish corn to persons that are not responsible for any thing and they do the s[t]illing while the weathy man reaps the benefit. they also get **lowdown** females to

Still for them. (T. J. Bicknell, Vance Papers, NCSA) Wilkes County

May 20, 1863: Phillips Was the meanest Looking White man You Ever saw. he Could not raise his head hardly. the men Curses him for all the Dam rascals that Ever Lived. after I Was almost unanimously Elected the Colonel Come and shook hands With me and said he hoped that I Would Live to Enjoy the honours that Was due me for the Bravery that I Displaid. he also said that Phillips acted **Lowdown.** I Cant tell You all the Particulars of it But I Come Out the Nisest You Ever Saw. (G. J. Huntley, Huntley Papers, WCU) Rutherford County

luck well *verb phrase* To have good luck. [*OED* **luck,** verb, 1.a., "usually with adverb complement *well, ill,* obscure except dialectal"]

Feb. 22, 1863: Too more of our boys have sent up their furloughs. William Murphy. And J. F. Fox is the next too: They will bee at home soon if they **luck well**. (W. M. Patton, Patton Family Letters, SHC) Buncombe County

M

ma, mar, maw *noun* Mother; see Overview § I.1.1.

July 30, 1861: Mar I waunt you and Sister to rase Hettie good and ceep her out of the Sun. (K. W. Coghill, Coghill Papers, Duke) Granville County

Feb. 7, 1863: a few lines for sissey & Buddy. you must be purty children for **maw.** you most toat chips and water for **maw** and you most not fite nor hurt the sweat little Baby and mind it good for **maw**. (Isaac Lefevers, Lefevers Papers, NCSA) Catawba County

Feb. 8, 1863: I want you and **Ma** if they ever come thare again to do your best in trying to kill them fer they are worse than A yankey. (J. F. Coghill, Coghill Papers, Duke) Granville County

Apr. 16, 1863: tell your **Mar** & Par that I would Be more then Glad to see them. (John Futch, Futch Letters, NCSA) New Hanover County

Feb. 26, 1865: ask **ma** to read this to you. your pa wants you to be good boys and if your pa dies without seeing you any more be good boys and repent of your sins. (Isham Upchurch, Upchurch Papers, Duke) Chatham County

mail, male *noun* An occasion or time at which mail is sent or delivered.

Aug. 10, 1861: Tell my friends to write to me Every chance they have So that I Can give them the Corr.,ect news. Tell wood sides to send my paper next **male** So that I Can here from that striped place called Newton where I have lived. (W. R. D. Bost, Gibson Papers, Duke) Catawba County

Oct. 1, 1861: They Stated that you arrived saft and sound. I was very anxious to hear from you. We haven receive but one **mail** since you left. (K. W. Coghill, Coghill Papers, Duke) Granville County

Feb. 2, 1862: It apears that I dont write offtimes to you My Mollie. my dear girl I write you nearly by evry **maile**. I wrote you just as I was starting fore Raleigh. (A. W. Bell, Bell Papers, Duke) Macon County

Feb. 16, 1864: idont git Eny Letters from you By the male iwant you to rite a letter to me ever **male**. irite three Letters to you ever week. (Thornton Sexton, Sexton Letters, Duke) Ashe County

make *verb*

1. To raise a crop, gather fodder, or produce a commodity (in sentences with human subjects).

Sept. 14, 1862: We want to know how much wheat we **made** and how you all come on **makeing** brandy. it is worth Twenty dollers per gallon here. (James Zimmerman, Zimmerman Papers, Duke) Forsyth County

Oct. 10, 1862: Dear Wife you said that you was done **makeing** fodder but the newground and youwouldent make it your self. (W. F. Wagner, *Confederate Soldier,* 19) Catawba County

June 23, 1863: I am try ing to **make** corn for us to live on. we have got over the corn the first time and started over the second time. (Sarepta Revis, Revis Letters, NCSA) Henderson County

Mar. 18, 1864: I want you to **make** all the corn you can and I want you to rite to me and tel me how the wheate looks and oats. (Daniel Setzer, Setzer Papers, Duke) Catawba County

2. Same sense as 1, but in passive constructions with the active voice subject (agent) omitted.

Oct. 29, 1861: thir is good crops **made** in our county. (Elizabeth Watson, Watson Letters, WCU) Jackson County

June 9, 1862: I hope thair will be good crops **made** this year for we get but Little now and if crops fails we Shall come to suffer. (J. W. Williams, Williams Papers, Duke) Onslow County

3. Of a crop or farmland: to yield a particular amount, to be successful or productive (in sentences with nonhuman subjects).

Aug. 23, 1862: tell mee how the corn is for i saw bw[t] litle bee tween home an her. i saw bar fields that wont **make** nothin a tol. (T. F. Baggarly, Baggarly Papers, Duke) Iredell County

Aug. 8, 1863: the wheat must bin mity bad that hant half as much as it **made** too yares ago. (Daniel Setzer, Setzer Papers, Duke) Catawba County

make garden *verb phrase* To prepare and plant a vegetable garden for household use.

Feb. 11, 1864: wee ar now agon to **make gardon** and plant potatoes. (Susan Setzer, Setzer Papers, Duke) Catawba County

make out *verb* See Overview § II.4.7.

1. To get by, get along, fare.

Oct. 16, 1861: tell Sister Elizabeth that She need not to Send me no bed clothing for I will **make out** with out them. (Charley Futch, Futch Letters, NCSA) New Hanover County

Feb. 26, 1863: if i git a plenty to eat and to ware a Somthing to drink and a five Shinplasters i Can **make out** verry well. (Isaac Copeland, Copeland Letters, NCSA) Surry County

Mar. 25, 1863: a young man bey Name of Jasper crook was taking sick an sent to Ralegh NC an was put in tha houspitatal a bout 7 weaks a goe and his pople has not heard from him sence. he is from Bumcombe co[unty] in J. R. Young companey in tha 11 Reagment of State Troops of NC volenteers an Mr vance his Mother qu<??>hes [= inquires?] of you if tha is a man bey tha name of Jasper crook in tha Houspital at Roligh. She wants you to you to make an inqury a bout him an if he is thar she wants youe to goe an see him an see how he is **a making out** an rite what you thinck is the matter with him. (M. P. Lytle, Vance Papers, NCSA) Buncombe County

June 4, 1863: we are faring very Well now. we got as mutch fat bacon as we can eat and **make out** with the flour and crackers tolerable well. (Joel Howard, Brotherton Papers, Duke) Lincoln County

Dec. 31, 1863: I want to no how you are **making out** for Provisions and whether you have moved or not. (Daniel Abernethy, Abernethy Papers, Duke) Catawba County

2. Followed by *like, as if:* To act (like), act (as if); to pretend.

Nov. 24, 1862: they are trying to slip around and get to Richmond and **make out** like they are yet at Fredricksburg. (James Zimmerman, Zimmerman Papers, Duke) Forsyth County

Dec. 15, 1864: you rote to no how my head was and I rote to you the docter was a going to cut it out but he gave me some thing to squirt up my nose but that did not do any good as I could tel. but the doctor said he would pool it out some time. he **makes out** as if it hant nothing much no how but it has not got no worse since I left home. (Henry Bowen, Bowen Papers, NCSA) Washington County

male see **mail**

mam *noun* Mother; see Overview § I.1.1. [*OED* **mam**, noun[1]]

Apr. 13, 1862: I think that I can make a niser Biscuit than you Or **mam** Either. if I Ever git home We Will try it at any rate. (G. J. Huntley, Huntley Papers, WCU) Rutherford County

July 20, 1862: tell **mam** not to be oneasy about me and Brother. we are all right on the Goose. (K. W. Coghill, Coghill Papers, Duke) Granville County

Jan. 21, 1864: tel **mam** hody for me and all the rest of the famles. i cant write to al of them. I hant got time tel them to write to me. (R. C. Caldwell, Caldwell Coll., ECU) Cabarrus County

mamma *noun* Mother; see Overview § I.1.1. [although common today throughout the South, *mamma* is the least common word for *mother* in the North Carolina sample, with the examples below being the only occurrences; *DARE* widespread but less frequent North, North Midland]

Jan. 9, 1862: pleas **mama** Send me A peace of fresh meet and bread by bryant basden and A potato. (J. W. Williams, Williams Papers, Duke) Onslow County

July 14, 1863: he has Left Rutherfordton But he sliped a Little. the signes Didnt Sute him and he Left with out going to See my **mama**. (W. A. E. Roberts, Vance Papers, NCSA) Rutherford County

mammy *noun* Mother; see Overview § I.1.1.

June 22, 1861: tell your **mamy** and dady that I am well and that I would like to harvest for them. (Harrison Hanes, Hanes Papers, Duke) Davie County

Sept. 7, 1861: Hannah please go over to paps and see my military ambrotype and you will say it is one of the best you ever saw. I had it taken in Raleigh and sent it to my **mamy**. (C. L. Moffitt, Caldwell Coll., Duke) Randolph County

Apr. 6, 1864: i want you to bea good boys and do what your **mammy** tells you to do. (Franklin Setzer, Setzer Corr., UVA) Catawba County

Nov. 24, 1864: you all so wrote to your **mamy** to not let your children suffer. if we dont keep our selves from suffering with out help from any plase we will perish. I think it makes me look very small for you to write the like to her when you know that she wont help them. (Martha Poteet, Poteet-Dickson Letters, NCSA) McDowell County

man *verb* To master, subdue, manage. [*DSME* **man**, B verb; *OED* **man**, verb, III.8.]

Nov. 21, 1863: I Was Glad to get my Box. I think I can **man** it this time. I can eat any thing. nothing cums rong to me. you ot ce [= ought to see] how I can eat. (R. C. Caldwell, Caldwell Coll., ECU) Cabarrus County

man *noun* A husband.

May 3, 1863: I Can inform you that the folks is A Dieing Pouerfull A bout her. thare was too wennon [= women] Buried this week that thare **men** was in the army. (Keziah Hefner, Hefner Papers, NCSA) Catawba County

man person *noun* A man, a male person. [*DSME* **man person**, noun; *DARE* chiefly South Midland]

Nov. 2, 1862: I have thrwee brothers in the armey with other relaten tow [= relations too]. so ther is know **man person** belonging to the famelys. (John L. Webb, Vance Papers, NCSA) Rockingham County

mar see **ma**

mast *noun* Fallen nuts from trees, especially acorns and (in the nineteenth century) chestnuts; an important feed for hogs which were let loose in the woods to forage in the late summer and early fall. [*OED* **mast**, noun[2], with citations going back to Old English *mæst*]

Sept. 27, 1863: Dear husband Ican say to you that I hav got my hogs up. ther is no **mast** and I thot that I had beter put them up in time. I hav fore up. I hav got for out yet and I hav got anuf old corn to do tel I gether mi corn. (Catherine Lefevers, Lefevers Papers, NCSA) Catawba County

Nov. 4, 1863: write whether uncle George is in the home guard and whether thar is any **mast** this fall. (J. M. Frank, Frank Papers, Duke) Davidson County

maul rails *verb phrase* To split fence rails with a maul. [*DARE* chiefly South, South Midland]

Jan. 5, 1864: I would be very glad to se all of you. Tel Charles and Ben to Be sure to take care of Bet until I come home. [tell] lige [= Elijah] I had much rather their with him **Maling** rales. (T. C. Wester, Wester Coll., NCSA) Franklin County

maw see **ma**

maybe can *auxiliary verbs* Might be able to (similar to *may can, might could*).

Oct. 4, 1864: I want you to send me sum cabetch potatoes and peper and sum of our homade tobacco.

send what you can. you **maby can** think About what I want. (F. M. Poteet, Poteet-Dickson Letters, NCSA) McDowell County

me *pronoun* Used reflexively instead of *myself* as an indirect object, or redundantly before a direct object (the two are not always distinguishable). [see *DSME* **me**, pronoun 1; *DARE* **me**, pronoun, 3a and 3b]

Dec. 6, 1862: we have Drawn clothing and I Drawd **me** a over coat and one pr pants and one shirt and pr Drawers and 1 pr shoes and I want you to send me them two shirts and that comfort the First chance you get. (William Tesh, Tesh Papers, Duke) Yadkin County

Feb. 27, 1863: I hav got **mee** A pone on to Rais then I think I can Eat my Supper. (J. W. Reese, Reese Papers, Duke) Buncombe County

Oct. 8, 1864: I have succeeded in getting **me** an old broken down horse, with which I have succeeded in making **me** a crop. (Jack Williamson, Whitford Papers, Duke) Jones County

Mar. 12, 1865: tell Mary Etter that I got up this moring a bout two ours be fore day and backed [= baked] **me** a grate big pon[e] of bread. (J. W. Joyce, Joyce Papers, MHI) Stokes County

meanness *noun* Mean-spirited behavior, a spiteful act.

June 17, 1863: I Pay for all the Letters I start. it is Jest **meanness** of the Post Masters that you have to pay for the Letters I send to you. (Sarepta Revis, Revis Letters, NCSA) Henderson County

May 17, 1863: I hate to hear of **meanness** Agoing on in my natif Countrey for if thair Ever was A time that peple wood lay off **meanness** and Ceace to doo wicked is not this the time. (J. W. Reese, Reese Papers, Duke) Buncombe County

meat house *noun* An out-building where meat is cured, smoked, and/or stored; same as or similar to *smokehouse*. [*DARE* chiefly South Midland]

May 25, 1863: there are a number of deserters Lerking about in this County and the malitia are making no effort to arrest them and they are a doing agreat deal of mischief Robing **meat houses** and Breaking open Mills and Stealing meal and flower and I have bean told that along this mountain they have Broke and carried off all the farming tools wash pots and kettles. (G. W. Dobson, Vance Papers, NCSA) McDowell County

meeting *noun* A worship service.

Aug. 8, 1861: I wish you a good **metin** for it is needed there. not there only but evry wher els for it is for the lack of good **meetins** and good people the reason this trouble is com a pon the land. (Harrison Hanes, Hanes Papers, Duke) Davie County

Aug. 23, 1863: I have binne goine to **meatin** day an nite fore some time ther hase binn aprotack [= protracted] meatin every sens I Came hare. I am glade to tell you of the nuse thar hase binn some Eighty soles Con varty[= converted] sense this **meating** Coments [= commenced]. (Phillip Walsh, Proffit Family Letters, SHC) Wilkes County

Aug. 4, 1864: Sunday we have good Preaching to Day and Pray **Meeting** this Eavning and So nearly Evry day. (Wade Hubbard, Hubbard Papers, Duke) Anson County

meeting house *noun* A church. [*DSME* **meeting house**, "used in the 18th and 19th centuries especially by Baptists and Methodists in church names and in general reference"]

July 16, 1861: they was meny Balls Went into the **meting house**. our old Colonel Was in all of the mexicin War And he says that he never Saw Such abattle in his travels. (Peter Poteet, Poteet-Dickson Letters, NCSA) Burke County

Aug. 19, 1864: I expect they will hav a protracted meeting at the Baptis **meeting house**. (Martha Poteet, Poteet-Dickson Letters, NCSA) McDowell County

meet up with *verb* To meet by chance; see Overview § II.4.7.

Feb. 6, 1863: I got A letter from Cousin Amie this weeak and she said that Brother was going from thare the other day and he **met up with** two of the Conscrips and one was Charles Edwards. (J. F. Coghill, Coghill Papers, Duke) Granville County

melon *noun*

1. variant forms *milon, milin.*

   Aug. 21, 1862: we had a heap of fun. we got plenty to eat. chickens rosenyears [= roastin ears] to eat water **milons** to eat. (S. E. Love, Love Papers, Duke) Henderson County

   Aug. 2, 1863: i want you to com and Sea Me and fetch Me a warter **Milin** and rite Me word how your garden is and how your crop is. (John Futch, Futch Letters, NCSA) New Hanover County

2. variant forms *milion, million.*

   Aug. 18, 1862: tell Miles Sherrill & Salley houdy for me. tell them I would like to see them all & be thir to eat Appels & Peaches & **water milions**. (James Fisher, Fisher Papers, Duke) Catawba County

   Sept. 10, 1862: well gorge you must plant them water **millions** Seed but I think that we will git home in time to eat them. (R. C. Love, Love Papers, Duke) Henderson County

   July 20, 1864: we ar geting plenty of Bred and meat to eat. and we Can Steel as many **watermilions** as we want. So the 6 Cav. will not starve while eney Body els has eney thing to eat. (James W. Horton, Councill Papers, Duke) Watauga County

mend *verb*

1. To heal, recover from an illness, injury, or wound.

   Oct. 15, 1861: I walk all the time passing to and froe evey whare and is **mending** fast. (J. W. Williams, Williams Papers, Duke) Onslow County

   Aug. 21, 1863: A. H. Eliott is **mending**. he is not Able to git About mutch yet. (Larkin Kendrick, Kendrick Papers, NCSA) Cleveland County

   Sept. 29, 1863: I was truley proud to here that poer litle Hugh was **mending** (A. A. Jackson, Jackson Family Corr., Notre Dame) Moore County

   Apr. 30, 1864: my horse has **mended** since I left home. (Albert W. Blair, Blair Letters, NCSA) Caldwell County

2. To repair.

   Nov. 1, 1864: on thursday night the 27 of October it was very dark and rainy the yankees sliped up on the iron clad and threw torpeders under her and blew a hole in her. I heard they took the men that done it. they dident injer her so but what she could of bin **mended**. (Ann Bowen, Bowen Papers, NCSA) Washington County

mend up *verb* To gain weight, become healthy; see Overview § II.4.7.

Sept. 9, 1863: I was in hops you was a mending by this time. if you can eat harty I think you will **mend up** before long if you dont get sick. (Molly Tesh, Tesh Papers, Duke) Yadkin County

Sept. 5, 1864: the filly ihave got her in your uncle bill pasture. She is thin in<??> but has **mended up** Som and has grod Smartly. (Thomas Brotherton, Brotherton Papers, Duke) Catawba County

mess[1] *noun* A sufficient quantity of some kind of food; an amount consumed at a single meal. [*DARE* chiefly Northeast, South, South Midland]

July 27, 1862: I would like prety well to take a **mess** of greens over some Saturday & Se how they are getting a long. (C. S. McCurdy, CS Army, Misc., Duke) Cabarrus County

Sept. 14, 1862: I had a fine **mess** of fish this morning I caut yestarday. (James Zimmerman, Zimmerman Papers, Duke) Forsyth County

Aug. 2, 1863: I have had one **Mes** of beanes and and squashes but I had to pay 1 dollar for them. (John Futch, Futch Letters, NCSA) New Hanover County

June 16, 1864: the sweet potatoes is very prety and the irish potatoes is the pretyest I ever seen. I hav a **mess** today. I wish you was hear to eat some with me. (Martha Poteet, Poteet-Dickson Letters, NCSA) McDowell County

Oct. 18, 1864: the beef that we get for one days rations only makes one Small **mess**. (William H. Horton, Councill Papers, Duke) Watauga County

mess[2] *noun* A group of soldiers who band together to pool resources in the form of rations they have been issued, or sometimes provisions sent from home or purchased or foraged locally. The number of members in a mess varied from five or six to as many as eight or ten.

Mar. 20, 1862: I and Mathew is well and all of my **mess** is well. (J. W. Love, Love Papers, Duke) Henderson County

Dec. 27, 1862: William litterl was shot for Runing A way from us at greenvill. he was A Brother to tom litterl. he was in my **mess**. I saw him neel down By his coffen and tha was putin A hankerchief on his hed. (J. W. Reese, Reese Papers, Duke) Buncombe County

Nov. 18, 1863: Dear I was captured the 7th of this inst and my hole **Mess** was captured on the Rapihancock. (W. F. Wagner, *Confederate Soldier,* 79) Catawba County

mess *verb* To belong to a mess. [*OED* **mess**, verb, 3.a.]

Mar. 22, 1864: We are in tolable good Quarters I Can tell you who I am **messing** With. B F Wood Tim Wood Henary Smith Jessey Kidd John Badgett. (Isaac Copeland, Copeland Letters, NCSA) Surry County

Aug. 19, 1864: me and William hawkins has bin **messing** to gether all the time this summer. (J. W. Joyce, Joyce Papers, MHI) Stokes County.

middling *adverb* About average, moderately; sometimes with more negative connotations (see citations).

Jan. 12, 1862: I think we will fare beter thare then we do hear for we fare but **Midling** at this plase. (James Keever, Keever Papers, Duke) Lincoln County

Jan. 17, 1864: he had the punish ment put one me and if I live to git out of this ware he will fare but **Midlen** I tell you. (J. S. Councill, Councill Papers, Duke) Watauga County

middling *noun* The side meat of a hog. [*DARE* chiefly South, South Midland]

Oct. 17, 1863: I will tel you Sumthing about our fair [= fare] doun [= down here?] it is ruff Scillit cake. cold at that. verry often burnt on the outside an raw in the midle. fat **middlin** Sum times. beef and pickeld pork that not good. (R. C. Caldwell, Caldwell Coll., ECU) Cabarrus County

Feb.14, 1865: I will name the things that I want. some buter a polk of flower [= a poke of flour] a pese of meet of a **middling** and some sower crout and a pese of Soap and a few buiscuits. (James A. Smith, J. A. Smith Papers, Duke) Cabarrus County

might *auxiliary verb*

1. variant forms *mought, mout.*

Oct. 19, 1862: you **mout** look for me thare if you get very bad and have to go to the hosptle. (Adaline Zimmerman, Zimmerman Papers, Duke) Forsyth County

Apr. 16, 1863: you had Better keep your money your Self for if you was to lend it out you **Mought** never get it Back. (John Futch, Futch Letters, NCSA) New Hanover County

Oct. 26, 1863: I have bin thinking that it **mout** be Some advantag to him to go to the Minerl Springs a while. (A. A. Jackson, Jackson Family Corr., Notre Dame) Moore County

Jan. 1866: we was all regler discarge and had the privledge of bying us Shot guns to take home with us to use on our farms and when we all landed at Winton the 20 day December with our Shot guns. Some 1 or 2 **mought** had pistols [. . .] and when we got to the Boat and Started up the hill all Sober we meet with Col Joshua garrett in command of the malisha. (John Bizzell, *Freedom,* ser. 2: 801) Hertford County

2. In a complex, multiple modal construction indicating possibility, with *it might be* followed by a subordinate clause introduced by *that* and a pronoun subject with *could, would* + a verb.

Apr. 9, 1863: If now one comes out of Weavers neighborhood it **mite Be** that **you could** Bring Fed a small Trunk or a a Box. Samel Jarrett is comen after he gets his corn planted and it **mite be** that **you could** al come to geather. he could assist you in getten a long as he is a fine man and understanding al about traveling. (Isaac Lefevers, Lefevers Papers, NCSA) Catawba County

Apr. 27, 1863: if the men colde Oneley Stay at home tell they colde Made thair cropes it **mite be** that **they colde** make breade enogh for another year. Provesions is very scearse her at this tim. (Wilburn Garren, Vance Papers, NCSA) Henderson County

Apr. 22, 1864: I also send my Over Coat. I thought that it **might be** that I **would** loose it and it was too Valuable to loose. (Christopher Hackett, Hackett Papers, Duke) Guilford County

mightily *adverb* Exceedingly, very much.

Nov. 25, 1862: I am sorry that the company did not get the Provisions that was sent in the boxes for they would a relished them **mitely**. (J. W. Lineberger, *Gaston Ranger*, 27) Gaston County

July 18, 1863: my tobacco it is drowned out **mitly** and dont grow atall hardly it keeps so wet. (James Broach, Broach Papers, Duke) Person County

Apr. 24, 1864: we have got plenty of men here if the yanks dont surprise our Troops at some week point. our Brigade has sufferd **mitely**. they aint 6 feald officers in the Brigade. they is two compa[n]ys in o[u]r regt that has not got nary officer. (S. E. Love, Love Papers, Duke) Henderson County

mighty *adverb* Very.

Sept. 8, 1862: I Want to hear from home **mighty** bad. I Want you let me know if littel martha matilda can crall yet or not. (G. C. Dickson, Poteet-Dickson Letters, NCSA) McDowell County

Dec. 23, 1863: Dare loving husban I haf to live a **mity** loncom soryfull life in this world. (Susan Setzer, Setzer Papers, Duke) Catawba County

Jan. 26, 1864: we have hed sume **mity** purty wether fore the last week. (W. P. Cline, Cline Papers, SHC) Catawba County

Apr. 13, 1864: There is **mighty** apt to be a big battle near Richmond. (C. A. Walker, Walker Papers, WCU) Cherokee County

Oct. 7, 1864: Cousin Albert Redfearn has been **mighty** good to come and see us. (Huldah Hubbard, Hubbard Papers, Duke) Anson County

mighty nigh, might nigh *adverb phrase* Very nearly.

Mar. 31, 1863: I am trubled to deth **mite ny** b[e]case I can not be at home at work. (Daniel Revis, Revis Letters, NCSA) Henderson County

Dec. 5, 1863: Father I cant get You no caps [= percussion caps] to save my life. I have tried **mighty nigh** every wher but I will keep a trying. (William Tesh, Tesh Papers, Duke) Yadkin County

milch *noun* variant form of *milk*. [see *DARE*, **milch cow**, scattered, but chiefly Northeast, Great Lakes]

Aug. 20, 1862: my stomache is very good and I have lots to eat and that is good. I have **milch** 3 times a day and butter and molases once and all sorts of vegetables &c. (Alfred N. Proffit, Proffit Family Letters, SHC) Wilkes County

Nov. 27, 1862: The ladys are very kind to me since I got acquaint with them. they send me **milch** evry day. I got a large pitcher full to night. (James A. Patton, Patton Letters, Emory) Granville County

Apr. 13, 1864: I hear you have lost all your meat and some person has stole your **milch** Cows. (C. A. Walker, Walker Papers, WCU) Cherokee County

mill tail *noun* Similar to or the same as *mill race, mill run;* a strong current of water which turns a mill wheel; also the channel of water downstream after it has passed through the wheel. [*OED* **mill-tail**, noun, 1]

Oct. 16, 1864: the water is salt here. the tide ebs and flowes evry six ours and runs as strong as a **mill tail**. (Henry Bowen, Bowen Papers, NCSA) Washington County

mind *noun* An intention, inclination (to do something); in the phrase *have a mind to.*

July 28, 1864: you can write to her in a friendly way if you have **a mind** to do so. (Hannah Smithwick, Smithwick Papers, Duke) Martin County

minie ball *noun* The common type of lead bullet, conical in shape, used in rifled muskets during the Civil War; named after co-developer Claude Étienne Minié.

Mar. 16, 1862: the Yankees wer in about 32 yards of me. the **meny balls** flying around thick as hale. (C. F. Mills, Mills Papers, Duke) Iredell County

Jan. 11, 1863: on our approached to a fence the yanks had Shelled us on our way & had wounded Several. W G Thomas of my Co was one. at the fence they give us a voley of **minie balls** Wounded several. Will Roane. Thompson of my Co. here Col Coleman was wounded. (A. W. Bell, Bell Papers, Duke) Macon County

Nov. 24, 1864: Sydney Poteet got badly wounded in his arm. the ball went in below his Elbow went through his Elbow and the ball lodged in his arm above his Elbow. it was a large **minie ball**. (Martha Poteet, Poteet-Dickson Letters, NCSA) McDowell County

misery *noun* A bodily ache or pain.

Dec. 18, 1863: your Son Wm. Carpenter went to the Hospittle yestarday he was Rite Sick with his old camplaint of bad cof & **misrey** in his head & brest & his Bowells Runing off freely. (James Ennis, Carpenter Family Papers, ECU) Chatham County

Nov. 22, 1864: I am about well al too [= except for] **misery** in my brest and the hard [= heart] burn. (J. C. Owens, Confederate Papers, SHC) Wilkes County

Mississippi rifle *noun* A common name for the Model 1841 Harpers Ferry rifled musket. The name had its origin in the Mexican War, during which a Mississippi regiment was equipped with this particular weapon.

Sept. 29, 1861: I think that we will Be in a fight Before any one Elce. and I hope So. We Drawd our guns to Day and tha ar the **Missisppi Rifels**. We ar Ready for them now and any other time. (R. P. Crawford, Estes Family Papers, WCU) Jackson County

Dec. 24, 1862: we carried our guns back and got whats cauld the **missippy rifle**. the best guns that I ever Saw. thair is no bayonet on them. So we Shall not fight with bayonets. (J. W. Williams, Williams Papers, Duke) Onslow County

mob *verb* To attack, molest, or harass others. [*OED* **mob**, verb[2], 1.a.]

June 19, 1863: we take this method to inform your honor that ther is a company of over a hundred men about here pretending to be hunting conscripts a going a bout **mobing** Sivel peopel and women and Children. taking up women and hanging them and threatning to Shoot women and threatening to whip children. ("Meny Citizens," Vance Papers, NCSA) Randolph County

Mar. 9, 1865: the next is Concerning of our White Soldiers. they Come to our Church and we treat them with all the Politeness that we can and Some of them treats us as though we were beast and we cant help our Selves. Some of them brings Pop Crackers and Christmas devils and throws a mong the woman and if we Say any thing to them they will talk about **mobin** us. (Richard Boyle, *Freedom*, ser. 1: 233) Tyrrell County

molasses *noun*

1. variant forms *lasses, lases*.

Apr. 19, 1863: wee draw some <bea?> & beef & som fish an some **lasses** an rice some sugar some times fruite & some times peas. (T. F. Baggarly, Baggarly Papers, Duke) Iredell County

Jan. 21, 1864: the last leter I got from you was dated the 12. I wold like to get one a week. I wood lik if you cod Send me a botle of **lases** and Sum ink. (R. C. Caldwell, Caldwell Coll., ECU) Cabarrus County

2. treated as plural.

June 8, 1863: we Send you alitle floure and Some fruit. **a few molases** and a little buter and a litle vinegar. it is not good but it is the best we have. (Sally Hackett, Hackett Papers, Duke) Guilford County

Oct. 7, 1863: I am glad to hear that you got such good **Molasses.** Dear Belovid you stated if I onely could be at home and help you Eat **them**. (W. F. Wagner, *Confederate Soldier*, 76) Catawba County

Feb. 10, 1865: some days we draw some meat and Som days we draw none. so when we get no meat we get **afew molasses**. (R. C. Love, Love Papers, Duke) Henderson County

mole, mole plow *noun* A plow with a pointed iron shoe for making drainage channels in the subsoil. [*EDD* **mole**, *sb*[4]]

Jan. 3, 1864: you will have to buy Sum plous. maby you can by Sum Share [plow Shares] from C.A.Caldwell if you can buy them right of[f]. if you cant you must by 2 or 3 **moles.** one horse **moles.** See Charles about them. (R. C. Caldwell, Caldwell Coll., ECU) Cabarrus County

morner, moner, mourner *noun* A person struggling with his or her spiritual condition while attending revival services, often over a period of days or even weeks; some eventually profess their faith and request baptism. [*OED*

mourner, noun[1], 3; see also *DSME* **mourner**, "one who seeks religion but is not yet converted"; *DARE* chiefly South, South Midland]

Aug. 30, 1863: my dear friends we have had meeting hear in camp for nearly two weaks and it is Still going on yet every day and night. I am also a **morner** and have bin for the last thee or four days and ant through yet. they have bin Some 8 or 10 profest and they air twenty Some odd out for **morners**. (John Hartman, Hartman Papers, Duke) Rowan County

Sept. 10, 1863: I must tell you something about our big meetings which has ben going on for several weeaks. A great meny has profest religion and A good meny **morners** yet I saw 27 baptise last sunday. (J. F. Coghill, Coghill Letters, SHC) Granville County

Sept. 11, 1863: we have some fine meetings now in camp by Mr. Andrews a methodist preacher and has had great revivals in the other regiment. the work commenced last night in our regiment. I think he had some thirty or forty **moners**. (J. W. Lineberger, *Gaston Ranger,* 66) Gaston County

Sept. 17, 1863: There were about 25 **mourners** last night and the whole congragation paid verry good attention. superior to what I almost ever saw at home. (C. A. Hege, Hege Papers, MHI) Davidson County

Mar. 11, 1864: their is sum few **moners** here which I am glad to se for I no we must dy and if we are not prepaird for deth what will become of us. (Daniel Abernethy, Abernethy Papers, Duke) Catawba County

mortify *verb* Of body tissue: to decay, decompose. [*OED* **mortify**, verb, 1.d. "To become necrotic or gangrenous. Now *rare* or *hist.*"]

July 14, 1864: He was wounded in the left hand slightly and was sent to Coventon Ga in the Hospital where he died the 9th of July. from all accts [= accounts] his Doctor and nurse both neglected him and his hand **mortified** and killed him. (E. H. Hampton, Bailey Letters, MHI) Yancey County

ND [Nov. 1864]: I expect it was a tooth Canker that the baby had come by her not cutting her teeth sooner. it come from her jawbone and **morterfied** as it went. if I had of had some of your water I could cured her but I couldent get it and she is ded and gone to heaven. out this troublesom world in heaven with her brother and Jesus her savour. (Martha Poteet, Poteet-Dickson Letters, NCSA) McDowell County

mosquito see **musketer**

most see **a most**

mought, mout see **might**

mourner see **morner**

muley *adjective* Of a cow: hornless.

Jan. 23, 1862: da befor yestorday was verry warm and this day is Cold anough to freeze a **muley** Bools [= bull's] horns off. we have got moved into our Cabin But wee have not got all the Chimneys Bilt. (J. T. Hamilton, Davison Papers, Duke) Gaston County

muscadine *noun* A variety of wild grape native to the southeastern states.

Oct. 2, 1863: I found some apples & graps and **muskadines** and chickapines though I walked a good peace for to get them. (J. W. Lineberger, *Gaston Ranger,* 68) Gaston County

mush *noun* A porridge made from boiled cornmeal.

July 13, 1863: I would lik to have been at home and got after Sam with the cradle or grass cythe, I think I would have made him earned his **mush**. (C. A. Hege, Hege Papers, MHI) Davidson County

mushmelon *noun* A muskmelon.

Feb. 10, 1863: I want you to plant a heap of watermelon & **mushmelon** seed and I hope that I will be at home when they get ripe. (C. A. Hege, Hege Papers, MHI) Davidson County

Jan. 8, 1864: Samuel Maxwell is to start home to morrow and I will send this By him and I will [send] you and George some **mush melon** Seeds in it and I want you to plant them in a good place for they are the Best I ever Saw. the **mush melon** waid 28 lbs. I think they will make Busters certain. (J. W. Love, Love Papers, Duke) Henderson County

musicianer *noun* A musician. [*OED* **musicianer**, "Now *colloq.* and *regional* (chiefly *U.S.*, *Sc.*, and *Irish English*)," earliest citation is from 1540; *DARE* chiefly South Midland, formerly also New England]

Mar. 31, 1863: you will oblige me by riting to me and Col jarett and having it arraing So I Can go back to the Company. pleas rite in hast. your ould **musisioner.** Eliha Chambers. of the ruf an redy guards. (Elihu Chambers, Vance Papers, NCSA) Buncombe County

musketer *noun* variant form of *mosquito.*

June 12, 1864: i will tel you alittle about the insects here. when wee are on post wee sit on our horses all nite and fites the nats and **musketers**. when we lay down on the ground to Sleep the frogs is gumping over us. when wee go through the brush wee get full of ticks. when wee go to eat wee cant hardly keap the flys out of our mouth. you never saw the like of such things in your life. (Silas Stepp, Stepp Letters, UNCA) Buncombe County

N

name *verb* To mention, say, talk about, inquire. [*DSME* **name**, B verb, "To mention, tell, call"; *OED* **name**, verb[1], 6.b.; *DARE* chiefly South Midland, especially Southern Appalachians]

Aug. 2, 1856: the people has ben vary well behaved Since master left as could be expected master to me an has worked well. nelson **named** to me that master wished mee to white wash magnolia an Belgrade. (Henry [Pettigrew slave], Pettigrew Family Papers, SHC) Washington County

Jan. 21, 1862: ther has Ben So Mutch talk of a fight ihav got tiard of hering it **namd**. (Abraham Maxwell, Love Papers, Duke) Henderson County

Mar. 9, 1862: you **namd** a bout your ditching. I dont now how it will be don for dinker is volunteerd and is gone but ef I cant get no bodey els I will try to doet my Self. (Austin Brown, Confederate Papers, SHC) Johnston County

Jan. 22, 1865: you **named** something a bout going to school. if you will take yore penn and rite a bout three times a Day at home you will lern faster than you will at school. (W. D. Smith, W. D. Smith Papers, Duke) Davie County

nary *adjective* Never (a), any, not any. [*DSME* **nary**, B, adjective, adverb]

Aug. 7, 1861: We hant had **nary** battle sense the battle at Bethel Church. (Peter Poteet, Poteet-Dickson Letters, NCSA) Burke County

Sept. 6, 1862: I want you all to write to mea as soon as you can. I have not recevd **narry** leter yet. (Bardin Brown, Brown Family Papers, Duke) Johnston County

Nov. 17, 1862: I had the jaundice lite. they never made me sick but a few days. I was not confined **nary** day. (J. W. Lineberger, *Gaston Ranger,* 5) Gaston County

June 16, 1863: I hant had the chance to send him **nairry** presant yet I had nothing that I cood send him in a letter handy. (J. H. Hundley, Hundley Family Letters, SHC) Stokes County

nary one *pronoun phrase* Not one, none; (following a negative) any (one). [*DSME,* **nary one,** B]

Dec. 17, 1862: we were lucky in our Company we lost **nary one** kild nor wounded. (J. W. Lineberger, *Gaston Ranger,* 29) Gaston County

Dec. 10, 1864: I heard he had some Letters but I dident get **nary one**. (Ann Bowen, Bowen Papers, NCSA) Washington County

near about *adverb phrase* Nearly.

Aug. 14, 1862: we ainte station yet ner [= nor] I dont now when we shal bee for we tra[v]el day & night **nere a boute** and when we stop we quite down like hogs & slepe. (Austin Brown, Brown Family Papers, Duke) Johnston County

necessaries *noun plural* Necessities; items needed for survival or comfort.

May 24, 1861: the real means of procuring the **nessesaries** of life are hard to come at most of the time. (Rhoda Hawn, Peterson Papers, Duke) Catawba County

July 31, 1861: tell me if you can get aplenty sutch as stockens and all **nesessaryes** that yu neade. (Letty Long, Long Family Papers, SHC) Alamance County

Oct. 29, 1861: thir is good crops made in our county. I think corn can bea bought at 50 cts all through the winter and now the people is debard of halling off thir meat. I dont now how wee will git our **nessaryes** for money is scerce here. (Elizabeth Watson, Watson Letters, WCU) Jackson County

neck comfort *noun* A "neck comforter," a woolen scarf. [*DARE* **comfort**, noun, 3]

Dec. 24, 1862: I recieved my **neck comfert** and my gloves and socks and half Dosen aples. (W. F. Wagner, *Confederate Soldier,* 29) Catawba County

necklace *noun* A scarf, usually made of wool. [All but one of the citations collected came from Catawba County, and given the ancestry of the letter writers, the term may be of Pennsylvania German origin.]

Dec. 12, 1863: the articles that I got is these. One good wit [= white] yarn blanket One pair of bron yarn socks one mixt **nekless**. (Harrison Hanes, Hanes Papers, Duke) Davie County

July 25, 1862: i wont you to make me too Culard [= colored] shurts as sune as you Can and i wont A good warme Jackshit [= jacket] tel [= before] fall and wod like to have A **neakles.** you Can git salm Parker wife to nit it. (W. P. Cline, Cline Papers, SHC) Catawba County

Dec. 1, 1862: I would like to have what I have named above. I also would like to have a good **necles** nit if you can get it or eny thing to make it out of. I think this is all I will have Sent at this time. (Isaac Lefevers, Lefevers Papers, NCSA) Catawba County

Dec. 12, 1863: I also received the Sacel you Sent with brother paul and the things you Sent in it. one blanket and one pair of pants and **necklis** and gloves and socks and something god to eate. (Daniel Setzer, Setzer Papers, Duke) Catawba County

need *verb*

1. negative form is regularly without auxiliary *do,* especially following *you.*

Oct. 2, 1862: I want you if its conventist [= convenient] to send me some little thing to eate but you **kneed not** put you self to much trubel a bout it. (James Patton, Patton Letters, Emory) Granville County

June 2, 1863: my hors is in very good fix. he mends dayly. I wrote to you to get another horse but you **need not** put your self to any Trouble unless you think it will pay. (Jesse Shipman, Shipman Family Corr., Notre Dame) Henderson County

June 24, 1863: It was said that many marched until they fell dead on this march. you **need not** be uneasy that I will do that. (A. J. Proffit, Proffit Family Letters, SHC) Wilkes County

Aug. 25, 1863: the opinion is universal in Camps that North Carolina Troops ort to Protect N.C. Soil & you **need not** be surprised if this thing is cared out before long. (Stephen Whitaker, Whitaker Papers, NCSA) Cherokee County

2. present participle after *it,* instead of *needs* with infinitive *to be done.*

Feb. 4, 1864: I am Sorrow to hear that you can not get that fens made. I know it is **kneeding** badly. (Alexander Keever, Keever Papers, Duke) Lincoln County

needsessity *noun* Necessity. [*DARE* "Brit, esp Scots, folk-etym for *necessity*"]

Mar. 16, 1862: if I cant be so happy as to be at home I know that I feel **needsesity** that compells me to be out. (Larkin Kendrick, Kendrick Papers, NCSA) Cleveland County

Feb. 17, 1863: Nothing but **needsesity** induces me to trouble you with this little account at present. (G. W. Shackleford, Vance Papers, NCSA) Buncombe County

June 15, 1863: I hope you will grant our request as our **neede sesetys** ar sever at this time and will no doute get worse if thear ant some done for the people in this naborhood. ("the female Sect," Vance Papers, NCSA) Rutherford County

negro buster *noun* See citation; obviously produce of some kind. See **buster**.

Mar. 22, 1862: have the Slips [= sweet potato sprounts] beded. bed all the yams and **negrobusters** and plant the rest and get five bushel from mrs Southerland. (Ichabod Quinn, Quinn Papers, Duke) Duplin County

nervious *adjective* Trembling or having spasms; variant form of *nervous*. [In *Tarheel Talk*, Eliason includes a Burke County, North Carolina, example of *nurvious* from 1836]

June 1, 1862: you must Excuse my Bad Writing for I am **nervious** and hant taken any pains you can tell that By my Writing. Writ soon. I must quit for there is coming up a heavy thunder storm. (G. J. Huntley, Huntley Papers, WCU) Rutherford County

June 5, 1863: I will close for I feel very week and **nervious** so that I dont whether you can read what I have wrote. (John Bachelor, Brown Coll., NCSA) Duplin County

Oct. 8, 1863: my hand is quite **nervious.** I will soon close. (Andrew J. Proffit, Proffit Family Letters, SHC) Wilkes County

newborned *noun* variant form of *newborn*.

June 3, 1862: as for my giving you a name for the **new Borned.** I dont suppose I can give any Better a name than you can. (G. J. Huntley, Huntley Papers, WCU) Rutherford County

newground *noun* Land newly cleared for cultivation. [*DARE* chiefly Central and South Atlantic, Gulf States]

June 18, 1862: you rote to mee that it was sow mutch wet that you could hardly get the chance to work the corn. if you get behinde with it by the wet wether you most try and get some one to help plant and ketch up again. I think when it comes to laying by you had maby better lay buy the **new ground** first as it is sow Ruty. (Isaac Lefevers, Lefevers Papers, NCSA) Catawba County

May 3, 1863: joe fullbright has got his Coarn all Planted to his **neu groun** an that A bout one Acker. (Keziah Hefner, Hefner Papers, NCSA) Catawba County

July 15, 1864: I would be glad to know how the Seasen is at home and how the Corn in your **new ground** looks and whether it got ploud or not. (Alexander Keever, Keever Papers, Duke) Lincoln County

newmony, newmoney see **pneumonia**

nicknack, nicnac *noun* A snack, food item, delicacy. [*OED* **knickknack | nicknack**, noun, 2.a.; *DARE* **knickknack** noun[1], especially South, Mississippi Valley]

Dec. 18, 1862: Tell Julius and Mary to send me some chestnuts, grassnuts, and ground peas and pies. I hope that you will not think hard of me for writing for more clothing &c because I need them very much here and as to eatables [and] **nicnacs**. they are very scarce here. (C. A. Hege, Hege Papers, MHI) Davidson County

Nov. 18, 1864: we will have Short & rough fare this winter but there is tapisters going threw the camp with **nicknacks** for sale. the Sell Sweet potaters at a dollar a pound. Irish potaters a dollar a quart. two turnups Small ones for a dollar. appels 4 little ones for a dollar. pies as big as a hand for a dollar. (John Peterson, Peterson Papers, Duke) Catawba County

nigh, ny, nie *adverb* Near, nearly, close; comparative *nigher*. See also **might nigh** and **well nigh**

Sept. 29, 1862: we cant get no furlow untel we get **nigher** home. (Austin Brown, Brown Family Papers, Duke) Johnston County

June 23, 1863: you ought to come home and see your fine son. it is agrate big felow. if you dont get to come home very soon it will be as big as you. it is petty **ny** as big as ujene now. (Joseph Ward, Revis Letters, NCSA) Henderson County

Oct. 8, 1863: Serg West came very **nigh** Being Capturd too or three times again. (William Tippett, Bell Papers, Duke) Macon County

Nov. 3, 1863: I am about thirty five miles **nigher** than when I was at Weldon. (F. M. Poteet, Poteet-Dickson Letters, NCSA) McDowell County

June 1, 1864: oh how **nie** I did come a bing tuck prisoner the other day. (L. W. Griffin, Griffin Papers, NCSA) Rutherford County

nigh-sighted *adjective* Near-sighted.

June 2, 1863: Wm Mc Master is well and harty and I want you to send and git him in my sons place for he is better able to be in the army than my son is for he is **nigh sighted** and Cant see hardly any and I think you are the one that Can Send him home. (Margaret Holder, Vance Papers, NCSA) Randolph County

nocount *adjective phrase* Worthless (from *no account*). See also **account**.

June 22, 1862: Crops is A **nocont** hire and i heard that the[y] was A **nocont** dire [= there] but i hope that mine will make sume. (W. P. Cline, Cline Papers, SHC) Catawba County

Aug. 21, 1863: if you want a milk cow and can git a good one buy one I dont care what it costs for they money is **nocount** nohow. (W. F. Wagner, *Confederate Soldier,* 68) Catawba County

Feb. 21, 1864: I think wee may as well pay it now for mebby this war mite end and then the money will bee **nocount**. (Susan Setzer, Setzer Papers, Duke) Catawba County

nock about, nock along, nock around see **knock about,** etc.

node see **know**

no how *adverb phrase* Anyway, anyhow, in any case. [*OED* **nohow**, adverb and adjective, 1.b., "*U.S. regional* (esp. *South Midland*)"]

Oct. 3, 1862: If I cant send some of my cloath [= clothes] home I cant carritt them **no how**. (W. F. Wagner, *Confederate Soldier,* 17) Catawba County

May 8, 1863: I left the money with a friend in Knoxvill to pay him when the [tomb] Stones is Shipt. they will be shipt to Sweet water unless I direct diferantly. I dont want you to pay eny thing **no how** till I see you. (Stephen Whitaker, Whitaker Papers, NCSA) Cherokee County

May 17, 1863: I never was as tired of any things in my life as I am of this old war for thare is no Jestus in this old war **no how**. (H. T. Ward, Revis Letters, NCSA) Henderson County

no odds see **odds**

nor, ner *conjunction* following a negative construction and without correlative *neither.* [*DSME* **nor**, B conjunction, 2, "without the form *neither* preceding"]

Aug. 14, 1862: I hante never hern **ner** I dont now how many of ourn is lost. (Austin Brown, Brown Family Papers, Duke) Johnston County

Dec. 17, 1862: we were lucky in our Company we lost nary one kild **nor** wounded. (J. W. Lineberger, *Gaston Ranger,* 29) Gaston County

Mar. 17, 1864: I cant Rite every week. if I could I would Rite oftiner. I cant git paper **nor** invellopes with out money. (F. M. Poteet, Poteet-Dickson Letters, NCSA) McDowell County

Jan. 9, 1865: She has been very helpless. not able to stand alone **nor** feed herself but she is better now. (Ann Bowen, Bowen Papers, NCSA) Washington County

nose hole *noun* A nostril. [*OED* **nose-hole**, noun, 1. "Now chiefly *Eng. regional* and *colloq.*, and *Caribbean*" (citations from ca. 1450 on)]

June 24, 1863: There is a yoong calf in Fredericks burg with 2 heads 3 years 4 eyes 4 **nose holes** & 2 mouths. there is a Sick georgia Soldier here who has Seen it & examined it. it sucks with either mouth & it 3d year [= ear] is between its heads. (Andrew J. Proffit, Proffit Family Letters, SHC) Wilkes County

notion[1] (also *noshen. nosing*) *noun;* see also **take a notion**.

1. An inclination, desire, intention, idea, opinion. [*OED* **notion**, noun, II.8.a.]

Feb. 1, 1862: tel marts Salley litle did I think of her getin maried untel I had been gon twelve months. but if that is her **notion** of cours I hav no obgections but I realy do think that she could av got a beter looking man than the one she is a goin to get. (Harrison Hanes, Hanes Papers, Duke) Davie County

July 13, 1863: if we can get the chance I want to Join the caveraldry. that is the **notion** of us hear. (J. M. Revis, Revis Letters, NCSA) Henderson County

Mar. 27, 1864: my **notion** is that this Fuss will end by the first of next Septtember But the most of us may be kild by that time and it never will doo us aney good.

(Isaac Copeland, Copeland Letters, NCSA) Surry County

Apr. 21, 1864: We had A Strong **notion** to go Tennessee To work in the Rail rode But ma did not want us to go & she was rite for 40 Cts A day & Bourd our selvs would not pay us. no sir. (Elias Peterson, Peterson Papers, Duke) Burke County

Sept. 21, 1864: I think thay ame at take the danvill rode and holde it when thay git evr thing fixt to ther **notion**. (Arthur Putnam, Kendrick Papers, NCSA) Cleveland County

2. In the phrase *in the notion:* inclined, in the mood (to do something); in favor of (some course of action).

Mar. 23, 1858: I can in form you that we recevid a letter from yo to day wich giv us grate satis fac tion to hear from you all wonst more an that you was stil **in the noshen** of mooving to the west. (David Headrick, Frank Papers, NCSA) Davidson County

June 22, 1858: I would like to know how your crops are coming on and whether you expect to git of[f] to Mo [= Missouri] this fall and whether eney of the rest hav got **in the noshing** to move. (William Boss, Frank Papers, NCSA) Davidson County

Mar. 6, 1862: try to get the peopell **in the notion** of putting fops and drunkards out of power and put in men in all publick matters that Will discharge their duty and go for the interest of Our Country. (G. J. Huntley, Huntley Papers, WCU) Rutherford County

3. In the phrase *out of the notion:* no longer inclined (to do something).

Feb. 14, 1862: I recievd your leter this morning and was glad to hear from you for it had been som time sence I heard from you and I had com to the conclusion that you had got **out of the notion** of write-ing. (Harrison Hanes, Hanes Papers, Duke) Davie County

4. In the phrase *to my notion:* in my opinion, in my judgment.

Nov. 24, 1864: you dont need to Send my any turn-ups nor no cook or bakeing tools. you may Send if you Send by cook about half of my Silver as I can doe Something with it as **to my notion** better then with Confederate money. (John Peterson, Peterson Papers, Duke) Catawba County

notion[2] *noun* Small, inexpensive items, wares. [*OED* **notion**, noun, II. In *pl.*, "Chiefly *N. Amer.* Small wares, *esp.* cheap, useful articles. Now chiefly: *spec.* haberdashery; buttons, hooks, ribbon, thread, etc."]

May 15, 1863: I sent 4 letters to you with Jane Hege and some other little **notions** and some of my old letters. (C. A. Hege, Hege Papers, MHI) Davidson County

no use, no youse *noun phrase* No liking or respect (for a person or group of people).

Apr. 21, 1864: Tell the girls the yankees is up here & thare are Best mounted men i Ever seen But I have **no youse** for them in this world. (Elias Peterson, Peterson Papers, Duke) Burke County

now, nowd see **know**

no ways *adverb* By no means, in any way.

Nov. 10, 1862: you Must live content and not grive for me. I hant **no wais** on easy a tall but what I will git home agin but hit Ma[y] be a good while yet. (Robert Spainhourd, Spainhourd Papers, Duke) Forsyth County

Jan. 10, 1864: I hope this war will close Sum day But wee dont no who will See the end of it time will prove all things. I Dont feel **no ways** on esy about the yankes kiling me But I cant tel but I feel like tha wold. (R. C. Caldwell, Caldwell Coll., ECU) Cabarrus County

nowheres *adverb* Nowhere, anywhere.

Aug. 18, 1863: some has nothing but thare Blankeds and so you can gess what sort of tents we have and nothing to ly on onley the ground and Dear Wife thare is no chance to git in a house **no whares**. (W. F. Wagner, *Confederate Soldier,* 67) Catawba County

O

obliged *past participle, adjective* Obligated; variant form *ablege.* [*DSME* **obliged**, past participle, A, variant form *obleeged; DARE* chiefly South, South Midland]

Oct. 5, 1862: they time is not fare distent that the north will be **ablege** to acnoledge our independance. (S. E. Love, Love Papers, Duke) Henderson County

Apr. 14, 1863: I shall start to wilmington a tusday to git me a pear of shose. I am **a blege** to have them. (Martha Futch, Futch Letters, NCSA) New Hanover County

odds *noun plural*

1. Favors. [*OED* **odds**, noun, 5.d. "Chiefly *U.S. regional.* ***to ask*** (formerly ***beg***) ***no odds:*** to desire no advantage; to seek no favours or special consideration. Now *rare.*"]

Feb. 27, 1863: we dont aske him **eny odds**. we are abel to bare all he can poot on us. he poot John in the garde house and left others out that was to blame worse than John. (Jonas Bradshaw, Bradshaw Papers, Duke) Alexander County

July 24, 1864: we are all down hear in one little hole with all the cesech a round us. <Drey?> is gone home and [he] dont ask the details **no ods**. he is as black is ever. he says he had rather see you than any body in this world. (Cassie Davenport, Hundley Family Letters, SHC) Stokes County

2. Difference (after *no*). [*OED* **odds**, noun, 2.c.]

July 12, 1862: tell him to try mackuntush if he sees proper to do so or any one makes **no ods** who so he can get. (J. W. Williams, Williams Papers, Duke) Onslow County

Aug. 15, 1862: I Waunt you to Write often and if you put hills Division Penders Brigaid I Will git the Letter **no Ods** Whare We are. (G. J. Huntley, Huntley Papers, WCU) Rutherford County

of *preposition*

1. to indicate the time when habitual or typical activity occurs. [*DSME* **of** preposition, A]

Oct. 26, 1862: I think mi back and Legs is A giting write smart beter. I can wrest pretty wel **uv** knights now. (B. C. Jackson, Jackson Family Corr., Notre Dame) Moore County

Feb. 13, 1863: thay are going about **of** a night a stealing horses and runing them off and shuting [= shooting] hogs. (Thomas M. Walker, Vance Papers, NCSA) Polk County

Sept. 1, 1863: the weather is vary cool for this season of the year. we haft to ware our coats **of** mornings. (Alfred N. Proffit, Proffit Family Letters, SHC) Wilkes County

Sept. 29, 1863: he will send you his Boots for the Wether is geting cold and he is sorry for you Bare Foot when the frost is glitering so strong **of** mornings. (A. A. Jackson, Jackson Family Corr., Notre Dame) Moore County

Sept. 21, 1864: we cod make our litel rashions go further than what thay do. we have men to cock and bring it in to us **of** night. (Arthur Putnam, Kendrick Papers, NCSA) Cleveland County

2. used redundantly after present participles or gerunds. [*DARE* chiefly South, South Midland]

July 5, 1856: I take a great plesure of sending a few lines back to master an h[o]pe it may be a great comfort to master in reading **of** them. (Moses [Pettigrew slave], Pettigrew Family Papers, SHC) Washington County

July 19, 1863: we had to fall back and they wer troubling **of** us all the way back threw marland. (Neill McLeod, McLeod Letters, SHC) Moore County

Aug. 24, 1863: you cannot imagine how much good it dun me to See Pappy and to eat the good things that he brought. nor I cannot discribe the pleasure that I took in eating **ove** them. (J. F. Coghill, Coghill Papers, Duke) Granville County

Sept. 29, 1863: This lieves my self & Burjes well except he is taking **of** a Cold which causis him to feel dull. (A. A. Jackson, Jackson Family Corr., Notre Dame) Moore County

3. used redundantly after past tense and past participle of verbs.

Aug. 21, 1861: we got to a spring whair some of the cmpanys got water but we got non. we then was marched on. we come to an old branch whair we just broke out of ranks and got some water that was thick with mud but we drunk **of** it like it was good. (James W. Overcash, Overcash Papers, Duke) Rowan County

Sept. 1, 1863: I am well and harty at the presenttime and I am also happy to State to you that I have profest **of** my Sins and I am going to Jine the church and be baptised. (John Hartman, Hartman Papers, Duke) Rowan County

4. following *glad* or *sorry* with the sense of *for*.

Mar. 3, 1863: he told us that the 4th reg Was on picket or wee wold of went an Seen them. i was **sorey of** it. (T. F. Baggarly, Baggarly Papers, Duke) Iredell County

Feb. 8, 1864: I was **glad of** the tobaco that you Sent me. (F. M. Poteet, Poteet-Dickson Letters, NCSA) McDowell County

June 20, 1864: I was very **glad of** the five dolars you Sent me though I did not nead as I have Sold my wach. you kneed not Send me any more money till write for Som. (J. H. Baker, J. H. Baker Papers, Duke) Rockingham County

5. after *better* or *well* in the sense of having recovered from an illness or injury.

Aug. 21, 1861: their is a g[r]ate deal of sickness heir now. Eli upright and Davie Sloop is very bad off with the mesils. Eli is geting beter. I had a lite tetch of them. Charl Atwell has got **well of** them. (James W. Overcash, Overcash Papers, Duke) Rowan County

Aug. 25, 1862: I now Seat my Self this the 25th day of Aug. to let yew no how I am. I am nerly **well of** the rumatis. but I hav bin Sick for the last few days. (John Hartman, Hartman Papers, Duke) Rowan County

Nov. 26, 1862: I hav had avry bad sore throat but i am **beter of** it. (Daniel Revis, Revis Letters, NCSA) Henderson County

Dec. 26, 1864: she has got **better of** the thrash but her mouth is not well yet. (Ann Bowen, Bowen Papers, NCSA) Washington County

offen, aufan *adverb* variant form of *off of*.

Sept. 16, 1862: he put A thunderan grad [= great] big blister aun mi back but [I] daunt think that it dun it any guod. only it taken the Skin **aufan.** yeu may gues whither that dun me mutch gwod or naugh [= not]. (B. C. Jackson, Jackson Family Corr., Notre Dame) Moore County

Jan. 27, 1863: Elizabeth yow can take them botons **offen** my coat and then yow will be awarion and then father can ware it if he wants. (W. H. Brotherton, Brotherton Papers, Duke) Catawba County

office *noun* A post office.

Mar. 12, 1862: we went to the **ofice** last mondy an was very sory that we did not get A letter but I am in hopes we will get one to morow evning from yow. (Jane Williams, Williams Papers, Duke) Onslow County

May 3, 1863: I can say to you that I never git too bisey to rite to you nor to go to the **ofice** for I rite to you evry week or too. I sent wone by tom young and has mald one or too sence. (George Robertson, Confederate Misc., Emory) Yancy County

Apr. 9, 1864: I sent a dozen kneedles in the letter. he sed he left it at pervard station to be put in the **offis** for you & I want to no if you got it or not. (Daniel Abernethy, Abernethy Papers, Duke) Catawba County

often *adverb*

1. variant form *ofent*.

Jan. 20, 1864: Dare love. I must Close for this time I want you to rite so[o]n and **ofent**. Susan Setzer to hir Dare husban Daniel Setzer. (Susan Setzer, Setzer Papers, Duke) Catawba County

2. comparative forms *oftener, ofttiner*.

Oct. 5, 1861: look over my not writing no **ofttiner** for I have to write to Som 20 or 30. (Job Cobb, Cobb Papers, Duke) Pitt County

Apr. 25, 1863: I now that I dont get all the leters you rite and for that reson you must rite **oftener**. (Daniel Revis, Revis Letters, NCSA) Henderson County

Nov. 22, 1863: I wood like to get a letter twiste a weeake enny how an **oftener** if I cood. (A. S. Harrill, Civil War Coll., TSLA) Rutherford County

Mar. 13, 1864: I think it apoor come off that you

cannot see them **oftener**. (W. L. Bleckley, Bleckley Papers, Duke) Catawba County

old *adjective*

1. used before the name of a general or politician, often indicating dislike.

Dec. 2, 1862: I dont think **old** Jeff Davis can feed us much longer and we will all have to starve or come home. (James Zimmerman, Zimmerman Papers, Duke) Forsyth County

Mar. 26, 1863: I wood Bee A draw Back in stid of A help to you and the children well if caut up in this kind of A fix while under **old** Bragg. he wood hav mee put to deth. (J. W. Reese, Reese Papers, Duke) Buncombe County

Mar. 28, 1863: I cant tell what **old** Jo Hooker will do. he had better go home and stay thare fur all the good that he is a doing. (Jonas Bradshaw, Bradshaw Papers, Duke) Alexander County

Sept. 11, 1863: maby they will quit harboring deserters and let them come back to the army wherethey belong and stop the idea of reconstruction for **old** holdens press is tore up and I hope it will remain so. (J. W. Lineberger, *Gaston Ranger,* 66) Gaston County

Oct. 7, 1863: The yankees are comeing over most every day two and sometimes three come over a day and sware They will fight no longer for **Old** Abe. (James Zimmerman, Zimmerman Papers, Duke) Forsyth County

Feb. 2, 1865: old vance Says that if they dont Make peace and let the men come home in time to make a crop that starvation will be at evry mans door. (Martha Poteet, Poteet-Dickson Letters, NCSA) McDowell County

2. used before the name of a state or home county, usually indicating affection.

Aug. 3, 1861: give my love to all the girls tell them I am coming back to See them I am agoing to ketch one when I git back in **old** rutherford. (L. W. Griffin, Griffin Papers, NCSA) Rutherford County

Nov. 25, 1861: I would like to bee in **old** Catawba to go to the corn shucking to fly around amongst the girls. (L. L. Houk, Fisher Papers, Duke) Catawba County

Feb. 27, 1863: if you node how mutch good it dus mee to git A letter from **old** Buncomb you wood keep one on the Rode to mee. (J. W. Reese, Reese Papers, Duke) Buncombe County

Aug. 7, 1863: if i liv to git back to **old** north Carline. i no that i will stay dire [= there] but i dont no if i will ever git back are not. (W. P. Cline, Cline Papers, SHC) Catawba County

Aug. 17, 1863: I want you to right to mee and let mee know how times is agoing on in **old** Caroliner. (O. C. Morgan, Revis Letters, NCSA) Henderson County

Feb. 21, 1864: write soon and give me the news in **old** Gaston for you no that I want to hear from you. (J. W. Lineberger, *Gaston Ranger,* 85) Gaston County

Old Christmas *noun* January 6, the older date of the holiday as calculated by the Julian calendar.

Dec. 2, 1864: the fattning hogs eats very well so far. they dont fatten northing extra. I hope you will get home time anof [= enough] to help kill them a little after **old christmas**. (Ann Bowen, Bowen Papers, NCSA) Washington County

Jan. 8, 1865: fore of our mareins [= marines] runaway on **old christmas** day and it makes our gard duty harder now. (Henry Bowen, Bowen Papers, NCSA) Washington County

old field *noun* and *adjective* A field which has been under cultivation for an extended period of time or has been fallow for a period of time.

Mar. 22, 1862: I want you to plant my **old field** corn as Soon as you get the land prepaired. (Ichabod Quinn, Quinn Papers, Duke) Duplin County

Mar. 8, 1863: I want that new field poot in corne over at ole Johns and that new peese over in the **ole field** unless you needed that for paster. (W. F. Wagner, *Confederate Soldier,* 39) Catawba County

Apr. 26, 1863: you wanted to Know whether any Boday had helped me about plant my corn. H F procter Laid off the **old feild** fer me. (Amanda Murph, Murph Papers, Duke) Catawba County

old horse *noun* A mildly pejorative term for an older male.

Sept. 4, 1864: I wont you to Send me all the news about it and about the box. I reckon the **old**

horse [= his father] will try and Send it to us as you Say you cant get down thare to help fix the box. (John Hartman, Hartman Papers, Duke) Rowan County

old lady *noun*

1. A mother; see Overview § I.1.1.

   Mar. 1, 1864: I was glad to here from you all but was Sorry to here of my Mothers affliction but the Lords Will be dun not mine nor thine. I hop She will recuver. that is all I can do for hur. I hope the rest of the famely will take good care of hur. I cant git home. I wold like to see the **old lady** very much but it is out of my power to do so. (R. C. Caldwell, Caldwell Coll., ECU) Cabarrus County

2. A wife.

   ND [1862]: you no how the **old lady** is a bout things that is concerning me. I am placed in a bad fix and you know that I cant help my self &c. if She was able to get about I wood not Say a word but she is placed in a condition that you know that she will need good attention. (W. D. Smith, W. D. Smith Papers, Duke) Davie County

   July 2, 1863: I am Seventy four years of age and my wife is Seventy and all three of my sones are in the army and me and the **old lady** are left a lone and I am blind and has been for ten years. (Joseph Harper, Vance Papers, NCSA) Cherokee County

old man *noun*

1. A father; see Overview § I.1.1.

   Sept. 29, 1862: tell the **old man** i want him to write to me wether he can get along with the hors i left there or not. (John Ingram, Ingram Papers, Duke) Forsyth County

   Jan. 10, 1863: if you and the **old mans** folks would Send me and Jackson a box a piece it it would not take so powerfull long. (James Zimmerman, Zimmerman Papers, Duke) Forsyth County

   Oct. 2, 1864: I want you to rite as so[o]n as you get this letter and let me no how tims is thar. if you dont no ask the **old man** and he can tel you. (Jesse Hill, Hill Letters, NCSA) Forsyth County

2. A husband.

   Feb. 1, 1862: tel her to not get mared untel the war is over for fear they coms a drafft and they take her **old man**. tel her that is my advise to all the young girls. (Harrison Hanes, Hanes Papers, Duke) Davie County

   Apr. 13, 1863: if yo cante doe nothing fore me I Shal Sende my **old mane** word and there is ahepe ind my fix. yo may depend they is no farnes in the way they doe. (Elizabeth Thrower, Vance Papers, NCSA) Moore County

3. God.

   Aug. 7, 1863: i put my hope in the **old man** i hope that he will fetch me thru safe. he is all my dependes. (W. P. Cline, Cline Papers, SHC) Catawba County

Old Master *noun* God.

Jan. 17, 1864: the Siner must repent bfore the war Stops. before **old master** rases his rod of afflicton. when the peple acnoleg god to be the Lord then we ma look for pece. not before. (R. C. Caldwell, Caldwell Coll., ECU) Cabarrus County

old Nead *noun* Fat pork, bacon. [*DSME* **old Ned**, noun, 1]

Dec. 21, 1862: I have to gow to put on some of **old Nead** to cook to pursurve life. (Phillip Shull, Councill Papers, Duke) Watauga County

Old North State *noun phrase* North Carolina.

June 1, 1863: we have not drawed any money yet nor I dont know when we will. I thought we were agoing to get our money before we left the **old North State**. I wish they would pay us for we stand in need of it. (Christopher Hackett, Hackett Papers, Duke) Guilford County

Sept. 3, 1863: I say Hurrah Boys at home and do all you can for the good **old North state** and the quicker she goes back in the Union the quicker we will have peace. (C. A. Hege, Hege Papers, MHI) Davidson County

July 10, 1864: I am thinking long of the time cince I heard from you and the rest of my friends if any in the **old North State**. (A. N. Proffit, Proffit Family Letters, SHC) Wilkes County

old woman *noun* A wife.

May 23, 1862: i want you to take care of the **old woman** till i come home and when you wright how she is agiting along and when i come home i am a going to come over and stay with your **old woman** about a week or ten days for yow have got the advantage of me now but i will make it up when i come home. (Christopher Sherrill, CS Army Misc., Duke) Catawba County

Mar. 8, 1863: well **old woman** you said that Mother saide she wished That I was thare to eate diner with her. (John Ingram, Ingram Papers, Duke) Forsyth County

on *preposition*

1. with the sense of *about*. [*DARE* scattered, but chiefly South, South Midland]

Sept. 1, 1864: I wrote Mother a letter a fu days ago. I hant got a leter from hur since I left home, only one. I under Stand She has bin complaning **on** me very much. tha cant write to me til I write to them. (R. C. Caldwell, Caldwell Coll., ECU) Cabarrus County

2. with the sense of *by*.

Oct. 10, 1864: I herd the Reasin we came wp [= up] hear was they yankes takin our cavelary **on** serprise And capterd some of them And we was sent hear to hold this place. (W. H. Brotherton, Brotherton Papers, Duke) Catawba County

on a scout see **on the scout**

once *adverb* variant forms including *onst, wonsed, oncet.*

May 4, 1862: I Would Like to see you all **Onst** more But it is uncertain Whether I git home this summer Or not and the prospect Is fair for my Boddy to Be Left in Old virginia. (G. J. Huntley, Huntley Papers, WCU) Rutherford County

Jan. 17, 1864: My Dear Wif if just could see you **wonsed** more and talk with you a while I would be better Sadesfid. (Jordon Councill, Councill Papers, Duke) Watauga County

Feb. 21, 1865: My dear I Suppose the yankeys air comeing to Salisbury. if they do my dear take care of your self the best you can. I exspect if they do get thair they will insult the ladys more than **oncet** but dont give up to them and let them do with you what they pleas. (John Hartman, Hartman Papers, Duke) Rowan County

Feb. 28, 1865: may god grant us the privalig of comeing hom onst more in peace to injoy the sweet privalige of home and its Surrounding beauties **onst** more. (James Cowand, Cowand Papers, Duke) Bertie County

one *pronoun* One or the other; *one* placed at the end of the two alternatives without *or the other.* [*DSME* **one**, pronoun, 2]

Apr. 3, 1863: you said that you would have to sell some of pigs or buy corn **one**. (Edgar Smithwick, Smithwick Papers, Duke) Martin County

Apr. 4, 1863: Sallie I wish it was So that Mary ur Murther **one** chold [= could] come and Stay with you. (Elizabeth Wagoner, Hundley Family Letters, SHC) Stokes County

Apr. 19, 1863: we cant git one bit of coten yarn. the big men buis it for 6 dolars abunch and Sells [h]is for 12 and we Shall hav to go and take it or beg **one** and I dont like to take nor beg. (Fereby Core, Vance Papers, NCSA) Cumberland County

May 13, 1863: old Hooker Ses that he intends to brake up our army or his **one**. (Hardy Matthews, Hefner Papers, SHC) Moore County

onease *verb* To cause unease, trouble, distress; variant form of *unease*. [*OED* †**unease**, verb]

Feb. 15, 1864: Well Mother you said that you was affraid that I was on sufferance when I writen hom for somthing to eate. you kneed not **oneas** yourself a bout that for I get a plenty to eate all the time. (D. R. Barnhill, Military Coll., Civil War, NCSA) Bladen County

Oct. 16, 1864: thare is one thing that **oneases** me a litle the yellow fever over in the town but I hope it wont get on the ship. (Henry Bowen, Bowen Papers, NCSA) Washington County

oneasy *adjective* variant form of *uneasy*.

Nov. 10, 1861: I told our captain that I was **oneasy** a Bout him. I told him I feard that they would not take good cear of him. (John B. Lance, Lance Papers, LSU) Henderson County

Feb. 22, 1863: I tell you that I am veary **oneasy** about you. I would be the glades to see you in the world. (Martha Futch, Futch Letters, NCSA) New Han-over County

May 28, 1863: I knew that You would be **oneasy** a bout me as soon as You heard tell of the Fight. (William Tesh, Tesh Papers, Duke) Yadkin County

Jan. 8, 1865: I could not heare frome you in time off the fight and I was **on easy** a bout you. (Flora Ann Campbell, Campbell Papers, Duke) Moore County

only *preposition* Except, except for. [*DARE* scattered, but especially South, South Midland]

June 6, 1863: we have afew Run Mad hot headed Secessionest that thinks every Body Aught to be gone to the Wars only them and they would have you Believe that every Body is Dis Loyal **only** them. (Stephen Collis, Vance Papers, NCSA) Mitchell County

Apr. 8, 1864: my dear wife and children. i rite you aline to let you now i am well **only** abad cole. (Silas Stepp, Stepp Letters, UNCA) Buncombe County

Sept. 25, 1864: I seat my self down to Rite you afew lines to let you now that I am well **only** my side and my hips and knees. (F. M. Poteet, Poteet-Dickson Letters, NCSA) McDowell County

on (one's) head *adjective phrase* Anxious. [*DARE* **head**, noun, D 3]

Jan. 26, 1862: if nothing happens I think I will get to come home when John comes. he is **on his head** to go home in Febuary. (Jonas Bradshaw, Bradshaw Papers, Duke) Alexander County

Jan. 30, 1862: if these toreys resest ther arest he will send force enough to wipe out the overt act. my boys are **on thir heads** to goe. (A. W. Bell, Bell Papers, Duke) Macon County

Aug. 21, 1864: you Rote to me to not Runaway. if it is the will of my loving Wife I wont Runaway god nows that it tis hard times hear. I want you to send me somthing to eat by sumbody if Pery Walkerdont fetch it. you Rote that you would all mose be **on your head** till Higgins Come back. (F. M. Poteet, Poteet-Dickson Letters, NCSA) McDowell County

on (one's) own hook *prepostional phrase* Without help, without permission, on one's own authority. [*OED* **hook**, verb[2], 16.a.]

Oct. 20, 1855: I will move my propertey to some outher point and leat him try on his **one hooke** and see what he will do. (Hugh McGregor, Jackson Family Corr., Notre Dame) Moore County

Feb. 5, 1865: if they dont let me Come home i am going to come on my **own hook**. (Wade Hubbard, Hubbard Papers, Duke) Anson County

on shares *prepositional phrase* An arrangement in which a landowner or shop owner receives a portion of a crop or other products in exchange for the use of the land or shop.

June 14, 1863: Dear wife you Rote to me that Bil had not paid you yet. If Stamy wil not settle it in that way I want you to Be shore and kee[p] what wair [= stoneware] and clay is their and dont allow him to move it. it may be that some one wil turn it up for you **own shears** and burn it [in a kiln]. (Isaac Lefevers, Lefevers Papers, NCSA) Catawba County

ont *verb* variant form of *want*.

Sept. 8, 1862: Dear Wife I **ont** you to write wether you have reseived aney leter from me or not and I **onte** you to git me a pair of shous fo my old ones ar nery give out. (Robert Spainhourd, Spainhourd Papers, Duke) Forsyth County

May 31, 1863: you Stated in your leter that you had severl galons of brandy and at last Stated you didnt get one galon. I do not **ont** none to drink. I would liked to had it Hear. I Could get A hundred dolers for one galon to retail it. that was what I wanted you to Save it for. (Marcus Hefner, Hefner Papers, NCSA) Catawba County

on the goose see **all right on the goose**

on the mend *prepositional phrase* In the process of healing, becoming healthy again.

July 16, 1862: I hav bin Sick A 2 weekes I am glad that I am **on the mend** Some. (Leonard Alman, Alman Papers, Duke) Cabarrus County

Aug. 20, 1863: Arthur is **on the mend** and says

he will be able to go to his company in a few days. (Mary C. Kendrick, Kendrick Papers, NCSA) Cleveland County

Aug. 22, 1863: E W Blair has bin sick and poke [= Polk] has bin sick and I thought tha wood die. tha had the bludey flux but thay ar **on the mend**. (Francis Blair, J. H. Baker Papers, Duke) Rockingham County

on the scout, on a scout *prepositional phrase* On a military expedition or patrol; also used figuratively for foraging.

Nov. 23, 1862: the rest of our catawba squad is all well at this time but not very well satisfied. i have bin in Va **on the Scout** & i dont want to go their no more soon. (T. B. Litten, Fisher Papers, Duke) Catawba County

Mar. 25, 1863: I was at the S Planes [= Strawberry Plains] 2 days but did not git to See David as he was out **on a Scout**. (Stephen Whitaker, Whitaker Papers, NCSA) Cherokee County

Oct. 2, 1863: I was out **on a Scout** yesterday and I did enjoy my self verry much. I got a fine dinnerwhile on scout. I found Some apples & graps and muskadines and chickapines though I walked a good peace for to get them. (J. W. Lineberger, *Gaston Ranger,* 68) Gaston County

Mar. 16, 1864: tha picked out about 65 of the Stoutes men and one capt and two lieutenants and went **on the Scout** for four days and nights and we had to travel thrugh Swamps and Slep in the Swamp and not a thing to Sleep on nor to cover with. (Jesse Hill, Hill Letters, NCSA) Forsyth County

onst, oncet, wonst see **once**

ontil *preposition* variant form of *until.*

Oct. 26, 1862: So nothing more at presant. only Remain your afectionate Husband **ontil** death. (Marcus Hefner, Hefner Papers, NCSA) Catawba County

onwell *adjective* variant form of *unwell.*

Jan. 10, 1864: I will try to finish my leter 12 in [= instant] of the month as I Stopt the 10 on acount of being **on well** and two cold I coldent write. (R. C. Caldwell, Caldwell Coll., ECU) Cabarrus County

orster *noun* variant form of *oyster.*

Nov. 21, 1863: tel uncle Jo to eat his **orsters**. (R. C. Caldwell, Caldwell Coll., ECU) Cabarrus County

ort to *auxiliary verb* variant form of *ought to.*

Feb. 17, 1862: ef you ant mared yet i think that you **ort to** wait tell i com back for i want to eat sum of the crust. (Evin Smith, E. Smith Papers, Duke) Stanley County

July 14, 1862: we **ort to** pray to god for the meny Blesing he has Be stod upon us. (Marion Sexton, Sexton Letters, Duke) Ashe County

Apr. 3, 1864: father you **ort to** be hear to help mee eat chese an coffey. (Alfred Cowand, Cowand Papers, Duke) Bertie County

ourn *possessive pronoun* Ours. [*OED* **ourn**, pronoun, (citations as early as 1382); *DARE* chiefly South, South Midland, New England]

Nov. 28, 1861: jerushea R Parker brouth his letter here and we had **ourun** wrought [= wrote] and put them all in one in vealop. (Dena Stack, Confederate Papers, SHC) Union County

Mar. 11, 1862: let me know how wheat looks up thare and Especially **ourn**. I think if I should Live I Will git a furlow to come home about harvest and cut wheat. (G. J. Huntley, Huntley Papers, WCU) Rutherford County

ourselfs *reflexive pronoun* variant form of *ourselves.*

Sept. 2, 1863: I hope you all will be purmited to com hom soon and we can haf the privlige of injoy **our selfs** as we haf in tim past and goan. (Thomas Brann, Tesh Papers, Duke) Yadkin County

out *adverb*

1. To the point of completion, completely. [*DARE* **out**, adverb, 6]

Mar. 16, 1863: Francis thay was too twenty Dollar Bills I sent them to you to pay you for the Bottle of Brandy an pound Cake. you Rote to me that I must drink the Brandy **out** and Send you the Bottle. (J. W. Joyce, Joyce Papers, MHI) Stokes County

2. In the expression *time is out:* when a soldier's period of enlistment is at an end.

Oct. 26, 1861: I hop I wil See you all Be fore long at leas[t] be for my **time is out**. I am vary well sattsfied aheap better than I expected. (D. M. Carter, Culberson Papers, Duke) Chatham County

Dec. 22, 1861: I dont think a fifty dollar furlow is no indu cement to me. if I have to stay until my **time is out** it will Be all Right with me. I think if nothing happens an I Can live till my **time is out** and then I know that I Can go and stay. (James W. Gibson, Gibson Papers, Duke) Catawba County

Feb. 2, 1862: all that hurts us is leaveing the fair sects [= sex] that is the girls that we left in old catawba. as for being at home I do not care if that was all that pestered me. I dont think I would come home until my **time is out**. (P. S. Whitner, Whitner Papers, Duke) Catawba County

Feb. 26, 1863: some seemes to think that pees [= peace] will be mad shortly but i dont Cal Culate on gitting to Come home before lincons **times is out** my self. (Isaac Copeland, Copeland Letters, NCSA) Surry County

outen *preposition* Out of. [*OED* **outen**, preposition, 1.b. "*regional* [*Sc., Eng. regional* (*north.*), and *U.S. regional* (chiefly *South.*)"]

Aug. 5, 1862: I want you to make me Some Shirts **outen** tha Calico what I got at germington. (A. J. Spease, Zimmerman Papers, Duke) Forsyth County

Feb. 6, 1863: father I want yow to try and get **owtten** Dept [= debt] if yow can. I will try and help yow all I Can. (W. H. Brotherton, Brotherton Papers, Duke) Catawba County

outlier *noun* A deserter or someone avoiding military service by hiding out. [*OED* **outlier**, noun, 1.c.; *DSME* **outlier**, noun, "a marauder, especially a deserter from Civil War service who hid out in the mountains, preyed on the local population for food and supplies, and often became a **bushwhacker**"]

June 24, 1863: the Militia was orderd by you or som other person to serch fore those **outlyers**. they went on one night an came a cros sume four or five conscripts the[y] say thy holted them. they run some of them. shot and kild one of them. (Wesley Jones, Vance Papers, NCSA) Chatham County

out of heart *adjective phrase* Downhearted, hopeless. [*DARE* especially South Midland]

Aug. 25, 1863: I am **out of hart** about writing as I have writen you Several leters Since I left home & has got no anser yet nor but 2 leters from Cherokee Since I left thar. (Stephen Whitaker, Whitaker Papers, NCSA) Cherokee County

Nov. 19, 1863: dont git **out of hart**. you no that it wood hav Bin A Bad chance for mee to hav stad at home. (J. W. Reese, Reese Papers, Duke) Buncombe County

Nov. 23, 1863: I have got **out of hart** that I ever Will git home any more till this War ends. (F. M. Poteet, Poteet-Dickson Letters, NCSA) McDowell County

Oct. 10, 1864: you muste note gite **out of hart** about mee cumeing home for I wille come ase soone ase I cane. (Daniel Abernethy, Abernethy Papers, Duke) Catawba County

owing to *preposition* Because of. [*DARE* scattered, but especially South, South Midland]

Nov. 19, 1862: mi Legs hav bin paning me writ smart fur the last few dase but it is **owing to** the weather. (B. C. Jackson, Jackson Family Corr., Notre Dame) Moore County

Mar. 8, 1863: Me and Nancy intended to go to see you last week but **owing to** so much water we had to give it out. (Betty Thomas, Quinn Papers, Duke) Duplin County

July 31, 1863: I have not had any letter from you in a good while But I reckon it is **owing to** our Marching we do not get the mail only once in a great while. (John Futch, Futch Letters, NCSA) New Hanover County

May 25, 1864: I cannot write eny more as time will not admit. I intended writing A long letter but **owing to** the move ment [of troops] I am complelled to stop. (J. F. Coghill, Coghill Letters, SHC) Granville County

owls have caught him *idiomatic expression* To go missing at night; to desert while on picket.

July 9, 1864: A compney out of the 54 verginia Regmant Belonging to ouer Bregad one nite whil on picket the liutenant in Command of the Companey he went over an mad airraingmet with the yankeys pickets and Cum Back and tuck the Companey over with him and sum has went sence and sevril has went out of the 58 N C Regmant. the Boys Calls this when on[e] Runs A way or is miss ing that the **owls has Cout him**. (J. W. Reese, Reese Papers, Duke) Buncombe County

own *verb* To admit. [*OED* **own**, verb, 5.a.]

Feb. 2, 1865: the sesesh men dos hate to **own** that we are whiped. they wont talk about it if they can help it. it dos me good to tell it to them but they hav to **own** it. (Martha Poteet, Poteet-Dickson Letters, NCSA) McDowell County

own hook see **on (one's) own hook**

P

pa, par, paw *noun* Father; see Overview § I.1.1. [*DARE* **pa**, noun, widespread, but especially Northeast, North Central, Upper Midwest; **paw** widespread except Northeast]

1. variant forms *pa* and *paw*.

Oct. 28, 1862: I will close this letter by saying kiss my sweet little babe fur its **Paw**. (Jonas Bradshaw, Bradshaw Papers, Duke) Alexander County

Mar. 4, 1863: I expect **pa** will not write for a few days & you must not be uneasy about Jim iny for he is wel sadisfied. (Elizabeth Kendrick, Kendrick Papers, NCSA) Cleveland County

Dec. 3, 1864: I send George Pinkney this Bill of money. you can tell him that his **paw** sent it to him. (F. M. Poteet, Poteet-Dickson Letters, NCSA) McDowell County

2. variant form *par.* [this form not listed in *DARE*]

June 12, 1862: Give my love and reSpect to **Par** and family and tell them as I am as well and heartty as I ever was. (J. W. Whitfield, Whitfield Papers, Duke) Nash County

Apr. 16, 1863: tell your Mar & **Par** that I would Be more then Glad to See them. (John Futch, Futch Letters, NCSA) New Hanover County

Oct. 21, 1864: Henry Cleophus ses he would be glad if **par** would come back if he could. he knows you cant and the poor little fellow appears to be resigned to it. (Ann Bowen, Bowen Papers, NCSA) Washington County

pantaloons *noun* Pants, trousers; underpants. [*OED* **pantaloon**, noun, 2.f. (after a sixteenth-century theatrical character of the name)]

Oct. 22, 1861: As for clothing Mother I am tolerably well off though if you get a good oppertunity to send anything you may send me a pair of woollen **pantaloons** and a pair of drawers. (H. J. Davis, WPA Transcripts, TSLA) Yadkin County

Oct. 16, 1863: I want you to send me some cloths by him. the coat that I wore of before and my boots and one par of **pantaloons** and some socks and a cag of Brandy and some honey. (Isaac Copeland, Copeland Letters, NCSA) Surry County

pap *noun* Father; see Overview § I.1.1. [*pap* is the most common term used in the North Carolina letters other than the formal term, *father; OED* **pap**, noun[3], *U.S. colloq; DARE* chiefly Midland, South Atlantic]

Nov. 28, 1861: uncle Lee, **pap** baut a galon of Whiskey for you an mother went to g[r]anmother and put it in your box and soad it up in your blanket. (Laura Stack, Confederate Papers, SHC) Union County

Feb. 18, 1863: Mat Clayton said he saw **pap** last Friday when he went over to Solamons Huffmans. (A. J. Spease, Zimmerman Papers, Duke) Forsyth County

Mar. 3, 1863: Tell **pap** an mam an all of the rest howdy for mee an to wright to mee. (T. F. Baggarly, Baggarly Papers, Duke) Iredell County

May 1, 1863: Pap if you and Elyzabeth goes to git maried you must Let me no it in time to giv you an ansuer. (Jesse Shipman, Shipman Family Corr., Notre Dame) Henderson County

May 1, 1864: Sorey to hear that **pap** was ded. I did want to see him one time more in this life. (J. W. Reese, Reese Papers, Duke) Buncombe County

pappy *noun* Father; see Overview § I.1.1. [*DARE* chiefly South Midland]

Oct. 1, 1861: Pappy we have not recieve our Money and it will be a long time befour we are do. (K. W. Coghill, Coghill Papers, Duke) Granville County

Aug. 1, 1863: Pappay aint vary well but is up and a bought [= about] and mother a bought as Common and all of the rest is as well as common at this time. (James Broach, Broach Papers, Duke) Person County

Mar. 6, 1864: we was glad to hear from you and the baby says **pappy** is gone. (Caroline Setzer, Setzer Corr., UVA) Catawba County

Nov. 2, 1864: far well well children. you cante see you[r] **papy** no more on erth. (J. R. Redmond, Military Coll., Civil War, NCSA) Buncombe County

parsel, passel *noun* A group, crowd, bunch. [*OED* **parcel**, noun, 6.a., "Now Eng. regional and U.S. colloq. (esp. in form passel)"]

Aug. 8, 1861: tel Jim he must have a corn shucken and hav a **parsel** a girls there for I know all the boys a round a bout there want him to. (Harrison Hanes, Hanes Papers, Duke) Davie County

Mar. 10, 1862: I never saw a moar peassiable **pasel** of men in my life. we hoald pray meeting twise a weak. (James A. Patton, Patton Letters, Emory) Granville County

June 12, 1862: their was a whole **parsel** of Boxes sent to some of the company from Newton & it was all spoilt. they was own the road Two weaks. (Isaac Lefevers, Lefevers Papers, NCSA) CatawbaCounty

Nov. 5, 1862: i ame a pore woman with a **pasel** of litle children. (Lydia Bolton, Vance Papers, NCSA) Guilford County

Apr. 7, 1864: they dont want to come for there aint any thing to come for but a **parcel** of half perished women and children. (Martha Poteet, Poteet-Dickson Letters, NCSA) McDowell County

par see **pa**

partake *verb* variant past participle *pertuck*.

Aug. 7, 1861: there is aheep of wekeedness going on here But thank God I never have have **pertuck** with none of it nor I never intend to as long as I live. (Peter Poteet, Poteet-Dickson Letters, NCSA) Burke County

partridge *noun* A quail; also variant form *patter-age*. [see *DSME* **partridge**, noun, A]

Sept. 11, 1862: ever things is high. chickens is worth 75 cent the sise of **patterage.** theas half sise pys is 25 cents for two. (W. H. Brotherton, Brotherton Papers, Duke) Catawba County

Dec. 21, 1862: Tell Julius that I am glad to hear that he has caught a possome and 12 rabbits and tell him to catch all the Rabbits and **partriges** that he can. (C. A. Hege, Hege Papers, MHI) Davidson County

pass *verb*

1. Of currency: to be accepted as legal tender. [*OED* **pass**, verb, 44.]

Feb. 25, 1863: If I finde out that the confederit Money wont **pass** no more then I shall try and run a way too. (W. F. Wagner, *Confederate Soldier,* 38) Catawba County

Mar. 7, 1864: we cant buy nothing her[e]. the money wont **pas** no more. (Daniel Setzer, Setzer Papers, Duke) Catawba County

Jan. 9, 1865: I send you theas little bill. they wont **pass** heare. it is some abisha got from the soldiers be-fore plymouth fell. perhaps they will **pass** thar. (Ann Bowen, Bowen Papers, NCSA) Washington County

2. Of mail: to be conveyed, delivered (often in the sense of being delivered without disruption or obstruction).

Aug. 19, 1864: the yankees hav Bin in perseertion [= possession] of the Weldon Rail Road for the last ten days So that the mail did not **pass**. (Edgar Smithwick, Smithwick Papers, Duke) Martin County

Nov. 6, 1864: I expect it is a bad chance to **pass** Letters but I shal try to send you one as often as I can. (Henry Bowen, Bowen Papers, NCSA) Washington County

passel see **parsel**

passenger *noun* A traveler, a visitor. [see *OED* **passenger**, noun, 3.a., "A person who passes by or through a place; a traveller, esp. a traveller on foot."]

Aug. 15, 1862: We are about 80 miles from Richmond in Orrange County close to gordons ville. I still hear from **pasengers** that you are Coming to see us. (G. J. Huntley, Huntley Papers, WCU) Rutherford County

patterage, patridge see **partridge**

paw see **pa**

peach leather *noun* A kind of preserved fruit made from peach puree spread on a flat surface and dried. [see *DARE* **leather**, noun, 3]

July 13, 1863: Tell Sam and Julius to make some **peach Leather** for me. (C. A. Hege, Hege Papers, MHI) Davidson County

peart, peert, pirt *adjective* Lively, healthy, recovered from an illness (usual pronunciation is *peert*). [*OED* **pert**, adjective, 4, "*Eng. regional* and *U.S. regional* (esp. in form peart)"; *DARE* chiefly South, South Midland]

Mar. 3, 1862: Sister margrat and hir child is very sick with the mezals. mother says that thar is all of them and too at home and she thinks that hir case is hard but she is **peert** yet. (Martha Futch, Futch Letters, NCSA) New Hanover County

May 3, 1863: you wanted mee to rite how your bulls look. I can Say to you that tha are thin but is **pirt** and harty. (George Robertson, Woody Letters, Confederate Misc., Emory) Yancey County

Sept. 5, 1864: the mule colt is in very good order an larg anuf of it age an well forme an mity **peart**. (Thomas Brotherton, Brotherton Papers, Duke) Catawba County

Jan. 21, 1865: some days she can set up and seem rite **peart** and others she keeps her bed most all day. (Ann Bowen, Bowen Papers, NCSA) Washington County

peg *noun* A tooth, in the expression *wet your peg* (with a sense similar to *wet your whistle*): to take a drink of whiskey or brandy. [*OED* **peg**, noun[1], III.6.a.]

Sept. 1862: me an Isaac go out some times an wet our **peg** but it is not so good as me an you are use to. (David Sherrill, Robinson Papers, Duke) Catawba County

pegging awl *noun* An awl used for repairing shoes.

Nov. 24, 1862: I want you to send me a **pegin all**. the largest I have got. they have a doller for putting on a heel to a shoe. I could mend mine if I had an all. (James Zimmerman, Zimmerman Papers, Duke) Forsyth County

pensman *noun* A person who writes letters for someone else.

Feb. 4, 1864: you asked to no how [= who] was my **pensman**. he is one of my mes mates that I have found acquantence with Hwo disiers [= who desires] pease un[s]tid of war. though I will not tel his name at this tim he is a native of N.C. (Daniel Abernethy, Abernethy Papers, Duke) Catawba County

people *noun* Family. [*DARE* **people**, noun, B 2; scattered but chiefly South, South Midland]

July 16, 1861: I Was happy to receive your kind letter today for it dose me so mutch good to here from eny of my **People** in this troublesum place. (Peter Poteet, Poteet-Dickson Letters, NCSA) Burke County

Dec. 28, 1862: i think of yow all evry day. thare is nothing pesters my mind onlly abowt my **people**. (T. F. Baggarly, Baggarly Papers, Duke) Iredell County

Oct. 26, 1863: I would be very glad to hear of him and I am sure his **People** would like to hear. if you see aney of them you tell them if I hear of him I will writ to them imediatley. (A. A. Jackson, Jackson Family Corr., Notre Dame) Moore County

June 4, 1864: if you git any Letters from your **People** or mine I want you to write how they are gitten along. (James Davis, Robinson Papers, Duke) Catawba County

perish *verb*

1. To die.

June 11, 1862: you wrote my hogs were about to dy. please dont let them **perish**. (Ichabod Quinn, Quinn Papers, Duke) Duplin County

2. To starve to death; suffer from hunger.

Sept. 27, 1862: I allways can get as much meat and bread as we have had. we will not **perish**. (James Zimmerman, Zimmerman Papers, Duke) Forsyth County

Dec. 19, 1862: Father you Requested to no how I faird When i was in Maryland. Sir mi fair was varybad for we had to Steal Rosten years [= roastin ears] to Eat to keep from **parishing**. (William Carpenter, Carpenter Family Papers, ECU) Chatham County

July 18, 1863: my dear wife I am glad to hear that yews has good crops at hom. I think. we began to need it for we dont draw but one rasions Sometimes for Six days. we all but **perish**. (John Hartman, Hartman Papers, Duke) Rowan County

3. In the phrase *perish to death:* to die from hunger. [see *DARE* **perish**, verb, 3]

Mar. 19, 1865: the men in richmon sais the Solgers famelys is **perishing to death** for something to eat and to ware and god only knows how soon it may the case with many others. (F. A. Bleckley, Bleckley Papers, Duke) Catawba County

4. As a phrasal verb with *out,* in both transitive and intransitive constructions: to starve completely, to starve into submission. [see *DARE* **perish**, verb, 2]

Mar. 3, 1863: if Our big lande o[w]ners & slave hol ders ante stopt from ma ken such large crops of tobaco our countrey will **Perrish oute** in a nother year & Whipt oute for the wante of Breade & meate. (Pleasant Black, Vance Papers, NCSA) Rockingham County

Apr. 25, 1863: the yankeys on picket the other daysed they understood we had A new Jeneral over hear Jenerel Starveation. old Jo hooker ses he only wants 4 weke to **perish us out**. (James M. Amos, Amos Papers, Duke) Rockingham County

5. To cause to starve, suffer from hunger.

Sept. 19, 1863: I hav had Six Sunes in this wor and thre is [in] it yeat an the pri[c]es of meete And bred Stuf will **parish** thar famlys to death without giving them moer or bring doun the price of purvishion. (Jesse Coppedge, Vance Papers, NCSA) Nash County

perished *adjective* From past participle of *perish:* starved, suffering from hunger, desiring a particular kind or quality of food.

Apr. 28, 1863: I have to Buy half I get to eat and then go a half **parished**. (Joseph Cowand, Cowand Papers, Duke) Bertie County

Dec. 12, 1863: I want you to Send me Some good dride froot. I am most **perrisht** for Som. (Daniel Setzer, Setzer Papers, Duke) Catawba County

pester *verb* To bother, afflict. [*OED* **pester**, verb[1], 4.a. (earliest citation from 1566)]

June 16, 1861: I havent sufferd forany thing yet. all that **pesters** me is beeing a way from you. (Harrison Hanes, Hanes Papers, Duke) Davie County

May 24, 1862: if eny body **pester** you i wont you to let mey now it. i wont ever body tend to dar [= their] one bisnes. if da [= they] dont i will kill dem [= them]. (W. P. Cline, Cline Papers, SHC) Catawba County

Dec. 2, 1862: I am sorter **pestered** this morning. I lost $20.00 a twenty doller bill some how. (James Zimmerman, Zimmerman Papers, Duke) Forsyth County

Dec. 28, 1862: i think of yow all evry day thare is nothing **pesters** my mind onlly abowt my people. (T. F. Baggarly, Baggarly Papers, Duke) Iredell County

Feb. 27, 1863: my Eys and knees **pesters** mee vary Bad. my eys is A little Better But tha **pester** mee A good deel A Bout Riting. (J. W. Reese, Reese Papers, Duke) Buncombe County

Aug. 7, 1863: he had the diarear for sometime. I am **pesterd** with that some times. (John L. Putnam, Kendrick Papers, NCSA) Cleveland County

physicianer *noun* A physician, medical doctor. [*OED* †**physicianer** noun (citations from 1598 through 1848)]

Oct. 8, 1861: as Soon as you and his **phisioner** thinks he can come home I want you to Send him. (F. H. Williams, Williams Papers, Duke) Onslow County

piazza *noun* A covered porch, veranda. [*DARE* chiefly Northeast, South Atlantic]

Dec. 26, 1864: I went to bring in a stick of wood out of the **piza** in the dark thar was several sticks piled up and one about Six inches through rolled down on my big toe and mashed it bad. (Ann Bowen, Bowen Papers, NCSA) Washington County

pick *verb* To play a stringed instrument, especially a banjo. [*DSME* **pick**, verb, 1; *OED* **pick**, verb[1], 10]

Dec. 3, 1861: thare is a Littell of a most every thing Carried on hear But more of Evil than any thing Eles. We have Fidling. Dancing. **Picking** the Banjo. Cursing plenty. preaching. praying. Singing and other things that is as mean as any. (G. J. Huntley, Huntley Papers, WCU) Rutherford County

picter *noun* variant form of *picture*. [*DSME* **picture**, *noun*, variant form *picter*]

July 13, 1863: Sarepta is well and Jack is as prety as a **picter**. (John Revis, Revis Letters, NCSA) Henderson County

piece, peace *noun*

1. A distance. [*DARE* widespread, but more frequent South, Midland, Texas]

Feb. 4, 1862: the water is bad an we have to tote it a good **pese** a bout a half mile. (J. S. Councill, Councill Papers, Duke) Watauga County

July 21, 1862: we marcht on a**peice** and then we Double quick a **pease** and formed our line and marcht up A little closer. (J. W. Love, Love Papers, Duke) Henderson County

Oct. 10, 1862: thare is a talk of our mooving back a **peace** to Ward old NC in afew das. (J. E. McFee, McFee Letters, SRNB) Buncombe County

Oct. 2, 1863: I found some apples & graps and muskadines and chickapines though I walked a good **peace** for to get them. (J. W. Lineberger, *Gaston Ranger,* 68) Gaston County

2. An amount or portion of land, ground, woods.

May 10, 1863: when we got their we form in lins of battle And charge the enemy. we charge them threw A **piece** of woods Abowt one mile And A half. (W. H. Brotherton, Brotherton Papers, Duke) Catawba County

June 15, 1863: now our Pickets are on the Banks of the Rhappohannock and we are a laying back in a **Piece** of wood about a half a mile From the Breast work. (William Tesh, Tesh Papers, Duke) Yadkin County

Oct. 16, 1864: i want to sow the haw tree **peas** [= piece] and them Bottoms in wheat and the new bares **peas** in oats. i did intend to sow All that **peas** of grond on the Road from the Cotton patch to the Long Slipe in wheat and oats. (Wade Hubbard, Hubbard Papers, Duke) Anson County

pig *verb* Of a sow: to have a litter of pigs. [*OED* **pig**, verb, 1.a.]

Apr. 5, 1863: I want to no whether your slippes is rotten or not and if yow are going to Gett enny boddy to plow for you or not and whether your sow has **piged** or not and how menny she has. (Daniel Brown, Brown Coll., NCSA) Duplin

piles *noun plural* Hemorrhoids.

Apr. 26, 1862: My der Partha i now Seate my Self to right yew afew lines that i am not well. I have got the **piles** verry bad but i hope that when theas few lines reach yew they will find yew enjoying good helth. (John Hartman, Hartman Papers, Duke) Rowan County

Feb. 25, 1863: he has got the **piles** sorty at this time but I hope he will get shet of it a gain before long. (W. F. Wagner, *Confederate Soldier,* 37) Catawba County

July 14, 1863: I am not Able to go through the hardships of a Solder in Camps. I am aflicted with the Rumitism and **Piles** so that I aint able half my time for Duty allthough I have Bin on every march save 3 since I have Bin in this Regt. (W. A. E. Roberts, Vance Papers, NCSA) Rutherford County

pill *noun* Figuratively: a bullet. [CACWL data suggest that the figurative use of *pill* for *bullet* was in widespread use during the war]

Feb. 17, 1863: All I dred her[e] is Linkons **pills** for tha will pass thru a man in less than no time. (Lee Hendrix, Hendrix Corr., VPI) Forsyth County

Nov. 4, 1863: Dear Sisters I hav nothing of interest to write to you this time only that I wont to see you very much. I also want to go home to talk to them fellows about my honey bees. I think I could make them eat something a little harder than honey and not quite so deliteful to there taste. a little **pill** smoked with sulphfer and salt peter. (J. M. Frank, Frank Papers, Duke) Davidson County

piller *noun* variant form of *pillow*. [*DARE* especially South Midland]

Sept. 16, 1862: yew was A saing that it was the straw **pilers** that was A making yore neck sore. (B. C. Jackson, Jackson Family Corr., Notre Dame) Moore County

Jan. 18, 1863: I send ten dollars in this letter and send a few Buttingis [= buttons] in the **Piller** Sleirp [= slip]. (P. W. Broach, Broach Papers, Duke) Person County

pilot *noun* A guide, especially a person who could guide Union recruits from Western North Carolina and East Tennessee through territory occupied by Confederate troops. [*OED* **pilot**, A. noun, I.2. "A person who acts as a guide through an unknown or hazardous area of land; an escort. Now *rare*."]

Dec. 27, 1862: tena thair was fore men Shot and hung one man by the name of gray. he had Bin A **pilet** for the yankeys. he was hung or hung him self. he jumpt off of the gales [= gallows] Be fore tha Cood nock him off. (J. W. Reese, Reese Papers, Duke) Buncombe County

pink *noun* Any of several flowering plants of the genus *Dianthus;* in the western part of North Carolina may also refer to rhododendron.

Apr. 3, 1863: my little Jwlarkey is as pretty as a **pink** and as a Rose. oh how I wold like to see her smille it would be the greatis of pleasur. (James Keever, Keever Papers, Duke) Lincoln County

June 17, 1864: when this you see remember mee though many miles apart wee bea. houdy my sweet **pink**. (Silas Stepp, Stepp Letters, UNCA) Buncombe County

pint *verb* variant form of *point*.

May 4, 1862: some times I Become vary mutch depressed in spirits then again hope Revives me up and **pints** me to something Bright in the future. (G. J. Huntley, Huntley Papers, WCU) Rutherford County

Oct. 28, 1862: i Send you this Letter to Let you knoo that wellington is at the **pint** of Death. the Doc tor give him over on yestidy But he has not Bin to see him yet on to Day. (William H. Thurber, DeRosset Family Papers, SHC) New Hanover County

pitch in *verb* To eat greedily, with gusto; see Overview § II.4.7.

Aug. 3, 1863: I will tell you the boys was played off on at Pettersburg. the old Negroes brought a chicken pie out to camp. they **pitched in** heavy but when they found out it was a mixture hog chicken & mostly dog. they even had the head of the dog. (J. W. Lineberger, *Gaston Ranger,* 61) Gaston County

pitch into *verb* To fight, attack furiously; see Overview § II.4.7.

July 24, 1864: old Hampton **pitch in to** them & taken 25 Hundred prisners & all their artillery & waggons .&.c. (Thomas B. Litten, Fisher Papers, Duke) Catawba County

pitiful *adjective* Pathetic; superlative form *pitifulest*.

Nov. 2, 1864: it was the **pittifullest** looking little Mortal you ever saw. (Martha Poteet, Poteet-Dickson Letters, NCSA) McDowell County

plague *verb* To pain, torment, harass. [*OED* **plague**, verb., 1.a. (earliest citation 1481)]

Aug. 2, 1856: all the people are well an wishes thare love to master. Molly is **pleged** with the rumatism. (Henry [Pettigrew slave], Pettigrew Family Papers, SHC) Washington County

Oct. 21, 1864: my caulf **plages** me yet and I am very week. I havent bin able to be out much in a week. (Ann Bowen, Bowen Papers, NCSA) Washington County

plagued *adjective* Bothersome, cursed. [*DSME* **plagued**, adjective, A]

Nov. 6, 1862: Send me one Shirt one pair Drawers one pair socks one good thick pair gloves. please sow the seames down close as the **pleged** Body bugs pesters us a good deal. (Isaac Lefevers, Lefevers Papers, NCSA) Catawba County

June 18, 1863: i am not fit for camp lif let alon the duty of the man for i hav Bin gevin to hart pluricey and the consuption and i am fity By spells 4 or 5 tims in a weeck. this i have haid for the last 8 or 10 years now. you now that a man that is so **plegued** is not fit for sirves. (Bluford Lucas, Vance Papers, NCSA) Harnett County

plat, plad *noun* A braid of hair; variant form of *plait*. [*DARE* chiefly South, South Midland]

June 12, 1862: my Dear wife I want you the next letter you rite to send mee a lock of your purty Black hair put it in a **plat** sow it will gow own my vest. (Isaac Lefevers, Lefevers Papers, NCSA) Catawba County

Dec. 23, 1862: yow dont know how glad i was to her from yow all for i had recvd none from yow since that one yow sent that **plad** of hair in. (T. F. Baggarly, Baggarly Papers, Duke) Iredell County

May 31, 1864: I got the **plat** of hear that you Sent me. I left your Brother in Richmond Monday Eavning. he hated to See me start. I had to get to My Redgment and he had to go to his. When I got to my Redgment I got that other letter that had the **plat** of hear in hit. (F. M. Poteet, Poteet-Dickson Letters, NCSA) McDowell County

plat *verb* To braid or weave hair or other material, the citation below suggests weaving a straw hat; variant form of *plait*.

July 24, 1862: I Waunt you to git martha Hamilton **to plat** me a summer hat and send it By Wm Jones. One that Will Fit pap Or a Littell Larger Will suit me you can pay her for it. a summer hat her is Worth 10 Dollars. (G. J. Huntley, Huntley Papers, WCU) Rutherford County

play *noun* A play party, a party with games and dancing.

Nov. 5, 1861: I want to come home about Christmas and I want you to have a big Quilting and a **play** if I dont get home then I will get home when my time is out. (J. L. Groves, Davison Papers, Duke) Gaston County

Sept. 21, 1863: I want to come home about christmas if I live. I want you to tell Davy that she must have a fine quilt as I shall expect her to have a fine quilting a **play** & a heap of fun &c. tell lilly to keep on begging and maby peace will be made sometime. (William Walsh, Proffit Family Letters, SHC) Wilkes County

play off on *verb* To deceive, trick; see Overview § II.4.7. [*DSME* **play off on**, verb phrase]

Aug. 3, 1863: I will tell you the boys was **played off on** at Pettersburg. the old Negroes brought a chicken pie out to camp. they pitched in heavy but when they found out it was a mixture hog chicken & mostly dog. they even had the head of the dog. (J. W. Lineberger, *Gaston Ranger,* 61) Gaston County

play on *verb* To fire on with massed muskets; to attack with artillery; see Overview § II.4.7. [*OED* **play**, verb, 8.b.]

Nov. 10, 1862: we have been in to a fight two days and a parte of one Night. the fight commence foremiles of watshing ton. an laste sunday fore compiny of our Reg **plade on** the yankes and keep them from coming to the Railroad. (W. D. Carter, Culberson Papers, Duke) Chatham County

Jan. 11, 1863: the yankees **played on** us with 2 Batterys & had 2 Ky leagons and 2 Indiana Regt clostto us & about 6 or 8 thousand in line of battle some 8 hundred yds form us. (A. W. Bell, Bell Papers, Duke) Macon County

Dec. 6, 1863: ouer Canons was plast in ouer Rear on top of the mish nary Ridg and ouer Brest works was at the foot of the Ridg in front of Chat tanoogia. ouer Batters Cood **play on** the yankeys Clean over us. (J. W. Reese, Reese Papers, Duke) Buncombe County

play out *verb* To become exhausted, quit; see Overview § II.4.7.

Apr. 25, 1864: if we can only whip the Yankees this fight I think tha[t] their army of the Potomac will **play out**. (G. W. Rooker, Newsom Papers, Duke) Halifax County

play the mischief *verb phrase* To cause trouble, harm, "play the devil." [*OED* **mischief**, noun, Phrases, P2, c. "*euphem.* The devil (in phrases including *play the mischief*)"]

Dec. 26, 1864: I heard they had taken a battery of six guns at poppler point below rainbow banks. I also hear that the yankees say the sharp shooters is **playing the mischief** with thar men. (Ann Bowen, Bowen Papers, NCSA) Washington County

plenty *adjective* Plentiful, in abundant supply. [*OED* **plenty**, B. adjective.]

May 17, 1858: I think if you come out hear you cant help but like the contry. Every thing is **plenty** hear. people dont work half thare time & have everything **plenty**. (John Frank, Frank Papers, Duke) Davidson County

July 27, 1861: Coffe is skerse on the account of the rivvers being blockaded but we think that navaggashen will be opend be fore long and salt and Coffee will be Cheep and **plenty**. (J. C. Haltom, Frank Papers, Duke) Davidson County

Apr. 12, 1863: allegater are **plenty** here in the ponds I hav Saw young ones. (J. M. Frank, Frank Papers, Duke) Davidson County

plenty *noun* A great or sufficient amount (of something); reduced form of *in plenty;* sometimes noun and adjective forms are indistinguishable. See also **aplenty**.

Oct. 7, 1861: it is bread and meat her one day and meat and bread the next but wee have plenty to eat wee have Coffee **plenty**. (James Fisher, Fisher Papers, Duke) Catawba County

July 13, 1863: there is Men **plenty** in the Cuntry that is Surrounded with Ever thing **plenty** and wont help apore woman to one hands turn. (William Martin, Vance Papers, NCSA) Burke County

plentiful *adverb* Plentifully.

Nov. 10, 1862: people gave **plentifull**, and it was heart braking to see the distress amongst the fair ones. I Saw more tears, than a few then would Shout when thay would see us Coming. (Dinson Caldwell, Caldwell Coll., ECU) Cabarrus County

plow stock *noun* The wooden frame of a plow.

July 13, 1863: Soldiers wives and widows work is done with neatness and Sent home, whether paid for or not as they must live and be Seen to, he make plows, and **plowstocks**, Swingletrees, Stocks Sythes for mowing and Cradling purposes, mends waggons & Carts, or any thing belonging to farms, or kitchens. at low prices. (John Livingston, Vance Papers, NCSA) Henderson County

plug (of tobacco) *noun* A flat, square cake of compressed chewing tobacco, from which a portion (a *chew* or *chaw*) could be cut with a pocket knife. [*OED* **plug**, noun, II.6.]

Oct. 13, 1862: you wrote that you was a gowing to send me 2 **plugs** Tobacco and some paper by Lt Neal. (William Tesh, Tesh Papers, Duke) Yadkin County

Apr. 28, 1863: eatables are scarse an dear. peas sell here for one dollar a quart. bacon one dolar a pound. tobacco two an a half dollars per **plug.** not good at that. I can chew half of my weadges up by chewing tobacco. (James Keever, Keever Papers, Duke) Lincoln County

Apr. 22, 1864: I recived your most welcom letter with a bit of meat and cake and 3 **plugs** of tobacco. (Christopher Hackett, Hackett Papers, Duke) Guilford County

plumb, plum *adverb* Completely, entirely.

Aug. 15, 1862: We have taken it all. Just Lie down and Lie in the rain all night Without eny thing over us. such hardships as that has Worn me **plum** out. (G. J. Huntley, Huntley Papers, WCU) Rutherford County

Nov. 16, 1862: the was some snow hire last week and i was **plume** bare futit but i bot A paire of shews. (W. P. Cline, Cline Papers, SHC) Catawba County

Jan. 11, 1863: I Cant rite to day. I hant in the rit fix for riting. I wold like to rite you along letter but I am

plum upside down to day. (John Hartman, Hartman Papers, Duke) Rowan County

plunder *noun* Baggage, gear, equipment.

July 27, 1862: I sent all thear **Plunder** <to ??> care. they dont know whare they are going. (C. S. McCurdy, CS Army Misc., Duke) Cabarrus County

May 9, 1863: they left any quantity of **plunder**. I could have gotten any thing I wanted but could not cary any thing. (John Futch, Futch Letters, NCSA) New Hanover County

pneumonia *noun* variant forms *newmony, newmoney.*

Nov. 26, 1861: we have but one man in the hospitle at this time that is R..L Baily. he has had the **Newmony** but is smartly on the mend. I think he will come out in a few days. (P. S. Whitner, Whitner Papers, Duke) Catawba County

Jan. 19, 1862: we have one verry Sick man in the hospital John Kelley is verry sick with the **new money** but I thank he is A mending. (Williford Upchurch, Upchurch Papers, Duke) Chatham County

point see **pint**

poke, polk *noun* A bag or pouch. [see *OED* **poke**, noun[1], for the complex etymology (earliest citation ca. 1300); *DARE* **poke** noun[1], chiefly Midland, especially Appalachians]

Mar. 7, 1864: I will Send you a bout one lb of coffee and a little **poke** of Shugar. the Shugar I send Expressly for the Baby But I want you to give each of the children a little tast of it and tell them that paw sent it to them sow they Should be purty children. (Isaac Lefevers, Lefevers Papers, NCSA) Catawba County

Apr. 22, 1864: A. G. Causey arrived yesterday evening. he brought me a **poke** of victuals and a letter. (Christopher Hackett, Hackett Papers, Duke) Guilford County

Nov. 18, 1864: David Barger got here last Saturday night. he brought me a Small **poke** of Some thing to eat which come verry good. (John Peterson, Peterson Papers, Duke) Catawba County

Feb. 14, 1865: I will name the things that I want. some buter. a **polk** of flower. a pese of meet of a middling and some sower crout and a pese of Soap and a few buiscuits. (James A. Smith, J. A. Smith Papers, Duke) Cabarrus County

poke greens, po(a)lk greens *noun plural* Edible greens (*poke salad*) of the pokeberry or pokeweed, *Phytolacca americana.*

July 5, 1863: we sometimes gather a mess of **poalk** for **greens** and sometimes gat[h]er blackberies and stue them. I have just been a taking a verry good mess of huckleburies. (C. A. Hege, Hege Papers, MHI) Davidson County

poke root *noun* The root of the pokeweed (pokeberry), *Phytolacca americana,* once used to treat skin rashes and infections. [*DSME* **poke**[2]]

Mar. 12, 1865: I am tolable well at this time all but the Each [= itch]. tell Davy and Josy that I have got the old Each the wost sort. tell thim they must bring Down me a pot full of **poke root** for I think I Shal haft to be gin to Docter fort it. (J. W. Joyce, Joyce Papers, MHI) Stokes County

pomace, pumis *noun* In cider making: crushed apples before the juice is pressed out; also, the pulp remaining after the juice is pressed out; variant form *pumis.* [*OED* **pomace**, noun, 3.a., 3.b.]

Dec. 26, 1864: I have had six barrels of cider stilled and half barrel of grape and half barel of beer but som of them dident make much beat [= crushed pulp] out of all them rotten apples and kept in the **pumis** two long. it lost its strength I have to say but little and let them do as they pleas about squeasing it out. I think it is better to have a little done than northing. (Ann Bowen, Bowen Papers, NCSA) Washington County

pone (of bread) *noun* A flat loaf or cake of cornbread. See also **corn pone**. [*OED* **pone**, noun[2], from "Virginia Algonquian *apones, appoans* bread (with -s taken as the plural ending)"; *DARE* chiefly South, South Midland]

Aug. 19, 1862: thair was thirteen apples four cowcumbers and nineteen iserspotatoes [= Irish potatoes] so you know how many you sent. the **pone of bread**

was sower to [= sour too]. (J. W. Williams, Williams Papers, Duke) Onslow County

Jan. 10, 1863: I wish you could send me a box with something if it was only a **pone** of corn bread. (James Zimmerman, Zimmerman Papers, Duke) Forsyth County

Feb. 27, 1863: I hav got mee A **pone** on to Rais. then I think I can Eat my supper. (J. W. Reese, Reese Papers, Duke) Buncombe County

Apr. 21, 1864: the boys at the camp is very kind. they come two or three every day. Lieutenant Allison Stefen Clark and two others come to day Stephen Clark baked a very nice **pone of bread** and fetched to me and W W Allison sent me a piece of bacon. it is as good **pone** as I ever eat. (Alvira Taylor, Taylor Papers, Duke) Orange County

Nov. 18, 1864: we get about half Pound of Bacon for two Days and corn bread ready baked with the brand [= bran] in it. we get a **pone** Some biger then one hand for one day rashens. that is about all that we get. (John Peterson, Peterson Papers, Duke) Catawba County

ponken see **punkin**

poor, po *adjective* Sick, unhealthy, malnourished, underweight; also in the phrase *poor as a snake*. [*DARE* chiefly South, South Midland, West]

Nov. 24, 1861: when that big batle is over it will stop ameny **po** fellow from coming home at Christmas. (L. W. Griffin, Griffin Papers, NCSA) Rutherford County

Mar. 21, 1862: he was sick three weaks with the typhored feaver. he suferd more then tong can tell he was the **porest** person I ever saw. (James Keever, Keever Papers, Duke) Lincoln County

Apr. 7, 1863: you rote to me that you was as fat as apig. I am not fat b[u]t as **pore** as a snake. (Daniel Revis, Revis Letters, NCSA) Henderson County

Aug. 24, 1863: I am afraid that your health is not good as it has ben by your being so **poor.** but your having to take such long hard marches I recon is the reason you have got so **poor**. (Molly Tesh, Tesh Papers, Duke) Yadkin County

Nov. 20, 1864: you Rote that you haint bin as **pore** in five years as you are now. (F. M. Poteet, Poteet-Dickson Letters, NCSA) McDowell County

poorly, poly *adjective* Sick, unhealthy. [*DARE* chiefly South, South Midland]

May 3, 1857: I am in the land of the living at this time and in hopes this fins you in the same as state. all the rast is will exept may mother. she is very **porly** at this time. (Anguish Darroch, Jackson Family Corr., Notre Dame) Moore County

June 1, 1862: I Seat my self onst more but under unfaverable circumstances to drope you a a few lines to lette you now that I am still **Porely**. (Isaac Lefevers, Lefevers Papers, NCSA) Catawba County

Mar. 13, 1863: I seat my self this morning to let you no that we are all yet A living though very **poly**. (Sally Bauldin, Hundley Family Letters, SHC) Stokes County

June 1, 1863: i was Sorry to here that your Pap was so **poorly** and had no one to do work on the farm. (James Zimmerman, Zimmerman Papers, Duke) Forsyth County

pop cracker *noun* A firecracker. [*DARE* Virginia, North Carolina]

Mar. 9, 1865: the next is Concerning of our White Soldiers. they Come to our Church and we treat them with all the Politeness that we can and Some of them treats us as though we were beast and we cant help our Selves. Some of them brings **Pop Crackers** and Christmas devils and throws a mong the woman and if we Say any thing to them they will talk about mobin us. (Richard Boyle, *Freedom*, ser. 1: 233) Tyrrell County

portion see **potion**

possum *noun* An opossum.

Oct. 5, 1861: tell gorge Baley that I think I Will Return Shortly A Bout **posom** time. (Jesse Shipman, Shipman Family Corr., Notre Dame) Henderson County

Dec. 28, 1863: tell tode an Sis to ceep bwdys [= Buddy's] little dog fat an when i come home i will lern it to hwnt **possoms** for him. (T. F. Baggarly, Baggarly Papers, Duke) Iredell County

Nov. 20, 1864: I want you to send me sum dride beans and sum cabetch and that **possum** that I Rote to you to git. (F. M. Poteet, Poteet-Dickson Letters, NCSA) McDowell County

Jan. 6, 1865: tel dock he must lern his dog to tree **possoms** and Squirles So that me and him can go hunting when I get home. (Jesse Hill, Hill Letters, NCSA) Forsyth County

pot *noun* A derogatory term for a person. [*DARE* **pot**, noun, 8]

Feb. 6, 1864: I had like to had afight last night and the pore **pot** bedgd [= begged] off and I pittyed the fellow els I wolddo anoct [= would have knocked] his boath eyes into one. (John Hartman, Hartman Papers, Duke) Rowan County

potato *noun* See also Irish potato and sweet potato.

1. variant form *potaters.*

Dec. 30, 1861: I sent for a box of **potaters.** I want you to see to it an I want som whisky fo[r] sid has to drink it reglar. (G. T. Beavers, Upchurch Papers, Duke) Chatham County

Sept. 26, 1862: potaters Sweete is worth From $4 to 7 Dollars per busual and and other things in per porshon. (Isaac Copeland, Copeland Letters, NCSA) Surry County

Mar. 31, 1864: plant All the **potaters** you Can and so[w] All the seeds you Can. (J. W. Reese, Reese Papers, Duke) Buncombe County

2. variant forms with deleted first syllable.

Mar. 31, 1864: if you could hav seen or eat som of the slice **tator** pyes that I made the other day you would give me the praise. (Harrison Hanes, Hanes Papers, Duke) Davie County

July 31, 1863: I bout a coupel aquarts of irish **taters** Sence I have bin Sick. I pade one dollar a quart for them. (Daniel Setzer, Setzer Papers, Duke) Catawba County

Sept. 21, 1864: i get plenty to eat such as it is. i dont get **taters** and chickns and pise like yo have. (Franklin Setzer, Setzer Corr., UVA) Catawba County

Oct. 10, 1864: I Receivd that Pervisione you send By Danile and was glad to gite ite but it wase alle spilte [= spoiled] excepte the **tatoes.** they was good. the Bread was moleded but I eate and was thaught it wase good. aman cane eate iney thang heare. (Daniel Abernethy, Abernethy Papers, Duke) Catawba County

potato pudding *noun* A sweetened cake made from grated potatoes or sweet potatoes. [see *DARE* **potato pone**, noun]

Dec. 14, 1862: you would laugh to have seen me & Mr. Linsley making a **potatoe pooding** for dinner. the Stuard [= hospital steward] said it was very nice but I did not relish it much. (J. A. Patton, Patton Letters, Emory) Granville County

Oct. 6, 1863: send me som butter A[nd] som swet pottatoes. 1 quart of brandy if you have got it And A good hed or toowo of Cabeg An som appeles An A Larg **tato puddin**. (Joseph Wright, Wright Papers, Duke) Alamance County

potion *noun* variant form of *portion.*

May 23, 1862: give my love to all of my enquiring frinds. keepe a larger **potion** for your self. (Joseph Cowand, Cowand Papers, Duke) Bertie County

Apr. 28, 1863: I am enjoying a Reasenable **potion** of health truly hop this may Reach you in due time and find you all the same blessing. (James Keever, Keever Papers, Duke) Lincoln County

Apr. 30, 1863: I must close By asking of you to give My Respects to all inquiring Freinds if any after heaving a large **potion** for your self. (W. R. Best, Quinn Papers, Duke) Duplin County

power *noun* A large quantity or amount. [*DARE* chiefly South, South Midland]

July 16, 1861: there is a **pour** of sickness here at this time and agreate many Deaths. (Peter Poteet, Poteet-Dickson Letters, NCSA) Burke County

June 3, 1862: Our Forces Drove the yankies Back at the point of the Bayonet But We Lost a **power** of men. (G. J. Huntley, Huntley Papers, WCU) Rutherford County

June 22, 1863: I can in form you that thay is a **power** of litel childern and Wiming a liven ner mea and no men to ad [= aid] them nor asis[t] them and hit ape pers [= appears] lik thay hav ruther pitch on mea for a frend. (H. A. Davis, Vance Papers, NCSA) Ashe County

Oct. 6, 1864: it has raind nearly all the time for 3 weeks. it is raining now. there is a **power** of fodder lost. I hav saved the crib full of fodder. (Martha Poteet, Poteet-Dickson Letters, NCSA) McDowell County

powerful *adjective* Big, great, considerable; superlative form *powerfulest*. [*DARE* chiefly South, Midland]

Aug. 7, 1861: they had a **pourful** Battle there. they fit one hole day they only kiled about 5 hundred of our men. (Peter Poteet, Poteet-Dickson Letters, NCSA) Burke County

Dec. 29, 1861: We left Lincolnton on Wednesday morning and Reached Charlott about one a clock. it Was a **powerful** Time in charlott all day. hundreds of peopell and all in a frollick. (G. J. Huntley, Huntley Papers, WCU) Rutherford County

Mar. 18, 1862: the peple is in a **powerful** distress hear at this time. (Dicy Ann Jackson, Jackson Family Corr., Notre Dame) Moore County

May 17, 1863: we air at fair feeld in 4 miles of war trace [= Wartrace] in 18 or 20 of murfrees Boroo one [= on] prong of duck River. this is A good Country hear. grate land and the **powrfulst** plac I Ever Saw for pasture. (J. W. Reese, Reese Papers, Duke) Buncombe County

powerful *adverb* Very; very much, considerably.

Jan. 11, 1862: there is no nuse worth relating. One thang we had a fight between two of our boys Mark Wimbly & Q. J. Hudson. Mark stuck him with his knife in front of his left hip 2 or 3 inches deep. he bled **powerful** but he is now beter. (G. T. Beavers, Upchurch Papers, Duke) Chatham County

May 1, 1864: my lipps needs kissing **pawrrful** Bad. (J. W. Reese, Reese Papers, Duke) Buncombe County

powerfully *adverb* Very much.

June 26, 1863: I would like **powerfully** to see her and the Children. (C. L. Proffit, Proffit Family Letters, SHC) Wilkes County

praise see **the praise, have the praise**

preaching *noun* A religious service with a sermon. [*DARE* chiefly South, South Midland]

Nov. 22, 1863: My Dear Wife I cant tell how mutch I would give to be at home this morning to go With you to **Preachin** and stay With you as long as I live. (F. M. Poteet, Poteet-Dickson Letters, NCSA) McDowell County

Aug. 4, 1864: Sunday we have good **Preaching** to Day and Pray Meeting this Eavning and So nearly Evry day. (Wade Hubbard, Hubbard Papers, Duke) Anson County

Jan. 8, 1865: Sunday is a lomsom day with me. evry body goin to **preachin** and I hav to stay at home. (Flora Ann Campbell, Campbell Papers, Duke) Moore County

press *verb*

1. To force someone into military service; to conscript (someone). [*OED* **press**, verb², 1.a.]

Mar. 20, 1862: they say the law is now to **press** us and make us stay 2 years. (J. W. Love, Love Papers, Duke) Henderson County

June 16, 1863: if wants fight So Bad we will **press** him in Servis and let him try the yanks a while. (John Futch, Futch Letters, NCSA) New Hanover County

2. To take, requisition goods, grain, and livestock from civilians. [*OED* **press**, verb², 1.c.]

Aug. 11, 1863: some says thear is a talk of men coming round to **pressing** brandie and jest giving 3 dollars a gallon. (Mary Kinsland, Kinsland Letter, UGA) Haywood County

Dec. 14, 1863: we are rideing all over the country **presing** and takeing propty of all kinds. (Franklin Setzer, Setzer Corr., UVA) Catawba County

Dec. 26, 1863: tha Sa tha are a goint to **press** all our things and if tha Dow I Dont no how wee will live. (Susan Setzer, Setzer Papers, Duke) Catawba County

Feb. 4, 1864: all the honest men is gone and a set of speckalating dogs is left to **press** the lives out of the poor Women and children. (Martha Poteet, Poteet-Dickson Letters, NCSA) McDowell County

press master *noun* The leader of a detail sent to *press* (requisition) livestock or farm produce.

Aug. 30, 1864: you wrote to me that the **press master** was going to press your Cows and Sheep and you wanted advise to know whether to break the hiefer or not. (Alexander Keever, Keever Papers, Duke) Lincoln County

Oct. 25, 1864: Dont give up any of your Stock to the **pres master** if you can help it. I Dont think he will take a Soldiers horses. (R. C. Caldwell, Caldwell Coll., ECU) Cabarrus County

press out *verb* To squeeze the juice from apples or other fruit; see Overview § II.4.7.

Oct. 16, 1864: we have picked up all the apples but havent got all **prest out** yet. I dident have barrels but I sent the honey beer and one barrel of cider to the still. (Ann Bowen, Bowen Papers, NCSA) Washington County

pretty *noun* A small, inexpensive present; often as variant form *purty*. [*DSME* **pretty**, C, noun; *DARE* chiefly South, South Midland, especially Southern Appalachians]

July 12, 1862: tel mark and James and elen and robard that must be good boys And when i Come home i will fech them A **purty** far them. (W. P. Cline, Cline Papers, SHC) Catawba County

Sept. 22, 1862: tel jonas and jimia [= Jimmy] I want them to be good boys and I will send them some **purtys** When I Can get the Chance. (Marcus Hefner, Hefner Papers, NCSA) Catawba County

June 25, 1863: tell mary I got her **purty** and that I am glad She has not forgot me. tell her I want to know if her head and hear [= hair] has got well. i will send her a **purty** ring. (Daniel Murph, Murph Papers, Duke) Catawba County

Feb. 25, 1865: here is a little **pretty** for little Jane that I fixt when I was Sick. be Shore and giv it to her and tel her her pap Sent it to here [= her]. (Jesse Hill, Hill Letters, NCSA) Forsyth County

pretty *adjective*

1. variant form with metathesized /r/, especially *purty*.

ND: tell him theat he is ugly if he is like that pictur. iwant a **purity** man than that is when igit aman. (Mary Cole, Jackson Family Corr., Notre Dame) Moore County

May 25, 1863: I am in 2 miles of a Station on the railroad by the name of hamlingtons crossing. I have ben here 4 or 5 days. it is the **pertises** place I have ever camped. we have cleaned it up and the oaks mitley shads the ground. (Neill McLeod, McLeod Letters, SHC) Moore County

Oct. 4, 1864: I would love to kiss that littel one that I haint never seen. you Rote that it had taken astart to grow and it was very **purty** and smart. (F. M. Poteet, Poteet-Dickson Letters, NCSA) McDowell County

Sept. 21, 1864: how glad i would bee to sea you all and eat some fresh pork with you and to kis my **purty** little baby. (Franklin Setzer, Setzer Corr., UVA) Catawba County

2. Of a child: well behaved, obedient, helpful.

Apr. 3, 1862: I want you to give the childrean all howdy for me and tell them to bee **Purty** tell paw comes home. (Isaac Lefevers, Lefevers Papers, NCSA) Catawba County

Dec. 23, 1862: Tell Tody and Sis to Bee **prety** girls an when i com home i will bring them some thing. (T. F. Baggarly, Baggarly Papers, Duke) Iredell County

pretty *adverb* Very, rather, fairly; variant form *purty*.

Apr. 13, 1862: times here are dull all tho we are in **purty** good hart. (Jonas Bradshaw, Bradshaw Papers, Duke) Alexander County

May 21, 1862: we will haft to stay here tell we mak a regment and I want it to **purty** soon for it is no place her for a white man to stay at. (R. C. Love, Love Papers, Duke) Henderson County

Mar. 29, 1863: martha is wevin She can weve three and fore yards a day. I think it is **purty** smart fore the first but she has got hirn out and wevin on a nother pece. (Catherine Ramsey, Futch Letters, NCSA) New Hanover County

pretty near *adverb phrase* Nearly; variant forms *pritner, pritenere*. See also **purt near, purt nigh**.

Mar. 8, 1863: I am **pritenere** out of hart Evere Seeing pease maid. (John Ingram, Ingram Papers, Duke) Forsyth County

Feb. 7, 1865: thay are [c]ampt for the winter and thay hav **pritner** eet us out of house and home. (Selena Colby, Bleckley Papers, Duke) Catawba County

prevail with *verb* To succeed in influencing, persuading; similar to *prevail upon*); see Overview § II.4.7. [*OED* **prevail**, verb, 2.c.]

July 13, 1863: the Col **pervailes with** the Doctor and wants him to Doe about as he pleas ther was Discharges Rote out for Men and the Col wolddent Give them to the men. Some Men Could Give in the Best Surtificate of Diseases and woulddent Bee listened at. (William Martin, Vance Papers, NCSA) Burke County

prices *noun plural* Following a number to indicate inflated prices; several times the normal value of an item or commodity (e.g., *four prices* = four times what it used to be).

July 12, 1862: We cannot get anything here but Bread and meat without paying **four prices.** Eggs is 25 cents a dozen. Chickens 40 to 50 cents a piece Bacon 35 to 40 cents a lb. Other thing in proportion. (James Zimmerman, Zimmerman Papers, Duke) Forsyth County

Sept. 12, 1862: we dont have any fruit in this country But what is Brought in this camp and them that Buys them has to pay **ten priceses** for them. (John Ingram, Ingram Papers, Duke) Forsyth County

Dec. 9, 1862: this confederate Money wont be good long for the prices of things. Shoes that it aint Counted much now for we have to pay **two prices** for all we bye. (Marcus Hefner, Hefner Papers, NCSA) Catawba County

prize, prise *verb* To pry. [*DARE* chiefly South Midland; also South]

June 8, 1863: I received a letter from my wife last week Stating that the deserters had come to hir House one night **prised** off one corner of the roof of the Smoke House went in drawn as much hard Sider as they wanted. taken 16 or 18 of the largest peaces of Bacon they could pick out. (James Tyson, Vance Papers, NCSA) Randolph County

protracted meeting *noun phrase* A religious revival lasting several days or weeks. [*DSME* **protracted meeting**, noun, B; *DARE* chiefly South, South Midland]

Aug. 8, 1861: Nancy I wish I could hav been at Bethlehem at the **protracted meetin**. (Harrison Hanes, Hanes Papers, Duke) Davie County

Aug. 23, 1863: I have binne goine to meatin day an nite fore some time ther hase binn **aprotack meatin** every sens I Came hare. I am glade to tell you of the nuse thar hase binn some Eighty soles Con varty [= converted] sense this meating Coments. (Phillip Walsh, Proffit Family Letters, SHC) Wilkes County

Aug. 19, 1864: there was a **protracted meting** at Trinity last week the greatest Meeting I ever was at and Mary and Thomas profesed Religeon. (Martha Poteet, Poteet-Dickson Letters, NCSA) McDowell County

proud *adjective* Pleased, happy, glad. [*DARE* chiefly South, South Midland]

Apr. 27, 1862: I am **proud** to here that you are getting Along so well About farmin. (J. W. Williams, Williams Papers, Duke) Onslow County

Aug. 15, 1862: I recived a letter from you yesturday Eeavning the one you sent with James Seagle. I also Received the little Jug of Honey. I was verry **proud** to get it. I eat some of it for my breakfast this morning. (Isaac Lefevers, Lefevers Papers, NCSA) Catawba County

Apr. 5, 1863: you stated that nel had a fine coalt. I am **proud** to hear it. I would be a heep **prouder** yet if I could be at home and see it my self. (W. F. Wagner, *Confederate Soldier,* 46) Catawba County

May 1, 1864: you dont no how **proud** I was to git your letter. I was as **proud** as A little girle with red shoos. (J. W. Reese, Reese Papers, Duke) Buncombe County

proudly *adverb* Gladly, with pleasure.

Nov. 6, 1863: he arrived heare last evening and I got the things that you sent by him thay ware **proudely** received by me. (J. F. Coghill, Coghill Papers, Duke) Granville County

pudding *noun* A form of sausage; a mixture of spices, bread, meat scraps and organ meats, chopped finely, cooked, and stuffed into casings. [*OED* **pudding**, noun, I.1.a., "Now *Sc., Eng. regional,* and *Irish English (north.)*"; *DARE* scattered, but chiefly Midland, Middle and South Atlantic]

Nov. 6, 1864: Mary Jane i woud lick to be with you to help you eat Beaf **puding**. i would lick to hav a ba[i]t [= a meal] of them but we git a plenty to eat. Mary Jane they boyes is a cucking diner. some is a cucking dumplins. (Gorry Jackson, Jackson Family Corr., Notre Dame) Moore County

Feb. 2, 1865: you sed if you had a mess of **pudding** you would be glad. I haint made non this winter. I kept one hot till after Camp went back to make you some **pudding** and sausage but he don so mean that dident get to send you any thing. (Martha Poteet, Poteet-Dickson Letters, NCSA) McDowell County

puke *noun*

1. A wretch, a despicable person. [*OED* **puke**, noun^2, 4.a.]

Feb. 8, 1862: I told him in plain English that if Smith suceeded in gitting him apointed that he could not drill not one of my men & that I was oposed to him out & out. so he left with his collers at half mass & the union Down. poor deluded **puke.** pobaly he will finde it wont do to follow Ruff Siler. I defeated Ruff for the Same office about 3 weeks ago & I glory in defeeting just such dogs & traiters. (A. W. Bell, Bell Papers, Duke) Macon County

2. An emetic. [*OED* **puke**, noun^2, †2.]

Oct. 29, 1862: I am un well and. has Bin vary sick an yester day I was vary Bad But thank god I am Bet ter this morning. I am afflicted with Rumatis and cald I am still on the sick list not Able for duty. the docttor giv mee A **puke** yester day and I am Rite smart Better this morning. (J. W. Reese, Reese Papers, Duke) Buncombe County

pullback *noun* A hinderance or setback. [*OED* **pullback**, noun, 1]

Jan. 21, 1865: it is a great **pulback** to me. I havent had the chance to do a dayes work since christmas. (Ann Bowen, Bowen Papers, NCSA) Washington County

pull down *verb* To shoot; to take aim at someone with the intention of shooting; see Overview § II.4.7.

June 27, 1864: tell Davy that I said if heneeley got arra [= ever a] one of his Rosenyears [= roasting ears] that he must take the old Shoot gun and fil it in Bout hafe full of Shoot and powder and take it up clost to his head and then **pull Down** at him. (J. W. Joyce, Joyce Papers, MHI) Stokes County

pull fodder *verb phrase* To strip the leaves from corn stalks so they can be tied in bundles and dried for cattle feed. [*DSME* **pull fodder**; *DARE* **pull**, verb, 1a]

Sept. 28, 1862: I want to now how you are git ing long **pulling fodder** and how mutch wheat and rie you have sowed. (R. C. Love, Love Papers, Duke) Henderson County

Oct. 1, 1863: I want to no whether you ons has made your molasses ornot and how much you made and whether you ar dun **pulling foader** or not. (Daniel Setzer, Setzer Papers, Duke) Catawba County

pumis see **pomace**

punkin *noun* variant form of *pumpkin.*

June 13, 1852: I hav cleard 12 acors of new ground this Spring and got don plantin it on the 24th day of may. I have got a good Stand of corn **punkins** and wattermilians in my newground and my old ground corn lokes well. (Neill McGregor, Jackson Family Corr., Notre Dame) Moore County

Sept. 28, 1860: I comencnd picking cotton last Friday. I have picked over 70 acors an have got 11.9.53 [= 11,953] pownds. **Punkins** scars [= scarce] Peas backword. Potates Sorry. they all depnd on whether we have earley or late fall. (Thomas Harding, Blount Papers, NCSA) Beaufort County

Dec. 14, 1864: Send me Some wry cofea [= rye coffee] and Some peas one peck 20 lbs flour Some baked Sweat potatoes Some **ponken** and Sweat potatoes. (Alexander Keever, Keever Papers, Duke) Lincoln County

puny *adjective* In poor health, sickly, weak. [*DARE* widespread, but especially South, South Midland]

June 22, 1861: I have not been down Sick nar a day Since I have left home But I have been Some what **puny** Several thimes. (J. N. Cunningham, Cunningham Letters, NCSA) Haywood County

Aug. 11, 1863: the baby has not groad much since yow have bin gon. it has bin mity **puney** this summar and is yet. (Mary Kinsland, Kinsland Letter, UGA) Haywood County

Feb. 4, 1864: I was right **puny** when James left hear to go home but I am able to drill again. (Alexander Keever, Keever Papers, Duke) Lincoln County

Apr. 3, 1864: unkle ned is not well. he is a little **puny** but I hope he will get well. (Alfred Cowand, Cowand Papers, Duke) Bertie County

pu(r)t near, pu(r)t nigh *adverb phrase* Pretty nearly, nearly, almost.

Oct. 23, 1862: I have quit Swearing **put near** Some times I git out of hart and git made and I Say dam be fore I think. (W. H. Horton, Councill Papers, Duke) Watauga County

May 25, 1863: igite **puteny** oute of harte of harin frm home any moar. (J. H. Hundley, Hundley Family Letters, SHC) Stokes County

purty see **pretty**

put (to) *verb* To breed, to bring livestock together for the purpose of breeding them, e.g., a mare and a donkey to produce a mule. [*OED* **put**, verb, 11.e.]

Feb. 16, 1863: I want to know how yow are getting Along And what yow are gowing to do with your mare And mion [= mine]. weather yow low [= plan] to **pwt** them or not. (W. H. Brotherton, Brotherton Papers, Duke) Catawba County

Mar. 23, 1863: Farther I to know how you are getting along with your farm and if can tend all your land or not. tell Mr Lockman Dock is well. he is a sp[l]ended fellow. I want yow to **put** my mare to some Jack [= donkey] this Spring. (W. H. Brotherton, Brotherton Papers, Duke) Catawba County

put away *verb* To prepare a body for burial, to bury; see Overview § II.4.7.

Mar. 11, 1863: they Sent for A.J. and I fourth with and we went and Saw him deseantly **put a way**. we had him washed and dressed in white. his officers has a good coffin made for him and **put him a way** with thare own hands. (Alfred N. Proffit, Proffit Family Letters, SHC) Wilkes County

June 28, 1863: as to the way he was put a way I no nothing for as soon as a man dies here he is taken out to what they call the ded house and no boddy seas how they are **put a way**. (John Bachelor, Brown Coll., NCSA) Duplin County

put off *verb* To sell; see Overview § II.4.7. [*OED* **put off**, 9.†b. "To dispose of by selling, *Obs.*"]

Dec. 1, 1862: I had rote in the other Letters that I thought you had better **put off** one of the horses some way or nother and I want you to keep the one you rather. fan would bee the most valable as thier could be another colte Raised from hur But I want you to Keep the one you like beast and the one that you think will Suit you the best in work it is sirten we cant keep them all the way corn and stuff is sellen. (Isaac Lefevers, Lefevers Papers, NCSA) Catawba County

put over *verb* To endure, experience, live through; see Overview § II.4.7. [*OED* **put**, verb, **to put over**, 5. "Chiefly *Sc.* and *Irish English* (*north.*)"]

July 24, 1861: We had a hard time here last Sunday. the hardest Sunday I ever **put over**. we fought eight hours without seasing. the Cannon balls flew over and amongst but as good luck would they all mist me. (Levi Festerman, Festerman Papers, Duke) Rowan County

putrid sore throat *noun phrase* A severe infection of the throat usually caused by a strep infection or diphtheria. [see *OED* **putrid**, adjective, **putrid sore throat**, "now *hist.*"]

Mar. 19, 1863: Margaret Lindseys little daughter Rebecca departed this life last tuesday morning her complaint was the **putrid soar throt** but I hear of now other haveing it. (John Kendrick, Kendrick Papers, NCSA) Cleveland County

put up *verb* See Overview § II.4.7.

1. To make, produce. [see *OED* **put**, verb, **to put up**, 1.a.]

Nov. 6, 1862: i Can **put up** as good Shoes and Boots as any man. (Archibald Curlee, Vance Papers, NCSA) Union County

2. To preserve, save for future use. [*DARE* **put up,** 1; chiefly South, South Midland]

July 24, 1862: I want you to **put up** some pickels this fall and if we are moved out any place where we can get any thing you can send us som of them. (W. M. Patton, Patton Family Letters, SHC) Buncombe County

Q

quilting *noun* A social gathering at which quilts are made.

Nov. 5, 1861: I want to come home about Christmas and I want you to have a big **Quilting** and a play if I dont get home then I will get home when my time is out. (J. L. Groves, Davison Papers, Duke) Gaston County

Dec. 25, 1863: I will have a **quilting** when you get home and ask your gal if you will tell me who it is. (E. E. Lindsay, Taylor Papers, Duke) Orange County

quinsy *noun* An inflammation of the throat. [for etymology, see *DSME* **quinsy**, noun; *OED* **quinsy**, noun]

Dec. 14, 1864: Cornelia Ann has a sore throat something like the **quinsey** but she is not bad off. (Ann Bowen, Bowen Papers, NCSA) Washington County

quire (of paper) *noun* Twenty-four or twenty-five sheets of writing paper (one-twentieth of a ream).

Feb. 23, 1862: I want you to Send me Some of the best paper that you can get this is So bad that I can not writ on it. Send it by Starrett if he is comeing Soone and if not Send it by mail. a half **quire** of Small and half of as large as this. (James W. Overcash, Overcash Papers, Duke) Rowan County

Apr. 3, 1862: I shall haft to quit Writing so mutch for paper is Worth a ful One dollar and half a **quire** at this place. (G. J. Huntley, Huntley Papers, WCU) Rutherford County

Apr. 16, 1863: Martha Every thing is very high up here Tobacco is 5 dollars a pound and paper is 5 dollars a **quire**. (John Futch, Futch Letters, NCSA) New Hanover County

R

raise *noun* A rise, hill, mountain. [*DARE* **raise**, noun, 3]

Aug. 21, 1861: we had nothin fowr or five days before the battle and we never will get over the **raises** across the mountains from Strawsburg to winchester then to then across the blue ridg to peadmont Station whair we took the train for manassas. (James W. Overcash, Overcash Papers, Duke) Rowan County

raised biscuit *noun* A biscuit leavened with sour dough or yeast rather than with baking soda and allowed to rise before baking (see citation).

Feb. 25, 1863: Dear I must tell you that I am still cook yet I wish you could see me make up dough. I ginerly Bake **raste Biscuits.** I always save a lump of dough from one time to a nother that away I can have my dough rased. (W. F. Wagner, *Confederate Soldier,* 37) Catawba County

rasher *noun* A portion of bacon or other provision; perhaps also confused with *ration*. [*OED* **rasher**, noun[1], 1.a. and 1.b. (origin uncertain; earliest citation from 1583); see also *DARE* **rasher** noun[1], "a slice of some foodstuff"; *DSME* **rash**, noun "Esp of foodstuffs: a spate, sudden or ample supply"]

Mar. 18, 1862: he got ten crackers and one **rasher** of meat a day. (Dicy Ann Jackson, Jackson Family Corr., Notre Dame) Moore County

Mar. 28, 1862: we have orders this eavning to cook 3 days **rashers**. (B. Y. Malone, *Malone Diary,* 17) Caswell County

ration *noun* A regular allowance of provision, a fixed amount of food; numerous variant forms, especially *rashing.* See also **rasher**. [*OED* **ration**, noun, 3.a. (earliest citation from 1687)]

May 17, 1862: I got the orders we were to leave there Sunday morning at eight oclock. I got them Saturday evening and to let the Company know it so they would have three meals **rashnels** by morning and to be ready to march. (J. W. Lineberger, *Gaston Ranger,* 7) Gaston County

Dec. 29, 1862: you tell them I have Ben Living on half **Racherns** of steer untwel I am as fat as you no what. (Joseph Cowand, Cowand Papers, Duke) Bertie County

Feb. 27, 1863: we hold prayr meetings in the companey a cashenly and are doing well considern our small **rashings**. (Jonas Bradshaw, Bradshaw Papers, Duke) Alexander County

Apr. 25, 1863: Old Jef giv us A ba[i]t [= a meal] or two of fresh fish and they surd [= served] me like they did yeu and I am naught supris at it for it was extry **rashings**. (B. C. Jackson, Jackson Family Corr., Notre Dame) Moore County

June 16, 1863: We are a going on after the yankes to Wards martinsburg. We have stop to cook **rasherins**. (J. H. Hundley, Hundley Family Letters, SHC) Stokes County

real see **reel**

receipt *noun* A recipe. [*OED* **receipt**, noun, IV.14. "A statement of the ingredients and procedure required for making a dish or an item of food or drink"]

Jan. 15, 1863: My Dier Wife. I will giv you A **Recpt** how to make that Apple Bwtter. in the first place you make some sweet cider and pwt it in citle or pot and let it get to boil and the yow hav your apples nicely peild and yow put them in an boil them ontill tha boil soft an then poor in moor an so on till they bee come to Jelly. yow stir them all the time. Just like makin molasses the sweeter the Jwse the beter it is. I seen it makin an hav eat of it. it is ver good. (T. F. Baggarly, Baggarly Papers, Duke) Iredell County

Apr. 27, 1863: I have got **Receipts** how to make Soap of all Sorts. I can make one Barrel of Soft Soap Every day and with some hands I can make Eny amount required. (John Caddell, Vance Papers, NCSA) Robeson County

reckon (also *recken, recking, reaking, recond*) *verb* To think, believe, suppose. [*DARE* scattered, but more frequent South, South Midland]

Dec. 21, 1862: well I **reaking** you have hurd all about our travels in Valley. (Philip Shull, Councill Papers, Duke) Watauga County

Mar. 3, 1863: Mag i hav got some thing i **reckon** yow want. i an affe got an order an went to hamelton crossen yesterday an had our likness taken an it is exactly like mee they all say. (T. F. Baggarly, Baggarly Papers, Duke) Iredell County

May 9, 1863: the Brigade male [= mail] boy was [ar] rested and confined for braking open leters. he is to be shot i **recken**. (L. W. Griffin, Griffin Papers, NCSA) Rutherford County

July 14, 1863: you Know my traid. I **Recond** if you havent forgot. I am a tailor that Lives in Old Rutherfordton. I **Recond** you Recollect me very well. (W. A. E. Roberts, Vance Papers, NCSA) Rutherford County

Mar. 17, 1864: I **Reckin** that you think that I have for got you. I dont want you to think Such A thing About Me for I think of you at any time in the day. (F. M. Poteet, Poteet-Dickson Letters, NCSA) McDowell County

recollect *verb* To remember, recall.

June 10, 1861: I **recolect** the last time I stade with you for it was such a pleasure to me that I cant forget it. (Harrison Hanes, Hanes Papers, Duke) Davie County

July 1, 1863: he is the saim man that sent you a list of subcribers when you cald for volinters when you was at kingston if you **Recklect** his naim. he sent you a good Rickmendation for you to give him athority to

Rais a compny. (Josiah Coats, Vance Papers, NCSA) Johnston County

Aug. 21, 1864: my dear if you cant Send nothing to me you can help pap fix Something for us. we must **reckolect** that we cant live allways and So live while you do live. (John Hartman, Hartman Papers, Duke) Rowan County

recruit, recruit up *verb* To regain strength, improve in health. [*OED* **recruit,** verb, 3.a. "*intr.* To return to strength, health, etc.; to recuperate, recover. Also with *up*"]

Aug. 17, 1862: I shall try to git Lt Anderson of[f] home tomorrow. he is sick & looks very bad & I think he ought to go home awhile & **recruit** his health. (A. W. Bell, Bell Papers, Duke) Macon County

Aug. 18, 1862: I am in A bad state of health some way but I hope I shall **recruit up** soon. (J. W. Williams, Williams Papers, Duke) Onslow County

Sept. 6, 1862: our horses is all broken doun and wee are stoped fore a few dase to **recrut up**. (Bardin Brown, Brown Family Papers, Duke) Johnston County

Aug. 27, 1863: I was sent to the hospittel and staid ther tell the 19 of may 1863 and then was sent home on a sick furlough to **recruit** my helth and am still at home not abel to do eny thing at home nor in the Camps. (John Roberts, Vance Papers, NCSA) Caldwell County

reel *noun* A device for winding yarn after it has been spun on a spinning wheel. [*OED* **reel**, noun[1], 1.a.]

Mar. 30, 1863: I have raised Robert Hall and learnt him his trade. he is Well Skild in the trad. he can make plans [= woodworking planes] hoes axes knives Spinning Wheels **reals** Bedstids cubbords Beauros fine tooth combs Wageons Besides many other things. I hope you will permit him to stay at home and Work for the public as I think he is badly needed. (Benjamin Hall, Vance Papers, NCSA) Wilkes County

regular *adverb* Regularly.

Jan. 5, 1864: tell margrett to rais us sum to bacco for I hav got to Smoking **Reglear**. (J. W. Reese, Reese Papers, Duke) Buncombe County

Jan. 17, 1864: you wrote that you wanted to hear from m[e] if you could not see me. I supose I do too. we dont get the mail **regular**. it is time I had another letter but dont know when I will get it. (Martha Poteet, Poteet-Dickson Letters, NCSA) McDowell County

repeater *noun* A repeating firearm; a clock or watch with a chiming mechanism (not always clear which is being referred to in the citations).

Sept. 22, 1861: I dont no of any **repeter** that I can bye, I hav ben looking around since I got your leter but thay hav Sent the most of them home, for the pertection of these folks. (G. T. Beavers, Upchurch Papers, Duke) Chatham County

Oct. 4, 1862: andy Magee has traded for him a **repeater** But he did not Keep it Many days be fore he tradeed it for a Watch. (John Ingram, Ingram Papers, Duke) Forsyth County

Apr. 16, 1863: I cent my **Repetor** home the other day I thot I could do without it here I could have got $40 for it but I thot Id Rather have it than the worth of it in confederte. (C. F. Mills, Mills Papers, Duke) Iredell County

Dec. 22, 1862: I want you to go down to John Poindexters and enquire for Robert Walkers and get my overcoat and when Wm Richmond get home or the first chance I wan you to get my Pistole a **Repeter.** He has got Johns money and watch also. get them and take care of them. (A. J. Spease, Zimmerman Papers, Duke) Forsyth County

rheumatism *noun* variant forms, especially *rumatis*.

Aug. 25, 1862: I am nerly well of the **rumatis** but I hav bin sick for the last few days. (John Hartman, Hartman Papers, Duke) Rowan County

Oct. 2, 1862: he is got the **rumtis** pains in his limbs. i am sum times two in mi sholders an lages. (Henry Baker, Henry Baker Papers, Duke) Catawba County

July 19, 1863: my little boy was sick and Elizia was give out werk with the **rumitiz**. (Neill McLeod, McLeod Letters, SHC) Moore County

rheumatized *adjective* Afflicted with rheumatism.

Oct. 15, 1863: I am **Rhumitised** very Bad. I Wood Like to have a transfur to Captin Buces caverly company for I cant stand marching. I am Nearley allways be hind my Company on a ma[r]ch. (David West, Vance Papers, NCSA) Gaston County

ride *verb* past tense *rid.*

Dec. 24, 1864: i can te[ll] you we have cold weth[er] here now. we **rid** all nite last nite. i never was as cold. (Franklin Setzer, Setzer Corr., UVA) Catawba County

ridgment, rigment *noun* A regiment; several variant forms.

Feb. 10, 1862: Our **Rigment** is in fine spirits and seems anchious to meet the yankies. (G. J. Huntley, Huntley Papers, WCU) Rutherford County

Nov. 10, 1862: we hav lost thirteen men out of this **Rigment** Sence we hav Bin hear. mils snider is ded. he died yesterday. Send word to his wife if you Can. he died with A Brest Complant. (J. W. Reese, Reese Papers, Duke) Buncombe County

July 5, 1864: i can tell you we hav a run the yankes 25 or 30 miles. we taken thear camps. John the first charg i want in i lost my hat. i got me a cap and went on. our **ridgment** is small. it dont contain 2 hundred men that is present. som ded some wounded. i do not no hoo wars kild ded. (G. W. Lawrence, Joyce Papers, MHI) Stokes County

rifle gun *noun* A rifle or rifled musket as opposed to a smoothbore musket or shotgun; also applied to artillery with rifled barrels.

Sept. 8, 1862: tewl [= tell] them to all to come hear if tha ont [= want] to Join a god regement but not dissaisfy them self. we have drod **rifel gones.** tha will hold up from three to five hundreth yeards. (Robert Spainhourd, Spainhourd Papers, Duke) Forsyth County

Jan. 2, 1865: this is the strongest iron clad that I ever saw. she is three feet thick of oak and six inches thick of iron. they say thare is 4 hundred tuns of iron on her. I suppose including her guns and amonetion. She will way one million and a half pounds. she carrys six guns. all **rifle guns** and has a bout 150 men on her now I beleave. (Henry Bowen, Bowen Papers, NCSA) Washington County

right *adverb* Rather, very. [*DARE* chiefly South, South Midland]

Nov. 2, 1862: I hav bin **write** sick fur the last few dase. (B. C. Jackson, Jackson Family Corr., Notre Dame) Moore County

Nov. 25, 1862: it rained on us all the time and we had a **rite** hard time of it. (J. W. Lineberger, *Gaston Ranger,* 27) Gaston County

Apr. 19, 1863: you owgh [= ought] to see mee an aff setin up eatin our eggs an fish. we hav baked seven pies. wee can bake a **rite** nice pie. (T. F. Baggarly, Baggarly Papers, Duke) Iredell County

July 25, 1864: I dont think it is **right** fare to [keep] us one day over are time but thay want us an th[e]y will keep us. (Lewis Moore, Moore Letter, CACWL) Cumberland County

right *adjective* True, proper, genuine. [*DARE* **right**, D, adjective]

Apr. 24, 1862: some say it is very Doubtfull whether there is a Battle her or not But I tell you there is Eny amount of troops heir on Boath Cides and if we Do have a Battle heir it will Be a **Right** one. it will Be the Bloodiest Battle Ever faught in the united States. (James W. Gibson, Gibson Papers, Duke) Catawba County

Apr. 21, 1863: he has some little marks in his fase and on his hands I dont think it was the **rite** small pox. he wasent at the hospittle more than a bout 2 weeks. (W. F. Wagner, *Confederate Soldier,* 47) Catawba County

rightly *adverb* Exactly, correctly. [*DSME* **rightly**, adverb]

Sept. 1, 1863: I am also happy to State to you that I have profest of my Sins and I am going to Jine the church and be baptised in afew days but I dont no **ritely** what day. (John Hartman, Hartman Papers, Duke) Rowan County

right mind see **in (one's) right mind**

right off *adverb phrase* Immediately, right away.

Dec. 3, 1862: tell mam an Elin an ant Sarah all to send mee some thing any thing bwt mollasses an bwtter yow must Direct it to Danvill va. Sowtherlan factory in car of Doct Williamson an put my name on it. if yow send it send it **rite off**. (T. F. Baggarly, Baggarly Papers, Duke) Iredell County

June 15, 1863: I recived a letter From You last week and I answerd it **Right off** but I was a Fraid that You would not Git my letter. (William Tesh, Tesh Papers, Duke) Yadkin County

right on the goose see **all right on the goose**

right smart *noun phrase* A large amount or quantity, a great deal. [*DARE* chiefly South, South Midland]

Oct. 25, 1861: Wee hav A **Right Smart** of Sickness her. they is Ben onely one Deth in this Riagment Sence Wee hav Ben her. One of Capten Crumplers men Died this morning. (Jesse Shipman, Shipman Family Corr., Notre Dame) Henderson County

July 16, 1862: we draw meet flour and some peas. that is what we get to eat and I would give A **right Smart** for somthing fresh an A peace of corn bread. (J. W. Williams, Williams Papers, Duke) Onslow County

Dec. 2, 1862: I am sorter pestered this morning. I lost $20.00 a twenty doller bill some how in changing when I had my pocket book out I droped it. I expect that is the way I lost it. it come light and went the same way I won it. easy. so it didnot do me any good though. it was a **right smart** to loose. I was a going to send it home the first chance. I guess I cant now. (James Zimmerman, Zimmerman Papers, Duke) Forsyth County

right smart *adjective phrase* Considerable, large, high, intense. [*DARE* chiefly South, South Midland]

Mar. 11, 1862: I can inform you that they had a **right Smart** little battle at Newport News. (H. J. Davis, WPA Transcripts, TSLA) Yadkin County

Aug. 18, 1862: I have got **A right Smart** fever but I hope I shall get better soon. (J. W. Williams, Williams Papers, Duke) Onslow County

Oct. 5, 1864: we have **a rite Smart** croud here. Some two hundrd. (Henry Bowen, Bowen Papers, NCSA) Washington County

right smart, right smartly *adverb phrase* Quite a bit, considerably; very. [*DARE* chiefly South, South Midland]

June 24, 1863: I am broken down, my feat wory [= worn] out & my head pains me **right smartly** All of which make me quite weak. (Andrew J. Proffit, Proffit Family Letters, SHC) Wilkes County

Apr. 28, 1864: I hav Been vaxinated in the arm an it is don fine. it is **rite smart** sore. (J. P. Culp, Culp Papers, Duke) Cabarrus County

rip (around) *verb* To rush around recklessly; to use strong language, swear. [see *OED* **rip**, verb[1], extended senses 5.a., 5.c., and 6.b.]

Oct. 8, 1861: I want to know how Wallas Lowrance is getting a long now his crowd is nearly all gon that us[e] to **rip around** with him. (James W. Overcash, Overcash Papers, Duke) Rowan County

Feb. 27, 1863: we are abel to bare all he can poot on us. he poot John in the garde house and left others out that was to blame worse than John. this is the way he dose buisness but he can just **rip**. we dont aske him eny boot So dont be oneasy a bout us. (Jonas Bradshaw, Bradshaw Papers, Duke) Alexander County

risban(d) see **wristband**

rise *verb* To swell, suppurate; variant past tense *rise*. [*OED* **rise**, verb, 16, a.; *DARE* **rise**, verb, B 1]

Feb. 16, 1863: he told Jo Allen he tended two him two weaks and he dide at winchester. he Said that his thoat **Rise** under boath Sides and broke open. so that is nuf on that. (W. H. Brotherton, Brotherton Papers, Duke) Catawba County

(the) rise (of) *noun phrase* More, more than. [see *DSME* **(the) rise of**, noun phrase; *DARE* chiefly South, South Midland]

June 13 1852: I am behind in my cotton crop. I have choped out 13 acors and have 8 or **the rise** to chope. I have cotton nea hie and full of formes [= buds?] nearly ready to blosom. (Neill McGregor, Jackson Family Corr., Notre Dame) Moore County

Mar. 16, 1863: I hav Bin in Survis **the rise of** twelve mownths and I gwt woonded at the fite of Malvun hill witch Disables [me] from dwty. (William Newell, Vance Papers, NCSA) Mecklenburg County

rising *noun* An abscess, boil, or infected swelling. [*DARE* chiefly South, South Midland, Texas, OK]

Apr. 26, 1863: we lost our beloved friend John E Webb. he was loved by all the company and hily esteemed as a soldier. he dide on the night of the Eight of april last. he was sick some two weeks with the feaver and then he had a **rising** on him that was suposed kill him. (Ervin Q. Davis, McNeill Papers, Duke) Robeson County

June 28, 1863: Dear father I take my Seate to let you no i am gitting nearly well only i have a very bade **Risen** under my arm hoping these few lines when comes to hand may find you and family all well. (Robert Carpenter, Carpenter Family Papers, ECU) Chatham County

Aug. 5, 1863: I have had adreadful **risin** on my leg under my Knee [u]pon back side of my leg and in havin it lanced I had one of the Cinures [= sinews] Cut and it Drawed it up very Bad in Deed. (Jesse Pouns, Vance Papers, NCSA) Brunswick County

May 22, 1864: I have a **risen** on my neck rite in frunt. I cant buten my Shirt color and my Bow[e]ls is Deranged So I feel like I am aflicted this morning. (R. C. Caldwell, Caldwell Coll., ECU) Cabarrus County

road, rode *noun* A way, manner, method; a way, course, path. [*EDD* **road**, *sb.* 2., *fig.*; see also *OED* **road**, noun, 5.b. and 9]

Feb. 28, 1864: som of the boyes is gon to the yanks an sens they went we git meet aplinty. they feed yus betr to keep us her. they are A fraid if they dont give us more meet we will go the same **rode**. (James Hackett, Hackett Papers, Duke) Guilford County

Apr. 3, 1864: tena has giv mee more un Easness than any thing that has Cum my **Rode** Senc I left home. (J. W. Reese, Reese Papers, Duke) Buncombe County

Feb. 23, 1865: it dont Seem like I ever can git to cum home with out I cum home like I did when I was at home before [by deserting] and. if I dont git to cum home before long I will take mi oald **roade** and try and git home one time more. (Daniel Setzer, Setzer Papers, Duke) Catawba County

roasting ear (also *rosten ear, rosten year, rosen ear, rosen year*) *noun* Immature corn suitable for cooking, roasting (in the shuck, as in the ashes of a fire).

Aug. 17, 1861: Rosenyears are geting so they will do to eat but cant get them at any price. (D. N. McCorkle, Military Coll., Civil War, NCSA) Catawba County

Oct. 2, 1862: we had to eat what we cold get. we mad the **Rosen ears** fly. it wold take a large fild of corn to make us one one mess. (James Keever, Keever Papers, Duke) Lincoln County

Dec. 19, 1862: Father you Requested to no how I faird When i was in Maryland. Sir mi fair was vary bad for we had to Steal **Rosten years** to Eat to keep from parishing. (William Carpenter, Carpenter Family Papers, ECU) Chatham County

May 1, 1864: They have not planted very much corn here yet. the first I saw planted was the 26th. They said that tha was a going to plant the next week. they was a planting a **rosting neer** patch then. (P. J. Peterson, Peterson Papers, Duke) Catawba County

June 27, 1864: tell Davy that I said if heneeley got arra one of his **Rosenyears** that he must take theold Shoot gun and fil it in Bout hafe full of Shoot and powder and take it up clost to his head and thenpull Down at him. (J. W. Joyce, Joyce Papers, MHI) Stokes County

rob oneself *verb phrase* Used reflexively: to deprive one's self, to suffer for the lack of something.

Nov. 9, 1864: rubin Hoil is going to hall boxes all winter he told me and I want a box every time he Comes if you Can Send me one but do not **rob your Self** and Children. Such as peas potatoes corn meal and flour Such as you can Speare will do. pies. (Alexander Keever, Keever Papers, Duke) Lincoln County

robing *noun* Clothing; an outergarment or coat; a robe. [*OED* **robing**, noun, 1.a.]

ND [1862]: I will tell you what I have Drawd. one pair of Drawers and one shirt and a **Robin** and a pare of pant. they [are] good yarn geans and a Cap and a pare of cotin socks. (W. D. Smith, W. D. Smith Papers, Duke) Davie County

Nov. 24, 1863: Tell John I Said if he wants to he may take that **Robin** of mine and wair it out. (William Tesh, Tesh Papers, Duke) Yadkin County

rock *verb* To throw rocks at a dwelling in order to intimidate the occupants. [*DSME* **rock**, B verb; *DARE* chiefly South, South Midland]

Jan. 25, 1863: thay ar **rocking** houses and Burning Bildings and steeling evry few nights. (B. B. Marley, Vance Papers, NCSA) Randolph County

rockaway *noun* A type of American four-wheeled carriage.

Dec. 1862: if you aint sold the **rockway** in newton you can tell unkel walter hevner he may sell it much as he can for mea. doant take in less an 130 Dollars for it if you Doant wantet and sell the coach if he can for as much as he can. Doant take iny less an 250 Dollars for it an sell mi old carrige in newton as much as he can. (Henry Baker, Henry Baker Papers, Duke) Catawba County

rogue *noun* A scoundrel, outlaw. [*DSME,* **rogue**, A, noun; *DARE* chiefly South, South Midland]

July 8, 1863: Bryson Essued a capeous [capias warrant] for me for stiling I supose. Sent A croud After me one half **rogs** and lyers followed me in to S. C. tuck me and one of my stils out of greenvill S.C. Came back and took A nother one from my house. (Charles Cison, Vance Papers, NCSA) Transylvania County

rogue *verb* To steal, cheat, swindle.

Dec. 9, 1862: I can inform you that Captain vine and lieutenient yont is out of office. they got Disonerly dis charged and I can say that that vine has **rogade** the goverment out of about $ 600 Dolers and he is one of the bigist raskels in this world. (Marcus Hefner, Hefner Papers, NCSA) Catawba County

roguish *adjective* Thieving; superlative form *roguishest.*

Mar. 16, 1864: I hope the army will never hav to com thrugh wher you liv for tha wuld Steal every thing you hav. the Soldiers is the **rogishist** people that livs. (Jesse Hill, Hill Letters, NCSA) Forsyth County

rosen ear, rosen year, rosting neer see **roasting ear**

roughness, ruffness *noun* Coarse fodder. [*DSME* **roughness**, noun; *DARE* South, South Midland, especially Appalachians]

Apr. 20, 1857: I have nothing very strange to rite. Corn Sells at 75 cts. **Ruffnus** is verry scerce. Anderson Sherrill froze to Death the 1st Day of march. (Laban Cline, Hefner Papers, NCSA) Catawba County

Jan. 28, 1864: tell mr beal that I have not any fodder to sell. I may Come home this Spring and if I doI will have use for all my **ruffnss** and if I do not come I do not want to Sell any fodder or Corn. (Alexander Keever, Keever Papers, Duke) Lincoln County

Oct. 4, 1864: I would like to now how your **Ruffiness** held out for the Mare. you Rote that it nearly broke your heart. it hurt me when I could not git to come home. I dont now how you are agoing to save your fodder but I am in hopes that god will provide sum way to save it. (F. M. Poteet, Poteet-Dickson Letters, NCSA) McDowell County

roundabout *noun* A men's work jacket. [*OED* **roundabout**, noun, 7.a. "Chiefly *U.S.* = roundabout jacket"]

Oct. 17, 1863: Mag I hav a Suit of Clouths. a **roundabout** pants cap C[l]oths Shous cotton Socks. Shirt. Slips [= men's underpants] I wil [send] Sum of them home the first opetunity tha ar verry corse and ruff. (R. C. Caldwell, Caldwell Coll., ECU) Cabarrus County

Dec. 4, 1864: I have just drawn a large lot of clothing. 2 Shirts pr of drawers 1 **roundabout** 1 pr of pants 1 pr of Socks and a Splendid Woolens Shirt. (John M. Black, Sexton Letters, Duke) Ashe County

ruffness, rufnus see **roughness**

rumatiz, rumatis, rumtis see **rheumatism**

run *verb*

1. past tense *run.*

Oct. 6, 1861: we fought there picets 11 miles **run** them in to there trenches taken som provisins. (W. B. Carden, Carden Papers, WCU) Macon County

Oct. 13, 1862: we Fell Back across the potomac and then we got in a Fight at Sheppardstown and **runn** them in the river. (William Tesh, Tesh Papers, Duke) Yadkin County

Nov. 9, 1862: on the 8 nov the yankers **run** our pickets in culpeper. (Henry Baker, Henry Baker Papers, Duke) Catawba County

Feb. 25, 1863: they was too steamers **run** the blockade and come in last night. (J. W. Lineberger, *Gaston Ranger,* 41) Gaston County

2. past tense *runned.*

July 16, 1862: wee fout 4 days. we **rund** them A Bout 25 miles. (Leonard Alman, Alman Papers, Duke) Cabarrus County

Oct. 21, 1864: I run a bout 5 milse and tha **rund** me through the river twise. the river was about 50 yards wide and it was waist deep to me but tha never got me. (Jesse Hill, Hill Letters, NCSA) Forsyth County

run *noun* The amount of alcohol produced in a distillation cycle.

July 8, 1863: as to my stiling I sufferd the neighbours to make A fu **runs** but all that was stild was not Enought to Keep my hogs from suffering. som died. there fore I did not stil or sufferd to be stilled more grain then I would have had to fed to my stock or lost them. (Charles Cison, Vance Papers, NCSA) Transylvania County

runaround *noun* A swelling or infection of a finger, usually involving the nail. [*DARE* scattered, but chiefly South, South Midland, Southwest]

Aug. 26, 1863: the boys is all well except A W Smith and bob. I heard from them yesterday. they area most well. steve has three Sore fingers with **runarounds**. (R. C. Love, Love Papers, Duke) Henderson County

Dec. 26, 1864: I have a **run round** on my rite thum that prevents me from sewing or nitting and I dont know how long it will last. it bothers me rite smart about my work. (Ann Bowen, Bowen Papers, NCSA) Washington County

runaway *noun* A deserter. [*OED* **runaway**, noun, 1.a.]

June 4, 1863: I Can now State that our **runaways** is Come back. they got taken up. they Come in yesterday. (Marcus Hefner, Hefner Papers, NCSA) Catawba County

June 9, 1863: tha say that the **runaways** sends word to Col <????>ned that tha wil meet him in any old field and take afight with him and his men but tha aint done it yet nor I dont beleive tha will. (Sarepta Revis, Revis Letters, NCSA) Henderson County

runaway *verb* To desert. [*OED* **run**, verb, **to run away**, 2. *intr.*, a.]

July 31, 1863: I would like to come home But I do not know when I will get the chance to come again But I am going to come before long if I have to **Runaway** to do it. (John Futch, Futch Letters, NCSA) New Hanover County

June 1, 1864: there was a yankey come to us the other day from newbern. S[e]veral has come to us cence wee have bin here. they are **runing away** as well as our men. (Silas Stepp, Stepp Letters, UNCA) Buncombe County

Dec. 25, 1864: I saw Something yesteday that looked vary Bad to me. I saw two men Branded on the left hip in aletter D. it looked vary hard. Boath of them **Runawy** from the army. one of them never got home before thay Catch him and he never got home a tol and thay Boath of them will half to wrid a wooden horse two ours every day for 84 days. (J. W. Joyce, Joyce Papers, MHI) Stokes County

runaway match *noun phrase* An elopement. [*OED* **runaway**, adjective, 1.b. "Relating to, connected with, or accompanied by running away or (esp.) elopement. Freq. in **runaway marriage, runaway match**"]

Feb. 27, 1865: my dear you Sead that yous had a **runaway match** at home. Jacob trexler and Mary kerns. I recon they have Sweat times now like I and you had ounst [= once]. (John Hartman, Hartman Papers, Duke) Rowan County

runlet *noun* A small keg or cask. [*OED* **rundlet**, noun[1], 1.; *DARE* chiefly New England]

Aug. 24, 1861: I want som cider worse than any thing in the world. it looks like you mite com for your. expence would only be about $15 dollars an if I was there I would give twenty to com. I should like to see you an papy coming up with a long **runlet** of cider Just from the pres. (G. T. Beavers, Upchurch Papers, Duke) Chatham County

run mad *adjective* Rabid, hot-headed. [Two of the three citations in *DARE* are from NC]

June 6, 1863: we have afew **Run Mad** hot headed Secessionest that thinks every Body Aught to be gone to the Wars only them and they would have you Believe that every Body is Dis Loyal only them. (Stephen Collis, Vance Papers, NCSA) Mitchell County

runner *noun* The upper, rotating millstone of a pair, the lower (the bedstone) being stationary. [*OED* **runner**, noun[1], 11.a.]

July 25, 1863: I have one other set of **runners** at my mill which I could soon fixt up if I had one other white man to attend to grinding that had some experience in milling. (Jesse Brown, Vance Papers, NCSA) Edgecombe County

run out *verb* Of a lease: to lapse; see Overview § II.4.7. [*OED* **to run out**, 2.b. *intr.*]

July 13, 1863: There is one thing, I wish you to have done, in the Call Session of the Legislator, and that is all entrys made from the Beginning of 1850 to Stand good till the 1 day Jan. 1865 So that all Soldiers wives and widows and all Concerned Can Get Rights for Land while money is flush, and women have Bad Chances to Get Land **Run out,** the Ladies will thank you, and hollow hurrah for Vance. (John Livingston, Vance Papers, NCSA) Henderson County

run over *verb* To harass, take advantage of (someone); to treat with disrespect; see Overview § II.4.7.

June 19, 1863: they are giting no deserters nor conscripts scarcley and are layin a bout here in the way of Sivil peapel and in truding on them and eating up all the Serpelas [= surplus] provision from they pore Soldiers wives and Childern which had a hard time to git along at best without being **run over** and troden down with such lawless mob. ("Meny Citizens," Vance Papers, NCSA) Randolph County

Apr. 24, 1864: he told the old man that he had **Run over** him as long as he intended for to do it. so he pick up A verry large Stick And Strwck the old man By the side of they head And the old man never spoke from the time he don it tell he died. (W. H. Brotherton, Brotherton Papers, Duke) Catawba County

rust *noun* A fungal disease of wheat or other grain crops. [*OED* **rust,** noun[1], 6.a.]

Dec. 5, 1858: our wheat Crop was hardely a half Crop & oats now cilled Entirely by the **rust**. (Francis Amos, Amos Papers, Duke) Rockingham County

June 3, 1862: I Was Glad to hear from home but sorry to hear that the Wheat had the **Rust**. (G. J. Huntley, Huntley Papers, WCU) Rutherford County

May 2, 1864: wheat look verry sorry as yet. It is to wet for it. It turned yellow for the last fiew days as if it was going to take the **rust**. (James Zimmerman, Zimmerman Papers, Duke) Forsyth County

June 1864: wheat crops Looks tolerable well if they are not too Late & the **Rust** takes it there will be tolerable crop made. My corn crop Look fine & I have it in as good fix I want it. (Ninion Edmonston, Edmonston-Kelly Family Papers, WCU) Heywood County

rusty *adjective* Of bacon: rancid. [*DARE* especially South]

Oct. 4, 1862: We have got a plenty of old Jef **rusty Bacon** here yet and flourer and a little Rise and Shugar. (John Ingram, Ingram Papers, Duke) Forsyth County

June 1, 1863: we poor soldiers stand up or lay down to **rusty bacon** and musty flower and hardly time eat it. (James Zimmerman, Zimmerman Papers, Duke) Forsyth County

rye coffee *noun* A coffee substitute made from parched rye. [*OED* **rye**, noun[1], **rye coffee** "*U.S.* a drink resembling coffee, made from roasted rye" (citations as early as 1766)]

Jan. 12, 1862: we are going down to wilmington. I think we will fare beter thare then we do hear for we fare but midling at this plase. I will tell you what we have to eat. beef and bread an **Rhy Coffee.** some time a few molasses an some none. (James Keever, Keever Papers, Duke) Lincoln County

Jan. 17, 1864: we dont get bread anuf. we draw bread loof So mucha day. wee:get half a pound of meet a day it is So Stinkin I cant go it and **ry coffe**. that is our ras [= ration]. (R. C. Caldwell, Caldwell Coll., ECU) Cabarrus County

S

sad bread *noun* Bread that is heavy, dense, or soggy. [*DSME* **sad**, *adjective; DARE* chiefly Midland, South]

Nov. 7, 1861: the living is so hard that I am nerly Starved owt on it. ole bacon mene beef and **Sad bread**. (C. F. Mills, Mills Papers, Duke) Iredell County

saft *adjective* variant form of *safe*.

Oct. 1, 1861: They stated that you arrived **saft** and sound. I was very anxious to hear from you. We haven receive but one mail since you left. (K. W. Coghill, Coghill Papers, Duke) Granville County

Apr. 25, 1863: Dear brother I recieved yore kind leter on the 21 inst which giv me grat plesure to hear that yew A rived home **saft** and that yore trip dident hurt yew any wirse than it did. (B. C. Jackson, Jackson Family Corr., Notre Dame) Moore County

Nov. 27, 1864: Francis I can Say to you that I have got Back to my company this mor[n]ing **Saft** as acoon. (J. W. Joyce, Joyce Papers, MHI) Stokes County

salet, sallet *noun* Edible greens, including those that grow wild. [*DARE* chiefly South, South Midland, Texas]

Apr. 5, 1863: we are Going in the plantations Getting weeds for **Salett.** we are Getting creeses. they are like turnups and we are Getting a wede like ole Gueading [= garden?] dock. (Daniel Brown, Brown Coll., NCSA) Duplin County

Apr. 21, 1864: I want you to have plenty of good eating tell I come Such as eggs and ham and crout and milk and butter and **Sallet** & Sweat potatoes and So on. (Alexander Keever, Keever Papers, Duke) Lincoln County

salivate *verb* Of a medicine: to cause unusual or excessive salivation. [*OED* **salivate**, verb, 1]

June 25, 1863: I took soom calomel when I first took sicke. we have no docter here and the put me on duty too soon and it fell into my head and teeth and **salivated** me a little. I feel a little better today. I think if i dont improve tolerable fast i will go to the hospitle. I have no stomach to eat any thin at all hardly. (Daniel Murph, Murph Papers, Duke) Catawba County

sapsucker *noun* A contemptible person (see citations). [*DARE* **sapsucker**, noun, 4]

Nov. 27, 1863: Maranda was well last Friday. I herd rite from her. well sal the **sapsucker** is gone. all the southcarolina soldiers is gone down in onslow. keninsvill. the last company left yesterday. they didnt like to leave by nomeans. well I will change the subject. (Betty Thomas, Quinn Papers, Duke) Duplin County

Mar. 28, 1864: I have bin to onslow since I saw you. I enjoyed mi viset finely. old miss Jorden was verry glad to see me. wuld you a believe it I wente to the consert to the richlanas two and we had A very fine time of it. tel Amanda that I saw the **sap sucker** ther two but he didnt look so hansom a mung so meney. (N. M. Thomas, Quinn Papers, Duke) Duplin County

sarvice *noun* variant form of *service*.

Aug. 5, 1863: Sir I am a Solgar 7 Seventeen years old. I have Bin in three Batels. I entered the **Sarvis** at the beginin of the war and I have done my Duty as near as any Solgar in the war. (Jesse Pouns, Vance Papers, NCSA) Brunswick County

Aug. 10, 1863: I dont think I ever shal be able to attend to wore enny more an I want you to send me a free discharg if you plese. I have bin in **sarvis** two yaers an hant receive enny thing only my bounty yet.

I hant receve no close nor enny thing eltes. (Elijah Ange, Vance Papers, NCSA) Pitt County

sarvice tree *noun* The serviceberry tree, *Amelanchier laevis.* [*DSME* **service**, noun, B]

Feb. 2, 1863: Tell Julius to take care of all of my tools and to use them if he needs them but not to spoil them and to tak good care of my grape vines and **sarvice trees**. (C. A. Hege, Hege Papers, MHI) Davidson County

sass, sause *noun* Fresh or preserved fruit and vegetables. [*DSME* **sauce**, A *sass,* B noun, 2; *DARE* **sauce**, noun, B 1]

Apr. 2, 1863: men is starved out an Bred and meet So Bad that tha will giv aney price for aney kind of **Case** [= sass]. (J. W. Reese, Reese Papers, Duke) Buncombe County

sat see **sot**[2]

satifide (also *sadifide, satfide, satafid*) *adjective* variant forms of satisfied.

July 1861: I am veary well well **Satfide** but I would be better **Satfide** home. (Charley Futch, Futch Letters, NCSA) New Hanover County

Aug. 3, 1861: sisters I want you to not greave after us for it Cases us to not be **satifide**. (L. W. Griffin, Griffin Papers, NCSA) Rutherford County

Apr. 21, 1862: I think it is hard for to press men who volenteer Their servis frely. if I Cood had the pleaure to come home when my [time] is out and Stay thirty or forty days I wood bin better **sadified** but I hafter put up with as it is. (G. L. Cunningham, Cunningham Letters, NCSA) Haywood County

Mar. 26, 1863: i never in dured so much oneasness in my life before and I want to hir from you the worst in the world I have not bin **satafid** in my mind. (Martha Futch, Futch Letters, NCSA) New Hanover County

sausage *noun* numerous variant forms, especially *sassege, sasege.*

Dec. 24, 1861: Mother I received thoes **Sorcerges** you Sent to me thankfuly and has got one more fry yet. (J. W. Williams, Williams Papers, Duke) Onslow County

ND [1862]: I have wrote home what I wanted but I will it agane. I want 2 or 3 galens of brandy and 15 or 20 pound of butter and a bout 2 galens of molases and about 2 hames of meat some drid fruit and drid beanes gren aples some unions and some sweet bred and if Paw has Kiled his hoges [and] they have any **saseges** I want a mess or 2. (J. S. Council, Councill Papers, Duke) Watauga County

Dec. 1, 1862: I wish you wold send me A few pouns of buter and a pint of Salt and when you butcher Send Me some **sosheses** for we dont get any thing fat to eat At this time. We get beef and Crackers and not A nuff of them. (Marcus Hefner, Hefner Papers, NCSA) Catawba County

Nov. 4, 1863: I suppose you hav the bacon to spare. I dont suppose you will hav **sauchedgs**. if you have send some. (J. M. Frank, Frank Papers, Duke) Davidson County

Jan. 1, 1864: Dear loveing wife want you to Send me Some dride froot and I want Some brandy to if you can Sendit and I want Some **Sassige** if you have enny and enny thing that is good to eate. (Daniel Setzer, Setzer Papers, Duke) Catawba County

Dec. 22, 1864: I want you to send me some flower and some fat meat. some molases and some **Sasengs** and peas an beanes any thang so to eat. (A. J. Spease, Zimmerman Papers, Duke) Forsyth County

sausage meat *noun* Sausage; perhaps minced meat and spices cooked and preserved with fat rather than stuffed into casings.

Jan. 3, 1863: if you git the chance I wood like to have som cabbedg and som **sashed m[e]at** an so on. (C. M. Mendenhall, Fonvielle Coll., MHI) Randolph County

Mar. 23, 1863: I got one mess of Jack['s] **sassege meat** and he cook the owther wp [= up] and eat it him Self and never seaid nowthing to no boddy els. (W. H. Brotherton, Brotherton Papers, Duke) Catawba County

save *verb*

1. To harvest, gather a grain crop, especially wheat. [*DSME* **save**, verb; *DARE* South, South Midland]

June 1, 1862: When you Write tell me how your Wheat is. I thought I Would git to come home at harvest and help **Save** the wheat But thare is no chance of it. **Save** all you can of it. (G. J. Huntley, Huntley Papers, WCU) Rutherford County

May 29, 1863: ha[r]vest is approaching as you know for which my object is to know of you if I may be permitted to **Save** my own grain and grass as heretofore by my own labor not having no person to do the same for me. (Asa Clapp, Vance Papers, NCSA) Guilford County

June 8, 1863: Dear Sir I take the privolidge of writing you a few lines requesting you to grant me the privelidge of going Home to **Save** my wheat crop that is now ready for the Sithe. (James Tyson, Vance Papers, NCSA) Randolph County

June 11, 1863: wheat crops ar as good as we evr had and half or one third will Be oblige to Be lost on the account of Scarcity of hands to cut. some can **save** there crops where they are small. (Mark Nelson, Vance Papers, NCSA) Randolph County

2. To be preserved, to keep.

July 28, 1862: i want you to send me some pear vishion [= provision] such as you think will **Save** the firs Chanc you have. (Larkin Kendrick, Kendrick Papers, NCSA) Cleveland County

Aug. 15, 1862: If you send a box have it bord full of small auger holes and have every thing cool before put in the Box. I would like to have a few good apples if you think they will **save** tell they get hear. (Isaac Lefevers, Lefevers Papers, NCSA) Catawba County

Feb. 2, 1863: I made about 40 bushell of potatoes last year they are **saving** very well so far. (Mary Driskell, Caldwell Coll., ECU) Cabarrus County

saving *adjective* Thrifty, economical (with money, crops, provisions). [*OED* **saving**, adjective, 4]

Jan. 19, 1864: Emoline I want you to mind and be **saving** with your pervision and ever thing that you hav got for thar is nothing to eat here. (Jesse Hill, Hill Letters, NCSA) Forsyth County

Mar. 7, 1864: I stil have a bout a half off my meet yet. I am very **Saven** with it. (Isaac Lefever, Lefevers Papers, NCSA) Catawba County

Aug. 7, 1864: you Sed you made fifty one and a half bshels of wheat. thats better then i expectd. tel me hou thrashed it. i only take good care of it and bea as **saveing** as you can. (Franklin Setzer, Setzer Corr., UVA) Catawba County

Nov. 24, 1864: See that the mule has fare play and other Stock but be as **Saveing** with corn as you can. (John Peterson, Peterson Papers, Duke) Catawba County

say *verb* Narrative or "historical" present tense *says*, used to report something which has been said in the past. [*DARE* **say**, verb, B 1a]

Apr. 28, 1863: the man come back and **sais** Boys we will have a fight hear to reckly [= directly] and I comenced geting up. (B. Y. Malone, *Malone Diary*, 32) Caswell County

Jan. 14, 1865: he ast Rofe what was the news. he **ses** if you want to be sunk in the middle of hell you stay here fifteen minut longr for the yankees is rite after me. (Ann Bowen, Bowen Papers, NCSA) Washington County

scarce *adjective*

1. variant forms *scearce, scerce, skerse.*

July 27, 1861: Coffe is **skerse** on the account of the rivvers being blockaded but we think that navaggashen will be opend be fore long and salt and Coffee will be Cheep and plenty. (J. C. Haltom, Frank Papers, Duke) Davidson County

Feb. 3, 1862: I hant rote to you in som time. I recived your leter an paper was **scerse**. I put it of till I got som paper. (G. T. Beavers, Upchurch Papers, Duke) Chatham County

Aug. 11, 1862: we started last wendesday morning. I was not well at the time we started & the wether was sow hot & water **scears** & bad at that that I think overheatin and drinken sow much bad water is what has brot mee to what it has. (Isaac Lefevers, Lefevers Papers, NCSA) Catawba County

Apr. 27, 1863: if the men colde Oneley Stay at home tell they colde Made thair cropes it mite be that they colde make breade enogh for another year. Provesions is very **scearse** her at this tim. (Wilburn Garren, Vance Papers, NCSA) Henderson County

2. variant form without initial *s.*

Mar. 22, 1864: Provisions is very **carce** in this country tho we git tolerable rations flower not bolted tho it dose very well neads no sodey. the boys dos not grumble & seems content. (Stephen Whitaker, Whitaker Papers, NCSA) Cherokee County

scarce in, scarce of *adjective phrase* Lacking in, in short supply of. [*DSME* **scarce of**, predicate adjective phrase; *DARE* **scarce**, B, as adjective]

Nov. 26, 1862: I can tell you it was the hardest march I ever have taken since I have bin out. we was very **scearse in** Provisions at the time and we air still tolerable **Scearse in** Provisions. (Isaac Lefevers, Lefevers Papers, NCSA) Catawba County

Feb. 27, 1865: if you cant keep things Safe in the corn houses you would better move it in the house. if you get too **Scarce of** corn the mule must doe with out corn and all the other Stock. (John Peterson, Peterson Papers, Duke) Catawba County

scarcely *adverb*

1. variant form *scearcely.*

Aug. 11, 1862: I eat **scearsly** nothing all the march & still have now stomache to eat enny thing **scearsly**. I am Just as weak as ever I was in my life. (Isaac Lefevers, Lefevers Papers, NCSA) Catawba County

2. variant form without initial *s.*

Mar. 23, 1858: I have not saw a sick purson ner herd tel of any won a bean sick sence I hav ben in Missouri an pople tels me that there is **casley** enny sickness at all in this nabor hood. (David Headrick, Frank Papers, Duke) Davidson County

scare *verb* variant forms *scear, skear.* [*DARE* chiefly South, South Midland]

May 25, 1862: They said they was a bout one Thousand yankey cavalry in 1 1/2 miles of us but they Got **Skerd** and turnd around and went back. (William Tesh, Tesh Papers, Duke) Yadkin County

Oct. 15, 1863: I have not Done nothing more since I have Bin at home only I shot some squirls. shot at the malishia But Did not heart no one as I Know off. I Dune this to **skeare** them. (David West, Vance Papers, NCSA) Gaston County

June 18, 1864: thay had to send ever old criple man out of the Sitty that thay cold find to healp keep thay yankes back. when we come thrugh the sitty the people was **sceard** vary bad. thay give me as mutch meat and bread as I cold Eat. I tell you that thay was vary glad to see us a coming. (J. W. Joyce, Joyce Papers, MHI) Stokes County

scary *adjective* variant form *skeery.* [*DARE* scattered, but chiefly South, South Midland; also Northeast]

May 25, 1862: I tell you it made some of them Look mighty **Skeery** but it didant Frighten me a bit. (William Tesh, Tesh Papers, Duke) Yadkin County

scear see **scare**

scearce see **scarce**

scholar *noun* A student, pupil. [*DARE* scattered, but especially Atlantic, North Central]

Dec. 21, 1860: ther was a graet meny out ther to hear the **scholler** make ther speaches and a fine table sat. (Catherine Strickland, Quinn Papers, Duke) Duplin County

June 16, 1863: tell lisa that I recieved hur letter but I hant never got **scoller** a nuff to make it all out yet it was so badly rote. (J. H. Hundley, Hundley Family Letters, SHC) Stokes County

scout *noun* A scouting expedition. See also **on the scout**.

Mar. 16, 1864: now I will tel you about the **scout** that me and felt had to take a while Sam was at home. (Jesse Hill, Hill Letters, NCSA) Forsyth County

scratch of a pen *noun phrase* Figurative usage indicating the lack of letters from home.

Mar. 21, 1862: I will now close by Seying to you Rite to me as so[o]n as thes few lines comes to you for I have never got one **scratch of a pen** from you yet. (James Keever, Keever Papers, Duke) Lincoln County

Feb. 26, 1863: Just to think that you have got as good a looking son in the army as i am and haint never got a **scratch of a pen** from his father yet after beeing gon eight months. (Isaac Copeland, Copeland Letters, NCSA) Surry County

Mar. 3, 1863: Tell pap an mam an all of the rest howdy for mee an to wright to mee an tell Asenith howdy to. i herd that she was a staing with yow now tell her i thawght she wold of Sent mee howdy once bee for now. thar has not one of them even sent me the **scrach of a pen**. (T. F. Baggarly, Baggarly Papers, Duke) Iredell County

script *noun* A piece of writing, something written. [*OED* **script**, noun[1], "Now *rare*"]

Apr. 2, 1863: I hope that this poor pitiful **script** will be acceptable with you. I am realy ashamed to let you read such a **script** from me for such a hyly & esteemed cosin to read but it is a poor soldiers chance. (W. R. Best, Quinn Papers, Duke) Duplin County

scrouge *verb* To crowd, squeeze into a space. [*DARE* chiefly South Midland]

June 6, 1862: we have got six more tents to day for our recruts to stay in So this tent will not be **schrougd** Like it has been. (J. W. Williams, Williams Papers, Duke) Onslow County

scrumish, scrumage Earlier, variant forms from which present-day *skirmish* and *scrimmage* are descended. [see *DARE* **skirmish**, noun and verb; *OED* **skirmish**, noun and verb (from Middle English *skarmuch, skarmushe*); see also *OED* **scrimish**, noun and verb; **scrimmage, scrummage**, noun]

1. *noun.*

July 6, 1862: My dear Partha I have been in two battles. I was in alittle **Scrumage** at west point and below rich mond at the Seven pines. thats the first battle of richmond. (John Hartman, Hartman Papers, Duke) Rowan County

Apr. 26, 1863: We have bin in 7 small **scrumages** though have never got a man in our campanie killed yet though We have had som Wounded. (Joseph Wright, Wright Papers, Duke) Alamance County

Nov. 15, 1863: wee hav been in to a little **Scrumedg** Since I writen to you. (T. F. Baggarly, Baggarly Papers, Duke) Iredell County

Dec. 6, 1863: They are a fiting ever day. **Scrumish** fiting. we never got in a reglar fite. (A. J. Spease, Zimmerman Papers, Duke) Forsyth County

2. *verb* and *verbal noun.*

Oct. 17, 1861: I am prepy [= pretty] well driled both from squad Company Battalion **Scrumageing** and Briggade Drills also in the Manuel of Arms. (Amzi Harris, Caldwell Coll., ECU) Cabarrus County

July 19, 1863: we got to the potomock and threw up brest werk and lay thare 3 days for our wagens to cross the river and the yankes was in site and **a scrumishing** all the time. (Neill McLeod, McLeod Letters, SHC) Moore County

June 11, 1864: We are in line of Batle yet But has not Binn no Regle [= regular] in gagement in a Week But **scrumish** evr Day an has Binn evr sense the 4 of May. (Phillip Walsh, Proffit Family Letters, SHC) Wilkes County

July 15, 1864: I Can Say to you that thear is but little fighting going on Since I have bin hear. only **Scumeshing** a long the river. (Alexander Keever, Keever Papers, Duke) Lincoln County

secesh (also *sesesh, cesesh, cesech, secess*) *noun* and *adjective* Short form of secessionist, a Confederate; sometimes used to refer to soldiers, but in the North Carolina letters, usually used in reference to civilian supporters of the war; often used as a collective noun. [*OED* **secesh**, noun and adjective]

May 2, 1864: the hot head **secess** about here glory in the duration of the ware as long as they can keep out. god help the contentions ignorant creturs. (James Zimmerman, Zimmerman Papers, Duke) Forsyth County

July 24, 1864: we are all down hear in one little hole with all the **cesech** a round us <Drey?> is gone home and [he] dont ask the details no ods. he is as black is ever. he says he had rather see you than any body in this world. (Cassie Davenport, Hundley Family Letters, SHC) Stokes County

Sept. 1864: rations that the goverment allows the contrabands are sold to the white **secech** citizen's, and got out the way at night. its no uncommon thing to see weman and children crying for something to eat, Old clothes sent to the Island from the North for contraband's are sold to the white **secesh** sitizen's. (Ned Baxter, *Freedom,* ser. 1: 203) Tyrrell County

Feb. 2, 1865: the **sesesh** men dos hate to own [= admit] that we are whiped. they wont talk about it if they can help it. it dos me good to tell it to them but they hav to own it. (Martha Poteet, Poteet-Dickson Letters, NCSA) McDowell County

Mar. 9, 1865: the Gentlemen that ration the Contrabands had Gone a round to all the White School-Teachers and told them to Give the boys orders to goe and get they ration on a Cirtain day. So the negros as we are Call are use to the **Cesesh** plots Suspicion the Game they was Going to play and a Greate many never Sent they Children. (Richard Boyle, *Freedom,* ser. 1, vol. 2: 233) Tyrrell County

secessioner *noun* A Confederate, a secessionist.

July 31, 1862: they was not **secessioners** for they was for the younion. I hate the name of secession for hit has cased so meny to see truble when hit cood ben hope [= helped] if they had atride. (L. W. Griffin, Griffin Papers, NCSA) Rutherford County

sech see **such**

sect *noun* Sex; possibly a euphemism or back formation (see citations). [*OED* **sect**, noun[1], 1.d. (citations from 1386 to 1861, mostly with female referents)]

Feb. 2, 1862: all that hurts us is leaveing the fair **sects**. that is the girls that we left in old catawba. as for being at home I do not care if that was all that pestered me. I dont think I would come home until my time is out. (P. S. Whitner, Whitner Papers, Duke) Catawba County

June 15, 1863: We the female **Sect** off .NC. Rutherfordton. doo Sertify that we are unwilling to put up with the treatment that theas Spectulaters are treating us with. ("the Female Sect," Vance Papers, NCSA) Rutherford County

Oct. 11, 1863: we had <??> meeting at Bales creeke. as for Rocspring I was not there. you said your meeting did not hav much affect for want of the femaile **sect**. (L. M. Bleckley, Bleckley Papers, Duke) Catawba County

section *noun* A part of a state or county.

Feb. 25, 1862: I can inform you that thare is a grate many peopell in this **section** that is in favor of appealing to england for help. (G. J. Huntley, Huntley Papers, WCU) Rutherford County

Aug. 19, 1862: write how you a getting along and write all of the news in that **section** of Country. (J. H. Hundley, Hundley Family Letters, SHC) Stokes County

Jan. 20, 1864: I was very Sorry to hear of So much Sickness through our **Section** of country. (Thornton Sexton, Sexton Letters, Duke) Ashe County

see *verb* See Overview § II.4.1.7.

1. past tense *seen.* [*DARE* widespread]

Sept. 29, 1861: our Boys went over on a littel istand this morning and **seen** them in a small Distance. (R. P. Crawford, Estes Family Papers, WCU) Jackson County

Dec. 25, 1862: i dident have nothing to drink nor no young ladies to talk too so I **seen** but little fun. (B. Y. Malone, *Malone Diary,* 27) Caswell County

June 19, 1863: tel John that I Cold ov got him some of the best Drums in this last fight he ever **Seen**. (John Futch, Futch Letters, NCSA) New Hanover County

2. past tense *seed.* [*DARE* chiefly South, South Midland]

Feb. 6, 1862: it reigns ever day or snows hear and is the muddiest plase you ever **seede** and the worst water to use I ever **seede** allthough wee ar willin to stay till the war ends. (Jesse Shipman, Shipman Family Corr., Notre Dame) Henderson County

Oct. 5, 1862: I thought I **seed** hard times when I wase at home but I did not see any thing to Whate I see here. (Isaac Copeland, Copeland Letters, NCSA) Surry County

Mar. 1, 1863: Francis I **sead** a man Shot yester day for runing way. he had run away three time in the time of fighting. the hole brigade was muster out and then tha fetch him out with his coffin and tha tide a white honkercheif over his eyes and tuelve men shot him. (J. W. Joyce, Joyce Papers, MHI) Stokes County

3. past tense *see.*

Sept. 1863: I tell you the truth I never **See** the like of Rock in my life. theay is Some as Bige is a house. (William Strickland, Quinn Papers, Duke) Duplin County

4. past participle *seed.* [*DARE* chiefly South, South Midland]

June 4, 1863: I had like to be with you and talk over all our past trubels and seans [= scenes?] sens we have **sead** each other. (Arthur Putnam, Kendrick Papers, NCSA) Cleveland County

Jan. 10, 1864: I have **Seede** more troble sence youe was at hom than I ever saw before in all the worl. (Susan Setzer, Setzer Papers, Duke) Catawba County

Mar. 1864: they Said that they had **Seed** the wounded men a going to the horse pital. (W. H. Horton, Councill Papers, Duke) Watauga County

5. past participle *saw.* [*DARE* widespread, but less frequent Northeast, Great Lakes, California]

June 3, 1862: i Cant rite hafe to you what i have **saw.** if i Cood See you i cood tell you more in one day and i Can rite to you in A week. (W. P. Cline, Cline Papers, SHC) Catawba County

June 1, 1863: I have **saw** nearly all the neighbor boys. they are in camp in the neighborhood of this place. (Christopher Hackett, Hackett Papers, Duke) Guilford County

June 29, 1863: Dear wife I can Say to you that I have **Saw** Sits Sens I lefte virginia. (Leonard Alman, Alman Papers, Duke) Cabarrus County

see the elephant *idiomatic expression* To experience battle, extreme hardship.

Nov. 23, 1862: I can inform that it was the Mud[i]est time and the Slickest time I ever Saw. as the Saying is I have **saw** some part of **the elephant**. (Marcus Hefner, Hefner Papers, NCSA) Catawba County

see the monkey *idiomatic expression* Same meaning as *see the elephant.*

Jan. 11, 1862: I recived a leter from charles the other day which stated that he had bin in one fight an was taken prisener. I recon he thought that he was in the very den of ——. he hant **seen the monkey** yet. by the time he stays out 2 years he can hav more to talk of than he has now. (G. T. Beavers, Upchurch Papers, Duke) Chatham County

sermond, sermont *noun* variant forms of *sermon.* [*DARE* chiefly South, South Midland]

June 6, 1862: I heard A fine **surmant** preached the seckond one that I have heard Sence I Left home. (J. W. Williams, Williams Papers, Duke) Onslow County

Oct. 4, 1862: I would give all Ihave in this world to get to See you and the childrean one time more and if I only could bee with you and them at the next meaten I can not tell you my fealings about that. I have not heard a **sermont** preached in the last three months. (Isaac Lefevers, Lefevers Papers, NCSA) Catawba County

Dec. 25, 1862: I havent herd but one **sermond** Since I left there. (J. W. Lineberger, *Gaston Ranger,* 31) Gaston County

Apr. 3, 1864: tell Joseph that I hearn A fine **surmet** the other day. (J. W. Reese, Reese Papers, Duke) Buncombe County

serve *verb* To treat in an unpleasant or unfair manner. [*OED* **serve,** verb[1], 47.a. "Now chiefly *colloq.*"]

Jan. 14, 1865: they have **served** the people round town rather worse than they use to. (Ann Bowen, Bowen Papers, NCSA) Washington County

service see **sarvice**

set *verb* To sit. See also **sot.**

Aug. 7, 1861: I am so weake that I Cant hardley **set** up to Rite. But I will try to give you alittle histry of the battle At Manases Junction. (Peter Poteet, Poteet-Dickson Letters, NCSA) Burke County

Nov. 24, 1861: I went up on the side of the mountain and was **seting** on a log. thar was two gons fired on the other mountain. they shot at me. one of the balls went in about 2 feet of me and the other 4 feet. they both miss me. I then got oup and got behind the tree. (L. W. Griffin, Griffin Papers, NCSA) Rutherford County

Apr. 16, 1863: I can Buy 7 & 8 dollars worth [of food] and **Set** down and Eat it all at one time and you may know By that it is not very Cheep. (John Futch, Futch Letters, NCSA) New Hanover County

set in *verb* To begin, start; of weather: to turn; see Overview § II.4.7. [*OED* **set**, verb[1], **to set in**, 5]

Mar. 8, 1858: we had a mild winter tell febuary then it **Set in** Cold and it has been Cold Ever Since. (David Headrick, Frank Papers, Duke) Davidson County

setler, settler *noun* variant forms of *sutler*.

May 28, 1863: We Dont get A Nuff to eat yet but we can buy little things from the **Setlers** but we have to pay mity high for it. (John Futch, Futch Letters, NCSA) New Hanover County

Mar. 8, 1864: the **Settler** Shop at lynsays turn out was charged afew nights ago by twelve of our compny and nine of potses compny. the provose guard has tacon them and they will be cortmarseld to morrow. I exspect it will go pretty hard with them. (John Hartman, Hartman Papers, Duke) Rowan County

settlement *noun* A community or neighborhood.

Dec. 8, 1862: rite all the nuse that is in the **Setlement** that you now that would be of intrust. (J. H. Hundley, Hundley Family Letters, SHC) Stokes County

Dec. 25, 1863: I want You to write when You think the Home Guard will have to go in camp a gain and if their is anny talk of takeing them out and all the nuse that is a stiring through the **Settlement**. (William Tesh, Tesh Papers, Duke) Yadkin County

May 20, 1864: well now I most close. I will give you the names of thoes that has bin kiled in our **Settlement.** Henry Workman. Wm. Warlick. Jos Richey. I beleave that is all in our neighborhood. (Isaac Lefevers, Lefevers Papers, NCSA) Catawba County

Sept. 21, 1864: we have got the nicest turnip patch there is in the **Settlement**. (Huldah Hubbard, Hubbard Papers, Duke) Anson County

set up see **sit up**

shade *noun* A slight degree. [*OED* **shade**, noun, 4.b. *fig.*]

Oct. 20, 1864: the Docer think Henry ise a **shade** beter to day. I think soe my selfe. hise case ise abad one but hee may git upe agane with close atten-tion. with out that he ise gon. (Malcom Murchison, Albright Papers, NCSA) Chatham County

shake *verb* variant past tense *shuck*.

Aug. 4, 1862: a bout midnight our artilry commence Firing on them and They Throwd Bums all Around us and I tell you they **shuck** the grown. (Joseph Cowand, Cowand Papers, Duke) Bertie County

shall *auxiliary verb* [According to CACWL data, first-person *shall* instead of *will* to indicate the future was still common in American English in the mid-nineteenth century]

1. *shall* used to indicate the future with first-person subjects.

Dec. 16, 1861: Just as Soon as I can get a furlough to Come I **Shall** do So. (Charley Futch, Futch Letters, NCSA) New Hanover County

Dec. 20, 1861: give my best respects to Father Mother Brothers & Sisters. tell them I **shall** neve[r] forgit them. (Larkin Kendrick, Kendrick Papers, NCSA) Cleveland County

Apr. 7, 1863: I dont now whether I **Shal** ever see you any more or not. (Daniel Revis, Revis Letters, NCSA) Henderson County

July 27, 1864: I **Shall** go to Richmond to Knight then take the boat down the James River to Drewry's Bluff. (Alfred N. Proffit, Proffit Family Letters, SHC) Wilkes County

2. contracted with the negative particle *not*.

Sept. 25, 1861: if I fare as good all the time as I have so far I **shant** grumble. (J. W. Williams, Williams Papers, Duke) Onslow County

June 10, 1863: Father You can do Just as You Please a bout that money. I **shant** say a word. (William Tesh, Tesh Papers, Duke) Yadkin County

Feb. 26, 1865: we have not bin in aney fight yet and I hope I **shant**. (Henry Bowen, Bowen Papers, NCSA) Washington County

3. *should* with first-person subjects indicating a wish, desire, or other senses in which present-day English uses *would.*

June 12, 1862: you said something in your letter about sinding me some sugar and vinergar. I **should** be very glad to get the vinergar. (J. W. Whitfield, Whitfield Papers, Duke) Nash County

Oct. 5, 1862: I **should** like to see you but if never see you any more I hope We will meete one canonse [= on Canaan's] bless[ed] shore. (Isaac Copeland, Copeland Letters, NCSA) Surry County

Jan. 21, 1865: I **should** think as good as you love dumplins you would want Some. (Ann Bowen, Bowen Papers, NCSA) Washington County

Shanghai *noun* A breed of large domestic fowl with feathered shanks, introduced from China in the 1840s (also known as a *Chochin*). [*OED* **shanghai**, noun, 1]

Apr. 29, 1862: I must close. give my love to all, write when you can. direct to Smithfield. Tell Jane that She kneed not save her **shangi** for it is uncertain when we will come to eat it. (W. M. Patton, Patton Family Letters, SHC) Buncombe County

shanty *noun* A crude, temporary shelter constructed of logs or scrap lumber, usually built by members of a mess to serve as winter quarters. See also **cabin**.

Jan. 1, 1862: their is nothing new in our Camp at this time only Still working on the **Shantys**. (C. F. Mills, Mills Papers, Duke) Iredell County

Jan. 15, 1863: I hant got mutch time to Right for I am engage in bilding a **Shanty**. I have got it all done bwt the chimly. we are all bilding winter qwarter. (W. H. Brotherton, Brotherton Papers, Duke) Catawba County

Nov. 18, 1864: we are ordered to put up winter quarters along the line here and every body is busy working on little **Shanties**. (John Peterson, Peterson Papers, Duke) Catawba County

shark *noun* A person who takes advantage of others for financial gain, a predator in the economic sense. [*OED* **shark,** noun[1], 2. *fig.*]

Dec. 8, 1862: the people could not git Salt to Salt their poark and here was **Sharks** that thought the[y] had the people pend. (Samuel C. Wilson, Vance Papers, NCSA) Burke County

sharpshoot *verb* To take careful aim with a rifle with the intention of killing or wounding an enemy; probably by back formation of *sharpshooter.*

July 8, 1864: us and the yanks is from two to 7 hundred yards apart. We are all the time **Sharp Shooting** and Shelling each other. (S. E. Love, Love Papers, Duke) Henderson

July 29, 1864: the yankees is lying Still only they **Sharpe Shootet** Some. (Edgar Smithwick, Smithwick Papers, Duke) Martin County

sheaf *noun* A bundle of fodder. [*DARE* widespread, but especially Pennsylvania, Maryland, West Virginia, Ohio]

Sept. 27, 1863: I hav mi foder all made and hald in I made abot twelve hundred **sheves** and I toped that at manuels the[y] do not hav to pay tool [= toll] out of the tops but we hav to pay o[u]t of the foder. it semes like hard times to pay tolde out of evry thing but I recon we hav it to do and So we nead not to say eny thing abot it. (Catherine Lefevers, Lefevers Papers, NCSA) Catawba County

shellot, shelot *noun* A green or spring onion, a scallion; variant form of *shallot.* [see *DARE* **shallot**, noun; chiefly South, South Midland, Texas]

Mar. 15, 1863: John I am a lokin fore you every day. I want you to come and eat **shelots** and turneps grens and I shall soon have peas and I want you to come and help me to eat them. (Catherine Ramsey, Futch Letters, NCSA) New Hanover County

shet of In the phrase *get shet of:* to get rid of, be free from; variant form of *shut of.* [*DSME* **shut**, B]

Feb. 2, 1862: as to the Negroes steeling meat. I am glad it [is] from McCoy for he will make them suffer for it & maby they will keep away from town. I Want Tom Well Whiped if he is guilty. I think we had best **git shet of** him any how. (A. W. Bell, Bell Papers, Duke) Macon County

Apr. 3, 1862: I seat my Sef to drop you a few lins to lette you now that I am a getting Able for drill a gain but I ant **got Shet of** the Boul Complaint yet. (Isaac Lefevers, Lefevers Papers, NCSA) Catawba County

Feb. 25, 1863: he has got the piles sorty at this time but I hope he will **get shet of** it a gain before long. (W. F. Wagner, *Confederate Soldier,* 37) Catawba County

June 29, 1863: the confederate Stats has **got Shet of** feading us now. (Leonard Alman, Alman Papers, Duke) Cabarrus County

shet up *verb* variant form of *shut up;* see Overview § II.4.7.

Feb. 27, 1865: as to manageing things you must look at the fences and **Shet up** holes and lay up the rails where the are down. all ways see to that in time be fore Stock of any kind finds out any thing. (John Peterson, Peterson Papers, Duke) Catawba County

shew see **shoe**

shifty *adjective* Changeable, unpredictable.

Jan. 2, 1865: we have had two or three days very cold but that is as long as we have it cold at at a time for the weather is verry **shifty** hear. (Henry Bowen, Bowen Papers, NCSA) Washington County

shinplaster *noun* A piece of paper currency of small denomination or of little value. [*OED* **shin**, noun[1], compounds, **shinplaster** noun (b)]

Oct. 12, 1862: I wil now tell you the price of things in Mariland. bacon 8cts Coffe 10. butter 12 ½. Shugar 10–12 1/2. Soda 25. Molasses 15 cts to 18 pur qt. Shoes from $1.50 cts to 4.00. Corse boots 2.50. Chicken 10 to 12d. We could not get any thing with our **Shinplasters**. every thing is as cheap as ever it was their. (James W. Overcash, Overcash Papers, Duke) Rowan County

Feb. 26, 1863: if i git a plenty to eat and to ware a[nd] Somthing to drink and a few **Shinplasters** i Can make out verry well. (Isaac Copeland, Copeland Letters, NCSA) Surry County

shit house *noun* An outdoor privy.

June 13, 1862: W N Swann is mad & I am glad. he put A F in the gard house one time & he got drunk a goin from Wilmington to Golesborro on the Train & we put him in The **Shit house** So we are even. (A. F. Harrington, Hubbard Papers, Duke) Moore County

shoat *noun* A young hog, usually less than a year old.

Jan. 3, 1862: I Will inform that we have not kild non of our largest hogs yet. we have only kild five **Shotes** and we have got 16 hogs in a pen. (F. H. Williams, Williams Papers, Duke) Onslow County

Oct. 16, 1864: cousin penny wanted to buy a **Shoat.** She ses She talked to you about it and you partley promist to let her have one. (Ann Bowen, Bowen Papers, NCSA) Washington County

Jan. 4, 1865: I want you to put up a **Shoat** and have it fat a ginst I git home. I ex pect to come home some time this winter if nothing happens to me. (Joseph Wright, Wright Papers, Duke) Alamance County

shock *noun* A sheaf of grain set together, tied in a pile. [*DSME* **shock**, A noun, 2]

May 31, 1863: I saw corn in silk and Tasels and I saw lots of wheat cut and in **shocks** and som stacked and as we com on the steam boat. I eat my diner on the Boat and I had green Beens fish Boild ham soop &c. I only paid two Dollars for it. (W. B. Lance, Lance Papers, LSU) Henderson County

June 22, 1863: Tel Arch not to lay By the corn two soon. it wil not do as well By laying it By two soon. Dear wife I hope tel you answer this letter you can lette me now how menny **shocks** of wheat you made and how it is. (Isaac Lefevers, Lefevers Papers, NCSA) Catawba County

July 13, 1863: I hear that the small grain is injurd very bad. tha sa that the wheat is in the **shock** yet and is green by the wet wither. (John Revis, Revis Letters, NCSA) Henderson County

shocking *adverb* Very, extremely.

Aug. 4, 1862: Archy they hav bin the prettest red color in your likeness face ever since you hav bin sick. it is **shocken** pretty. (Dicy Ann Jackson, Jackson Family Corr., Notre Dame) Moore County

shoe *verb* To supply people with shoes; variant form *shew*.

June 15, 1863: the[y] say the[y] never did go to church beare footted sence they weare grone and they will haft to stay or go beare footted for they cant ge[t] Shoes. the people in this nabor hood says theas speckulators Shant have thear hides. the[y] have treatte us so mean. thears hides a nough in this nabor hood to **Shew** the people if we cold get them tand on fare termes. ("the female Sect," Vance Papers, NCSA) Rutherford County

shoe-mouth deep *adjective phrase* Of snow, mud, sand: an indication of depth by comparing it to the opening at the top of a shoe. [*DSME* **shoe-mouth deep, shoe-top deep**, adjective phrase; *DARE* chiefly South Midland]

Oct. 8, 1861: This is a very Sandy place. most too Sandy to drill. The sand is **Shoe mouth deep** most any where. (J. T. Groves, Davison Papers, Duke) Gaston County

Nov. 25, 1862: it was a awful time I tell you the mud was **Shewmouth Deep** all the way. I can tell you it was the hardest march I ever have taken since I have bin out. (Isaac Lefevers, Lefevers Papers, NCSA) Catawba County

Nov. 4, 1862: we have hade some snow here. it wase a bout **shoe moth deep**. (Isaac Copeland, Copeland Letters, NCSA) Surry County

May 1, 1864: clover is about **shoo mouth deep** in the fields here now. (P. J. Peterson, Peterson Papers, Duke) Catawba County

shore *adverb* and *adjective* variant form of *sure*. [*DARE* chiefly South, South Midland]

Oct. 16, 1861: fold it up in a Sheat of paper and Back it to me and do be **Shore** and Send it. (Charley Futch, Futch Letters, NCSA) New Hanover County

July 31, 1862: Give my love to all of the enquiring frinds be **shore** to give Miss Matti G my love. (L. W. Griffin, Griffin Papers, NCSA) Rutherford County

Oct. 14, 1862: I want yu to be a good Son and be **shore** to meat me in heaven when yu die. (Letty Long, Long Family Papers, SHC) Alamance County

Oct. 29, 1863: thair is one thing **Shore.** Ganerril Brag Cammanding the suthern Boys got A tree mends whiping over thair the other day. (J. W. Reese, Reese Papers, Duke) Buncombe County

shortened biscuit *noun* A biscuit made with lard or other cooking fat.

Jan. 17, 1863: I want you to be sure and come to see us now and bring me a box of provisions as soon as you can because we may leave here in a couple weeks. I want a hat and the pair of socks, ink &c a pint cup, tin plates, coffee pot, knife, fork & spoon, sody, **shortened biscuits** & several pounds of butter, pies, dried peaches &c&c and any thing else that is good. (C. A. Hege, Hege Papers, MHI) Davidson County

shote see **shoat**

shrub *verb* To clear underbrush; verbal noun *shrubbing*. [*DARE* chiefly South Midland]

Dec. 28, 1863: tell Lewis to be a good boy and get his **S[h]rubing** don as soon as he Can so he can make Corn next Summer. (Alexander Keever, Keever Papers, Duke) Lincoln County

shuck *noun* Figuratively: the skin.

Aug. 7, 1862: I tell you my dear friend wee hav Such hard tims it is no yous for mee to tell you eney thing a bout it. this thing of drinking water out of pudel hols in the rode. it Sorteer gits into the boys **shucks**. (A. P. Ward, Whitner Papers, Duke) Catawba County

shuck *verb*

1. To remove outer cover of an ear of corn. [*DARE* scattered, but chiefly South, South Midland]

Oct. 7, 1861: tel Jim that I would A liked mity to a helpt him a **shucked** his corn but it was So I couldent. (Harrison Hanes, Hanes Papers, Duke) Davie County

Nov. 4, 1863: I could not write when the rest was writing and I hardly hav time to writ now. we are **shucking** corn. we have all of our corn getherd but that down about the meadow. (Sarah Overcash, Overcash Papers, Duke) Rowan County

2. To discard, throw away. [see *DARE* **shuck**, verb[1], d 3]

Apr. 18, 1862: there was Some of the boys that Started with grate loades but after travling some to or three miles it commense raning and the boys commensede **Shucking** thare goods. Some of them th[r]ode thare napsacks a way. (James W. Overcash, Overcash Papers, Duke) Rowan County

shucking, corn shucking *noun* A gathering or party of neighbors where the outer husks of newly harvested corn would be removed. The event would be followed by a celebratory meal, often accompanied by music and dancing.

Aug. 8, 1861: tel Jim he must have a **corn shucken** and hav a parsel a girls there for I know all the boys a round a bout there want him to. (Harrison Hanes, Hanes Papers, Duke) Davie County

Nov. 25, 1861: I would like to bee in old Catawba to go to the **corn shucking** to fly around amongst the girls. (L. L. Houk, Fisher Papers, Duke) Catawba County

Sept. 29, 1863: The Wether is plesent but very cool of nights. ther has bin a plenty of Frost her. It puts me in mind of **Corn-shucking** times. (A. A. Jackson, Jackson Family Corr., Notre Dame) Moore County

Nov. 3, 1863: you Rote that if I could be at home to go with you to the **shucking** that you would be glad. If I could I would give Ever thing that I am worth to be with you. (F. M. Poteet, Poteet-Dickson Letters, NCSA) McDowell County

shuck stable *noun* Apparently an outbuilding for storing fodder; see citation. [see *DARE* **shuck**, noun[1], b (5) *shuck house* and (6) *shuck pen*]

Dec. 2, 1864: he ses they fare verry hard. he would swap his place with his dog. he does have **shuck stable** to sleep in. (Ann Bowen, Bowen Papers, NCSA) Washington County

shumake *noun* One of several species of small trees or shrubs belonging to the genus *Rhus;* variant form of *sumac.*

Dec. 25, 1858: as you requested to know what kind of timber we have in this country. thare is white oke. black oke. red oake. Spanish oake and hickrey black white and scaly barke. black walnut white walnut. mulbery. cotton wood. wile [= wild] chery. elum and lin wood. shugar trees. sicamore and buckei. buroake. severl other kinds too tedous to mention. the under groth is mostley hasle and **shumake**. (William Boss, Frank Papers, Duke) Davidson County

shun *verb* To protect, shelter. [*OED* **shun**, verb, 7, "Now only *dial.*"]

Mar. 3, 1864: may God in his infnite mercy be with you and watch over you and shield and **shun** you from all danger and harm and return you safe home. (Elizabeth Phillips, Phillips Papers, Duke) Robeson County

shut of see **shet of**

sich see **such**

sick at the stomach see **at**

sight *noun* A large amount or number, a great deal. [*DARE* chiefly South, South Midland, New England]

Sept. 7, 1861: We are not very well fixed here yet though we have done a good eal of work here and I expect we will have to do a **sight** more yet. (C. L. Moffitt, Caldwell Coll., Duke) Randolph County

Oct. 17, 1861: We distroyed an amence **sight** of property for them. we burnt evry thing that was worth spending any time with Such as tents, the Commssary, sutlers &c. (Amzi Harris, Caldwell Coll., ECU) Cabarrus County

July 3, 1862: our men has whipt them evry fite and has drove them Severl miles and has taken a **Site** of prisners. (M. W. Parris, Parris Papers, WCU) Jackson County

Apr. 3, 1864: I just thought you could make a Little Snack and bake me some cakes and send me some butter and it wouldant be much Trouble to him and would help me a **sight**. (William Tesh, Tesh Papers, Duke) Yadkin County

Apr. 14, 1864: he was sent to a hors pitle the second day of April and died the 4. I tell you poly is in a **sight** of trouble about him. (Molly Tesh, Tesh Papers, Duke) Yadkin County

signify *verb* To talk indirectly, suggest.

Jan. 14, 1865: I ses wats the news. he sed bad news. I am sorry to tel you the yankees has bin out last night and they will be out again to night. I ast him how far they come. he couldent tel me. he sed they dident come as far as my hous but talk like the[y] would that night. he sed if they did they wouldent hurt me. I neadent be afraid of them but **signefied** like they would hurt somthing else. (Ann Bowen, Bowen Papers, NCSA) Washington County

simblin *noun* A variety of squash; variant form of *cymling*. [*DARE* chiefly South, South Midland]

Aug. 19, 1864: I hope peas [= peace] will be Made so you can come home. I had a mess of **simblins** for supper. dont you wish you had some. (Martha Poteet, Poteet-Dickson Letters, NCSA) McDowell County

singing *noun* A gathering, often in the evening, for the purpose of group singing, often of hymns.

Jan. 5, 1862: you can tell Dobbins folks that Calloway is Well. me and him and tolliver had a pretty smart **singing** Last night. (G. J. Huntley, Huntley Papers, WCU) Rutherford County

Jan. 8, 1865: tha had **singin** yesdrday and the docter McDonal and gorge robson was all the men tha had. (Flora Ann Campbell, Campbell Papers, Duke) Moore County

sink *verb* past tense *sunk*.

Mar. 11, 1862: thei have had abatle at nofork last weeke thei fout four days and **sunk** three yankys vesels. (Thornton Sexton, Sexton Letters, Duke) Ashe County

Apr. 22, 1864: our men **sunk** two Gun Boats and captured one thousand Lbs. of Bacon and any amount of ther commissary stores. (C. A. Walker, Walker Papers, WCU) Cherokee County

sink *noun* A latrine; usually as plural *sinks*. [*OED* **sink**, noun[1], I 1.a. "A pool or pit formed in the ground for the receipt of waste water, sewage, etc.; a cesspool; a receptacle for filth or ordure. Now *rare*."]

Dec. 2, 1862: If I was at home and could get some milk and butter and chicken and a little brandy I soon would fee[l] like a live person. there was a man died last night going to the **sinks** with the diarear. that is two that has died very sudden in a short time. (James Zimmerman, Zimmerman Papers, Duke) Forsyth County

sircuit preacher see **circuit preacher**

sit see **sot**

sit up, set up *verb* To keep company with the deceased before burial, as at a wake; to assist and provide comfort for someone who is gravely ill; see Overview § II.4.7.

Aug. 14, 1861: I am sorry to say that he is dangerously sick. he has ben sick ever since we have ben here. he is now out of his head all the time. I and Brother **set up** with him all night last night. he has got the Typhoid Fever Wee think. (J. N. Coghill, Coghill Papers, Duke) Granville County

Apr. 14, 1863: he had bin dead a weke before I hird of it tha never let me no a word of it. tha feched him to yours fathers and **saut up** with him one night. (Martha Futch, Futch Letters, NCSA) New Hanover County

Aug. 16, 1864: I have to go to Monroe [a family member whose youngest child had just died] to **set up** and I am A fraid that it is A going to Bee A Bad old go with me. [. . .] I was A **seting up** Last night at Monroe and I am very Sleepy. I cant half write for Agoing to sleep. (Nancy Howard, Brotherton Papers, Duke) Catawba County

skear see **scare**

skearce see **scarce**

skedaddle *verb* To run away, flee, make a hasty retreat (unknown origin, first used at the beginning of the Civil War). [earliest citation in the *OED* is from 1861]

Jan. 11, 1862: I recon you hav hird what he was in the guard hous for. Mark rote that he was in for **skiddadling** in the time of the fight here which was so.

(G. T. Beavers, Upchurch Papers, Duke) Chatham County

Aug. 17, 1862: the most of my boys has **skiddadled** & gone home. all on the account of our staff officers. (A. W. Bell, Bell Papers, Duke) Macon County

Nov. 10, 1862: I donte no wither this place will be our winter quarters or not. I think it likley so if they donte make us **Skedadle** from here. (Dinson Caldwell, Caldwell Coll., ECU) Cabarrus County

May 31, 1863: we left Fairfield Tennessee last Sunday morning the 24th day and got to chattanooga monday morning and then to Dalton gia [= Georgia] monday evening and thear fed Israel [= Frederick Israel] Sam Tow Wilson Ruth and Mathew Corn **Skedadeld** for home. I guess theay are nearly home by this time if theay had good luck. (W. B. Lance, Lance Papers, LSU) Henderson County

skeer see **scare**

skerse see **scarce**

skillet *noun* and *adjective* A frying pan. [*DARE* widespread, but somewhat more frequent Midland, Gulf States, Texas]

May 21, 1862: we haint got nothing to cook in only one **skillet** and a old buckit of a thing of a thing to boil our meet in. (R. C. Love, Love Papers, Duke) Henderson County

Oct. 17, 1863: I will tel you Sumthing about our fair [= fare] doun [= down here?]. it is ruff **Scillit** cake. cold at that. verry often burnt on the outside an raw in the Midle. fat middlin Sum times. beef and pickeld pork. (R. C. Caldwell, Caldwell Coll., ECU) Cabarrus County

skin *noun* A punch made with whisky or brandy to which sweetening is added. [*OED* **skin**, noun, IV, 24. *U.S.*]

Nov. 1862: I would like to be thar to take Chrismus with you an take alittle brandy an honey or brandy is good anuff with out the honey. Jim **skin** is scarce here an I no you need help an I would like to assist you the best I aught. (David Sherrill, Robinson Papers, Duke) Catawba County

skin *verb* To cheat or swindle. [*OED* **skin**, verb, 4.a.; *DARE* skin, verb, B 1, scattered, but somewhat more frequent South Midland, West]

Apr. 14, 1863: susen muney and franceny lee dresed thear selves in mens close and went to a sick mands house and trid **to Skin** him out of his house. (Martha Futch, Futch Letters, NCSA) New Hanover County

skinned eye see **keep a skinned eye**

skipper *noun* A kind of maggot that infests poorly preserved meat. [*OED* **skipper**, noun[1], 2.d.; *DARE* chiefly South, South Midland]

Mar. 16, 1863: I must let you no what we git to eat and how mutch we git. a pound of flour thats a loud for us and some times we dont git more than three quarters of a lb a day and a quarter of a pound of rotten Baken and that old and rank and some of hit nairly eat up with the **skippers**. (Noah Wike, Setzer Papers, Duke) Catawba County

skirmish see **scrumish**

slapjack cakes *noun* A pancake made with cornmeal. [*DARE* **slapjack**, noun, 1; scattered, but chiefly North, North Midland]

Sept. 21, 1862: we get nothin to eat escepting fresh beef and **slapjack cakes**. (C. A. Hege, Hege Papers, MHI) Davidson County

slip *noun* A sweet potato sprout.

Mar. 22, 1862: have the **Slips** beded. bed all the yams and negrobusters and plant the rest and get five bushel from mrs Southerland. (Ichabod Quinn, Quinn Papers, Duke) Duplin County

Apr. 3, 1863: rite to me how the **Slips** kep that I put up before I left thare. (John Futch, Futch Letters, NCSA) New Hanover County

Apr. 5, 1863: I want to no whether your **slippes** is rotten or not and if yow are going to Gett enny boddy to plow for you or not and whether your sow has piged or not and how menny she has. (Daniel Brown, Brown Coll., NCSA) Duplin County

slipe *noun* A strip or long, narrow piece of ground. [see *EDD* **slipe**, *sb.*, 20; *OED* **slipe**, noun[2], "Now *dial.* (and *U.S.*)"]

Oct. 16, 1864: i want to Sow the haw tree peas [= piece] and them Bottoms in wheat and the new bares peas [= piece] in oats. i did intend to Sow All that peas of grond on the Road from the Cotton patch to the Long **Slipe** in wheat and oats. So you may do as you think Best if you think you Can Sew it all Sow the Best of it in wheat and the porest in oats. (Wade Hubbard, Hubbard Papers, Duke) Anson County

slips *noun* A pair of men's underpants; the term appears to have been particularly common in western North Carolina.

Dec. 29, 1861: Caldwell Blair arrived safe to our camps this night a week ago with all there boxes I received mine very gladly it had Some apples Some butter and my **Slips** in it but I have got so big or Something else down here that my **Slips** is to Small for me I had to let them out the full bigness and then they were as tite on me as the Skin. every time I go to draw a long breath I can hear them tear. So if you are very plenty of cloth you may make me another pair and Send to me but make them larger round, they are long anough. (Robert M. Blair, Blair Letters, NCSA) Caldwell County

July 28, 1862: i want you to make me tow pair of pan[t]s and tow pair of **slips** and keap them and i will rite when i neade them. (Larkin Kendrick, Kendrick Papers, NCSA) Cleveland County

Feb. 5, 1863: the shirt and **slips** had some apples rolled up in them and they had rotten and spoiled the cloths. (D. R. Hoyle, Kendrick Papers, NCSA) Cleveland County

May 24, 1863: I can tell you I drawed my cloths yesterday. I got 1 cap 1 coat. 2 Shirts. 2 pair of **slips** 1 pair of pants. 2 pair of cotton socks. 1 pair of shoes. (Daniel Murph, Murph Papers, Duke) Catawba County

Nov. 26, 1863: i am here with one sute of close. i left my yarn **slips** and gloves socks shirt and belt and one pare of pants i drawd all at cam[p] vanc. (Franklin Setzer, Setzer Corr., UVA) Catawba County

small grain *noun* Wheat, rye, oats; grain other than corn.

May 4, 1863: give me all the newes yu Can. i want to no how you Come on farming of it and how yor **small grain** looks. (Isaac Copeland, Copeland Letters, NCSA) Surry County

July 13, 1863: I hear that the **small grain** is injurd very bad. tha sa that the wheat is in the shock yet and is green by the wet wither. (John Revis, Revis Letters, NCSA) Henderson County

July 10, 1864: I want you to write me a long letter as soon as you git this give me a full account of our affars at home the **small grain** the corn crop the fruit and in form me how those trees don. (Alfred N. Proffit, Proffit Family Letters, SHC) Wilkes County

small money *noun phrase* Paper currency of small denominations.

Jan. 5, 1864: I wish we cwod [= could] a bin pad off before Mr Flynt Started back home then I cwod a Sente **Small mony**. (A. J. Spease, Zimmerman Papers, Duke) Forsyth County

small people *noun phrase* Slave children.

Aug. 2, 1856: nelson named to me that master wished mee to white wash magnolia an Belgrade an I will white wash magnolia. master will pleas to wright me whether nellson will white wash Belgrade or no as I need him very bad among my **Small people**. (Henry [Pettigrew slave], Pettigrew Family Papers, SHC) Washington County

smallpox *noun* treated as a plural.

Dec. 24, 1862: I dont want you to come on the the count of the **small pocks**. they say that Barnhart in our Co has got **them**. he is in abou 8 feete of wheare i stay now. I think we will have harde worke to miss **them**. (J. S. Overcash, Overcash Papers, Duke) Rowan County

Feb. 13, 1863: I want you to try and come and see me if it can be in your power. But as the **smallpox** air Still about I will not Insist own you comen tell after their Is a change in **them**. (Isaac Lefevers, Lefevers Papers, NCSA) Catawba County

small rations *noun phrase* Reduced or inadequate rations; same as *short rations*.

June 12, 1862: We halv plenty to Eat and Ware but our **rashones** of whiskey is quite **Small**. we got a dram the other Morning. is the Second drop I hav had Since I Saw you. (Alfred Walsh, Proffit Family Letters, SHC) Wilkes County

Oct. 2, 1862: corn crops is tolerab good. the most of the plases I have ben but we have eat up all the corn whare we have ben and evry thing els that wold do to eat as our **rashens** was very **small** we had to eat what we cold get. we mad the Rosen ears [= roasting ears] fly. (James Keever, Keever Papers, Duke) Lincoln County

Feb. 26, 1863: we ar under marching orders now but whear to i cant tell. we get very **small rations**. hardly a nuff to make out on. (John Futch, Futch Letters, NCSA) New Hanover County

Feb. 27, 1863: we hold prayr meetings in the companey a cashenly [= occasionally] and are doing well considern our **small rashings.** we dont get a nuff to eat but I hope times will get better and I hope to get a furlow when the ware ends. (Jonas Bradshaw, Bradshaw Papers, Duke) Alexander County

smart *adjective*

1. Of children: good, well-behaved, helpful, obedient (this sense not always distinguishable from sense 2 below).

June 12, 1862: Mary kiss William Sarah John Jackson for me, tell them to be **smart** and I will bring them some candy as ther is a pleanty in Wilmington. (J. W. Whitfield, Whitfield Papers, Duke) Nash County

Feb. 15, 1863: tel him to be A **smarte** boy tel i come home. i hope that i will git to come home dis [= this] spring and i will fetch him A nife. (W. P. Cline, Cline Papers, SHC) Catawba County

May 3, 1863: my Dear little Boys. I Rote to sis and in A few days you Shal hear from me. I Sent you some fishooks las week. Be **Smart** and help your mother all you Can. (Green B. Woody, Woody Letters, Confederate Misc., Emory) Yancy County

Nov. 2, 1864: you must Bee a **Smarte** Boy and obey your mother. al So Sissey you must be Bee A **Smarte** little girl and bee good to the Baby and call it Jobey. (J. R. Redmond, Military Coll., Civil War, NCSA) Buncombe County

2. Industrious, diligent, effective or productive in working. [*DARE* chiefly South, South Midland]

Nov. 16, 1856: I beleive my Children All keeps even with the world and sum to speair. tha was All poor an marred poor but all mared **smart** men. (Stephen Phillips, Phillips Papers, Duke) Robeson County

July 28, 1864: hear martha is wevin she can weve three and fore yards a day I think it is purty **smart** fore the first but she has got hirn out and wevin on a nother pece. (Catherine Ramsey. Futch Letters, NCSA) New Hanover County

July 28, 1864: she is a good girl but she is not **smart** nor she wont work if she can help it and that wont do for you. if you ever com home you you will need some one to help you work. (Hannah Smithwick, Smithwick Papers, Duke) Martin County

Sept. 21, 1864: Papa I was about the best hand there was in the Fodder field So you may know I am a **smart** girl. (Eliza Hubbard, Hubbard Papers, Duke) Anson County

3. Healthy, well. [*DARE* especially New England]

Oct. 23, 1864: tel george Mary is rite **smart.** she has had some chils with her milk but she ses she is rite **smart** now. (Ann Bowen, Bowen Papers, NCSA) Washington County

4. Considerable, big. See also **right smart**

Jan. 5, 1862: you can tell Dobbins folks that Calloway is Well. me and him and tolliver had a pretty **smart** singing Last night. (G. J. Huntley, Huntley Papers, WCU) Rutherford County

smartly *adverb* Quickly.

Nov. 26, 1861: we have but one man in the hospitle at this time that is R..L Baily. he has had the Newmony but is **smartly** on the mend. I think he will come out in a few days. (P. S. Whitner, Whitner Papers, Duke) Catawba County

Feb. 15, 1864: I must Say to you that father has been very porley But he is improving **smartly** at this time. (J. W. Edwards, Keever Papers, Duke) Catawba County

Sept. 5, 1864: the filly ihave got her in your uncle bill pasture. She is thin in<??> but has mended up Som and has grod **Smartly**. (Thomas Brotherton, Brotherton Papers, Duke) Catawba County

smell *verb* variant past tense *smelt.*

Sept. 9, 1862: I saw more ded men than I ever saw before. they **smelt** aufull bad. the lost of the yankes ware seventeen thousand so they acknowledge that number in thare Papers. our loss I do not know. (J. F. Coghill, Coghill Papers, Duke) Granville County

snaps *noun plural* Snap beans, green beans. [*DSME* **snap, snap bean** *noun; DARE* scattered, but chiefly South, South Midland]

June 11, 1864: I would like to be at home A bout the time Irish potatoes gits larg Enough to Eat and **snaps.** I hope that I shal get home by that time If I live. (T. C. Wester, Wester Coll., NCSA) Franklin County

so *adverb* and *conjuction*

1. following the verb *be,* and expressing uncertainty about whether a particular event or circumstance is true or not. [*OED* **so**, adverb and conjunction, I, 3.a.]

   Sept. 25, 1861: you need not believe what you here for one halfe of it is not **so**. (J. W. Williams, Williams Papers, Duke) Onslow County

   June 24, 1863: Sally I Heard that Brother George was dead and I reckon from all accounts its **so**. (Sally Bauldin, Hundley Family Letters, SHC) Stokes County

   July 8, 1863: it was reported hear this morning that the yankees have Taken Vixburg which I hope is not **so** and I rather think it is **so**. (Alfred N. Proffit, Proffit Family Letters, SHC) Wilkes County

   Aug. 11, 1864: hit is raported that the yankes is foleing back now but I dont no whither hit is **so** or not but we will fine out to morrow. (Gorry Jackson, Jackson Family Corr., Notre Dame) Moore County

2. following the verb *be* in a conditional subordinate clause.

   June 22, 1861: you wanted to know how I am satisfied. I would be better Satisfied if it was **so** that I Could be back in old haywood. (J. N. Cunningham, Cunningham Letters, NCSA) Haywood County

   Nov. 3, 1862: iwill stay at home tell you come if it is **sow** ican. (Sarepta Revis, Revis Letters, NCSA) Henderson County

3. following *get* and indicating a change in circumstances that allows or will allow something to take place.

   Aug. 13, 1862: I went over to see the boys day befor yesterday and they wer well. Hardy is geting **so** he can be up and about agin. (Neill McLeod, McLeod Letters, SHC) Moore County

   Feb.10, 1863: I think there will be another battle here as soon as the wether and the ground gets **so** the yankeys can advance. (James Zimmerman, Zimmerman Papers, Duke) Forsyth County

   Jan. 9, 1865: my toe that I spoke of droping the stick of wood on has got **so** I can wear my shoe and my thumb has got well. (Ann Bowen, Bowen Papers, NCSA) Washington County

so as *conjuntion*

1. So that, in such a way, in such a manner (that). [*DSME* **so's**. conjunction; *OED* **so**, adverb and conjunction, 20.a.]

   Mar. 23, 1858: if you come to the west & com by land starte the fist [= first] days of september **so as** you can get her be fore the wther gets so cold. (David Headrick, Frank Papers, Duke) Davidson County

   Aug. 14, 1862: I hope the lord wil provid some way for me & you all **so as** we may see one another one more time. (Austin Brown, Brown Family Papers, Duke) Johnston County

   Mar. 25, 1863: he is A giting **sow as** he can walk A bout wright smart now. I daunt think they is any danger but what he wil git over it now if he daunt take the relaps A gane. (B. C. Jackson, Jackson Family Corr., Notre Dame) Moore County

2. followed by an infinitive.

   Oct. 2, 1862: I want you to write to me as soon as you get this **so as** to lett me know if you got the money. (James A. Patton, Patton Letters, Emory) Granville County

   Nov. 24, 1862: I am verry sore from marching so hard, and have a severe pain in my sholder. the rest is **so as** to be about. (James Zimmerman, Zimmerman Papers, Duke) Forsyth County

sody, sodey *noun* Baking soda; variant form *sody*. [*DARE* chiefly South, South Midland, Northeast]

Nov. 3, 1862: tell mother to send me 2 pair of gallasses, some soap and a little **sody** if she can. (C. A. Hege, Hege Papers, MHI) Davidson County

Mar. 22, 1864: Provisions is very carce [= scarce] in this country tho we git tolerable rations. flower not bolted tho it dose very well. neads no **sodey.** the boys dos not grumble & seems content. (Stephen Whitaker, Whitaker Papers, NCSA) Cherokee County

some *adjective*

1. before numbers. [*OED* **some**, B. adjective, 9.a. "Used with numbers to indicate an approximate amount or estimate, and passing into an adv. with the sense 'about, nearly, approximately'"]

Aug. 19, 1862: we expect to drill here **some** three or four weeks and go on to the regular Army. (John H. Hundley, Hundley Family Letters, SHC) Stokes County

Sept. 1, 1863: the sick has been cawled on to defend the Town of Stanton **some** three or fawr times. (Alfred N. Walsh, Proffit Family Letters, SHC) Wilkes County

Nov. 10, 1864: if they will get up a partition tha[t] it is nessary to hav such a machanic at home as I am and get **som** ten 10 or 12 siners [= signers] or as many as they can and hav them swern and get the county seal to it and get the Enroling offiser to sine it and send it to Jeneral homes [= Holmes] at raleigh. they may get me off. (F. A. Bleckley, Bleckley Papers, Duke) Catawba County

2. before *few*. [*OED* **some**, B. adjective, 8.c.]

Nov. 26, 1861: Our healt is tolerable good. we have **some** few mesels cases but I think they are about ofer. we have but one man in the hospitle at this time. (P. S. Whitner, Whitner Papers, Duke) Catawba County

June 12, 1862: I had the plasure of seeing our Noble president **Some** few days ago. (Alfred Walsh, Proffit Family Letters, SHC) Wilkes County

Nov. 20, 1864: I Sent you **some** few stamps in the last two or or three Letters. (Henry Bowen, Bowen Papers, NCSA) Washington County

somewheres *adverb* Somewhere.

Aug. 26, 1862: Dear Wife. Link tole me that Elija Hoffman and Marcus and John was all dead. Elija dide since they come back and Marcus on the Isleand and John a bout Richmond **Some whares**. (W. F. Wagner, *Confederate Soldier,* 11) Catawba County

song ballat see **ballat**

sop *verb* To soak up gravy, syrup, honey, or molasses with bread. [*DSME* **sop**, B verb]

Sept. 29, 1863: your make of surop was first rate sure. I would like to have about forty dropes of it now to **sop** my gressy Bisquet in. (A. A. Jackson, Jackson Family Corr., Notre Dame) Moore County

sop *noun* A sodden tuft of grass in a hayfield. [*OED* **sop,** noun[1], 3; *EDD* **sop**, *sb[1]*, 3]

Feb. 15, 1863: we march fore days in the snow and Rain and lay out every night in it. it was the hardist time I ever saw in my life. I lay one night in the snow 7 inches deep in a old field and the next night I lay on a peace of **sop** in the Water whair it was three or fore inches deep. (Joseph Cowand, Cowand Papers, Duke) Bertie County

sorrow *adjective* Sorry. [*OED* **sorrow**, B. adjective, "Now *arch.* and *U.S. regional*"]

May 26, 1862: I was varry **sorrow** to hear that ant Jane was ded. (Jesse Shipman, Shipman Family Corr., Notre Dame) Henderson County

Mar. 2, 1863: I am **sorrow** to have to frank my letter but I Cant git stamps hear an they aint no post office hear for me to pay postage at. (G. H. Hundley, Hundley Family Letters, SHC) Stokes County

Mar. 15, 1863: I receved your kind and affectionly letter on the 6 day of March and was glad to hir from you but was **sorrow** to that you was not well. (Martha Futch, Futch Letters, NCSA) New Hanover County

June 10, 1863: I recieved Your Kind letter Yisterday and was Truly glad to hear From You but I am **sorrow**

to tell You what a Condition it Found me in. (William Tesh, Tesh Papers, Duke) Yadkin County

sorter, sorty *adverb* variant forms of *sort of.*

Jan. 15, 1863: i can make out very well i Suppose for we live **sorty** hog fashion Any how. (James Hackett Hackett Papers, Duke) Guilford County

June 15, 1863: ther had like to bin alitlet batel her the other day with the boys that runaway an the melishey but tha got hit **sorter** seteld. (J. A. W. Revis, Revis Letters, NCSA) Henderson County

Mar. 24, 1864: we heard that Cate was married. it **sorty** got me when I heard it. I thaught she might of tole me if she had any such notion. (Noah Wagner, *Confederate Soldier,* 88) Catawba County

Oct. 18, 1864: we can buy Sweet potatoes and get some pumpkins and we can buy flour and we we can **sorter** make out to live. (W. H. Horton, Councill Papers, Duke) Watauga County

Jan. 11, 1865: you must Excuse me for not writing To you sooner for I have bin at the hospitle parteof the tim and had a ball cut out of my hand. it was lodged against the bones in the back of my haind. it nearly made me twist my tale when the doctors was cuting it out but it is nearly healed up. I can **sorty** rit. that is all that I do. (J. W. Parlier, Military Coll., Civil War, NCSA) Wilkes County

sot[1] *verb* variant form of *sat.*

May 4, 1864: I just came of gard and got your leter and read it and **Sot** doun and answerd it. So I was glad to here from you all. (R. C. Caldwell, Caldwell Coll., ECU) Cabarrus County

sot[2], **sat** *verb* variant forms of *set.*

June 15, 1862: Could I just see you and them just one our it would do me more good [than] the bes thing that ever could be **Sot** before me wen I was hungry. I never have craved enny thing as mutch in my life as I have craved to see you and the little Childrean. (Isaac Lefevers, Lefevers Papers, NCSA) Catawba County

Mar. 10, 1863: the rail road bridge was **sot** on fire by Some one but thank god It never done any harm. (J. W. Williams, Williams Papers, Duke) Onslow County

Sept. 1, 1863: I have profest of my Sins and I am going to Jine the church and be baptised in afew days but I dont no ritely what day for the minesters has not **Sot** the day yet. (John Hartman, Hartman Papers, Duke) Rowan County

Mar. 16, 1864: they was some of them negros got in a house and they Shot till the las. the[y] **Sot** the house on fire and they Staid in till they Burnt up 5 of them. (J. W. Love, Love Papers, Duke) Henderson County

Dec. 1870: in 1861 the manspation had not taken place but I was in the prtection By the youion Troops an **Sat** free by Presadence Lincon at the manspation I think in 1863 if I mis Stake not. (Charles Jones, *Freedom,* ser. 2: 798) Craven County

souse *noun* A food item made primarily from the meat picked from a cooked hog's head (and sometimes feet), often seasoned with vinegar (*sour souse*). Same as *headcheese.* [*DSME* **souse**[1], **souse meat** noun; *OED* **souse**, noun[1], 1.a. "Now chiefly *dial.* and *U.S.*"]

Jan. 17, 1863: If Henry comes I want him to fetch me a Box of provision. I want sosedg inpoticlar & some good sower **souse**. I Recken you will have now [= no] hash to send. you nead not send much Pork for fear it may be that we will have to move & then I could not take it. (Isaac Lefevers, Lefevers Papers, NCSA) Catawba County

Spanish oak *noun* Usually referring to *Quercus falcata,* southern red oak. [*OED* **Spanish oak**, in quote, "1852 C. Morfit [. . .] (1853) 98 *Quercus Falcata* [is] known in Delaware, Maryland and Virginia by the name of Spanish oak"]

Dec. 25, 1858: as you requested to know what kind of timber we have in this country. thare is white oke. black oke. red oake. **Spanish oake** and hickrey black white and scaly barke. black walnut white walnut. mulbery. cotton wood. wile chery. elum and lin wood. shugar trees. sicamore and buckei. buroake. severl other kinds too tedous to mention. the under groth is mostley hasle and shumake. (William Boss, Frank Papers, Duke) Davidson County

spare ribs *noun plural* Pork rib bones with meat attached.

Dec. 4, 1863: we is agoing to send you boath some bred if we can hav room and wold send grate meney more things if we had they chance to do so. our hogs is nerley fat. we will have a plenty of backcann and **spear ribs** by Christmast. (Effie Jane Jackson, Jackson Family Corr., Notre Dame) Moore County

Dec. 5, 1863: I wish I was at home now to get some Back bones and **Spar ribs** and Cabage. (William Tesh, Tesh Papers, Duke) Yadkin County

Dec. 1863: Tell Hugh that I hope he will continew to Improve and be well soon so he can fly round sevierley and help me eat **spare ribs** and Potatoes if I get home this winter. (A. A. Jackson, Jackson Family Corr., Notre Dame) Moore County

specie *noun* Money in the form of coins. [*OED* **specie**, noun, II 6.]

July 9, 1864: the yankeys is a Diserting and comeing over to us. Some of the yankes sa that **specie** is three Dollars and 15 cts, and this will brake up the ware if nothing else Dont. (W. D. Smith, W. D. Smith Papers, Duke) Davie County

Nov. 30, 1864: they went to plundering the house so aunt Betsy had her **specia** in a matteras. she caught it to put it in her pocket and they snached it away from her and she got down on her nees and beged them and cryed to them and they gave her back 11 dollars. (Ann Bowen, Bowen Papers, NCSA) Washington County

spell *noun* A period or attack of an illness. [*DSME* **spell**, noun, 2]

Jan. 15, 1863: I had A verry hard **spell** of Tyfoid Fever last Winter spring and summer. I got no corn planted hardly. I could not hire any person so I made no corn. (B. B. Marley, Vance Papers, NCSA) Randolph County

Aug. 8, 1863: I am a volenteer in the Confedeate Servis and is not abel for the Servis by having a hard **Spell** of the feaver about 10 monts a go. (J. H. Hudson, Vance Papers, NCSA) Burke County

Apr. 8, 1864: i was truly glad to here from you and here you was all alive and well. i am sorry to here bille has them **spels** yiet. ithink hee had better wash his head 2 or 3 times aday in cold water. (Silas Stepp, Stepp Letters, UNCA) Buncombe County

spile, spilt *verb* and *adjective* (from past participle); variant forms of *spoil, spoiled.* [*DARE* chiefly South, South Midland; formerly also New England]

Dec. 25, 1862: I want you to send me some pie and custers if you can. the weather is cole and the[y] wont **spile** soone. (W. F. Wagner, *Confederate Soldier,* 31) Catawba County

July 16, 1863: it raines her everyday and some time day and nite. the water has **Spilt** evry thing along the water corses her. (Daniel Setzer, Setzer Papers, Duke) Catawba County

Oct. 10, 1864: I Receivd that Pervisione you Send By Danile and was glad to gite ite but it wase alle **spilte** excepte the tatoes. they was good. (Daniel Abernethy, Abernethy Papers, Duke) Catawba County

Mar. 6, 1865: tell me how there shoes is lasting and whether they take care of theme or not and dont let them **spile** for want of fixen. (Franklin Setzer, Setzer Corr., UVA) Catawba County

spill *verb* variant past participle *spilt.*

Feb. 25, 1862: it appears that the tide of war is about to turn against the south yet I Waunt to right nothing discourging for thare Will haft to Be Lots of Blood **spilt** Before We are subjugated. (G. J. Huntley, Huntley Papers, WCU) Rutherford County

spite *noun* A negative, sometimes hateful feeling directed at someone, especially in the phrase *to have a spite at.* [*OED* **spite**, noun, 3.a.]

Oct. 12, 1863: wee wais tuck prisoners at Roan oak. after the perroal wais out I went Back to the old Co[mpany] again and thare wais only one man in the Campany that I ever sawe bee fore and hit seamid like the[y] had a **spite** at ous as wee wais from Columbus [County]. (Jacob Herring Vance Papers, NCSA) Columbus County

sponge bread *noun* Bread leavened with yeast. [*EDD* **sponge**, *sb.*, 2., "Leaven; leavened dough; any preparation used for raising dough"]

Jan. 21, 1864: Standing out in the rain and win day and knigh is a nuf to kill a mule and not half fed at that a litle **Spung bred** and a quarter of a pound of

Stinkin meet a day. about a nuf of bread for one mele. (Robert Carpenter, Carpenter Family Papers, ECU) Chatham County

spree *noun* A drinking bout, boisterous frolic, prolonged period of carousing. See also **take a spree**. [*OED* **spree**, noun.]

May 20, 1862: When you Write a gain give the fool purticulars of the booys Success on that **Spree** you Spoke of. (Alfred Walsh, Proffit Family Letters, SHC) Wilkes County

Oct. 1863: I will go Back & Leave no more without Permission as I am sorry I Ever Left which I never would if I had not of bin in a **spree**. if you will be so good as to try to Help me out of this case I never will be caught in such an other. (W. Quick, Vance Papers, NCSA) Richmond County

sprout *noun* A young child, infant, newborn. [*OED* **sprout**, noun, 3. *fig.*, b. "*U.S. colloq.* and *Slang*. A young person, a child."]

June 10, 1861: thers is good helth all over the country. old Jimy Deaton got tite and fell out of the bugy and broke his thy and two ribs and is very bad off. your cozen terisa has gote a **sprout** and youre aunt Sarah has a fine Sone. (Joseph Overcash, Overcash Papers, Duke) Rowan County

sprout *verb* To clear ground of small saplings, suckers, and brush in preparation for plowing. [*DARE* chiefly South Midland]

Feb. 6, 1862: you Can put him to **Sprouting** and Cleaning up grond tel time to plow. (M. W. Parris, Parris Papers, WCU) Jackson County

Aug. 30, 1864: try and get lackes to Sowe it and you find the Seed and the plows to breake the ground and Lewis can **sprout** it. (Alexander Keever, Keever Papers, Duke) Lincoln County

spung bread see **sponge bread**

spunk *noun* Spirit, courage, fortitude. [*OED* **spunk**, noun, 5.a.]

Oct. 13, 1862: I tell you we Saw hard times. Some times we would have to do with out rations 2 days at a time and march all day and mabe half the night and then Start next morning By day light. I tell you that tries a Fellows **Spunk** certain. (William Tesh, Tesh Papers, Duke) Yadkin County

Mar. 27, 1863: you Sead Some thing about the Wimen presing flour. I glory in the ladyes **Spunk**. (John Hartman, Hartman Papers, Duke) Rowan County

Apr. 5, 1863: I heard last week in sals bary NC thare was a potion of soldiers wives armed themselves and went to the flower speclaters and demanded flower. he gave them twenty three bbls th[e]n they went to the man that had Salt. he Gave them one sack and they went to the man that had molases and he Gave them all he had and they <Said?> they would be back when they eat what they had. Dear wife I Glory in ther **Spunck**. (Daniel Brown, Brown Coll., NCSA) Duplin County

squally *adjective* Troubled, uncertain, threatening. [*OED* **squally**, adjective[2], 3. *fig.* "Chiefly *U.S.*"]

Feb. 15, 1863: the times is also a geting very **squally** in this Cuntry. there is a Strong talke of the hole Malishey a being ordered oute and it has causd a mity Confusion amung the people. (Samuel C. Phillips, Woody Letters, Confederate Misc., Emory) Mitchell County

June 1, 1864: times is very **Squaly** her. fighting is going on her yet. we ar in our Ditches and have to ly low to keep out of the way of the bulets. (L. W. Griffin, Griffin Papers, NCSA) Rutherford County

Jan. 2, 1865: I hope the time well soon come when I can come to see you all again but I cant tel you when i can get a furlow for the times is so **squaley** now. (Henry Bowen, Bowen Papers, NCSA) Washington County

start *verb* To send (a letter, money, or other items). [*EDD* **start**, verb, 2, "to dispatch, send off"; *DARE* chiefly Southern Appalachians]

Jan. 22, 1862: me and Wm Jones and Tolliver Hughes and James Wood **started** some money home to day By David Harrill. he promised to Take it to Berry Mcdaniels and Leave it thare. (G. J. Huntley, Huntley Papers, WCU) Rutherford County

Feb. 6, 1862: I **Started** a leter last monday morning and I want to now what days my leters gits thar. (M. W. Parris, Parris Papers, WCU) Jackson County

June 17, 1863: I Pay for all the Letters I **start**. it is Jest meanness of the Post Masters that you have to pay for the Letters I send to you. (Sarepta Revis, Revis Letters, NCSA) Henderson County

June 26, 1863: for fear you dident git the letter I **started** from Gordonville I will tell you some thing a bout A J. (Alfred N. Proffit, Proffit Family Letters, SHC) Wilkes County

Jan. 28, 1864: all that you **started** in the box it was all rite as you **started** it. only the potatoes was partly spoilt. (Alexander Keever, Keever Papers, Duke) Lincoln County

start naked *adjective phrase* Completely naked; earlier form of *stark naked*. [*OED* **start naked**, adjective; *DARE* South, South Midland]

Nov. 11, 1864: my dear you disapointed me verry mutch about that Soldier [= a male child] and it is agirl at last. I am verry Sorry that you air geting all the help and me none. I will hafto renigg trumps and Start anew game. I reckon the next time I must Strip **Start naked** and then it will Sertnly be aboy. that is the old Saying. my dear you Sead that I Shold Send it aname. I cant think of no name for it. you name the girls and I will name the boys. (John Hartman, Hartman Papers, Duke) Rowan County

start up *verb* To have, begin, take notice of; see Overview § II.4.7. [perhaps related to *OED* **start**, verb, 13. **start up**, d.]

Dec. 25, 1863: have you all got any christmas down your way. there is none about here. I wish that you could come home and we would **start up** christmas. (E. E. Lindsay, Taylor Papers, Duke) Orange County

starver *noun* One who suffers from hunger, starvation. [*OED* **starver**, noun, 1.b.]

Feb. 9, 1863: wee hav seen the time when wee cod call our Little Childen and our Husban to our tables an hav a plenty an now wee hav Becom Beggars and **Starvers** an now way to help our Selvs. (Margaret Harrel, Vance Papers, NCSA) Wayne County

steady see **study** *adverb*

steal *verb*

1. past tense and past participle *stoled.*

Aug. 9, 1862: the close that you Sent to me got **Stold** before they got here. (J. W. Williams, Williams Papers, Duke) Onslow County

Jan. 7, 1864: Pery Walker sed you had Washs gloves blanket and to send them to him. I want you to tell him if he was as willing for other people to hav there oune as he was for Wash to hav his I would got my ring in the place of some one els. he talked like you had **stold** the Blanket and gloves. (Martha Poteet, Poteet-Dickson Letters, NCSA) McDowell County

2. past participle *stole.*

Dec. 18, 1862: I have heard since I commenced this letter that the boxes have been broken open and the things **stole**. (C. A. Hege, Hege Papers, MHI) Davidson County

Apr. 13, 1864: I hear you have lost all your meat and some person has **stole** your milch Cows. (C. A. Walker, Walker Papers, WCU) Cherokee County

Dec. 1870: I Enlested for three years Sooner Discharge. that was in the case if the war Should End in Side of three years the 35 US [= 35th USCT] Sould be Discharge. My Discharge was **Stole** in the city of Charleston S.C. (Charles Jones, *Freedom,* ser. 2: 798) Craven County

still *adjective* Quiet; superlative *stillest.*

Oct. 9, 1862: there is no talk of a fight now. it is the **stillist** time I most ever saw. (G. T. Beavers, Upchurch Papers, Duke) Chatham County

still *verb* To distill alcohol, especially to distill brandy from fruit and whisky from corn. [*DSME* **still**[2], A, verb]

Feb. 15, 1863: thare is Som men **Stilling** right a way and has not stoped at all sence tha got done **Stilling** fruit tha comenced on corn and is selling thare whiskey as fast as tha can make hit. (E. D. Hawkins, Vance Papers, NCSA) Rutherford County

July 8, 1863: as to my **stiling** I sufferd the neighbours to make A fu runs but all that was **stild** was not Enought to Keep my hogs from suffering. som died. there fore I did not **stil** or sufferd to be **stilled** more grain then I would have had to fed to my stock or lost them. (Charles Cison, Vance Papers, NCSA) Transylvania County

June 15, 1864: I want you to **Still** our one [= own] froot this year if you have enny to **Still**. (Daniel Setzer, Setzer Papers, Duke) Catawba County

Nov. 15, 1864: that brandy is not **stilled** yet an as soon as it is **stilled** i will send you som. (Hannah Peterson, Peterson Papers, Duke) Catawba County

stiller *noun* One who distills alcohol. [*DSME* **stiller**, noun]

Feb. 15, 1863: you know when the stills is boling hit up that the **stiller** can aford to give all most Eny prise for corn. (E. D. Hawkins, Vance Papers, NCSA) Rutherford County

May 7, 1863: these persons that furnish this corn to **stillers**, willnot sell a grain to the poor for love or money. I want to know how a Justice will see that the law is put inforce, when the **Stillers** say that if a Justice issues a warrant they will burn their houses and barns. (T. J. Bicknell, Vance Papers, NCSA) Wilkes County

still house *noun* A shed built over a still. [*DSME* **still house**, noun]

May 3, 1863: [I] Can inform you Brother jeffer left one monday an one [= on] wendsday thare **still house** burnt A way an all that was in it. (Keziah Hefner, Hefner Papers, NCSA) Catawba County

stout *adjective* Healthy, strong, in good health. [*OED* **stout**, A. adjective, II Physical senses, 6.a., "Strong in body; of powerful build. Now only *U.S. dial*" and 6.b. "In robust health, 'strong,' esp. with reference to recovery from illness. *Obs.* exc. *Sc*"]

Jan. 22, 1863: I have bin sick ever sins the fite. I have ben in the hospitle ever sinse. I hav got **stout** A nuf to go to the redgt. (J. C. McFee, McFee Letters, SRNB) Buncombe County

Aug. 20, 1863: since I last wrote you I have had a vary savear attact of disintary which weakened me vary mutch but I am now over it and tolearble **Stout**. (Alfred N. Proffit, Proffit Family Letters, SHC) Wilkes County

Nov. 24, 1863: I Feel a heap **stouter** and Look better than I did but my Legs is a little stiff Yet. (William Tesh, Tesh Papers, Duke) Yadkin County

June 16, 1864: My baby will be 4 weeks old Saturday Night. she was born the 21 of May. write to Me what to name her. I had the best time I ever had and I hav bin the **stoutest** ever sens. I haint lay in bed in day time in two Weeks today. (Martha Poteet, Poteet-Dickson Letters, NCSA) McDowell County

Sept. 11, 1864: i have bin verry bad of with the Collick A few dayes back But thanks Be to god i have Recoverd and **Stout**. (Wade Hubbard, Hubbard Papers, Duke) Anson County

straight *noun* The truth. [*OED* **straight**, B. noun, e. **the straight**]

June 13, 1862: hope that I never will see a nuther such a time as Long as I live but I Recond I will have to face the Musick a gin in a few days I want to see you all myty bad but you know that it is out of my power to do so. I will give you the **strate**. (James A. May, Military Coll., Civil War, NCSA) Guilford County

strange *adjective* Newsworthy (a common convention in nineteenth-century letter writing).

May 17, 1863: I have nothing **strange** to rite to you at presant. (H. T. Ward, Revis Letters, NCSA) Henderson County

July 27, 1864: Thare is no **strange** news. times are tolearbly Still along the lines. (Alfred N. Proffit, Proffit Family Letters, SHC) Wilkes County

strike hands *verb phrase* To stroke, caress hands. [*OED* **strike**, verb, II 3.a., To stroke, and VIII 69.a. **To strike hands**; *EDD* **strike**, verb, II 13, "To touch gently, to stroke"]

May 29, 1864: i wood give any thing i have got to get home and stay with you the rest of my days. i will doo the best ican. you must doo the same. i hope wee will see each other again. i wood bea sow glad to **strike hands** with you. (Silas Stepp, Stepp Letters, UNCA) Buncombe County

strip fodder *verb phrase* To remove leaves from corn stalks in order to dry for cattle feed; same as **pull fodder**.

Sept. 17, 1860: I have just finish **Striping fodder** to day. ther will be 50 Stax. (Thomas Harding, Blount Papers, NCSA) Beaufort County

strong *adjective* Of meat and butter: rancid, having an unpleasant odor. [*DSME* **strong**, A, adjective]

Aug. 2, 1863: We have verry warm weather now and plenty of **strong** bacon and wormy crackers to eat. (C.A. Hege, Hege Papers, MHI) Davidson County

Dec. 5, 1863: I eat the Last of my butter the 28th of last month but it was a geting sorta **strong**. but I wish I had some more Like it. (William Tesh, Tesh Papers, Duke) Yadkin County

strop *noun* A heavy strip of leather used for sharpening razors or other cutting edges, a *razor strop*.

Nov. 15, 1864: i will send you that **strop** an som turnips an som other things when ever i get the chance. (Hannah Peterson, Peterson Papers, Duke) Catawba County

strow, strew *verb* variant past tense *strowed*.

Sept. 9, 1862: when wee get to the edge of a field wee saw A few yankes but when wee got whare wee could see ded yankes. I suppose thare was several hundred of them for they ware **streod** all along for about 5 miles. (J. F. Coghill, Coghill Papers, Duke) Granville County

strumpet *noun* A woman of low moral character, a harlot.

May 3, 1863: I Can inform you that old adam Lenze think that thare is no world for he will just will run after his **strumpet** an he will never will quit it in this world. (Keziah Hefner, Hefner Papers, NCSA) Catawba County

study *verb* To think, ponder, consider, worry. [*DARE* chiefly South, South Midland, Texas]

June 18, 1862: I dont dout but what you **Study** as mutch a bout mee as I do about you but you have the the childrean with you and they air a great Sattesfaction to you while I am absent from you and them all. (Isaac Lefevers, Lefevers Papers, NCSA) Catawba County

July 12, 1862: I want you to take evry thing fare an easy an dont **Study** About me too much for I hope the Lord will take care of us all. (J. W. Williams, Williams Papers, Duke) Onslow County

Oct. 20, 1862: try and bare yure tobles and dont **study** too mutch. but we cannot helpe **studing** when we think of the loved ones thates lefte us. (Mary Long, Long Family Papers, NCSA) Alamance County

Oct. 4, 1864: you dont now how mutch I **Study** about you and my littel Children. I would love to kiss that littel one that I haint never seen. (F. M. Poteet, Poteet-Dickson Letters, NCSA) McDowell County

study *noun* A thought, preoccupation.

Mar. 5, 1862: my ingoyement ant much for my **study** is about you in the day and dreme of you at nite. (Martha Futch, Futch Letters, NCSA) New Hanover County

Dec. 26, 1864: it is my daily **study** to think of you and think and feel how glad I should be to see you. (Ann Bowen, Bowen Papers, NCSA) Washington County

study *adverb* Steadily, continuously, regularly; variant form of *steady*. [*DARE* **steady**, adjective and adverb, A 2; chiefly South, South Midland]

Sept. 6, 1862: wee have dun sum hard marching for the last thre weekes. we have marched **study**. our horses is all broken doun and wee are stoped fore a few dase to recrut up. (Bardin Brown, Brown Family Papers, Duke) Johnston County

June 3, 1863: I think this war wont last mutch longer for they are Runing off **Studdy**. Some Regment 35 And forty leaves at Atime. I think that is what will end this Cruel ware. (W. H. Brotherton, Brotherton Papers, Duke) Catawba County

May 6, 1864: I am well at this time but I am vary tired of marcheing. we bin marcheing four days right **Study.** we are clost to nubern. (J. W. Joyce, Joyce Papers, MHI) Stokes County

stuff *noun* Crops, provisions, garden produce. See also **breadstuff**. [*OED* **stuff**, noun[1], I, 1.e.]

Dec. 1, 1862: I had rote in the other Letters that I thought you had better put off one of the horses some way or nother and I want you to keep the one you rather. fan would bee the most valable as thier could be another colte Raised from hur But I want you to Keep the one you like beast and the one that you think will Suit you the best in work it is sirten we cant keep them all the way corn and **stuff** is sellen. (Isaac Lefevers, Lefevers Papers, NCSA) Catawba County

Oct. 7, 1863: tel me if the[y] have took the tenth of youer **stuf** ar not. i tel you not [to] let them have it. (W. P. Cline, Cline Papers, SHC) Catawba County

such *adjective, pronoun* variant forms *sich, sech.*

July 1, 1863: i think you ar A Man that hase Got A feling for all **sech** Wiming an for that resen i rite to you A bout my case an i shall be bound to have some help. (F. E. Proctor, Vance Papers, NCSA) Edgecombe County

Oct. 6, 1863: Dear Sir I request one faver of you as I am not ~~fit~~ able for Sirves and I want to no of you if the is any chance to git a detale in any publick work **Sich** as Shew making or any other worke that I can doe. (J. D. Baker, Vance Papers, NCSA) Cumberland County

Dec. 19, 1863: Sich men will See hard times when the Solders get home. (R. C. Caldwell, Caldwell Coll., ECU) Cabarrus County

such like *pronoun phrase* Such a thing or things. [*DSME* **such like**]

June 28, 1863: Ad Shepperd Be longs to this Reg mant But he has not Bin with us mutch. he has Bin on detail the most of his time to work on Brigges and **Sutch like**. (J. W. Reese, Reese Papers, Duke) Buncombe County

sufferance *noun* The suffering of trouble, pain, or hardship. [*OED* **sufferance**, noun, 2.a., *arch.*]

Feb. 15, 1864: Well Mother you said that you was affraid that I was on **sufferance** when I writen hom for somthing to eate. you kneed not oneas yourself a bout that for I get a plenty to eate all the time. (D. R. Barnhill, Military Coll., Civil War, NCSA) Bladen County

sugar tree *noun* A sugar maple, *Acer saccharum*. [*DARE* chiefly Midland]

Dec. 25, 1858: as you requested to know what kind of timber we have in this country. thare is white oke. black oke. red oake. Spanish oake and hickrey black white and scaly barke. black walnut white walnut. mulbery. cotton wood. wile chery. elum and lin wood. **shugar trees**. sicamore and buckei. buroake. severl other kinds too tedous to mention. the under groth is mostley hasle and shumake. (William Boss, Frank Papers, Duke) Davidson County

sumac see **shumake**

sundown *noun* The time when the sun sets. [*OED* **sundown | sun-down**, noun, "Chiefly *U.S., English dial.*, and *S. Afr., Austral.*, etc."]

Nov. 2, 1864: poor little Francis Emmer is dead. she died the 29 of oct last saturday a little while before **sundown.** I wrote to you about the sore in her Mouth. her chin rotted and come loos f[r]om its Jaw bone and 5 of her teeth come out and her toung turned black. it was the pittifullest looking little Mortal you ever saw. (Martha Poteet, Poteet-Dickson Letters, NCSA) McDowell County

sure *adjective* see **shore**

sure, shore, shure *adverb* For sure, for certain; commonly used at the end of a sentence.

Oct. 4, 1861: We had A mery time to get here **shore.** (J. W. Love, Love Papers, Duke) Henderson County

Feb. 26, 1862: if the yankees comes hear Wee Will giv tham the best that is in our Shop **Shore**. (John A. Long, Long Family Papers, SHC) Alamance County

Sept. 12, 1862: thare is lots of wounded soldiers comes heare on thar way home. they are pittiful looking persons **shure**. (John Ingram, Ingram Papers, Duke) Forsyth County

Mar. 22, 1863: before they had gone far they wore toll as Shure as they went back they would not be allowed any witness an be shot **shure**. (A. Zachery, Vance Papers, NCSA) Jackson County

Oct. 29, 1863: war is a hard place **Shore**. Soldiers fairs like hogs and cows. take wether Just as it cums. (R. C. Caldwell, Caldwell Coll., ECU) Cabarrus County

sure enough *adverb phrase* Following *and:* as expected, truly. [*DSME* **sure-enough**, B, adverb; *OED* **sure**, B. adverb, 4.b.]

June 3, 1862: We expected to be Ordered to the Fight evry minit and **sure enough** We got Orders a Sunday Eaving to march to the Field of action. (G. J. Huntley, Huntley Papers, WCU) Rutherford County

June 14, 1863: when I saw the mail Broat in I tolde the mes that I shorley had aletter in the pack and **shore anuf** I had. it don me that much good when I got it. (Isaac Lefevers, Lefevers Papers, NCSA) Catawba County

Aug. 30, 1863: my dear friends it Struck me as Soon as I Saw the envelops whitch the letter was in. I new thear was Something to matter. O it Struck me to the Midle of my hart. I new the moment I Saw it that Some of you ware dead and **Shore enuff** when I unfolded it thair the pale lines red that Annette was dead and buried in the cold and sylem dust of the earth. (John Hartman, Hartman Papers, Duke) Rowan County

surtain See **certain**

swap *verb* To exchange places (with a soldier), take the place (of a soldier).

June 1, 1864: if ben comes to **Swap** for mee after hee Starts dont rite any more tel you now [= know] whither i come or not. if i get away i dont want any more of your letters to come to the command. (Silas Stepp, Stepp Letters, UNCA) Buncombe County

sweet cider *noun* Freshly pressed apple cider that has not been allowed to ferment; non-alcoholic cider rather than **hard cider**.

Aug. 24, 1861: I hope yoo will bring me a pech of[f] of that tree an som of your best **sweet cider**. if I cood get a blly full of cider an peches I think I should be redy to die. (G. T. Beavers, Upchurch Papers, Duke) Chatham County

Jan. 15, 1863: My Dier Wife. I will giv you A Recpt [= recipe] how to make that Apple Bwtter. in the first place you make some **sweet cider** and pwt it in citle or pot and let it get to boil and the[n] yow hav your apples nicely peild and yow put them in an boil them ontill tha boil soft an then poor in moor an so on till they bee come to Jelly. yow stir them all the time. Just like makin molasses the sweeter the Jwse the beter it is. (T. F. Baggarly, Baggarly Papers, Duke) Iredell County

sweet milk *noun* Fresh milk (rather than buttermilk). [*DARE* especially South, South Midland]

Mar. 17, 1862: I Would Like to Be at home and git some milk and Butter. I crave that more than any thing else. I am Worn out on meet. I Went out yesterdi evning and Baught me a quart of **Sweat milk**. it hope me vary mutch. I think if I could git milk and Butter that I Would git fat. (G. J. Huntley, Huntley Papers, WCU) Rutherford County

sweet potato *noun* various forms with deleted first syllable in *potato*.

Oct. 16, 1862: I must come to a close by giving you the prise of some things. **sweet taters** Sells at 25 cents a quart. half groing [= grown] chickens 1.00 Dollar. (W. F. Wagner, *Confederate Soldier*, 22) Catawba County

Dec. 23, 1862: Mag i Will tell some thing abowt the prices of things her. aples $3 per bw [= bushel] **Swete tatos** do [= ditto]. polk 50 ct per lb small onions .2. 10cts. (T. F. Baggarly, Baggarly Papers, Duke) Iredell County

Dec. 20, 1863: i want you to tri and git afurlo and come home and eat beaf and **sweat taters**. (Caroline Setzer, Setzer Corr., UVA) Catawba County

swell *verb* variant past tense *swoled* and present participle/verbal noun *swollen*.

Feb. 15, 1864: he has had A very bad Coff And his feet and Legs **swoled** very mutch but the **swollen** nerly all left him now. (J. W. Edwards, Frank Papers, Duke) Catawba County

swingletree *noun* Of a wagon: the pivoting crossbar to which traces are attached; variant form of *singletree*. [*OED* **swingletree**, noun, 2; *DARE* chiefly Central and South Atlantic, Appalachians]

July 13, 1863: Soldiers wives and widows work is done with neatness and Sent home, whether paid for or not as they must live and be Seen to, he make plows, and plowstocks, **Swingletrees**, Stocks Sythes for mowing and Cradling purposes, mends waggons & Carts, or any thing belonging to farms, or kitchens. at low prices. (John Livingston, Vance Papers, NCSA) Henderson County

swop off *verb* To trade for something; variant form of *swap off;* see Overview § II.4.7. [see *OED* **swap, swop**, verb, 7a. and 7b.]

Feb. 11, 1864: that nife i had when you was at home i broke and **Swoped off**. (Carr Setzer, Setzer Papers, Duke) Catawba County

T

tackey *noun* A worthless person; a poor white. [*DARE* **tacky**, noun, 2; Eliason's *Tarheel Talk* includes a citation from 1836]

Feb. 6, 1864: my dear I am Sorry to tel that I will not get home this winter. they air Sending the triflen edgcome [Edgecombe County] **tackeys** and the conscripts. So that will throw me back that I wont get home this winter. (John Hartman, Hartman Papers, Duke) Rowan County

tadpole *noun* The larval stage of a frog or toad. [*DARE* widespread, but somewhat less frequent North Atlantic, West]

Feb. 4, 1862: Nere Newbern Camp **Tad Pol**. febuary 4th 1862. Deare Mother I seet my self with grate Plesur to drope you a few lines to in form you that I am well at this Time. (Jordan Councill, Councill Papers, Duke) Watauga County

July 24, 1864: I had a fin time Saturday at Hartgroveses with Sallie C and Nan C you ever saw eating June appels. the girls is all as lively as **tadpoles**. (T. B. Edmonston, Edmonston-Kelly Family Papers, WCU) Haywood County

take[1] *verb* To convey, be transported (on); to capture, arrest; to steal, confiscate; to happen (with *place*); see Overview § II.4.1.8.

1. past tense *taken.*

June 11, 1862: we left Chickahominy And went to Richmond and **taken** the cars and went to the Junction. (B. Y. Malone, *Malone Diary*, 21) Caswell County

Apr. 26, 1863: I **taken** the stage Thirsday evning at 6 O-clock for Raleigh & got thar Friday morning at 9 O-clock. (A. A. Jackson, Jackson Family Corr., Notre Dame) Moore County

May 31, 1863: we broght afine drove of catel and all so afine lot of hogs that we **taken** from the bush whackers. (Daniel Revis, Revis Letters, NCSA) Henderson County

June 16, 1863: We **taken** a great many prisners & property & captured a great many comisary stores. (J. H. Hundley, Hundley Family Letters, SHC) Stokes County

2. past tense *tuck.*

Apr. 12, 1863: I will tell yow what **tuck** place in Richmon the other day. the women rased a mob and tha armed them selvs with axes and bowenives and suoards and they went to work. they went in the comisaryes stoars and all others that they come to. thare ase [was] six hundred of them. old Jef davis ordred our troops to fiar on them and our troops just come to a order arms and did not fiar on them. (Daniel Brown, Brown Coll., NCSA) Duplin County

June 9, 1863: Liutenant garron **tuck** sevral men with him and went after ruben and Ambers Staton and one of them shot garron and kill him. (Sarepta Revis, Revis Letters, NCSA) Henderson County

Feb. 8, 1864: we drove them Back and **tuck** one peace of artilrey from them and kild severl yankeys. (Thornton Sexton, Sexton Letters, Duke) Ashe County

Aug. 19, 1864: thay was foure Letters come to the Ridgment while I was gon to the hospital. William hawkins said that he got them and **tuck** care of them untill he Star[t]ed in to the fight and then he tourned them up for fear the yankeys wold get them. (John W. Joyce, Joyce Papers, MHI) Stokes County

3. past participle *took, tuck.*

Aug. 7, 1861: gineral Mcgrooder has **tuck** 10 thousand men down there And is agoing to attact newport news. (Peter Poteet, Poteet-Dickson Letters, NCSA) Burke County

Sept. 1, 1862: we have **took** one prisner and too Stills and 34 gallons of Brandy. (R. P. Kelly, Edmonston-Kelly Family Papers, WCU) Haywood County

Oct. 1, 1863: he will bee in newton the 14 of October and will take all the boxes that is **tuck** ther and bring them to us. (Daniel Setzer, Setzer Papers, Duke) Catawba County

June 1, 1864: oh how nie I did come a bing **tuck** prisoner the other day. (L. W. Griffin, Griffin Papers, NCSA) Rutherford County

June 19, 1864: It is reported that the yankees has **took** our breast works at peters burg. (J. H. Baker, J. H. Baker Papers, Duke) Rockingham County

take[2] *verb* To contract an illness or physical complaint. See also **take sick.**

1. infinitve, present tense.

Mar. 25, 1863: he is A giting sow as he can walk A bout wright smart now. I daunt think they is any danger but what he wil git over it now if he daunt **take** the relaps A gane. (B. C. Jackson, Jackson Family Corr., Notre Dame) Moore County

2. present participle.

Oct. 10, 1862: Since I rote last I think I am **taking** the yellow Janders. (W. F. Wagner, *Confederate Soldier,* 18) Catawba County

June 15, 1863: the folks is as well as comon as far as I know but gimey. he has got to **taking** fits. he toock one the other day. (J. A. W. Revis, Revis Letters, NCSA) Henderson County

Aug. 30, 1864: the children is complaining. I expect they are **taking** Measels. (Martha Poteet, Poteet-Dickson Letters, NCSA) McDowell County

3. past participle.

Mar. 5, 1862: fathers famly is all well exsep fracney and sis. tha have the mezals very bad. I have not **takin** it nor John have not yet. (Martha Futch, Futch Letters, NCSA) New Hanover County

Jan. 12, 1863: I hav no news to write of importance more than [there are a] good many cases of small pox about here. I hav been with several cases myself but hav not **taken** it yet. (J. H. Hundley, Hundley Family Letters, SHC) Stokes County

4. followed by *on:* to be affected in some way.

Dec. 2, 1862: the smallpocks has been about here and the army has ben vaccinated and it has **taken on** me very well. (J. F. Coghill, Coghill Papers, Duke) Granville County

5. with a function the same as *become.*

Sept. 6, 1863: I **took** very unwell the day after James left & did not get to this regt. till yesterday. (C. F. Mills, Mills Papers, Duke) Iredell County

take a highlow *verb phrase* To desert; perhaps formed on the model of *furlough.*

Sept. 7, 1863: I will again try to get a pass or permit to go home and if they wont then give me one, I think I and several more will **take a highlow**. (C. A. Hege, Hege Papers, MHI) Davidson County

take a/the notion *verb phrase* To decide on a parti cular course of action (followed by an infinitive).

Jan. 29, 1863: I think if you **tak a notion** to Com you must com by her too. (E. M. Phillips, Phillips Papers, Duke) Robeson County

June 26, 1863: if you **take the notion** to write me a letter please put in a good Knidle [= needle] and as much thread as you can. (C. L. Proffit, Proffit Family Letters, SHC) Wilkes County

Aug. 26, 1863: Mr. John Null **took a notion** to steele Rosenears and went out 2 nites and stole some. (W. F. Wagner, *Confederate Soldier,* 71) Catawba County

take a spree *verb phrase* To go on a lively and boisterous frolic, often featuring courting, dancing, and drinking alcohol. See also **spree**.

Sept. 2, 1863: Bill I would be glad to see you and **take a spree** with you. the girls ar all well a bout hear and as fancey as ever. tha all wanto see you all com hom. (Thomas Brann, Tesh Papers, Duke) Yadkin County

Jan. 24, 1864: they had **took a Sprey** last night a week a go and in there fight broak one mans leg and struck another one on the head with a pole so that they had to send two to the hospital and the rest ware in the guard house waiting to be cort marcheld. (John A. Smith, J. A. Smith Papers, Duke) Cabarrus County

take Christmas *verb phrase* To celebrate Christmas.

Dec. 30, 1861: I would like to hav ben there **to tuck chrismas** with you all. we had a livly time here. we had about 20 fites on that day but no body was hirt bad. (G. T. Beavers, Upchurch Papers, Duke) Chatham County

Jan. 1, 1862: I would like to be at home now **to take Christmas** and new years But it may be Christmas a time or two yet before we get to go. (J. W. Overcash, Overcash Papers, Duke) Rowan County

Dec. 8, 1862: I Wold like to be at home to eat Som God crackling bred and Wold like to **take crismas** With you all but I See tha is no chance for hit. (Robert Spainhourd, Spainhourd Papers, Duke) Forsyth County

take dinner *verb phrase* To have dinner (with someone).

Mar. 8, 1863: tell here I wold like to be thare to **take Diner** with Her the Best in the world but tell Her that times is Just So that I cant be thare now. (John Ingram, Ingram Papers, Duke) Forsyth County

Mar. 16, 1863: Gorge was hear yesta day an me an him **tuck dinner** to gether. (J. W. Joyce, Joyce Papers, MHI) Stokes County

June 28, 1863: mother i should like to **take dinner** with you next Sundy if you would have a big dish of greens. (Robert Carpenter, Carpenter Family Papers, ECU) Chatham County

take down *verb* To become ill with a disease; see Overview § II.4.7.

Aug. 8, 1861: I am sory to say but will hav to say I hav seen one of our company deposited in the grav. it was Henry Hall. he was **taken down** with the tifoid feaver a few weeks a go and died the sixt of this month. (Harrison Hanes, Hanes Papers, Duke) Davie County

take on (about) *verb* To grieve, moan, make a fuss; see Overview § II.4.7. [*DSME* **take on**, verb phrase]

Dec. 23, 1862: one thing i like to for got what will bill moor do if he has to go off. i reckin tha ar **takin on abowt** him. (T. F. Baggarly, Baggarly Papers, Duke) Iredell County

take sick *verb phrase* To become ill.

June 5, 1863: I take the plesure or righting you A fiew lines to let you now that I am not w[e]ll at this time. I **taken Sick** this moring I am not bad of[f] but I am not abel to drill but I hope that I may get stout A gaine. (Julius Seitz, Whitner Papers, Duke) Catawba County

June 5, 1863: I bee long to the 31. Regt and was at Charlston all the time the Reg was thare until the eighteen of April and I was **taken Sick** and was Sent to Hos pitel at Charlston and then to Columba South Carlina and they Sent me home on a Furlow. (Samuel Garrard, Vance Papers, NCSA) Orange County

June 25, 1863: I took soom calomel when I first **took sicke**. we have no docter here and the put me on duty too soon and it fell into my head and teeth and salivated me a little. I feel a little better today. I think if i dont improve tolerable fast i will go to the hospitle. (Daniel Murph, Murph Papers, Duke) Catawba County

Aug. 5, 1864: Dear Father I write you a few lines tho I am in a bad fix to write. I **took sick** some 2 weeks ago. first a savier cold & then disentary. I stade with the army till I got so weak that I could hardly walk. (Stephen Whitaker, Whitaker Papers, NCSA) Cherokee County

take the shine off *verb phrase* To outshine, surpass.

Mar. 2, 1859: I was at a frolic yesterday. where there were some clever looking young ladies. but ah, I Saw one done the country that that **took the shine off** of them. (John McGregor, Jackson Family Corr., Notre Dame) Moore County

take to the brush *verb phrase* Of deserters, conscripts: to hide out in the woods to avoid arrest.

Sept. 21, 1863: I heard the gard had taken up Jesse J Bull. I wonder what they will do with him. What has gone with Hump Noris. has the gard got him to. I reckon Noah Brookshir has **taken to the brush** again. (William Walsh, Proffit Family Letters, SHC) Wilkes County

take up *verb* See Overview § II.4.7.

1. To apprehend, arrest. [*DSME* **take up**, verb phrase, 2; *OED* **take**, verb, **to take up**,12]

Sept. 29, 1862: two of them was **taken up** and fetcht back this morning they formed a line of all the men here in camp and ran them threw and every man had a hickory and had to hit each of them one lick. (John Ingram, Ingram Papers, Duke) Forsyth County

Feb. 13, 1863: I have not Dun a day work at home in about five monts for **taking up** Deserters and Bying corn and haling to the volenteears wives. (Thomas M. Walker, Vance Papers, NCSA) Granville County

Oct. 16, 1863: I received yours of sept 28 and was glad to hear from you and to hear you was all well and sorry to hear of our own country boys doing so bad as to be hand cuft and sent to the army but we are **take-ing** them **up** every day more or less. (R. C. Love, Love Papers, Duke) Henderson County

Mar. 5, 1865: their was a man left our Company last week and he was **taken up** and braut back and put in the gard house and he may be Shot. (Alexander Keever, Keever Papers, Duke) Lincoln County

2. To establish, occupy. [*OED* **take**, verb, **to take up**, 22.a.]

Sept. 22, 1861: we traveld about eight miles and then **tuck up** camp and stade til morning then started and came here. (J. S. Beavers, Upchurch Papers, Duke) Chatham County

June 12, 1862: they marched in one mile of the Battle ground and night over taken them and they was orderd back about Two miles wheir they **taken up** camp untell nex morning. (Isaac Lefevers, Lefevers Papers, NCSA) Catawba County

3. In the phrase *take up a note:* to receive payment for a loan, settle a debt. See also **lift a note**.

ND [1862]: I Sent a hundred and five Dollar home by Sam Naylor and I want to no wheather it has got home or not. if you have not got it I want you to go and get it and pay Bowden off and **take up** that not[e] and give Bet the balance if they is any left. (W. D. Smith, W. D. Smith Papers, Duke) Davic County

Oct. 11, 1863: Dear Brother you wanted to know if i was willing for Girken **to take up** the note that i had a gain him as he wanted to pay it. you can do just as you think best. i want you to doo just like you wold for you self. (Alfred Roberson, Roberson Family Papers, ECU) Martin County

talk *verb* To say, report; in a passive construction with *it* as the impersonal subject (as in *it is said, reported, rumored*).

June 9, 1862: it is **talked** that we shall go to petersburg va but do not know it for surtain. (J. W. Williams, Williams Papers, Duke) Onslow County

(a) talk *noun* A report or rumor. [The CACWL data indicate this usage was limited mainly to the South, South Midland]

Apr. 13, 1862: thar has bin **a talk** of keeping us in longer than our time but I don't think that will be don. (M. W. Parris, Parris Papers, WCU) Jackson County

Sept. 16, 1862: there is **a talk** of our leaving this place but I dont know when we will leave nor where we will go to. (J. H. Hundley, Hundley Family Letters, SHC) Stokes County

Mar. 9, 1863: Dear wife tell me in your next letter wheather Thomas litle auctiley lay out or not or wheather it onley was **a talk**. (W. F. Wagner, *Confederate Soldier,* 40) Catawba County

Dec. 26, 1863: I Dont no how wee will live if tha take all our things from us and tha have **atalk** of taking our beds from us and clothing. (Susan Setzer, Setzer Papers, Duke) Catawba County

talk short *verb phrase* To speak rudely or curtly (to someone). [see *DARE* **short talk** noun, "Quarrelsome talk; hence v phr *short talk* to speak rudely"; *OED* **short**, adjective, 10.a.]

Feb. 4, 1864: you stated that Bulinger **talked very short** to you when you ast him for my pistol. (Daniel Abernethy, Abernethy Papers, Duke) Catawba County

tapister *noun* Older form of *tapster,* a tavern keeper, but in this case a person passing through camp selling food items, a peddler. [*OED* **tapster**, noun, 3, "one who sells retail or in small quantities"]

Nov. 18, 1864: we will have Short & rough fare this winter but there is **tapisters** going threw the camp with nicknacks for sale. the[y] Sell Sweet potaters at a dollar a pound. Irish potaters a dollar a quart. two turnups Small ones for a dollar. appels 4 little ones for a dollar. pies as big as a hand for a dollar. (John Peterson, Peterson Papers, Duke) Catawba County

tarheel *noun* A North Carolinian; naval stores, including tar, were principal products during the state's early history. [The first recorded occurrences of *tarheel* apparently date from the time of the Civil War (see Powell, *Encyclopedia of North Carolina,* 1104; the earliest citation in the *OED* is from 1864). The citation below is from a letter Susanna Frank wrote to her husband, who was serving in the Confederate army. She appears to have copied part of her letter from a newspaper or other firsthand account of the siege of Petersburg.]

Sept. 4, 1864: I have no news of importance to writ So I will Say a little more about the boys at Petersburg from Sunday 21. they <gave?> the Yanks around the railrode near Petersburg but did not succeed much. took one line of works so we left them. came out after night. rested monday tuesday Wednesday. started went round Some 15 miles thursday afternoon. went in to them near Reams Station. Gen Heath had taken ours and Mc rays Brigads as they are the **tar heels**. (Susanna Frank, Frank Papers, Duke) Davidson County

tarnal see **tornal**

tater see **potato**

tear down *verb* variant past participle *tore down;* see Overview § II.4.7.

Jan. 17, 1862: I can inform you that Our Rigment Left Raleigh Last Monday. We got Orders Last sunday to have Our tents **tore Down** and Ready for moving By day light next morning. (G. J. Huntley, Huntley Papers, WCU) Rutherford County

tear up *verb* To damage, destroy; see Overview § II.4.7.

1. past tense *torned up.*

Aug. 19, 1864: thay was foure Letters come to the Ridgment while I was gon to the hospital. William hawkins said that he got them and tuck care of them untill he Star[t]ed in to the fight and then he **tourned** them **up** for fear the yankeys wold get them. (J. W. Joyce, Joyce Papers, MHI) Stokes County

2. past participle *tore up.*

June 26, 1864: the yanks have **tore up** the rail Road some place betwn here and Richmond. (Franklin Setzer, Setzer Corr., UVA) Catawba County

July 15, 1864: I had to walk 22 miles on the danvill road whear it was **tore up**. (Alexander Keever, Keever Papers, Duke) Lincoln County

Jan. 14, 1865: they have just come from down the country and have taken all of some peoples meat and poltry and have **tore up** rite smart and bad. (Ann Bowen, Bowen Papers, NCSA) Washington County

3. past participle *tore up* as an adjective: damaged, disabled, in distress.

July 28, 1862: we ar undear marching ordars and ar all **tor up**. we dont no whear we ar going too. (Larkin Kendrick, Kendrick Papers, NCSA) Cleveland County

Jan. 12, 1863: sence i have got home **tore up** my famly is a lowed nothing. (William Core, Vance Papers, NCSA) Guilford County

tedious *adjective* variant forms including *teajus, teagious, dedas.*

Sept. 16, 1862: our men toock the place yesderday and we toock 14 thousand prisners and evry thing to **teagious** to mension. (J. W. Williams, Williams Papers, Duke) Onslow County

Nov. 10, 1862: Jackson Record is not heart. George Bridges is in camp was lefte with the sick. D. M.

Carter is well was lefte in camp also. and a Good many outhers two **teajus** to meson. (W. D. Carter, Culberson Papers, Duke) Chatham County

May 10, 1863: we lost Some of our best men. we lost John car and corprel dobson and Cirtas Sandlin and the wonded is to **dedas** to menchan. we whiped the yankeys and run them over the river a gain. (Daniel Brown, Brown Coll., NCSA) Duplin County

tell *verb* To say, recite. [*DARE* **tell**, verb, 2 a]

Feb. 7, 1863: I want to now If Bud can **tell** his abcs or not and tell me how fair Sissey has got in hur Boock. (Isaac Lefevers, Lefevers Papers, NCSA) Catawba County

tell see **till**

tetch *noun* and *verb* variant form of *touch*.

Aug. 21, 1861: their is a g[r]ate deal of sickness heir now. Eli upright and Davie Sloop is very bad off with the mesils. Eli is geting beter. I had a lite **tetch** of them. Charl Atwell has got well of them. (James W. Overcash, Overcash Papers, Duke) Rowan County

May 7, 1863: I went with them on the charge And I give owt and fell down. I nevver was **tech**. I got my belt shot in two. (W. H. Brotherton, Brotherton Papers, Duke) Catawba County

Nov. 14, 1863: Mother I had a plenty to do me Till I got to camp without **Tetching** My butter or molasses. (William Tesh, Tesh Papers, Duke) Yadkin County

thang *noun* variant form of *thing*.

Jan. 11, 1862: I recived som **thangs** from home the other day. I was mutch pleased for them but I want to com home just as bad as ever. geting **thangs** dont sadesfie me. (G. T. Beavers, Upchurch Papers, Duke) Chatham County

Apr. 24, 1862: how glad would I bea if this Wair was over and I could get back to you and our dear little childrean onst more and I do hope they time is not a fair distance off when this **thang** will come to a close. (Isaac Lefevers, Lefevers Papers, NCSA) Catawba County

Dec. 22, 1864: I want you to send me some flower and some fat meat. some molases and some Sasengs and peas an beanes. any **thang** so to eat. (A. J. Spease, Zimmerman Papers, Duke) Forsyth County

thank see **think**

thanky *exclamation* Thanks, thank you.

Aug. 25, 1861: So nothen Moor at present. rite to Mee as Soon as you git this Onley I got them too Shurts that you sent Mee By Mr Muray and I Cant Sent you **thankey** a nuff for them. (John A. Long, Long Family Papers, SHC) Alamance County

Apr. 19, 1863: I was very glad to the provision you sent to mee. tell ant [= aunt] vi an crees **thanky** for what tha Sent me. (T. F. Baggarly, Baggarly Papers, Duke) Iredell County

than what see **what**

that *relative pronoun* reduced form *at*.

Jan. 16, 1863: I am in ten miles of the Rail road **at** leades from Richmond to fredickes burge. (Evin Smith, E. Smith Papers, Duke) Stanley County

July 24, 1864: they Just tore up every thing that was in their House & broke all the fine furniture & Delf [= delft dinnerware] **at** was in they houses. (Thomas B. Litten, Robinson Papers, Duke) Catawba County

that *conjunction* used redundantly following *like*, especially with verbs *seem* and *look*. [*DSME*, **that**, C, conjunction]

Dec. 2, 1862: It looks like **that** wee will never draw eny more money. (J. F. Coghill, Coghill Papers, Duke) Granville County

Jan. 8, 1864: I here the torys and yanks are near Asheville now. I tell you I hate for them to come in that cuntory But it looks like **that** we cant keep them Back at all places. (J. W. Love, Love Papers, Duke) Henderson County

July 24, 1864: Ben I think that this cruel war will end this fall and I hop that we will all live to see the end of it. let it be long or short. but it dont look like **that** som of us can live when you are exsposed evrey day as you are but I hope you boath will come through Saf. (T. B. Edmonston, Edmonston-Kelly Family Papers, WCU) Haywood County

Aug. 30, 1864: I try to pray for every body and peace. it seems like **that** tha wont be any More peace in this life but I still hope and pray for it. (F. M. Poteet, Poteet-Dickson Letters, NCSA) McDowell County

that *adverb* So. [*DARE* **that**, B, adverb; chiefly South, South Midland]

May 28, 1863: I think the weather was as hot and Dry as ever I felt for the time of year in my life. it was **that** Dust[y] and Dry that we hardly could tel one a nother for the Dust that Settle[d] awn us. (Isaac Lefevers, Lefevers Papers, NCSA) Catawba County

May 7, 1864: i am **that** tired and Sleepy i cant hardly rite. my health is good and has bin all the time what agreat blesing it is. (Silas Stepp, Stepp Letters, UNCA) Buncombe County

thataway *adverb* That way, in that manner.

Sept. 19, 1861: I saw litle Joe Howel the other day and talked with him. he said that Mary Jane and Hanor is maryed but Ann is not nor dont entend to untel he gets back. I hope that som body els is **that away** a bout me. (Harrison Hanes, Hanes Papers, Duke) Davie County

Aug. 15, 1863: Dear I will tell you how they done. the held a Election and the most of the Solegers voted for peese and now they got it published that we had voted to keepe on the war. we never voted **that a way**. (W. F. Wagner, *Confederate Soldier,* 65) Catawba County

the *definite article*

1. before a place.

Jan. 12, 1863: I found John hier at **the straw bery plains** 15 miles from knoxville. (Daniel Revis, Revis Letters, NCSA) Henderson County

July 15, 1863: we still staid at Darksvill untell about a hour by sun and marched to **the Alagater mountain**. (B. Y. Malone, *Malone Diary,* 38) Caswell County

Oct. 24, 1863: we expect to go to ashville or to **the warm Spring** in tennessee. (Franklin Setzer, Setzer Corr., UVA) Catawba County

Nov. 19, 1863: we air on the norwest Cide of **the mishnary Ridg** in Cite of Chat ta nooga. (J. W. Reese, Reese Papers, Duke) Buncombe County

Oct. 18, 1864: you sed you had a good meeting at **the Rock springs**. (L. W. Griffin, Griffin Papers, NCSA) Rutherford County

2. before illness or disease.

Oct. 22, 1861: That young man that was sick when you was here has been down ever since with **the tyfoid fevor**. (H. J. Davis, WPA Transcripts, TSLA) Yadkin County

Sept. 16, 1862: I had **the tooth ache** too days but I had it taken out. (R. P. Kelly, Edmonston-Kelly Family Papers, WCU) Haywood County

Nov. 10, 1862: thair is A heep of Sickness hear with **the Brane feaver**. (J. W. Reese, Reese Papers, Duke) Buncombe County

Dec. 7, 1862: I herd he had **the sore thrat**. (Daniel Revis, Revis Letters, NCSA) Henderson County

3. with indefinite pronoun *most.*

June 1, 1863: my feet is as tender as a childs and **the most** of the boys feet is sore. (James Zimmerman, Zimmerman Papers, Duke) Forsyth County

June 28, 1863: he has not Bin with us mutch. he has Bin on detail **the most** of his time to work on Brigges and Sutch like. (J. W. Reese, Reese Papers, Duke) Buncombe County

Oct. 30, 1864: they didrent hav time to cary their ded out. they left **the most** of they woundid one the batle field. (Gorry Jackson, Jackson Family Corr., Notre Dame) Moore County

Dec. 1, 1864: i got the money for the mare i sold and now i wil send **the most** of it home. (Franklin Setzer, Setzer Corr., UVA) Catawba County

4. with *half.*

June 11, 1862: i wod as sune fite as to stay hire. we liv like dogs. not hafe nufe to eat **the hafe** of our time. (W. P. Cline, Cline Papers, Duke) Catawba County

theirn, thern, tharn *possesive pronoun* Theirs.

Dec. 19, 1863: he Jest had aparte thare at the odom branch to make and the boys ses the half of that other is **tharn** to make. (Susan Setzer, Setzer Papers, Duke) Catawba County

Apr. 22, 1864: our boat sunk one of **thern** & they was one hundred and fifty went down with it to their long homes. (J. W. Lineberger, *Gaston Ranger,* 96) Gaston County

theirselves (also *thereselves, thearselves, therselves, thirselves) reflexive pronoun* Themselves. [*DARE* chiefly northern New England, South, South Midland]

Aug. 8, 1861: tel them to take good car of **there selves** and not mary to soon for they dont know but what there husbens would hav to go to the war. (Harrison Hanes, Hanes Papers, Duke) Davie County

Apr. 14, 1863: susen muney and franceny lee dresed **thear selves** in mens close and went to a sick mands house and trid to skin him out of his house. (Martha Futch, Futch Letters, NCSA) New Hanover County

Apr. 27, 1863: thir is sevrial stout able bodyd men in Henderson ville that ant duing any thing but Speculating of[f] of the Pore who cant helpe **their selvs**. (Wilburn Garren, Vance Papers, NCSA) Henderson County

Oct. 5, 1863: I Recvd a letter yesterday from capt Turner. he sais Thomas heath an maden has giv **thirselvs** up. (T. F. Baggarly, Baggarly Papers, Duke) Iredell County

May–June 1865: the white soldiers break into our houses act as they please steal our chickens rob our gardens and if any one defends **their-Selves** against them they are taken to the gard house for it. (Richard Etheredge, *Freedom,* ser. 2: 730) Tyrrell County

the like *noun* So large a number or amount, so many, such a thing; often with verb *see.* [*DSME* **(the) like**]

Aug. 7, 1861: We whipt them Badley and tuck every thing they had. the[y] say when they did Retrete that they run over one another & women & Children and kiled lots of them selves. I supose **the like** never was knowd in the world. (Peter Poteet, Poteet-Dickson Letters, NCSA) Burke County

June 1, 1862: We have Just any amount of troops Round Richmond. I never saw **the Like** of artillery infantry and Cavalry in all my Life. (G. J. Huntley, Huntley Papers, WCU) Rutherford County

July 12, 1862: the Like of ded men an horses I never saw before. (J. W. Williams, Williams Papers, Duke) Onslow County

Oct. 3, 1862: the fever Dont sem to Bate [= bad] sum Days. et stops for A while and then Sped A gain. i never saw **the Like** Bee for of our toon [= town]. ef you walk in the street et Look Like A sory ful time all Day Long. (William H. Thurber, DeRosset Family Papers, SHC) New Hanover County

them *demonstrative adjective* Those. [*DARE* scattered, but chiefly South, South Midland; also New England]

Oct. 16, 1862: I carried them though the 3d regement and they was not a one that could read them so I can not answer **them** Letters. (Charley Futch, Futch Letters, NCSA) New Hanover County

Feb. 5, 1863: Martha please make hast and get **them** gloves done and send them out to Burgaw So Sergeant W.A. Bloodworth can Bring them to me. (John Futch, Futch Letters, NCSA) New Hanover County

Nov. 23, 1863: I want you to tell Joseph Landis to pay you for **them** coffins. (F. M. Poteet, Poteet-Dickson Letters NCSA) McDowell County

Dec. 21, 1863: Car I want you to take the tire off of **them** cart wheals and work them up if you neede iron. (Daniel Setzer, Setzer Papers, Duke) Catawba County

them *demonstrative pronoun* Those.

Mar. 25, 1863: I can have the tom [= tomb] stones Letered & I hope you or Some one else will See that **them** & Mothers is put up in their proper place. (Stephen Whitaker, Whitaker Papers, NCSA) Cherokee County

May 7, 1863: Lieut Breedlove was wounded and Robbert Champien and Bil Cheatham and Ben Dun. **them** is all that I know ove and I tell you that wee whiped them good and gained A glorious victory. (J. F. Coghill, Coghill Papers, Duke) Granville County

July 31, 1863: you have never rote to me yet how your gardens is adoo ing and you potatoes. I want to no how **them** dun we planted last fall. (Daniel Setzer, Setzer Papers, Duke) Catawba County

Mar. 16, 1864: I hav ben rite Sick but I am better but I did not take any medison only three pills. I would not hav it and I got well as quick as **them** that takeing the medison. (Jesse Hill, Hill Letters, NCSA) Forsyth County

the praise, prase *noun phrase* The highest degree of approval in comparison with other individuals or other groups (especially companies or regiments)

July 24, 1861: the Cornel must have been excited the way he went on but the pore fellow losed his life in the opperration. [. . .] But he killed eight men before he was killed. he died with his sored [= sword] in a man. he wanted his Riment to get **the pras** and I think they faught as hard as any one in the field. (Levi Festerman, Festerman Papers, Duke) Rowan County

Dec. 17, 1861: he Sed that the 34th was the best Regt he had ever inspected and he seed [= said]. it should be Equipt Right a way and paid off. the Col gives our Company **the Prais** of being the best drilled company. (James Overcash, Overcash Papers, Duke) Rowan County

Dec. 30, 1861: out of three thousand men our company got **the prase** by the revewing oficer in marching to day. (J. W. Williams, Williams Papers, Duke) Onslow County

the rise of see **rise** *noun*

they (also *thay, tha, the*) *existential subject* There.

1. *they + is.*

Sept. 29, 1861: tha is from six to ten thousand yankees in the fleete. (R. P. Crawford, Estes Family Papers, WCU) Jackson County

Mar. 20, 1862: they is so much camp nuse that we do not know what to write. (J. W. Love, Love Papers, Duke) Henderson County

June 1, 1864: I wood give the worl if I cood git out of this fight but **the** is no chanc. (L. W. Griffin, Griffin Papers, NCSA) Rutherford County

Nov. 30, 1864: I hope and trust to god that **they** is a day a coming when poor privats will be as free as big ritch officers. (W. H. Horton, Councill Papers, Duke) Watauga County

2. *they + was* or *were.*

July 16, 1861: they was meny Balls Went into the meting house. our old Colonel Was in all of the mexicin War And he says that he never saw such abattle in his travels. (Peter Poteet, Poteet-Dickson Letters, NCSA) Burke County

Mar. 22, 1862: thay was a party at Gorge Gilekrist a thursday Night thay saye **thay** was a heape there. I think thay had better stay a way from partys. (Effie Jane Graham, Jackson Family Corr., Notre Dame) Moore County

May 17, 1862: last Saturday **they** wer too regaments went to the river to wash for sunday morning inspection. (J. W. Lineberger, *Gaston Ranger,* 7) Gaston County

3. *they + are.*

Jan. 21, 1862: they ar one Regament hear frome Lusiana and they mostly all arishmen and **they** ar no doing any thing with them. (D. C. Johnson, Jackson Family Corr., Notre Dame) Moore County

Apr. 5, 1862: I under stand that **tha** are five reg ment orderd to vagina from this place. (Jonas Bradshaw, Bradshaw Papers, Duke) Alexander County

Apr. 18, 1862: they are four company on the newbern roade and the others are on the dovers roade. (J. W. Lineberger, *Gaston Ranger,* 5) Gaston County

4. *they + has.*

July 16, 1862: thay has bin A dredfull Battle fout her At richmond. (Leonard Alman, Alman Papers, Duke) Cabarrus County

5. *they + will.*

Mar. 22, 1862: I am a fraid **thay** will bee a heape of men kill. (Effie Jane Graham, Jackson Family Corr., Notre Dame) Moore County

thing see **thang**

think *verb*

1. variant present tense *thank.*

Jan. 11, 1862: there is no nuse worth relating. One thang we had a fight between two of our boys Mark Wimbly & Q. J. Hudson. Mark stuck him with his knife in front of his left hip 2 or 3 inches deep. he bled powerful but he is now beter. I thought yestady that he would die befour now but I now **thank** he will get well after while. (G. T. Beavers, Upchurch Papers, Duke) Chatham County

Jan. 19, 1862: we have one verry Sick man in the hospital John Kelley is verry sick with the new money but I **thank** he is A mending. (Williford Upchurch, Upchurch Papers, Duke) Chatham County

2. variant past tense *thort.*

Nov. 24, 1861: he **thort** he ought to got one to. (L. W. Griffin, Griffin Papers, NCSA) Rutherford County

Dec. 28, 1862: i **thort** of you all that day an whare wee was last christmas day. (T. F. Baggarly, Baggarly Papers, Duke) Iredell County

Feb. 20, 1864: mi rite leg was Sweld what the skin would hold and I **thort** it would brake open but it dident. (Daniel Setzer, Setzer Papers, Duke) Catawba County

think hard *verb* To have a negative opinion of someone; see Overview § II.4.7.

July 24, 1861: you must not **think hard** for me not writing sooner for I had no chance. we have been trav-ling about for too weaks and are still travling yet. (Levi Festerman, Festerman Papers, Duke) Rowan County

Sept. 17, 1862: I think you have forgot me interely. I **think** mity **hard** of you for it for I love you And would give enny thing in this world if I could se your purty sweete cheeks one time mor. (Joseph Cowand, Cowand Papers, Duke) Bertie County

Jan. 11, 1863: I under stand by Your Letters that granmother Ingram **thinks hard** of my not Writing to her. I have a bad Chance to write. (John Ingram, Ingram Papers, Duke) Forsyth County

thort see **think**

thout see **without**

thrash see **thrush**

threw *noun* A spell, episode, brief period of time; perhaps from Scots, Middle English *thraw.* [see *DSME* **through**, B noun, 1]

Sept. 14, 1861: we were tolerable sick a few days but are about well now. We expect to go to drilling in the morning. Our company has had a prety good **threw** of the chills for the last week or too but all are get-ting better. there were only about twenty men of our co able for duty for several days There is a greateal of sickness in our regiment now. it is mostly chills an fever and mumps. (W. M. Patton, Patton Family Letters, Duke) Buncombe County

throw *verb* See Overview § II.4.1.9.

1. past tense *throwed, throde* (including *throwed away*).

July 12, 1862: the yankes **throde** their bums at us but tha did not hurt eny of us. (W. P. Cline, Cline Papers, SHC) Catawba County

Aug. 4, 1862: And a bout midnight our artilry commence Firing on them and They **Throwd** Bums all Around us and I tell you they shuck the grown. (Joseph Cowand, Cowand Papers, Duke) Bertie County

Sept. 27, 1862: at one place we **throwed** away over two hundred garments pants coats shirts drawers. (James Zimmerman, Zimmerman Papers, Duke) Forsyth County

May 25, 1863: I **throwed** away my yarn pants but I have put down for some more. (Neill McLeod, McLeod Letters, SHC) Moore County

2. past participle *throad.*

Mar. 20, 1864: wee had some bome Sheles **throad** here yesterda. (A. S. Harrill, Civil War Coll., TSLA) Rutherford County

3. past participle *threw.*

June 20, 1864: we air in site of the yankeys. we air on this side of the river and the yan keys is on theo-ther side. the yankeys has **threw** some Bumshells in the town. (Joseph Wright, Wright Papers, Duke) Alamance County

throw out *verb* To dismiss, remove from office, lose one's job; see Overview § II.4.7.

May 24, 1861: they searched all the storers & a great many dwelling houses for the secession flag & arms amunition &c. a great many have bin **thrown out** of employments. (Rhoda Hawn, Peterson Papers, Duke) Catawba County

Oct. 25, 1861: Blasingame is **throwed out** of his ofice. he Went out one Sundy and Jump one [= on] A Boy and Beate him Badly so I herd. he was **throwd out** to Day. (Jesse Shipman, Shipman Family Corr., Notre Dame) Henderson County

throw up *verb* See Overview § II.4.7.

1. To relinquish, abandon, quit. [*OED* **to throw up**, 7.]

   June 2, 1863: if you will Send me a Repreave I will go Back to my Company & dy with them sertin & Send me Orders to take J. C. Parks who was Majestrate of Iredell Couny & there he **throwd up** & went to Wilkes C O & Stad thare a Bout Twelve Month & then went to the Armey. (A. R. Harris, Vance Papers, Duke) Iredell County

   Oct. 10, 1864: men say that has tried both say they had rother be a private here then to be a lutenant in the in fantry. two lutenants left campe homes [= Holmes] with us and **threw up** there cumishions to come with us to this place. (Henry Bowen, Bowen Papers, NCSA) Washington County

2. To make, construct (usu. by digging); variant past tense and past participle forms. [*OED* **to throw up**, 4]

   Dec. 17, 1862: on mundy night wee **throwd up** breast works with our hands and bug up the dirt with our bayonets. (J. F. Coghill, Coghill Papers, Duke) Granville County

   May 7, 1863: they had their brest works **threw wp**. we flank them And come Rownd in their Rair. (W. H. Brotherton, Brotherton Papers, Duke) Catawba County

3. To vomit; variant past tense.

   Aug. 20, 1862: I feel better this eavening then I did yesderday for I had A high fever and **throwed up** all day. (J. W. Williams, Williams Papers, Duke) Onslow County

thrush, thrash *noun* An infection of the mouth, especially of children. [*DSME* **thrush**, noun]

Dec. 10, 1864: the baby is not rite well she has the **thrash** and her chin broke out in Festers which makes her more fretful than she ever was. (Ann Bowen, Bowen Papers, NCSA) Washington County

thundering *adverb* Very; immensely, tremendously. [*OED* **thundering**, adjective (and adverb), 4 .b.]

Sept. 16, 1862: he put A **thunderan** grad [= great] big blister aun mi back but [I] daunt think that it dun it any guod. only it taken the Skin aufan. yeu may gues whither that dun me mutch gwod or naugh [= not]. (B. C. Jackson, Jackson Family Corr., Notre Dame) Moore County

tick *noun* A mattress cover. See also **bed tick**.

Oct. 5, 1861: I would be glad hee bring mi **tick** and two Shirts wooling for I need them. (C. F. Mills, Mills Papers, Duke) Iredell County

Nov. 22, 1861: I have got my **tick** stuft with oak Leaves. (J. W. Williams, Williams Papers, Duke) Onslow County

ticket *noun* An invitation.

Aug. 17, 1859: Cousin Archibald we is geting tired a wating for that **tickit** to you and Miss Mays weding. (Isabella Johnson, Jackson Family Corr., Notre Dame) Robeson County

Aug. 20, 1863: tell her that I want her to <???> & Give me A **Tickit** to her wedding. (Mary Wagoner, Hundley Family Letters, SHC) Stokes County

tight, tite *adjective*

1. Strict. [*OED* **tight**, adjective, 6.b. *fig.*]

   ND: our fear is but ondifearnt and **tite** laws tha will not let a man pass out with out commision ofecr with him. (Charley Futch, Futch Letters, NCSA) New Hanover County

2. Intoxicated, tipsy. [*OED* **tight**, adjective, 7]

   June 10, 1861: old Jimy Deaton got **tite** and fell out of the bugy and broke his thy and two ribs and is very bad off. (Joseph Overcash, Overcash Papers, Duke) Rowan County

   Feb. 11, 1862: Capt barry is under A rest at the

presant for getting **tite** but he is A man I Like as A Captain and I intend to Stick up to him. (J. W. Williams, Williams Papers, Duke) Onslow County

July 9, 1864: Weevr was in Charg of of the picket that and after he was Run in he was Reposting his pickets and this yankey was **tite.** he Sed he was orderd to advanc his post and he was so drunk he did not no what he was dooing and advanct two fur and Cum throu ouer lins. (J. W. Reese, Reese Papers, Duke) Buncombe County

till preposition

1. By, before. See also **till** *conjunction*, 3. [*DARE* especially Pennsylvania German area]

July 25, 1862: i wont you to make me too Culard Shurts as sune as you Can and i wont A good warme Jackshit [= jacket] **tel** fall and wod like to have A neakles [= Scarf] you Can git salm Parker wife to nit it. (W. P. Cline, Cline Papers, SHC) Catawba County

July 25, 1862: Dear Husband I want you and lamuel to try and come home **till** Tuesday. I think they thrashers will come **till** Wednesday. (Nancy Wagner, *Confederate Soldier*, 7) Catawba County

Sept. 28, 1862: we have had the teroblest fiting for the last cupely weaks and I look for tireble Strugles yet. old abe Ses **til** the first of Jan. the negros will be freed. he aims to whip us yet but I hope and trust in god that we may Sucksead. (John Hartman, Hartman Papers, Duke) Rowan County

Dec. 5, 1863: Tell bet and Fanny They must bake me a sweet cake and send it to me **Till** Christmas. (William Tesh, Tesh Papers, Duke) Yadkin County

Mar. 8, 1863: Dear I all along thaught and was in hopes this war would End **til** Spring but it apears like it was poore hopes. (W. F. Wagner, *Confederate Soldier*, 38) Catawba County

2. Until.

Nov. 22, 1861: I left Lincolten at 9 o clock a tuesday morning and got to charlet at a 11 and Remainded in Charlott **till** a bout one hour after dark. I had the oppertunity of seeing a good deal in charlott that I never saw before. (G. J. Huntley, Huntley Papers, WCU) Rutherford County

Dec. 17, 1861: we drill so much hear that we cant get Time to write we heave to drill from .9. oclock in the morning **tell** .11. and from .1. oclock **till** sun set. (Reuben Overcash, Overcash Papers, Duke) Rowan County

Feb. 4, 1862: I think that we will stay here **till** Spring an then we will leave here an goe to Cantuck or tenisee. (J. S. Council, Councill Papers, Duke) Watauga County

May 17, 1862: I never heard that my child was ded **till** yesterday and tongue cant express my feeling about it. (Larkin Kendrick, Kendrick Papers, NCSA) Cleveland County

till *conjunction*

1. Before, by the time. [*EDD* **till**, conjunction, 11; *DARE* "Calque of (Pa)Ger *bis*"]

Feb. 13, 1863: tell Bud that he most larn his Boock purty **tell** paw comes home and he will Bring him some little Briches and some candy. (Isaac Lefevers, Lefevers Papers, NCSA) Catawba County

Jan. 26, 1864: Bet Said She was Feeding her Chickens to mak them fat **till** Billy come home. (Molly Tesh, Tesh Papers, Duke) Yadkin County

Apr. 21, 1864: I want you to have plenty of good eating **tell** I come Such as eggs and ham and crout and milk and butter and Sallet & Sweat potatoes and So on. (Alexander Keever, Keever Papers, Duke) Lincoln County

2. Until.

Aug. 12, 1863: I laid on the battle field with Daniel that Night and outhers of our compinay. he was brange to winchester thirty miles this side of pertomack river. I stade with him **till** he died. he died in Winchester on the 21 of July. (W. D. Carter, Culberson Papers, Duke) Chatham County

Oct. 18, 1864: you must rite Soon and often. no more only I remain your Brother **til** deth parts us good bey. (W. H. Horton, Councill Papers, Duke) Watauga County

Feb. 20, 1865: dont let your Cows get So pour then they will die. try and get thear horns opened and Serch thear tails and See if they aint holler and try to do the best you Can **till** I Come home. (Alexander Keever, Keever Papers, Duke) Lincoln County

3. So that, in order that; not always distinguishable from sense 2. [*DSME* **till**, B. conjunction, "In order that, with the result that, to the point that"; see also *OED* **till**, B. conjunction, e.]

July 6, 1862: I had the dierear and it grew worse on me **till** I were oblige to give up an stop. I laid up til yesterday. (W. M. Patton, Patton Family Letters, SHC) Buncombe County

Sept. 8, 1862: I hope the lord Will bless and keep us alive **til** We can See each other agin is my praayer for christ Sake. (G. C. Dickson, Poteet-Dickson Letters, NCSA) McDowell County

Feb. 10, 1863: we air the funneyest looking sit you ever saw. we air all lousey and smoked **til** you cold not tell whether we was a bacon side or a human. (Daniel Revis, Revis Letters, NCSA) Henderson County

June 22, 1864: I would like we could all be at home a while **till** we could all get to rest a while. (S. E. Love, Love Papers, Duke) Henderson County

time about *adverb phrase* By turns, alternately; same as **turn about**.

May 8, 1863: Scot was drunk & was quarling with welsh & dave was trying to git them to quit & Scott turned his pistol from welch & Shot at dave wounding him in the arm. I supose they then shot **time about**. Scott is badly wounded. some Say dangerous. (Stephen Whitaker, Whitaker Papers, NCSA) Cherokee County

time is out see **out**

tite see **tight**

titty *noun* The breast, especially that of the mother. [*OED* **titty**, noun[3]; *EDD* **titty**, *sb.*[3] 1., "A teat; the nipple of the breast; a mother's breast"]

Feb. 13, 1863: I [would] be glad to see the sweat little Babe. please lette me now in your next letter whether it can talk or not and whether it still sucks **titey** yet or not. (Isaac Lefevers, Lefevers Papers, NCSA) Catawba County

Jan. 9, 1865: Olivia ses how do pa make her a ring and put her name on it and one for henry two and one for Cornelia. I say and dont no what little Mary etter [= the baby] wants. something pretty pa for I is smart anoughf to get up in a big chair and fall down some times and say **titta**. (Ann Bowen, Bowen Papers, NCSA) Washington County

to *preposition*

1. With the sense of *at, in (a place)*. [see *DARE* **to**, B, preposition, 1a; scattered, but especially frequent North]

Dec. 20, 1861: I landed **to** this place last thurs day morning. We are located fore & half miles from Rahley. (Larkin Kendrick, Kendrick Papers, NCSA) Cleveland County

Mar. 5, 1862: you must not greve after me for I am deter mined to be **to** my post as long as I am able. (Ichabod Quinn, Quinn Papers, Duke) Duplin County

Aug. 25, 1862: I Stoped over **to** Richmon the other day to get one d dram & I did not get but little over a gill & had to pay one dollar for it. (Elijah Gatewood, Amos Papers, Duke) Stokes County

May 3, 1863: joe fullbright has got his Coarn all Planted **to** his neu groun an that A bout one Acker. (Keziah Hefner, Hefner Papers, NCSA) Catawba County

Jan. 14, 1865: She hasent bin able to comb her head in ten days until to day nor sit **to** the table. (Ann Bowen, Bowen Papers, NCSA) Washington County

2. With the sense of *for*. [see *DARE* **to**, B, preposition, 4. "Scots, nIr dial"]

Apr. 19, 1863: I was very glad **to** the provision you sent to mee. tell ant vi an crees thanky for what tha sent me. (T. F. Baggarly, Baggarly Papers, Duke) Iredell County

3. With the sense of *with*. [see *DARE* **to**, B, preposition, 5 (Pennsylvania German, "Calque of German *zu*"), 7; South, South Midland]

Aug. 24, 1863: I paid a half a dollar for a quart of milk last evning and eat it for my breakfast this morning **too** [= with] some warm corne bread. (W. F. Wagner, *Confederate Soldier*, 70) Catawba County

to boot see **boot**

tolerable (also *tolabel, tolerbul, tolerbill*)

1. *adjective* Common, fair, average (especially in reference to one's health).

   Mar. 1, 1863: I am yet A mon the living and in Joying **tolerbill** helthe. (J. W. Reese, Reese Papers, Duke) Buncombe County

   Feb. 4, 1864: I Can Say to you that my helth is only **tolerable** but right Smart better than it was last weeak. (Alexander Keever, Keever Papers, Duke) Lincoln County

2. *adverb* Rather, somewhat, fairly (exact meaning depends on the context).

   Sept. 19, 1861: I will writ you a **tolerable** long leter. (Harrison Hanes, Hanes Papers, Duke) Davie County

   Sept. 24, 1861: hall and Brown got to Drinking and hall kicked Brown and hurt him **tolerabile** Bad. (Jesse Shipman, Shipman Family Corr., Notre Dame) Henderson County

   Dec. 21, 1862: the health of camp is **tolabel** good at this tim. (Philip Shull, Councill Papers, Duke) Watauga County

   May 25, 1863: I have had **tolerbul** plenty to eat sence I have ben here such as it is. (Neill McLeod, McLeod Letters, SHC) Moore County

tolerably *adverb* Rather, fairly.

Sept. 12, 1862: we get coffey for breakfast and supper and other vittls **tolerabley** plenty. (A. D. McBride, McBride Family Papers, SHC) Bladen County

Mar. 4, 1864: this leves me in **tollerably** good health. better than when I first came here. (John Futch, Futch Letters, NCSA) New Hanover County

toll *noun* A portion of grain, meal, or fodder given as a share in exchange for some service, especially to a miller for grinding grain.

July 25, 1863: I am the owner of Public mills grinding for **toll** (the eighth) which mills are nearly always crowed [= crowded?] having to grind partly of nights to keep up which at present will have to run both day and night for a while to relieve the suffering with meal. (Jesse Brown, Vance Papers, NCSA) Edgecombe County

Sept. 27, 1863: I hav mi foder all made and hald in I made abot twelve hundred sheves and I toped that at manuels the[y] do not hav to pay **tool** out of the tops but we hav to pay o[u]t of the foder. it semes like hard times to pay **tolde** out of evry thing but I recon we hav it to do and So we nead not to say eny thing abot it. (Catherine Lefevers, Lefevers Papers, NCSA) Catawba County

tore up see **tear up**

tornal, turnal *adjective* Infernal; variant form of *eternal*. [*DSME* **tarnal**, adjective]

Aug. 7, 1862: tha all say tha ar all tierd of eating crackers and tha all ar in the dough up to thar elbows and I reckin I had beter git at it too or tha mite mak the boye chew crakers and my teeth is all brouk out now eating the **turnel** things. (A. P. Ward, Whitner Papers, Duke) Catawba County

Mar. 16, 1864: I hav not drawd one cent and but mity little of any thing and I hant a going to Stay at no Such a dam plase because I can make more at home in the bushes amakeing brooms than I can here in this **tornel** war. (Jesse Hill, Hill Letters, NCSA) Forsyth County

torpeder *noun* An explosive device attached to a boom or spar projecting from the bow of an attacking vessel and detonated against the hull of an enemy vessel, usually at or below the waterline; variant form of *torpedo*. [*OED* **torpedo**, noun, 2.a.]

Nov. 1, 1864: on thursday night the 27 of October it was very dark and rainy the yankees sliped up on the iron clad and threw **torpeders** under her and blew a hole in her. I heard they took the men that done it. they dident injer her so but what she could of bin mended. (Ann Bowen, Bowen Papers, NCSA) Washington County

tory *noun* A derogatory term used by Confederates to label Union sympathizers in Southern or border states. See also **Lincolnite**.

Jan. 30, 1862: I suppose my boy[s] is having some difficulty in arresting those traitors & Deserters. the Maj. will write Lieut Bird this evening & if these **toreys** resest ther arest he will send force enough to wipe out the overt act. (A. W. Bell, Bell Papers, Duke) Macon County

May 13, 1863: we cotch a **tory** as we came on and kild him and the **tories** shot at our boys and shot one threw the hat. (Daniel Revis, Revis Letters, NCSA) Henderson County

June 24, 1863: if I wer to arrest I Should b cald a Lincconite and a **tory** by all good sitisons of my own of cunty and I had rather Suffer a most any thing than to be Cald a **tory** or a Linconite. (Wesley Jones, Vance Papers, NCSA) Chatham County

Jan. 8, 1864: I here the **torys** and yanks are near Asheville now. I tell you I hate for them to come in that cuntory. (J. W. Love, Love Papers, Duke) Henderson County

tote, toat *verb* To carry. [*DSME* **tote**, verb; *DARE* "Perh of Afr orig"]

Feb. 4, 1862: the water is bad an we have to **tote** it a good pese. a bout a half mile. (J. S. Councill, Councill Papers, Duke) Watauga County

May 17, 1863: I have got me shirts and Drawers more than I can **toat** this summer. (William Tesh, Tesh Papers, Duke) Yadkin County

Aug. 2, 1863: he was shot in the head and sufered Mity Bad before he died. I **toted** him of[f] of the feald and stade with him tel he died. (John Futch, Futch Letters, NCSA) New Hanover County

May 31, 1864: tha giv mee a gun to **tote** But this morning colonel weaver had it turned over so I hav no gun to **tote**. (J. W. Reese, Reese Papers, Duke) Buncombe County

to the (man/horse) *prepositional phrase*

1. Of rations: a specified amount of provisions for each man.

Apr. 17, 1863: we only draw three cracker and a quarter of a pound of meat **to the man** a day. (Henry Brotherton, Brotherton Papers, Duke) Lincoln County

May 17, 1863: we draw 1 ½ lb Flour **to the man** and sugar enough to sweeten or coffee and Rice. we get splendid Baccon. (William Tesh, Tesh Papers, Duke) Yadkin County

Mar. 16, 1864: we get tolerble plenty now Such as it is. it is corn choping the roughest Sort and fat mete a third of a pound **to the man** for a day. (Jesse Hill, Hill Letters, NCSA) Forsyth County

2. Of horse feed: a specified amount issued for each horse.

May 23, 1864: iwas on the post 24 hours of it all nite without fire. set on my horse every 5 and 6 hour of the time and wee get 2 bundles of fodder aday **to the hors** and one half galon of corn a day. (Silas Stepp, Stepp Letters, UNCA) Buncombe County

tother *pronoun* Other, the other.

Dec. 18, 1862: Miles Drum was Shot in his head above his tempel and lodged against the skin on **tother** Side and I hope [= helped] to bery him. (Marcus Hefner, Hefner Papers, NCSA) Catawba County

Dec. 21, 1863: I hope my **tother** two little ones will be the same way when they get big a nuff to go to scool. (Neill McLeod, McLeod Letters, SHC) Moore County

July 15, 1864: I think the most of the fighting is over at this plase. the yankeys is on one Side of the river and us on **tether** Side. (Alexander Frank, Frank Papers, Duke) Davidson County

touch see **tetch**

tow *noun* Coarse fabric, usually made from flax. [*DSME* **tow**, noun]

Nov. 18, 1864: we want some good **tow** to wipe our guns as we have to keep them in good fix. (John Peterson, Peterson Papers, Duke) Catawba County

to what *conjunction* Compared to what (two sets of conditions).

Jan. 1, 1862: we are fixed hier now So that we can do as wel as if we was at home almost. we have a good close cabbin and beads fixed up off the ground so it looks like home **to what** It did when we was in our old tent Smoked half to Death. (James W. Overcash, Overcash Papers, Duke) Rowan County

Sept. 14, 1862: We had no tent to lay tell last night. it Seem like home now **to what** it did. (W. H. Brotherton, Brotherton Papers, Duke) Catawba County

Oct. 5, 1862: I thought I seed hard times when I wase at home but I did not see any thing **to Whate** I see here. (Isaac Copeland, Copeland Letters, NCSA) Surry County

Mar. 24, 1863: I am faring very well **to what** I have ben for I am Getting yust to my fear [= fare]. Daniel Brown, Brown Coll., NCDA) Duplin County

trafling see **trifling**

trash *noun*

1. A worthless or disreputable person. [*OED* **trash**, noun[1], 4]

Feb. 25, 1862: I expect she drove us off because you were not with us. I dont know what els She got mad A bout. I never was drove off from any bodys house before & called **trash** before. that was A time long to be remembered. (Florah Ann Campbell, Jackson Family Corr., Notre Dame) Moore County

Nov. 6, 1863: well it is useless for me to spend my time in Writing about such lowlife **trash** and tharefore I will not say enything farther concerning those that runaways from thare Country call. (J. F. Coghill, Coghill Papers, Duke) Granville County

Sept. 4, 1864: you Sead Some thing about my farthers having Sutch aroudy Set that you cold not Stay thare. I wont you to tel me who he has lying thare. me and Daniel wonts to no verry bad. I hope he hant got apassle of **trash** lying round him liveing off of what me and Daniel worked hard for. (John Hartman, Hartman Papers, Duke) Rowan County

2. Of food: poor quality.

July 5, 1861: we eate too much **trach** an backen [= bacon] but I think that we will get uste to it after wile. (Julius Seitz, Whitner Papers, Duke) Catawba County

tree *verb* To use dogs to run game up a tree.

May 1, 1864: tell john to feed yard [= dog's name] well so he Can **tree** Sqirls. (J. W. Reese, Reese Papers, Duke) Buncombe County

Jan. 6, 1865: tel dock he must lern his dog to **tree** possoms and Squirles So that me and him can go hunting when I get home. (Jesse Hill, Hill Letters, NCSA) Forsyth County

trembles *noun* A condition characterized by involuntary trembling or shaking, especially of the hands. See also **weak trembles**

May 10, 1863: dear wife I have lot more to wright than I could right in a week bwt I shant right much now for I cant right. I have Got the **trimbles** So bad I doant feele like setting up. (Daniel Brown, Brown Coll., NCSA) Duplin County

July 12, 1863: she sais that she can not rite to yo she has got the **trimbles** so bad. (Sarah Bell, Murph Papers, Duke) Catawba County

Nov. 12, 1863: you dont now how bad that I want to see you and My littel Babes. I had to stand gard last night and I hav got the **Trimbles** so bad that I cant Hardly Rite. (F. M. Poteet, Poteet-Dickson Letters, NCSA) McDowell County

trick *noun* A small, inexpensive item. [*OED* **trick**, noun, 6.b. "A trifling ornament or toy; a trinket, bauble, knick-knack; hence *pl.*, small and trifling articles; 'traps,' personal belongings or effects (*U.S.*)"]

June 25, 1863: I here send a few little **tricks** with E. Fishel to Julius which were pickked upp on the battle ground. (C. A. Hege, Hege Papers, MHI) Davidson County

Oct. 21, 1864: I will tel you what I capturd. I got a pocket book with 44 dollars of green back and a nap sack and a blanket and a good oil chloth and pare of boots and severl other little **tricks** and little pocket knife. (Jesse Hill, Hill Letters, NCSA) Forsyth County

trifling *adjective* No account, lazy, good-for-nothing; small, lacking promise. [*DARE* chiefly South, Midland]

May 7, 1863: they persons that have the corn stilled hire people to still it that are so **trifeling** that the good Citizans think it unnesissary to take them to Court, as non but the stiller suffers according to the act of the legislature on stilling. (T. J. Bicknell, Vance Papers, NCSA) Wilkes County

Feb. 6, 1864: my dear I am Sorry to tel that I will not get home this winter. they air Sending the **triflen** edgcome tackeys and the conscripts. So that will throw me back that I wont get home this winter. (John Hartman, Hartman Papers, Duke) Rowan County

June 18, 1864: I tell you that thay was vary glad to see us a coming and I think it was a nuf to make them glad for the **trafling** yankes Jest tars up evry thing whare thay go. thay Destroy all the propety thay can find. thay eaving to[t]e oute people fethers beads and tare them all to peaces. I Do wish that thay [would] go back and let us a lone. (J. W. Joyce, Joyce Papers, MHI) Stokes County

Dec. 2, 1864: I have just taken the pigs from the red sow. she dident save but three. they are very **trifling**. (Ann Bowen, Bowen Papers, NCSA) Washington County

trimbles see **trembles**

truck[1] *noun* Mainly vegetables grown for use by a family but may also include small crops such as cotton, flax, and cane raised for use by a household or crops in general. [*DARE* **truck**, noun[1], 1]

Jan. 17, 1862: I Waunt you to make all the **truck** you can this coming year for it will Be Worth something. (G. J. Huntley, Huntley Papers, WCU) Rutherford County

Mar. 3, 1863: I Can inform you that we hav rain A Plenty hear at this time. I have all my **truck** Plante[d] but my Cabage. (Keziah Hefner, Hefner Papers, NCSA) Catawba County

Nov. 18, 1864: Send that least pot. we need it to cook turnups and other **truck.** Send a small pan and lid to bake corn bread in. (John Peterson, Peterson Papers, Duke) Catawba County

truck[2] *noun* Househould goods, clothing, supplies. [*DSME* **truck**, noun, *DARE* **truck**, noun[1], 4]

Aug. 21, 1861: we have a grate deal of raine for the last three or four weeks. it is very disagreeabel hier our tents leaks when it raines hard. we have to pile our **truck** up in the middle and sit on them till it is over. (James W. Overcash, Overcash Papers, Duke) Rowan County

Aug. 20, 1863: I want to know if you sold the bonnet **truck** that you took or not and what you sold them at. (Mary C. Kendrick, Kendrick Papers, NCSA) Cleveland County

Mar. 13, 1864: we charged upon the negro cavalry in the Town of Suffolk. we killd abowt 30 Negroes and Capturd several horses over coats and other cloathing and other **truck**. (W. L. Bleckley, Bleckley Papers, Duke) Catawba County

truck patch *noun* A garden for raising vegetables for household use. See also **truck**[1]. [*DSME* **truck patch**, noun; *DARE* chiefly Midland, Lower Mississippi Valley]

June 18, 1862: I most now fix to come to a close by asken you to rite as soon as you can find out wheir the company is and lette me now how you and the childrean is geten a longue and how your garden is doing and your potatoes is doing and all your **truck patches**. (Isaac Lefevers, Lefevers Papers, NCSA) Catawba County

June 1, 1863: you wrote and that the Garden and **truck patches** looked flourishing. (James Zimmerman, Zimmerman Papers, Duke) Forsyth County

June 4, 1863: Francis I wold like to hear how your little corne crop looks and **truck paches**. (J. W. Joyce, Joyce Papers, MHI) Stokes County

turkle *noun* variant form of *turtle*. [*DARE* chiefly South, South Midland]

May 24, 1863: I will send some of you 75 cts as I cant get any thing here for it. I got 25 from J.M. Kids and I think I got the other from J Clark. I caught a water **turkle** the other day and sold it for $1.50 cts. (Daniel Murph, Murph Papers, Duke) Catawba County

turn *noun*

1. An amount of grain that can be ground with one turn of a millwheel. [*DSME* **turn**, noun, 2]

Feb. 2, 1863: wheat is 6 dollars per bushel. I have one **turn** to grind yet then I dont know whether I will ever taste biscuit again or not. (Mary Driskell, Caldwell Coll., ECU) Cabarrus County

2. A load. [*DARE* chiefly Middle and South Atlantic; also Gulf States]

Sept. 27, 1862: I am very sore from marching and carrying such a heavy **turn** and can eat as harty as I ever could. (James Zimmerman, Zimmerman Papers, Duke) Forsyth County

Dec. 15, 1864: We have comenced drawing wood. we get two smawl shoulder **turns** a day to a Company. (B. Y. Malone, *Malone Diary,* 55) Caswell County

turn about *adverb phrase* By turns, alternately. See also **time about**.

Nov. 11, 1861: as to cooking we take it **turn about** a mongst us and stand guard also. (W. P. Burns, Peterson Papers, Duke) Catawba County

Feb. 8, 1863: Dear Wife I can say to you that I still cook some yet. I cook one week and Monro Miller one week. we take it **turn a bout**. (W. F. Wagner, *Confederate Soldier,* 36) Catawba County

turnal see **tornal**

turn off *verb* To dismiss, release, discharge; see Overview § II.4.7.

Apr. 26, 1862: My dear Partha rite as Soon as yo get this letter for i mite meet your letter on the road for i dont know but wat imay be **turned off**. (John Hartman, Hartman Papers, Duke) Rowan County

turn out *verb* See Overview § II.4.7.

1. To defeat in an election; as past participle, to be *turned out* of a political or military office; to fail in a bid for reelection.

June 13, 1862: we see hard times & good times But that is the way to git a long. Co H is givin up to be the best Company in the Regiment But Some Rascal thare too. We hav a good set of officers Sence Swann left. he was **turned out** & I was glad. (A. F. Harrington, Hubbard Papers, Duke) Moore County

Oct. 26, 1863: Old Capt Swann is Enroling officer in that County and I expect he he will bare down on him as he is my Brother. I being an officer in his Old Companey and helped **to turn him out** of Office. (A. A. Jackson, Jackson Family Corr., Notre Dame) Moore County

2. To enlist.

Aug. 18, 1862: if i wase in thomas and James place i Should Stay as long as i could before i should **turn out** any more. (Robert Carpenter, Carpenter Family Papers, ECU) Chatham County

3. To drive livestock out to pasture; of hogs: to drive out to forage on their own.

May 17, 1864: mi cow does verry well. to of mi hens has got chickens. i **turned out** mi pig and it is doing verry well now. your hog is growing finely. (Sarah Wester, Wester Coll., NCSA) Franklin County

twist *ordinal number* variant form of *twice*.

Mar. 6, 1862: we had orders today from General Whiten to drill **twist** every day. (B. Y. Malone, *Malone Diary,* 16) Caswell County

Nov. 19, 1863: tena we air on the norwest Cide of the mishnary Ridg in Cite of Chat ta nooga. tena it is A Cite to Be hold from the top of this Ridge. you Can see Chat A noogia and yankys A plenty. tena wee hav A Baut seventy fiv thousan men hear and the feds has A Baut **twist** that A maunt. this is A awful Cit to loock A pon. (J. W. Reese, Reese Papers, Duke) Buncombe County

Nov. 22, 1863: I wood like to get a letter **twiste** a wee-ake enny how an oftener if I cood. (A. S. Harrill, Civil War Coll., TSLA) Rutherford County

Nov. 23, 1863: we had preachen hear **twist** Sunday But I would of been mutch glader to of bin at home to of went to with you. (F. M. Poteet, Poteet-Dickson Letters, NCSA) McDowell County

twist (of tobacco) *noun* Leaves of tobacco twisted or braided before it cures.

Feb. 4, 1864: I sent you somthing to eat by Marion Higins five pies and five ginger Cakes, one doz unions, two custerds, 1 ham of Meat, and three **twists**

of tobaco. (Martha Poteet, Poteet-Dickson Letters, NCSA) McDowell County

type, tipe *noun* A photograph; short form of *daguerreotype, ambrotype, tintype.*

Sept. 16, 1862: you wrote to me to send you my **type** But never have Been to any place where I could have it taken yet. I am agoing to have it taken the first chance that I can get and send it to you. (J. H. Hundley, Hundley Family Letters, SHC) Stokes County

Aug. 3, 1863: my dear wife you Sead Some thing about my dear little daughters cising [= kissing] my **type.** god bless hur little hart. how I wold like to Se hur. (John Hartman, Hatman Papers, Duke) Rowan County

June 20, 1864: you wrote to me to have my **type** taken if I could. I can say to you that I have tried to have it taken but did not succeed in getting it done. (J. H. Baker, J. H. Baker Papers, Duke) Rockingham County

typhoid fever *noun* numerous variant forms.

Mar. 21, 1862: he sead he was going to heven to see his dear old farther. I had hem bured nise and deasant he dyde in the colege hospital in goldsboro N C and was bured in the pispacaling [= Episcopalian] grave yard. he was sick three weaks with the **typhored feaver**. he suferd more then tong can tell. he was the porest person I ever saw. (James Keever, Keever Papers, Duke) Lincoln County

Oct. 13, 1862: I herd today that he is at home and has the **tifored fever** and is verry low. (J. W. Lineberger, *Gaston Ranger,* 23) Gaston County

Apr. 14, 1863: I under stant that he had the **tiberdfored** fever and the munps and his Legs both war sore and eat to the bone so I sopose he dide turebl deth. (Martha Futch, Futch Letters, NCSA) New Hanover County

Sept. 5, 1864: ther is Rite Smart of Sickness in our cuntry. **ty forred fevever** an Scarlet fever. munrow howard has lost 3 children in avery short time with the Scarlet fever. (Thomas Brotherton, Brotherton Papers, Duke) Catawba County

U

ult. *adverb* A specific day of the previous month; abbreviation for *ultimo.*

June 1, 1863: We left Kinston the 20th **ult.** and come as far as Richmond on the cars and from there here. we had to foot it. (Christopher Hackett, Hackett Papers, Duke) Guilford County

July 21, 1863: i went to kinston on the 16th **ult** and when I got thare i could not be examind. it tuck me five days to go to kinston and home agane. (John Roberts, Vance Papers, NCSA) Onslow County

unease see **onease**

uneasy see **oneasy**

unhandy *adjective* Inconvenient.

Dec. 29, 1861: the Camp is about four miles from Town on a high pinney Ridge. I think in a vary healthey place But it is vary **unhandy** about Wood and Water. (G. J. Huntley, Huntley Papers, WCU) Rutherford County

until see **ontil**

unwell see **onwell**

up *adverb* used redundantly to extend or intensify the action of verbs.

May 11, 1863: I live in Transylvania on french Broad and is A Mill Rite and the people wants Mee to Come and **Repair up** Mills if I am A lowd to for I am Neaded Badly they Say. (James Caul, Vance Papers, NCSA) Transylvania County

Aug. 16, 1863: Doctor A.A. Scroggs ses he can help the dropsy but cant help my eys. I have had it all winter and spring in my Legs and their and now it is up in my boddy. I want you to let me stay at home awhile and be **doctord up** and without being interupted if you pleas and then I will be willing to go Back. (M. D. Laney, Vance Papers, NCSA) Caldwell County

Nov. 4, 1863: if you have any old socks or any old thing that can be **mended up** I want you to send it home if you have a chance and have it **mended up**. (Sarah Overcash, Overcash Papers, Duke) Rowan County

Oct. 30, 1864: I understand the day before he was killed, he **shaved up** nicely. looked so promising for life as likely to live as any body else. (Washington Wills, Wills Papers, SHC) Halifax County

up the spout see **go up the spout**

upward *adverb* variant form *uperd.*

Sept. 25, 1861: I am going down in the town next saterday morning to have my Liknes taken I can get it taken for one dollar and **uperd**. (J. W. Williams, Williams Papers, Duke) Onslow County

us *pronoun* used reflexively instead of *ourselves.*

Jan. 1866: we was all regler discarge and had the privledge of bying **us** Shot guns to take home with us to use on our farms and when we all landed at Winton the 20 day Dec. with our Shot guns. Some 1 or 2 mought had pistols. (John Bizzell, *Freedom,* ser. 2: 801–2) Hertford County

use see **no use**

V

victuals, vittles *noun plural* Rations, provisions, food; from Middle English/Old French *vitaile, vitayle.*

May 24, 1862: I received the **vitles** you sent to me an is going to eat some this morning. (J. W.Williams, Williams Papers, Duke) Onslow County

Sept. 12, 1862: we get coffey for breakfast and Supper and other **vittls** tolerabley plenty. (A. D. McBride, McBride Family Papers, SHC) Bladen County

Aug. 6, 1863: Father is A fixing to start in the morning and Mother is A fixing **vitles** to send to him. (Sally Bauldin, Hundley Family Letters, SHC) Stokes County

Sept. 11, 1864: the time will Soon Come wen i can Come home and Be with my Dear wiefe and childern once more in this woorld and eat some of your good **vittles**. (Wade Hubbard, Hubbard Papers, Duke) Anson County

Dec. 31, 1864: I went to See newton mackinsy last Sonday and got the poake of **victuals** you Sent to me in his box and it was all wright and good. (Alexander Keever, Keever Papers, Duke) Lincoln County

W

wagers *noun plural* Wages, pay.

Aug. 7, 1861: We hant got no Cent of our **wagers** yet. (Peter Poteet, Poteet-Dickson Letters, NCSA) Burke County

Jan. 15, 1863: the Cornel Red owt orders for All men over thirty five years of age Could Pay Back thare Bounty and Loose thare **wagers**. (McCoy Johnson, Vance Papers, NCSA) Johnston County

June 28, 1863: I will also inform you that there is one month and four days **wagers** due be sides his bounty which you are entitled to and which I hope you will git. (John Bachelor, Brown Coll., NCSA) Duplin County

Nov. 19, 1863: tha air owing mee 77 dollars for **wagers** and A Baut 60 dollars of comppotishing money that was A lowed for my Clothing that I never tuck up. (J. W. Reese, Reese Papers, Duke) Buncombe County

wair see **ware**[2]

waistcoat see **wescoat**

wait on *verb* To tend to, care for; to nurse someone who is ill or wounded; see Overview § II.4.7. [*DARE* South, South Midland]

Mar. 16, 1862: I am in goldsbur at the hospital **waiting on** the wounded. (C. F. Mills, Mills Papers, Duke) Iredell County

July 24, 1862: Mr Merrell come to our camp yesterday eavening. I was truly glad to see him for I like to see any of our friends he has been in Richmond several days **waiting on** his son henry. poor ben and henry. they will kneed no more **waiting on**. Ben died before his father got here. Henry died in a few days afterwards. (W. M. Patton, Patton Family Letters, SHC) Buncombe County

Aug. 4, 1862: we wants him to com home & stay until he will get well & you come with him **to wate on** him a coming home. (Dicy Ann Jackson, Jackson Family Corr., Notre Dame) Moore County

Aug. 13, 1862: the mess is well except James vaughn. he went to the hospital yesterday at golsburough. he is purty bad of with relaps of mesels. woody went **to wate on** him. (R. C. Love, Love Papers, Duke) Henderson County

wake (up) *verb* variant forms *waked, waked up, woked up.*

Aug. 14, 1862: one of our company got his fingr cut off one night in his sleep and he or nobody els knows what or who done it, it never **waked** him when it was done. he **waked up** in the night and complained of his hand hurting him, they got a light and saw that his finger was cut. (James Zimmerman, Zimmerman Papers, Duke) Forsyth County

Aug. 17, 1862: in the morning we are **waked** by the sound of the drumb. then the roll is called. (C. A. Hege, Hege Papers, MHI) Davidson County

June 3, 1863: tell her that I have just **woked up** frome a knap of sleep. (James A. Patton, Patton Letters, Emory) Granville County

Aug. 21, 1864: I dreamed about you this morning. I thought that I was at home and as well satsfide as I ever was in my life but when I **waked up** I was laying on my blanket. (F. M. Poteet, Poteet-Dickson Letters, NCSA) McDowell County

wamus (also *wamis, womis, warmas*) *noun* A jacket. [*DARE* "Du *wambuis, wammes,* dial Germ and PaGer *wammes* (Ger *wams*)"; chiefly North Central, Pennsylvania]

Aug. 26, 1862: we drawed some cloathing we drawed **wamises** and pants and draws and shirts and caps each of us a soot all but shoose and sock. (W. F. Wagner, *Confederate Soldier,* 11) Catawba County

Dec. 28, 1863: you wanted to now whether I had drawd any Clothing or not. I have draud janes shirt and **warmas.** I do not lack for clothing to wear but I kneed one blanet yit. (Alexander Keever, Keever Papers, Duke) Lincoln County

Jan. 26, 1864: I want you To bring me one Shirt one pare of drawers and A blanket and A comfert tel you return. I havant had any blanket this winter. I drawd two par of pants and one **womis**. (Marcus Hefner, Hefner Papers, NCSA) Catawba County

Nov. 5, 1864: I drawed apare of pants and Shirt & **wamis** and drawer and a cap. I Sent the cap home for Rufus. it was too little for me. (John Peterson, Peterson Papers, Duke) Catawba County

want *noun* A lack, need (of something); followed by preposition *of.*

Oct. 26, 1862: You stated somthing about writing about every bodies children. if I had the paper I would not mind it but by the time I get started I hav to stop for the **want** of Space. (G. T. Beavers, Upchurch Papers, Duke) Chatham County

Mar. 3, 1863: if Our big lande o[w]ners & slave hol ders ante stopt from ma ken such large crops of tobacco our countrey will Perrish oute in a nother year & Whipt oute for the **wante** of Breade & meate. (Pleasant Black, Vance Papers, NCSA) Rockingham County

Aug. 15, 1862: Dear wife I was sorrow to hear you was sow dry up their and that every thing was burning up for the **want** of Rain. (Isaac Lefevers, Lefevers Papers, NCSA) Catawba County

Sept. 10, 1863: I intended to write you A longer letter than this but for the **want** of paper and time it is so that I cannot. (J. F. Coghill, Coghill Letters, SHC) Granville County

want *verb* To need, lack. [*OED* **want**, verb, 2.a. and 2.d.]

Apr. 25, 1863: old Jo hooker ses he only **wants** 4 weke to perish us out. (James M. Amos, Amos Papers, Duke) Rockingham County

July 28, 1863: I aint laid by no corn yet but a bout three days plowing and it is raining now and evry thing **wants** work. (James Broach, Broach Papers, Duke) Person County

want see **be**, 9, *weren't*

ware[1] *noun* variant form of *war.*

June 12, 1862: old Stone Wall Jackson has Whiped out the yankees thare and got Lots of prisners also Lots of Amunition comisaries stores & Munitions of **ware.** camp Equipage &c &c. (Alfred Walsh, Proffit Family Letters, SHC) Wilkes County

Oct. 5, 1862: the yaller feever is fearfully rageing at wilmington and I fear it will git in our regt. I wish that this cruel **ware** will soon end for we are all giting tird of it. (S. E. Love, Love Papers, Duke) Henderson County

Nov. 29, 1862: gravs ses the north is thriving fast on this war. <we?> hav herd they was starving. he tels a defernt tail to that. he saw thousandes of men drilling and preparing to come on. he sayes they have fifteen iron clad vesels now ready to travel. it is the genral belief of the people that the **ware** cannot last much longer. (J. T. Revis, Revis Letters, NCSA) Henderson County

ware[2] *noun* Earthenware and stoneware.

May 30, 1863: I want to no whether there will be any chance to get a Contract to make **ware** for the government or a detail. Mr Govonor vance I will State to you that I am tolerable bad Corr.,uptureed [= ruptured]. I can stand making **ware** beter then marching for instans for chamber Mugs for Hospital use also galon pitchers and too gallon pitchers would be Necessary for Hosptial use. also three half pint bottels for puting Medicean in and also wash boals Dishes Mugs and all kind of ware from one gallon upto five. (Joseph Richey, Vance Papers, NCSA) Lincoln County

June 14, 1863: Dear wife you Rote to me that Bil had not paid you yet. If Stamy wil not settle it in that way I want you to Be shore and kee[p] what **wair** and clay is their and dont allow him to move it. it maybe that some one wil turn it up for you own shears [= on shares] and burn it [= fire it in a kiln]. (Isaac Lefevers, Lefevers Papers, NCSA) Catawba County

warmas, warmis see **wamus**

warter *noun* variant form of *water.*

June 12, 1862: it is rumerd hear that our reg. is orderd away from hear. I do Not know and I dont care if it is for the Strong Limstone **Warter** is Not good for No 1 [= no one]. (Alfred Walsh, Proffit Family Letters, SHC) Wilkes County

Aug. 2, 1863: i want you to com and sea Me and fetch Me a **warter** Milin and rite Me word how your garden is and how your crop is. (John Futch, Futch Letters, NCSA) New Hanover County

Aug. 9, 1863: We are Camped in alarge oake Grov about ahalf mile from kenansville. We hav a splendid Well of **Warter**. (Edgar Smithwick, Smithwick Papers, Duke) Martin County

waste *verb* To spoil. [*OED* **waste**, senses †6, *Obs., rare,* and †13]

Aug. 30, 1864: he sed that the apels was **wasted** Roten that tha wasant no acount. he sed that he would try to save the dried fruit for me till I got well. (F. M. Poteet, Poteet-Dickson Letters, NCSA) McDowell County

water million, water millon see **melon**

ways, a long ways *noun* A distance, usually a considerable distance.

Aug. 14, 1862: I want to se you mighty bad but I dont now when I shal for I am **a long ways** from you. (Austin Brown, Brown Family Papers, Duke) Johnston County

Aug. 28, 1862: I am **a long ways** from you now. I am 15 miles a bove gordinvill in Cite of the blue Ridge. (A. D. McBride, McBride Family Papers, SHC) Bladen County

June 9, 1863: I am afraid I never will get to See you any more on earth for I hear that the yanckeys has run you all back agood **ways**. (Sarepta Revis, Revis Letters, NCSA) Henderson County

Aug. 2, 1863: he was kild at getties burg P N. pore feler he got kild **a long wase** from home. (John Futch, Futch Letters, NCSA) New Hanover County

ways *noun* A means of accomplishing something, a way.

June 20, 1864: tell her I would send a pound of soda if I had any **wais** to send them. (J. H. Baker, J. H. Baker Papers, Duke) Rockingham County

weakly *adjective* Weak, sickly, debilitated, chronically ill. [*OED* **weakly**, adjective]

Aug. 2, 1862: I have Went through Lots and is **Weakly** and vary pore and puny But I Can Curl my tail a Little yet. (G. J. Huntley, Huntley Papers, WCU) Rutherford County

Nov. 18, 1862: I allso have A Brother which is allso A very **weekly** man or was when he went in to sirves. (Thomas Rogers, Vance Papers, NCSA) Duplin County

Jan. 4, 1863: I am 48 years old in Febuary next and has 4 litle children and My wife which is vary **weekly**. (J. C. M. Justice, Vance Papers, NCSA) Cumberland County

July 28, 1863: I am a verry pore **weakley** man and has a family of seven Small childern the oldest is only Eight year and a fue days old. (A. D. Bracy, Vance Papers, NCSA) Robeson County

weak trembles *noun* An uncontrollable trembling of the hands because of illness, hunger, or exhaustion. See also **trembles**

June 22, 1862: i cant rite A bout eny more for i have got the **week trimels**. (W. P. Cline, Cline Papers, SHC) Catawba County

wearious *adjective* Weary.

Mar. 21, 1863: after a long and **Wearious** march We returnd to Camp a gain. (Isaac Copeland, Copeland Letters, NCSA) Surry County

wear out see **wore out**

week *noun* In various phrases used to fix a date.

1. in reference to past event, usually following *last* and a day of the week.

Feb. 4, 1864: there has bin several deaths in the last two or three weeks. your Aunt Barbry died last sunday **week**. (Martha Poteet, Poteet-Dickson Letters, NCSA) McDowell County

Aug. 5, 1864: I left the army ner winchester last saturday **week**. they had a fight next day drove the yankes 10 miles took about 2000 prisoners. (Stephen Whitaker, Whitaker Papers, NCSA) Cherokee County

2. in reference to a future event, usually following *next* and a day of the week.

Nov. 24, 1862: I dont know what I ame a getting yet and wont know untill pay day Comes. thats **next tusday weak**. (John J. Taylor, Taylor Papers, Duke) Orange County

Apr. 5, 1863: Dear wife this day & **to morrow one weak** wil Be your communion meaten and I should be glad to Be their with you one time more. (Isaac Lefevers, Lefevers Papers, NCSA) Catawba County

3. in the phrase *a week ago*.

May 17, 1862: we havent got news to write. we left camp mangum last monday **a week ago**. (J. W. Lineberger, *Gaston Ranger,* 7) Gaston County

Jan. 24, 1864: they had took a Sprey last night **a week a go** and in there fight broak one mans leg and struck another one on the head with a pole. (John A. Smith, J. A. Smith Papers, Duke) Cabarrus County

4. in the phrase *was a week (ago)*.

Dec. 24, 1861: I received your Letter with gladness whitch come to hand Last Sunday **was A week Ago**. (J. W. Williams, Williams Papers, Duke) Onslow County

Feb. 6, 1862: Dear Aunt I have not got much of importac to write to write you at present only I can inform you that we have lefte More head citty. we lefte thare laste Sunday **was a week a go**. (W. D. Carter, Culberson Papers, Duke) Chatham County

Sept. 10, 1863: I left the hospital this day **was one week ago** and am geting along as well as could be expected. (C. F. Mills, Mills Papers, Duke) Iredell County

well *adjective* Healthy (in attributive position rather than after a linking verb). [*OED* **well**, adjective, 5, c.(a)]

June 28, 1863: our fair hear is not very good it is not fit for **well** men to eate. (Robert Carpenter, Carpenter Family Papers, ECU) Chatham County

Jan. 7, 1864: the children is sick with bad colds and I haint seen a **well** day since you left. (Martha Poteet, Poteet-Dickson Letters, NCSA) McDowell County

well as common *adjective phrase* In generally good or average health.

Jan. 15, 1863: i am **well as common** and hope you and family is the Same. (James Hackett, Hackett Papers, Duke) Guilford County

Mar. 8, 1863: you can tell Henrys folkes that He is **well as comon** and Allso Andy Magee is well and fater then he ever was before. (John Ingram, Ingram Papers, Duke) Forsyth County

Apr. 20, 1863: I take the presant opertunitey to drop you a few lines to in form you that I am as **well as common**. (Daniel Revis, Revis Letters, NCSA) Henderson County

Oct. 7, 1864: your Mother & Brother is well as usual and getting on as **well as common**. (Huldah Hubbard, Hubbard Papers, Duke) Anson County

well nigh *adverb phrase* Very nearly. See also **nigh**.

Apr. 25, 1863: I think the con federsy is **wel ny** lat out. (Daniel Revis, Revis Letters, NCSA) Henderson County

went up see **go up (the spout)**

wescoat *noun* A vest; a short, sleeveless under jacket; a jersey; variant form of *waistcoat*.

June 8, 1861: Tell uncle Penland that George has sent his coat and **wescoat** and for him to get them. (W. M. Patton, Patton Family Letters, SHC) Buncombe County

what *relative pronoun* in place of *that, who,* or *which*.

Oct. 7, 1861: the docter says it is the fever and ague **what** ales me. (J. W. Williams, Williams Papers, Duke) Onslow County

June 15, 1863: we would give any thing in the world if I could see yo come home agane. I cant go to A M Smith till I cut my wheat **what** is ripe. then I will go an see what he sais. (Amanda Murph, Murph Papers, Duke) Catawba County

Jan. 5, 1864: you wanted to know a bout James Clothing **what** he left in camp. I cwooden find out what wente with them. (A. J. Spease, Zimmerman Papers, Duke) Forsyth County

what *adverb* used redundantly after *than*. [see *DARE* **what**, adverb]

Feb. 3, 1862: The helth of the redge is beter than **what** it has ben for som time we hant had nary deth in Som time. (G. T. Beavers, Upchurch Papers, Duke) Chatham County

Mar. 16, 1863: Francis you Rote to me that I must write to you oftenr than **what** I do. I write vary offten to. I dont think you git all of my Letters. (J. W. Joyce, Joyce Papers, MHI) Stokes County

Sept. 21, 1864: we cod make our litel rashions go further than **what** thay do. we have men to cock and bring it in to us of night. (Arthur Putnam, Kendrick Papers, NCSA) Cleveland County

what all *pronoun phrase* What (items, things).

Dec. 25, 1862: he wants butter and onions and litle liquer and some other things he ditent say **what all**. (W. F. Wagner, *Confederate Soldier,* 30) Catawba County

what for *adjective phrase* What kind of (a). [see *DSME* **what for**, B; *DARE* **what for (a)** adjective phrase, "In some areas obviously a claque of Ger *was für (ein),* but in others perh from the same idiom in Scots and Engl (Kentish) dial"]

Aug. 23, 1862: I should like to know **what for** time you had getting home and if you got home safe. (James Zimmerman, Zimmerman Papers, Duke) Forsyth County

Dec. 20, 1863: So you must write Soon and often and fail not in So doing and gave me all of the news in Ashe and whether the people in Ashe thinks this war will ever end or not and write how all of my connection is coming on and **what for** times there is in Ashe. (Thornton Sexton, Sexton Letters, Duke) Ashe County

Oct. 10, 1864: I have not received any news from home saince I left. I should be glad to here from you all and **what for** cropp you made &c. (James Zimmerman, Zimmerman Papers, Duke) Forsyth County

what for a looking *adjective phrase* Of a person: having what appearance. [*DSME* **what for**, adjective phrase; see also *DARE* **what for**, adverb phrase, 2]

Nov. 6, 1862: I was a garden Genrl Long Streets head Quarters. the man you have heard sow much talk a bout. he is a bout the sise of J.W. Bandy only a heaver man. he wais about 2 hundread 25 lbs. he has Large whiskers & mostach. fair complection & blew Eyes. we air all under his command at this time. I just thought that I would tell you **what for a loocken** man he is as you have heard sow much talk a bout him. (Isaac Lefevers, Lefevers Papers, NCSA) Catawba County

what went with see **go with**

whenever *conjunction* As soon as. [*DARE* South, South Midland, western Pennsylvania]

Nov. 15, 1864: i will send you that strop an som turnips an som other things **when ever** i get the chance. (Hannah Peterson, Peterson Papers, Duke) Catawba County

where abouts *adverb* Where.

June 12, 1862: I would like to hear from Brother Dave as he is some weir in Va but I dont now **whier abouts** he is Stationd. (Isaac Lefevers, Lefevers Papers, NCSA) Catawba County

whether see **whither**

which *relative pronoun* Who. [*OED* **which**, pronoun and adjective, III. Relative uses, 9. "Used of persons. Now only *dial.*"]

Jan. 4, 1863: I am 48 years old in Febuary next and has 4 litle children and My wife **which** is vary weekly. (J. C. M. Justice, Vance Papers, NCSA) Cumberland County

Mar. 9, 1865: we want to know from the Secretary of War has the Rev Chaplain James **which** is our Superintendent of negros affairs has any wright to take our boy Children from us and from the School and Send them to newbern to work to pay for they ration without they parent Consint. (Richard Boyle, *Freedom*, ser. 1, vol. 2: 233) Tyrrell County

whilst *conjunction* While.

Aug. 8, 1861: he was taken good car of **whilst** sick and was buryed acordin to miletary orders. (Harrison Hanes, Hanes Papers, Duke) Davie County

June 8, 1863: whilst we was a passen threw the 6th N. C. Brass Ban plaid the Bonnie Blew Flag. (B. Y. Malone, *Malone Diary,* 34) Caswell County

whip *verb,* To win (a battle); to defeat (an enemy).

1. transitive.

Sept. 21, 1861: I think the time long to see your lovly face one time more. I hope we will **whip** old abe and come home sone and then I will hav to leave you no more. (J. T. Groves, Davison Papers, Duke) Gaston County

Dec. 19, 1862: Dear father I have bin in a nother hard Battle at Fedrecks Burg. I was not In gaged in the firs but I was under the Shelling for 3 dayes. we **whiped** the yankeys & Ran them a cross the River. (William Carpenter, Carpenter Family Papers, ECU) Chatham County

June 18, 1864: the yankes is the meanest people that I ever saw in my lif. thay make us travil and fight a heap when we **whip** them at one place thay will run a round at another and then we will have to Start a gain. (J. W. Joyce, Joyce Papers, MHI) Stokes County

2. intransitive.

June 24, 1862: our men has been in Line of battle five days at Richmond. it is thought that the fight will come of soon. if we can **whip** thair I think the war will close soon. (J. W. Williams, Williams Papers, Duke) Onslow County

July 31, 1862: I am so tierd of this war I wish one side wood **whip** so we cood Come home. (L. W. Griffin, Griffin Papers, NCSA) Rutherford County

Apr. 28, 1864: we **whipped** when they outnumbered us so far and we did not lose a single man. (C. A. Walker, Walker Papers, WCU) Cherokee County

3. past participle/adjective.

Feb. 2, 1865: the sesesh men dos hate to own that we are **whiped**. they wont talk about it if they can help it. it dos me good to tell it to them but they hav to own it. (Martha Poteet, Poteet-Dickson Letters, NCSA) McDowell County

Feb. 25, 1865: tha is houndreds a going to the yankeys every week and as Soon as warm wether coms nearly all our Brigade Say tha will go home or Som where elce. tha Say it hant of any use to Stay here and be kild for nothing. tha all Say we ar **whiped** and tha all no it. (Jesse Hill, Hill Letters, NCSA) Forsyth County

whip out *verb* To defeat badly, rout completely; often with *out* moved to a position after the object; see Overview § II.4.7.

May 23, 1862: we have got Some yankes prisners down here and they say that they are agoing to **whip** us **out** til some time in June. (Christopher Sherrill, CS Army Misc., Duke) Catawba County

Feb. 23, 1863: I am in hopes that the most of the Big fighten is over But if we Stil have to Keep fighten the Sooner it is don the sooner the War will close for it appears that neather side will give up tell one or the other is **whiped out**. (Isaac Lefevers, Lefevers Papers, NCSA) Catawba County

May 8, 1863: I Come out saft but I dont know how I Dunit. the yankees Shot Down our boys right around me. I thought that I wold be kill evry minit. we lost one hundred and forty men killed and wounded. we **whip** them **out** an run them back. (J. W. Joyce, Joyce Papers, MHI) Stokes County

June 16, 1863: We **Whooped** the yankes **out** & takin Winchester & We gaind a great victory hear. (J. H. Hundley, Hundley Family Letters, SHC) Stokes County

white swelling *noun* An abnormal swelling of the joints or limbs, apparently without redness, although the exact nature of the illness is not certain. [*OED* **swelling**, noun, 2.a. (one citation for *white swelling* from 1803); *DSME* **white swelling**, noun, "Apparently bone erysipelas"]

Sept. 30, 1863: I am in my twenty Third year and Have Had the **White Sweling** in my Leg and Foot about twenty one yeares Which Has taken away all my foot or very neare it. (J. W. Ellis, Vance Papers, NCSA) Chatham County

Mar. 7, 1864: Some ses that it is the **white Swellin** in mi leg. the doctor never Sed what he thort was the matter with it. (Daniel Setzer, Setzer Papers, Duke) Catawba County

white walnut *noun* An alternate name for the butternut tree, *Juglans cinerea*.

Dec. 25, 1858: as you requested to know what kind of timber we have in this country. thare is white oke. black oke. red oake. Spanish oake and hickrey black white and scaly barke. black walnut **white walnut.** mulbery. cotton wood. wile chery. elum and lin wood. shugar trees. sicamore and buckei. buroake. severl other kinds too tedous to mention. the under groth is mostley hasle and shumake. (William Boss, Frank Papers, Duke) Davidson County

whither *conjunction* variant form of *whether*.

Sept. 16, 1862: he put A thunderan grad big blister aun mi back but daunt think that it dun it any guod only it taken the Skin aufan. yeu may gues **whither** that dun me mutch gwod or naugh [= not]. (B. C. Jackson, Jackson Family Corr., Notre Dame) Moore County

June 1, 1864: if ben comes to Swap for mee after hee Starts dont rite any more tel you now [= know] **whither** i come or not. if i get away i dont want any more of your letters to come to the command. (Silas Stepp, Stepp Letters, UNCA) Buncombe County

who all *pronoun phrase* All of whom. [*DSME* **who all**, pronoun phrase]

July 3, 1862: A W parris is with the rest in the fite. I hant heard any thing a bout him. parker did not now **hoo all** was mising this is all I Can find out a bout the fite. (M. W. Parris, Parris Papers, WCU) Jackson County

Aug. 8, 1863: I want you rite to me and tel me **whoo all** has to go to the war. (Daniel Setzer, Setzer Papers, Duke) Catawba County

Dec. 8, 1864: I would like to here from all the neighbors **whoe all** has to go to the army yet &c &c. and what the People say about this war. by now here in the army the most of the soldiers Say tha wont fight an other compaign. (John Peterson, Peterson Papers, Duke) Catawba County

widder *noun* variant form of *widow.*

Dec. 8, 1864: Give my love to the **widder** Culberson and Mr Coles family and all enquayng friends. tell sister if she is thare howdy for me. (D. M. Carter, Culberson Papers, Duke) Chatham County

Apr. 10, 1863: we beleave that otho Cauble will do his duty and has promise to work Cheap fo[r] the Solders wifes and **widders** as we are not abel to pay Specerlating prises for there is many **widders** and Solders wives in this neighbur hood that is not abel to pay for thear work. (Elnori Cauble, Vance Papers, NCSA) Rowan County

wiggletails *noun plural* Mosquito larva. [*OED* **wiggle**, verb, derivatives, **wiggletail** noun]

Sept. 29, 1861: The water we have is the very worst of water. Such as you never Drank in your Life. the **wigeltails** is as thick as Bees in gum [= beehive]. (R. P. Crawford, Estes Family Papers, WCU) Jackson County

winder *noun* variant form of *window.*

July 10, 1863: they were sticking there heads out at the **winders** laughing and holering. (J. W. Lineberger, *Gaston Ranger,* 56) Gaston County

Aug. 22, 1863: we liv in fine house. the[y] is fif tene **winder** in the house. (Francis Blair, J. H. Baker Papers, Duke) Rockingham County

Jan. 14, 1865: I am sorry to learn that W H has lost his beas and to heare they have broke out all of the **winders** at my place on long ridge. (Henry Bowen, Bowen Papers, NCSA) Washington County

winder light *noun* A windowpane. [*DSME* **window light**, noun]

Dec. 14, 1864: some boddy went thar and broke out every **winder lite** in the house and stold his leather. (Ann Bowen, Bowen Papers, NCSA) Washington County

without *conjunction* Unless. [*DSME* **without**, A]

Feb. 11, 1862: thei wont gave a furlow **without** we inlist fur the ware and I dont intend to dooit. (Thornton Sexton, Sexton Letters, Duke) Ashe County

May 9, 1863: they have run lots of troops her from NC. for what I cant tell **without** we ar agoing to cross the river. (L. W. Griffin, Griffin Papers, NCSA) Rutherford County

Sept. 11, 1864: i want to git someting f[r]ome home to eat if i Can But the Chance will be Bad i expect **with ought** some person wer passing to Wilmigton. (Wade Hubbard, Hubbard Papers, Duke) Anson County

Nov. 24, 1864: I dont look for this war to stop for 4 years yet **without** the soldiers all comes home. (Martha Poteet, Poteet-Dickson Letters, NCSA) McDowell County

wonderful(ly) *adverb* Extremely.

Oct. 20, 1864: I hav giv him close attention sence I Come. he rested purty well now. I want you to come ase soone ase you can and if he livese tele then I think wee can git astruch [= stretcher?] and pute him on and bring him home. hee semes sencelesse yeat. he seames to know no body but me and seamese **wonderfle** taken upe with mee. (Malcom Murchison, Albright Papers, NCSA) Chatham County

wore out *verb, adjective* Of people: exhausted; of clothing or shoes: no longer usable; variant form of past participle *worn out.*

Jan. 27, 1863: my over coat is about **wore out** but I think I can draw one before long. (W. F. Wagner, *Confederate Soldier,* 33) Catawba County

Jan. 1, 1864: I want you to Send me apar of Shoes if you can for I cant git non her and mi old Shoes is **wore out**. (Daniel Setzer, Setzer Papers, Duke) Catawba County

May 15, 1864: I am well thogh nearly **wore out** of fighting and marching. (John A. Smith, J. A. Smith Papers, Duke) Cabarrus County

Feb. 25, 1865: you Sed your shous was **wore out**. tel Emoline She must look a round and try and get you Some. (Jesse Hill, Hill Letters, NCSA) Forsyth County

work on *verb* Of a disease or medical condition: to affect, cause a deterioration of health; see Overview § II.4.7.

June 16, 1863: My dispepcia Complant is **working on** mee vary strong. I throd aup alarg quonety of bludy looking stuf the other day. (J. A. W. Revis, Revis Letters, NCSA) Henderson County

worry *verb* To pester, afflict, trouble.

Oct. 29, 1863: I have bin in bad health for ten days with my bowels. Sumthing like flux and fevar. I am sum beter now but not well yet. I have bin on the Sick list for a week. I am taking Spirits of terpin [= turpentine] ons [= once?]. lodnum all the time. I am not confin to bead. I think i am over the worst but it has **worred** me bad. (R. C. Caldwell, Caldwell Coll., ECU) Cabarrus County

worse *adjective* comparative form *worser.*

Nov. 28, 1861: he new that he had to go. the longer they put it [off] the **worsser** it is. (Dena Stack, Confederate Papers, SHC) Union County

Dec. 4, 1864: I want To see you **woser** then I ever did in my life. (Daniel Abernethy, Abernethy Papers, Duke) Catawba County

worse *verb* To make worse, exhaust, damage, injure. [*OED* **worse**, verb, 2]

Sept. 14, 1862: I am well at present though I am a little **worsted** by a hard march from which we returned night before last. (S. A. Patton, Patton Family Letters, SHC) Buncombe

June 6, 1863: the boys is all tolerable well except captin bening field. he is gon to the horspitel. that trip to caintuck **worsted** all the boys. (Daniel Revis, Revis Letters, NCSA) Henderson County

Sept. 10, 1864: I will be on gard to morow garding goverment Stores guns cotin corn powder bots [= boats] prisners. every thing that belongs to the goverment. it taks 50 men to make one gard. when I go on I Stay 24 hours. I hope the chills wont cum back on me badely again. tha **worsted** me badley. (R. C. Caldwell, Caldwell Coll., ECU) Cabarrus County

wristband *noun* The part of a shirt sleeve that covers or fastens around the wrist; a cuff. [*OED* **wristband**, noun.]

Oct. 5, 1862: tell Edward and Chalie and Salie howdy. tell all the boys howdy for me and tell them my fare and tell Bety also I have to pay 10cts to get one shirt washed and after it is done it is not a bit beter than I can do in cold water. stripes al over the back and colar and **ris bands**. (W. D. Smith, W. D. Smith Papers, Duke) Davie County

write *verb* See Overview § II.4.1.10.

1. past tense *written.*

Sept. 19, 1861: I thought yesterday when I **writen** that I had beter not close it. (Harrison Hanes, Hanes Papers, Duke) Davie County

Jan. 11, 1863: Dear Wife this is a small letter but I **ritten** One yesterday. (W. F. Wagner, *Confederate Soldier,* 31) Catawba County

July 22, 1863: I havent heard frum A A senc I **writen** to you but I heard thay hav got back in to Dixey A gane. (B. C. Jackson, Jackson Family Corr., Notre Dame) Moore County

2. past participle *writ, rit.*

Dec. 3, 1862: my dear Partha me and Daniel has **rit** to our farther to Send us abox of provishons and I wont yew to fix me Somthing good and Send it to me. (John Hartman, Hartman Papers, Duke) Rowan County

May 4, 1864: I have **writ** three Letters Since I Recevd one from you. (F. M. Poteet, Poteet-Dickson Letters, NCSA) McDowell County

3. past participle *wrote, rote.*

Mar. 20, 1862: I would of **wrote** oftainer but I hav a Bad chance. (J. W. Love, Love Papers, Duke) Henderson County

Sept. 16, 1862: I have **wrote** three Letters to home and I have not received any from home yit. (R. P.

Kelly, Edmonston-Kelly Family Papers, WCU) Haywood County

Feb. 24, 1863: I hav **rot** and **rote** and I hav not received but this one leter Since i left home. (Daniel Revis, Revis Letters, NCSA) Henderson County

Nov. 30, 1864: the last letter that I got from Carry was **rote** the 22 of may. (W. H. Horton, Councill Papers, Duke) Watauga County

Y

yaller fever *adjective* variant form of *yellow fever.*

Sept. 28, 1862: I can tell you this is a vary sickly place they have got the **yaller feever** and smallpocks both in wilmington. (R. C. Love, Love Papers, Duke) Henderson County

Oct. 3, 1862: Kitty and [= Ann] has Bin very sick with the **yaller fever** for sevel Days pass and the peapel that she stay with ar Driv ing hir out all the time to wurk and she is not abbel to wurk for she can had Ley [= hardly] stand on hir foot. (William H. Thurber, DeRosset Family Papers, SHC) New Hanover County

yam, yam potato *noun* A sweet potato. [*DARE* **yam potato**, noun; chiefly Gulf States]

Oct. 20, 1861: I have not seen any thing a growing here but goobers and **yam potatoes**. (William Featherston, Love Papers, Duke) Henderson County

Mar. 22, 1862: have the Slips [= sweet potato sprounts] beded. bed all the **yams** and negrobusters and plant the rest and get five bushel from mrs Southerland. (Ichabod Quinn, Quinn Papers, Duke) Duplin County

yan, yander *adverb* Yonder.

Sept. 25, 1862: I will rite a little something in this letter a bout the big Ba<ttle?> that was foght the 17th Day of this month. I can tell you that it was a awful fight. the fight was own **yan** side of the potomace River own the Mariland Side. (Isaac Lefevers, Lefevers Papers, NCSA) Catawba County

Sept. 2, 1863: yander goes Wily Cumbo with a load of water melons. (Molly Tesh, Tesh Papers, Duke) Yadkin County

Apr. 22, 1864: the Grounds is dried off here but **yander** 30 or 40 miles the ground is coverd with snow. we can see it when the sun shines. (J. M. Frank, Frank Papers, Duke) Davidson County

yankeedom *noun* The Union states.

July 18, 1863: I have got back to my Company. I hav been over in **yankeedom**. I saw a grate deal while I was gon. wee was treted very well over thare. wee get a planty of bred and meat to eate tho I wold like to bee thar with you to eat sum beans and potaters. (James Teer, Wright Papers, Duke) Alamance County

Apr. 6, 1864: tell Marion E Newsom that I expect William will come from **yankey dom** in a few days. they have a greed to exchang all prisioners. (J. W. Newsom, Newsom Papers, Duke) Halifax County

Jan. 1, 1865: Dear friend I will Bid you farewell till the war ends for I am A going to the Yankees in A day or too. Dear friend I want you to give this letter that is in here to Sarah A Beck. Dear friend. I Am A going to **Yankdom** and I dont think that I will come home till the ware ends. (George Lenard, Frank Papers, Duke) Davidson County

yankee land *noun* The Union states.

July 27, 1863: you rote something a bout Henry Jones. it is so. I saw his grave and John Hanes saw him and saw where he was shot. he was shot in the head and in the brest. some of my Company buried him but I Did not see him but he is cirtainly Dead and buried and left in the **yankey land**. (W. D. Smith, W. D. Smith Papers, Duke) Davie County

yarn *adjective* Of clothing, especially pants: woven or knitted from wool yarn.

May 16, 1862: I was going to send my new pants home but Capt told me to keep them. they are nice black **yarn** pants. (J. W. Williams, Williams Papers, Duke) Onslow County

May 25, 1863: I throwed away my **yarn** pants but I have put down for some more. (Neill McLeod, McLeod Letters, SHC) Moore County

year *noun* variant form of *ear*. See also **roasting ear**. [*DARE* frequent South Midland]

Sept. 17, 1860: I have had the white corn halled down to the mill in the **year**. an will be reddy to comence as soon as mr Myers sends me word. I Shal have to Bey a new corn Sheller. (Thomas Harding, Blount Papers, NCSA) Beaufort County

Aug. 3, 1861: Nancy I want to know if you got your **year** bobs and brest pin I sent. (L. W. Griffin, Griffin Papers, NCSA) Rutherford County

June 24, 1863: There is a yoong calf in Fredericks burg with 2 heads 3 **years** 4 eyes 4 nose holes & 2 mouths. there is a Sick georgia Soldier here who has Seen it & examined it. it sucks with either mouth & it 3d **year** is between its heads. (Andrew J. Proffit, Proffit Family Letters, SHC) Wilkes County

Sept. 9, 1863: sam fanny and bet was all sick last weake with colds and **year** ache. sam and fanny has got well but bet hant well yet. (Molly Tesh, Tesh Papers, Duke) Yadkin County

yearn *verb* variant form of *earn*. [see *DSME* **earn**, verb; *DARE* **earn** verb; chiefly South Midland]

ND [1862]: if bet['s] shoes is give out I want you to get her a pare if you please for if She has wove as mutch Cloth as She says she has I think that she has **yernt** one pare. (W. D. Smith, W. D. Smith Papers, Duke) Davie County

yeast see **east**

yellow janders, yaller janders *noun* variant forms of *yellow jaundice*. See also **janders**.

Aug. 11, 1862: I have the **yellow Janders** at this time. they have come own me since I got back to camp. I never had enny thing to weken me as faist in the same le[ng]the of time. (Isaac Lefevers, Lefevers Papers, NCSA) Catawba County

Oct. 24, 1862: i have bin sick for two week and i haint mutch better yet. i have got the **yaller janders** and the liver complaint. (T. B. Litton, Fisher Papers, Duke) Catawba County

Nov. 22, 1862: I Seat my self to drop you a few lines to let you know that I am well at present. I have had the **yelow janders** but I am well of them now. (Elbert Carpenter, Carpenter Family Papers, ECU) Chatham County

you all *pronoun* You; second-person plural.

June 10, 1861: Nancy I would like to see **yuall** ver well. you in particular. (Harrison Hanes, Hanes Papers, Duke) Davie County

Dec. 30, 1861: I would like to hav ben there to tuck chrismas with **you all**. we had a livly time here. we had about 20 fites on that day but no body was hirt bad. (G. T. Beavers, Upchurch Papers, Duke) Chatham County

Feb. 2, 1862: you rote that Wm Long & Miss Emline Fisher wose a gowin to git mared new year day I wod like to bin thare with **you all**. I hope **you all** had a hapy time. (L. L. Kale, Fisher Papers, Duke) Catawba County

Feb. 25, 1862: I expect we will have no more fun untill **you all** gets back again and I wish that time was here now. (Flora Ann Campbell, Jackson Family Corr., Notre Dame) Moore County

May 16, 1863: I have once more received A letter from you dated the 13 and I was certanly glad to hear from **you all** and to hear that **you all** was well. (J. F. Coghill, Coghill Papers, Duke) Granville County

yourn *possessive pronoun* Yours. [*DARE* especially New England, South, South Midland]

Apr. 1860: my pen is bad my ink is pale my love to you shal never fail. Just as sure as a grape grows on a vine I will be **yourn** if you will be mine. (James Fisher, Fisher Papers, Duke) Catawba County

Apr. 26, 1862: My dear Partha i wont yew to have your likeeness tacon and Send it to me if yew can have **yourn** and my Sweat babs tacon to gether. (John Hartman, Hartman Papers, Duke) Rowan County

May 3, 1864: I cant See why it is my Letters all Seam to gow threw and wile **yourn** dont come more Regelar. I cant Say their is Something not Rite a bout the mail betwixt hear and home. you dont no how uneasy it makes me when I cant hear from you for sow long. (Isaac Lefevers, Lefevers Papers, NCSA) Catawba County

Nov. 24, 1864: if the war dont stop there will be moor children that will perish besids **yourn**. (Martha Poteet, Poteet-Dickson Letters, NCSA) McDowell County

youns (also *youens, yowns, youons, younes) pronoun* You; second-person plural.

Nov. 10, 1861: I thought of **youns** at home and me here on the lonesom Sea Side. (John B. Lance, Lance Papers, LSU) Henderson County

Jan. 22, 1863: I have not got much to rite to **youns** at this time. (J. C. McFee, McFee Letters, SRNB) Buncombe County

Feb. 20, 1863: I have wrote my sister A Song And I want **yowns** and her to learn it agance I come home so that yow can sing it to me. (W. H. Brotherton, Brotherton Papers, Duke) Catawba County

June 1, 1863: I have inquired of the other boys who have been geting Letters if they spoke any thing concerning **youens**. (Christopher Hackett, Hackett Papers, Duke) Guilford County

Oct. 1, 1863: I want to no whether **you ons** has made your molasses ornot and how much you made. (Daniel Setzer, Setzer Papers, Duke) Catawba County

Dec. 19, 1863: Sum thinks tha will cill **youns** yet leavin tha cepe **youns** So long in the gard house. (Susan Setzer, Setzer Papers, Duke) Catawba County

Oct. 1, 1864: if Benton Dont come **youns** can com throw if one of us can mee[t] **youns** at goldsburu. that is the only place **youns** will have to change. (R. C. Caldwell, Caldwell Coll., ECU) Cabarrus County

yous (also *youse, yews) pronoun* You; second-person plural.

Dec. 22, 1861: I Just thought I would write you a fiew lines to let **yous** know that I am well at present and hope when thees fiew lines Comes to hand they may find **yous all** in the same state of health. (James W. Gibson, Gibson Papers, Duke) Catawba County

Dec. 20, 1862: my dear Partha I want yew and my farther to Send me and Daniel abox between **yews**. Send me adram for my crismas. (John Hartman, Hartman Papers, Duke) Rowan County

Dec. 24, 1862: it seems to me lik **yous** is living at home and dont care for us any mor but if **yous** thinks tha it is rite go ahead. **yous** has pleanty and we have nothing. (John S. Overcash, Overcash Papers, Duke) Rowan County

June 25, 1863: i will send her a purty ring. it is not horn. it is a button of some kind. I will send each one of **yous** a button in this letter. the little one is for Susan. (Daniel Murph, Murph Papers, Duke) Catawba County

Aug. 18, 1863: Dear cousin I Seat myself to informe **youse** that we are all tollable well at present (Mary E. Gibson, Overcash Papers, Duke) Iredell County

Jan. 8, 1864: I here the torys and yanks are near Asheville now. I tell you I hate for them to come in that cuntory But it looks like that we cant keep them Back at all places I tell you I am uneasy for **yous** for they will Steal any thing that they lay hans on. (J. W. Love, Love Papers, Duke) Henderson County

Appendix A

The North Carolina Letter Writers

Daniel Abernethy [Catawba], Co. C, 16th NC Inf., Abernethy Papers, Duke

Mary Alderman [Duplin], McBride Family Papers, SHC

Bartlett Y. Allen [Person], Co. H, 24th NC Inf., Vance Papers, NCSA

Henry Allen [Lincoln], Co. K, 23rd NC Inf., Brotherton Ppers, Duke

Joseph Allen [Lincoln], Co. K, 23rd NC Inf., Brotherton Papers, Duke

Martha A. Allen [Orange], Vance Papers, NCSA

M. E. Allen [Edgecomb], Vance Papers, NCSA

Beady M. Alley [Franklin], Vance Papers, NCSA

Leonard Alman [Cabarrus], Co. D, 7th NC Inf., Alman Papers, Duke

Francis Amos [Stokes], Amos Papers, Duke

James M. Amos [Stokes], Co. L, 21st NC Inf., Amos Papers, Duke

Peter Amos [Stokes], Amos Papers, Duke

William Amos [Stokes], Amos Papers, Duke

Richard Anderson [county unknown], Vance Papers, NCSA

Elijah Ange [Pitt], Co. D, 44th NC Inf., Vance Papers, NCSA

Fed Arrington [Chowan], Hayes Collection, SHC

John Averett [Pitt], Co. D, 44th NC Inf., Vance Papers, NCSA

John D. Bachelor [Duplin], Co. B, 3rd NC Inf., Brown Collection, NCSA

Tilmon F. Baggarly [Iredell], Co. I, 5th NC Inf., Baggarly Papers, Duke

Harvey Bailey [Yancey], Co. G, 29th NC Inf., Bailey Letters, CW Doc. Coll., MHI

Henry Baker [Catawba], Co. E, 57th NC Inf., Henry Baker Papers, Duke

James H. Baker [Rockingham], Co. D, 4th Batt., NC Jr. Res., J. H. Baker Papers, Duke

J. D. Baker [Cumberland], Co. C, 2nd NC Art., Vance Papers, NCSA

J. N. Ballenton [New Hanover], Co. C, 30th NC Inf., Vance Papers, NCSA

John C. Barnes [Robeson], Co. A, 31st NC Inf., Phillips Papers, Duke

Duncan R. Barnhill [Bladen], Co. H, 2nd NC Art., Military Coll., Civil War, NCSA

Rhoda Bateman [Washington], Bowen Papers, Military Coll., Civil War, NCSA

Sally Bauldin [Stokes], Hundley Family Letters, SHC

Ned Baxter [Tyrrell], Berlin, et al., *Freedom,* ser. 1, vol. 2: 202–3

C. E. Beavers [Chatham], Co. I, 6th NC Inf., Upchurch Papers, Duke

G. T. Beavers [Chatham], Co. I, 6th NC Inf., Upchurch Papers, Duke

J. S. Beavers [Chatham], Co. I, 6th NC Inf., Upchurch Papers, Duke

Alexander Beck [Davidson], Co. F, 1st NC Art., Vance Papers, NCSA

Alfred W. Bell [Macon], Co. B, 39th NC Inf., Bell Papers, Duke

Samuel H. Bell [Macon], Co. H, 16th NC Inf., Bell Papers, Duke

Sarah Bell [Catawba], Murph Papers, Duke

W. R. Best [Duplin], Co. B, 51st NC Inf., Quinn Papers, Duke

T. J. Bicknell [Wilkes], Vance Papers, NCSA

George P. Bird [Buncombe], Co. K, 11th NC Inf., Patton Family Letters, SHC

John Bizzell [Hertford], Co. C, 14th USCHA, Berlin, Reidy, and Rowland, *Freedom,* ser. 2: 801–2

James M. Black [Mecklenburg], Vance Papers, NCSA

John H. Black [Yadkin], Co. D, 62nd GA Cav., John Black Letters, UVA

John M. Black [Ashe], Co. A, 37th NC Inf., Sexton Letters, Duke

Pleasant Black [Rockingham], Vance Papers, NCSA

John W. Blackburn [Robeson], Co. A, 5th NC Inf., Vance Papers, NCSA

Albert W. Blair [Caldwell], Co. D, 1st NC Cav., Blair Letters, NCSA

Francis E. Blair [Rockingham], J. H. Baker Papers, Duke

Robert M. Blair [Caldwell], Co. I, 26th NC Inf., Blair Letters, NCSA

F. A. Bleckley [Catawba], McLean's Batt., NC Lt. Duty Men, Bleckley Papers, Duke

J. M. Bleckley [Catawba], Co. I, 49th NC Inf., Bleckley Papers, Duke

L. M. Bleckley [Catawba], Bleckley Papers, Duke

William L. Bleckley [Catawba], Co. I, 49th NC Inf., Bleckley Papers, Duke

Michael Bollinger [Catawba], Vance Papers, NCSA

Lydia Bolton [Guilford], Vance Papers, NCSA

Sarah Boon [Franklin], James Boon Papers, NCSA

William Boss [Davidson], Frank Papers, Duke

W. R. D. Bost [Catawba], Co. F, 23rd NC Inf., Gibson Papers, Duke

Hester Bowden [New Hanover], Vance Papers, Military Coll., Civil War, NCSA

Ann L. Bowen [Washington], Bowen Papers, Military Coll., Civil War, NCSA

Cornelia Ann Bowen [Washington], Bowen Papers, Military Coll., Civil War, NCSA

Henry H. Bowen [Washington], Bowen Papers, Military Coll., Civil War, NCSA

Sophia Bowen [Washington], Vance Papers, NCSA

William J. Bowen [Washington], Bowen Papers, Military Coll., Civil War, NCSA

John A. Boyett [Duplin], Co. B, 51st NC Inf., Vance Papers, NCSA

Mahata Bell Boykin [Johnston], Vance Papers, NCSA

Richard Boyle [Tyrrell], Berlin et al., *Freedom,* ser. 1, vol. 2, 231–35

Alexander D. Bracy [Robeson], Vance Papers, NCSA

Jonas Bradshaw [Alexander], Co. G, 38th NC Inf., Bradshaw Papers, Duke

John H. Brann [Yadkin], 9th Batt., NC Sharpshooters, Tesh Papers, Duke

Thomas H. Brann [Yadkin], Tesh Papers, Duke

Eli H. Brewer [Martin], Co. F, 31st NC Inf., Hardison Family Papers, ECU

Malcom Brewer [Moore], Co. H, 26th NC Inf., Jackson Family Corr., Notre Dame

Nicholas Brinkle [Rowan], Co. D, 23rd NC Inf., Vance Papers, NCSA

G. W. Bristol [Clay County], Vance Papers, NCSA

Augustin V. Broach [Person], Broach Papers, Duke

James G. Broach [Person], Broach Papers, Duke

Pleasant W. Broach [Person], Co. A, 50th NC Inf., Broach Papers, Duke

John W. Brock [Wayne], Co. G, 55th NC Inf., Vance Papers, NCSA

Henry Brotherton [Lincoln], Co. G, 52nd NC Inf., Brotherton Papers, Duke

James Brotherton [Lincoln], Co. G, 52nd NC Inf., Brotherton Papers, Duke

Thomas Brotherton [Catawba], Brotherton Papers, Duke

W. H. Brotherton [Catawba], Co. K, 23rd NC Inf., Brotherton Papers, Duke

Austin Brown [Johnston], Co. F, 13th Batt., NC Light Art., Brown Family Papers, Duke

Bardin Brown [Johnston], Co. F, 13th Batt., NC Light Art., Brown Family Papers, Duke

Daniel M. Brown [Duplin], Co. B, 3rd NC Inf., Isaac Brown Collection, NCSA

G. T. Brown [Catawba], Fisher Papers, Duke

James M. Brown [Orange], Co. D, 1st NC Inf., Vance Papers, NCSA

Jesse Brown [Johnston], Brown Family Papers, Duke

Jesse P. Brown [Edgecomb], Vance Papers, NCSA

Lucian Brown [Chatham], Co. I, 32nd NC Inf., Vance Papers, NCSA

William W. Buchanan [Mitchell], Co. C, 13th TN Cav. (Union), Vance Papers, NCSA

Ezra Bullock [Edgecombe], Co. E, 1st NC Art., Vance Papers, NCSA

James Burke [Catawba], Co. B, 26th NC Inf., Vance Papers, NCSA

William P. Burns [Catawba], Co. A, 22nd NC Inf., Peterson Papers, Duke

John L. Caddell [Robeson], Vance Papers, NCSA

Dinson Caldwell [Mecklenburg], Co. H, 35th NC Inf., Caldwell Collection, ECU

Nancy Caldwell [Catawba], Vance Papers, NCSA

Robert C. Caldwell [Cabarrus], Co. C, 10th NC Heavy Art., Caldwell Collection, ECU

W. L. Caldwell [Cabarrus], Caldwell Collection, ECU

Robert F. Calloway [Wilkes], Co. K, 5th NC Senior Reserves, Vance Papers, NCSA

George W. Cameron [Cumberland], Vance Papers, NCSA

Flora Ann Campbell [Moore], Campbell Papers, Duke

Flora Ann Campbell [Moore], Jackson Family Corr., Notre Dame

John K. Campbell [Moore], Campbell Papers, Duke

John M. Campbell [Moore], Co. H, 30th NC Inf., Jackson Family Corr., Notre Dame

William Carden [Macon], Co. H, 16th NC Inf., Carden Papers, WCU

Elbert Carpenter [Chatham], Co. D, 61st NC Inf., Carpenter Family Papers, ECU

Robert Carpenter [Chatham], Co. E, 3rd NC Inf., Carpenter Family Papers, ECU

Thomas Carpenter [Chatham], Co. D, 61st NC Inf., Carpenter Family Papers, ECU

William Carpenter [Chatham], Co. G, 1st NC Inf., Carpenter Family Papers, ECU

Daniel M. Carter [Chatham], Co. E, 26th NC Inf., Culberson Papers, Duke

Joshua C. Carter [Catawba], Co. C, 28th NC Inf., Murph Papers, Duke

Sallie A. Carter [Hertford], Vance Papers, NCSA

William D. Carter [Chatham], Co. E, 26th NC Inf., Culberson Papers, Duke

Elnori Cauble [Rowan County], Vance Papers, NCSA

M. P. Caudle [Anson County], Vance Papers, NCSA

James H. Caul [Transylvania], Co. E, 25th NC Inf., Vance Papers, NCSA

Alphonso G. Causey [Guilford], Co. D, 45th NC Inf., Hackett Papers, Duke

Elihu Chambers [Buncombe], Co. L, 16th NC Inf., Vance Papers, NCSA

Calvin Childers [Ashe], Co. A, 37th NC Inf., Sexton Letters, Duke

Charles Cison [Transylvania], Vance Papers, NCSA

Asa Clapp [Guilford], Vance Papers, NCSA

Laban Cline [Catawba], Hefner Papers, NCSA

William P. Cline [Catawba], Co. K, 46th NC Inf., Cline Papers, SHC

Josiah Coats [Johnston], Vance Papers, NCSA

Job Cobb [Pitt], Co. I, 15th NC Inf., Cobb Papers, Duke

Armistead Coffey [Caldwell], Co. H, 58th NC Inf., Vance Papers, NCSA

David C. Coggins [Buncombe], Co. D, 8th Ala. Inf., Vance Papers, NCSA

Ann E. Coghill [Granville], Coghill Papers, Duke

J. F. Coghill [Granville], Co. G, 23rd NC Inf., Coghill Papers, Duke, and Coghill Letters, SHC

J. N. Coghill [Granville], Co. G, 23rd NC Inf., Coghill Papers, Duke

Joseph W. Coghill [Granville], Co. G, 23rd NC Inf., Coghill Papers, Duke

K. W. Coghill [Granville], Co. G, 23rd NC Inf., Coghill Papers, Duke

Selena Colby [Catawba], Bleckley Papers, Duke

Mary Cole [Moore], Jackson Family Corr., Notre Dame

Martha Coletrane [Randolph], Vance Papers, NCSA

Stephen M. Collis [Mitchell], Vance Papers, NCSA

William F. Condrey [Iredell], Vance Papers, NCSA

Robert T. Conley [Jackson], Co. F, Inf. Reg., Thomas Legion, CW Soldiers' Letters, ADAH

James Cook [Guilford], Vance Papers, NCSA

Isaac Copeland [Surry], Co. B, 2nd Batt. NC Inf., Copeland Letters, NCSA

Jesse Coppedge [Nash], Vance Papers, NCSA

Fereby J. Core [Cumberland County], Vance Papers, NCSA

William Core [Guilford], Co. E, 2nd NC Inf., Vance Papers, NCSA

A. P. Corn [Henderson], Co. G, 1st NC Cav., Shipman Family Correspondence, Notre Dame

Jesse M. Corn [Henderson], Co. E, 6th NC Cav., Vance Papers, NCSA

A. L. Corpening [Macon], Co. A, 7th NC Cav. Batt., Vance Papers, NCSA

Jordon S. Councill [Watauga], Co. B, 37th NC Inf., Councill Papers, Duke

Alfred E. Cowand [Bertie], Co. B, 2nd NC Inf. (Union), Cowand Papers, Duke

James R. Cowand [Bertie], Co. B, 2nd NC Inf. (Union), Cowand Papers, Duke

Joseph J. Cowand [Bertie], Co. G, 32nd NC Inf., Cowand Papers, Duke

Isaiah Craven [Randolph], Vance Papers, NCSA

R. P. Crawford [Jackson], Co. B, 25th NC Inf., Estes Family Papers, WCU

Abetha Crowell [Guilford], Vance Papers, NCSA

Jane Culberson [Chatham], Culberson Papers, Duke

John W. Culberson [Chatham], Co. G, 26th NC Inf., Culberson Papers, Duke

James P. Culp [Cabarrus], Co. B, 20th NC Inf., Culp Papers, Duke

Catherine Culpepper [Franklin], Vance Papers, NCSA

George L. Cunningham [Haywood], Co. I, 16th NC Inf., Cunningham Letters, NCSA

John N. Cunningham [Haywood], Co. I, 16th NC Inf., Cunningham Letters, NCSA

Archibald Curlee [Union], Co. I, 53rd NC Inf., Vance Papers, NCSA

Martha Curtis [Buncombe], Vance Papers, NCSA

Anguish Darroch [Harnett], 3rd NC Cav., Jackson Family Corr., Notre Dame.

Cassie Davenport [Stokes County], Hundley Family Letters, SHC

James R. Davenport [Pitt], Co. B, 33rd NC Inf., Van Nortwick Papers, ECU

Ervin Q. Davis [Robeson], Co. D, 51st NC Inf., McNeill Papers, Duke

H. A. Davis [Ashe], Vance Papers, NCSA

H. J. Davis [Yadkin], Co. B, 14th NC Inf., WPA Transcripts, TSLA

James Davis [Catawba], Co. K, 5th NC Cav., Robinson Papers, Duke

Martin Davis [Yadkin], Co. F, 18th Ark. Inf., WPA Transcriptions, TSLA

George Dearmon [Iredell], Co. D, 42nd NC Inf., Mills Papers, Duke

Bella DeRosset [New Hanover], DeRosset Family Papers, SHC

Jimmy DeRosset [New Hanover], DeRosset Family Papers, SHC

George Dewese [Mecklenburg], Co. K, 56th NC Inf., Fonvielle Coll., MHI

Sarah E. Dicken [Halifax], Vance Papers, NCSA

Harriet Dickey [Orange], Vance Papers, NCSA

G. C. Dickson [McDowell], Co. I, 18th NC Inf., Poteet-Dickson Letters, NCSA

G. W. Dobson [McDowell], Vance Papers, NCSA

Tabuna Downs [Beaufort], Vance Papers, NCSA

Mary Driskell [Cabarrus], Caldwell Collection, ECU

James R. Duncan [Columbus], Co. D, 20th NC Inf., Vance Papers, NCSA

Andrew Eaves [Rutherford], Co. C, 50th NC Inf., Vance Papers, NCSA

George M. Eaves [Granville], Co. A, 1st NC Jr. Reserves, Coghill Papers, Duke

Ben F. Edmonston [Haywood], Co. F, 25th NC Inf., Edmonston-Kelly Family Papers, WCU

Ninion Edmonston [Haywood], Edmonston-Kelly Family Papers, WCU

T. B. Edmonston [Haywood], Co. I, 62nd NC Inf., Edmonston-Kelly Family Papers, WCU

Lydia Edmundson [Wayne], Whitfield Papers, Duke

J. W. Edwards [Catawba], Keever Papers, Duke

Caleb Eller [Rowan], Co. F, 7th NC Inf., Vance Papers, NCSA

Joshua Eller [Rowan], Co. D, 23rd NC Inf., Vance Papers, NCSA

Mariah Eller [Wilkes], Vance Papers, NCSA

Moses Eller [Rowan], Co. D, 23rd NC Inf., Vance Papers, NCSA

J. W. Ellis [Chatham], Vance Papers, NCSA

James Ennis [Wake], Co. G, 1st NC Inf., Carpenter Family Papers, ECU

Richard Etheredge [Hyde], Co. F, 36th USCT, Berlin, Reidy, and Rowland, *Freedom,* ser. 2, 729–730

Charles Evans [Cherokee], Vance Papers, NCSA

John W. Evans [Alleghany], Co. K, 37th NC Inf., Vance Papers, NCSA

William C. Featherston [Henderson] Co. A, 25th NC Inf., Love Papers, Duke

The "Female Sect" [Rutherford], Vance Papers, NCSA

Levi Festerman [Rowan], Co. G, 6th NC Inf., Festerman Papers, Duke

James Fisher [Catawba], Co. F, 23rd NC Inf., Fisher Papers, Duke

Margaret Fisher [Catawba], Murph Papers, Duke

William Fisher [Catawba], Co. I, 49th NC Inf., Fisher Papers, Duke

G. P. Formyduval [Columbus], Vance Papers, NCSA

Penelope Forrest [Greene], Vance Papers, NCSA

Alexander Frank [Davidson], Co. I, 6th NC Senior Reserves, Frank Papers, Duke

George W. Frank [Davidson], Co, B, 48th NC Inf., Frank Papers, Duke

Jessie M. Frank [Davidson], Co, B, 48th NC Inf., Frank Papers, Duke

John Frank [Davidson], Frank Papers, Duke

Susanna Frank [Davidson], Frank Papers, Duke

Jacob E. Fronberger [Cleveland], Co. F, 34th NC Inf., Kendrick Papers, NCSA

Mary Fuller [Granville], Vance Papers, NCSA

Charley Futch [New Hanover], Co. K, 3rd NC Inf., Futch Letters, NCSA

John Futch [New Hanover] , Co. K, 3rd NC Inf., Futch Letters, NCSA

Martha Futch [New Hanover], Futch Letters, NCSA

Enoch Garner [Randolph], Jackson Family Corr., Notre Dame

Samuel Garrard [Orange County], Co. D, 31st NC Inf., Vance Papers, NCSA

Wilburn Garren [Henderson County], Mallet's Company, NC Camp Guards, Vance Papers, NCSA

Elijah Gatewood [Stokes], Co. D, 45th NC Inf., Amos Papers, Duke

Phebe Gaultney [Alexander], Baggarly Papers, Duke

Thomas J. Gentle [Wilkes], Vance Papers, NCSA

Alfred Gibson [Caldwell], Vance Papers, NCSA

Elender Gibson [Caldwell], Vance Papers, NCSA

James C. Gibson [Union], Co. C, 10th Batt. NC Heavy Art., Vance Papers, NCSA

James W. Gibson [Catawba], Co. F, 23rd NC Inf., Gibson Papers, Duke

Joseph F. Gibson [Iredell], Co. C, 4th NC Inf., Overcash Papers, Duke

Mary Gibson [Iredell], Overcash Papers, Duke

Jeremiah Glover [Rowan], Co. K, 4th NC Inf., Vance Papers, NCSA

Eliza Godward [Martin], Vance Papers, NCSA

J. A. Goode [Rutherford], Vance Papers, NCSA

Nancy Grady [Burke], Vance Papers, NCSA

Effie Jane Graham [Moore], Jackson Family Corr., Notre Dame

Elias Green [Cleveland County], Co. K, 50th NC Inf., Vance Papers, NCSA

Hiram Green [Watauga], Vance Papers, NCSA

Lorraine Griffin [Rutherford], Co. D, 16th NC Inf., Griffin Papers, NCSA

Thomas Griffin [Rutherford], Co. I, 34th NC Inf., Vance Papers, NCSA

J. L. Groves [Gaston], Co. B, 28th NC Inf., Davison Papers, Duke

Benjamin Gurley [Stanley], Co. H, 42nd NC Inf., Vance Papers, NCSA

Samuel J. Guy [Cumberland], Co. I, 51st NC Inf., Vance Papers, NCSA

Christopher Hackett [Guilford], Co. D, 45th NC Inf., Hackett Papers, Duke

James Hackett [Guilford], Hackett Papers, Duke

Sally Hackett [Guilford], Hackett Papers, Duke

Benjamin Hall [Wilkes], Vance Papers, NCSA

James W. Hall [Cumberland], Co. G, 19th Ark. Inf., Hall Collection, NCSA

John Hall [Wilkes], Vance Papers, NCSA

John G. Hall [Cumberland], Co. G, 51st NC Inf., Hall Collection, NCSA

Robert Hall [Wilkes], Vance Papers, NCSA

J. C. Haltom [Davidson], Frank Papers, Duke

J. T. Hamilton [Gaston], Co. B, 28th NC Inf., Davison Papers, Duke

Ezekial H. Hampton [Yancey], Co. G, 29th NC Inf., Bailey Letters, CW Doc. Coll., MHI

Harrison Hanes [Davie], Co. G, 4th NC Inf., Hanes Papers, Duke

Hugh C. Hardin [Moore], Vance Papers, NCSA

Thomas G. Harding [Beaufort], Blount Papers, NCSA

Clayton Hardison [Martin], Co. H, 61st NC Inf., Hardison Family Papers, ECU

Joseph Harper [Cherokee], Vance Papers, NCSA

Margaret Harrel [Wayne], Vance Papers, NCSA

A. S. Harrill [Rutherford], Co. I, 1st NC Cav., Civil War Collection, Confederate, TSLA

Abner Harrington [Alexander], Co. G, 38th NC Inf., Vance Papers, NCSA

A. F. Harrington [Moore], Co. H, 30th NC Inf., Jackson Family Corr., Notre Dame

T. H. Harrington [Moore], Co. I, 2nd NC Cav., Jackson Family Corr., Notre Dame

Amzi Harris [Cabarrus], Co. C, 9th Miss. Inf., Caldwell Collection, ECU

A. R. Harris [Iredell], Co. C, 16th NC Inf., Vance Papers, NCSA

Jesse Harrison [Beaufort], Co. A, 1st NC Inf. (Union), Jesse Harrison Papers, Duke

Daniel Hartman [Rowan], Co. D, 1st NC Art., Hartman Papers, Duke

John H. Hartman [Rowan], Co. D, 1st NC Art., Hartman Papers, Duke

Edward Hawkins [Rutherford], Vance Papers, NCSA

Rhoda Hawn [Catawba], Peterson Papers, Duke

David Headrick [Davidson], Frank Papers, Duke

Keziah Hefner [Catawba], Hefner Papers, NCSA

Marcus Hefner [Catawba], Co. E, 57th NC Inf., Hefner Papers, NCSA

Constantine A. Hege [Davidson], Co. H, 48th NC Inf., Hege Papers, Lewis-Leigh Coll., MHI

John Helms [Union], Vance Papers, NCSA

James Hemby [Greene], Vance Papers, NCSA

Anderson Henderson [Rowan], Henderson Papers, SHC

Lee Hendrix [Forsyth], Hendrix Corr., VPI

Elizabeth Herrell [Randolph], Vance Papers, NCSA

Jacob Herring [Columbus], Co. I, 8th NC Inf., Vance Papers, NCSA

John Herring [Wake], Vance Papers, NCSA

J. C. Hill [Catawba], Co. I, 49th NC Inf., Fisher Papers, Duke

Jesse Hill [Forsyth], Co. K, 21st NC Inf., Hill Letters, NCSA

Samuel Hinson [Columbus], Co. E, 2nd NC Art., Civil War Documents Coll., MHI

L. F. Holder [Randolph], Co. M, 22nd NC Inf., Vance Papers, NCSA

Margaret Holder [Randolph], Vance Papers, NCSA

Willis J. Holland [Duplin], Quinn Papers, Duke

Jerry Hooper [Orange], John DeBerniere Hooper Papers, SHC

Betty Horner [Orange], Vance Papers, NCSA

J. W. Horton [Watauga], Co. A, 6th NC Cav., Councill Papers, Duke

Nathan Horton [Watauga], Co. B, 37th NC Inf., Councill Papers, Duke

William H. Horton [Watauga], Co. I, 58th NC Inf., Councill Papers, Duke

L. Lawson Houk [Catawba], Co. D, 6th NC Inf., Fisher Papers, Duke

Joel Howard [Lincoln], Co. G, 52nd NC Inf., Brotherton Papers, Duke

Nancy Howard [Lincoln], Brotherton Papers, Duke

William B. Howard [Chatham], Co. G, 7th NC Inf., Williams-Womble Papers, NCSA

D. R. Hoyle [Cleveland], Co. F, 34th NC Inf., Kendrick Papers, NCSA

Huldah Hubbard [Anson], Hubbard Papers, Duke

Wade Hubbard [Anson], 6th NC Senior Reserves, Hubbard Papers, Duke

John D. Hudson [Burke], Co. F, 55th NC Inf., Vance Papers, NCSA

George H. Hundley [Stokes], Co. H, 58th VA Inf., Hundley Family Letters, SHC

John H. Hundley [Stokes], Co. C, 21st NC Inf., Hundley Family Letters, SHC

Catherine Hunt [Randolph], Vance Papers, NCSA

George J. Huntley [Rutherford], Co. I, 34th NC Inf., Huntley Papers, WCU

John Ingram [Forsyth], Co. D, 21st NC Inf., Ingram Papers, Duke

Lucinda Ingram [Forsyth], Ingram Papers, Duke

Archibald A. Jackson [Moore], Co. H, 30th NC Inf., Jackson Family Corr., Notre Dame

Burgess C. Jackson [Moore], Co. H, 30th NC Inf., Jackson Family Corr., Notre Dame

Dicy Ann Jackson [Moore], Jackson Family Corr., Notre Dame

Effie Jane Jackson [Moore], Jackson Family Corr., Notre Dame

Gorry Jackson [Moore], Co. I, 2nd NC Cav., Jackson Family Corr., Notre Dame

James Jackson [Moore], Jackson Family Corr., Notre Dame

Thomas Jackson [Davidson], Co. A, 21st NC Inf., CSA, Army. Misc., Duke

Phillip James [Forsyth], Co. D, 52nd NC Inf., Spainhourd Papers, Duke

Amos Johnson [Martin], Co. B, 33rd NC Inf., Vance Papers, NCSA

D. C. Johnson [Moore], Co. A, 5th NC Inf., Jackson Fam. Corr., Notre Dame

Henry Johnson [Forsyth], Vance Papers, NCSA

Isabella Johnson [Robeson], Jackson Fam. Corr., Notre Dame

John L. Johnson [Henderson], Co. F, 1st SC Inf. (Butler's), Vance Papers, NCSA

McCoy Johnson [Johnston], Co. C, 53rd NC Inf., Vance Papers, NCSA

Charles Jones [Craven], Co. A, 35th USCT, Berlin, Reidy, and Rowland, *Freedom,* ser. 2, 798–799

Stephen H. Jones [Lenoir], Co. D, 66th NC Inf., Vance Papers, NCSA

Wesley Jones [Chatham], Vance Papers, NCSA

John W. Joyce [Stokes], Co. L, 21st NC Inf., Joyce Papers, Harrisburg CW Roundtable Coll., MHI

Perrin Joyce [Stokes], Joyce Papers, Harrisburg CW Roundtable Coll., MHI

John Justice [Cumberland], Vance Papers, NCSA

L. L. Kale [Catawba], Co. D, 6th NC Inf., Fisher Papers, Duke

Alexander Keever [Lincoln], Co. E, 34th NC Inf., Keever Papers, Duke

Henry Keever [Lincoln], Co. G, 57th NC Inf., Keever Papers, Duke

James Keever [Lincoln], Co. E, 34th NC Inf., Keever Papers, Duke

Ruth Keever [Lincoln], Keever Papers, Duke

R. P. Kelly [Haywood], Co. I, 62nd NC Inf., Edmonston-Kelly Family Papers, WCU

Elizabeth Kendrick [Cleveland], Kendrick Papers, NCSA

John Kendrick [Cleveland], Kendrick Papers, NCSA

Larkin S. Kendrick [Cleveland], Co. F, 34th NC Inf., Kendrick Papers, NCSA

Mary C. Kendrick [Cleveland], Kendrick Papers, NCSA

Bellfield King [Chatham], Co. G, 11th NC Inf., King Papers, Duke

Jesse Kinley [Davidson], Vance Papers, NCSA

Mary Kinsland [Haywood], Kinsland Letter, UGA

Letitia Kirkpatrick [Alamance], Long Family Papers, SHC

John B. Lance [Henderson], Co. H, 25th NC Inf., Lance Papers, LSU

William B. Lance [Henderson], Co. D, 60th NC Inf., Lance Papers, LSU

M. D. Laney [Caldwell], Co. I, 26th NC Inf., Vance Papers, NCSA

H. P. Langley [Edgecombe], Co. G, 31st NC Inf., Vance Papers, NCSA

Nathan Langly [Johnston], Co. E, 50th NC Inf., Vance Papers, NCSA

George W. Lawrence [Stokes], Co. H, 22nd NC Inf., Joyce Papers, Harrisburg CW Roundtable Coll., MHI

William Lawrence [Chatham], Co. I, 6th NC Inf., Upchurch Papers, Duke

William H. Leazer [Rowan], Co. G, 42nd NC Inf., Overcash Papers, Duke

Catherine Lefevers [Catawba], Lefevers Papers, NCSA

Isaac Lefevers [Catawba], Co. K, 46th NC Inf., Lefevers Papers, NCSA

William D. Lefevers [Catawba], Co. A, 22nd NC Inf., Peterson Papers, Duke

George Lenard [Davidson], Frank Papers, Duke

E. E. Lindsay [Orange], Taylor Papers, Duke

James W. Lineberger [Gaston], Co. H, 49th NC Inf., Pitts, *Letters of a Gaston Ranger*

James M. Lineberrier [Iredell], Co. H, 5th NC Inf., Vance Papers, NCSA

J. A. Lipe [Iredell], Co. C, 48th NC Inf., Mills Papers, Duke

Thomas B. Litten [Catawba], Co. K, 5th NC Cav., Fisher Papers, Duke, and Robinson Papers, Duke

John S. Livingston [Henderson], Vance Papers, NCSA

Levi A. Lockman [Lincoln], Co. K, 23rd NC Inf., Brotherton Papers, Duke

Benjamin N. Long [Alamance], Co. I, 57th NC Inf., Long Family Papers, SHC

Jacob S. Long [Alamance], Co. E, 1st NC Inf., Long Family Papers, SHC

John A. Long [Alamance], Co. E, 13th NC Inf., Long Family Papers, SHC

Letty B. Long [Alamance], Long Family Papers, SHC

Mary C. Long [Alamance], Long Family Papers, SHC

John Lonon [Cherokee], Vance Papers, NCSA

George W. Love [Henderson], Co. G, 56th NC Inf., Love Papers, Duke

John W. Love [Henderson], Co. A, 25th NC Inf., Love Papers, Duke

Robert C. Love [Henderson], Co. G, 56th NC Inf., Love Papers, Duke

Samuel Ervin Love [Henderson], Co. G, 56th NC Inf., Love Papers, Duke

Bluford Lucas [Harnett], Vance Papers, NCSA

Betsey Lury [Anson], Vance Papers, NCSA

M. P. Lytle [Buncombe], Vance Papers, NCSA

Joseph F. Maides [Jones], Co. I, 27th NC Inf., Maides Papers, Duke

Bartlett Yancey Malone [Caswell], Co. H, 6th NC Inf., *The Diary of Bartlett Yancy Malone*

B. B. Marley [Randolph], Vance Papers, NCSA

Cass Marlow [Wilkes], Vance Papers, NCSA

William Martin [Burke], Vance Papers, NCSA

Hardy Matthews [Moore], Co. H, 30th NC Inf., McLeod Letters, SHC

Abraham T. Maxwell [Henderson], Co. A, 25th NC Inf., Love Papers, Duke

James A. May [Guilford], Co. E, 22nd NC Inf., Military Coll., Civil War, NCSA

R. S. May [Pitt], Co. F, 61st NC Inf., Tom W. Johnson Coll., ECU

Alexander D. McBride [Bladen], Co. G, 48th NC Inf., McBride Family Papers, SHC

G. S. McClintock [Guilford], Vance Papers, NCSA

David M. McCorkle [Catawba], Co. F, 23rd NC Inf., Military Coll., Civil War, NCSA

Ann McCormick [Guilford], Vance Papers, NCSA

Intha McCraw [Polk], Vance Papers, NCSA

Caleb S. McCurdy [Cabarrus], Co. K, 28th NC Inf., CS Army, Misc., Duke

Kenneth M. McDonald [Moore], Co. D, 49th NC Inf., Vance Papers, NCSA

William S. McDonald [Cumberland], Co. D, 26th NC Inf., Vance Papers, NCSA

John C. McDowell [Burke], Vance Papers, NCSA

Jeptha McFee [Buncombe], Co. E, 60th NC Inf., McFee Letters, SRNB

John McFee [Buncombe], Co. E, 60th NC Inf., McFee Letters SRNB

Hugh McGregor [Moore], Jackson Fam. Corr., Notre Dame

Neill McGregor [Moore] Jackson Fam. Corr., Notre Dame

Duncan McLeod [Moore], Co. I, 2nd NC Cav., Jackson Fam. Corr., Notre Dame

Neill McLeod [Moore], Co. E, 3rd NC Inf., McLeod Letters, SHC

Francis M. Medlin [Wake], Co. I, 47th NC Inf., Williams-Womble Papers, Duke

C. M. Mendenhall [Randolph], Co. A, 10th NC Art., Fonvielle Coll., MHI

"Meny Citizens" [Randolph], Vance Papers, NCSA

Isaac Miller [Davidson], Vance Papers, NCSA

Jesse Miller [Wilkes], Co. K, 53rd NC Inf., Proffit Family Letters, SHC

Charles F. Mills [Iredell], Co. I, 7th NC Inf., Mills Papers, Duke

R. W. Mills [Iredell], Mills Papers, Duke

Elizabeth Mock [Yadkin], Tesh Papers, Duke

Charles L. Moffitt [Randolph], Co. C, 1st NC Art., Lawrence Papers, Duke

Lewis H. Moore [Cumberland], Co. G, 33rd NC Inf., Moore Letter, CACWL

Randall Moore [Johnston], Vance Papers, NCSA

Anthony W. Morgan [Pasquatank], Co. A, 8th NC Inf., Vance Papers, NCSA

John E. Morgan [Henderson], Co. B, 64th NC Inf., Revis Letters, NCSA

O. C. Morgan [Henderson], Co. D, C, 6th NC Cav., Revis Letters, NCSA

David G. Morrow [Rutherford], Co. I, 24th NC Inf., Vance Papers, NCSA

Malcom Murchison [Chatham], Albright Papers, NCSA

Amanda Murph [Lincoln], Murph Papers, Duke

Daniel W. Murph [Lincoln], Co. C, 1st NC Art., Murph Papers, Duke

Julius A. Myers [Cabarrus], Co. B, 7th NC Inf., Alman Papers, Duke

Ralph D. Myers [Bertie], Co. F, 4th NC Cav., Cowand Papers, Duke

Elizabeth Nance [Randolph], Vance Papers, NCSA

Mark Nelson [Randolph], Vance Papers, NCSA

William Newell [McDowell], Co. B, 35th NC Inf., Vance Papers, NCSA

Jesse F. Newsom [Halifax], Co. A, 14th NC Inf., Newsom Papers, Duke

Peter Newton [Lincoln], Co. H, 1st SC Inf. (Butler's), Vance Papers, NCSA

Archibald Nicholson [Moore], Co. I, 2nd NC Cav., Jackson Family Corr., Notre Dame

John Nicholson [Moore], 26th NC Inf., Jackson Family Corr., Notre Dame

Hackley Norton [Madison], Vance Papers, NCSA

Martha Ann Oakay [Granville], Vance Papers, NCSA

James W. Overcash [Rowan], Co. G, 6th NC Inf., Overcash Papers, Duke

John S. Overcash [Rowan], Co. G, 6th NC Inf., Overcash Papers, Duke

Joseph Overcash [Rowan], Overcash Papers, Duke

Sarah Overcash [Rowan], Overcash Papers, Duke

John C. Owens [Wilkes], Co. E, 26th NC Inf., Confederate Papers, SHC

J. G. Page [Iredell], Fisher Papers, Duke

Solomon Page [Stanley], Co. C, 42nd NC Inf., E. Smith Papers, Duke

J. W. Parlier [Wilkes], Vance Papers, NCSA

James W. Parlier [Wilkes], Co. I, 26th NC Inf., Military Coll., Civil War, NCSA

M. W. Parris [Jackson], Co. B, 25th NC Inf., Parris Papers, WCU

Jacob E. Patton [Buncombe], Co. F, 14th NC Inf., Patton Family Letters, SHC

James A. Patton [Granville], Co. G, 47th NC Inf., Patton Letters, Emory

John B. Patton [Buncombe], Co. K, 60th NC Inf., Patton Family Letters, SHC

Samuel A. Patton [Buncombe], Co. H, 29th NC Inf., Patton Family Letters, SHC

William M. Patton [Buncombe], Co. F, 14th NC Inf., Patton Family Letters, SHC

Fannie Perry [Franklin], Person Papers, Duke

Sam Perry [Pitt], Grimes Family Papers, SHC

Aaron Peterson [Sampson], Vance Papers, NCSA

Elias Peterson [Burke], Peterson Papers, Duke

Hannah Peterson [Catawba], Peterson Papers, Duke

John Peterson [Catawba], Co. D, 28th NC Inf., Peterson Papers, Duke

Peter J. Peterson [Catawba], Co. H, 28th NC Inf., Peterson Papers, Duke

Henry Pettigrew [Washington], Pettigrew Family Papers, SHC

Lissy Pettigrew [Washington], Pettigrew Family Papers, SHC

Moses Pettigrew [Washington], Pettigrew Family Papers, SHC

Margaret Phelps [Brunswick], Vance Papers, NCSA

Betsy Phillips [Robeson], Phillips Papers, Duke

Edmund M. Phillips [Robeson], Co. A, 31st NC Inf., Phillips Papers, Duke

John H. Phillips [Henderson], Co. E, 62nd NC Inf., Love Papers, Duke

N. G. Phillips [Cherokee], Co. D, 25th NC and Thomas Legion, Phillips Papers, WCU

Roseann Phillips [Lenoir], Vance Papers, NCSA

Samuel C. Phillips [Mitchell], Co. A, 58th NC Inf., Woody Letters, Confederate Misc., Emory

Stephen Phillips [Robeson], Phillips Papers, Duke

Stephen H. Phillips [Henderson], Co. G, 56th NC Inf., Love Papers, Duke

William N. Pierce [Wilkes], Vance Papers, NCSA

William H. Pilkinton [Johnston], Co. E, 24th NC Inf., Vance Papers, NCSA

John H. Pless [Haywood], Co. F, 14th NC Inf., Vance Papers, NCSA

Francis M. Poteet [McDowell], Co. A, 49th NC Inf., Poteet-Dickson Letters, NCSA

Martha Poteet [McDowell], Poteet-Dickson Letters, NCSA

Peter Poteet [Burke], 1st NC Inf. (6 months), Poteet-Dickson Letters, NCSA

Jesse J. Pouns [Brunswick], Co. G, 20th NC Inf., Vance Papers, NCSA

Alfred N. Proffit [Wilkes], Co. D, 18th NC Inf., Proffit Family Letters, SHC

Andrew J. Proffit [Wilkes], Co. D, 18th NC Inf., Proffit Family Letters, SHC

Calvin L. Proffit [Wilkes], Co. H, 13th NC Inf., Proffit Family Letters, SHC

Arthur Putnam [Cleveland County], Co. C, 15th NC Inf., Kendrick Papers, NCSA

John L. Putnam [Cleveland County], Co. C, 15th NC Inf., Kendrick Papers, NCSA

William R. Quick [Richmond], Co. A, 13th Batt. NC Light Art., Vance Papers, NCSA

Ichabod Quinn [Duplin], Co. C, 51st NC Inf., Quinn Papers, Duke

William R. Raby [Caldwell], Co. H, 58th NC Inf., Vance Papers, NCSA

Catherine Ramsey [New Hanover], Futch Letters, NCSA

Pleasant B. Ray [Stokes], Co. L, 21st NC Inf., Amos Papers, Duke

Job R. Redmond [Buncombe], Co. A, 5th NC Cav. Batt., Military Coll., Civil War, NCSA

John W. Reese [Buncombe], Co. F. 60th NC Inf., Reese Papers, Duke

J. G. Reynolds [Madison], Vance Papers, NCSA

Daniel Revis [Henderson], Co. B, 64th NC Inf., Revis Letters, NCSA

J. A. W. Revis [Henderson], Revis Letters, NCSA

J. M. Revis [Henderson], Co. B, 64th NC Inf., Revis Letters, NCSA

John Revis [Henderson], Revis Letters, NCSA

Sarepta Revis [Henderson], Revis Letters, NCSA

Henry Rhodes [Lincoln], Lefevers Papers, NCSA

Edward Rice [Bertie], Co. B, 2nd NC Inf. (Union), Cowand Papers, Duke

Robert Rice [Alamance], Vance Papers, NCSA

William Richardson [Ashe], Vance Papers, NCSA

Joseph C. Richey [Lincoln], Co. I, 11th NC Inf., Vance Papers, NCSA

John Riddle [Moore], Jackson Family Corr., Notre Dame

Daniel E. Ridenhour [Stanley], Co. F, 5th NC Inf., Vance Papers, NCSA

Catherine M. Riley [Alamance], Vance Papers, NCSA

Joseph Robason [Martin], Vance Papers, NCSA

Alfred Roberson [Martin], Co. B, 40th NC State Troops, Roberson Family Papers, ECU

L. A. L. Roberson [?], Vance Papers, NCSA

John Roberts [Caldwell], Co. D, 23rd NC Inf., Vance Papers, NCSA

John L. Roberts [Onslow], Co. B, 24th NC Inf., Vance Papers, NCSA

William A. E. Roberts [Rutherford], Co. K, 50th NC Inf., Vance Papers, NCSA

George Robertson [Yancy], Green Woody Letters, Confederate Misc., Emory

John H. Robinson [Catawba], Co. K, 5th NC Cav., Robinson Papers, Duke

Thomas V. Rogers [Duplin], Vance Papers, NCSA

George W. Rooker [Warren], Co. A, 14th NC Inf., Newsom Papers, Duke

Charles Rothrock [Forsyth], Co. I, 33rd NC Inf., Rothrock Papers, Duke

William C. Rough [Davidson], Co. I, 42nd NC Inf., Vance Papers, NCSA

Charlotte Rowell [Brunswick], Vance Papers, NCSA

H. F. Rudasil [Davie], Co. G, 4th NC Inf., Confederate Misc., Emory

Jane Sandlin [Duplin], Williams Papers, Duke

Roxy A. Sandlin [Duplin], Williams Papers, Duke

Julius Seitz [Catawba], Co. F, 23rd NC Inf., Whitner Papers, Duke

Caroline Setzer [Catawba], Setzer Correspondence, UVA

Carr Setzer [Catawba], Co. K, 46th NC Inf., Setzer Papers, Duke

Daniel A. Setzer [Catawba], Co. K, 46th NC Inf., Setzer Papers, Duke

Franklin Setzer [Catawba], McRae's NC Cav. Batt. and 1st NC Cav., Setzer Correspondence, UVA

Susan Setzer [Catawba], Setzer Papers, Duke

Marion Sexton [Ashe], Co. A, 37th NC Inf., Sexton Letters, Duke

Thornton Sexton [Ashe], Co. A, 37th NC Inf., Sexton Letters, Duke

George W. Shackleford [Buncombe], Vance Papers, NCSA

Dougal C. Shaw [Moore], Co. H, 30th NC Inf., Jackson Family Corr., Notre Dame

Christie H. Sherrill [Catawba], Co. K, 46th NC Inf., CS Army, Misc., Duke

David H. Sherrill [Catawba], Co. K, 5th NC Cav., Robinson Papers, Duke, and Vance Papers, NCSA

James Sherrill [Catawba], Co. D, 18th NC Inf., Robinson Papers, Duke

Moses O. Sherrill [Cabarrus], Co. E, 33rd NC Inf., Vance Papers, NCSA

James K. P. Shipman [Buncombe], Co. G, 1st NC Cav., Shipman Family Corr., Notre Dame

Jesse Albert Shipman [Henderson], Co. G, 1st NC Cav., Shipman Family Corr., Notre Dame

Benjamin C. Shull [Watauga], Co. A, 6th NC Cav., Councill Papers, Duke

Phillip Shull [Watauga], Co. E, 37th NC Inf., Councill Papers, Duke

J. E. Sigmon [Catawba], Co. I, 49th NC Inf., Fisher Papers, Duke

C. F. Sikes [Orange], Co. A, 3rd NC Cav., Taylor Papers, Duke

Caroline Smith [Davidson], Frank Papers, Duke

Evin Smith [Stanley], Co. K, 28th NC Inf., E. Smith Papers, Duke

Isaac Smith [Alexander], Vance Papers, NCSA

James A. Smith [Cabarrus], Co. E, NC Jr. Reserves, J. A. Smith Papers, Duke

John A. Smith [Cabarrus], Co. F, 1st NC Cav., J. A. Smith Papers, Duke

John C. Smith [Robeson], 1st Batt. NC Heavy Art., McNeill Papers, Duke

Samuel L. Smith [Davie], Co. H, 5th NC Cav., W. D. Smith Papers, Duke

William D. Smith [Davie], Co. H, 5th NC Cav., W. D. Smith Papers, Duke

Edgar Smithwick [Martin County], Co. H, 61st NC Inf., Smithwick Papers, Duke

Hannah Smithwick [Martin], Smithwick Papers, Duke

Robert Spainhourd [Forsyth], Co. D, 57th NC Inf., Spainhourd Papers, Duke

A. J. Spease [Forsyth], Co. D, 57th NC Inf., Zimmerman Papers, Duke

Dena Stack [Union], Confederate Papers, SHC

Silas H. Stepp [Buncombe], Co. D, 6th NC Cav., Stepp Letters, UNCA

Catherine Strickland [Duplin], Quinn Papers, Duke

Isaac J. Strickland [Duplin], Co. E, 30th NC Inf., Quinn Papers, Duke

Jeremiah Strickland [Duplin], Co. B, 51st NC Inf., Quinn Papers, Duke

William H. Strickland [Duplin], Co. E, 30th NC Inf., Quinn Papers, Duke

Isaac Suttles [Rutherford], Vance Papers, NCSA

Dista Swindell [Hyde], Vance Papers, NCSA

Samuel Tate [Burke County], Vance Papers, NCSA

Alvira Taylor [Orange], Taylor Papers, Duke

John J. Taylor [Orange], Co. E, 31st NC Inf., Taylor Papers, Duke

Mary M. Taylor [Orange], Taylor Papers, Duke

James P. Teer [Alamance], Co. G, 44th NC Inf., Wright Papers, Duke

Jane Tesh [Yadkin], Tesh Papers, Duke

Molly Tesh [Yadkin], Tesh Papers, Duke

William A. Tesh [Yadkin], Co. I, 28th NC Inf., Tesh Papers, Duke

Berry Thomas [Pitt], Co. G, 21st NC Inf., Vance Papers, NCSA

Betty Thomas [Duplin], Quinn Papers, Duke

Calvin Thomas [Duplin], Co. A, 38th NC Inf., Williams Papers, Duke

Daniel Thomas [Duplin], Co. A, 38th NC Inf., Williams Papers, Duke

Jemima Thomas [Iredell], Vance Papers, NCSA

Lewis Thomas [Duplin], Co. A, 38th NC Inf., Williams Papers, Duke

N. M. Thomas [Duplin], Quinn Papers, Duke

Zilpha Thomas [Duplin], Williams Papers, Duke

Elizabeth Thrower [Moore County], Vance Papers, NCSA

William Henry Thurber [New Hanover], DeRosset Family Papers, SHC

William Tippitt [Macon], Co. B, 39th NC Inf., Bell Papers, Duke

Joseph Turner [Alamance], 7th Reg. NC Sr. Reserves, Wright Papers, Duke

Lucinda Tweed [Madison], Vance Papers, NCSA

James Tyson [Randolph], Co. H, 26th NC Inf., Vance Papers, NCSA

Isham Upchurch [Chatham], Co. G, 16th NC Inf., Upchurch Papers, Duke

Williford Upchurch [Chatham], Co. I, 6th NC Inf., Upchurch Papers, Duke

Oliver Varnum [Robeson], Co. D, 1st Batt. NC Heavy Art., McNeill Papers, Duke

Pattie Vernon [Rockingham], Vance Papers, NCSA

Nancy Wagner [Catawba], Hatley and Hufman, *Letters of William F. Wagner, Confederate Soldier*

Noah Wagner [Catawba], Co. C, 28th NC Inf., Hatley and Hufman, *Letters of W. F. Wagner, Confederate Soldier*

Thomas J. Wagner [Catawba], Co. C, 28th NC Inf., Hatley and Hufman, *Letters of W. F. Wagner, Confederate Soldier*

William F. Wagner [Catawba], Co. E, 57th NC Inf., Hatley and Hufman, *Letters of W. F. Wagner, Confederate Soldier*

Elizabeth Wagoner [Stokes], Hundley Family Letters, SHC

Mary Wagoner [Stokes], Hundley Family Letters, SHC

Samuel H. Wagoner [Stokes], Co. G, 42nd VA Inf., Hundley Family Letters, SHC

C. A. Walker [Cherokee], Co. I, Love's Regt., Thomas Legion, Walker Papers, WCU

Levi Walker [Guilford], Vance Papers, NCSA

Lucy Walker [Orange], Vance Papers, NCSA

Mary A. Walker [Cumberland], Vance Papers, NCSA

Thomas M. Walker [Polk], Vance Papers, NCSA

Nathaniel A. Waller [Granville], Co. E, 23rd NC Inf., Vance Papers, NCSA

Alfred Walsh [Wilkes], Co. B, 1st NC Inf., Proffit Family Letters, SHC

Phillip Walsh [Wilkes], Co. F, 37th NC Inf., Proffit Family Letters, SHC

William Walsh [Wilkes] , Co. K, 53rd NC Inf., Proffit Family Letters, SHC

Ellen Walters [Chatham], Vance Papers, NCSA

Thomas Walters [Nash], Co. A, 51st NC Inf., Vance Papers, NCSA

A. Pinkney Ward [Catawba], Co. K, 35th NC Inf., Whitner Papers, Duke

H. T. Ward [Henderson], Revis Letters, NCSA

Joseph Ward [Henderson], Revis Letters, NCSA

Elizabeth Watson [Jackson], Watson Letters, WCU

Elizabeth Weadon [Rockingham], Vance Papers, NCSA

G. M. Webb [Rutherford], Vance Papers, NCSA

John Webb [Rockingham], Vance Papers, NCSA

David F. West [Gaston], Co. H, 37th NC Inf., Vance Papers, NCSA

Ichabod C. West [Sampson], Vance Papers, NCSA

Sarah E. Wester [Franklin], Wester Collection, NCSA

Thomas C. Wester [Franklin], Co. B, 66th NC Inf., Wester Collection, NCSA

J. P. Whisnant [McDowell], Vance Papers, NCSA

Stephen Whitaker [Cherokee], Walker's Batt., Thomas Leg., Whitaker Papers, NCSA

John W. Whitfield [Nash], Co. I, 30th NC Inf., Whitfield Papers, Duke

Daniel Whitner [Catawba], Co. K, 35th NC Inf., Whitner Papers, Duke

P. S. Whitner [Catawba], Co. K, 35th NC Inf., Whitner Papers, Duke

John W. Whitworth [Cleveland], Vance Papers, NCSA

Noah Wike [Catawba], Co. C, 18th NC Inf., Setzer Papers, Duke

C. L. Williams [Chatham], Co. I, 6th NC Inf., Upchurch Papers, Duke

George A. Williams [Orange], Co. G, 7th NC Inf., Wiliams Womble Papers, NCSA

F. H. Williams [Onslow], Williams Papers, Duke

Jane Williams [Onslow], Williams Papers, Duke

John Williams [Craven], Co. E, 37th USCT, Berlin et al., *Freedom,* ser. 1, vol. 2, 182–84

John F. Williams [Chatham], Co. I, Co. I, 6th NC Inf., Upchurch Papers, Duke

John Wesley Williams [Onslow], Co. A, 35th NC Inf., Williams Papers, Duke

Marianne Williams [Onslow], Williams Papers, Duke

Mary H. Williams [Wake], Vance Papers, NCSA

Jack Williamson [Jones], Whitford Papers, Duke

Edward Wills [Halifax], Co. K, 2nd NC Jr. Reserves, Wills Papers, SHC

Washington Wills [Halifax], Wills Papers, SHC

Alfred Wilson [Jackson], Watson Letters, WCU

J. L. Wilson [Catawba], Co. K, 46th NC Inf., Setzer Correspondence, UVA

Samuel C. Wilson [Burke], Vance Papers, NCSA

James G. Wiseman [Mitchell], Co. A, 58th NC Inf., Vance Papers, NCSA

Marion Womack [Chatham], Co. D, 61st NC Inf., Carpenter Family Papers, ECU

Richard Womble [Wake] Co. G, 7th NC Inf., Williams-Womble Papers, NCSA

Green Woody [Yancy], Co. C, 58th NC Inf., Woody Letters, Confederate Misc., Emory

Joseph Wright [Alamance], Co. G, 44th NC Inf., Wright Papers, Duke

Louis S. Wright [Alamance], Wright Papers, Duke

A. W. Zachery [Jackson], Vance Papers, NCSA

Adaline Zimmerman [Forsyth], Zimmerman Papers, Duke

James C. Zimmerman [Forsyth], Co. D, 57th NC Inf., Zimmerman Papers, Duke

Appendix B

Information from the Federal Census of 1860

* Indicates the person listed was not the head of household; thus real and personal estate are that of the parent. The occupation in parentheses indicates that none was listed; the occupation is that of the head of household.

Name	Age	Occupation	Family	Real estate	Personal estate
Daniel Abernethy	20	farm laborer	married, no children	0	0
Bartlett Y. Allen	24	farmer	married, 2 children	0	400
Henry Allen	22	farmer	married, no children	0	0
Joseph Allen*	20	farm laborer	in father's household	0	270
Leonard Alman	30	farmhand	married, 2 children	0	0
James M. Amos*	22	farm laborer	in father's household	2,450	8,000
Peter Amos*	21	farm laborer	in father's household	2,450	8,000
William Amos*	25	farm laborer	in father's household	2,450	8,000
Elijah Ange	38	laborer	unmarried	0	0
John D. Bachelor	28	farmer	married, 2 children	500	375
Tilmon F. Baggarly	27	farmer	married, 2 children	50	100
Harvey Bailey	34	farmer	married, 5 children	1,200	638
Henry Baker	31	carriage maker	married, 2 children	1,400	2,300
Duncan R. Barnhill*	36	farmer	in brother's household	2,000	2 ,000
C. E. Beavers*	19	laborer	in father's household	1,500	500
G. T. Beavers*	22	laborer	in father's household	1,500	500
J. S. Beavers*	24	laborer	in father's household	1,500	500
Alfred W. Bell	30	dentist	married, 2 children	0	3,090
Samuel Bell*	21	laborer	in father's household	2,000	4,225
George P. Bird*	16	(farmer)	in father's household	0	1,600
John H. Black*	14	farm laborer	in father's household	4,000	1,325
Albert W. Blair*	13	farmer	in father's household	1,000	600
Robert M. Blair*	21	mechanic	in father's household	1,000	600
F. A. Bleckley*	35	millwright	in father's household	400	800
J. M. Bleckley*	26	house carpenter	in father's household	400	800

Name	Age	Occupation	Family	Real estate	Personal estate
William L. Bleckley	32	millwright	married, no children	1,000	350
Henry H. Bowen	37	farmer	married, 3 children	2,000	5,470
William J. Bowen	38	farmer	not married	5,300	6,800
Jonas Bradshaw	25	farmer	married, 1 child	0	210
John H. Brann*	22	laborer	in mother's household	1,500	1,140
Eli H. Brewer*	20	not listed	in grandmother's household	240	0
Nicholas Brinkle	34	day laborer	married, 4 children	85	65
Pleasant W. Broach*	27	farm hand	in father's household	3,000	1,850
W. H. Brotherton*	19	(farmer)	in father's household	500	360
Austin Brown	32	farmer	married, 3 children	95	220
Bardin Brown	25	farmer	married, no children	170	150
Daniel Brown	31	farmer	married, 3 children	400	300
James Brown	26	harness maker	married, 2 children	0	0
Jesse Brown	35	farmer	married, 5 children	716	696
Ezra Bullock	30	farmer	not married	0	0
William D. Burns*	16	(farmer)	in father's household	2,500	900
Robert C. Caldwell	37	farmer	married, no children	200	700
Robert F. Calloway	41	farmer	widower, 4 children	500	200
John K. Campbell*	25	farmer	in father's household	2,000	6,000
John M. Campbell	23	shoemaker	married, no children	600	300
William Carden	26	farmer	married, no children	0	187
Elbert Carpenter*	20	laborer	in father's household	300	300
Robert Carpenter	25	laborer	not married	0	0
Thomas Carpenter	24	laborer	not married	0	0
Daniel M. Carter*	20	farmer	in father's household	0	130
Joshua C. Carter	23	farm laborer	not married	0	0
William A. Carter*	27	farmer	in father's household	0	130
James H. Caul	39	carpenter	married, 4 children	0	100
Elihu Chambers	24	farmer	married, 3 children	500	150
Calvin Childers*	15	not listed	in mother's household	500	100
William P. Cline	26	farmer	married, 3 children	50	300

Name	Age	Occupation	Family	Real estate	Personal estate
Job Cobb*	21	farm hand	in father's household	11,700	26,250
David C. Coggins*	20	not listed	in father's household	0	2,100
J. F. Coghill*	18	farmer	in father's household	1,162	900
J. N. Coghill*	19	farmer	in father's household	1,162	900
Joseph W. Coghill*	21	farmer	in father's household	1,162	900
K. W. Coghill	25	farmer	married, 1 child	0	100
Robert Conley*	16	(farmer)	in father's household	800	850
Isaac Copeland*	18	farmer	in father's household	3,000	756
Jesse M. Corn	38	blacksmith	married, 6 children	500	300
A. L. Corpening	31	farmer	married, 3 children	3,000	2,525
Jordon S. Councill*	21	farmer	in father's household	1,250	0
Alfred E. Cowand*	15	(farmer)	in father's household	1,000	600
James R. Cowand*	14	(farmer)	in father's household	1,000	600
Joseph J. Cowand	23	farmer	not married	0	125
R. P. Crawford	21	farmer	married, 1 child	300	120
John W. Culberson*	13	farmer	in mother's household	700	700
Archibald Curlee*	17	farmer	in father's household	1,200	2,959
Anguish Darroch	25	overseer	not married	0	1,000
Ervin Q. Davis*	20	not listed	in father's household	2,000	11,500
H. J. Davis*	26	laborer	in mother's household	600	481
George Dewese*	14	(stone mason)	in father's household	400	560
G. C. Dickson	31	miner	married, 1 child	0	0
Ben F. Edmonston*	23	farmer	in father's household	2,500	3,200
T. B. Edmonston*	18	"at school"	in father's household	2,500	3,200
Andrew Eaves	28	farmer	married, no children	200	100
John W. Evans	22	farmer	married, 2 children	0	100
James Fisher*	17	(farmer)	in father's household	0	185
William Fisher*	14	(farmer)	in father's household	950	496
George W. Frank*	20	farmer	in father's household	500	900
Jessie M. Frank*	17	farmer	in father's household	500	900
Charley Futch*	30	farmer	in father's household	1,000	250

Information from the Federal Census of 1860

Name	Age	Occupation	Family	Real estate	Personal estate
John Futch*	28	farmer	in father's household	1,000	250
Samuel Garrard	24	(farmer)	in father's household	0	1,600
Wilburn Garren	35	farmer	married, 4 children	240	200
Thomas J. Gentle*	23	farmer	in father's household	200	150
James W. Gibson	30	day laborer	not married	0	0
Jeremiah Glover*	16	farmer	in father's household	1,000	600
Elias Green	34	farmer	married, 7 children	225	135
Thomas Griffin	40	farmer	married, 6 children	0	200
Benjamin Gurley	33	farmer	married, 4 children	250	0
Samuel J. Guy	28	cooper	married, 2 children	0	50
Christopher Hackett*	21	farmer	in father's household	1,500	200
James Hackett*	16	farmer	in father's household	1,500	200
John G. Hall*	21	farmer	in father's household	0	0
E. H. Hampton	25	minister	married, 1 child	3,700	595
Clayton Hardison	25	farmer	unmarried	300	0
A. S. Harrill	40	farmer	married, 4 children	1,100	200
T. H. Harrington	24	farmer	married, no children	500	500
Jesse Harrison*	24	(farmer)	in father's household	400	200
John H. Hartman*	19	day laborer	in father's household	3,300	1,000
Marcus Hefner	27	farmer	married, 3 children	0	350
C. A. Hege*	17	(farmer)	in father's household	2,000	3,200
Lee Hendrix	25	miller	not married	0	200
Jacob Herring	27	turp. distiller	married, 1 child	0	200
J. C. Hill*	15	(farmer)	in mother's household	2,500	3,800
Jesse Hill	32	farmer	married, 2 children	250	300
Samuel Hinson*	14	(farmer)	in father's household	2,500	800
L. F. Holder*	16	blacksmith	in father's household	0	75
William H. Horton	25	farmer	married, 1 child	1,900	600
Jackson Howard*	17	(farmer)	in father's household	1,200	715
William B. Howard	34	farmer	married, 5 children	1,100	400
Wade Hubbard	42	farmer	married, 3 children	1,600	5,000

Name	Age	Occupation	Family	Real estate	Personal estate
John H. Hundley	27	farmer	married, 3 children	0	100
John Ingram	29	farmer	married, 1 child	135	100
Archibald A. Jackson	26	turp. distiller	not married	1,000	750
Gorry Jackson*	14	farmer	in father's household	400	600
James Jackson	45	farmer	married, 5 children	400	600
Thomas Jackson	19	farmer	not married	0	0
Amos Johnson*	21	day laborer	in father's household	1,400	0
McCoy Johnson	34	farmer	married, 5 children	500	345
Stephen H. Jones	25	painter	married, no children	600	200
John W. Joyce	24	farm renter	married, 2 children	0	150
Alexander Keever	38	miller	married, 4 children	0	150
James Keever	23	miller	not married	200	100
Larkin S. Kendrick	23	farmer	married, 2 children	0	0
Bellfield King*	14	farmer	in father's household	0	30
John B. Lance*	22	farm laborer	in father's household	3,000	1,000
William B. Lance*	24	farm laborer	in father's household	3,000	1,000
Isaac Lefevers	30	farmer	married, 2 children	1,000	500
Benjamin N. Long*	17	farmer	in father's household	1,000	400
Jacob S. Long	21	laborer	married, 1 child	0	150
John A. Long*	16	farmer	in father's household	1,000	400
George W. Love*	14	farmer	in father's household	300	100
Robert C. Love*	16	farmer	in father's household	300	100
Samuel Ervin Love*	18	farmer	in father's household	300	100
Alexander D. McBride*	27	farmer	in father's household	5,000	1,240
David M. McCorkle	30	farmer	married, 2 children	0	6,200
William S. McDonald	21	distiller	not married	400	600
Jeptha McFee	22	farmer	not married	200	100
John McFee	25	farmer	married, 3 children	0	225
Duncan McLeod	31	not listed	not married, 2 children	300	1,000
Neill McLeod	25	cooper		300	15
Joseph F. Maides*	21	farmer	in father's household	0	0

Information from the Federal Census of 1860

Name	Age	Occupation	Family	Real estate	Personal estate
Bartlett Y. Malone*	21	farmer	in father's household	2,000	3,500
Hardy Matthews*	20	farmer	in father's household	600	200
Abraham T. Maxwell*	16	farmer	in father's household	1,500	1,200
C. M. Mendenhall*	20	farmer	in mother's household	300	100
Jesse Miller	35	farmer	married, 5 children	0	150
Charles F. Mills*	21	farmer	in father's household	200	190
Charles L. Moffitt*	20	carpenter	in father's household	0	0
Anthony W. Morgan	30	farmer	married, 3 children	1,200	2,330
John E. Morgan*	24	farm laborer	in father's household	600	200
Oliver C. Morgan	27	farmer	married, 2 children	300	200
David G. Morrow	34	farmer	married, 7 children	0	125
Daniel Murph	31	day laborer	married, 5 children	0	185
Jesse F. Newsom*	16	farmer	in father's household	720	350
Peter Newton	19	laborer	unmarried	0	0
Archibald Nicholson*	20	(farmer)	in father's household	500	500
John Nicholson	30	house carpenter	not married	350	300
James W. Overcash	21	laborer	not married	0	0
John S. Overcash*	20	farmer	in father's household	2,000	950
John C. Owens*	25	farmer	in father's household	500	100
James W. Parlier	30	farmer	married, 4 children	100	50
M. W. Parris	36	farmer	married, no children	700	150
James A. Patton	23	farmer	married, no children	0	900
Jacob E. Patton	23	miller	not married	0	0
John B. Patton*	16	(farmer)	in father's household	4,500	1,650
Samuel A. Patton	26	farmer	not married	0	0
William F. Patton*	21	(farmer)	in father's household	4,500	1,650
John Peterson	39	farmer	married, 8 children	450	350
Peter Peterson*	14	(farmer)	in father's household	450	350
Edmund M. Phillips*	21	(farmer)	in father's household	1,226	600
Samuel C. Phillips	42	farmer	married, 7 children	460	1,370
William N. Pierce	44	farmer	married, 5 children	200	400

Name	Age	Occupation	Family	Real estate	Personal estate
John H. Pless*	20	farming	in father's household	500	650
Francis M. Poteet	33	farmer	married, 8 children	0	0
Peter Poteet	38	farmer	married, 3 children	0	65
Alfred N. Proffit*	18	school teacher	in father's household	100	500
Andrew J. Proffit*	24	farm laborer	in father's household	100	500
Calvin L. Proffit*	18	farm laborer	in father's household	100	500
Arthur Putnam	27	farmer	married, 4 children	231	55
Ichabod Quinn	33	farmer	married, 3 children	1,460	4,822
Job R. Redmond	28	farmer	married, 3 children	0	661
John W. Reese	31	miller	married, 3 children	0	95
Daniel Revis*	24	farm laborer	in father's household	2,500	1,000
Edward Rice*	25	(farmer)	in father's household	100	200
Daniel Ridenhour	24	farmer	married, 1 child	650	850
Alfred Roberson	37	farmer	married, 2 children	550	100
W. A. E. Roberts	34	tailor	married, 2 children	0	100
Thomas V. Rogers	52	farmer	married, 2 children	1,000	500
George W. Rooker*	20	carpenter	in father's household	1,200	200
Charles Rothrock	31	farm laborer	married, 2 children	0	100
William Rough	41	carpenter	married, 7 children	0	200
H. F. Rudasil	23	farmer	married, no children	0	200
Julius Seitz*	16	farmer	in father's household	1,300	445
Carr Setzer*	11	farm laborer	in father's household	1,500	1,000
Daniel A. Setzer	36	farmer	married, 4 children	1,500	1,000
Franklin Setzer	38	farmer	married, 4 children	2,000	3,000
Thornton Sexton*	17	farmer	in father's household	0	50
Marion Sexton*	19	farmer	in father's household	0	50
Christie H. Sherrill	26	farmer	married, 1 child	0	75
James K. P. Shipman*	15	farmer	in father's household	3,500	2,300
Jesse Albert Shipman*	16	farmer	in father's household	0	100
Phillip Shull*	16	farmer	in father's household	3,500	4,315
Evin Smith*	27	day laborer	not married	0	140

Information from the Federal Census of 1860

Name	Age	Occupation	Family	Real estate	Personal estate
James M. Smith*	13	farm hand	in father's household	2,034	1,458
John A. Smith*	25	farm hand	in father's household	2,034	1,458
William D. Smith*	19	laborer	in father's household	3,000	7,110
Edgar Smithwick*	28	farmer	in mother's household	555	0
Robert Spainhourd	17	farmer	unmarried	0	0
A. J. Spease*	22	day laborer	in father's household	500	300
Silas Stepp	37	farmer	married, 5 children	1,000	1,900
John J. Taylor*	15	farmer	in father's household	3,000	2,300
Berry Thomas	22	farmer	unmarried	0	300
Calvin Thomas*	18	laborer	in father's household	1,000	650
Daniel Thomas*	21	laborer	in father's household	1,000	650
William J. Tippitt*	21	laborer	in father's household	600	618
James Tyson	28	farmer	married, 2 children	1,500	6,500
Isham Upchurch	35	farmer	married, 5 children	900	300
Oliver Varnum*	14	not listed	household of guardian	8,000	38,900
William F. Wagner	29	blacksmith	married, 1 child	800	840
C. A. Walker*	14	farmer	in father's household	5,000	3,500
Alfred Walsh*	18	farmer	in father's household	1,200	400
Phillip Walsh*	22	farmer	in father's household	350	350
William Walsh	21	farmer	married, 1 child	10	60
Thomas C. Wester*	18	not listed	in father's household	2,700	6,205
Stephen Whitaker	46	farmer	married, 9 children	10,000	10,000
John W. Whitfield	26	overseer	married, 1 child	0	0
Daniel Whitner*	19	farmer	in father's household	2,800	9,825
John W. Whitworth*	17	not listed	in mother's household	600	112
George A. Williams	30	miller	married, 3 children	0	100
John Wesley Williams*	17	farm laborer	in father's household	3,000	2,500
James Wiseman	37	farmer	married, 7 children	800	436
Green B. Woody	30	farmer	married, 7 children	200	450
James C. Zimmerman	27	farmer	married, 3 children	1,300	550

Sources of Letters

Archival Sources

Alabama Department of Archives and History

Robert T. Conley Letter

CACWL Collection

Lewis Moore Letter

Duke University, David M. Rubenstein Rare Book and Manuscript Library

Daniel Abernethy Papers
Leonard Alman Papers
Richard Amos Papers
Tilmon F. Baggarly Papers
Henry Baker Papers
James H. Baker Papers
Alfred W. Bell Papers
F. A. Bleckley Papers
Jonas A. Bradshaw Papers
James G. Broach Papers
William H. Brotherton Papers
Brown Family Papers
Daniel K. Campbell Papers
Job Cobb Papers
James O. Coghill Papers
Confederate States of America, Army, Miscellany, Officers' and Soldiers' Letters
Mary A. Councill Papers
Winifred A. Coward Papers
John Culberson and Samuel J. Culberson Papers
J. P. Culp Papers
Mary F. Davison Papers
Julia Deane Papers
Levi A. Festerman Papers
Jane Fisher Papers
Alexander Frank Papers
James W. Gibson Papers
John C. Hackett Papers
Harrison H. Hanes Papers
Jesse Harrison Papers
John H. Hartman Papers
Wade H. Hubbard Papers
John Ingram Papers
Alexander Keever Papers
Willis H. King Papers
Hannah R. Lawrence Papers
Mathew N. Love Papers
James F. Maides Papers
Mary Margaret McNeill Papers
Elizabeth Amanda Mills Papers
Daniel W. Murph Papers
Jesse F. Newsom Papers
Joseph Overcash Papers
Person Family Letters
John Peterson Papers
Jesse Phillips Papers
Sally G. Quinn Papers
John W. Reese Papers
James T. Robinson and John H. Robinson Papers
Charles Rothrock Papers
Daniel Setzer Papers
Thornton Sexton Letters
Evin Smith Papers
John A. Smith Papers
William D. Smith Papers
Edgar Smithwick Papers
Robert Spainhourd Papers
John J. Taylor Papers
William A. Tesh Papers
Isham Sims Upchurch Papers
John W. Whitfield Papers
Eliza Whitner Papers
John Wesley Williams Papers
J. D. and Joseph Wright Papers
James C. Zimmerman Papers

East Carolina University, Joyner Library Special Collections

Robert C. Caldwell Collection
Carpenter Family Papers
Hardison Family Papers
Tom W. Johnson Collection
Roberson Family Papers
Van Nortwick Papers

Emory University, Manuscript and Rare Book Library

James A. Patton Letters
Rudasil Letter, Confederate Miscellany
Woody Letters, Confederate Miscellany

Louisiana State University, Hill Memorial Library Special Collections

Samuel J. Lance Papers

North Carolina State Archives, Raleigh

Henry Clay Albright Papers
Duncan R. Barnhill, Military Collection, Civil War
John Gray Blount Papers
James Boon Papers
Henry H. Bowen Papers
Blair Letters

Isaac Brown Collection
Isaac Copeland Letters, Military Collection, Civil War
Cunningham Letters
Futch Letters
Lorraine Griffin Papers
W. P. Hall Collection
Marcus Hefner Papers
Jesse Hill Letters
Larkin S. Kendrick Papers
Isaac Lefevers Papers
James A. May, Military Collection, Civil War
David McCorkle, Military Collection, Civil War
James Parlier, Military Collection, Civil War
Poteet-Dickson Letters
Job R. Redmond, Military Collection, Civil War
Daniel W. Revis Letters
Zebulon Baird Vance, Governor's Papers
T. C. Wester Collection
Steven Whitaker Papers
Williams-Womble Papers

Southern Historical Collection, University of North Carolina, Chapel Hill

William Pickney Cline Papers
John Fuller Coghill Letters
Confederate Papers
DeRosset Family Papers
Grimes Family Papers
Hayes Collection
John Steele Henderson Papers
John DeBerniere Hooper Papers
Hundley Family Letters
Long Family Papers
McBride Family Papers
Neill McLeod Letters
Patton Family Letters
Pettigrew Family Papers
Proffit Family Letters
William H. Wills Papers

Stones River National Battlefield, Murfreesboro, Tennessee

McFee Letters

Tennessee State Library and Archives, Nashville

Civil War Collection, Confederate
WPA Transcripts, Civil War Correspondence

United States Army, Military History Institute, Carlisle, Pennsylvania

Harvey Bailey Letters, Civil War Document Collection
Christopher Fonvielle Collection, Civil War Document Collection
Constantine A. Hege Papers, Lewis-Leigh Collection
John W. Joyce Papers, Harrisburg Civil War Roundtable Collection

University of Georgia, Hargett Library Special Collections

Mary Kinsland Letter

University of North Carolina, Asheville, Special Collections Department

Silas H. Stepp Letters

University of Notre Dame, Hesburgh Libraries, Rare Books and Special Collections

Jackson Family Correspondence
Shipman Family Correspondence

University of Virginia Library Special Collections

John Thomas Black Letters
Franklin Setzer Correspondence

Virginia Polytechnic Institute and State University Libraries, Special Collections

Lee Hendrix Correspondence

Western Carolina University, Hunter Library Special Collections

William Carden Papers
Edmonston-Kelly Family Papers
Estes Family Papers
M. W. Parris Papers
George Job Huntley Papers
N. G. Phillips Papers
William Walker Papers
Watson Letters

Published Sources

Berlin, Ira, Joseph P. Reidy, and Leslie S. Rowland, eds. *Freedom: A Documentary History of Emancipation, 1861–1867.* Ser. 2, *The Black Military Experience.* Cambridge: Cambridge Univ. Press, 1982.

Berlin, Ira, Steven F. Miller, Joseph P. Reidy, and Leslie S. Rowland, eds. *Freedom: A Documentary History of Emancipation, 1861–1867.* Ser. 1, vol. 2, *The Wartime Genesis of Free Labor in the Upper South.* Cambridge: Cambridge Univ. Press, 1993.

Hatley, Joe M., and Linda B. Huffman, eds. *William F. Wagner, Confederate Soldier.* Wendell, N.C.: Broadfoot's Books, 1983.

Pierson, William Whatley, Jr., ed. *The Diary of Bartlett Yancy Malone.* James Sprunt Historical Publications, vol. 16, no. 2. Chapel Hill: Univ. of North Carolina, 1919.

Pitts, H. Douglas, ed. *Letters of a Gaston Ranger.* Richmond: Museum of the Confederacy, 1991.